THE COMICS JOURNAL

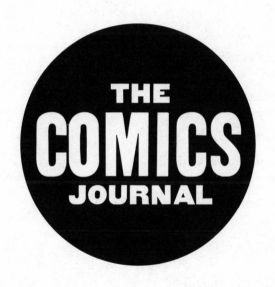

301 Contents

The Comics Journal 301
7563 Lake City Way NE
Seattle, Washington 98115

The Comics Journal 301 is
copyright ©2011 Fantagraphics
Books. All images/photos/text ©
their respective copyright holders.
All rights reserved. Permission to
reproduce material must be
obtained from the editor
or publisher.

Distributed in the U.S. by W.W.
Norton and Company, Inc.
(800-233-4830)

Distributed in Canada by
the Manda Group
(800-452-6642 x 862)

Distributed in the United Kingdom
by Turnaround Distribution
(44-(0) 20 8829-3002)

Distributed in the comics specialty
market by Diamond Comics
Distributors (800-452-6642 x 215)

ISBN: 978-1606992913

Second Fantagraphics printing:
June 2011

Printed in China

The Comics Journal

PUBLISHER
Fantagraphics Books

EDITOR IN CHIEF
Gary Groth

MANAGING EDITORS
Michael Dean
Kristy Valenti

ART DIRECTOR
Eric Skillman

SCANMASTER
Paul Baresh

INTERNS
Jenna Allen
Ian Burns
Andrew Davis
Melissa Gray
Jamie Hibdon
Michael Litven
Chi-Wen Lee
Christine Texeira

DESIGN INTERN
Kayla Carpitella

ADVERTISING
Matt Silvie

For advertising
information, e-mail
silvie @fantagraphics.com.

Visit us at tcj.com
for submission
guidelines and more.

Our Contributors

Warren Bernard is an independent scholar of comics history, contributing both materials and research to over a dozen books on the subject. He has lectured on comics history at the Library of Congress, where as a volunteer he has cataloged over 1000 pieces of original cartoon art in their holdings. Warren is also the Executive Director of the Small Press Expo.

Rob Clough has written about comics for Sequart.com, the Poopsheet Foundation, his own blog at highlowcomics.blogspot.com and now at tcj.com. In his spare time, he writes about women's college basketball and hangs out with his wife and daughter.

Tom Crippen is a writer who lives in Montreal.

Gene Deitch is a respected and influential animator, illustrator and comic-strip artist. His more-than-50-year career in animation included work for Terrytoons, UPA and MGM. The father of underground cartoonist Kim Deitch, he has resided in Prague since 1960.

R. Fiore is a longtime contributor to *The Comics Journal*.

R.C. Harvey is a comics historian and critic. Visit http://www.rcharvey.com/ for more.

Jeet Heer is co-editor of *Arguing Comics: Literary Masters on a Popular Medium* (University of Mississippi Press).

Timothy Hodler is the co-founder and co-editor of *Comics Comics*, and has written for publications including *New York*, *Bookforum* and *Details*. To his own great surprise, he lives in New Jersey.

Ryan Holmberg is a scholar of modern and contemporary Asian art and culture, currently based in Tokyo. He is the author of *Garo Manga: The First Decade, 1964-1973* (New York: The Center for Book Arts, 2010).

A collection of **Tim Kreider**'s political cartoons and essays, *Twilight of the Assholes*, is due out this year from Fantagraphics.

Chris Lanier is a cartoonist, artist and an assistant professor of Digital Art at Sierra Nevada College.

Rick Marschall has written 62 books, mostly on popular culture and Christian apologetics. He was comics editor of three newspaper syndicates, a writer/editor at Marvel Comics and a writer for Disney Comics. Several recent books include *Johann Sebastian Bach: Christian Encounters* (Thomas Nelson) and *Drawing Power: A Compendium of Cartoon Advertising* (Fantagraphics).

Robert Stanley Martin is a freelance writer and editor. His blog Pol Culture (polculture.blogspot.com) is devoted to commentary on the arts, literature and politics, with comics reviews featured every Sunday.

Donald Phelps has been writing about the arts for 40 years. His collection *Reading the Funnies* earned him an American Book Award.

Kenneth R. Smith has written books about late-modern culture and provides e-mail commentaries to subscribers from kensmith@texas.net. He has been a self-published artist and writer since 1971, when his *Phantasmagoria* series appeared. He is a former professor of philosophy.

Marc Sobel is a writer and critic whose work has appeared in a variety of publications and websites, including *The Comics Journal*, *Sequart Research and Literacy Organization* and *Comic Book Galaxy*.

Alexander Theroux is a novelist, essayist and poet. His latest work is *The Strange Case of Edward Gorey*, a memoir/biography.

Kent Worcester is co-editor of *Arguing Comics: Literary Masters on a Popular Medium* (University Press of Mississippi, 2004).

4

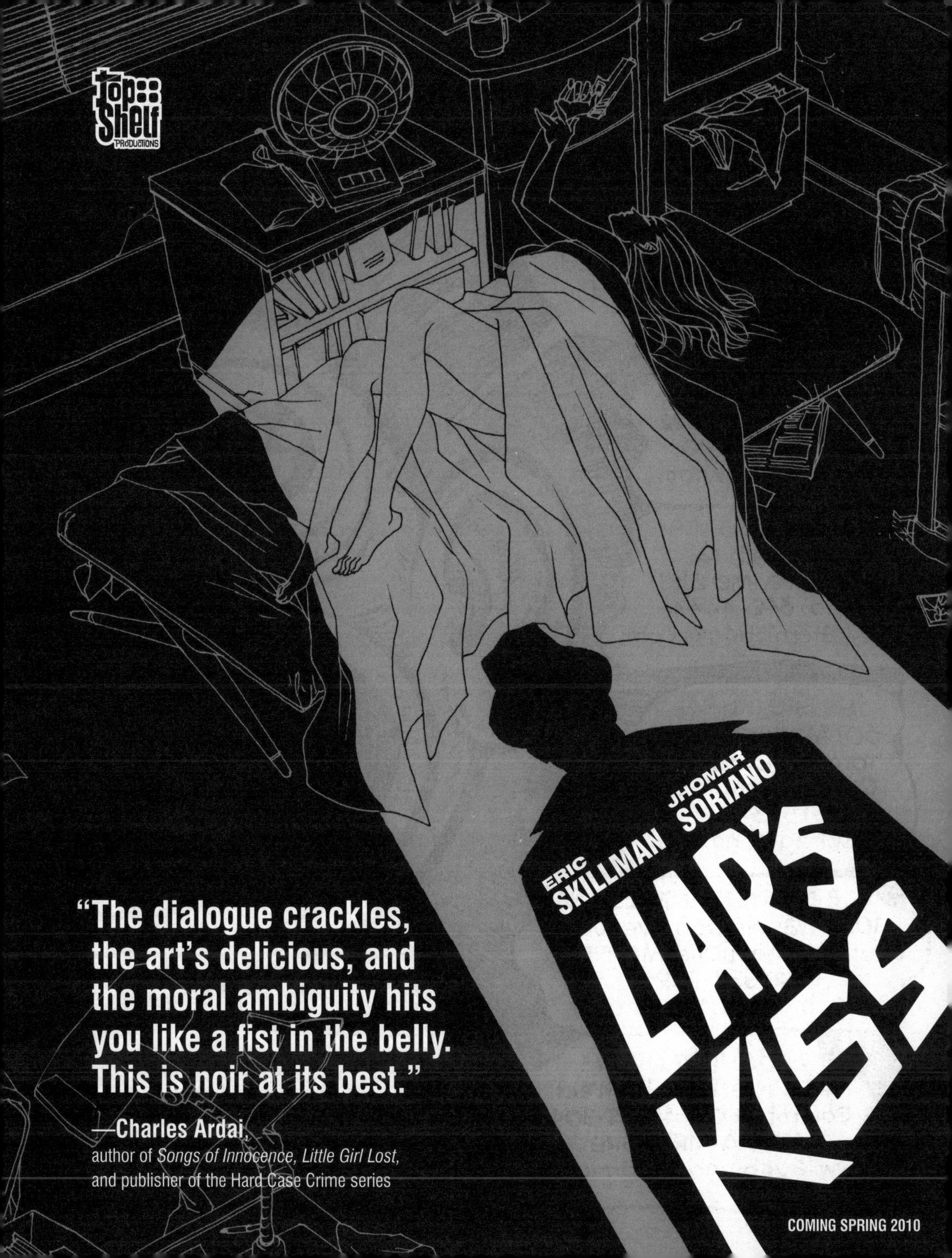
Top Shelf Productions
"The dialogue crackles, the art's delicious, and the moral ambiguity hits you like a fist in the belly. This is noir at its best."
—Charles Ardai,
author of Songs of Innocence, Little Girl Lost, and publisher of the Hard Case Crime series
ERIC SKILLMAN
JHOMAR SORIANO
LIAR'S KISS
COMING SPRING 2010

Comics Country

PAT MORIARITY

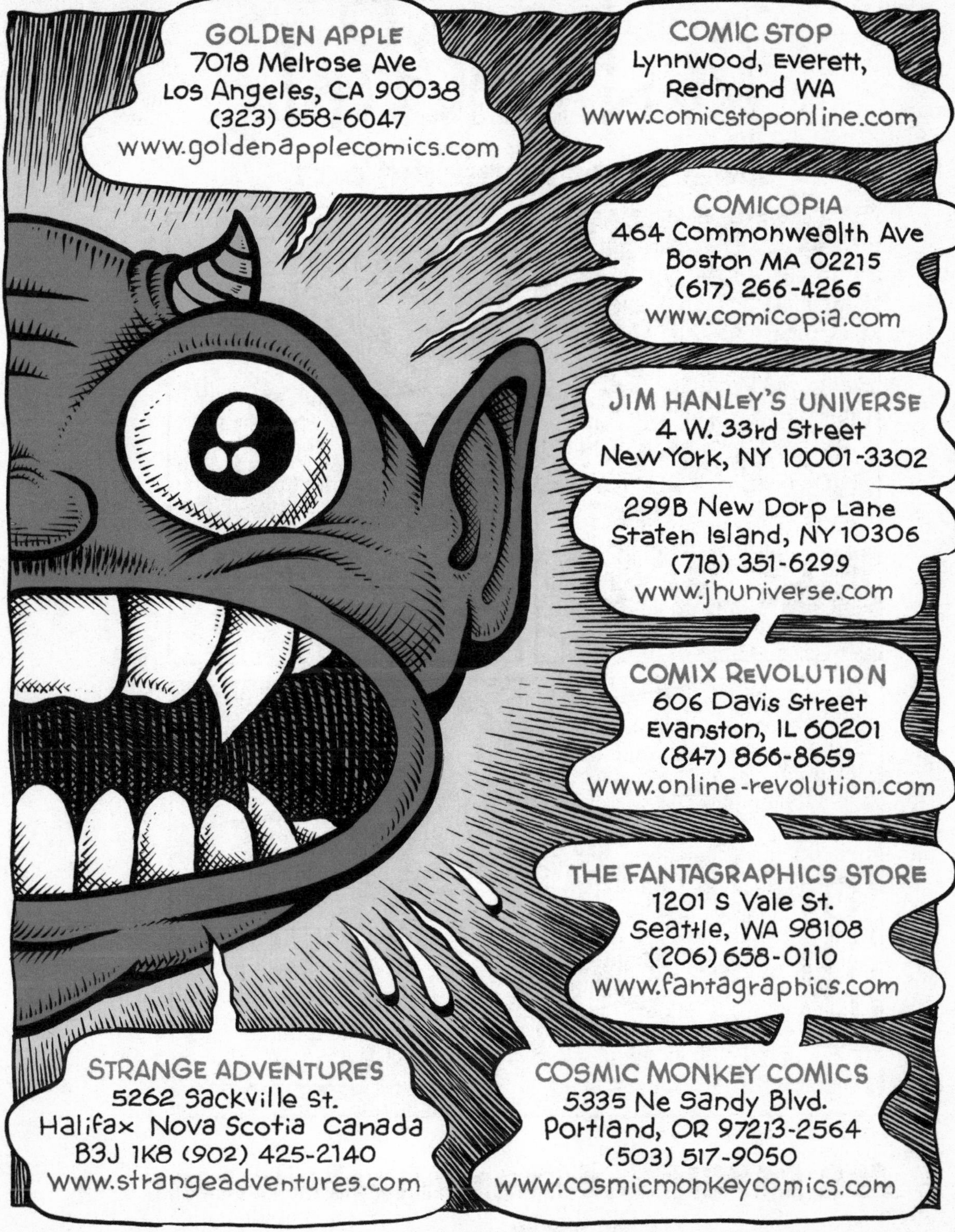
GOLDEN APPLE
7018 Melrose Ave
Los Angeles, CA 90038
(323) 658-6047
www.goldenapplecomics.com
COMIC STOP
Lynnwood, Everett,
Redmond WA
www.comicstoponline.com
COMICOPIA
464 Commonwealth Ave
Boston MA 02215
(617) 266-4266
www.comicopia.com
JIM HANLEY'S UNIVERSE
4 W. 33rd Street
New York, NY 10001-3302
299B New Dorp Lane
Staten Island, NY 10306
(718) 351-6299
www.jhuniverse.com
COMIX REVOLUTION
606 Davis Street
Evanston, IL 60201
(847) 866-8659
www.online-revolution.com
THE FANTAGRAPHICS STORE
1201 S Vale St.
Seattle, WA 98108
(206) 658-0110
www.fantagraphics.com
STRANGE ADVENTURES
5262 Sackville St.
Halifax Nova Scotia Canada
B3J 1K8 (902) 425-2140
www.strangeadventures.com
COSMIC MONKEY COMICS
5335 Ne Sandy Blvd.
Portland, OR 97213-2564
(503) 517-9050
www.cosmicmonkeycomics.com

DoN MARTiN ®

AN EVENING IN THE BIG CITY

FOR LAUGHS...donmartinwebsite.com

TAKE A TRIP FROM HELL TO HEAVEN WITH DANTE AND SEYMOUR CHWAST

"Chwast's adaptation is infused with his original comic style."
—*Huffington Post*

"Diabolically witty, devilishly expressive cartoon drawings ... an accessible introduction to *The Divine Comedy*—a sort of high-end, WHAM-POW *Cliff's Notes* ... fiendishly entertaining."
—*NPR.org*

"A clever reimagining of a classic...the lamentations of the damned were never so much fun."—*Entertainment Weekly*

"The protagonists' journey through Inferno, Purgatory and Heaven is transformed by Chwast into a feast of illustrative noir."
—*Eye Magazine*

"With all due respect to Dante, this is Chwast's *Divine Comedy* ... [He] makes the *Divine Comedy* irresistibly comic and inspirationally transcendent."—*Kirkus Reviews* (starred review)

"Chwast's version is not your grandmother's *Divine Comedy* ... [He] has succeeded in making this classic into something timely and just as vital today as it has ever been—and more engaging."
—*The Daily Heller*

"Mighty nice graphic design."
—*Comics Alliance*

"Dante + Seymour = Heaven."—Maira Kalman, author of *The Principles of Uncertainty*

"Seymour's take on this timeless classic is not only charming and clever, it is so cannily rendered that it makes Dante's complex masterwork easily understood for any reader. Divine."—Chip Kidd, author of *The Cheese Monkeys*

"I have to say, seen through Seymour Chwast's eyes, Hell doesn't look so bad. I'm almost looking forward to floating in pools of excrement or being tossed about carelessly by furious winds. Seymour Chwast has put the comedy back into the divine in this fiendishly heavenly extravaganza."—Marian Bantjes, graphic artist

"Seymour Chwast! Oh, how I hate him! He's already the top artist! He's already the top designer! Now he's gonna be the top graphic novelist! Seymour Chwast can go to Hell!"—Craig Yoe, author of *The Art of Steve Ditko*

Journal of
Graphic Novels
and Comics

NEW IN 2010

SUBMIT YOUR RESEARCH

Journal of Graphic Novels and Comics is a peer reviewed journal covering all aspects of the graphic novel, comic strip and comic book, with the emphasis on comics in their cultural, institutional and creative contexts. Its scope is international, covering not only English language comics but also worldwide comic culture. The journal reflects interdisciplinary research in comics and aims to establish a dialogue between academics, historians, theoreticians and practitioners of comics. It therefore examines comics production and consumption within the contexts of culture: art, cinema, television and new media technologies.

The journal will include all forms of 'sequential imagery' including precursors of the comic but in the main emphasis will be on twentieth and twenty-first century examples, reflecting the increasing interest in the modern forms of the comic, its production and cultural consumption.

NEW ISSUE ALERTS

Would you like to receive an email telling you when a new issue of the journal is published, with links to the online articles? Register for Table of Contents Alerting at the website

FIRST ISSUE

We will be offering free online access to the inaugural issue throughout 2010. Visit the website regularly to find out more.

www.tandf.co.uk/journals/rcom

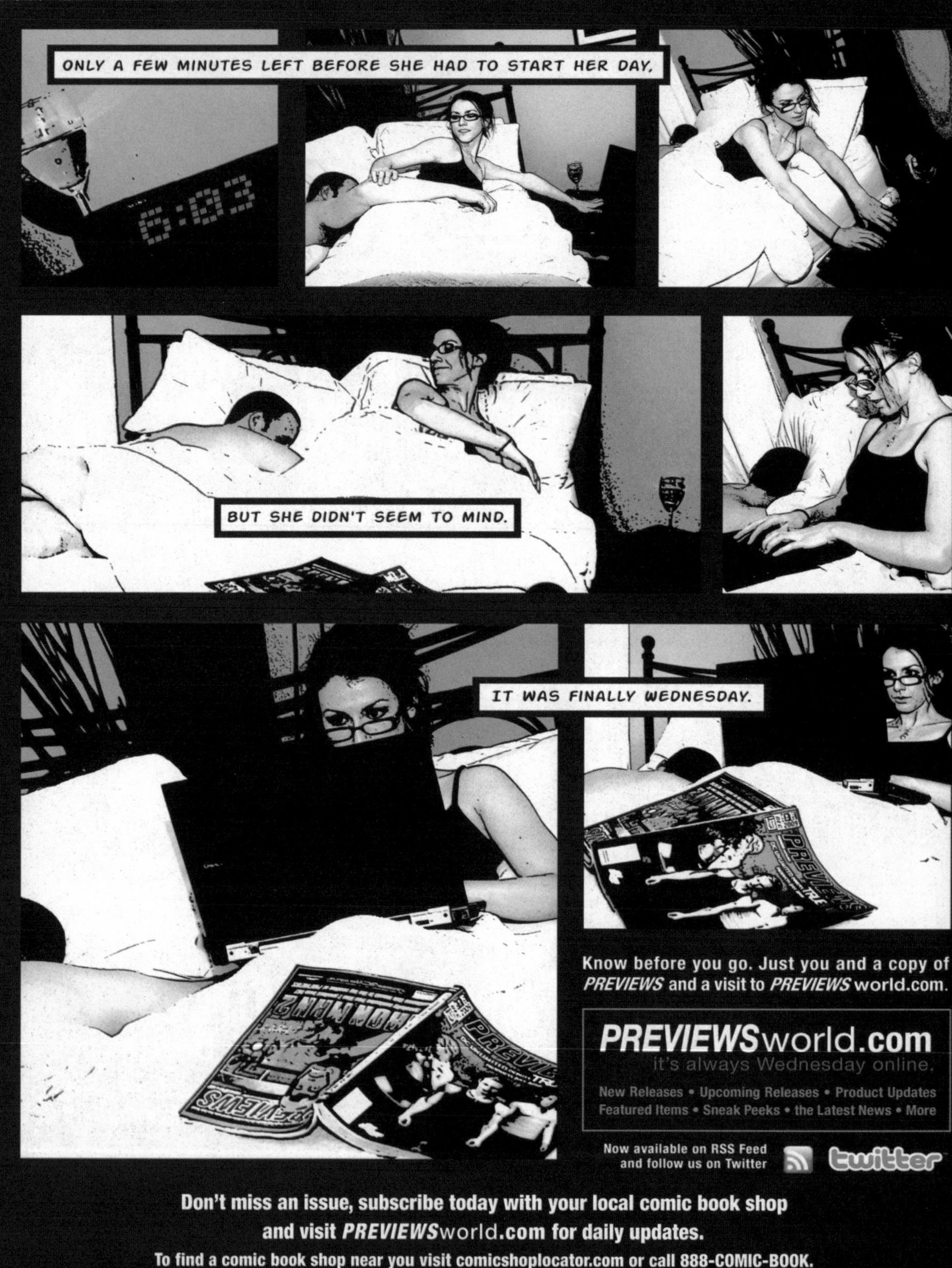
ONLY A FEW MINUTES LEFT BEFORE SHE HAD TO START HER DAY,
6:03
BUT SHE DIDN'T SEEM TO MIND.
IT WAS FINALLY WEDNESDAY.
Know before you go. Just you and a copy of PREVIEWS and a visit to PREVIEWSworld.com.
PREVIEWSworld.com
it's always Wednesday online.
New Releases • Upcoming Releases • Product Updates
Featured Items • Sneak Peeks • the Latest News • More
Now available on RSS Feed and follow us on Twitter
twitter
Don't miss an issue, subscribe today with your local comic book shop
and visit PREVIEWSworld.com for daily updates.
To find a comic book shop near you visit comicshoplocator.com or call 888-COMIC-BOOK.

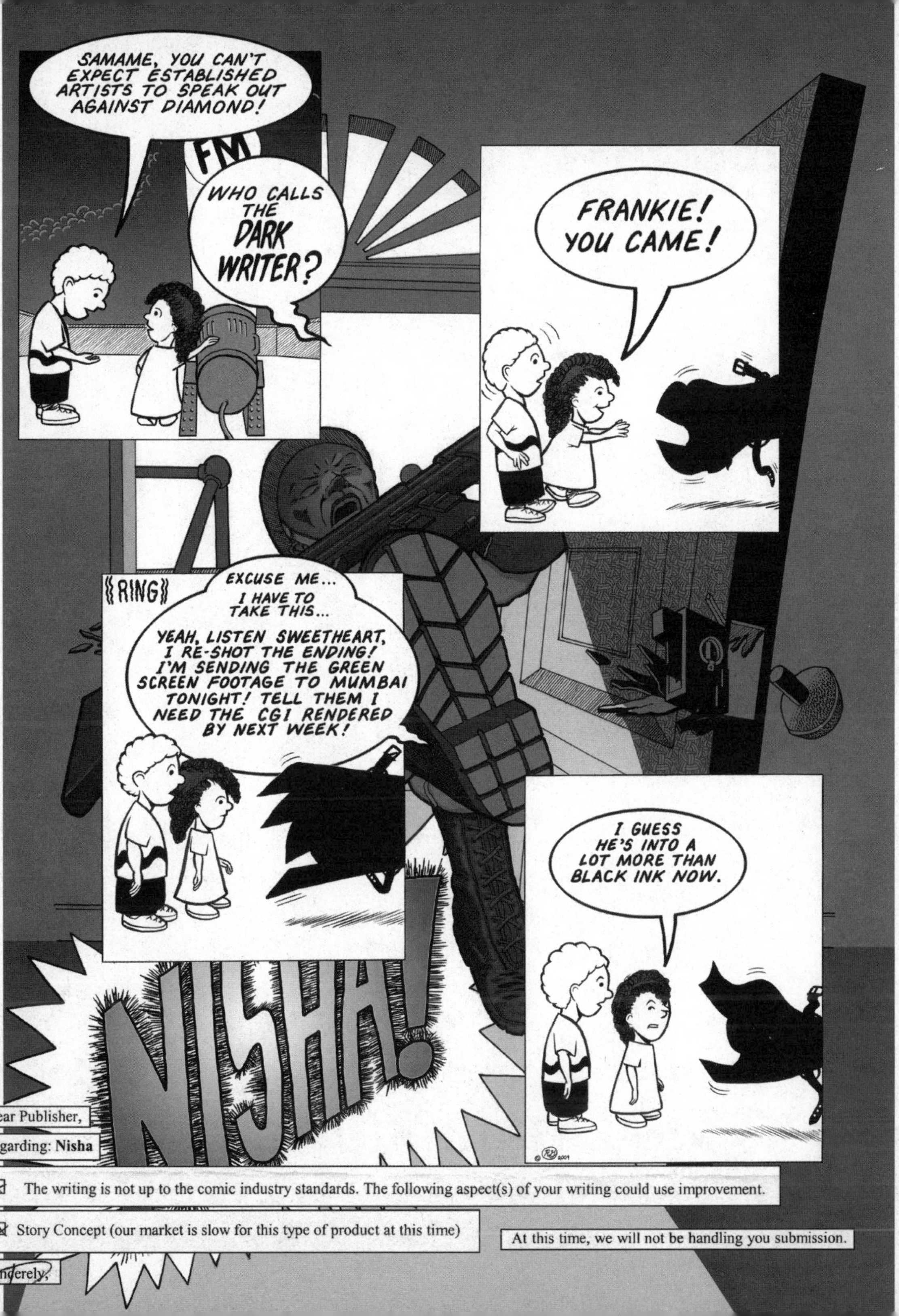
SAMAME, YOU CAN'T EXPECT ESTABLISHED ARTISTS TO SPEAK OUT AGAINST DIAMOND!
FM
WHO CALLS THE DARK WRITER?
FRANKIE! YOU CAME!
RING
EXCUSE ME... I HAVE TO TAKE THIS...
YEAH, LISTEN SWEETHEART, I RE-SHOT THE ENDING! I'M SENDING THE GREEN SCREEN FOOTAGE TO MUMBAI TONIGHT! TELL THEM I NEED THE CGI RENDERED BY NEXT WEEK!
I GUESS HE'S INTO A LOT MORE THAN BLACK INK NOW.
NISHA!
Dear Publisher,
Regarding: **Nisha**
☒ The writing is not up to the comic industry standards. The following aspect(s) of your writing could use improvement.
☒ Story Concept (our market is slow for this type of product at this time)
At this time, we will not be handling you submission.
Sincerely,

WILLIAM AYERS
RYAN ALEXANDER-TANNER

Ayers · Alexander-Tanner

TO TEACH
the journey, in comics

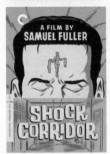 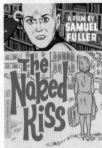   

THE CRITERION COLLECTION CELEBRATES
THE ART OF CINEMA

Leo McCarey's *Make Way for Tomorrow* cover art by **Seth** • Alexander Mackendrick's *Sweet Smell of Success* cover art by **Sean Phillips** • Byron Haskin's *Robinson Crusoe on Mars* cover art by **Bill Sienkiewicz** • Pietro Germi's *Divorce Italian Style* cover art by **Jaime Hernandez** • Pietro Germi's *Seduced and Abandoned* cover art by **Mike Allred** • Samuel Fuller's *Shock Corridor* cover art by **Daniel Clowes** • Samuel Fuller's *The Naked Kiss* cover art by **Daniel Clowes** • Yasujiro Ozu's *The Only Son/There Was a Father* cover art by **Adrian Tomine** • Terry Zwigoff's *Crumb* cover art by **R. Crumb** • Terry Zwigoff's *Louie Bluie* cover art by **R. Crumb** • Allen Baron's *Blast of Silence* cover art by **Sean Phillips** • John Huston's *Wise Blood* cover art by **Josh Cochran** • Francesco Rosi's *Hands over the City* cover art by **Danijel Zezelj** • Guillermo del Toro's *Cronos* cover art by **Mike Mignola** • Monsters and Madmen box set art by **Darwyn Cooke** • And many more at **criterion.com**

R. CRUMB

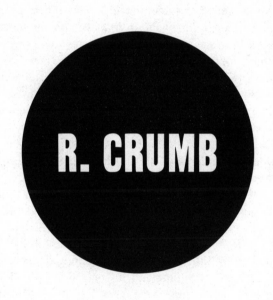

R. Crumb is regarded by critics, historians and cognoscenti generally — the occasional contrarian notwithstanding — as one of the greatest cartoonists to emerge in the second half of the 20th century (or thereabouts), a judgment I share. But what makes him stand shoulder to shoulder with Charles Schulz, Harvey Kurtzman and Carl Barks, among a tiny handful of others? Why has he become such an iconic presence in the history of cartooning? Part of the answer resides, I think, in his protean, creative restlessness, the fact that he's maintained an aesthetic vitality by evolving in technique and content while retaining his trademark visual style. Artistically, he's never stood still, yet his essential voice and point of view have been unwaveringly consistent.

He and his comics have continually evolved, from his earliest Fritz comics (told in cleanly delineated, detailed, cluttered drawings and reflecting the influence of 1940s funny-animal comics combined with the 1950s *Mad* comic) to his LSD-fueled visions, with a looser (he would say sloppier) line that segued into a more exuberant big-foot approach and a grungier, more urgently expressive line where he let loose his own sexual demons and ridiculed social mores. In the '80s and '90s, especially in the fecund *Weirdo* period, his stories became more focused and reflective, his line-work more controlled and his pages denser. He learned to use a brush for the first time and put it to good use by adapting prose into comics and illustrating biographical vignettes of favorite blues musicians. His work lost some of its exaggeration and became more representational, as befitted the subject matter. In the same vein, he illustrated Charles Bukowski short stories, as well as a long Kafka biography in the '90s, both of which required more realistic rendering.

When it became public knowledge that Crumb had embarked upon the adaptation of Genesis, the reaction among my acquaintances was one of curiosity mixed with puzzlement. This did not sound like a Crumb project, ether in terms of subject matter or length. Biblical study had not played a role in his art previously, he belonged to no organized religion, he was scarred by his Catholic upbringing; and the longest story he'd written and drawn, at 22 pages, was "Fritz Bugs Out," and that was when he was 21 years old. Why would he start work on a 200 page "graphic novel" version of one of the foundational texts of Christianity at age 62? Had he lost his mind?

The jury is still out on that question, but in retrospect, his Genesis project should not necessarily have come as a shock; a surprise, maybe, but not a shock, given Crumb's need to set new challenges for himself, expand his range and not coast creatively. Admittedly, this wasn't as gradual as shifts he's made in the past, which were more organic, one moving seamlessly into the next, but a gigantic leap and one which required him to dramatically

adapt his drawing to suit what he felt were the aesthetic requirements of the project — a more visually sober and less cartoony approach than he's heretofore employed.

This was a gigantic undertaking that consumed four years of his life, and insofar as a new 200-page graphic novel by R. Crumb is a bona fide event and ought to be given its critical due, I asked six critics to assess the book and, in a second round, each other. If they all agreed, I could've run a summarized consensus in a few pages, but fortunately for those of us who crave intellectual stimulation — and even a little intellectual fireworks — they did not, and they proceed to disagree on the merits of Crumb's *Genesis* in the pages following the interview with Mr. Crumb.

This is the longest critical symposium the *Journal* has ever run. Rarely does a single comic deserve this level and intensity of critical attention, and even more rarely does it get it. Crumb's *Genesis* is one that does.

Robert Crumb graciously consented to an interview on the subject — after feeling like he'd been interviewed to death on the subject over the previous 12 months; nonetheless, this is the most comprehensive one on the subject that I've seen and I think we were able to cover a lot of territory that was left untouched in those other interviews.

—*Gary Groth*

R. Crumb
IN HIS
LOUNGE PANTS,
MANDAGOUT,
AUGUST 26, '05

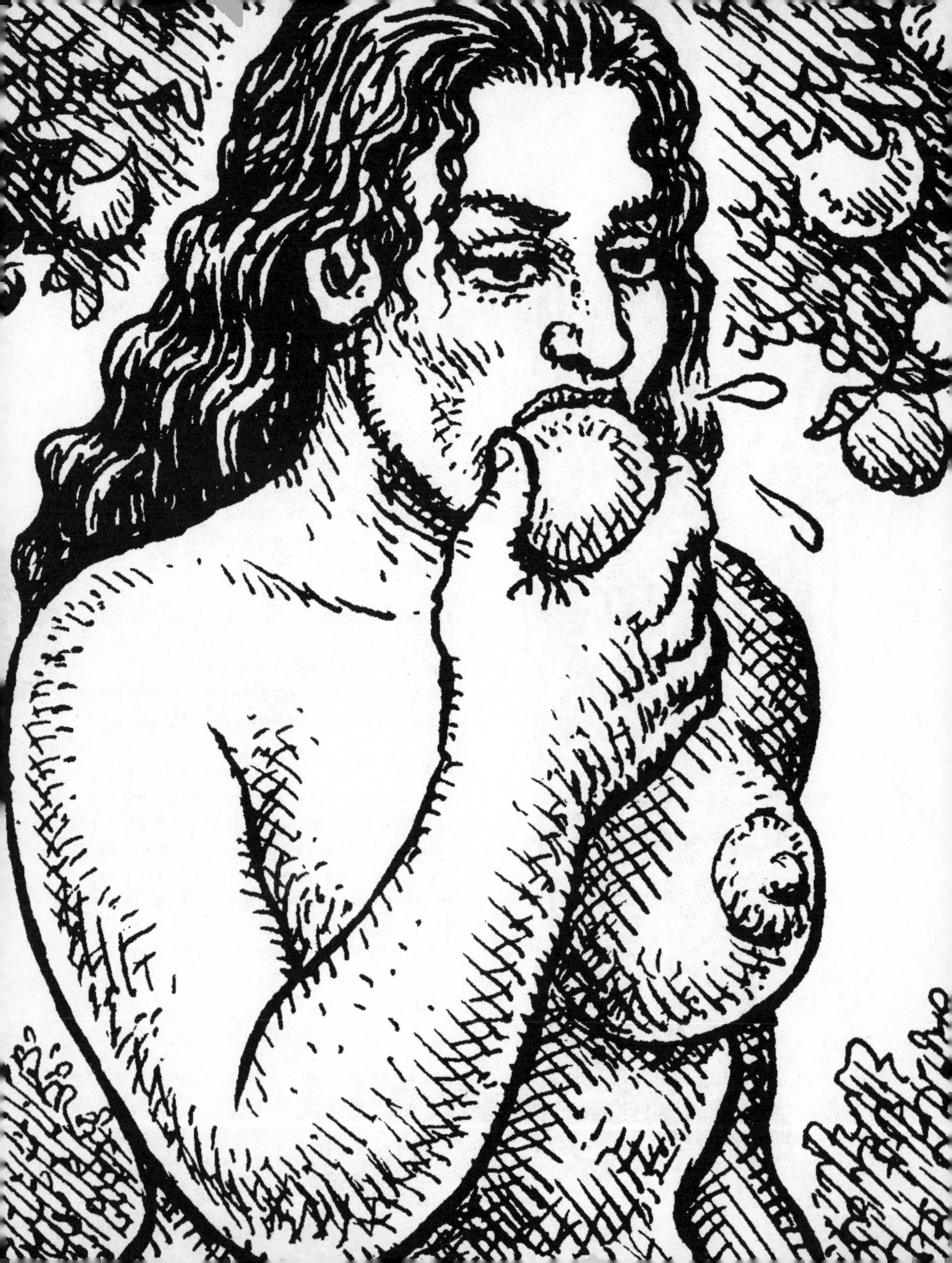

THE GENESIS INTERVIEW

Gary Groth: I'd like to talk to you about the road that led to Genesis. But I also want to ask you why you chose Genesis. And you tend to say provocative things ...

R. Crumb: Have you read a lot of these things I've said about that?

Groth: Oh yes.

Crumb: They're all true; they're all true, actually. In one interview, I said I did it for the money.

Groth: Yes, I was just about to quote that and ask you if you were serious.

Crumb: It's true, I did. Denis Kitchen shopped it around. He first proposed this. He said, "Why don't you do all of Genesis instead of just Adam and Eve?"

I said, "Jeez, well, that's a huge amount of work."

He said, "Well, what if I can get some publisher to pay you a lot of money?"

I said, "OK, well, see what you can do." So he came back with a couple offers. One was for $150,000 from some publisher and I said, "Eh, I don't know, maybe."

Then he said, "Well, maybe I can get more." So he got the offer of, I think, $250,000 from Norton. $50,000 of which goes to him and various other middlemen, Lora Fountain and others, and Judy Hansen and all them.

All images from *The Book of Genesis Illustrated* by R. Crumb [©2009 R. Crumb] unless otherwise noted.

They divide up $50,000 of it.

But that sounded like a lot of money to me at the time, so that was motivating. "OK, all right." That was a stupid decision. "OK, I'll do it, yeah": Four fucking years later and hundreds of hours of labor, it barely seems worth it.

Groth: In retrospect you indeed think it was a stupid decision?

Crumb: Yeah [*laughs*]. It was a dumb decision. But at the same time I thought, "Well, it'll be an interesting project, it's never been done before, and it'll have some significance." I think any good comic illustrator worth his salt could've pretty much done the same thing I did.

Groth: Well now, it was stupid in the sense that it wasn't gratifying artistically or economically? Or both?

Crumb: Well, it was stupid because I didn't take into consideration how much time it was going to take. Once I got started working on it, 20 pages into it, I realized, "Oh my God, this is gonna take me years." I had no idea [*laughs*]. When I said, "Yeah, sure, OK, $200,000, yeah." I thought, y'know, maybe six months or something. By the time I got to The Flood, Noah's Ark, I said, "Oh shit." [*Groth laughs.*] That's only like chapter six or something [*laughs*]. I said, "Oh my God, now I've done it." And there was no turning back at that point.

Groth: Were there moments when, in fact, you would have preferred not to have taken the job as you were working on it?

Crumb: Once you get rolling on it, you can't even think that way. Y'know, once it gets rolling, then you're just into it. You have committed yourself to, as

I've said somewhere before, laying the tracks for the Trans-Siberian Railroad, and you're not going to start having second thoughts about it once you're out there in the middle of the fuckin' Gobi Desert layin' those tracks [*Groth laughs*]. You just gotta see it through, that's all. See it through to the end.

And it was interesting. There were many things about it that were positive. One was it just really honed my drawing skills. That was like back to the woodshed for me as far as the technical aspects of drawing skill go. I upgraded my abilities by doing that, and anything I attack now, any project I do now, I can see the result, how that slave labor on *Genesis* has made me a better and more facile artist.

Groth: Considering that you were already a pretty good artist, how significant is that?

Crumb: As I progressed on the project, I kept going back to the beginning, to the early pages and making corrections because they looked too crude —they looked really crude to me by the time I got halfway through. I had to go back and fix 'em up, and make them better. The first photocopies

"All my previous work looks crude to me now."

I made of the first few pages, the first 10 or 20 pages, I looked at 'em, I saved 'em, and compared them to after I made the corrections. They're really upgraded.

Groth: But insofar as you were already an excellent drawer, how significant is the improvement?

Crumb: Well, to me it's very significant. All my previous work looks crude to me now.

Groth: Is that right?

Crumb: All of it. God almighty, I should've gone back to school and really learned correct anatomy and stuff like that. I never learned to draw anatomically correct — never. Until I hit *Genesis*, and then I had to get a copy of that Muybridge's *The Human Figure in Motion*. It's all photos. It's a great, great book. Justin Green turned me on to that book. Muybridge also made one of animals that I used; those books were like the Bible, I had them next to me at all times. You can find a human figure in almost any position in that book, male and female.

Groth: And you hadn't studied that book previously?

TOP
Whoa Nellie! [©2000 Jaime Hernandez]

BOTTOM
The Arcane Eye of Burne Hogarth [©1992 Burne Hogarth]

Crumb: No. I had it for years and I never did much with it. Maybe used it a couple times before, but y'know, what I learned in my earlier years, before *Genesis*, was what a lot of cartoonists do: just fake your way through. Just kind of fake it, and it works. It's all tricks and sleight of hand. But then again, you look at the Hernandez brothers: Those motherfuckers learned how to draw the human figure. They know how to draw. And it's marvelous: it's uncanny how good they are at it. And all kinds of figures, not just an ideal Burne Hogarth figure, but any kind of figure, all kinds of shapes and sizes of different types of people. They're great at that, just great at it.

Groth: And do you feel that you previously couldn't draw as well as they could?

Crumb: I couldn't draw the human figure as well as they could, no way. Nothing close to what they could do — and many others, too, many other cartoonists. As I was working on *Genesis* I came to greatly respect a lot of those guys that draw action comics and stuff. I mean, some of them I think are ridiculous, but some of them obviously have slaved to learn that stuff, to learn anatomy and to learn to draw the human figure and the musculature: animals and humans both.

Pete Poplaski lent me this big comic from the '70s — a comic version of the Bible — and a quarter of the way through Genesis they gave up on it. They put out one issue, I think. And boy, I just studied that and came to really respect the guy's skills. The thing about a lot of those guys is they don't know how to make something funky and personal, it all looks very standard heroic style. So in a certain sense it's not very interesting, it doesn't have much individual

personality. You might admire their inking technique or something, but there's not much individualization there.

Groth: There always seems to be the danger that an academically perfect drawing can be devoid of any real personality or quirkiness.

Crumb: That's right. I much prefer a crude drawing; Aline [Kominsky-Crumb] has lots of personality and crazy intensity compared to this kind of slick, facile Marvel/DC type art. That doesn't interest me generally.

Groth: Is there a fear that you can draw better but you may lose some of your wildness or stylistic idiosyncrasy as a cartooonist?

Crumb: No, uh-uh. I think if you start from where I started from, you're never gonna lose that. If you're crazy, you're crazy, that's it. [*Laughter.*] But when you have to show two men wrestling on the ground it helps to know what you're doing.

Groth: Right, it facilitates executing your vision. So money was a motivating factor, but presumably not the only one. Did you have an a priori interest or fascination with Genesis or the Bible?

Crumb: For many years I'd been studying ancient Mesopotamian civilization. And for some reason that interested me more than ancient Egypt, I don't know why. We're talking Sumer, Akkadia, Babylonia, Assyria, Hittites, the Mitanni, the Elamites, all those people. That really interests me. I was studying that for years. At the same time I had another line of interest which was basically the Old Testament, and the Hebrews and how they evolved their whole monotheistic thing, that interested me also. I spent time studying the Old Testament — the Torah, basically, the first five Books of Moses. Stuff like that.

I played around with this idea of making a take-off on Adam and Eve for years and years, and I drew stuff in my sketchbook about it, and made jokey stuff about Adam and Eve, and it never was satisfying somehow. I mean, the original text is so strange in and of itself, it doesn't really need to be joked on. Why not just illustrate it as it is written? The jokes I made seemed lame to me. They didn't seem as interesting as the original text itself.

Groth: Your interest was not from a theological or religious point of view, right? It was from more of an historical point of view?

Crumb: Well it's hard to separate. Obviously, I'm not a believer. As I said in the introduction, I believe it's the words of men. It's not the word of God. It's not inspired by God. It's a heavy text. It's a very powerful folk artifact, and any folk artifact like that is a collective phenomenon. You cannot credit one person as the creative genius behind it. There's probably no genius behind Genesis or the Adam & Eve story; it's something that evolved over a long period of time, and took on weight as it was passed down through the generations before it was even written down, I think. It was told over and over again, so it acquires, as fairy tales do, collective layers of meaning for people. There are just layers of meaning in Adam & Eve; it's still a powerful story. It's not just a lightweight made-up story; if one person had made it up, it wouldn't have that weight.

Groth: So you're saying it's powerful even to a non-believer.

Crumb: Yeah, it's powerful stuff: all of it. But a lot of people told me since they've read my book, they could never make it through the original text, but my book helped them get through it. Even though it's not written as entertainment. Although I think probably in its original form, some of those stories were told with a certain entertainment edge to them. There're classic literary devices in a lot of those stories of suspense and resolve and violence, and lurid details, and all that stuff, which were probably enjoyed when they sat around in the tents telling the stories originally. But then later, when it became the sacred text of the Hebrew peoples, and into the possession of the priests, then they added all their stuff to it, which makes it quite tedious. [*Laughs*]. A lot of it. You've got all the begots, and you've got all this legalistic and religious doctrinal stuff stuck in there, which messes up the original excitement of the stories a lot of the time, so a lot of people just can't wade through that — unless you're a real fanatic true believer, but even they skip over lots of it. And a lot of people who were brought up reading the Bible tell me, "Wow, I never read that part!" or "We used to skip over the part about Lot and his daughters; I didn't know about that." [*Laughs.*] In illustrating everything, every detail of the actions described, then it's all brought out

AND HE DROVE THE MAN OUT, AND SET UP EAST OF THE GARDEN OF EDEN THE CHERUBIM AND THE FLAME OF THE WHIRLING SWORD TO GUARD THE WAY TO THE TREE OF LIFE.

and it makes it much easier for a modern person to read through it. You can actually see what's written there.

Groth: So in a way you've secularized Genesis.

Crumb: In a way you could say that, yeah. That's a good way to put it: "secularized." Without putting any obvious kind of polemic on it there ...There's no attempt to make a philosophical statement on top of the text. Of course, my drawings are my own personal interpretation to a degree, but I also very consciously and scrupulously avoided putting any kind of snide comments in the drawings that might be taken as pointing at the text and saying, "Isn't this ridiculous?" or "Isn't that an outlandish thing to say?" or anything like that. I tried to respect the text in that I just wanted to interpret it as literally as I possibly could, and not make even the most subtle ridicule of it. Because then people would be looking for that, and that would alter the entire sense of the whole thing.

Groth: Even as literal a transformation of the text as you've attempted, you can't help but impose an interpretation onto it. And as you've just said,

yours is a secular interpretation, which means that you couldn't imbue it with that kind of transcendent perception that —

Crumb: Can you think of any artist in history who's done paintings or illustrations of the Bible and has succeeded in doing that? Without becoming very schmaltzy and corny — even Michelangelo in the Sistine Chapel: very schmaltzy. I looked at a lot of the old European art to see if I could get any ideas from it for how to draw certain scenes, but everything was too over the top. It was so overplayed and melodramatic. Have you ever looked at Gustave Doré's Bible illustrations?

Groth: Yes, I was going to mention Doré.

Crumb: They're so schmaltzy! And also the mid-19th century is very ignorant historically about what people dressed like, and what things really looked like. So it was very unhelpful, as far as swiping ideas.

Groth: You think Doré's Bible illustrations were schmaltzy?

Crumb: Totally. Take a look. They are dripping with melodrama. Doré did other stuff that's great and not at all schmaltzy: His drawings of London, did you ever see those?

Groth: No.

Crumb: Oh man, they're great. They're really great. He captured the sordidness of the slums of London in the 1870s. Fabulous.

Groth: Do you think it would literally be impossible to visually depict the Bible in —

Crumb: In a transcendental religious manner?

Groth: Yeah — without being schmaltzy.

Crumb: I can't imagine. You'd have to go all the way back to the iconographic stuff of the early Middle Ages or really crude, primitive visualizations of religious stuff to get anything close to what you might call "magical art." You know, communication of something beyond the mundane world. Like the Book of Kells or something, where it's just mystical. It's very iconographic and not narrative. It's just intricate, mesmerizing symbolic images. You'd have to go to that level, old African art and stuff like that. Or some of the stuff in India: the temples in India, like those Krishna things you see. Those approach that. Even the modern versions of that stuff get schmaltzy. It gets overdone, melodramatic. Robes blowing in the wind, and shit like that: beautiful images of Moses and God or whatever. I tried to avoid that. But at the same time I walked a line because I wanted to put in some of that old, lurid comic-book aspect. I didn't want to lose that.

Respect Without Reverence

Groth: Speaking of the lurid comic-book aspect, it seemed to me that there were two opposing strains in your adaptation, and the first is that you were paying homage to the more lurid comics of the '40s and '50s, especially with the covers for example. And you actually see the book in terms of those comics. You once said, "The original is so strong and strange in its own right, there's so much in there that's lurid and lends itself to comic-book adaptation."

Crumb: That's right, there are lurid things in the text.

Groth: But then, the problem is its stature as a divine document of religious

TOP
Gustave Doré's
*Prisoners Exercising
at Newgate Prison,*
engraving from
London: A Pilgrimage
by Blanchard Jerrold
(London, 1872).

history, considered by its adherents as a monumental touchstone of civilization, and how reverently and respectfully you adapted it. So you have these opposing strains within the work — lurid mass-produced comics and reverence toward the original document.

Crumb: I did not adapt it reverently. I respected the text insofar as I did not want to ridicule it. But I see the text as actually a quite primitive document. It's primitive; it's full of ancient, very old, ritualistic ideas, which are very crude. And there's a lot going on there that is not consciously understood by the people who are telling the stories. And then you have pasted over that this really annoying religious priestly stuff, which is trying to nail the whole thing down so that people can't get out from under it. [*Laughs.*]

At a certain point while I was working on it, after about 25 pages, I actually started to despise the text. For a while I went through this phase of hating it. It is really a hateful thing actually. A hateful document that kept people down, kept people in ignorance and darkness, and from advancing intellectually or mentally. To hold a text like that over people as the only thing that they should take seriously, that that's their whole prescription for living and for morality and all that, is a terrible thing to do. It just proves how insane and crazy the human race is that still in this day and age, to take a text like that as a source of moral guidance. That just causes nothing but trouble. [*Laughs.*] And the same can be said of the New Testament, the Qur'an, all the Western religious stuff. The Eastern thing is different, the Buddhist and the Hindu things are very different. They're much more democratic and open, and not as rigid.

Groth: And more generous spirited?

Crumb: Well, they are not as hard-line. They're not as defined. Like the Hindu religion has 4,000 different gods and you can take your pick of which ones you want to revere according to how they appeal to you. You can worship this one or that one. You can worship Ganesh, symbolized by an elephant, whatever you want. So it's different, it's very different. But the Western religions are pretty awful, actually. All three of the major Western religions are contentious and antagonistic and aggressive.

Groth: Harsh.

Crumb: Yeah, hard-edged. All three of 'em: Islam, Christianity and Judaism.

Groth: Did you see a conflict between your wanting to pay homage to certain lurid conventions of comics and transcribing this?

Crumb: None at all. [*Laughs.*] No conflict whatsoever [*Groth laughs.*] Like if you wanted to illustrate an ancient folktale or a folk song. I did that, I did illustrations of an old Grimm's Fairy Tale, "Mother Hulda," and it's the same thing. It's full of lurid detail, incredibly, all the Grimm's Fairy Tales. Besides from the fact that the Bible is considered the word of God — Genesis particularly is full of the most harrowing, lurid goings-on. Chapter 34 is probably the ugliest chapter in the whole book. That's the one where the sons of Jacob decide they're gonna kill all the men of Shechem because the prince slept with their sister Dinah.

Groth: Yeah, that was a terrifying act of treachery and betrayal.

Crumb: Wasn't it, though? And what's the moral resolve of that? Jacob scolds them for it and says, "You have made me odious in the eyes of all the people

around here, and if they decide to attack us, they could kill us because we are few and they are many."

And the sons say, "What, our sister should be treated like a whore?" And that's the end of it. [*Groth laughs.*] So what lesson are we supposed to gain? What's the moral inspiration? What is God telling us there, if it's the word of God?

Groth: Have you come to a conclusion? Have you resolved that yourself?

Crumb: It's like, pay no attention to the man behind the curtain. It's obvious from the re-solve that it's not the word of God, it's some ancient crazy fuckin' tribal shit [*laughter*]: some guys defending their sister's honor.

Groth: I was quite taken aback by that.

Crumb: I think that when modern religious people read the Bible for inspira-tion, they just pass over stuff like that. I read a lot of commentary about Genesis. In the Jewish Publication Society version it's full of commentaries from different scholars over centuries. And like the story of Abraham tell-ing his wife Sarah to tell the pharaoh that she's his sister. The explanations by these scholars who are also religious believers, trying to give that story some moral justification, just bending over backwards trying to figure out what God meant to tell us in that story or what the real meaning of that is. Because it *has* to — it's the Bible; it has to have a higher moral purpose, right? When in fact it doesn't: How 'bout it?

So I would say in that way, by literally illustrating all of that stuff, there is a slightly subversive quality to it. As you say, secular interpretation. It's slightly subversive to *show* a story like that, illustrate it, literally show it. What it's really about. And it's very hard to give any moral rationale to a story like that. And then in my commentary in the back of the book I bring up Savina Teubal, this Israeli woman writer, and her explanation for those stories, for the "she's my sister" routine, and how her reasons make much more cogent sense than any of the previous explanations that I've come across, and she wrote this stuff in the 1980s. It's probably the first time any-one has ever examined that stuff from that matrilineal, matriarchal angle. I think she's probably right about it.

TOP

From *Weirdo* #19 (Winter 1986-1987) [©1987 R. Crumb]

33

...AND THEY KILLED EVERY MALE.

AND HAMOR AND SHECHEM HIS SON THEY KILLED BY THE EDGE OF THE SWORD.

Groth: Obviously the matrilineal angle interested you quite a bit. How much research did you do prior to finding her book, Sarah the Priestess?

Crumb: Well, I'd read a lot. And then there's this woman in Oregon, this really interesting woman — Kelpie Wilson is her name — I told her I was working on Genesis, and she's like this really strong feminist woman, and she sent me Savina Teubal's book, and said, "You should read this." And I read that thing and it really excited me. I was *shaking* when I read that book. It was so incredible what she reveals. I was turning the pages, reading as fast as I could the first time I read it, and I went back and read it over again two or three times. She really did her homework. For what it's worth, as far as the Bible's concerned, it's really significant what she comes up with. I haven't spent a lifetime studying the Bible so I'm not a Bible scholar or anything, but on the other hand, some of the stuff I've read, the scholarly stuff ... If people basically start from the point of believing it's the word of God, then right away I think they're very hampered and crippled from examining the text in a disinterested way and analyzing it correctly. It's a big handicap to start from that premise, that it's the word of God. Because then you have to constantly rationalize: "What does God mean here? What is God trying to tell us?" That's just ridiculous.

Groth: When you say you're a non-believer, does that mean you're an agnostic or an atheist, or what?

Crumb: I'm a Gnostic.

Groth: A Gnostic.

"I told a lot of reporters that I was a Gnostic and they'd never heard of it, so they'd write, 'Crumb says he's an agnostic.'"

Crumb: Yeah. I told a lot of reporters that I was a Gnostic and they'd never heard of it, so they'd write, "Crumb says he's an agnostic." [*Groth laughs.*] I'm not an agnostic, I'm a Gnostic. But that's only a loose definition. I'm sure there're official Gnostics out there who'd say, "You're not a real Gnostic! You're just throwing that word around!" And that's true, I am. I'm sure there's some very specific definition of a Gnostic, but my rough, crude definition of a Gnostic is someone who's interested in the idea of higher spiritual existence or being or reality — a greater reality that you could call divine, you could call it God, you can call it the great spirit, all-that-is, whatever you want. But I'm interested in that, and I spend time studying that and seeking that, and seeking communication with it, a connection with it: the higher reality. So I call that Gnosticism.

Groth: Gnosticism indicates that you do believe in a god or gods.

Crumb: A god?

Groth: A god or gods, yeah.

Crumb: Well, look at it this way. Would you agree that we live in a reality that's a unified field?

Groth: [Pause.] Sure. I'll go that far.

Crumb: Everything's interconnected, right? Every time you breathe you affect the universe.

Groth: That's right.

Crumb: So if it's all a unified field, it's all one. And that means that we are all part of some giant entity, some kind of organism, whatever you want to call it, and it's huge and vast, and beyond our comprehension because we can't know what's going on everywhere all the time. We can't. We can't even know what's going on in the house next door let alone out there in the billions of stars and planets. So it's bigger than we can possibly, in our little limited human existence, understand fully. But at the same time, something in us wants to know, something has a desire for knowledge. That's where "gnosis" actually comes from, "knowledge." So it's seeking after that knowledge that's interesting. We all have some interest in that, but we get stuck in dogmatic, doctrinal thinking, which makes us feel secure. It's like building a wall around yourself, against the unknown, you know? And people feel secure inside that wall. It's familiar, always the same. And then of course, you've got people who take advantage of that fear of the unknown to put themselves in positions of power. Something like the Catholic church, or any priesthood, or political entities, corporate entities that will use some kind of fixed beliefs to try to control people. I grew up in the Catholic Church, so I know what that's all about.

So that's a lot of what's happened to something like the Bible. A long time ago they started using that text as a way to clobber people over the head with these narrow, fixed beliefs. Since the time it was written down and turned into a sacred scroll, and became the *raison d'être* of the Hebrew people.

Groth: How do you think your Catholic upbringing affected your perception of Genesis?

Crumb: I'm not sure ... maybe. We had that standard image of God as the severe patriarch with the long white beard. That was in a lot of the books we looked at. But in the Catholic Church you're not actually encouraged to read the Bible. They teach you the catechism and the rules and regulations of the church, and the Sunday mass and all that, and the seven sacraments and blah blah blah. I remember we had a book when I was in fourth grade: *Stories From the Bible.* They rewrote the stories because it's too tedious to read the original and that's about the extent of familiarity with the Bible when you're raised Catholic.

Groth: You never read Genesis as a kid, right?

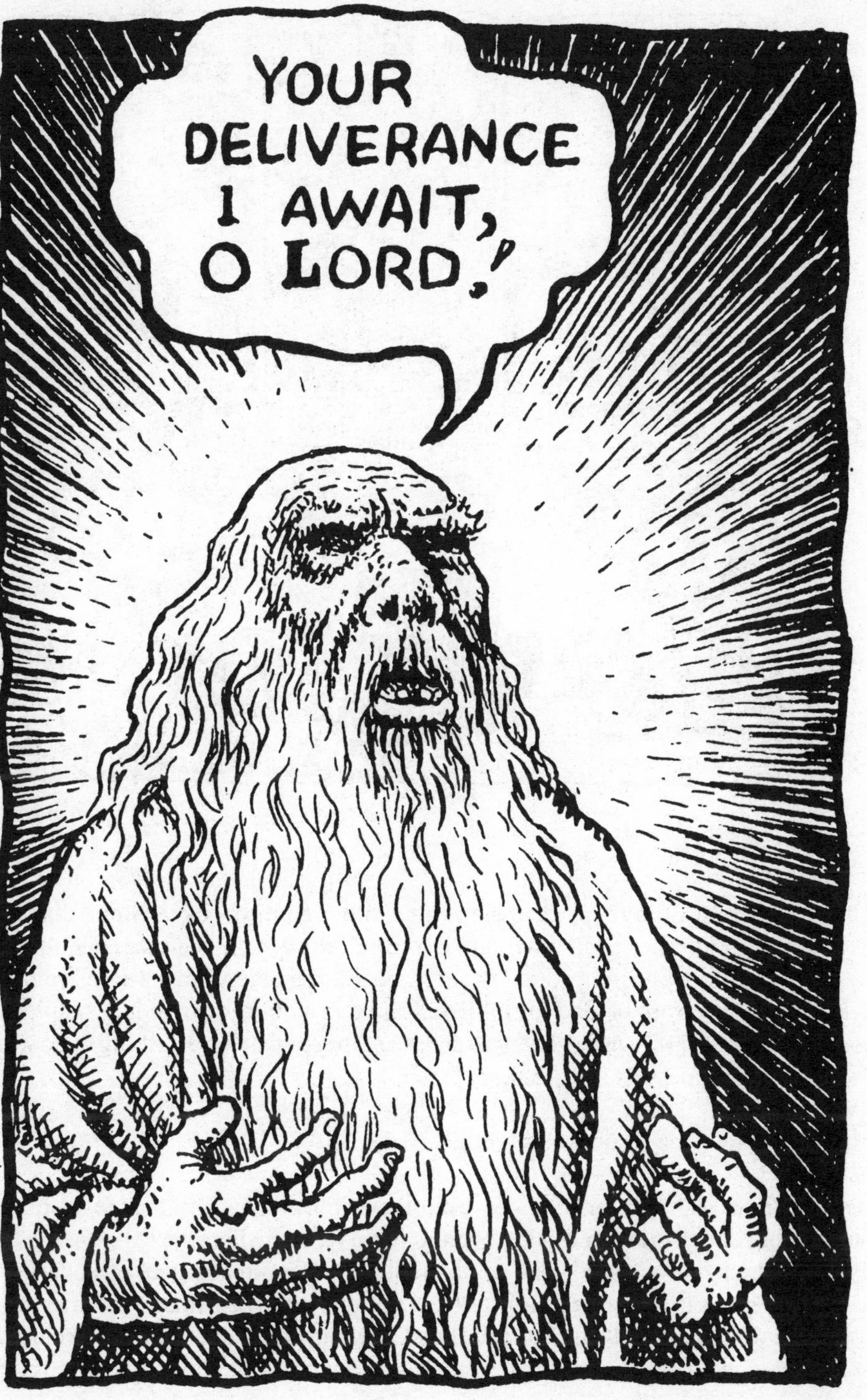
YOUR DELIVERANCE I AWAIT, O LORD!

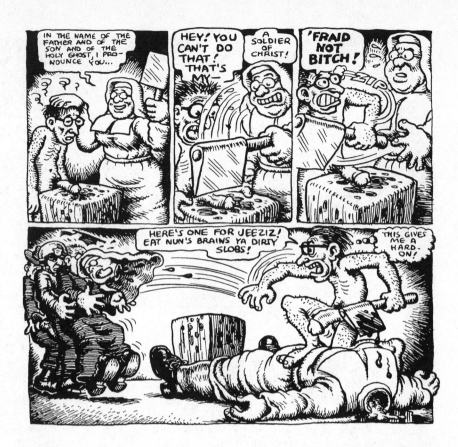

Crumb: No. It's funny that the various other comic book versions that I've seen of it, they're all rewritten. In the EC *Picture Stories From the Bible*, there's a big pompous introduction at the beginning about how "we're bringing the holy word of God to children," and then you read it and it's completely rewritten! [*Laughter.*] There're pages and pages that have nothing to do with the original text [*Groth laughs*].

Groth: And badly drawn as I recall.

Crumb: Yeah, it's terrible. I have another Bible comic from the '70s. Not the big one that Pete gave me, but another one, a smaller, thicker one. It's the whole thing, I think, the whole Bible, and I was reading an episode from Genesis in it, and I thought "Wait a minute, did I miss this in the original?" I went back and checked and there're whole pages of stuff that have nothing to do with the original at all. It's funny, this thing that I did seems like an obvious thing to do, but nobody's ever done it before: an unabridged, comic version following the original text; it's a simple, straightforward task to set yourself. You're on a track, you just have to illustrate the text as it's written to the best of your ability, as closely as possible, and in order to interpret it as closely as possible, you must read a lot of background material and understand something about the context of it, to some degree. And really study Cecil B. DeMille's *The Ten Commandments* very closely. [*Laughter.*]

Groth: You know, I was slightly appalled to have heard that you studied that movie closely.

Crumb: Oh, you snob.

Groth: C'mon, talk about schmaltz.

Crumb: Take a look at it closely. Freeze-frame the scenes from the Exodus, where they're leaving Egypt and look at the detail; it's marvelous. They did an incredible job on the details in that film.

Groth: Now, you're talking about the set designs?

Crumb: The set designs, the costumes, the clothing on the people: such a rich variety of people in the Exodus scene. There's a woman carrying a cage full of chickens on her head. There're mules pulling a cart with big terracotta urns tied to it: just great detail. Full of rich, very well-thought-out, very well-produced detail, the whole movie. All those sets in Egypt: those aren't computer generated, that's all fuckin' real. The only thing that's fake is the parting of the Red Sea. It looks very fake. But the avenue of the lion statues, or whatever, sphinx statues, they built all that! It's incredible. Incredible.

Groth: And do you think all that stuff was accurately recreated?

Crumb: I dunno. I dunno how accurate. [*Groth laughs.*] Probably as accurate as anybody could do. I thought that the scenes in the poor part of the village were pretty Disneyland-looking, pretty fakey-looking. They show these people that are supposed to be poor sitting at a table. I don't think poor people had tables then. They sat on the floor. Tables were for rich people only. But still, I studied very closely the costumes of the Egyptian people and used a lot of that for my illustrations. Pete Poplaski was very helpful. He freeze-framed and took hundreds of photos from that movie and a couple other biblical epics, a couple of later ones that he found that are really low-budget and chintzy-looking. Compared to Cecil DeMille they were really chintzy. But even there, it's a comic book so I thought, "There's no way to find accurate, historically precise pictures of how people really dressed then. There's no way to know. These movies, these Hollywood versions — it'll do, close enough. What the hell, it's just a comic book."[Laughs.]

Groth: I found it hard to believe that all that armor that Yul Brynner was wearing could possibly have been accurate. It just looked cheesy and Hollywoodized to me.

Crumb: Sure. Absolutely. But it's close enough; it works. I'm sure that in many ways, those illustrations I did were not historically accurate. In fact, as I progressed, I became more educated that way and I started to realize as I got toward the end and it was too late to go back and change it, that probably the early semi-nomadic Hebrews and other people who wandered around with their herds of animals and lived in tents — we're talking 2000 B.C. here, the time of Abraham and Jacob and all those people — I realized toward the end that, oh yeah, they didn't actually dress like modern desert-dwelling Arabs with those long robes and all that stuff as I depicted them. They probably dressed more like the ancient Aztecs.

Groth: Well, Teubal argues that Genesis is closer to myth than reality. And if that's the case, then that kind of historical perfection is probably less important.

Crumb: Yeah, that's right. That's one of the attitudes that I took on: that historical accuracy is not the most important thing actually.

Groth: You could drive yourself insane trying to get that right.

Crumb: Yeah, you could. It could take forever. I spent a lot of time looking at ancient visual imagery from Egypt and Mesopotamia. And in Mesopotamia there's not much going all the way back to 2000 B.C.; there's not much visual stuff. There's some Sumerian stuff, not much. Sumerian-Akkadian visual imagery is very limited. In all the books, you come across the same images over and over because there's a limited amount of it. Egyptian,

40

there's more, but it's so highly stylized, it's very hard to extrapolate, to apply it to illustrating scenes of everyday life.

Groth: The drawing in *Genesis* is so illustrative, it's so different from what a lot of people expect from you. One thing I wanted to ask you about is your slow evolution toward drawing more realistically. You said, in some interview I read that you "started trying to draw realistically in the late '70s. I was trying to learn to draw a more realistic style." And I remembered that you did a lot of proto-*Genesis* work in the '80s. You adapted *Psychopathia Sexualis* in '85, you drew a Charley Patton story in '85.

Crumb: I did classic-comic-type things, yeah.

Groth: Right. Jelly Roll Morton ...

TOP
From "Patton"
in *Zap* #11
[©1985 R. Crumb]

Crumb: Phillip K. Dick.

Groth: Phillip K. Dick in '86.

Crumb: I did the Kafka thing in the early '90s.

Groth: Right, so you seemed to be moving in that direction in fits and starts. You were also doing your more big-foot style and things like *Mystic Funnies* and *Hup*, but you were simultaneously working in a more realistic mode. So I assume it wasn't that discomforting for you to take that to the nth degree.

Crumb: No it wasn't, but I set myself a very hard task. I didn't realize how grueling it was gonna be when I said I would do it. It was very hard. No one will ever know. [*Laughter.*] They won't ever know how much white-out I used.

Groth: Was it hard to inhibit your more exuberant, cartoony side?

Crumb: No, uh-uh. Not at all. But I just had to learn fuckin' anatomy, that's all. [*Laughs.*]
In the first 50 pages I did, I was correcting anatomy with white-out *so often*, because I thought, "Oh shit, look at that, I made his arms way too long for the body," and "Oh my God, look how short I made his legs," etc., etc.. "Look how awkward that pose is, ridiculous." So I made a lot of corrections, lots of corrections.

Groth: As literal as you tried to be, you still had to do a lot of interpretation because there's ambiguity in the work.

Crumb: The text is often very terse. When they say that God was angry at the human race and its evil ways, and He was going to destroy them with a flood, it doesn't tell you what the evil ways are. It doesn't tell you what exactly made God so angry. What were people doing that was so bad? Well, I basically made it up. I'd just show some really bad shit, some bad behavior. I just had to think that up on my own. And there's lots of stuff like that where you just have to fill in the missing bits, and I was very careful about that; I didn't want to take too much liberty that way. I didn't want to get on any kind of polemic of my own in those instances, where I had that freedom of interpretation. I usually took the conservative route with that.

Groth: Right. But you obviously had to visualize that, and that does change the reader's reading experience. Because instead of him —

Crumb: … Imagining his own view of human evil.

Groth: That's right; you do it for him with your view of human evil.

Crumb: In that one version of Genesis that Pete lent me, that comic-book version illustrated by that Latin American guy, [*probably Nestor Redondo*] he shows the evils of Sodom and Gomorrah, why God is down on Sodom and Gomorrah, which is a big panel, a big splash panel showing a town square with lots of things going on, small figures doing bad things. And what are they doing? They're all just having fun. There's like a couple making out, there's some people gambling, there's some people that are drunk. So that's his interpretation of it. He's probably Catholic, you know? They're just enjoying themselves. [*Laughter.*] So my Sodom and Gomorrah, I mean the only way I could show bad stuff is to show people hurting each other: people doing really nasty shit to each other.

LEFT
Crumb is likely
referring to *Limited
Collector's Edition* Vol. 4
C-36 (Jun.-July 1975):
The Bible, written by
Sheldon Mayer, art by
Nestor Redondo and
Joe Kubert. [©1975
DC Comics]

AND THE EARTH WAS CORRUPT BEFORE GOD, AND THE EARTH WAS FILLED WITH OUTRAGE. AND GOD LOOKED UPON THE EARTH AND, BEHOLD, IT WAS CORRUPT, FOR ALL FLESH HAD CORRUPTED ITS WAYS UPON THE EARTH.

Groth: Well now, do you think that does some damage to the text in the sense that it forecloses people's imagination?

Crumb: That was one criticism that was given in one review. It was ... who was that guy?

Groth: I think it might have been Robert Alter's.

Crumb: It wasn't Alter. Who was it? This other old guy that —

Groth: Harold Bloom?

Crumb: Harold Bloom! Yeah, him. He said — maybe it *was* Alter — that it precludes people's own imagination of the text. Any illustrated text is gonna do that, sorry. Y'know? OK, go back and read the original then if you want to let your own imagination play out. [*Groth laughs.*] But I think that appropriating the imagination can be carried too far, like with Disney doing *Winnie the Pooh* or something: It really robs *Winnie the Pooh* of a lot of its original mood and feeling and charm. Putting the Disney take on something …Or *Alice in Wonderland*, you know? Although I thought Disney's *Alice in Wonderland* was a masterpiece in itself, but if you see that and then go back and read Lewis Carroll [*laughs*], if you grew up on the Disney version, it's hard to go to Lewis Carroll. So that can be taken too far, robbing people of their imagination. But comic books? I don't think so. But I thought about that while I was working on it, too.

Groth: I mean it's still reductionist. You're still reducing something that's open to multiple forms of …

Crumb: Imagining?

Groth: Imagination, yeah. And thereby restricting the reader's imagination, in a way.

Crumb: Yes, you are. You're right.

Groth: And you considered that an acceptable artistic risk.

Crumb: I don't think that that condemns the job, you know? But it is a downside, yeah. On the other hand, that's a hard text to get through. To read the text of Genesis all the way through, to have the patience for it, to let your imagination play with it is a hard job, too hard a job for most people. And most people are not going to bother to do that unless they have a scholarly interest or they're religious (and if they're religious, then their imagination has already been robbed by the people that pushed their face in it to begin with). There're things that they're not allowed to imagine, and if they're gonna continue to believe in the religious part of it, they have to stop themselves from thinking certain things. So already they're screwed. [*Laughs.*] So other than that, there's not a whole lot of people who are going to, in a disinterested manner, read the Bible and let their imagination go with it. So I don't feel too bad about robbing people's imaginations of the pleasure of thinking up their own ways that Sodom and Gomorrah were evil.

Groth: You illustrate every single passage in the book. Was it difficult to find an inspired image for each one of those? And how did you deal with the ones that were difficult to do?

Crumb: With a lot of them, at first it seemed impossible. I said, "How the hell am I going to illustrate this?" And I had to rack my brains, and I eventually came up with something for everything. The begots for instance, were very hard.

> "If every begot is illustrated, then people see the significance of that, too; a big significant part of the whole thing is this reading out of the generations, you know?"

Groth: I wanted to ask you about that. It seems to me like one of the dangers is that if you can't be excited about the visual potential of every passage or scene, and in the case of those you aren't, you're just going to slog your way through it. You're just going to come up with something because you've got to move on to the next passage, to the next panel. And that can result in images that you're not entirely satisfied with, or ...

Crumb: Well, you don't want any throwaway images; that's for certain, so you have to come up with something interesting for everything. If you're going to illustrate it, it's got to be interesting. So yeah, that was a challenge. That was the hardest stuff to get through. Stuff like the begots, the family lineages, trying to think of something interesting for each of those. I didn't want to have any really huge blocks of unillustrated text. Sometimes I was tempted to just have a half a page of text. So-and-so begot so-and-so, and he begot so-and-so — just make a big half-page of text there. But I thought, "No, no, that's cheating; don't do that." There were a couple times where I did make a large block of text that just listed names. But mostly I tried to force myself to think of some way to illustrate my way through that. And also I think that the begots are important enough to actually break it down so people have to read through it. They can't skip over it. If every begot is illustrated, then people see the significance of that, too; a big significant part of the whole thing is this reading out of the generations, you know? And when I got to the part where they're telling about those chieftains, boy that

AND THESE ARE THE CHIEFTAINS OF ESAU BY THEIR CLANS AND PLACES NAME BY NAME...

...THE CHIEFTAIN OF TIMNA...

...THE CHIEFTAIN ALVAH...

...THE CHIEFTAIN JETHETH...

...THE CHIEFTAIN OF O-HOLIBAMAH...

...THE CHIEFTAIN ELAH...

...THE CHIEFTAIN PINON...

...THE CHIEFTAIN KENAZ...

...THE CHIEFTAIN TEMAN...

...THE CHIEFTAIN MIBZAR...

...THE CHIEFTAIN MAGDIEL...

...THE CHIEFTAIN IRAM.

THESE ARE THE CHIEFTAINS OF EDOM BY THEIR SETTLEMENTS IN THE LAND OF THEIR STRONGHOLDS — THAT IS, ESAU, FATHER OF EDOM.

was tough. I had to make those little postage stamp-size portraits of each one of those chieftains. There's like 50 of 'em or something like that.

Groth: Yeah, and I noticed that each and every one of those was unique.

Crumb: Yeah, hell yeah. [*Laughs.*]

Groth: That must have been incredibly grueling.

Crumb: Well it was grueling in one way, and yet in another way not, because I didn't have to think of ways to have them doing anything. You just show their face. So I just sifted through all of my source material for faces.

Groth: Did you not find the redundancy between the captions and the dialogue somewhat frustrating?

Crumb: No, it didn't bother me.

Groth: It's in opposition to what you might call good cartooning, when you have someone saying something and then a caption saying, "He said, 'such and such.'"

Crumb: I made a conscious decision to keep in all the "and he said," "and she said," "and he said to him."

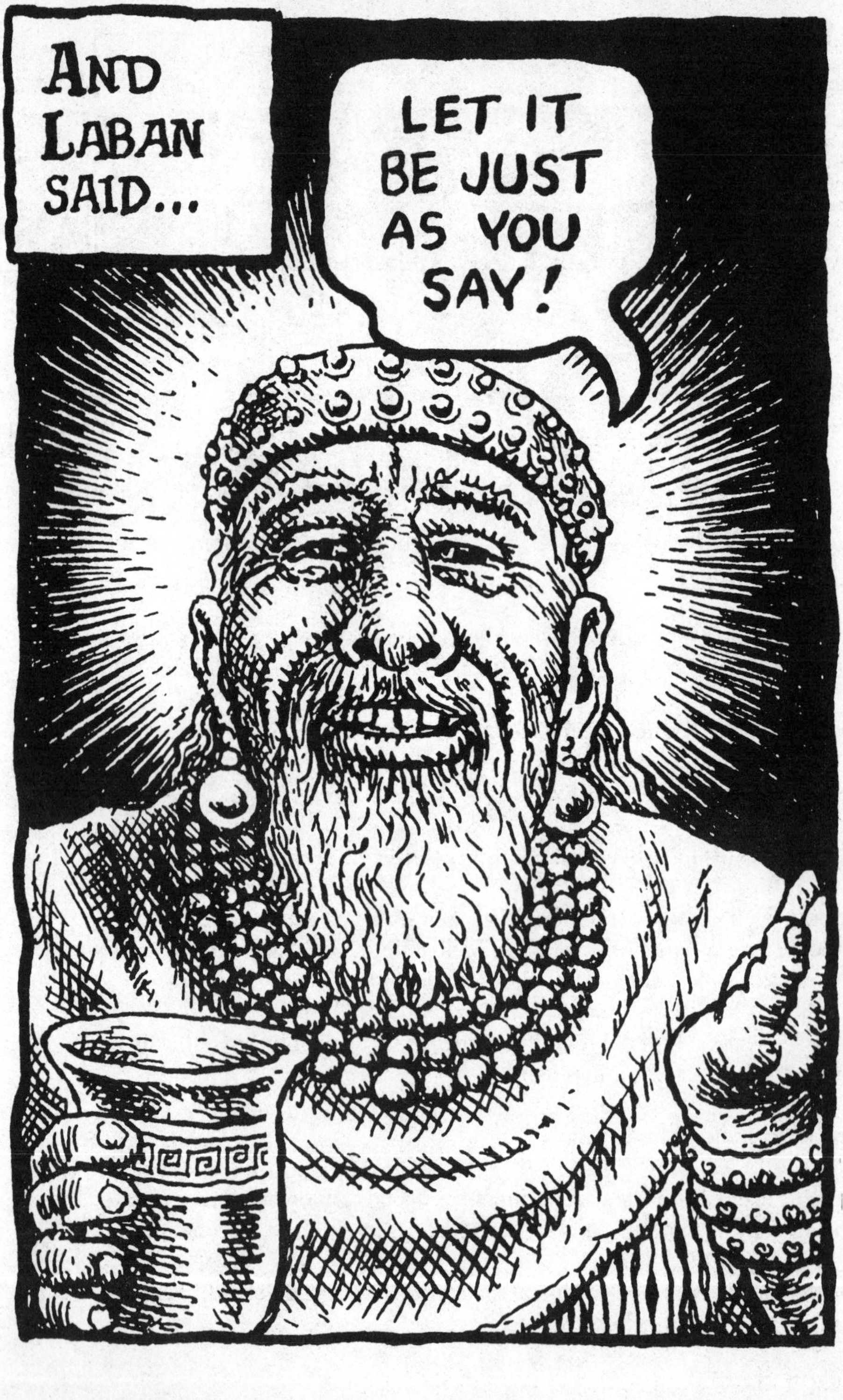
AND LABAN SAID...
LET IT BE JUST AS YOU SAY!

Groth: Why did you feel it necessary to do that? Since "he" clearly is saying it in your illustrated version.

Crumb: I decided to make a rule not to leave out any of the text. There's only one place in the book where I left out "And he said." It was where Jacob is wrestling with the angel. At the end he says something like, "Why do you ask me my name?" There's supposed to be a "he said" there and I just forgot, accidentally left it out.

Groth: Oh, I see, OK. [Laughter.]

Crumb: You don't notice when you're reading it, because as you say it's illustrated. You don't have to have "and he said."

Groth: Right. Well you also left out two words: "and Bethuel."

Crumb: That I left out deliberately for a different reason. That was not an accident: That was deliberate. Because in the notations it shows that Bethuel wasn't there. Obviously he wasn't there. It was a priestly insertion later to put Bethuel in there for their own reasons [*Groth laughs*], because the patriarchal imperative required that he be there.

Groth: Right, required a little copyediting.

Crumb: Yeah, that's right. I decided, "Fuck it, I'm going to leave that out. It doesn't belong there; it doesn't make any sense for it to be there." 'Cause he's not there.

Illustration Versus Cartooning

Groth: There's a school of thought that says that illustration is antithetical to cartooning. *Prince Valiant* is the quintessential example of something that's closer to an illustrated text than a comic, and your Book of Genesis is clearly in the *Prince Valiant* tradition of the illustrated narrative.

Crumb: Who says illustration is antithetical to cartooning? What do you call, let's say, Alex Raymond? What do you call Wallace Wood? Milton Caniff? I don't know. Where do you draw the line? What's illustration and what's cartooning? Where does the line exist?

Groth: You don't feel that way at all? You don't think there is any such demarcation?

THEY HURRY FROM THE ACCURSED PLACE....AND WHEN THEY LOOK BACK AGAIN THE EVIL TOWER IS CRUMBLING INTO THE FLAMES.

MOST OF THE NATIVE STOKERS ARE DAZED BY THE SUDDEN TURN OF EVENTS — BUT ONE HAS CREPT AROUND BEHIND TERRY AND PAT...

Crumb: I don't get it. I don't understand what they're talking about when they say that, "antithetical to cartooning." I mean, OK, Hal Foster is a little bit stiff, a little bit stilted-looking. He's a stiff illustrator, so his stuff looks illustrational. It looks like children's book illustration; it doesn't look like "comics." And he never used dialogue balloons, did he?

Groth: No, no, it was all captions underneath with quotation marks.

Crumb: So, yeah. He was just kind of stiff so his stuff looks very illustrational.

Groth: The argument is that someone like Foster is just not using the vocabulary of comics to the best advantage.

Crumb: Well, I like to look at Hal Foster's stuff. It's a little stiff, but I enjoy looking at it. Cartooning has a lot of leeway. It's a broad spectrum of approaches — huge. Could you say illustration is antithetical to painting? Y'know, cartooning, what is cartooning? Is it just putting images in a sequence? There's lots of ways to do that: lots of ways, from the crudest Aline Kominsky approach all the way up to Hal Foster.

Groth: But you wouldn't draw any qualitative distinctions — I mean in terms of cartooning itself — between someone like Roy Crane and someone like Hal Foster?

Crumb: Qualitative distinction? What do you mean? Like if one is better than the other?

TOP LEFT
Hal Foster's July 26, 1942 *Prince Valiant* strip [©1942 King Features Syndicate, Inc.]

TOP RIGHT
Milton Caniff's Jan. 30, 1936 *Terry and the Pirates* strip [©1936 Tribune Media Services, Inc.]

Groth: That one constitutes better cartooning than the other.

Crumb: They each have their strong points: like Milton Caniff, a great example of a masterful illustrator who took to the comic-book medium very well. I've also said a few times I'm not sure that in doing a really long work like *Genesis* that all that crosshatching is helpful. It might have been better if I had used a brush and done a lot of more stark black and white, you know? Reading pages and pages of all that heavy, detailed crosshatching, it's a lot to look at it; the eye might get fatigued, bogged down, I don't know. I'm not sure. And comic books and cartooning lends itself to abbreviated drawing styles, certainly. You have *Peanuts*: it's very minimal, but it certainly works.

Groth: That's one of its virtues, isn't it? That abbreviated style?

Crumb: Well, there're other people who use abbreviated styles that are stupid and lame and don't work at all. It just dumb-looking. Like *Dilbert* or something, it's terrible. So it's not just that it's minimal. Schulz certainly made it work. So again, there's a broad spectrum of different ways of doing cartooning. But all that crosshatching, it's very heavy. If Brueghel was gonna do a comic book, would he really bother with all that detail in every panel? I dunno. I guess there's something to be said for a more simplified and readable style when you're drawing comic pages. Black and white works really well: lots of black and white. Too much gray and detail and crosshatching, it's burdensome. Maybe. I dunno, maybe I'm wrong.

TOP LEFT
Charles Schulz' July 27, 1971 *Peanuts* comic strip [©1971 United Features Syndicate, Inc.]

TOP RIGHT
From Scott Adams' *Dilbert* collection *Journey to Cubeville* [©1998 United Features Syndicate, Inc.]

Groth: Well, when you say it's burdensome, I think that's what I'm trying to get at. That it's ...

Crumb: Hard on the eye, wearying to the eye.

Groth: Yeah, in the context of cartooning, that kind of thing can be oppressive, in a way.

Crumb: I don't know: I'm not sure. I can't help myself when I've got that pen in my hand. I doodle every fucking detail to death, but it might not be helpful to the reader.

Groth: But you have your big-foot approach too, which has so much less of that.

Crumb: Yeah, but I hardly ever do that any more. My drawing basically got increasingly baroque over the years. More and more detail, I kept working slower, and a certain simplicity and lightness got lost in the process.

Groth: Do you think that's a function of age, or what?

Crumb: Yeah, possibly, yeah. A certain spontaneity is lost. The early stuff looks much more light-hearted, and probably more fun.

Groth: A greater exuberance.

Crumb: Yeah. Yeah. Maybe, ultimately, that might be better. I don't know. When I first started doing *Weirdo* in the '80s, I got a lot of criticism from people saying that the drawing was heavy, and laden down with a seriousness and heaviness that my earlier stuff didn't have, and they didn't like that. People like Cat Yronwode didn't like it. Your pal [R.] Fiore didn't like it.

Groth: I thought that you still retained your essential cartooning center during your *Weirdo* period. You combined the two approaches felicitously.

Crumb: I hope so. I can't judge.

Groth: Which I don't think you did in *Genesis*, in which you very purposefully have made that decision. There're these fine distinctions between cartoony work. I don't want to say big-foot exactly, because it's more than that. But a more cartoony or elastic approach to drawing.

Crumb: It just doesn't apply in something like *Genesis*. If you're gonna do a serious illustrated version of Genesis...

Groth: It would've been inappropriate.

Crumb: Yeah, you gotta take the Classics Illustrated approach, basically.

Groth: It seems like you took particular delight in drawing landscapes.

Crumb: Yeah, I did.

Groth: I thought they were just exceptionally stunning.

Crumb: Yeah? Good, good. Well, you're the first person who said that.

Groth: Am I? [Laughs]. It seems pretty obvious.

Crumb: The landscapes were pleasing. I looked at lots of photos in *National Geographic* and other places of that region of the world. There are parts of Africa that are probably similar to Mesopotamia that I used for the vegetation and rocky hills and stuff like that.

Groth: It occurs to me that you could not entirely mitigate a certain essential Crumbness to your drawing, or your vision, in Genesis no

AND THE MEN AROSE FROM THERE AND LOOKED OUT OVER SODOM, AND ABRAHAM WALKED WITH THEM TO SEE THEM ON THEIR WAY.

matter how much you might've tried. And that was particularly true of the women.

Crumb: Harold Bloom said that "the women were dreadful." [*Groth laughs.*]

Groth: Both Harold Bloom and Robert Alter commented on this.

Crumb: [*Laughter.*] Sorry about that. The way I draw women is not the most popular way; not the cute little sexy nymphs, I hate to tell ya.

Groth: Did you try? Did you experiment and try to draw women differently than you normally do?

Crumb: Why would I do that? [*Laughs.*]

Groth: Well, to honor the text.

Crumb: The text doesn't — OK, the text does say that they were *comely*.

Groth: Right, there you go.

Crumb: But who's to say what their standards were? I mean if you look at the Venus of Willendorf, come on. [*Laughs.*] So I mean, their standards — they could have really liked thick-limbed and big-assed women, I dunno. Who knows. There's this movie made by a Mongolian director — did you see that? Written and made by Mongolians, it's the legend of Genghis Khan. And there are quite a few times when they talk about how they really like women with strong legs. [*Laughter.*]

Groth: A whole race of Crumbs.

Crumb: So yeah, who knows what their standards were, what was "comely" to the ancient Hebrews?!

Groth: Well, both Alter and Bloom had amusing things to say about that...

TOP
Photo of the Venus
of Willendorf [©Ali
Meyer, the Bridge-
man Art Library]

Crumb: Yeah, but they're both middle-class Jewish-Americans. And we all know that middle-class Jewish-American men like skinny women.

Groth: Is that true?

Crumb: Yeah. They all like skinny women. Basically they like what I call the "mousy shiksa." That's what they like. Virtually all of them!

Groth: I wasn't aware of that.

Crumb: They don't like their own zaftig big Jewish women, they don't like that. They're in flight from their Jewish mothers.

Groth: You were quoted as saying, "I'm not very good at drawing attractive women, actually."

Crumb: No, I'm not. It's hard. Actually there aren't very many artists who can really do it well. Not many. It's a science in itself. Again, the Hernandez brothers, you know? They're really right there with that.

Groth: Yeah, they sure are.

Crumb: And they can draw all types of women, all physical types of women. It's incredible what they do.

Groth: Yeah, yeah I agree.

Crumb: I admire that, but I have a problem with it. I've tried to figure out how to draw an attractive woman, God knows!

Groth: Let me ask you a little about the process. First of all, could you describe to me how you can be so undeviatingly focused on a single creative project? I remember you once commented to me — I don't know if you did this in an interview or just in a personal conversation — but you said something to me to the effect that you couldn't even conceive of doing a story more than 15 or 20 pages long.

55

TOP
From "Duck Feet Part Two" in Palomar: The Heartbreak Soup Stories [©1986 Gilbert Hernandez]

Crumb: It's true, when I was young, I couldn't.

Groth: And this is, obviously, the most monumental task you ever —

Crumb: Two-hundred-and-one pages. [*Laughter.*]

Groth: So how did you — I don't know if I'm asking you to tell me how you psychologically did this — but how did you bear down and focus on such an enormous project, something so different from anything you've done before?

Crumb: Well, I'm older. I have more patience. I went into isolation to get it done, and I really enjoyed that isolation. I enjoyed that, immensely.

Groth: Tell me about that. Aline found a *gite* [small French rental vacation house or apartment] near where you worked. You felt you couldn't do it in your studio at home?

Crumb: I tried. I realized: "There's too much going on here every day. This place is like a business office, and I just can't concentrate. This thing's gonna take so much concentration to do."
Aline figured out, "You're not advancing! You got five pages done in the last four months!"
I said, "Yeah, I know, I know."
"So I'm gonna find you a place up in the mountains so you can really get started on it." And she did, she found a place way up in the hills, and no one knew where I was. Only she knew. She brought me groceries on the weekends. It was a fully equipped little house. I loved it. I stayed there for months; it was great. So then I came home, had a bunch of business I had to attend to at home that took several weeks. Then I went back to another place in isolation. And basically I did that five times over the four-year period. Went to an isolated place where no one knew who I was.

Groth: For a month at a time each?

Crumb: Yeah.

Groth: [Laughs]. She would bring food and slip it under the door, or something?

Crumb: She'd bring food, and you know, hang out for the weekend or something and then go home. And the last place was in a village far away from here. So I could walk to this grocery store, but I didn't know anybody there, so I was basically for all practical purposes in isolation.

But that was the first time since I was quite young that I've experienced that much isolation. I really enjoyed it; it really cleared my head and I had so much more energy to work. Because there were no interruptions, there was no nothing. Took along a couple books to read. Of course, I had to take along boxes of stuff: art supplies, and all my source material, and books and shit. And work equipment. Otherwise, it was quite simple to do; it just cost some money. But it was well worth it. I never would have gotten the job done otherwise. Never would have got it done. And having that isolation really helped; I enjoyed it so much that it made it possible to get through the work. As I said, once I got into it I realized what a much larger task it was gonna be than I had assumed when I said yes to it. I felt almost a kind of dread at having to do it. And the years went by, and I plowed on and on and on, and I remember when I got to the last panel, the funeral procession of Joseph, [*Groth laughs*], I couldn't believe I was actually working on the last panel. I couldn't believe it. Of course there was still weeks of work making corrections after that, but when I actually got to the end of it. "Oh my God." It was like the meeting of the Union Pacific and Southern Pacific railroads in 1869.

HE HAD BARELY FINISHED SPEAKING WHEN, BEHOLD, REBEKAH WAS COMING OUT, WHO WAS BORN TO BETHUEL, SON OF MILCAH, THE WIFE OF ABRAHAM'S BROTHER, NAHOR, WITH HER JUG ON HER SHOULDER.

Groth: Right, you can see the light at the end of that tunnel.

Crumb: Yeah, it was incredible. And then I sent photocopies of the whole thing to Norton, and they had their proofreader — this guy named Trent Duffy — who was an incredible proofreader. He found hundreds of small textual errors that I had made. Including three places where I had accidentally left out blocks of text.

Groth: Oh my God.

Crumb: I know, so I had to go back. Fortunately, I was able to squeeze in all the text I had left out without having to redraw any pages. I was able to fix it by enlarging the dialogue balloons in several panels on one page and a couple panels on two other pages.

Groth: Were you tempted to take an occasional detour while you were working on the book and do something completely different?

Crumb: Well, I did. I did some small jobs in between working on it — nothing real big, actually a whole bunch of small jobs over that four-year period.

Groth: Were those necessary breaks?

Crumb: Well, yeah. It was good to take a break. I was, at several points, fairly sick of the text. When you work on anything that closely — you're taking some other text, somebody else's work, or something like that — and you examine it while you're working on it that closely, and it deconstructs itself. You see through it; it becomes transparent, what it's really about. And that kind of familiarity can be sickening [Groth laughs]. Nauseating.

Groth: As grueling as the regimen sounds, did you take, and do you take generally, pleasure in the act of drawing?

Crumb: I'm obsessive-compulsive; I don't really call that pleasure. It's like cleaning the sink with a toothbrush — is that pleasurable? I guess, in a way. [Laughs.]

Groth: Did you derive the same kind of pleasure drawing *Genesis* as you have drawing in the past?

Crumb: Of drawing comics?

Groth: Yeah.

Crumb: I don't know, I don't know if I can even answer that question. It's complicated. Did I used to enjoy drawing? I can't remember. [Laughter.]

Groth: Well, that would certainly indicate you don't now.

Crumb: I think that I was put at the task of drawing at such a young age by my brother Charles, and I'm such a dysfunctional geek in the world, that drawing was my lifeline to staying alive in the world. It was more like drawing out of necessity, not for fun so much, more like necessity.

Groth: I would assume also you don't want it to be a routine-ized habit. In other words, you want to derive some palpable pleasure or reward from of it.

Crumb: I don't know if it's pleasure so much as it has to stay interesting. It has to stay interesting and challenging. Pleasure? I derive pleasure from listening to music. [*Laughs.*] Or, you know, sex or something.

Groth: You can neither listen to music nor have sex while you're drawing, correct?

Crumb: No. [*Groth laughs.*]

Groth: I was surprised to learn, actually, that you don't listen to music when you draw.

Crumb: Really?

Groth: Yeah. It would just seem to be a beautiful accompaniment to drawing.

Crumb: Well no, it's a distraction. Because when I'm fully concentrating on drawing obviously I am not going to be listening to music. I can't enjoy music and concentrate on drawing at the same time. When I play records — I almost always play 78s, sometimes I play CDs, usually I'm playing 78s — I just fully concentrate on listening, I don't do anything else. I don't read or do anything else while I'm listening. I just listen. Often I close my eyes.

Groth: It's funny, but [my son] Conrad recently observed that I never just listen to music: I'm always doing something else while I'm listening to music — cooking, reading, driving, whatever. Since it was brought to my attention, I felt that it was some sort of defect ...

Crumb: Well, if it's a defect, it's a common one in the modern world. When I was a kid, I would go over to some relatives' house — working-class people on the East Coast there —and they would always have the TV on in the background. No one would be necessarily paying any attention to it, but they would just have it on. Noise box just going — what the hell is that about? Just have it on in the background like that, some obnoxious asshole

59

This complete Old Testament Edition of PICTURE STORIES FROM THE BIBLE offers for the first time in one volume, all of the glamorous, romantic stories of the old familiar heroes—told in faithful detail—carefully illustrated in fast-moving action continuity—brought to modern life in glorious full color.

Arranged in chronological order, every story in this Complete Old Testament Edition has been checked, edited and approved by the religious leaders of many denominations who comprise the Editorial Advisory Board.

Though especially designed to provide a religious background for children, men and women of all ages will be fascinated with PICTURE STORIES FROM THE BIBLE.
The Publishers.

with his image on the screen chattering on in the background. [*Groth laughs.*] I can't do that. I don't like having music in the background while I'm doing other stuff. I'm not like that.

Groth: I'm sure it's far better. Obviously you can appreciate the music at a far deeper level if you're —

Crumb: Yeah, you do. And also you become much more selective when you do that. You can't just put on any old thing if you're giving it your full attention. So you become a connoisseur and you gradually reject the stuff that's mediocre, that's less than great. If you're gonna give your full attention to it, it's gotta be the best. So, eventually you wade through all the sea of mediocrity and get to the really good stuff.

Groth: It's preferable when it's not just background noise.

Crumb: Yeah, or "easy listening."

Groth: It's hard listening. [Laughs.]

Crumb: But it's interesting — deriving pleasure from drawing. I guess it's pleasure. In a way it's pleasure in that you are focused, you are always at the edge of your game, you're always pushing the limit of what you can do and trying to do it better and there is a kind of pleasure in that, I suppose. I guess it's not the same sort of relaxing pleasure you get from the sensual enjoyment of music or sex, cause it's always kind of uphill, you know. It's always a push uphill.

Groth: Right, there's a pleasure at achieving mastery.

Crumb: Yeah, it's satisfaction from a job well done. When you look at the page afterward and it looks good, it's a great satisfaction. "Hey, he's good." [*Laughter.*]

Groth: It keeps you going, yeah.

Crumb: "Hey, that looks pretty good, not bad. But oh, wait a minute; that hand looks fucked up. I better change that. Okay, get out the white-out: Fix it. Shit, still doesn't look right! Put some more white-out on it; change it again. Oh, there's another detail that doesn't look right! How did I overlook that? Oh my God." It's endless.

Groth: You know, speaking of your use of white-out, I wish you had told me before you started Genesis, I would have bought some stock in the White-out corporation.

Crumb: Really, no kidding.

Groth: I saw the pages of Genesis up in the New York Gallery.

Crumb: Yeah.

Groth: And my God, there is a lot of white-out on those pages.

Crumb: You could tell, huh? Fortunately, a lot of people can't tell, they don't even see it; it takes somebody who really knows comics well to notice all that white-out.

Groth: Well, you can see it on the original art.

Crumb: Oh yes, it's heavy with white-out: especially the early pages. Some of those early pages, I corrected almost everything later. But the best white-out is that Cel-Vinyl stuff — that's the best. It's actually made for coloring animation cells, dries really hard so you can draw over it with pen and ink easily without it coming off and gunking up the pen.

Groth: I assume it dries quickly.

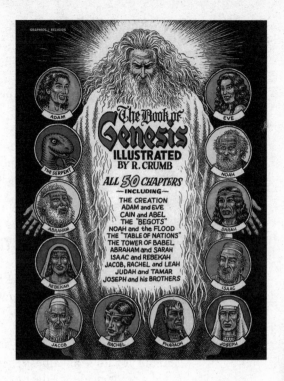

TOP
The Book of Genesis Illustrated by R. Crumb's back cover

Crumb: Fairly quickly. You have to wait a little bit, and you have to layer it. One layer won't do it, won't cover the original line enough. But it's great stuff and it's getting harder to find, too.

Groth: Well, that's possibly because you bought all of it.

Crumb: It's because computers have taken over animation color work. A woman employee at the Cartoon Color company that makes Cel-Vinyl told me it's mainly used in Latin American countries, now. The New York Central Art Supply store still stocks it. That's where I get it.

The Crumb Version

Groth: Why did you choose to use primarily the Robert Alter version, rather than the King James or another version? Did you study them carefully and then conclude that his was …

Crumb: I was originally going to use the Jewish Publication Society version and mix it with King James. Then Robert Weil, the editor at Norton, after I had already made the deal to do it with Norton, he said, "Do you know about the Robert Alter version?"

I said no, so he sent me a copy of it and I started reading it and I said, "Oh, yeah, this guy, he's really done his homework on it and gone back to the old Hebrew and really tried to figure out what these words mean. His version in a lot of ways is better than the Jewish Publication Society version, which is the older Jewish version.

Groth: Better in what sense?

Crumb: Probably more accurate. But at the same time, sometimes his wording was a little stilted and awkward. It's kind of a "throw mama from the train a kiss" type problem, where in the original Hebrew, often the object in the sentence precedes the subject kind of thing, you know. So, I sometimes used the Jewish Publication Society version because they had written it more in terms of modern English, for readability. But my version is completely mixed. I used stuff from King James to retain that sort of Biblical poesy, which is taken out of the modern translations. In King James they're always saying, "And behold!" and there's no "Behold!" at all in Alter or the Jewish Publication Society, that's all gone. All that stuff that we, in the English language West, think of as "biblical" language, that's the old King James, Elizabethan English we're talking about. And that's just all gone from the modern translations. They're very dry. In the modern versions, instead of saying, "And behold!" they say, "Look." That just doesn't do it, that doesn't sound biblical — "And look." [*Laughter.*] So, I retained some of that stuff. Even Robert Alter says that those English scholars in the 17th century did a very good job, considering the limits of their sources and all that. But, a lot of times they misinterpreted things and there're some garbled passages in King James because they just couldn't figure out what the original Hebrew meant. They had some good Hebrew scholars there in 17th century England, but often it's awkward and difficult to comprehend. The King James Version is really hard to get through. It's like trying to read Elizabethan Shakespeare, you know?

Groth: Did you change any words yourself?

Crumb: I did, yes. Sometimes.

Groth: And what was usually the rationale for that?

Crumb: The reason was that in some instances, in all the versions I had, there was no sense to what they were saying. So, I would read it over and over, and compare the three versions, trying to figure out, what the hell did they mean here? By reading the three different versions, you get a comparative perspective. That helps you come up with a possible meaning that could be underneath the three confused versions — because they each interpret the original Hebrew, or whatever it was, in their own way. So comparing these three different garbled versions, I just decided none of these really work and I'm going to have to come up with something that I think is workable. I have a friend, Betsy Sandlin, who reads Hebrew. She was visiting in Paris once and I had these problematic passages and I asked her to help me and she looked on the Internet for the Hebrew words and we broke it down. She kinda helped me figure out what they possibly could mean. Jews are much looser about interpreting than the Christians, you know. They have

AND THE LORD SCATTERED THEM FROM THERE OVER THE FACE OF ALL THE EARTH, AND THEY LEFT OFF BUILDING THE CITY.

the Talmudic tradition. Anybody who's really serious about studying the sacred text is allowed to come up with their own interpretation and you can argue endlessly about it. It's part of the pleasure Jewish Bible scholars have — to be able to hash out what they think it really means and what the point of it really is, and all that. It's different from the more dogmatic Christian attitude.

Groth: I did a little bit of comparing, your version with the Alter version, and I was trying to figure out if there was a consistent rationale ...

Crumb: No.

Groth: No. [Laughs.]

Crumb: There's no consistency. Sometimes I would use long passages from Alter without changing them at all and other times I would change them a lot, or use the Jewish Publication Society version because it just read better. And then sometimes I would mix the two together, select words from one and words from the other, put 'em together and sometimes even change the order around of the sentence to make it read, what I felt, was a better read than either of them. So, I just took some liberties that way, but I would not dare to ever alter it so much that it would change the meaning — only structural alterations to make it more readable. I didn't want to add anything or take anything out that would alter the meaning of it in any way.

Groth: I found that you usually changed vocabulary to a more common usage.

Crumb: Sometimes I did. When I started it ...

Groth: ... but not consistently.

Crumb: When I started it, the editor, Robert Weil, he started sending me back typed commentaries on the pages saying, "In this panel, instead of using this awkward, old, archaic way of talking why don't you word it this way, in a modern way," and at first I thought, I should please him by doing that. And he kept doing it and doing it, until finally I told him, "You know, you're going to change the whole mood of this, if you do this. I'm not going to make this all sound modern and colloquial." I turned down so many of his suggestions that would ... he just wanted to take such liberties with the original text, he thought I should take much more liberty than I was willing to take. And he claimed he's a Bible scholar, but then he was telling me stuff like, "In the beginning it's very confusing here to the reader, because you have these contradictory stories of the creation. Why can't we combine these somehow?"

I had already drawn the pages, so if I had conceded I would have to completely redraw it. I had to tell him, "Well, that's the way it's written and I'm not gonna mess with the way it was written."

He said, "Oh really, that's the way it was written?"

I said, "Yes! I'm just putting it exactly as it's written in there." Some Bible scholar.

Groth: And these editorial suggestions were all basically attempts to make it more contemporary-sounding?

Crumb: Yes. Make it easier for the modern person to read. He's an editor, you know, he's just going at his editorial job in his usual way as if I was the author of this text and he was going to help me make it more readable.

R. Crumb, Defender of the Universe

Groth: Let me ask you about your depiction of God. Very traditional, very Chuck Heston. You said that you actually were visited by God in a dream around the year 2000, I believe.

Crumb: Yeah.

Groth: And that influenced your depiction.

Crumb: Yes, it did.

Groth: Can you tell me a little about that?

Crumb: I only saw this image for an instant because it was too strong to look at for longer than that.

Groth: Can you describe the dream you had? This was in a dream, right?

Crumb: Yeah. It was in a dream where I foresaw terrible cataclysms happening to the Earth and then this being appeared. I was so distressed, this destructive force was killing me. I basically foresaw the tsunami from high up in the sky and this being appeared and I couldn't look at him and he spoke to me and told me that I could help. There was a rolling force coming towards this Earth, or this universe actually — it wasn't just the Earth, it was our whole material reality — that wanted to destroy it. And this force was coming in waves and that the waves were getting stronger and each time it came it was more powerful. And I asked this being, this God-being, I said, "Where is it coming from?"

And the God-being said, "We don't know." This God-being was the most powerful protective entity of this reality that we live in. He was the symbol of the preserver. Possibly the creator of it too, but the preserver, definitely. But not the great "all-that-is." That's why he said: "We don't know."

I said, "What is this destructive force? Where is it coming from?"

He said, "We don't know. But it's getting stronger, it's coming in waves; rolling waves of destructive force. You can join in a league of souls that commit themselves to protecting this reality from these destructive waves. And if we're strong enough, if we create a strong enough unified field, maybe we can protect this reality from this force."

I said, "Why do you want to preserve this reality?"

He said, "Because we love this reality. We want to preserve it. We want to save it."

And I saw that I could make this commitment, and I saw a kind of collection of spheres of light — all joined together like a honeycomb or a unified wall, protecting the reality that we live in from this rolling force of destruction. And the being that was telling me about this, from the instant that I looked at him, he had this severe but anguished face that was so extreme, so strong that I could barely look at it, couldn't look at it for longer than an instant. And he sort of looked a little bit like Charlton Heston or even Mel Gibson.

Groth: That's scary! [Laughs.]

Crumb: He had a little bit of that look, but even more anguished and severe and serious. But it was very masculine, extremely masculine and powerful.

Groth: Did you imagine rendering God any other way, or was that dream powerful enough for you to have just taken it and ....

Crumb: At the same time, I just thought I was going to go with the stereotype, the basically Michelangelo God. The patriarchal God, he's got longer hair and a longer beard than anybody. He's the ultimate patriarch. That's what comes across in Genesis: He's an angry, jealous, male God.

And he's also a commanding God and a judging God, he's really down on Adam and Eve. [*Laughter.*] He's also crazy. After the flood when he shows the rainbow to Noah and his sons, he says, "I created this rainbow so that I'll remember next time when it rains, that I don't want to completely destroy the human race ..." That's some crazy shit. But, you know, God can be crazy if he wants to. It's his universe. It's only we humans that impose ideas of consistency, rationality. [Laughs.] Those are human ideas. [Laughs.]

Groth: It occurs to me that there's a paradox in that the longest, most sustained single piece of work you ever did, is the least Crumbian work you ever did.

Crumb: Yeah, sure.

Groth: And I'm wondering where do you think Genesis resides within the Crumb oeuvre? Is it the work you're proudest of, or ...?

Crumb: I don't know. I guess when you say it's — what did you say? It's ironic that it's the longest thing I ever did?

Groth: Ironic because ...

Crumb: It's the least Crumbian?

Groth: Yes.

Crumb: Because "Crumbian" things are not long. The length was dictated by the task that I took on. I was forced to do the whole thing. Once I made the commitment to do it word for word then there was no turning back.

Groth: But by Crumbian, I meant more in terms of tone and subject matter and so forth.

Crumb: Yeah, when I'm just creating my own stories I don't think in terms of anything that epic, I just don't. For my own stories I just think of, you know, "Super Duck" or something. [Laughs.]

Groth: One of your dominant artistic characteristics is being a satirist and your distinct point of view and your critical disposition toward the contemporary world — and you eschewed all of that for four years to do this project.

AND TO ADAM HE SAID...,

BECAUSE YOU LISTENED TO THE VOICE OF YOUR WIFE AND ATE FROM THE TREE OF WHICH I COMMANDED YOU, "YOU SHALL NOT EAT FROM IT," *CURSED BE THE GROUND BECAUSE OF YOU!*

Crumb: Yes, I did. Yep. [*Laughter.*] There were many times where I was sitting there, slaving away, thinking, "Is this worth it? Does this text even merit this amount of slave labor?"

Groth: Would you call it labor? You know the ancient Greek distinction between work and toil. Was this more toil than work?

Crumb: Well, kind of both, you know. OK, it had its challenge: I was definitely working up, pushing the limits of my skills and trying to go beyond them and all that stuff. It was educational. But there was plenty of toil. There was toil.

Groth: Perhaps more toil than usual?

Crumb: A lot more than usual. Hell of a lot more than usual. But now I think it was a worthwhile task. If you're building a house and even though you've designed it yourself and you're putting all kinds of nice, pretty decorations that you want the house to have, it's going to be a pleasing house, a beautiful house when it's finished — there's still all that fucking brickwork to do, you still got to keep laying those bricks and putting down that mortar, putting in that framing. There's still lots of toil, and any cartoonist will tell you that. Cartooning's not all beer and skittles [*laughter*].

There's lots of labor in doing anything well. But there's something to be said, on the other hand, for this lighter, free and easy approach that I had

RIGHT
From "The Heartbreak of the Old Cartoonist" in *The R. Crumb Handbook* [©2005 R. Crumb]

when I was younger. I'm sure that you could look at my earlier work and get more pleasure out of it because it looked like it was more fun to do, that I was living a more fun lifestyle then. I was wild and having all kinds of crazy adventures. I was a cowboy. It's like listening to a hillbilly band that's having a good time playing for a square dance as opposed to, say, listening to a symphony orchestra playing Mozart. It's serious and heavy and the musicians are slaving away. They've spent hundreds of hours practicing these parts. It's two different things. There's a lot to be said for the hillbilly band, I think. [*Laughter.*]

   Myself, I'd rather listen to a good hillbilly band than Mozart.

Groth: Right, but *Genesis* is closer to Mozart than a hillbilly band.

Crumb: Yeah, that's the thing. I've gotten myself into this much heavier, more serious kind of task. I don't know, I can't make a value judgment about it.

Groth: Was it problematic or disturbing or painful to suppress that part of you? The part of you that comments on the modern world; the part that tries to make sense of sex and women.

Crumb: Make sense of sex and women? A hopeless task. I'm not at all sure that's what I was doing.

Groth: But you were compelled to do it.

Crumb: I was, yes. I was driven.

Groth: You couldn't do anything else.

Crumb: Yeah, it was a compulsion. That was a very masturbatory compulsion.

Groth: But *Genesis* doesn't seem like a compulsion, it seems like something else.

Crumb: Well, that's not up to me to decide. I'm just a compulsive person. There's plenty of compulsion in all that crosshatching. Like I said, cleaning the bathroom with a toothbrush.

Groth: Well, maybe a different kind of compulsion that comes from a different part of you, or something like that.

Crumb: I don't know. You tell me. ■

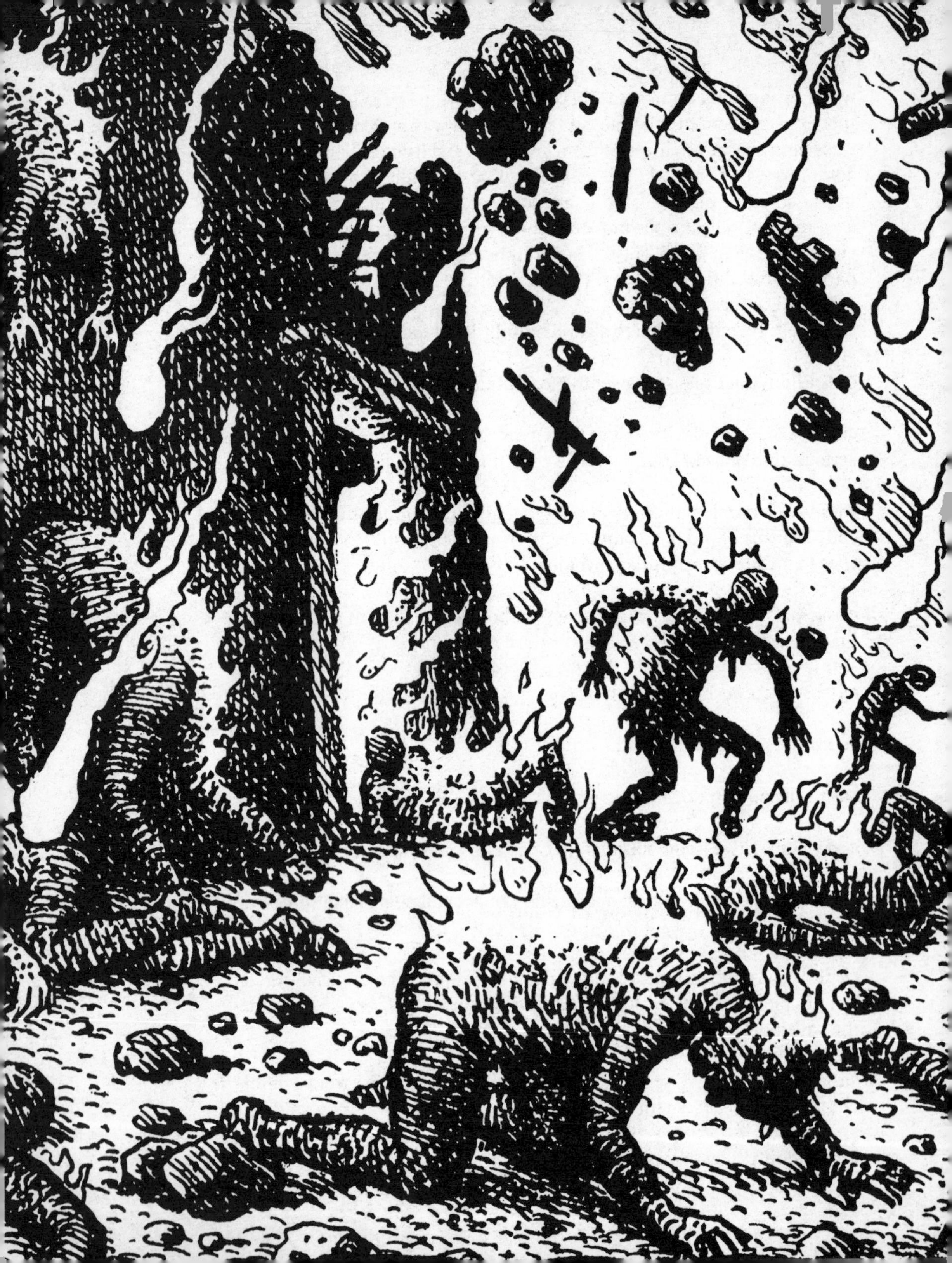

THE BOOK OF GENESIS

ROUNDTABLE

ILLUSTRATED BY R. CRUMB

"PILGRIM'S PROCESS"

A REVIEW OF R. CRUMB'S HAGIOGRAPHIC NOVEL

BY RICK MARSCHALL

"Scritch... scritch... scritch." When my son was a young film major, he produced a video documentary of the editorial cartoonist Tony Auth. The studio was quiet except for the incessant sound of pen scratches across the paper; the camera came in focus to show the pen lines being drawn — intricate shading (before Auth incorporated computer-aided tones in his work) — and then pulled back until he was shown in full, bent over the drawing board, Crafter of the Crosshatch.

I remembered this aural aspect of cartoon shading when I first leafed through R. Crumb's *Book of Genesis Illustrated*; and of course I recalled Crumb's own famous affection for "lines on paper." Here he seems to assume the omniscient powers of God Himself: readers feel like witnesses to every person, place, wrinkle, fold, shadow, texture, leaf, whisker, grain of sand and speck of dust since the creation of the world. In my imagination I peeked into Crumb's studio in the south of France, over the purported four years he worked on *The Book of Genesis*. Did he wear a burlap robe and squint by candlelight? Surely no monk, transcribing Holy texts or illuminating sacred manuscripts, ever worked harder.

Close eyes ... shake head ... rinse: repeat. No, another image intruded: something about Crumb's depiction of God Almighty. White beard, long robe ... one of His many biblical names is "The Great I AM." I couldn't get it out of my mind: "The Great I... 'Keep On Truckin'." Not fair, but actors are not the only people who get typecast. You decide to traffic in graven images, buddy, and you pay the price.

There are many highlights in this book to delight the Crumb fan, and a few that will interest people of faith. At the outset, so there is context to my essay: I am both a Crumb fan and a committed Christian. I have worked some in the comics field, as a political cartoonist, editor and historian. I have also worked in the Christian field, as author of devotionals, an "answer book" to *The Secret*, and a forthcoming treatment of J. S. Bach's faith life. I have worked in youth ministry, as editor of Mike Yaconelli's *Youth Specialties*; on projects connected to Saddleback Church and International Justice Mission; and was part of the editorial team that reissued the 1599 *Geneva Bible* (the "Breeches Bible"). I was Managing Editor of *Rare Jewel Magazine*, a Christian journal of culture and worldview; and I am a fundamentalist, evangelical, Pentecostal — three circles that are not always concentric, except, as with me, when tied together by beliefs like "New Earth" Creationism. Full disclosure.

To the highlights of Crumb's book: He has crafted some individual images that please, and sometimes sear, the mind. The Flood and its victims; the Ark itself, especially its interior; the destruction of Sodom and Gomorrah (the third of four panels is on a par with Basil Wolverton, one of the great Apocalyptic artists since Albrecht Dürer); Pharaoh's court; many evocative sandscapes — masterful, memorable. His depiction of the Garden's serpent is brilliant: on legs at first, so the curse to "crawl

the earth" resonates. The "great, dark dread" of Abram is a museum piece. It is impossible not to admire Crumb's craft, and certainly his industry, in the detail-work and crosshatching. By the end of the book, especially, it becomes less random and more disciplined, reminding one of classic woodcuts or even steel engravings.

Other features are impossible to miss, or dismiss.

I wonder whether Crumb rejects the Theory of Evolution, because the first women, from Eve forward, are exactly as Crumb draws them in other works, walking around city sidewalks and crowded rock concerts: mannish; um, zaftig; generally snarling and unkempt; often bent forward with hips somehow nine inches behind their anatomically correct position. They just grew leather boots and dungarees through the centuries ... OK, that has nothing to do with evolution. But some of his visual clichés, trademark representations, are here: the typical Crumb women's ubiquitous huge nipples, always threatening to burst through burlap robes; the sex scenes that, OK, are mentioned in Scripture, but seem to be drawn in neon-laced ink in this book; fevered copulation scenes that provide a high percentage of the splash panels (and some of the only smiles on characters' faces). Crumb drew The Book of Genesis, but I'll bet he'd trade his birthright to draw The Song of Solomon.

Are Crumb's men different from the stock Crumb man? Many in this book are hunched over, beat down, careworn, somewhat crazed ... and those are just the jubilant ones. There is the moment in the rivalry between Jacob and Esau where the latter observes, "My brother is an hairy man ..." If Jake had lived in a world devised by Crumb, he could not have made that distinction: every Crumb man here is furry, fuzzy and hairy, whiskers everywhere but from the eyeballs. (That is, every one of Crumb's Hebrew men. The Egyptians are as shiny as Yul Brynner's bottom.) Otherwise, an alchemist's goal has been realized; ink has been transformed into Rogaine in this book.

The cartoonist assures us in his Introduction that he will not make visual jokes. If this were 15th-century Catholic Europe, however, Crumb would need a couple of indulgences (my treat), because I think he strayed a bit on that one. I impute no offense; in fact I was tickled in at least one instance. Perhaps the touchstone was my own curiosity since childhood about the strange names of Noah's sons: Ham, Shem and Japheth. Is it me, or has Crumb drawn them to resemble Moe, Shemp and Larry? Their hairdos are the giveaways — at least Moe, Shemp and Larry as drawn in their dotage by Drew Friedman, and transcribed by Crumb. Here, I must confess, I considered it perfectly kosher to do this ("visual joke" or not), and I was grateful

for evidence that Crumb was having fun somewhere in there. I cannot feel certain he did, however, throughout.

Those were random impressions and questions, at the first leaf-through. The book itself presents enough substantial manna that it should be considered from three vantage points. I will address *The Book of Genesis by R. Crumb* as theology, as a comic strip and as history.

Theology

In the beginning, Crumb created a dilemma for readers of this book. The hefty comics portion recounts Genesis in a manner that appears somewhere between genuine and authentic. In crafting a costume-drama, a period piece, Crumb has been meticulous. Then in the Introduction, especially, and in the chapter-by-chapter Commentary at the end of the book, he substantiates the research and explains his choices in the representation of costumes, settings, architecture and artifacts. More, Crumb uses those essays to vitiate the veracity he labors so hard to convey in the vast majority of the book's pages.

TOP

"'The great, dark dread' of Abram"

HENCE A MAN LEAVES HIS FATHER AND MOTHER AND CLINGS TO HIS WIFE AND THEY BECOME ONE FLESH.

AND THE TWO OF THEM WERE NAKED, THE MAN AND HIS WOMAN, AND THEY WERE NOT ASHAMED.

Clearly, Crumb was eager to establish that he has not become a fundamentalist. He makes clear in his Intro and Commentary that he does not subscribe to Genesis as the literal account of Creation, nor anything like "the Word of God." He grants that "it seems indeed to be inspired," but he evidently means the common use of inspired — as a spring afternoon can inspire a young poetess — not in the etymological sense, "breathed in" by God.

There is one aspect of Genesis where I not only sympathize with a difficult editorial choice Crumb faced, but empathize with the manner in which he met it. A personal recollection:

One of the biggest leaps of faith in my life occurred when I was a young teen and our church youth group — not a hugely on-fire bunch in the first place — was on one of its occasional summer "retreats." We went to a camp where swimming, bonfires and hiking were more exercised than our faith was. At least it wasn't a weekend of "Kumbaya"; nevertheless it was closer to a Scouts' outing than it was to church.

Nevertheless, there were Bible studies and hymn-sings, and during this year, a few of us were spurred to break out and break in our spiritual hiking-boots, so to speak. In the boy's cabin one night, a few of us decided to go to the Main Hall and have a Bible-read. It was during "lights out," so technically we shouldn't have done this, but we felt led by God. So seven of us grabbed our Bibles, traipsed down dark paths to the Main Hall, turned on one light in the middle of the room, and awkwardly arranged ourselves in a circle underneath. Despite the impromptu boldness we were exercising, everyone was a little shy about taking the lead. After some silence, some sweating and a growing fear that the pastor would barge in and break up this infraction of the rules unless we did something religious, I suggested we read a passage from our Bibles.

Agreed. At least no one objected. All the guys stared at me, as if anyone who blinked was signaling to go first. "All right, I'll start," I said ... but, I thought, "Where to start? Genesis 1:1 might obligate us to keep going until, well, maybe past breakfast."

So I hit upon the very spiritual rule that if God led us to do this, He would also order the circumstances to read a proper passage. So without any further ceremony or prayer, I opened my Bible to a random page, pointed to a spot and read.

"The sons of Perez: Hezron, and Hamul. The sons of Zerah: Zimri, and Ethan, and Heman, and Calcol, and Dara; five of them in all ..." I got through this strange passage, grateful that it ended in some English words I knew.

"The sons of Carmi; Achar, the troubler of Israel, who committed a trespass in the devoted thing ..." I read quickly and a little louder, afraid one of the guys would ask me what a "devoted thing" was. "The sons of Ethan: Azariah. The sons also of Hezron, who were born to him: Jerahmeel, and Ram, and Chelubai. Ram became the father of Amminadab, and Amminadab became the father of Nahshon, prince of the children of Judah; and Nahshon became the father of Salma, and Salma became the father of Boaz ..." When are these semicolons ever going to end, I wondered. "... and Boaz became the father of Obed, and Obed became the father of Jesse; and Jesse became the father of his firstborn Eliab, and Abinadab the second, and Shimea the third, Nethanel the fourth, Raddai the fifth, Ozem the sixth, David the seventh; and their sisters were Zeruiah and Abigail."

I cleared my throat, nervously scanning ahead in Scripture, wondering how long this judgment was to continue. Verily, verily, I say unto thee that I was stumbling, mumbling and fumbling over those funky names.

> The sons of Zeruiah: Abishai, and Joab, and Asahel, three.
> Abigail bore Amasa; and the father of Amasa was Jether the Ishmaelite. Caleb the son of Hezron became the father of children of Azubah his wife, and of Jerioth; and these were her sons: Jesher, and Shobab, and Ardon. Azubah died, and Caleb took to him Ephrath, who bore him Hur. Hur became the father of Uri,

and Uri became the father of Bezalel. Afterward Hezron went in to the daughter of Machir the father of Gilead, whom he took as wife when he was sixty years old; and she bore him Segub.

Good for him, I'm thinking, while wondering — and rejecting — whether God would be pleased if we declare this midnight sneak-away a mistake, close our Bibles, and recite, "The Lord is my shepherd…" But didn't God lead us here?

Segub became the father of Jair, who had twenty-three cities in the land of Gilead. Geshur and Aram took the towns of Jair from them, with Kenath, and its villages, even sixty cities. All these were the sons of Machir the father of Gilead. After that Hezron was dead in Caleb Ephrathah, then Abijah Hezron's wife bore him Ashhur the father of Tekoa. The sons of Jerahmeel the first-born of Hezron were Ram the firstborn, and Bunah, and Oren, and Ozem, Ahijah. Jerahmeel had another wife, whose name was Atarah; she was the mother of Onam. The sons of Ram the firstborn of Jerahmeel were Maaz, and Jamin, and Eker. The sons of Onam were Shammai, and Jada. The sons of Shammai: Nadab, and Abishur. The name of the wife of Abishur was Abi-hail; and she bore him Ahban, and Molid. The sons of Nadab: Seled, and Appaim; but Seled died without children. The sons of Appaim: Ishi. The sons of Ishi: Sheshan. The sons of Sheshan: Ahlai. The sons of Jada the brother of Shammai: Jether, and Jonathan; and Jether died without children. The sons of Jona-than: Peleth, and Zaza. These were the sons of Jerahmeel.

One of my friends in the group was named Jeremy, and the similarity in the sound of these names made me look up, happily, and realize it was time to pass the ball! But Jeremy, and all the other guys, had their eyes shut tight. I knew why. Not one volunteer was amongst us, nor a sympathetic worship leader, not even a friend in time of trouble. Nope: I was the one ordained to share what God had for us in that enlightened circle in the large Hall in the middle of the dark, cold woods.

Whoops: My mind was wandering. Back to God's word:

Now Sheshan had no sons, but daughters. Sheshan had a servant, an Egyptian, whose name was Jarha. Sheshan gave his daughter to Jarha his servant as wife; and she bore him Attai. At-tai became the father of Nathan, and Nathan became the father of Zabad, and Zabad became the father of Ephlal, and Ephlal

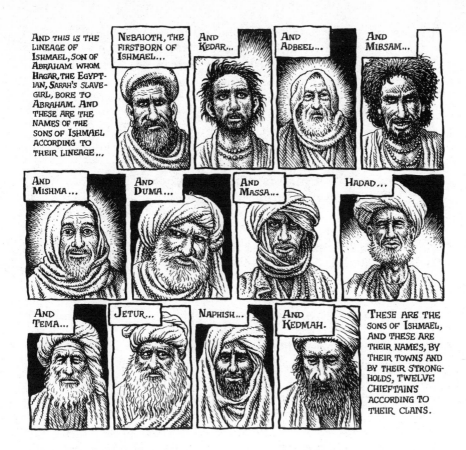

AND THIS IS THE LINEAGE OF ISHMAEL, SON OF ABRAHAM WHOM HAGAR, THE EGYPTIAN, SARAH'S SLAVE-GIRL, BORE TO ABRAHAM. AND THESE ARE THE NAMES OF THE SONS OF ISHMAEL ACCORDING TO THEIR LINEAGE...

NEBAIOTH, THE FIRSTBORN OF ISHMAEL...

AND KEDAR...

AND ADBEEL...

AND MIBSAM...

AND MISHMA...

AND DUMA...

AND MASSA...

HADAD...

AND TEMA...

JETUR...

NAPHISH...

AND KEDMAH.

THESE ARE THE SONS OF ISHMAEL, AND THESE ARE THEIR NAMES, BY THEIR TOWNS AND BY THEIR STRONGHOLDS, TWELVE CHIEFTAINS ACCORDING TO THEIR CLANS.

became the father of Obed, and Obed became the father of Jehu, and Jehu became the father of Azariah, and Azariah became the father of Helez, and Helez became the father of Eleasah ...

Why was the Bible repeating these names??? They were hard enough to try to pronounce the first times! ...

and Eleasah became the father of Sismai, and Sismai became the father of Shallum, and Shallum became the father of Jekamiah, and Jekamiah became the father of Elishama. The sons of Caleb the brother of Jerahmeel were Mesha his first-born, who was the father of Ziph; and the sons of Mareshah the father of Hebron. The sons of Hebron: Korah, and Tappuah, and Rekem, and Shema. Shema became the father of

Raham, the father of Jorkeam; and Rekem became the father of Shammai. The son of Shammai was Maon; and Maon was the father of Beth Zur. Ephah, Caleb's concubine, bore Haran, and Moza, and Gazez; and Haran became the father of Gazez. The sons of Jahdai: Regem, and Jothan, and Geshan, and Pelet, and Ephah, and Shaaph. Maacah, Caleb's concubine, bore Sheber and Tirhanah. She bore also Shaaph the father of Madmannah, Sheva the father of Machbena, and the father of Gibea; and the daughter of Caleb was Achsah. These were the sons of Caleb, the son of Hur, the firstborn of Ephrathah: Shobal the father of Kiriath Jearim.

There were even more branches on that family tree, I remember noting with dismay. I also definitely remember mispronouncing "concubine." What a mess. Suddenly I did what many a decent pastor probably has done in similar situations through the millennia.

I raised my decibel-level and declared: "Amen!"

None of the guys moved. Heads bowed, eyes closed, and if I didn't know better I would have thought they were stifling chuckles.

It was up to me, still. What to do? I could have prayed aloud, but that wasn't quite in my spiritual comfort zone ... and it was a challenge to wrap up this particular litany in a neat prayer that was relevant to this name-game. I could have taken up a collection, but that seemed presumptuous. So — still not wanting to offend God's evident direction for the excursion, which I still had troubling figuring out — I opened my Bible to another random spot and plopped the tip of my finger down.

I kid you not: more begats stared up at me! Dozens. Scores. A multitude of rods and cubits of them, to be biblical.

And Salmon begat Booz of Rachab; and Booz begat Obed of Ruth; and Obed begat Jesse; and Jesse begat David the king; and David the king begat Solomon of her that had been the wife of Urias; and Solomon begat Roboam; and Roboam begat Abia; and Abia begat Asa; and Asa begat Josaphat; and Josaphat begat Joram; and Joram begat Ozias ...

Wait a minute. Salmon? BOOZ? My eyes were skating all over the page. Oh, no ... a whole lot more begats. I noticed I was lingering s-l-o-w-l-y on the

AND THESE ARE THE NAMES OF THE CHILDREN OF ISRAEL WHO CAME TO EGYPT, JACOB AND HIS SONS...

JACOB'S FIRSTBORN, REUBEN, AND THE SONS OF REUBEN; ENOCH, AND PALLU AND HEZRON AND CARMI.

AND THE SONS OF SIMEON; JEMUEL AND JAMIN AND OHAD AND JACHIN AND ZOHAR AND SAUL, THE SON OF THE CANAANITE WOMAN.

AND THE SONS OF LEVI; GERSHON, KOHATH, AND MERARI.

AND THE SONS OF JUDAH; ER AND ONAN AND SHELAH AND PEREZ AND ZERAH —AND ER AND ONAN DIED IN THE LAND OF CANAAN.

AND THE SONS OF PEREZ WERE HEZRON AND HAMUL.

AND THE SONS OF ISSACHAR; TOLA AND PUVAH AND IOB AND SHIMRON.

AND THE SONS OF ZEBULUN; SERED AND ELON AND JAHLEEL.

THESE ARE THE SONS OF LEAH WHOM SHE BORE TO JACOB IN PADDAN-ARAM, AND ALSO DINAH HIS DAUGHTER, EVERY PERSON OF HIS SONS AND DAUGHTERS, THIRTY-THREE.

AND THE SONS OF GAD; ZIPHION, AND HAGGI, SHUNI AND EZBON, ERI AND ARODI AND ARELI.

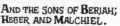

AND THE SONS OF ASHER; IMNAH, AND ISHUAH, AND ISHVI AND BERIAH AND SERAH, THEIR SISTER.

AND THE SONS OF BERIAH; HEBER AND MALCHIEL.

THESE ARE THE SONS OF ZILPAH, WHOM LABAN GAVE TO LEAH HIS DAUGHTER, AND SHE BORE THESE TO JACOB, SIXTEEN PERSONS.

first pronunciations of the names, and then zipping through their second readings. Right or wrong, I drew another breath and continued:

> Ozias begat Joatham; and Joatham begat Achaz; and Achaz
> begat Ezekias; and Ezekias begat Manasses; and Manasses begat
> Amon; and Amon begat Josias; and Josias begat Jechonias and
> his brethren, about the time they were carried away to Baby-
> lon: and after they were brought to Babylon ... they lived happily
> ever after? NO! Jechonias begat Salathiel; and Salathiel begat
> Zorobabel; and Zorobabel begat Abiud; and Abiud begat Eliakim;
> and Eliakim begat Azor; and Azor begat Sadoc; and Sadoc begat
> Achim; and Achim begat Eliud; and Eliud begat Eleazar; and
> Eleazar begat Matthan; and Matthan begat Jacob ...
>
> And Jacob begat Joseph the husband of Mary, of whom was
> born Jesus, who is called Christ.

My Bible loudly slapped shut, and I said, with eyes bowed and head closed, believe me, "The end thus says the Lord and we all pray that your Word is a lamp unto our feet as we return to our bunks and bless pastor and all the leaders and keep us safe Oh Lord we pray through the night and every day bless this food to our bodies for ever and ever Amen." Something like that.

We scurried to our bunks as swiftly as the pitch-black night would permit. You might think I slept quickly and soundly, but not so: I tossed and turned, wondering whether the Lord is a God of Practical Jokes. I had stepped out ... and felt like I stubbed my toe, big time.

What was there to learn in this not-so-genial genealogy? Can we know God through every passage in the Bible, or maybe not? The question is pertinent to the attention paid to the begats in *The Book of Genesis Illustrated by R. Crumb*. First, I take the interminable family trees as evidence of the Bible's literal reliability. Would idle oral traditions, or aggressive schemes to invent a religion, invest in so many names and relationships and places and events? (First-and-a-half point: recent biblical archaeology is reveal-ing the existence of many of these names and places, heretofore thought by "scholars" to be fictional.) Second, while many names never appear again in Scripture, some of them have spiritual significance — specifi-cally as the ancestors of Jesus. The New Testament traces every name on Jesus' family tree — his mother's side (bloodline from Adam; recounted in Matthew) and his father's side (legal lineage from Abraham; recounted in Luke). The Messiah's prophetic identity is confirmed, and the Adamic

"[The Book of Genesis Illustrated by R. Crumb] is a book that, to our eyes and ears, often has the literary élan of financial charts."

foundation of biblical creationism's timeline is substantiated. Those names are relevant after all.

Did Crumb need to show every face? That is a question that is pertinent to the dynamics of the comic-strip form (following): highlighting the "cast of thousands" crowds out drama, spectacle and miracles. Those characters are important, yet Crumb might have let a few longer captions (there are plenty already) do that work.

II Timothy 3:16 says, "All Scripture is given by inspiration of God, and is profitable for doctrine, for reproof, for correction, for instruction in righteousness." So I am grateful Crumb did not remove passages, but I regret that he leaned upon a translation that was more philological than spiritual … and certainly less poetic than the familiar King James version. Crumb says he referenced the King James version but "mostly" relied on Robert Alter's *Genesis: Translation and Commentary* (1996) and the incorporation/expansion *The Five Books of Moses* (2004).

Robert Alter's work, a jot-and-tittle examination and interpretation of ancient Hebrew texts, is literary and semantic more than creedal and spiritual. There are as many footnotes as the stars in the heavens, and the text — literal thought it *might* be — becomes disjointed, overshadowed and undercut by reference notes. To those who have tried to translate a foreign-language text by the Babel Fish computer program... that, unfortunately, is how many of Alter's passage read. It has lost its soul as well as, maybe, its spirit; and it is that text that Crumb uses. This is a book that, to our eyes and ears, often has the literary élan of financial charts; and they fall, like tables, from the Crumb. (At the other end of the spectrum is Eugene Patterson's translation, *The Message*, the most popular of the postmodern vernacular Bibles. Both these men dissect a precious butterfly — Holy Scripture — to study it better ... and kill it in the process.)

We take from Alter's books, for instance *The Pleasure of Reading*, that literary theory, literary criticism, properly divined and interpreted, can come as close to truth as truth itself. (And don't hold me to the revolving doors, as it seems to me, of the "in crowd" and "out crowd" between the old philology, the varieties of linguistic analyses, semantic critiques, literary theory, literary criticism. The head spins.) Language arises from contending with, and building upon, polemics. Discourse analysis is in fact useful to Alter's efforts to better translate and simultaneously interpret the Pentateuch. It can make for great scholarship ... but it almost insures a cold, inaccessible presentation of God's word in the 21st century. It elucidates words; it does not illuminate the Word.

We are presented with a robe that fits badly: Alter has applied himself to reconstruct Genesis; Crumb tends to deconstruct Genesis, line by line — lines of text, lines of his art: poetry, subtlety, mystery, all fall like the walls of Jericho in the *midrash*-of-sorts that is this collaboration. It makes for irony, since Alter, especially in his non-biblical works, is generally hostile to Deconstructionism. One of the labels festooned upon him (or that he invites, for instance as a contributor to *Commentary*) is that of a Cultural Neo-Conservative. Strange bedfellow for Crumb, I assume.

A reminder, not that we need it, that words profoundly have meaning, is found in the first words of *The Book of Genesis Illustrated by R. Crumb*, taken precisely from Alter's translation: "When God began to create heaven and earth ...". The difference from the familiar King James phraseology is pregnant with implications — about God before Creation; about Creation as an ongoing process; about the definitive events of the first six days. Crumb has adopted the Alter-ations, whether subtle or startling, without pausing at their nuances. Does he assume his readers do not need a commentary? Or has he not examined the questions himself? And since he *does* frequently speculate on similar and parallel pagan legends to accounts in Genesis, surely a discussion, even brief, of the deviations from passages familiar to most of us, and their implications, is proper. For all the notes in his Commentary, for

instance, Crumb includes information about other accounts of the Flood in diverse ancient cultures, as well as and "recent scholarship" rejecting biblical history ... but he does not discuss Alter's translation of the Bible's opening words. One sentence, such as the previous, would vastly assist the putative thrust of his work, or at least balance the points in the Commentary.

Alter's retranslation of Genesis, in short, makes provocative scholarship, frustrating reading and a frankly poor script for a comic strip. Alter seems to agree, at least regarding Crumb's reliance on his work; his book review of the *de facto* Alter-Crumb association in *The New Republic* shows him somewhat bemused by Crumb's request to use his text; and Alter's review of Crumb is an endorsement with qualifications (largely about the inevitable inappropriateness as graphic depictions, and opportunities Crumb might have missed). Alter's evident unease reflects a basic flaw in the narrative aspect of *The Book of Genesis Illustrated by R. Crumb*: By choosing one of most stilted and mechanical of translations, Crumb simultaneously rejected any of the more "artistic" texts to complement the artwork; and — God forbid — he sought a text whose language was somewhat awkward and stilted, as window-dressing, a literary prop, superficial evidence that remoteness equates with impregnable academic rectitude.

Regarding the appropriateness of Alter's text for a comic-strip scenario, there is the most fundamental consideration — and perhaps, I will admit, a fundamentalist consideration — that the translator does not believe in a personal God. He is a Relativist, more than he might allow, even more apparent in his Book of Psalms, where his social prejudices prevented him

TOP

To Marschall, the Alter translation used in *The Book of Genesis Illustrated* by R. Crumb is unnecessarily awkward.

from using the word, or the concept of, sin. To know such premises should forewarn the reader of Crumb's book, which relied so heavily on Alter that the indicia states: "Translation by Robert Alter, rev. by R. Crumb."

By stating that he incorporates opinions of "many scholars," Crumb clearly refers to what has informed his own opinions of theology, and presumably what assisted his visual research (since the actual words largely are Alter's). Further, by stating his acceptance of views of "most scholars" who reject biblical literalism, Crumb telegraphs a skepticism that does not inform his "literal, visual interpretation" as he calls it, but serves ambiguity instead. His book's unprecedented feeling of reality (the sandy, gritty, sweaty lives of these people of the Word) *could* have also embraced cryptic elements (the church suffers from a loss of mystery today); but it dares us to accept a counterfeit reality. Crumb does not ask us to believe his work, and here he refreshingly is humble. But the schizophrenia of his points of view in the total package (the comics, the Introduction and the Commentary)

peremptorily assures the reader a bumpy ride. He oddly offers a sort of oath: "I, R. Crumb, the illustrator of this book, have, to the best of my ability, reproduced every word of the original text..." Every word indeed seems to be accounted for. But beyond that he depicts not so much a group of God-encountering believers, but according to his Commentary, a group of deluded people. "BCE," the tedious neologistic acronym of recent coinage, might well mean, "By Crumb's euphemisms."

The book jacket trumpets, "Nothing Left Out!" but there are some clear "misses" that are as good as a mile. Alter, a dissenter from the faith of his own fathers, cannot be expected to include Christological elements in his several Bible translations. But Crumb could have done so, without having to endorse them. Just as he consulted a variety of sources for scholarship and reference, he could have referred to the vast, and interesting, body of work that sees in Genesis, the Pentateuch and the entire Old Testament, foreshadows and prophecies of the Christ. All the episodes in Genesis are saturated with these elements, as well as numerology, typology, etc., pointing to the Messiah. The curse to the tempting serpent, "He will trample your head, and you will bite His heel" is regarded as a picture of Jesus' death and resurrection. Such interpretations were not Alter's and likely not Crumb's, so these inclusions would have made a different book; I understand. But to cite ancient occult practices and postmodern feminist critiques as Crumb does, and not the reality — that is, the presence — of the New Testament, or the scholarship of its multitudinous scholars, is not to appear neutral but (needlessly) antagonistic.

Outside the comic's realm in the book, for instance — in the Commentary — Crumb skips any such biblical scholarship, whether of traditional beliefs or of recent interpretation. Chapter 22 of Genesis, where Abraham prepares to sacrifice his son, is a passage that has troubled many readers through the ages, until some of them consider the prophetic picture of God's willingness to sacrifice His own Son. Citing theories of a band of skeptics, folklorists and such "scholars," but not classical Rabbinic traditions, Christians, nor Messianic Jews, should constitute a warning label to readers who expect Crumb to have addressed Genesis with basic impartiality.

TOP
Marschall believes that the angel that wrestled Jacob was pre-incarnate Jesus.

FROM THE FOWL OF EACH KIND AND FROM THE CATTLE OF EACH KIND AND FROM ALL THAT CRAWLS ON THE EARTH OF EACH KIND, TWO OF EACH THING SHALL COME TO YOU TO BE KEPT ALIVE. AS FOR YOU, TAKE YOU FROM EVERY FOOD THAT IS EATEN AND STORE IT BY YOU, TO SERVE FOR YOU AND THEM AS FOOD.

In a similar, and puzzling, sequence, Crumb spends a bit of ink on the familiar account of Jacob's wrestling match. Expositors through the years have taken many meanings and lessons from this, for instance how Jacob — who many times was revealed to us as duplicitous and tricky — loses this marathon struggle by a trick of his opponent. But my crowd clearly believes that the opponent that night was the preincarnate Jesus (just as was the fourth man in the fiery furnace). Crumb's depiction of the "divine being," however, most notably in the sequence's last panel, is of a glowing face not merely angelic, but Holy — virtually a Hallmark-card portrait of Jesus. In his Commentary, without so much as a reference to this widely shared belief about the character's identity, Crumb writes a lengthy passage on occult parallels, stories from American Indian lore, etc. Surely a nod to the widely accepted, closely related, and obviously pertinent interpretation, would have been appropriate ... fulfillment of his pledge.

So it is *not* clear that "nothing is left out!" But it is clear that Crumb undertook a conscious effort to leave Christian scholarship out: likewise, prophetic passages and eschatology. Some would say (since Crumb regards his narrative as a collection of legends, many of them borrowed or bowdlerized from other traditions) that the Spirit of God is left out. I say this not judgmentally, despite how it sounds, but as an observation. Crumb says as much in his Introduction, that he has amalgamated the words of men who felt inspired through the centuries; the opinions of students and scholars; and the pollination of other cultures, pagan and religious, whose "stories" affect his own attitude toward Genesis. It is very significant that none (as far as Crumb indicates) of the scholars he cites are Hebrew or Christian scholars, biblical archaeologists or biblical creationists. Scientific and academic studies of the Bible — of Genesis — by Jews and Christians in recent years has far outnumbered studies by skeptics; and far outnumbered the faith communities' own previous scholarship. There has been an explosion of research *and* artifact discoveries in recent years. It is not just interesting but significant, as I say, that Crumb reveals that none of that was on his menu.

These omissions are so blatant that one of the promo-bursts on the book jacket could read, "Absolutely no references to the New Testament! Contains references to pagan, occult and dead religions!!"

Comic-Strip Technique

In this aspect R. Crumb has sinned.

Of all books in the Bible, even the Levitical rules in Deuteronomy, and the descriptions, symbols and numerology of Revelation, Genesis is abecedarian. We have just visited some the *begats*. There are specified instructions for ark-building; we have dreams recounted with more details than a therapist who charges by the hour could elicit. But God knew what He was doing; and He wants us too know, also.

But I continually wondered whether Crumb — that is, Crumb the comic artist — knew what he was doing, exactly, anent the excruciating details in his *Book of Genesis*. One of the graces of the comic-strip creator is the ability, virtually unique in the arts, to stretch or expand narrative elements, in the process not perverting the source material, but illuminating it. Given that his or any version of Genesis could not be completely free of personal interpretation — that is, in its "translation" to illustration and the dynamics of narrative expression — Crumb was under no obligation to highlight the relatively mundane elements, minimize the spectacles, or any creative choices in between. Yet the very *choices* he makes in the telling, before words or drawings are set to paper, say something. He truncates the Creation of the Universe to four pages, including the book's splash page: and the entire Noahic flood (the original Sedimental Journey) to six pages. To devote pages to dialogue exchange, which have been carried by captions, he elevates them disproportionately and diminishes the fantastic, dramatic, supernatural, compelling and yes, spiritual, significance of Creation, the Flood and other miracles. Yes, the detailed mug-shot characters are descendants of Adam and of Noah, and of the ancestry of Christ — let us visit the *begats* again. If they deserve portrayals for their godly pedigree, one would expect them to appear special or anointed or called out, because that is why Moses listed them; that is what they were. On the other hand, a detailed family album of Ishmael and company: Esau's children; Esau's grandchildren; even assorted chieftains and kings, goes beyond the lineage of the Messiah. Even if Crumb meant to say that these illustrious leaves on the Family Tree were in fact filled with folks like you or me — no halos nor Sunday-school-lesson tidiness — then we must ask why they are not even *normal* faces at all, but uniformly unpleasant, angry, gnarled, scowling or looking like the sheepherder off-screen just made a stinky.

In fact there are very few smiling faces in Crumb's *Book of Genesis*.

I mention this observation here, and not in the theological section of the essay, because Crumb has long been a master of the comic-strip art form. If 90 percent of humanity is miserable wretches (as Crumb's "potter's hands" have depicted them), then that is less "visual, literal" history (Crumb's pledge) than a theological postulate. Or it is an extra-biblical comment on human nature — redolent of what E. H. Gombrich called the psychology of pictorial representation — to serve ends apart from a "straight illustration job."

The disappointing delineations and the very narrative construction, I argue, do not disappoint because they stray from traditional representations, nor my own expectations, nor traditional Bible "stories" in frescoes or stained glass or tapestries or carvings or paintings or illustrations or comics or movies. He exercises free will to craft his exegesis; and that is not my problem here. There is a problem in this book of the comic strip *qua* comic strip. If one cannot escape the constraints of the form, if *some* interpretation is inevitable, one can nevertheless channel it, and not be exactly "faithful" (except to finish the phrase: "... to what"?) or purely "literal."

I once asked Al Capp a fawningly rhetorical question — "Do you consider cartoonists to be commentators?" — and he obliged with a brilliant answer: "When you draw a cat, there is no way you can *avoid* commenting on cats." Just so. That came to mind as I wrestled with Crumb's creation of *Genesis*. I am persuaded that this book comments (as, *per* Capp, unavoidably) not on the first book of the Bible, or even on the God who inhabits it, but ultimately comments more on Crumb himself: his view of life, his opinions of biblical traditions, his assessment of humankind. And *that* is not unavoidable.

It is hard, for the reader, to divorce Crumb's skepticism and rejection of textual elements of Genesis (especially revealed in the Commentary) from impressions to be gleaned from his comics. An outright rejectionist of biblical truth might draw a dozen sarcasm-flavored characters or scenes to produce an entertaining comic *and* to advance a point of view. To draw a version that *seems* literalist ... that in sum appears joyless ... that grinds out details and largely avoids narrative (and thereby, visual) excitement ... seems to lack purpose, to have an inchoate functionality.

Some of Crumb's sins of comic-strip syntax follow. Again, one can *read* the Bible and accept or reject, or imagine to various degrees, the narrative. But to *draw* (or otherwise depict, as movies have also done) the Bible accounts, you have not just an opportunity, but an obligation, to employ the tools at hand. (Especially when you are R. Crumb.) So, having kvetched about the peripheries of his *opus*; e. g., that all his Hebrew children look dyspeptic, my list of Crumb's (comic-strip) transgressions include:

The incessant march of minutia leaves the reader feeling like the Israelites, wandering 40 years in the desert. As a quasi-literalist (at least as appertains to actions and characters if not spiritual underpinnings) Crumb evidently was chary of excising words, passages, people and events. Yet he chose frequently to combine captions and balloons (more anon) — therefore *many* elements could have been carried by captions.

Comic-strip creators do not need to view Cecil B. DeMille epics to remind them that there are opportunities to spectacularly depict what is already spectacular: similarly, moments of extreme conflict or introspection, grief or joy. In the movies they are wide shots and close-ups, characters contemplating the pertinent themes, sound effects, the use of warping time and space for dramatic purposes, letting images serve narrative functions, contrasts and juxtapositions, parallel action and so forth. In the comic strip, the creator's opportunities are ... well, the same. And many more. I felt like a voice crying the wilderness with this book: there is one full-page drawing; no half-page drawings; three panels that fill two-thirds of a page; and 23 third-page panels (although some are compromised by captions). This in a book whose (unnumbered, *grrrr*) pages total 196. To paraphrase Jerry Seinfeld's exchange with Father Curtis in the "Yada Yada" episode: So this offends me as a Christian? No, it offends me as a student of the comic strip. This is not a procedural stolen-jewels mystery here — Crumb chose to depict the creation of the universe; humankind's origins; a Flood of, well, biblical proportions; the *Brit Bein HaBetarim* — the significant Abrahamic Covenant that had such profound effect on the world and three

major faiths; and all manner of God's physical, verbal interaction with humans. The book of Genesis also addresses sin, sex, mighty promises and mean betrayals, faith, temptation, revenge, retribution, repentance, sweet forgiveness, patience, incest, thievery, humor, grief and sacrifice — in fact, the first manifestations of all these things. One wishes that the cartoonist Crumb had honored the obvious dramatic highlights with double pages, longer sequences, and some appropriate graphic construction. Instead, except for the scorecard above, there is page after page of three-tiered grids and, often, small panels. Again, livelier architectonics would not have been a cheap trick of comix: expositors have followed the rules of homiletics — high points, dramatic effect — for centuries. It is a matter of being faithful, that is, logical, to the narrative.

All great stories (and even the secular, Literary Criticism crowd agree that Genesis is nothing if not a collection of great stories) subsist of conflict and resolution, dynamic tension and release, dilemmas and solutions. I am tempted to observe that, with Crumb's loping documentarianism, *The Book of Genesis* reserves its climaxes for the voyeuristic copulation scenes.

The captions in *The Book of Genesis* are maddening. Sometimes necessary, they often are also intrusive, or utterly superfluous. Crumb's book hearkens back, in this way, to the proto-comic British picture-stories... or before. Too many times there is a panel with a caption: "He said:" next to a balloon where he or she says something. To a reader already overwhelmed by an over-abundance of detail this seems, in the ancient Mosaic term, meshuga nah. If Crumb were absolutely faithful to one text, this would be understandable. However, he informs the reader in the Introduction (not even after the fact in the back-of-the-book Commentary), that he chose to judiciously pick and choose from more than one source. Choosing what "works" and what doesn't from various sources would seem to free Crumb from redundancies in captions and elsewhere. It really asks more questions that should not be questions in the first place: does he intend similitude, or verisimilitude? Is Truth (or an attempt to understand and present Truth) at the core of the book, or fiction clothed in the semblance of truth? A carefully-faithful-looking, but carefully-not-faith-filled, pictorialization?

In that sense, Crumb keeps kosher in his book, not to religious rules, but to the slogan of the Elvis Café in (believe it or not) Abu Ghosh, on the road to Jerusalem: "Not real but realistic."

In short, Crumb, whose career has revealed him as a master of intelligent design (pun intended), broke many of the form's commandments in this book.

History

Many of us accept the Bible literally, and Genesis (therefore) as an historical account. Does an individual's salvation depend on believing in six literal days (*yom*, always meaning a 24-hour day, used specifically in the original Hebrew) of Creation? Of the Noahic flood? Of the existence of an actual Sodom and its destruction (persuasive remains of which have recently been discovered, rattling skeptics)? Probably not. Yet it is dangerous thing — the famous "slippery slope" — to adopt a pick-and-choose approach to what one believes; that is, what one believes God says. There are dozens of examples, for instance, citing Jesus' literal acceptance of Genesis, in every aspect. Therefore one who accepts Jesus as God Incarnate must accept His understanding. There are no possibilities (quoting C. S. Lewis) other than Jesus being a liar, a fool or the Son of God.

Thomas Henry Huxley, who promoted Charles Darwin better than did Charles Darwin, accepted Jesus' challenge. When science clashes with the Bible, the result is the undermining of "Jewish Scriptures," "Messianic Doctrine" and "Paul's dialectic," he claimed. That is true ... in contemporary culture; that is, in a Nietzschean sense. Before 150 years ago, it was otherwise. In the postmodern ethos — in this post-Christian culture — secularism is becoming a religion and biblical beliefs are becoming anathema. Crumb looks to the First Book and finds questions;

"Does he intend similitude, or verisimilitude? Is Truth (or an attempt to understand and present Truth) at the core of the book, or fiction clothed in the semblance of truth?"

history wants us to look to the Last Book (indeed, the whole Book) and find answers.

The Book of Genesis Illustrated by R. Crumb could have been an illustrated history; Crumb did his homework for the historical trappings. Devoid of a belief of its essential veracity and relying on numerous interpretations, legends and theories about its reality — while rejecting the considerable body of biblical interpretation, effectively evincing a hostility to such — the book becomes a visit to a theme park, not, say, an archaeological dig. Not only theology, but history is ill-served.

But Crumb did not set out to do history? Like Capp's view of commentary, this cannot be escaped. It seems clear that Crumb did not set out to limn history, any more than he was convinced of the text's truth or falsity. Nor, probably, did he desire to address those questions. As the book has been assembled, however, it would properly be categorized for bookstore-placement, not as "Graphics" or "Religion" (as on the back cover) but as "Historiography" — the history of history. Everything Crumb has done in this book, whether on his own or as a disciple of Robert Alter, is the stuff of historiography: interpretation, analysis, literary criticism, "truth" vs. "fact," evaluation of competing myths, epistemology, questions of revisionism vs. tradition and so forth. (Historiography of the late 20th century encompassed semiotic theory ... oh, why did Crumb check that at the door?)

Although all of biblical history is the story of God's encounter with man (we are fond of saying that Religion is mankind reaching up to God; Christianity is God reaching down to mankind), there are certain points where the "vertical" intersects with the "linear" more than at other times. The Incarnation is one point; the Genesis story surely is another. That Crumb depicted one distinct interpretation, provided a concordance of other interpretations, rejected Christian interpretations ... all result in *The Book of Genesis Illustrated by R. Crumb* standing as a work of Historiography, more than as a religious book, even more than as a comic strip. Because it is provocative, it succeeds on that level.

Speaking of the book's jacket, I guess Crumb (or publisher W. W. Norton) hoped that some bookstores have a "hardback tabloid" section. The design and promotional copy might lead some scholars to deduce that ancient texts of EC Comics and various literary strains of the *National Enquirer* and *The Star* influenced this cover in subtle ways. What were they thinking of?

A promo-burst: "Adult supervision recommended for minors." What nonsensical, not to mention needless, pandering. I suppose the publisher will contend that some tepid booksellers needed to be mollified, but a) Norton could shrink-wrap the book; and b) any bookseller carrying an R. Crumb book, on whatever subject, is not equivocal about customers' sensibilities. No, the cover of *The Book of Genesis Illustrated by R. Crumb* is just T&A — Titillation and Artifice; and Crumb should be embarrassed. "The first book of the Bible graphically depicted!" continues the misuse of "graphic," to suggest, sigh, the prurient; and is redolent of the days when publishers would call a book's content "exotic," with a wink to customers seeking the "erotic" (and when the contents usually were neither). "NOTHING LEFT OUT!" another blurb reads, modestly using a single exclamation point. I will bet there are more kids who will ask, "Mommy, is that woman supposed to be pretty?" than will notice an occasional weenie, circumcised or not: even the be-fruitful-and-multiply scenes/incest category are no more salacious than Crumb's other depictions. Anyway, Barnes & Noble is not about to hide Crumb's *Genesis* behind last month's *Cosmo*, so the breathless warning labels on the cover are dopey ploys to attract the sweaty-palmed, I suppose. Better to have the serpent drop the F-bomb when banished from the Garden of Eden, and be done with it; happily slap the "R" rating on the cover.

(Also, scholars are needed to help me interpret the largest promo-burst on the cover: "ALL 50 CHAPTERS." Have there been previous comics versions expurgated to 47 chapters?)

Crumb makes a point in his Introduction and Commentary to assure readers of his fidelity to history, that is, history as revealed in his props, settings and costumes. His inclinations led him like a pillar of fire at night; and his friends, who are generously acknowledged, assisted with documentation. The flavor of these elements (whether accurate or not!) provides a powerful underpinning to the book's attractiveness. In fact they are remarkable evocations, in corpus, and might ultimately be a major legacy of the book, perhaps itself becoming a resource for scholars.

Unfortunately (returning to my basic disappointment that Crumb's work here flirts with banality) the textbook depictions of props, settings and costumes tends to envelop the characters and action, instead of providing a context or illuminating their environment. The book of Genesis contains, after all, the greatest collection of supernatural events in the world. Except for the unalterable script of Crumb's first chapters, he delineates mighty miracles in mundane ways. The reader longs for the images to propel the story — not just the story, but its graphic, frankly outrageous possibilities.

But perhaps we Crumb fans are bowing to a false idol. The book's jacket says "Illustrated" and "...graphically depicted." Crumb's Introduction clearly signals that he "approached this as a straight illustration job." So if we are disappointed that Crumb has eschewed many of the comic-strip cartoonist's techniques... we have failed to notice that, despite the panels and speech balloons, this is not a comic strip but an illustrated text, a picture-story reminiscent of the times that antedated the language and structure of the comic strip. I conclude that this project would be more satisfactory as a portfolio of his fabulous images, not this feast-nor-fowl creation.

Whether The Book of Genesis Illustrated by R. Crumb proves to be incunabulum — not simply as the first book of the Bible, wrapped in the swaddling clothes of apparent historicity, but as the genesis of a new thematic preoccupation of its translator — we must wait. Well, we waited at least 6,000 years for this exposition, so we can wait for an Exodus, a Revelation, or anything in between.

Anticipating the response to his four years' of work, Crumb writes a preemptive warning, if not an apology, in the book, presumably referring

to the text, not the art. If it "offends or outrages some readers. ... All I can say in my defense is that I approached this as a straight illustration job." We can take Crumb at his word (or His Word), but I — as a fan of Crumb and a fan of God — was not particularly offended or outraged. But I was disappointed.

Thou shalt not! ∎

AN EPIC VISUALIZED

BY DONALD PHELPS

Robert Crumb's transliteration of Genesis into paneled narrative emerges from his drawing board as a consummate triumph, in what — thanks to the earthy vitality and sheer passion with which he has invested it — amounts to a new genre. Lumbering to identify his triumph, I can only recall another genre viewed, by this writer, only meagerly. I recall the film triumphs of Carl Theodor Dreyer: *The Passion of Joan of Arc* and *Leaves From Satan's Book*. Crumb's vital earnestness of absorption in his subject revitalizes the comic-strip genre. His adaptation — the Bible's first book — is reinforced by the familiar textures of his fiercely earnest realism.

In this instance, Crumb makes us recall the humane skepticism of his worldly textures and the shabby vitality of his folk-heroes: Mr. Natural (the white bearded sage); Fritz (the female-fixated cat); and Etaoin Shrdlu (the brain-stagnant TV-addict). The mix of consummate hopelessness and ever-revived desire and resource has attained blazing identity in the Old Testament's battling, copulating, murdering, God-invoking Hebrews. And not to be forgotten: the zealous, sometimes raging, often heartsick faith of the Old Testament's cast.

Robert Crumb, in this graphic masterpiece, has effected a virtual new genre, a visual narrative that enlarges and re-electrifies its subject.

Accompanied by a procession of black-and-white illustrations, the texts of Hebraic history are unreeled: from Adam and Eve, to the Jews' settlement in Egypt under Joseph. The fusion of bodies, faces, costumes and settings produces a density at once historic and dramatic; the most powerful appeal being the sheer immediacy of Crumb's history, a narrative power fully as immediate and as poignant as any film (by D. W. Griffith, or Dreyer, say) might realize.

The stature of this beautiful work is confirmed by a postscript: an account, of some length, in which Crumb describes the progress of his own enlightenment about the progress of Hebraic and Mesopotamian cultures in the days described and represented. A treasure, this: in the advance of the graphic arts, and of biblical study.

II

Crumb's *Genesis* unreels — a fair term for the jostling, lurching rhythms, in a succession of black-and-white panels, of roughly hewn faces, bodies, garments — in a procession of writhing, glamorous, utterly functional postures: accompanied by the dry earnest murmur of (captioned) biblical narrative — now and then, half a page will offer an immense prospect: the building and launching of the Noah's Ark; the decimation of Sodom and Gomorrah — the sober magnitude of which arrests and, somewhat, relieves the eye. But the dominant tone is the fiercely focused rapture of Crumb's scholarly *and* artistic dedication. He contributes to the mission — religious and artistic — an intensity at once intellectual, whole-hearted and sublime. ∎

TOP

Crumb's rogue gallery (images [©1970, 1972, 1981 R. Crumb]): left; Fritz the Cat in "Superstar"; middle, Mr. Natural in "Meeting of the Minds"; and Etaoin Shrdlu in "TV Blues."

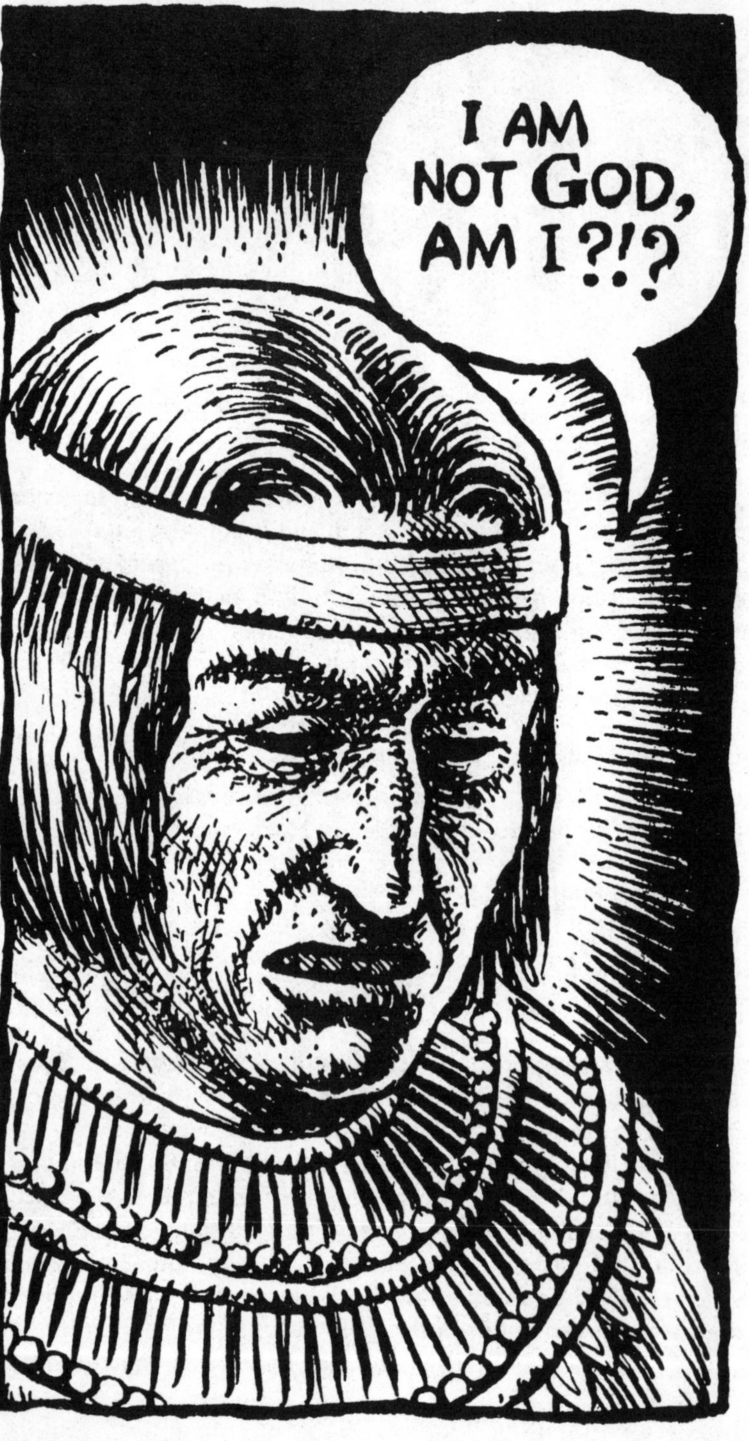
I AM NOT GOD, AM I?!?

CRUMB FINALLY FINDS HIS LIMITS

BY ROBERT STANLEY MARTIN

Robert Crumb is undeniably one of our greatest cartoonists. Before him, the best comics artists — for example, Winsor McCay, Harvey Kurtzman and Charles Schulz — were commercial entertainers before they were anything else; they always produced their work with one eye on the audience. If they had to make a choice between following their muse and alienating their readers, concern for their readers always won out. Crumb was the first to embrace the Romantic ideal of the artist. Following his muse was paramount, with self-expression and art for art's sake the highest goals. There were no limits on subject matter with Crumb. And he has used his freedom to develop a satirical eye and command of nuance that is unmatched by any of his peers. Each new Crumb strip has been an event for readers for more than four decades now.

Ironically, it has always been a challenge to recommend work by him to those unfamiliar with his œuvre. Most people need to get acclimated before being confronted with his more extreme material. There is also the problem of format. Crumb has always embraced the increasingly anachronistic magazine format for comics; he doesn't like thinking about his work in graphic-novel terms. (He once said the thought of the work involved in producing a book-length effort was enough to make him physically ill.) My usual solution has been to refer people to the *Kafka for Beginners* book he produced with writer David Zane Mairowitz. The underlying material is familiar to most readers to at least some degree, and Crumb keeps his excesses in check. Most importantly, his earthy, anxious artwork is very much at home with the adaptations of Franz Kafka excerpts, dramatizations of the writer's life and satirical pokes at Kafka's contemporary readership. My only reservation in recommending it is that Crumb was perhaps a bit too sympathetic to Kafka's work. A great adaptation would have had the two's sensibilities at odds to a degree; it would provide a great reading of both Kafka and Crumb as artists.

The Book of Genesis, when it was announced as a work-in-progress a few years back, was promoted as the magnum opus we have never gotten from Crumb. When considered relative to the Kafka effort, it promised to duplicate that book's strengths and transcend its shortcomings. Described as a comprehensive adaptation of the biblical material, the Genesis project would be a book-length effort. The material would make it accessible beyond the coterie of Crumb's readership. And best of all, it promised the enlightening discords readers didn't get from Crumb's handling of Kafka. The thought of Crumb's trenchantly satirical perspective illuminating this hoariest of ancient texts was irresistible. One hoped for the pot at the end of the artistic rainbow: a rich, defining statement from a great contemporary talent, and a brilliantly irreverent reading of a monolithic cultural touchstone. One anticipated a work that could redefine one's view of both artist and subject. This material has inspired it before; just think of John Milton and Paradise Lost.

Well, the book has now been published, and it is a strong reminder of the truism that one should never get one's hopes up in the arts. (I hasten to add that I didn't anticipate anything as accomplished as Milton.) Anyone expecting an imaginative retelling of the biblical material, or an inspired effort from Crumb, isn't going to find it here. In his introduction, Crumb writes, "I approached this as a straight illustration job, with no intention to ridicule or make visual jokes." He can say that again. His treatment of the material is grindingly literal-minded. It is barren of any hint of satire, irony or even allegory. In short, it is a plodding, R-rated Classics Illustrated rendering of the biblical text. Crumb often isn't even visually in especially good form.

Crumb's timidity in imposing his point of view on the material goes beyond eschewing a satirical or other conspicuously re-imaginative approach. He won't even give it his own narrative rhythms. One of the pleasures of Crumb's work is the loose, open pacing he employs; combined with his incomparable eye for detail, it gives his work a lifelike texture that few cartoonists can duplicate. However, in Genesis, he doesn't allow scenes to play out and find

their own shape. Instead, he largely adopts the monotonous, illustrated-text approach of *Prince Valiant* cartoonist Hal Foster: a panel that largely repeats the same information accompanies a snippet of exposition. No thought has been given to using the text as a counterpoint to the images. The dialogue scenes aren't much different. Talking heads and indifferently posed figures tediously expound at one another. Crumb's usually acute dramatic sense largely abandons him. He grossly overuses manic-eyed, raised-hair expressions for dramatic emphasis, numbing whatever effect they might have if used more sparingly. The rare, reasonably well-dramatized scene, such as Tamar's seduction of Judah in Chapter 38, isn't enjoyable so much as it is a relief from the rest of book's dramatically repetitive tedium.

The individual drawings aren't especially interesting, either. Crumb's figure drawing is frequently desultory, and his treatment of the characters' faces is often hackneyed. He makes an effort to individualize the men's faces, but the refusal to shape the scenes dramatically makes the characters largely indistinguishable from another. In one chapter, he models a trio of brothers after the Three Stooges, and it barely registers. The female characters fare even worse. The most prominent ones, including Eve, Sarah, Rebekah, and Rachel, all look like Crumb's Devil Girl. Crumb's vision of God is a retread of the Michelangelo cliché of the stern, robust old man with a long, flowing beard. The one character I was really looking forward to seeing Crumb's treatment of was the Garden of Eden's serpent. It's a letdown; Crumb makes the character an indifferently drawn rehash of one of Wallace Wood or Mark Schultz' lizard people.

TOP LEFT
Eve

TOP RIGHT
Devil Girl in "The Meeting" from *Hup #2*
[©1987 R. Crumb]

The drawing is probably at its most interesting when Crumb models it after the work of one of his idols, Pieter Bruegel the Elder. Crumb frequently falls back on Bruegel imagery when the text requires him to illustrate the more abstract verses. However, even that wears out its welcome. One can take only so many images of earthy peasants tilling the land, or herding livestock or sitting down at communal gatherings before the sight has one's eyes sliding off the page.

The overwhelming problem with *Genesis* is that Crumb doesn't seem to have thought it through as a dramatic piece. The scenes are not played off each other for dramatic effect, and he doesn't imagine the characters as distinct, idiosyncratic personalities whose interactions are greater than the sum of the parts. He just seems to have illustrated each verse, one after the other, without any consideration as to how they might contribute to a larger whole. When one reads the most accomplished graphic novels, such as *Maus*, *Watchmen* or *Black Hole*, one sees that the authors carefully weigh each moment with an eye on the reading experience of the entire book. It's the main reason the books are so understated dramatically; it makes the climactic passages all the more effective. At their poetic best, they take an idea, and seeing the need to present it in different terms for the sake of their

LEFT
The Hunt for Wild Hares, engraved by Pieter Bruegel (The Elder) himself.

RIGHT
Pieter Bruegel (The Elder) is an influence on Crumb.

and the reader's interest, reimagine it as a trope — a metaphor, an ironic moment or whatnot. As the books develop, they create new tropes out of the previous ones, and one reaches the end with one's view of the original idea transformed again and again. Compared to these books, *Genesis* seems creatively lazy. It comes across as hackneyed, and the saddest aspect of it is that it is hackneyed in Crumb's own terms. His unrelenting dramatic fortissimo makes the entire book feel flat, and he doesn't build his ideas into tropes — he lets them degenerate into clichés.

Genesis isn't a slothful effort; producing it took five years of Crumb's life, with the effort apparent in every intensively crosshatched panel. But it comes across as more of a test of his artistic endurance than an opportunity to expand his creative range. Perhaps he was right to once feel physically ill at the prospect of having to produce a book-length effort. The problem, though, has proved not to be the amount of work that would need completion; it's that he's not up to the creative challenges such a project entails. I should emphasize that there's no shame in being only a master of short pieces, as Crumb most assuredly is. I love Alice Munro and Ernest Hemingway's work, but I've never been that taken with their novels, either. ■

This essay is a revised and expanded version of a review published on the author's Pol Culture blog.

GENESIS REVISITED

BY JEET HEER

I published one of the earliest and most favorable reviews of Crumb's *The Book of Genesis Illustrated*, and in the ensuing months my opinion of the book has only risen. Below are some notes on the book and its response.

The stature of the book. Robert Crumb is one of the greatest cartoonists of the last century. His only real rivals in terms of producing comics that reach deep into the human concern are George Herriman and Charles Schulz. *The Book of Genesis Illustrated* is not Crumb's masterpiece; he's had too long and varied a career to be summed up in one work. But it belongs in the small pantheon of his other first-rank works, including "Let's Talk Sense About This Here Modern America," "That's Life," "Those Cute Little Bearzy Wearzies in 'Ain't It Nice,'" "Patton," "Boswell's London Journal," "Trash," "Uncle Bob's Mid-Life Crisis," "The Religious Experience of Philip K. Dick," a few of the Harvey Pekar collaborations, and Crumb's sketchbook from the mid-1970s. These are among the greatest comics anyone has ever done, and the *Book of Genesis* is a worthy addition to this canon. My sense is that most people don't rate the book that high, but I'll try and explain why through the course of this essay.

Commercial success, critical muddle. Crumb's *Genesis* has been a great commercial success. In North America, Norton didn't print enough copies and there were periods where you had to wait weeks for the next edition to arrive. But the critical response has been more muted. Robert Alter, the translator Crumb relied heavily but not exclusively on, wrote the most intelligent review, which ran in *The New Republic*. Alter's long essay was appreciative and full of keen observations, but marred by a theoretically confused discussion of the limits of comics.

"A visual representation of a character or an event is inevitably a specification," Alter argues.

> When we see Er as a cutthroat who
> gets his own throat cut, the meaning
> of 'was evil in the eyes of the Lord'
> and the mechanism of 'the Lord
> put him to death' are strongly stipulated, and other possible meanings are closed off. This foreclosure of ambiguity or of multiple meanings is intrinsic to the graphic narrative medium, and hence is pervasive in the illustrated text ... This disparity between how words and pictures work as narrative vehicles is by no means limited to the Bible. Imagine for a moment an illustrated version of *Anna Karenina* or *The Charterhouse of Parma*, in which there would be one or more graphic frame for every sentence of the novel. An artist with Crumb's inventive energy might provide many pleasures along the way, but what is enabled in the novel through words — the deft slide in and out of the point of view of the characters, the subtle play of irony, the nice discriminations of the narrator's analytic observations — would inevitably be flattened in the pictorial representation.

What Alter doesn't allow for is that pictures can be as ambiguous, as rich in meaning, as words. Nor is it clear why a graphic adaptation of *Anna Karenina* would need to use one panel (or frame) per sentence. Most adaptations are freer than that (see for example R. Sikoryak's extremely wild but also revealing adaptation of many classic works in his *Masterpiece Comics*). Crumb was more literal than most translators, but that's for the very good reason that he's dealing with a venerable and dense text. Someone adapting a novel would most likely do the job freestyle.

TOP

From "Uncle Bob's Mid-Life Crisis" in *Weirdo #7* [©1983 R. Crumb]

107

"People are trying to read the book as if it's a new graphic novel by Crumb. It's not and that frustrates them."

In talking about how the adaptation is inferior to the original, Alter failed to realize that every adaptation is by necessity not a replication of the original, but to some degree a commentary on the original work and also a fresh work in and of itself. Crumb's illustrated version can't replace the original but that's true of any adaptation of a great work. Benjamin Britten's *Billy Budd* opera doesn't overthrow Herman Melville's novella, but rather gives us another way of approaching the same story.

To put it another way, even if we had the Hebrew knowledge of a Robert Alter, we can't have an unmediated and unvarnished view of the Bible, a venerable text surrounded by layers of tradition and commentary. Each new adaptation is not a replacement of the original, but rather part of the millennium-spanning conversation about the original. Crumb is, in that sense, following in the Talmudic tradition, as is Alter himself with both his translation and the extensive exegesis that runs along the bottom of his translations. Still, Alter's review shines forth in its intelligence, especially when compared to Harold Bloom's boorish display of complacency and ignorance in *The New York Review of Books*.

The Comics World and the General Community. If Crumb is now being embraced by a general readership, the comics world remains divided about the new work and there have been many grumblings. I think the main objections to the book come from category errors about what Crumb is doing. People are trying to read the book as if it's a new graphic novel by Crumb. It's not and that frustrates them.

The Bible is not a novel, and the *Book of Genesis Illustrated* is not a graphic novel. I'm not a conventionally religious person, but I've read the Bible closely and repeatedly. In reading Crumb, I've particularly benefited from a reading group I belonged to a few years ago where we read the book of Genesis very slowly (about one page per week). This snail-pace reading is the only way you can really appreciate what the Bible is all about. The Bible is a puzzling book because it lacks the narrative propulsion found in many great works of literature, ranging from Homer's epics to the novels of Philip Roth. But the Bible is not a coherent work of literature the way the other classics are. It's a heavily edited tribal encyclopedia with a strong agenda created by a priestly caste over generations and then re-interpreted by Christians and Muslims.

The book of Genesis in particular is a real grab bag of a book, which starts with a cosmology, shifts into a fairy tale about a talking snake, morphs into a disaster story about a flood and eventually becomes a family saga, all of which is interspersed with genealogies. The coherence that comes from the book comes from attention to small details. To give you one example of how the Bible benefits from close reading: at first the story of Noah's Flood and the destruction of Sodom might seem very different. But as Robert Alter points out in his textual note, when examined closely, the stories mirror each other. "Moshe Weinfeld has aptly observed a whole series of parallels between the two stories," Alter observes. "In each case, God wipes out a whole population because of epidemic moral perversion, marking one family for survival. In each case, the idiom 'to keep alive seed' is used for survival. In each case, the male survivor becomes drunk and is somehow

AND NOAH, A MAN OF THE SOIL, WAS THE FIRST TO PLANT A VINEYARD. AND HE DRANK OF THE WINE AND BECAME DRUNK AND EXPOSED HIMSELF WITHIN HIS TENT.

sexually violated by his offspring, although only Lot is unambiguously represented as the object of an incestuous advance." Knowing the story of Lot allows us to reread the tale of Noah with fresh eyes and ask what it means when it says that Ham, Noah's son, "saw his father's nakedness" (clearly a euphemism). Many such discoveries await the patient reader who is willing to pay attention and occasionally avail herself of textual commentary. This is not the way we normally read a book of literature, but it's the best way to read Genesis.

In sum, if you want to fully appreciate Crumb's book, you have to be prepared to give it a lot of time, much more so than an ordinary book. But the payoff for the work is that you'll see the origins of many of the central myths of Western civilization.

Crumb the conservative, Crumb the radical. Crumb hasn't kept pace with the effort of younger cartoonists to create comics that capture the small texture of experience the way the best films and fiction does. Crumb is, and always has been, a deeply conservative artist, one that keeps returning to the mainsprings of his tradition. To this day, the way he organizes a page and has his people move around in it bears the mark of Carl Barks, John Stanley and Harvey Kurtzman. Crumb's indifference to the graphic-novel aesthetic can be seen in one of the book's major faults; the cover of the North American edition is garish and ugly: the attempts by artists like Ware and Seth to improve the standards of book design clearly don't interest Crumb. Yet it is precisely Crumb's devotion to traditional forms that also makes him so revolutionary. To take a stylistic licks from past masters like Barks and apply them to stories about sex and drugs was and remain a potently subversive act. To then adopt the famous Crumb style to the Bible adds another twist of the knife.

The genealogy of The Book of Genesis Illustrated. One reason Crumb's book is off-putting to the comics community is that Crumb is working in a very unfashionable tradition, the *Classics Illustrated* style of text-heavy, non-cinematic storytelling, where the pictures and text sit next to each other like two passengers on a bus, rather than blending smoothly in the way that always makes R. C. Harvey so happy. The *Classics Illustrated* approach was never much loved by comics fans or critics at large (Delmore Schwartz in particular hated these comic-book adaptations). I myself am not a big fan, but Crumb has shown just how flexible and deep this approach can be.

In particular, his pictures don't just replicate what's in the text, but often offer a sly commentary on it, as in the scenes where the text has the women following the orders of their husbands. Crumb often suggests that they are not doing so willingly. Instead of blending words and pictures, Crumb often has them quietly at war with each other, the pictures sometimes acting as a grumbling heckler that wants us to jeer at the text.

Other sources. Aside from *Classics Illustrated* and *Picture Stories from the Bible*, Crumb has surely looked at Basil Wolverton's Bible illustrations (now available in the great Fantagraphics book *The Wolverton Bible*). Crumb has often talked about his debt to Basil Wolverton, going back to the sacred cover of *Mad* Comics #11.

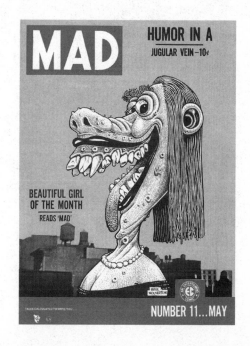

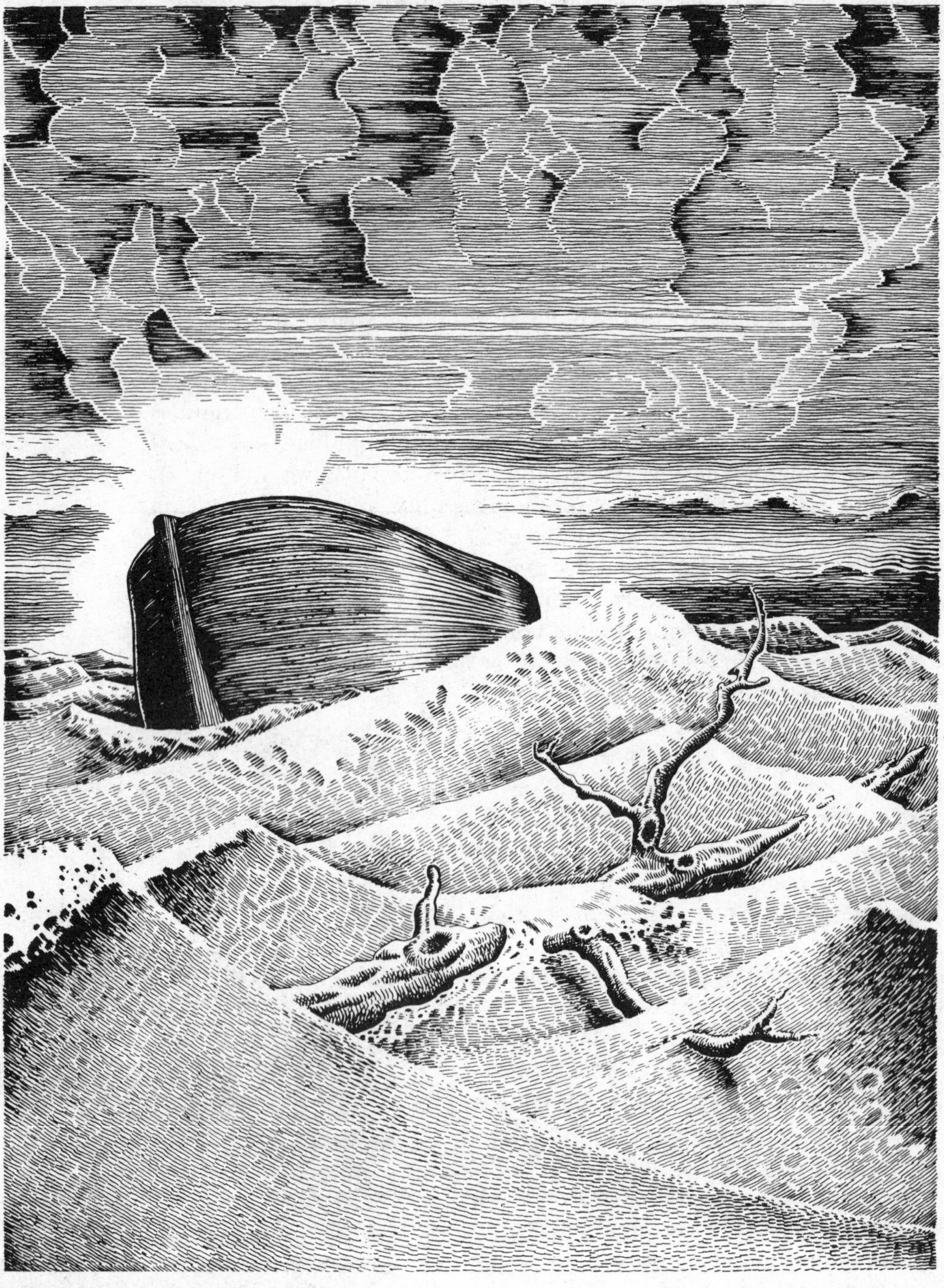

AND THE WATER SURGED OVER THE EARTH 150 DAYS.

At left is a scene from Wolverton's rendition of the Noah story.

And above is a panel from Crumb's *The Book of Genesis Illustrated*. Notice that in both Wolverton and Crumb, the choppy waves have an oddly static look, as if they were sand dunes rather than water.

Other adaptations. One day, a scholar will look at all of Crumb's adaptations in addition to Genesis — his renderings of Franz Kafka, Philip K. Dick, Jean-Paul Sartre, James Boswell, and Richard Freiherr von Krafft-Ebbing and others. Crumb has a common methodology in all his adaptations. He's always drawn to extreme texts, those that offer intense emotional states or unconventional behavior (certainly true of the incest-rich stories in Genesis). Also he's always very faithful to the text and tries to visualize each textual detail. Another fruitful project would be to compare Crumb to contemporary cartoonists who adapt the classics, notably R. Sikoryak and Kim Deitch (who did a memorable distillation of The Book of Job).

The two traditions. Crumb has often talked about what he sees as the two major traditions in Western representational art. On the one hand there

LEFT

From *The Wolverton Bible* [©2009 The Worldwide Church of God]

is the high, heroic tradition that runs from Michelangelo to Raphael, to Academic Painting to Burne Hogarth to Frank Frazetta and the modern superhero comic. On the other hand, there is the low comic tradition of Pieter Bruegel, William Hogarth (the good Hogarth), Will Elder and Crumb himself. Interestingly, illustrations of the Bible almost always come from the high heroic tradition, with the exception of Crumb's own work and that of Basil Wolverton.

The syntax of the Bible, the syntax of comics. One of the virtues of Robert Alter's translation is that it preserves as much as possible the syntax of the Hebrew original. As Alter notes, "biblical syntax is additive, working with parallel clauses linked by 'and'." Thus biblical syntax often looks like a train with a series of small phrases joined together by "and". An example from Genesis Chapter 24 (Alter translation): "... and she came down to the spring and filled her jug and came back up. And the servant..." It seems to me that the visual syntax of comics (breaking down action to discrete panels) is also "additive" and thus very similar to biblical syntax. This is especially true if you make the panels roughly the same size, as Crumb tends to do except for special occasion (great disasters, genealogies).

Ethnicity. Here is an example of how Crumb's book rewards close attention. Western Art often makes biblical characters look European, if not exclusively Nordic. Crumb is careful to make his characters look Middle Eastern. There is a tradition that Ishmael is the father of the Arabs. So when Crumb depicts the descendants of Ishmael (Chapter 25) they look Arabic.

The Devil is in the details. Many visualizations of the Bible glide over the difficult passages. For example, Sarah was 90 years old when she gave birth to Isaac, but it is rare for a painting or illustration of Sarah to actually depict her as that old, as Crumb does (Chapter 21). The sight of the haggard Sarah nursing a baby is one of the many visual shocks Crumb provides simply by paying attention to the text.

A book about people. Genesis starts with God creating the universe, but over the course of the book, the deity recedes and humanity takes the foreground. Eventually, in the story of Joseph and his brothers, God exists only as a dream-like visitation. Genesis thus is really a book about people as much as about theology. The most impressive aspect of Crumb's adaptation is his skill in drawing characters: the servile Noah and his stupid sons (who look, Paul Karasik has noted, like The Three Stooges), willful Sarah, Lot the sodden refugee from Sodom, the wild Ishmael, the sly Rebekah, the masterly Joseph. There are scores of characters in the book, and they are all individuated with care. To read the book is to spend time with a town-full of characters.

AND SHE SAID... WHO WOULD HAVE UTTERED TO ABRAHAM, "SARAH IS SUCKLING SONS!" FOR I'VE BORNE HIM A SON IN HIS OLD AGE!

Final judgment. The Book of Genesis Illustrated is a major work of comics. If we are playing the ranking game, I'd say it joins the small book shelf of essential comic books, next to Maus, Jimmy Corrigan, I Never Liked You and Palestine. As an adaptation, the value of Crumb's book can't be separated from the value of the book of Genesis itself. That's partially a matter of the length of the book and the investment in time and mental energy it requires. But there is no gainsaying the importance of Genesis and as I've tried to suggest here, the pleasures of the book are many and real for readers who are willing to make an effort. ■

STRAIGHT LINES

BY TIM HODLER

It all begins with God. The universe is a void without form, until a stern, virile, all-powerful and full-bearded man creates the heavens and the earth. In his comic-book adaptation of the Book of Genesis, Robert Crumb has chosen a remarkably conventional bodily form for God — this is the deity from the ceiling of the Sistine Chapel, Cecil B. DeMille and countless *New Yorker* gag cartoons — which has proven the subject of much discussion. Some, who apparently expected a more extravagantly imaginative depiction from "Mr. Sixties," have reported feeling shortchanged. But while considering this book, it is important to keep two things in mind. 1. Crumb claims to believe in God. 2. The God of Genesis is not the God he believes in. As he writes in the introduction, Crumb does "not believe the Bible is 'the word of God,'" but instead the words of men. "It is, nonetheless," he writes, "a powerful text with layers of meaning that reach deep into our collective consciousness, our *historical* consciousness, if you will." By illustrating Genesis, Crumb doesn't want to retell the true story of the origins of earth and humanity, but instead to illuminate the myth that Western man has told himself about those origins for millennia. And in the story Western man likes to tell himself (and his children), a big strong white man created the universe.

This blatant bit of anthropocentric self-congratulation is the kind of obvious-in-retrospect but often missed point that cartoonists were born to draw and everything about Crumb's *Genesis* is designed for just this purpose: to hold out for examination as many of these easily overlooked connections and ironies and discrepancies as possible, found in what is, after all, a very old and difficult-to-understand text. But against his reputed usual practice, Crumb has chosen to forgo the laughs this time. Instead, he claims to have taken on Genesis as a "straight illustration job" (a quote which I expect will be included in every essay in this roundtable, and about which more later); he's just drawing what's there, folks! Every word is right from the Bible, nothing added, nothing removed. You can't blame Crumb for any of it.

...AND SHE ALSO GAVE TO HER MAN, AND HE ATE.

Once you accept that premise, Crumb's decision to go with so much conventional biblical imagery — Adam and Eve are also straight out of central casting, and even the fruit they eat is the old storybook apple, rather than a fig or pomegranate, as is more likely accurate (if less familiar) — grows more understandable. If Crumb had chosen to portray God as a black woman (as he once contemplated doing), it would have focused the reader's attention too strongly on Crumb himself, and his artistic decisions. Using the old familiar Sunday-school images, on the other hand, allows readers to forget that Crumb is even there, making all kinds of choices in every panel about what they see and what they don't, and obscures the fact that he is not really doing a simple straight illustration job at all. Those critics who have complained that Crumb has been too faithful in his adaptation, that he hasn't added anything to Genesis, and that therefore the whole exercise is pointless, have fallen right into his trap.

Not that Crumb actually intends to mislead readers about the contents of Genesis; he just wants you to see the book the same way he does, and must know that if Mr. Natural popped up now and again to deliver commentary on the action, it would be counterproductive to his aim. But it is important to realize that Crumb's adaptation technique is much more complicated than it appears at casual glance, and far more so than most commentators have credited: this not his first literary adaptation (though it is the first, to my knowledge, which comics critics have so misunderstood). In his comic-book versions of Richard von Krafft-Ebing, Philip K. Dick, Jelly Roll Morton, Jean-Paul Sartre and James Boswell, Crumb uses exactly the same technique, matching verbatim phrases from an original text with images taken out of Crumb's own imagination and research. And in those cases, too, Crumb meant to draw out his source material's contradictions. "In all those literary things that I did, I saw something comic in the characters that was probably not intended to be there in the original," Crumb explained to Jean-Pierre Mercer in *Qui a peur de Robert Crumb?*

> There was something that lent itself to a comic-book rendition that was probably not intended by [Sartre]. The same thing with Philip K. Dick and his religious experiences: There's something absurd and comical about his paranoia and his religious visions and how he interpreted them. Boswell, also, with his pretensions to being a cultured gentleman whilst he was compulsively going out and looking for prostitutes in the park every night.

In a way, it is perhaps even possible to trace elements of Crumb's adaptation process back to his collaborations with Harvey Pekar; those stories must have posed a continual challenge in terms of devising visuals strong enough to accompany Pekar's very text-heavy and action-light stories. (Interestingly, Pekar himself has dismissed Crumb's *Genesis* in what appears to be a casually tossed off comic-strip review for the *Jewish Review of Books.* "So what I think the story is, is there's no story," writes Pekar. "Crumb said he used various translations of the bible literally, he didn't add or subtract. So the text, to me, is no big deal." (A strange attitude for a comics writer to take when discussing one of his own artistic collaborators; he presumably didn't want Crumb monkeying around too much with *his* words.)

But yes, Crumb has included the entire text of Genesis, and "merely" illustrated the words by portraying key actions. To several of Crumb's detractors, the results have looked as repetitive and word/image redundant as Al Feldstein-penned EC comics at their worst. But Crumb's process is almost never actually as simple as it first appears (and I am not just referring to Crumb's beautifully crosshatched art, perhaps the most accomplished and breathtaking of his career —Pekar again: "The illustration is wonderful, but you can count on Crumb for great drawing"). An example picked at random (honest!): A panel from Chapter 14 is captioned, "And he and his servants with him fanned out against them

by night and struck them and pursued them to Hobah, which is north of Damascus." In the drawing that accompanies this narration, Abram and two other robed men ride camels in pursuit of a group of men, apparently trampling some of their enemies and spearing others. Abram, in particular, impales a tribesman through his back. That Abram and his servants tracked down a group of foreign invaders, and reclaimed lost property and kidnapped kinsmen from them is information given in the text; that Abram and his servants did so this violently is not. (For that matter, that they were riding camels is not, nor that the ground was littered with bodies and discarded weapons and gore, nor that Abram is not above a little back-stabbing, etc.) Crumb's panel seems to me an entirely plausible interpretation of the Bible's words, as Abram's violent

TOP

From "Assaults the Media" in *American Splendor* #8

retribution is certainly implied, but a casual reader of the text quickly forgets just how much Crumb is in fact adding to the text (and guiding our thinking about it) at every moment, in each one of thousands of editorial and visual choices he makes for each biblical verse. The cumulative effect is enormous.

In a *New Republic* essay on Crumb's book (easily the most thoughtful and provocative one yet published, though misguided on some simple principles of comics aesthetics), Robert Alter, the Hebrew scholar whose translation of Genesis Crumb heavily relied upon, isolated two such meaning-altering (or, better perhaps, meaning-*creating*) instances. "There are even some exegetical insights in the way the reticences of the spare narrative are fleshed out visually," Alter writes.

> Of the first of Tamar's doomed husbands, all we are told is, "And Er, Judah's firstborn, was evil in the eyes of the Lord." Under these words, Crumb offers an image of a sinister-looking figure thrusting a dagger into an old man's belly as he seizes his victim's money bag. . . .

> ... [M]ost interestingly, when Dinah is led out by her brothers from the house of Shechem, the man who raped her, after they have massacred all the males of the town, Crumb shows her weeping, her feet dragging reluctantly as one of her brothers pulls her by the hand. This is by no means an inevitable reading of the story, but it is certainly a stimulating one. Shechem, after all, falls in love with Dinah after the rape; and only now, at the very end of the story, do we learn that ever since the rape she has been in Shechem's house — perhaps, as some interpreters imagine, in captivity, but perhaps, as Crumb suggests, of her own free will, because her feelings have been touched by the loving devotion of the man whose desire for her first expressed itself in an act of sexual aggression.

Alter's examples here are especially interesting in that they point to two of Crumb's constant concerns — horror at man's aggressive violence toward man, and, insofar as this can be separated from the first, a fascination with the more specific crime of sexual assault — as well as for what they reveal of the morality of Genesis as a whole. In fact, the Dinah story in particular is explicitly returned to near the end of the book of Genesis. In Chapter 49, as the elderly Jacob delivers his deathbed prophecies to

"But while considering this book, it is important to keep two things in mind. 1. Crumb claims to believe in God. 2. The God of Genesis is not the God he believes in."

his children, the dying patriarch rails at his sons Simeon and Levi, the vengeful brothers of Dinah just mentioned by Alter, proclaiming, "In their council let me never set foot, their assembly my presence shun! For in their fury they slaughtered men! At their pleasure they tore down ramparts! *Cursed* be their fury so fierce, and their wrath so remorseless!" You might expect Jacob to cut his sons some slack, considering they were rescuing his daughter Dinah. (Of course, they did go a bit far in their vengeance, especially since they tricked the entire doomed town into getting circumcised before they sucker-massacred them.)

Just prior to this diatribe, Jacob had already cursed his eldest son, Reuben: "For you mounted the place where your father lay! You profaned my couch! You mounted!" Years earlier, you see, Reuben had a clandestine liaison with his father's concubine. In general, throughout Genesis, the sexual violation of men is taken far more seriously than that of women. The rape of women occurs often, but is never given much weight, while every possible sexual offense against men is viewed with abject horror, from Noah being seen "in his nakedness" to a drunken Lot being seduced by his daughters to Joseph being sent to prison after being *falsely* accused of rape. Crumb, who is reputed to be a misogynist, pays careful attention to the relations between the genders throughout, and claims in the endnotes to have been guided by the feminist scholar Savina Teubal.

In fact, she and Alter are the only two scholars Crumb cites by name. Whether or not one is persuaded by Teubal's historical theories of a forgotten matriarchy (I for one am unequipped to comment with any authority on the matter), this focus on gender is an artistically fruitful one, and Sarah, Rebekah, Rachel and Leah, some of the most vibrant and complicated characters in the book, provide Crumb with much rich and ironic material.

Most of all, though, this book impresses for Crumb's constant artistic invention. Those who claim that Crumb has added little to nothing to the text should try to come up with visuals this powerful and compelling for a single page, much less for so consistently over such a sustained page count. One difference between *Genesis* and earlier Crumb literary adaptations is that this time, Crumb hasn't picked and chosen the phrases he wished to adapt — this book recreates the entire 50 chapters. "In illustrating everything and every word, everything is brought equally to the surface," Crumb explained to a *Vanity Fair* interviewer earlier this year. "The stories about incest have the same importance as the more famous stories of Noah and the Flood or the Tower of Babel or Adam and Eve or whatever. I think that's the most significant thing about making a comic book out of Genesis. Everything is illuminated."

This of course means that the rough edges of Genesis — which it should be noted, was most likely not a single narrative written by one author, but, as most scholars and historians believe, a collection of stories gathered together by ancient editors into a not-exactly-cohesive whole — are illuminated as well. But that's part of the book's beauty, too. This is an old, old text, and to smooth away entirely what Robert Alter calls its "mysteries" would be a significant mistake. The most notorious of all the Bible's rough spots arrives in the famous "begats" section of the book, and paradoxically, this is where the power of Crumb's method is perhaps displayed most clearly. Crumb has drawn an individual (and individuated) portrait of each and every one of the hundreds of people named in the text. Whatever one might believe about the truth of the narratives told in Genesis, there is no doubt that it is a book rooted in the story of a very real and very ancient people, scores of generations of human beings who lived and died centuries ago. The book of Genesis, flawed as it is, is the only literary record we still have of what they did and thought and believed. When one looks at the portraits Crumb has drawn of them, *imagined* of them, it is difficult not to be moved, both by what is inevitably lost through time, and by what, however insufficient it must be, can be regained through art. ■

CRUMB GOES TO CHURCH

BY ALEXANDER THEROUX

One way to judge an artist is whether or not you want to see his work over and over again, and to me, R. Crumb's work has always been and remains endlessly fascinating. I consider him matchless, inimitable, the nonpareil of daring illustrators. The reason for illustrating this seminal book, which many people consider inspired by God, he neither offers nor explains, which is only part of what may seen an enigma. Another is that this instantly recognizable and daring stylist, whose acidic drawings and amusing scatologies we all know, has chosen to pledge allegiance, inversely, to such a different ideal — many may find it as unlikely an about-face as Lenin playing the banjo!

I never thought illustrating Scripture was unlikely for Crumb, for nothing is unlikely with him, or beyond him, for neither does that apply. I have long treasured his range. He is an unbeliever. He was raised a Catholic. He boasted to me he was never an altar boy. In 1998, Crumb kindly sent me a copy to read of his father's book, Charles V. Crumb's *Training People ... Effectively* (1970), a grim title that might have been written by SS-Obergruppenführer Reinhard Heydrich, Deputy Protector of Bohemia and Moravia! "A true believer, the 'Organization Man' of his generation," Crumb described his father to me, adding, "I wonder if this book sold well ... probably not ... it's not entertaining enough." A man with 20-years active duty in the U. S. Marines, Crumb, Sr.'s book, one of several he wrote and replete with charts and diagrams, sets

down laws of control, repetition, instruction for "trainees." I can see he would have been a father who brooked no griping or guff. "My father was an openly preferred atheist," he wrote me on June 5, 1997 after the subject of faith came up:

He sent me to Catholic school, he claimed because he thought the 'discipline' was better than public schools. He attended church on Sundays out of social obligation and conformity. My mother was a 'lukewarm' Catholic — she basically had no belief system, really — she lived on an elemental level, taking each day as it came.

I confess that I have always considered Crumb's victimization tales and rug-chewing reasons for leaving the Catholic Church, at least the explanations he wrote to me about, to be only puerile and contrived, all of that grousing and hand-wringing about having been walloped by little nuns for minor infractions total bullshit, and as far as any festering wounds go — What? He got yelled at in the confessional for stealing a bag of M&Ms, berated for swearing at his mother, scolded for trying to look underneath a schoolgirl's dress? I have to say I would have my martyrs made of sterner stuff. Christianity and the requirements to follow it seriously and with honor have, of course, always been a particular bugbear, not only to the conveniently faithless, but also to bored and idle anti-intellectuals. Whenever Crumb would write to me with tall tales about having to study "Latin and crap like that," offered with anticlerical sallies and muttering insinuations about the dark lunacies of "Father McGuire's Baltimore Catechism with its diagrammatic milk bottles of sin," I could only laugh. Several times Crumb would bristle at my criticism of his respectful but xenophilic interests in Eastern thought, ayurvedic diets, Tharavada Sutras, and the chloroform-in-prose writings of nature mystics like Baba Ram Dass and Maharaji Ji and Swami Ramakrishnananda which make me only want to chew gum and cry. Crumb loves porkpie hats, sandals, riding on women's backs, France, 78 r.p.m. records. I prefer going hatless, loafers, watching a woman ride a horse, Germany and 45 r.p.m. records.

No funnier or hipper correspondent could be found, but I early found an anti-intellectual component in many of Crumb's arguments, a rather

muscular endorsement of populism (which I can't take) — he would para-doxically inveigh against Bruce Springsteen, but then go and puff Charles Bukowski, when they are both of them, let's face it, interchangeably bad and equally talentless — and an earnestness in regard to contradictory positions. People who did not go to college are always the ones to make a big issue of it, I have noticed, and bristle at systemic intricacy and always seem to act as if complexity is an indulgence of the formally educated alone. It is surely sociologically diagnostic (if not a matter for the psychiatric couch) that Crumb in correspondence always puts polysyllabic words in quotation marks. He is a complete original, but there has often been something of the stubbornly doctrinal in the man, so I was not at all flabbergasted when he told me he was illustrating this sacred book.

I was simply looking for fiercer grace.

TOP
From "Footsy"
in Weirdo #20
[©1987 R. Crumb]

I myself would have chosen, had I Crumb's brilliance for art and were looking toward Scripture, instead of the first book of the Bible — I was going to write the last book, Revelation or the Apocalypse, a daring sci-fi option forcing his own crazy dream, pictorial wit and illimitable interpretive genius, in spite of the fact that he is past his gonzo period, but clearly the correct choice should have been Job, a tale perfectly suited for his particular fret-patterns, endless griping, sweaty ultra-agitation, execrations, misery, false counsel, revenge and scabrous bitterness — by cursing his birth, Job sets in motion no end of destruction — all of it allowing for R. Crumb's patented sword-to-the-heart satire, delight in sexual foolishness, and the depiction of a howling string-band of weird God-botherers and freakazoids!

While Genesis can be dark, theatrical, and full of moiling and intrigue in places (the Serpent, Lot and his daughters, Abraham and Isaac, the fire and brimstone of Sodom and Gomorrah, etc.), it is mainly the pious if occasionally dramatic account of the Hebrew story with the usual if predictable contretemps: anger, jealousies, bitter rivalries, personal failures, love and betrayal and death, standard fare in the annals of human behavior. There is the phantasmagoria of the Creation and Garden of Eden, which as graphic possibilities do lend itself to fantasia, but in terms of illustration, R. Crumb charts familiar territory — a lot of Hebrew visages face to face: big noses, teeth, headbands, raiment — and gives us with his drawings, a very literal account of the book that recapitulates, on a Scoville scale of non-outlandishness, the sort of Sunday School images I have come across many times. The project is worse than failing to call up Crumb's specific talent — it ignores it.

One is able to discover the usual Crumb signifiers in these 175 or so closely worked pages (they are quirkily not numbered): round, buttocky women; a love of feral, toothy grins; the ongoing gallery of wonderful rubbery faces — the splendid lineage of Ishmael in Chapter 25 and the children of Israel who came to Egypt in Chapter 46 are two particularly splendid ones — and repeatedly, acts of sexual congress, always the missionary position ("And Shechem, the son of Hamor, the Hivite, prince of the land, saw her ... and took her ... and laid her ... and defiled her." Chapter 34) which comes as no surprise to any of R. Crumb's loyal fans, scenes — drawings, an equal surprise, that are as tasteful, subdued and chastely unveering from those of Moses' own brief references to them, for a respectful and obedient Crumb is staying strictly in bounds. "In a few places I ventured to do a little interpretation of my own," writes Crumb in his "Introduction," "if I thought the words could be made clearer, but I refrained from indulging too often in such 'creativity,' and sometimes let it stand in its convoluted vagueness rather than monkey around with such a venerable text."

Chapter 34

AND DINAH, LEAH'S DAUGHTER, WHOM SHE HAD BORNE TO JACOB, WENT OUT TO SEE SOME OF THE DAUGHTERS OF THE LAND. AND SHECHEM, THE SON OF HAMOR THE HIVITE, PRINCE OF THE LAND, SAW HER...

...AND TOOK HER...

...AND LAID HER AND DEFILED HER.

Crumb is scrupulous. Having worked so hard on this demanding project for so long is certainly proof of that. He is always graphically accurate. Certain panels show entire landscapes, travel narratives, hectic conflagration, court scenes and full assemblages. There is a stream of facial realizations and reactions so detailed, so specific, running through the panels of Crumb's *Genesis* as to constitute the creation of an entire people, an actually realized populace! Many of the Hebrew faces he draws one can see today on the New York City streets and subways. Abraham looks like Ed Asner, Leah Julie Kavner, Laban Mel Brooks, Shechem Adam Sandler, Sarah Molly Goldberg, and there is more than a hint of Norman Podhoretz in Noah! Isaac looks like an aging Victor Borge! Fumble through the pages and you can find in this or that face, panel to panel, the lineaments in Crumb's Old Testament faces — with shading here, a grimace there — the identifiable faces of people who resemble Don Rickles, Elie Wiesel, Barbra Streisand, Mandy Patinkin and other celebrity Jews. There seems to be enough force in Crumb's splendid images for the book, dispensing with the text — high praise for an illustrator of vivid scenes — to be passed around like those old wordless pictorial midget Bibles by missionaries to illiterate-but-impressionable aborigines in order to convert them! It is the different personalities in Genesis that one remembers more than anything. And Crumb brings to even the least celebrated figures on these pages, the smallest supernumeraries, a distinct uniqueness of face.

Let no one think, however, that the master of grotesque cannot draw a tender figure or a soulful one. Consider some of the profoundly realized women's faces and figures he has drawn so well in his series of *Sketchbooks* or, say, illustrated on a lot of those restaurant menus in his *Waiting for*

"...THE FEMALE IS NOT ONLY THE GUARDIAN OF THE MYSTERIES— SHE IS THE MYSTERY HERSELF."
— MARA FREEMAN
"THE GODDESS & THE BRITISH MYSTERY TRADITION," 1988

— A SEXIST REMARK IF EVER I HEARD ONE!
— R. CRUMB

DOLLY HENSLEY
INCREDIBLE BODY, LOW-LIFE HILLBILLY SEX-POT, PRIZED POSSESSION OF BIG MAN WAYNE PARKER

JEANETTE "JINNY" BETTS
FABULOUS LEGS — PLAYED FOOTSY IN AMERICAN HISTORY & MR. STOOPS' HOME-ROOM.

BRIGITTE COSCARELLI
VOLUPTUOUS ITALIAN, CONSIDERED "EASY" BY ALL THE GUYS, SWEET BUT SLIGHTLY SUBNORMAL

AH, DEAR GOD, THEY'RE ALL MIDDLE-AGED HOUSEWIVES NOW! SOME A' THEM ARE PROBBLY EVEN GRANDMOTHERS!! OH LORD?!

Food books which to me in instances are as sweet as any done by Raphael himself. Let me add here that I have seen in London at the Victoria and Albert Museum the Raphael "cartoons" (that is indeed their correct name) which were commissioned from the great Italian Renaissance painter and planned as full-scale designs for a set of 10 tapestries that Leo X intended to cover the lower walls of the Sistine Chapel in the Vatican — of the cartoons, which were sent to Brussels in 1517, several sets of tapestries were woven, 10 now exist — and Crumb's strong visual gifts, his innate depictive sense, the way he can bring out the structure of a face and animate it

TOP
From "The Girls in My Class" in ID #1
[©1990 R. Crumb]

with both the passion and the dimensional precision we can recognize, are not far behind Raphael Sanzio's.

Fans of the illustrator know the 2006 title *The Sweeter Side of Crumb*, which assembles a potpourri of drawings. It states on the dust-jacket flap that it purports "to help him establish a more positive public image with women," and compiles many of his softer drawings: pretty girls; former high-school classmates; blues singers; all sorts of amiable sketches; a lovely drawing of his son, Jesse, as a tyke; even "Women Singers from the Torrid Regions of the World." I do not need to be convinced of Robert Crumb's softer side. His confessions show humility, even if crude, and he conveys a spiritual sense in the role of seeker.

Crumb, a self-professed "unbeliever," also give us God the Father, who in white raiment and the long white beard that reaches down to his toes looks every bit like the conventional movie prototype that we can all identify from our collective unconscious, a big, tall, scolding electric-eyed aristarch of a Walt Whitman with a booming, firmament-loud voice, and hair till Tuesday, who appears from on high throughout the book with a dark scowl and a mood blacker than muscular dystrophy to chastise we poor inchlings. Crumb's Satan makes a brief, ludicrous appearance as a creature from the black lagoon. It is always a mistake and far too taxing to try to draw Satan or the Supreme Being. Writers, even the best of them, like Milton in his *Paradise Regained*, fail, having weakly resorted to jewel imagery to convey the concept of heaven and majesty — and artists are no different. I gotta tell ya, when I saw Crumb's conceptions of both God the Father and of Satan — the Jerry Falwell versions — I needed to reread a few of his early *Zap Comics* as an anodyne.

Crumb's commitment to the project was unswerving. It has been long in the making. He wrote to me about it almost five years ago, March of 2006. In a letter of April 19, 2006, he wrote, "I'm up to page 50 on the Genesis Project. I will enclose a few pages with this [letter], to give you some idea ... Man, it's a lot of work. I get so obsessed with the detail ... But it's a good challenge for me, and I think my drawing skills have been upgraded in the process ... I figure I've got about 125 or so pages left to do ..." Crumb was unswerving. But was he unsparing?

I have used the phrase "staying in bounds." But is that what we want from Crumb — self-editing, damping down, circumspection, being good, balance, sobriety and sense? Needless to say, that is not what we know the cantankerous godfather of underground comix by, certainly — not that misanthropic, sexually obsessed, madcap creator of Skutch, Fritz the Cat, Whiteman, Angelfood McSpade, or loonies like Snoid, Eggs Ackly, Shuman the Human or the Mr. Natural we know and love (who spent time in a loony bin in the 1970s) and his thumb-fumbling companion, Flakey Foont, who in their hysterical and profane madness chase Cheryl Borck, Devil Girl, and twist off her head and violate her in a hundred ways!

Let me ask then: Where is the sabotage, the satire, the spice, the scorn? Where in his rendering of this book of the Bible, first of the Pentateuch, can one find a rough-edged, revolutionary irreverence that for half-a-century now has animated Crumb's astonishing universe, one that is uniquely his? What can we find in this great anomaly of Crumb illustrating Moses to applaud? Can we honestly accept it as part of the Crumb oeuvre or is it apocrypha?

Does this book succeed or fail?

An old apothegm goes, "Sinners commit, saints omit." All literature depends on conflict — clashes, battle, antagonism, etc. Stories inherently need a state of opposition in the very way heat needs blister. Most actors (except Robert Redford, I gather, who repeatedly loves playing the hero) far and away choose to play negative parts — bedlam figures, heavies, rogues, marginals. Iago, Richard the Third, Captain Ahab, Uriah Heep, Dracula. The explanation is simple: such creatures *do* something — act, act up, act out. The wussy roles tend passively to do nothing. Take John Milton's *Comus* (1634), a masque presented at Ludlow Castle in honor of chastity. The plot concerns two brothers and their sister, called the Lady, lost in a journey though the woods. The Lady becomes fatigued, the brothers wander off in search of sustenance, and then, alone, she encounters the debauched and devilish Comus who is disguised as a villager and claims he will lead her to her brothers. Deceived by his amiable countenance, the Lady follows him, only to be captured, brought to his pleasure palace, cruelly taunted and victimized by his necromancy. Comus accosts her; she rebuffs him. With his guile and schemes and magical inventiveness, he uses his wiles, but she refuses, arguing for the virtuousness of temperance. She is too sedate.

In terms of drama — of pure theatrics — one commits, the other omits. In short, she is static, while he is kinetic. That is why, although the masque's actual full title is quite long and didactic, it is colloquially known as *Comus*, for Comus, as it were, gets all the good lines and hogs the best scenes.

What is missing in Crumb's *Genesis*? Salt. Spite. Satire — specifically, *his* salt, *his* spite, *his* satire! I mean, a *Mad* comics version of the book of Genesis, not

a polite Gustave Doré-esque simulacrum of the thing. Much of his work here is splendid. The 70 or so pages on the Joseph story, probably the richest lode to mine in Genesis, at least in terms of narrative, are amazing, almost as dramatic, all things considered, as the wood engravings done by the genius Lynd Ward for his supernal *Madman's Drum*, *Wild Pilgrimage*, *God's Man*. Crumb's line never flinches, the detailed root-work and scaling of his pen on these pages wonderful. The crosshatching! The guy can draw anything and never fails to get perspective right in backgrounds and settings, the vistas and views. He went to the trouble to be accurate; one can see that. Look at the nap in his drawings of stones, wood, cement, brick. Skies! He knows surfaces! The flow of water. The cast of trees, buildings. The shims, shadows and graininess of his black-and-white illustrations, the exactitude, never fail to ignite the many

TOP

Mr. Natural vanquishes the Devil in "Mr. Natural Takes a Walk," originally published in The Village Voice. [©1976 R. Crumb]

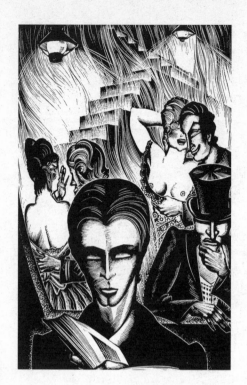

scenes. But the moralist in Crumb having taken over, even an over-reverential timidity, ultimately addresses a subject matter too intimidating even for him — who knows, maybe even his imagination — to dare to test it with the extravagances of revolutionary audacity or coldly satirical boldness or of rude, thumping innovation. There is not enough bite in Crumb's *Genesis*, is what I am saying, too much cozy reverence. Consider the brilliance, the untrammeled racy *insolence* of, say, "The Young Crumb Story" or "My Troubles With Women" in *Hup #1* or *Introducing Kafka* simply to compare genres. I prefer the work of the guy who had been coloring outside the lines since the 1960s!

Truthfully? I would have told Crumb to pass on the job. Not to accept the undertaking. Why did he do it? Did he do it for money? Was he paying penance for all of his lewd and blasphemous comic books of the past? Had this been a childhood goal? Was some kind of epistemological voyage involved, some kind of ethical *rites de passage*, whereby he set himself the task of drawing the images of such a book in order to study such a subject in order to learn something? Who knows? Was it somehow an act of contrition? Of conciliation? Is this an example by way of art of the man throwing himself down on his face with chest-thumping *mea culpas* to the very God he draws? Who can say? Do I want to keep this book on my shelf? I most certainly do. Can one say that this is R. Crumb's *capolavoro*? It is most definitely not. It is quaint, like those old biscuity Colonial hand stitched chapbooks with homely drawings of alphabets, animals, farm implements. It is not his A-game, not even close. Was he the perfect choice to manage this vast, four-year-long undertaking, to stay the course? Yes. For the resolve to bring it off? Indeed. For the exactitude required? Absolutely. For staying loyal to the Scriptural text? Without question. And why?

Crumb is a very literal person. He is literal because at bottom Crumb is a moralist. Satirists invariably are. Remember, satire is ridicule in order to correct. Oodles of fun they are not. Scapegraces, maybe. But the fact is, they all take themselves seriously. Alexander Pope, Jonathan Swift, Mark Twain. Scratch a caricaturist and find a didactician. If one were to choose to illustrate

TOP
Madman's Drum
[©1958 Lynd Ward]

"What is missing in Crumb's Genesis? Salt. Spite. Satire — specifically, *his* salt, *his* spite, *his* satire!"

something like the book of Genesis — and such a person would indeed do such a thing — he would rarely try to extrapolate or even innovate with a drawing, for the didactician is unbudgingly stubborn, one of the worse manifestations of the moralist who is of course a compulsive truth-teller. Who would deny in R. Crumb's work — and it is the major thrust of his work — that autobiography figures largely? I would venture to say that in the matter of confession in words alone never mind drawing, not one person — not St. Augustine, not Jean Jacques Rousseau, not Thomas Merton — has ever exceeded Crumb for his almost rabid and compulsive frankness, his bold, brutally impartial, pathologically relentless depth of exposure, self-deprecation, rudely raw and humiliating candor. So to find Crumb's slavish adherence to the word, in this case to the Word, does not surprise me in the least. I have seen it before. I once took the initiative to send him, with a view to his illustrating it, a manuscript of mine entitled *Truisms*. I was astonished to find it not only returned, but annotated by a Luddite, an earnest and flat-footed herbert, immune to irony, with neither a sense of humor nor a concept of either the tropological or the figurative. A few of my truisms follow — they were composed in quatrains — with Crumb's comments in brackets:

> A handshake's more than anything a code [-?huh??]
> You rarely see a pretty woman walking [not true! I seen lots of pretty women walking — thousands of them, so what are you talking about??]

Dryness never figures as a concept in a toad [silly]
There's lassitude in every rumpled stocking. [??]

Baseball writers are always sentimental [—?]
It is vulgar to smear jelly over bread. [snobbism]
Commitment is avoided by a rental [? not necessarily]
Texans like buckles as big as their heads. [silly]

Eating coffee-grounds will kill a dog [nah...]
Impotence is common among sports fans. [conjecture, snobbism]
The act of voting is like feeding hogs [who says?]
A ballerina's beauty's in her hands [No, in her legs!!]

Chaplin was a bore compared to Keaton. [opinion]
Mountains always range from north/south. [??]
A good biscuit's never overbeaten. [you don't beat biscuits]
Bad teeth slubber a pretty mouth. [slubber?]

I would hasten to point out that Crumb's low-brow humorlessness here, certainly not characteristic of him and by no means the essential Crumb, reminded me then, and does even now, of W. B. Yeats' theory of the "Anti-Self," by which the poet advances the unique idea that, as a deep, subconscious act of self-completion, the work that we do in art — the nature of the things we make — is inevitably the opposite of what we really are. Yeats convincingly offers that Dante Alighieri, being a sensualist, wrote spiritual poetry, that John Keats, an unhappy fellow, wrote joyous poetry, and so on. It is about paradox, all of it.

The mask, as it were, becomes the face.

"In setting out to illustrate the Book of Genesis," Crumb writes in a final "Commentary" to the book of *Genesis*, "I quickly learned that I had to read the text very carefully and closely in order to render as accurately as possible the words that were actually written there." *Render accurately?* But no artist is bound to any particular set of images when illustrating Scripture, for no such set of images exist. It is just that Crumb being so literal a fellow — and I will hasten to add, in the matter of approaching a sacred text, even slightly obsequious — decided to set aside the Yeatsian mask and give us, for whatever reason, the moralist's face. It is at least in one morph an act of anti-transformation. Christ "illuminated" himself in one dynamic instance. I would guess that this is Crumb's version of such a momentary transfiguration. It is his "coming forth" to show us

that he is more than just the comix creator who in his "fuzzy" acid-period back in the mid 1960s gave us so many creeps, inveterate self-loathers or unsavory little peckerheads like Mr. Snoid, and all those bulb-nosed, gross-booted little Zoot-Suiters who keep on truckin'. As Robert Browning wrote, "Ah, but a man's reach should exceed his *grasp*, or what's a heaven for?" ■

A BOOK FOR MAN RECOUNTED IN A BOOK BY/FOR/OF MAN

A REVIEW OF R. CRUMB'S *BOOK OF GENESIS ILLUSTRATED*

BY KENNETH R. SMITH

It is enough that our fathers have believed. They have exhausted the faith-faculty of the species. Their legacy to us is the skepticism of which they were afraid. –Oscar Wilde

For he to whom the present is the only thing that is present, knows nothing of the age in which he lives. –Oscar Wilde

Faith has not always been infantilism; even though ancient Christianity was a peasant or plebeian movement, a tide among the lowest victims of the Roman Empire, today it has been specially cretinized by the empire of modern materialism. In the ancient world—seated *in vivo*, in the awesome cosmos of nature —"faith" was above all else the passionate, sun-brilliant belief that this world and human existence truly *had a founding principle and force of rightful order*, and correlatively that humans had to harness their animality and self-centeredness and subordinate them to the truth of this spiritual insight. Such faith, like culture itself, functions as its own self-fulfilling prophecy, over centuries moralizing and spiritualizing humans into something relatively higher.

But in modernity — seated contrariwise, *in vitro*, in man's own artificial, abstracted and cloistered technosphere —"faith" has become en masse the antipode of what it anciently was, a *derivative/secondary*, "equal but opposite reaction" against the *primal fear* that modern behaviorist/evolutionary scientism and materialist/egocentric capitalism are ultimately objectively and rationally *correct*: Like "Communism," "faith" remains the crippled Siamese twin of that insidious world-order it struggles to revolt against, but against which it has, in truth, no radically independent principles to ground itself in. Faith's strategic "position," its Archimedean standpoint, is quite undermined: where once it liberated, now it far more commonly enslaves. Morality, spirituality, conscience, altruism, generosity, justice, "soulishness," have all proven themselves in the modern dispensation of "normality" to be the exception not the rule, an effete "symbolism" or token corrective against the Behemoth of "human nature." Modernity, and modern faith as well, lack any diagnostic higher-order perspective on themselves and certainly any penetrating sense of what they are systemically deprived of.

AND WHEN SHE SAW THAT SHE HAD CONCEIVED, HER MISTRESS SEEMED DIMINISHED IN HER EYES.

Modern world-order or our mechanically conceivable universe, insane or delusionary as it may be, demonstrably morally/socially/spiritually/naturally toxic as it may be, is the "Word" or "Utterance" of the Most Potent Principle that modern world knows, a terraforming and ecocidal, mass-organizing "militarization" of society and individual that puts all ancient slave-empires in the shade. Neither fecund Nature nor creative Divinity but rather self-amassing Capital is the reigning self-procreative force in the modern scenario. It is the mathematical and materialist/fiscal logic of Money that sets the base terms in which humans live and think and understand themselves and try not to get crushed by this juggernaut. In the modern enclosure of our mechanistic universe, "faith" is so far from being fully self-certain faith that it is overwhelmingly *bad faith*, i.e. hypocrisy and denial: "'Faith' means not *wanting* to know what is true" (Nietzsche), because the powers against which faith tries to be a countervailing truth are *so cogent or apodictic* that faith cannot afford to look them in their Medusa-face, lest it too be turned to stone like the heart of the capitalist and the souls of his technicians. For the "faithful," no matter how fervently they may try, truly have *no other* visceral or believed-in conception of existence than the one modernity has sold them, the demythologized and disillusioned, prosaic concentration-camp of verifiable Facts (and the less the faithful know about that world and its "reality-principles" the better for their morale). For between *"faith"* and *"would-be faith"* there is as gross a difference as Mark Twain observed between "lightning" and a "lightning-bug."

The most significant history of The Bible, as of every other great formative force in the *mythoi* and moralities of the world, would not be any work of factical scholarship scrutinizing how it came to be or was formed, but rather of what it has *meant*, how its peculiar *authority* organized and expended itself on personalities and societies. The "truth" about The Bible, as also of every other tradition- or *ethos*-shaping work, is its *normative* not its descriptive truth, its power to concentrate and orchestrate forms of *ought*: but just such a profile or diagnosis in literal fact *is not*, and no one could be more inept to gather such understanding than modern academics and intellectuals. Not to see this trans-factual and trans-rational potency is the cause of countless misplaced polemics, one side arguing past another, both sides equivocating on what The Bible (or the Quran, or other sacred Scripture) doctrinally "is." For shaping works are also, by no accident, distortive and deformative works that *interfere with* their own comprehension, the truthful presentation of their Truth.

What is directly at hand: the encyclopedic labor of Crumb's *Genesis*, a saga compressing as the original Bible did the currents of whole lives and peoples to postage-stamp terseness, and starkness. Like the original story, it is a powerful work of Judaic tragedy. It is a respectable culling of research, and classic or prime Crumb, but does it make palpable the meaning of an enduring *ethos* of the premodern world? Here or there is a scene redolent of Wolverton's work (e. g. the evacuation from Noah's Ark in ch. 8), and a jarring if inadvertent near-quote from popular culture (early in ch. 9 the faces of Noah's three sons smack of The Three Stooges). All in all a Herculean effort, and Crumb and his publisher correctly expect its promotion to reap bountiful results. Those glad to see Crumb still challenging himself will be delighted, and those broadly pleased to see the first book of the Pentateuch given a new lease on life will also rejoice in their way, neither of course seeing the same thing as the other in this book.

But as a critic, as a thinker concerned not about the epidermis of things but about their neurology, their *essential* genesis and teleology, I have to regard all of that as so much taken-for-granted bait dangled before wholesalers, retailers and consumers. What moves me to wonder about this book is the great but obscured discrepancy between what Crumb's version is *about* and what it itself *is*: By what kinds of chasms of *civilizational discord* are the Bible's

AND NOAH WENT OUT, HIS SONS AND HIS WIFE AND HIS SONS' WIVES WITH HIM. EVERY BEAST, EVERY CRAWLING THING, AND EVERY FOWL, EVERYTHING THAT STIRS ON THE EARTH, BY THEIR FAMILIES, CAME OUT OF THE ARK.

own reasons-for-being divided from the kinds of purposes this rendition has been produced to serve? Are there even names for this kind of culture-cleavage, this ideological "repurposing" from one worldview to another?

I bite my lip,
I buy what I'm told;
From the latest hit,
To the wisdom of old.
— Leonard Cohen

What the philosophers say about Reality is often as disappointing as a sign you see in a shop window, which reads: Pressing Done Here. If you brought your clothes to be pressed, you would be fooled: for the sign is only for sale.
— Kierkegaard, Either/Or I

This is not a pipe.
— Magritte, caption to a picture of a pipe

Crumb has to be saluted I suppose for taking up a daunting project, for setting his modern/anti-modern talents and perspective in contrast against millennial contents. But then we must ask also of this work the kinds of searching questions that a classical masterwork or archetype has had to prove itself against. What is the internal *life-impulse*, the surpassing need or "genetic" rationale for this present book? What does it *demand* of us, what does it *offer* us in the way of both visceral and higher-order life-resources, imperatives and axioms for living and understanding ourselves? Lacking such answers it becomes neither more nor less than any other contemporary book, the sort of automatic, myopic "chatter" into which the Great Conversation of World Culture has more and more degenerated. Here is how far Crumb is willing or able to enlighten us about what kind of drive or purpose begot his *Genesis*: in his introduction he calls the Book of Genesis "a venerable text," without of course signifying that he himself venerates it; he reviles "streamlined" and "modernized" versions that pander to the limitations of modern readers, at the same time he insists that in his own eyes this book is not "the Word of God." It is "a powerful text with layers of meaning that reach deep into our collective consciousness, our *historical* consciousness . . . ." It is indeed "inspired" but " . . . its power derives from its having been a collective endeavor that evolved and condensed over many generations," compiled and organized by a priestly caste who proclaimed the finished product "a sacred, holy document." The question why an entire people was receptive to this sacerdotal salesmanship is never asked, or how religion was rooted also in primitive intuition and *mythos*-cultures. It begs the question to blame priests without asking where *their* authority more primordially came from: priests are typically of a kind of character deft at exploiting faith and myth but singularly sterile at originating or inspiring them.

And what then *are* those "layers of meaning"? What exactly does the cogency or authority or contemporary value of this book specifically consist in, even if only as a sheerly "human" document, a moral or

"What moves me to wonder about this book is the great but obscured discrepancy between what Crumb's version is about and what it itself is: By what kinds of chasms of civilizational discord are the Bible's own reasons-for-being divided from the kinds of purposes this rendition has been produced to serve?"

spiritual manifesto? We get no substantive answer except for ethnological concepts of patriarchalism versus matriarchalism, and little in Crumb's treatment is novel or original enough to make even those particular matters more morally or psychically biting. In a way never fulfilled or evinced, he merely alludes to the depths of our "collective consciousness" in a nod to cosmopolitan or far-seeing cultural perspectives, and so his homage to the "greatness" of the Bible remains rather hollow and sterile no matter how earnest it may be. He goes on to offer a sort of "apologia":

> If my visual, literal interpretation of the Book of Genesis offends or outrages some readers, which seems inevitable considering that the text is revered by many people, all I can say in my defense is that I approached this as a straight illustration job, with no intention to ridicule or make visual jokes. That said, I know that you can't please everybody (this reviewer's italics).

Crumb is known and respected as a culture critic, a heterogeneous *idol of* but at the same time a *reviler* of popular media. I argue that he has revealed more of himself than he probably intended in his mundane and pro forma prefatory remarks, and revealed as well how much he is indeed *of* as well as in the belly of the beast, the Leviathan of modern culture.

LEFT
From "Snoid Goes Bohemian" in *Snoid Comics*
[©1980 R. Crumb]

He acknowledges that this rendition was to him a prosaic task, a "job." He denies (I gather) having any ulterior purpose beyond scrupulous illustration, and effectively denies that he is among those who revere this book. What is it to him, then, other than a pretext for exercising his talent and earning his bread as Genesis said we are condemned to, by the sweat of his brow? Is he then truly animating the significance of this text or only visualizing it, making it into a more literalist "narrative" of first-this and then-that, that is, *sequences of particulars* missing any grandeur of purpose, destiny or character? Crumb's *Genesis* has been realized to serve as "product" or "content," the same kind of thing that our media pipelines make of every other kind of precipitated event or act: what about it ought to set it apart from any other ploy of the marketing department? It has the virtues and "use-values," the assets that make it a significant "commodity," and Crumb's cachet makes it an "illustrational" event of note. But does it have any artistic or cultural or "moral" or "spiritual" substance of its own, beyond shining by the reflected light of a 3,000-year-old classic? Should we know better than to interrogate a merely and truly "modern" or "contemporary" work for its ultimate and substantive "meaning"? Is it simply a foregone conclusion that, in matters of ultimate truth or value, modern works of culture are routinely and presumptively vacuous and axiomatically vain, and only fools would expect otherwise?

How rich it was decades ago to see Basil Wolverton, father of Lena the Hyena and the Brain-Bats of Venus, naïvely but sincerely putting his nearly farcical stylistics upon the Bible, that Doré and his engraver had earlier raised to some visual grandeur and classicism. How exasperating in the past decade to see the idioms and tones of (for the most part) machismo-fantasism in Simon Bisley's renditions from the Bible, as saturated with bloody and terrifying emotionalisms but as generally feeble in spiritual sublimity as Mel Gibson's S&M-drenched *Passion of the Christ*. Enough modern sensualizations of the Old and New Testaments, and moderns will be esthetically seasoned to process them like hamburgers, to savor and then forget them the same way moderns grow fatigued and blasé about every other kind of transient blockbuster. But, in the case of creators and consumers alike, creatures of modern media and markets will inevitably *be* the creatures of modern media and markets, as surely as chickens yield eggs that yield chickens: if it weren't for their implacably inauthentic and indelibly alienated identities, most moderns wouldn't have any identities at all. We are what we eat.

And now, the master of Mr. Natural, Flakey Foont, the Snoid and the Devil Girl has given in to a confluence of our society's imperfectly finished credal business and his own need for an epic task: but how could the complex of idioms that is Crumb not eclipse from its own side the product-pretext that is his *Genesis*, the media event that is the true horizon of this work's meaning and purpose for existing? The more *oxymoronic* or paradoxical or counterintuitive the coupling of *countercultural icon* with *archaic Scripture*, the more prodigious the marketing "hook," of course. Incongruity and even rending or violent incommensurability are for moderns just poignant and torturous "teasers," not provocations to more penetrating self-understanding. As the Church Father Tertullian insisted, so too the modern consumer: "I believe *because* it is absurd"—but enough incomprehension and paradox-mongering and (all too obviously) one no longer knows what it even means to "believe." The most profound form of mind-fuck, heterologism or the Babel-conflict between utterly unlike and unrelated principles, is for moderns just a form of sauce, a different tactic of piquancy. At the quick of the modern psyche, there is no sensibility receptive to the organismic *gestalten* of cultural or spiritual forms and *archai*: all those pre-modern issues and concerns fall way outside the spectrum of visible light, to us. Nietzsche aptly named this vitamin-deficiency, this failure in our digestive fluids, "*amytheia*" or basal and congenital mythlessness, and Joseph Campbell confirmed a century later that this privation was enduring and pandemic.

Certainly in our value-eviscerated, utterly *extrinsicalized* dysculture, millions — neither blithe believers nor arrant iconoclasts — who see or hear about Crumb's book will find no "cognitive dissonance" in it: intuitively and critically oblivious to any vital distinction between intrinsic and extrinsic (useful, exploitable, circumstantial, profitable, divertible, self-promotional, or "commercial") meanings or "goods" or perspectives, moderns (most of all Americans) have long since acclimatized themselves to the omnipresent pollutants of *mercantile crassness* throughout our materialist economic and ego-interests. These are the now-ubiquitous psycho-manipulative and morally anesthetic intrusions of a species of personality the Greeks knew as *banausoi*, which is, a caste of the "utilitarian" or "means-minded" who respect or admire nothing but live only to exploit, to find an "angle" for profiteering (the reason, ultimately, that the Greeks relegated the *agora* to

such amoral personalities and cautioned all who entered there "buyer beware": "A market is a place set apart for men to deceive and to get the better of one another," said Anacharsis, in Diogenes Laertius). The U.S. seems to be beginning to wake up from a state of naïve sloth to realize that this sort of single-minded materialism is anything but innocuous; like virtually every dominant character-type it has the potential to extremize itself into a predatory cult, an organizedly nihilist worldview. Even the Bible itself may fall among thieving types: even Christianity in toto.

> What is man that thou art mindful of him?
> —Psalms 8:4

> Weighed, weighed in the balance and found wanting.
> —Daniel 5:25-28

Who can doubt that moderns, congenital starvelings in everything that has to do with soul/spirit/values/culture, will go on ravenously nibbling at the fat-saturated junk-food relics of what they are told is "religion," just like the fossil-forms and eviscerated norms of "education" and "politics"? "Curiosity" is that pathetic hybrid with concern that is the perfect mate of hypocrisy, a facile and deliberately superficial equivocation between "respect" and "contempt," "attraction" and "repulsion," "virtue" and "vice," "piety" and anarchic "nihilism": like the "liberal" virtue of "tolerance," which is

TOP
From "Euro-Dirty
Laundry" in The
Complete Dirty Laundry
[©1992 Sophie and
Robert Crumb]

far more frequently honored in the counterfeit and in the outright breach than in its actual core of principle, so too fence-straddling and dissembling "curiosity" is exactly the sort of pseudo-value or –virtue that a post-credal dysculture so irresolutely resolves upon when it no longer believes even in its own secular, "humanistic," Enlightenment-rationalist codes and norms. Moderns have a grave disability when it comes to admitting to themselves that they fundamentally cannot fathom what kinds of beliefs, perspectives, principles, or values once drove any of the *mythos*-cultures like the Hebrews or the Greeks, the archaic "founding fathers" who alas constituted the *last potent* firmament of principles or values in the Western lineage, the last time values were indeed grasped as values. It was from those archetypes that our Founding Fathers took their axiomatics of human nature and history; but we imagine we can maintain our stratified national cruise liner by aspiring to be nothing more than Know-Nothing ideologues and camp-following "hookers." Moderns live not in a strenuous self-athleticism of values and principles but rather in a self-soothing Jacuzzi of "ideals" and "idealisms," figments of a devout self-delusionality, a culture of/by/for slackers.

Since the ancients, we have so utterly fallen into a *pathos* of being *epigoni* — especially through the self-uncomprehending Hellenicism of Christianity, the crypto-Platonism of Catholic traditions and the egocentric and idiotist "cracker" self-righteousness that Protestantism has decayed into — that we cannot in the least recognize our evidentially and indisputably *witless derivativeness*, our constitutional ineptitude to confront and evaluate principles as principles. We are in truth the *other extreme from matriarchalism as well as from patriachialism*, we are *anarchicalists*, disbelievers *au fond* in any and all forms of *principles, authority, axiomatics*: we are soulishly comfortable only in a state utterly vacuous of principles, foundations, ultimates. We are "cynics" indeed, captives of a doglike instinctive suspiciousness: viscerally allergic to any kind of utterance with even the aroma of "deeper" or "higher" significance. We are by nature and by design *groundless and myopic opportunists*, "pragmatists" incompetent to differentiate between self-interest and principles, "private" and "public," short-term or smash-and-grab "easy money" and long-term and arduous "weal" and "wisdom." Life — beyond being an opportunity for the shallow to "play it by ear"— *means* nothing, and *meaning* means nothing, to moderns: we labor far more intensively at *resisting and repelling* questions than the ancients ever did pursuing their revelatoriness. We are on the one hand a caste of engineers/technicians and on the other a caste of sheep/swine, so naturally we lack all virtues of self-discipline or self-mastery that might enable us to perceive frontally our actual way of existing. If it was on its face absurd for the mountain to labor in order to produce an anticlimactic mouse, what then when all the eons of evolution and history have churned only to generate a species of civilizationally *suicidal idiot*, a creature as culturally sterile as a mule?

In section 23 of *The Birth of Tragedy*, Nietzsche 's first work, he threw down a gauntlet of savage diagnostic contempt before modern dysculture, and no one has ever yet imagined that modernity had some well-hidden "saving graces" with which to defend itself, in response to this critical fusillade:

> ... Without myth every culture loses the healthy natural power of its creativity: only a horizon defined by myths completes and unifies a whole cultural movement. Myth alone saves all the powers of the imagination and of the Apollonian dream from their aimless wandering. The images of the myth have to be the unnoticed omnipresent demonic guardians under whose care the young soul grows to maturity and whose signs help the man to interpret his life and struggles...

> By way of comparison let us now picture the abstract man, untutored by myth; abstract education; abstract morality; abstract law; the abstract state; let us imagine the lawless roving of the artistic imagination, unchecked by any native myth; let us think of a culture that has no fixed and sacred primordial site but is doomed to exhaust all possibilities and to nourish

itself wretchedly on all other cultures—there we have the present age, the result of that Socratism which is bent on the destruction of myth. And now the mythless man stands eternally hungry, surrounded by all past ages, and digs and grubs for roots, even if he has to dig for them among the remotest antiquities. The tremendous historical need of our unsatisfied modern culture, the assembling around one of countless other cultures, the consuming desire for knowledge—what does all this point to, if not to the loss of myth, the loss of the mythical home, the mythical material womb? Let us ask ourselves whether the feverish and uncanny excitement of this culture is anything but the greedy seizing and snatching at food of a hungry man—and who would care to contribute anything to a culture that cannot be satisfied no matter how much it devours, and at whose contact the most vigorous and wholesome nourishment is changed into "history and criticism"? (Walter Kaufmann tr. , pp. 135-6)

As an accomplished classical philologist Nietzsche was himself drawing in his charges on one of the most gnomic and prophetic of Greek *mythoi*: the story of Erysichthon, recounted by Tripp's *Meridian Handbook of Classical Mythology* —

Erysichthon was a ruthless man who scorned the gods. One day he cut down an oak tree that grew in a grove sacred to Demeter, ignoring the groans of the dryad nymph whose blood flowed from the wounds made by the ax. The other dryads of the grove prayed to Demeter to punish the culprit for the sacrilege and avenge their sister. At once Erysichthon was afflicted with an insatiable hunger. Having eaten all his food, he sold his daughter, Mestra, to buy more. . . . Unable to quiet the pangs of hunger, Erysichthon eventually fell to gnawing his own flesh and died. (Ovid's Metamorphoses, 8. 738-878) ∎

AND VOID, AND DAR
WAS OVER THE DEE
GOD'S BREATH HOV
OVER THE WATERS

ROUNDTABLE RESPONSES

Rick Marschall's Response

As far as I can tell, my fellow reviewers regard the Divine centrality of *Genesis* from a viewpoint similar to Crumb's: that is, a proposition somewhere between doubtful and infantile. Tim Hodler did recognize from the start that "1. Crumb claims to believe in God. 2. The God of Genesis is not the God he believes in." That clears part of the air for reviewers, yet it seems to me that the atmosphere is still foggy; a lack of sympathy with the source's essential message could interfere with Crumb's treatment. This is not fatal, but would leave a reviewer to concentrate rather on Crumb's comic-strip techniques in *Genesis* … and, I still maintain that, by this evidence that leaves Crumb defrocked as a high priest of the art form.

Reviewers tend to compare the first book of the Bible to Krafft-Ebing, Philip K. Dick, Jelly Roll Morton, et al., not only because Crumb has happened to address each of them, but agreeing with Crumb that Genesis is a tale, it is not uniquely inspired, that its narrative is bereft, no offense to Jelly Roll, of special implications for the lives of every reader (specifically, let me say, denying the supernatural claims *Genesis* makes for itself). Of course Crumb's attempt must fail: He treats the creation of the universe as one with a book of fairy tales (and so forth) elsewhere on a bookshelf, and it seems that members of this roundtable share that point of view. So the enormous task Crumb undertook, and the putative goal, largely are unplugged by Crumb (and virtually ignored by reviewers). We have nearly

AND THE LORD SAW THAT THE WICKEDNESS OF THE HUMAN CREATURE WAS GREAT ON THE EARTH, AND THAT EVERY SCHEME OF HIS HEART'S DEVISING WAS ONLY PERPETUALLY EVIL.

200 pages, then, not of significance but of banality – a He-said/ he-said transcript with pictures.

You don't have to agree that the Book of Genesis is the inerrant Word of God to recognize what Crumb decided to tackle: not just a formidable job but also one with massive and unavoidable responsibility. I am not talking about spiritual matters. I am talking about artistic, narrative, language-and-structure matters. You cannot step up to the plate in this particular game, the "game" of discerning and imparting Significance in such a book as *Genesis*, on its myriad levels ... and lay down a bunt. You must go for the grand slam. Michelangelo did not paint the Sistine Closet when he depicted Scripture.

I don't believe there can be a full assessment of Crumb's book without an acknowledgement that he castrated nearly everything that has made The Book of Genesis a vital story for 6,000 years.

Here is the test on which it may stand or fall: If a reader had never heard the Genesis accounts of creation, the flood and so forth, would Crumb's book persuade them of its heritage and influence through the millennia? Despite Crumb's announcement that it has been stories and legends that fueled whatever heritage and influence the Bible has had, he simply cannot sweep the inherent spiritual confrontations between God and reader aside. He can ignore that aspect; he can deny it; but it remains the undrawn picture behind every printed panel.

If Crumb's book was your only evidence that the Genesis has established nations, inspired the art and poetry of countless millions, served as the foundation-stone of three major religions composed of billions of believers through history and so forth ... would you know it from his version? Are such things plausible by the evidence he transliterates? I say no, and I'm not sure my fellow knights of this roundtable see it any way but Crumb's either. With few exceptions, to paint a stark contrast, Crumb's book portrays a few dramatic scenes with subtext-echoes of standard and standardized Sunday School leaflets, and otherwise reminds one of a catalog of costumes and snapshots.

Crumb's drawings seldom inform us. They scarcely illuminate the narrative inherent to the text (sorry, skeptics and rejectionists), and as interesting as they are, thanks to Crumb's commendable research, they parallel the narrative instead. Comics should combine elements of text and art, not make them separate but equal. More, thanks to an irreconcilable conflict in this book between text and art, Crumb's dismisses what, at its core, the text of Genesis asks of its readers. So I think Crumb's reviewers, here, whether largely approving or dissenting, miss the anomaly.

Alexander Theroux has, I think, properly identified an essential flaw in this book, and he stated it more clearly than I did in my essay: "The project is worse than failing to call up Crumb's specific talent — it ignores it." His friendship with Crumb informs his speculation: "Was [this book] somehow an act of contrition? Of conciliation? Is this an example by way of art of the man throwing himself down on his face with chest-thumping *mea culpas* to the very God he draws?"

I answer, by the evidence: No, because Crumb seems (I must say "seems" and I must ask, why is it ambiguous to us after 200 pages?) to reject the God whose story he tells. A: What is the point? And B: if the point is not spiritual... why not make it a better, more vivid, more interesting *comic-strip* version, as long as he bought all that ink and paper?

Robert Stanley Martin distilled this formal criticism, I think brilliantly, when he lamented: "... the saddest aspect of it is that it is hackneyed in Crumb's own terms. His unrelenting dramatic fortissimo makes the entire book feel flat, and he doesn't build his ideas into tropes — he lets them degenerate into clichés."

Crumb cannot escape being judged by what Martin calls "his own terms." The temptation of the reader is to respect the book because it is Crumb; trust it because the cartoonist attests to sweating blood in its creation; and invest sympathy because of the publicized four years of his life between those two

"I don't believe there can be a full assessment of Crumb's book without an acknowledgement that he castrated nearly everything that has made The Book of Genesis a vital story for 6,000 years."

covers. But we must judge it on its success as a comic strip — that is the name on the door of the house we enter. It is not a faulty comic strip because it lacks, say, laughs, as we have come to expect in spite of ourselves in many a Crumb project: it fails because it employs blessed few of the thousands of other comic-strip tools available.

As it surely is not meant to advance a point of view (except negatively, as I pointed out in my essay) and, with surprising awkwardness, traffics in a needless sterility to the point of abstraction (as, I take, Theroux implies and Martin sees even more clearly), one wishes for some evidence of why Crumb considered this a worthwhile project, and why he assumes we consider it worthwhile to read. Except for irreducible passages, he seems to have labored hard in order to make action, emotion, personality and profundity *anathema* — this, in history's pre-eminent book of action, emotion, personality and profundity.

To Jeet Heer's observation that Crumb's "only real rivals in terms of producing comics that reach deep into the human concern are George Herriman and Charles Schulz," I detect some hyperbole, or praising-by-faint-damns; I think of the pantheon of cartoonists — in a medium that enables exploration of the human condition better than most — and think the list can be long indeed. It is an open question, but threatens to be a silly question, unless Crumb suffers by that comparison. I think he does in this project; Jeet does not.

I am afraid that Brother Kenneth Smith's essay strikes me as a Tower of Babble: I suppose it is my shortcoming, not his. I have trouble with neologisms, especially so many, and I would like to address his review but I cannot.

It remains an important observation that all the essayists, in one way or another — indeed, almost everyone I spoke to for several months about Crumb's book — ask the same question: *Why did he do it?*

This is not a coincidence. We don't ask these questions of other artists and actors and poets. We seldom ask it even when a creator makes a radical departure: um, Linda Ronstadt doing operetta; Kelsey Grammer doing Shakespeare; E. Power Biggs playing ragtime; Benny Goodman performing Mozart's *Clarinet Concerto. Why* did *Crumb* do it?

Are we solicitous of his career — like baseball fans arguing about players' salaries as if they were the owners' relatives and heirs? No. What was in Robert Crumb that made him devote four or five years of his life to this? To me — and the roundtable has not persuaded me otherwise — what came *out* of Crumb keeps that question alive: *Why did he do it?*

This book could have been Mr. (Super)Natural, yet — please don't lead us there, Bob, in your next project! — I for one, as a reader, feel, as with the Hebrew children in Exodus, like I have wandered in the desert for 40 years. ∎

Donald Phelps' Response: Robert Crumb's Fugitive Laughter

The correspondence recently received by me, re. Robert Crumb's *Genesis*, reveals a strain of lamentation that recalls an artwork of c. 1946. Charlie Chaplin's *Monsieur Verdoux* elicited dismayed murmurs from diverse "movie critics." Chaplin had devised a Balzacian depiction of late 19th-century French society as reflected through the depredations of an urbane Parisian swindler and poisoner. Chaplin's reversal of his comic-vagabond tone evoked aggrieved chidings from some of the critical press. Such presumption and ill judgment: Abandoning the beloved buffoon for an urbane 20th-century predator.

To which James Agee in *The Nation* — engaged in bringing American film criticism to a new level of adulthood — remarked the penchant of small children for the repetition of familiar stories: a prescience brought back to

me by the recent cataract of plaints that Crumb has abandoned his satiric vein and, in so doing, his vocation (?).

As a longtime admirer of Robert Crumb and devotee of his unique Hobohemia, I have grown inured to the interplay of blatant buffoonery: cascading squalor, spiritual, erotic, esthetic and, via his implacable pen, an overarching equanimity. The earnestness of Crumb's style is its power — not rock 'em sock 'em Popeye stuff, but the serene integrity of America's groundbreaking authors and artists: Kenneth Patchen; Henry Miller; the Gershwins. The blanketing, roiling verisimilitude he invokes in his *Genesis* — what? Transliteration maintains the serenity, the heroic sangfroid, of the few artists named — as well as William de Kooning, Robert Motherwell, Mark Rothko, Manny Farber.

The cargo — precious contraband — of Crumb's trek is the granite-like serenity (forgive the cliché; but consider its redemption) of his homely toughness, which adds the catarrhal vigor of Andy Devine — the rip-snorting majesty of Wallace Beery — to a chorus grown more tame, and more urbane. Crumb's Old Testament cast radiates a natural majesty maintained by his prose, rather than his poetry. This, the province of Angelfood McSpade and Etaoin Shrdlu: whose strains of insolence and anguish, by the way, are not always far from the *esprit* of the aforementioned Chaplin. ∎

Robert Stanley Martin's Response

As for my differences with specific contributors, I would like to focus on Tim Hodler's and Jeet Heer's pieces, as they seem to disagree with me the most about the issues I raise in my review.

Hodler praises Crumb for avoiding a satiric (or, one infers, an allegorical) point of view in his adaptation. Those of us who have criticized the book on this basis aren't calling for Crumb to mock the material, as Hodler suggests. (We're certainly not faulting him for not including an absurdist character like Mr. Natural to comment on the material. It's hard to imagine such a move as coming off as anything but trite.) Our disappointment is that Crumb has not used the Genesis material as a foundation for a work that is distinctly and unmistakably his own. We wanted him to do what, in the broadest terms, Milton did with *Paradise Lost*: create an effective adaptation of the material that no reasonable person could ever see as a substitute for the original. We don't need Crumb's help to read the Scriptures, and if that's all he was going to offer us, the years he spent putting this book together were wasted time.

The achievement of the book, in Hodler's view, is that it fills out the narrative detail the Scriptures only imply. This might be valid if Crumb were illuminating aspects of the material that our present-day cultural assumptions blind us to. Unfortunately, that's not what Hodler is praising. What he seems to like is that Crumb has done his best to supplant even the slightest ambiguity in the text. Here is a moment that Hodler singles out for praise:

> ...a panel from Chapter 14 is captioned, "And he and his servants fanned out against them by night and struck them and pursued them to Hobah, which is north of Damascus." In the drawing that accompanies this narration, Abram and two other robed men ride camels and spear down their opponents' caravan, Abram in particular impaling a tribesman through his back. That Abram and his servants tracked down a group of foreign invaders, and reclaimed lost property and kidnapped kinsmen from them is information given in the text; that Abram and his servants did so this violently is not.

To think that Crumb's treatment adds anything, one would have to fail to understand from the text that Abram's decision to attack the invaders by night reflects an intention to terrorize them. Nor would one understand that the phrase "struck them" means — no trope here — that Abram's

AND HE AND HIS SERVANTS WITH HIM FANNED OUT AGAINST THEM BY NIGHT AND STRUCK THEM AND PURSUED THEM UP TO HOBAH, WHICH IS NORTH OF DAMASCUS.

attack was violent. The invaders being pursued into Hobah suggests that the attack was quite violent indeed — so much so that the invaders were apparently fleeing for their lives. Crumb isn't showing much of anything that a reasonably alert reader wouldn't pick up from the text. (Well, he provides details like the camel-riding and the spear to the back, but those are negligible.) Hodler isn't praising Crumb so much as he is displaying an apparent lack of affinity for the art of words — how they can be brought together in ways that create far more meaning than they explicitly say. I'm sure he just picked a bad example, because if this is a considered opinion on his part, he comes across as one who is completely lost when confronted with verbal tropes — at best a philistine. If you can't handle verbal tropes, you can't effectively read Scripture, poetry or prose fiction — you'd be somebody who needs Crumb's pictures because you couldn't read Genesis otherwise. Praising an artist for catering to a lack of imagination is pretty dubious praise. Crumb isn't enhancing Genesis with his treatment; he's dumbing it down.

Hodler is right when he notes that Crumb's adaptation techniques in *Genesis* are similar to the ones he has used in adaptations of Boswell, Dick and others. (Jeet Heer brings this up as well.) The previous adaptations, though, are short; I believe all are less than a dozen pages long. (Crumb's Kafka book is a collection of short adaptations.) Monotonous rhythms are nowhere as conspicuous in a shorter piece as they are in a long one; they don't have the room to get oppressive. And a limited dramatic palette is more tolerable as well; there isn't enough repetition for it to get tiresome. But to tackle a piece the length of *Genesis* effectively, Crumb needed to modify

TOP
Abram's backstab.

156

his techniques. In particular, he needed to come up with ways to vary the rhythms and expand his dramaturgy. As it stands, all he does is run his effects into the ground. A long piece requires different techniques than a short one, and Crumb didn't meet the challenge.

Jeet Heer writes that the objections of *Genesis* detractors like myself "come from category errors about what Crumb is doing. People are trying to read the book as if it's a new graphic novel by Crumb. It's not and that frustrates them." Heer states that it should be read the same way one reads the Scriptures. My response is that Heer's approach to reading it is the idiosyncratic one. For starters, I'm not sure quite what he means when he says the book isn't a graphic novel. My definition of that term — a standard one, I think — is a long comic book. The visual design of *Genesis* is that of a comic book — multiple panels per page, which readers are meant to read in narrative sequence. If it looks like a comic book, one would expect that it's intended to be read like one. If Crumb wanted the book read in the deliberate manner with which the text Scripture is traditionally handled, he should have designed it in a way that promoted that approach among readers, such as presenting the material with one panel to a page. Heer's admonition to readers like myself only makes the book seem like a greater failure.

Frankly, I'm not sure that Heer agrees with his own admonition. Later on in the essay, he writes that Crumb's page design and panel staging still reflect the approaches of Carl Barks, John Stanley and Harvey Kurtzman — which are comic-book approaches if ever there were ones. He then echoes my statement that Crumb repeats the *Classics Illustrated* approach to adaptation, which, again, is a comic-book style. (It's a tedious, unimaginative comic-book style, but still.) By the way, Heer again makes *Genesis* look worse with his defense. Crumb is enough of a student of comics history to know that the narrative style of *Classics Illustrated* made their adaptations a slog for readers; deliberately adopting it for his own project would be nothing less than self-sabotage. Personally, I prefer to think he blundered into it; I'd hate to think Crumb chose to make his book bad on purpose. And getting back to Heer's contradictory views about whether *Genesis* is a graphic novel or not, why does he write that it isn't a graphic novel when he ends his piece by identifying it with several examples of the form?

In looking over the rest of Heer's and Hodler's essays, as well as those of the other participants, the area in which I seem to be in the most disagreement is over the quality of Crumb's drawing. That disagreement appears greater than it actually is. I concede that a good deal of *Genesis* is pen-and-ink illustration of the first order, with visuals that are impeccably

"Crumb isn't *enhancing* Genesis with his treatment; he's dumbing it down."

researched. However, I don't feel it counts for a whole lot, and I sought to minimize it as much as I could. It's generally accepted that impressive production design, costuming and cinematography can't make a dramatically inert narrative into a worthwhile film. If anything, lavish production values make an audience resent a bad film more. ("Geez, with all the money they spent on the sets, couldn't they have put some aside for a decent script?") I don't think comics should be held to a different standard. If the work doesn't function effectively as a dramatic piece, the strength of the cartoonist's visual research and crafting of single images shouldn't be regarded as a saving grace.

And in the long run, I don't think it will be. Arguing that *Genesis* is a superb example of book illustration isn't making much of an argument for it at all. As a rule, the work of book illustrators, no matter how accomplished, ends up on the scrap heap of history. The only exception has been the work of Gustave Doré, and that's an example of an exception proving a rule. The efforts of John Tenniel, Howard Pyle and so on are of no interest today beyond the enthusiasms of a few cultist admirers and fans of the underlying books. As near as I can tell, Crumb's *Genesis* is going down the same road. Crumb's fan base seems to consider the book a treat, and biblical scholars appear to find it fascinating, but there just isn't enough there to make it compelling for anyone else. ∎

Jeet Heer's Response

As I noted in my earlier essay, the response to Crumb's *Genesis* has been a critical muddle. I'm not sure if this roundtable will do much to clear this muddle. I'm grateful to discover that Donald Phelps, one of the greatest of comics critics, shared my appreciation for Crumb's achievement, but dismayed to see the dismissive response of analysts as estimable as Rick Marschall, Alexander Theroux, Robert Stanley Martin and Kenneth Smith.

If I had to locate a common flaw in the negative response to Crumb's book, I'd say the critics are judging Crumb not by what he created, but by what they wished he had done. John Updike once offered a very useful "rule" for book reviewers: "Try to understand what the author wished to do, and do not blame him for not achieving what he did not attempt." In this case, each of the hostile critics brought to the work a prior sense of what they wanted, which is very different from what Crumb set up to do. For the religious believer Marschall, Crumb is not pious enough; for the wickedly witty novelist Theroux, Crumb is not satirical enough; for Martin, Crumb's fails to live up to the model of his co-created book on Kafka; and for Smith, a stern repudiator of modernity, Crumb is too tied to contemporary commercial civilization. This symposium, then, is very much a group of critics bringing their prized preconceptions to the table, where they hold forth on beloved bugbears while ignoring the poor cartoonist in the corner.

I'm going to have some fairly harsh things to say about Rick Marschall's essay, but before I do so, I do want to acknowledge my larger regard for his work as a comics scholar. Along with Bill Blackbeard and Lucy Shelton Caswell, Marschall has been one of the foundational comics scholars of the last century, a collector, historian and anthologist who has made it possible for subsequent scholars (myself very much included) to study the comics past. For me, *Nemo*, the comics history journal he edited in the 1980s and 1990s, is almost as important as Genesis itself, and my bookshelves overflow with volumes written and edited by Marschall.

Having said that, I've always found Marschall's theological and political views (which are connected) to be hair-raising. He once described Father Charles Coughlin as "one of my heroes." Well, Father Coughlin has never been my idea of a good man or a good Christian. On another occasion Marschall criticized an anti-apartheid comic book for being "anti-white," as if opposition to white supremacy were itself a form of racism. It has to be said that Marschall's religious/political views rarely seem to influence his comics scholarship, aside from a few stray cases such as his unwillingness to acknowledge Herriman's mixed race identity or McCay's anti-clericalism. But these are relatively minor issues. In reviewing Crumb's *Genesis*, Marschall has brought his own theological and political views much closer to the surface than in previous works.

Rick Marschall writes, he says, as a "committed Christian" as well as a "Crumb fan" and in both capacities expresses disappointment with Crumb's adaptation, seeing it as both theologically empty and ineptly constructed as a narrative (albeit with some well-rendered pictures). Now, of course, the views of religious believers are especially pertinent when it comes to Genesis, a foundational text not just for Jews but also Christians and Muslims. Aside from Marshall, there have been a number of interesting religious responses, notably a very respectful review by Gary A. Anderson, professor of Old Testament at Notre Dame, writing for *First Things*, the leading neo-conservative journal of religious thought. Anderson's generous response to Crumb should remind us that Christians come in many varieties (as do, of course, Jews, Muslims, pagans and non-believers).

I bring up Anderson (a Catholic theologian) because I want to make it clear that Marschall isn't speaking for all Christians, and indeed represents a distinct minority position among Christians. As Marschall makes clear, he is a "fundamentalist, evangelical, Pentecostal" and a believer in "New Earth" Creationism. For those unversed in the arcane shadings of Christian theology, that means that Marschall believes that the age of the earth is between 6 to 10 thousand years. That means Marschall rejects not just the theories of Darwin (which underwrite modern biology), but also all contemporary geology, paleontology and physics (to mention only a few of the many fields that are built on the truth that the age of the earth is more than 10,000 years). To be a "New Earth" creationist (or a Young Earth creationist, as it is sometimes called) is to reject almost all of modern science.

The issue of creationism is relevant because much of Marschall's critique of Crumb's *Genesis* is taken up with scholarly questions. Just as creationists reject most modern scientific scholarship, biblical fundamentalism is built around a rejection of almost all of historical scholarship done since the rise of the Higher Criticism in the early 19th century. Biblical fundamentalists are only interested in those narrow fields of study that confirm the historical accuracy of the Bible (i.e., some, but not all, archaeology). In general, biblical fundamentalists turn their backs on the many forms of scholarship

AND GOD SAID, "LET THERE BE LIGHTS IN THE VAULT OF THE HEAVENS TO DIVIDE THE DAY FROM THE NIGHT, AND LET THEM BE FOR SIGNS FOR THE FIXED TIMES AND FOR DAYS AND YEARS, AND THEY SHALL BE LIGHTS IN THE VAULT OF THE HEAVENS TO GIVE LIGHT UPON THE EARTH." AND SO IT WAS.

AND GOD MADE THE TWO GREAT LIGHTS, THE GREATER LIGHT TO DOMINATE THE DAY AND THE LESSER LIGHT TO DOMINATE THE NIGHT AND THE STARS.

AND GOD PLACED THEM IN THE VAULT OF THE HEAVENS TO GIVE LIGHT UPON THE EARTH, AND TO RULE OVER THE DAY AND OVER THE NIGHT, AND TO DIVIDE THE LIGHT FROM THE DARKNESS. AND GOD SAW THAT IT WAS GOOD. AND IT WAS EVENING AND IT WAS MORNING, A *FOURTH* DAY.

AND GOD SAID, "LET THE WATERS BRING FORTH SWARMS OF LIVING CREATURES AND BIRDS THAT FLY OVER THE EARTH ACROSS THE VAULT OF THE HEAVENS." AND GOD CREATED THE GREAT SEA MONSTERS, AND EVERY LIVING CREATURE THAT CRAWLS, WHICH THE WATER HAD BROUGHT FORTH IN SWARMS, AND ALL THE WINGED BIRDS OF EVERY KIND, AND GOD SAW THAT IT WAS GOOD.

AND GOD BLESSED THEM, SAYING, "BE FRUITFUL AND MULTIPLY AND FILL THE WATER IN THE SEAS AND LET THE BIRDS MULTIPLY IN THE EARTH." AND IT WAS EVENING AND IT WAS MORNING, A *FIFTH* DAY.

(notably philology, textual criticism, comparative religion and the study of the history and archaeology of the wider Middle East) that tend to undercut traditional religious ideas.

Tellingly, Marschall sometimes puts the word scholars in quotes without demonstrating why the people he's taking issue with are not real scholars. Equally characteristic is Marschall's disdain for Robert Alter's translation, described as "more philological than spiritual." Now, it's true that the King James Bible is unequalled in poetic power (which is why Crumb occasionally reverts back to it) but it's also the case that Alter has a much better command of ancient Hebrew than anybody in Tudor England possessed. There has been a renaissance of Hebrew scholarship in modern times, and Alter's translation, despite its occasionally stilted quality, is built upon a remarkable body of scholarship that allows us to understand the words of the Bible as they were originally intended to be understood, before the accretion of later religious traditions (be they Jewish, Christian or Islamic).

In my *Bookforum* review, I wrote: "Crumb describes his adaptation as being 'literal,' a rather loaded word in biblical circles. The idea takes many forms: There is the literalism of the fundamentalist, convinced that the Bible is the inerrant and inspired word of God, but there is also the literalism of modern scholars and translators, who use archaeology and philology to uncover what the words in this ancient text meant." The choice of Alter's translation was part of Crumb's literalism, his goal of trying to recover the primordial meaning of the words in Genesis. This goal is in some ways an impossible one: we can never fully recover the past, and we're always going to see Genesis through the prism of our times. Still, as with other noble attempts at historical reconstruction — say Margaret Yourcenar's novel *Memoirs of Hadrian* — Crumb's aim for authenticity helps orient his work and make it deeper and more thoughtful.

As a "fundamentalist, evangelical, Pentecostal" Marschall reads the Bible backward: He starts with Christ and then goes back to the Hebrew Bible to find stories and characters that prefigure the Nazarene messiah. While this hermeneutics might be useful for shoring up the faith of believers, it is not a very fruitful historical approach. If we're reading the Bible historically, we have to start with the simple fact that Genesis was written long before Christ lived, and the original Hebrew authors didn't know about Christ and were writing it for their own purposes. Therefore, someone who is doing a historically minded adaptation of Genesis, which is what Crumb is up to, has no obligation to include putative "Christological elements" in his work. This is especially true if the cartoonist is a non-Christian, as Crumb is. To put it another way, Crumb has also ignored the work of many Islamic exegeses, but Marschall doesn't upbraid him for that. No coherent Genesis could be done that incorporates all the competing religious and secular interpretations of the text that are available, so Crumb made a wise decision in simply trying to be as historically accurate as possible, which is in and of itself a difficult task.

In a superb critique of the biblical analysis of Northrop Frye, Robert Alter made a fundamental objection to the habit of some (not all) Christians who read the Hebrew Bible allegorically to find evidence of Jesus buried everywhere in the text.

> The revelatory power of the literary imagination manifests itself in the intricate weave of details of each individual text. On occasion it can be quite useful to see the larger frameworks of convention, genre, mythology, and recurring plot shared by different texts. The identification of overarching patterns was Frye's great strength as a critic, enabling him to make lasting contributions to the understanding of genre and literary modes. But the real excitement of reading is in the endless discovery of compelling differences. In the nineteenth-century novel, a Young Man from the Provinces may be the protagonist of a whole series of books, but Rastignac is not Raskolnikov, nor is Flaubert's Frédéric Moreau just a Gallic version of Dickens's Pip. The specificity of sensibility, psychology, social contexts, and moral predisposition of each is what engages us in the distinctively realized world of each of these novels, whatever the discernible common denominators. The Bible, as a set of foundational texts for Western literature, is an exemplary case for the fate of reading. Through centuries of Christian supersessionism, Hebrew Scripture was systematically detached from the shifting complications of its densely particular realizations so that it could be seen as a flickering adumbration of the Gospels that were understood to fulfill it. This is hardly a reading practice we want to revive, either for the Bible or for secular literature
>
> (Robert Alter, "Northrop Frye Between Archetype and Typology," *Semeia* #89, 2002).

Much of what Alter says about Frye applies with even greater force to Marschall's hunt for the Jesus in the pages of Genesis.

AND THE SONS OF RACHEL, JACOB'S WIFE, JOSEPH AND BENJAMIN.

AND TO JOSEPH WERE BORN IN THE LAND OF EGYPT, WHOM ASENATH, DAUGHTER OF POTIPHERA, PRIEST OF ON BORE TO HIM., MANASSEH AND EPHRAIM.

AND THE SONS OF BENJAMIN; BELA AND BECHER AND ASHBEL, GERA AND NAAMAN, EHI AND ROSH, MUPPIM, HUPPIM, AND ARD.

THESE ARE THE SONS OF RACHEL WHO WERE BORN TO JACOB, FOURTEEN PERSONS IN ALL.

THE SON OF DAN; HUSHIM.

Marschall is bored by Crumb's handling of the family genealogies. But it's possible that this is so because he reads these long "begat" lists simply through the prism of his own fundamentalist worldview. For Marschall, the genealogies in Genesis and elsewhere in the Hebrew Bible serve largely to ground the historical veracity of the text and also to provide a back-story for the life of Christ.

But there is another way to view those genealogies. The first book of the Bible is a seminal text in more ways than one, just as Crumb is a seminal cartoonist in more ways than one. Genesis is all about procreation, the seeding of the world, the birth and growth of the many tribes who make up the history of the people of Israel. In his *First Things* review, Gary Anderson provides a compelling defense of Crumb's handling of the genealogies. "Crumb shows deep attention to the biblical text at many other points along the way," Anderson notes.

For example, he handles the various 'begats' by listing the family members in a style that resembles a photo album of classmates or family. This is a beautiful way to depict a part of the Bible that many readers simply skip over because they are bored. But the family trees that are so basic to Genesis are anything but boring. They show us the relationships basic to the family God has elected to change the course of human history.

Anderson's appreciation shows that the division over Crumb's work doesn't have to fall along the line separating believers from free-thinkers. Rather, believers who are at ease with modern scholarship (Vatican II Catholics and liberal Protestants, Conservative and Reformed Jews, Islamic moderates) are likely to enjoy Crumb in a way that fundamentalists of all faiths aren't.

Aside from all these theological debates, which are no doubt boring to outsiders, there is the more basic question of whether Crumb has made a comic or not. Although they are sometimes willing to praise a small section here and there, the answer from Marschall, Theroux, Martin and Smith is no.

Again, I will ask if the critics aren't guilty of creating an imaginary Crumb in their mind and holding the real Crumb at fault for failing to measure up. "Where is the sabotage, the satire, the spice, the scorn?" Theroux asks. Well, it's easy to imagine a satirical take on the Bible. There's an old underground anthology titled *Outrageous Tales from the Old Testament* that does just that, with contributions by Alan Moore, Hunt Emerson and Kim Deitch, among others. But that's not the game Crumb chose to play: It's like criticizing Tiger Woods for not being a good swimmer when he's on the golf course. It's an irrelevant critique. (Theroux's essay, it must be said, is beautifully written and an excellent record of his friendship with Crumb, so I'm glad to have it, however misguided it is.)

Martin's objections to Crumb overlap with Theroux's. "His treatment of the material is grindingly literal-minded," Martin says. "It is barren of any hint of satire, irony or even allegory." Well, I think there is more irony in Crumb's drawings than Martin is willing to allow. As I noted in both my *Bookforum* review and previous contribution to this roundtable, Crumb is notably subversive on the issue of gender, incorporating a very serious feminist reading of the Bible into his storytelling. The other critics in this roundtable only glace at the issue of gender, which is of primary concern to Crumb. Again, we have a case of critics more attentive to their own agendas unwilling to look at what the artist is doing on the page.

Ken Smith's critique is an excellent example of this sort of critical myopia. Smith's essay is nearly 4,000 words long [*edited down for publication*], but only a small percentage of those words address Crumb's adaptation of Genesis. The vast majority of his essay consists of the typical Smithian screed against modernity. Now you may agree with this critique, but for it to be relevant it needs to be tied in some ways to Crumb's work. I suppose a case can be made that Crumb is a paradoxical figure: an anti-modernist who hates technology while working in a form (comics) that is deeply tied to modern mass communication. Smith hints at such a critique but doesn't pursue it. This is very much a shame since a man as erudite as Smith, with his longstanding interest in comics and skills as an illustrator, could have written a very interesting review of Crumb's book. Instead, Smith decided to belt out an old favorite, one we've heard many times before.

In sum, the hostile critics of Crumb have yet to come to terms with his book. Until they do so and offer a more compelling critique, I'll stand by my judgement that this intensely drawn and deeply researched adaptation of a text that helped create Western civilization, drawn by one of the world's greatest cartoonist, is a book that deserves to be read, reread and cherished. ■

Tim Hodler's Response

I will respond to the essays individually.

Rick Marschall: Aside from his aversion to the book's occasional sexual explicitness (which, to my mind, he overstates by some measure), Rick Marschall's problems with Crumb's version of Genesis can be divided into three major complaints: (1) He doesn't approve of the use of Robert Alter's translation, (2) he believes that Crumb's structural and formal approach is misconceived, a sin against comic-strip aesthetics, and (3) the book is insufficiently Christian.

Let's take them one at a time.

1. As regards Alter's text, of course intelligent and fair-minded people can reasonably disagree about which biblical translation is best. Wars have been fought over less contentious issues. Marschall believes Alter's efforts are disjointed, cold, overly literal and inaccessible, possessing the "literary élan of financial charts."

For what it is worth, in his own words, Alter set himself the goal of presenting Genesis in a language that conveys with some precision the semantic nuances and the lively orchestration of literary effects of the Hebrew and at the same time has stylistic and rhythmic integrity as literary English.

Marschall quite obviously has the right to argue that Alter hasn't achieved this goal. And Alter's language does in fact occasionally prove awkward and stilted — Crumb himself smoothed the prose into more readable form a handful of times, as Jeet Heer has generously demonstrated online at Comicscomicsmag.com. But while Alter's language rarely reaches the poetic

heights displayed in King James, I would argue that it offers its own beauties and mysteries and music. Opinions may and do differ. It is worth noting too that some of this linguistic awkwardness arises from the inevitable conflict of translation: whether to privilege accuracy over poetry, or vice versa. When forced to a decision, Alter seems to have most often chosen semantic accuracy. (Marschall should count his blessings that Crumb didn't opt for the more extreme literalist translation of Everett Fox: "no bush of the field was yet on earth, no plant of the field had yet sprung up, for YHWH, God, had not made it rain upon the earth, and there was no human/adam to till the soil/adama — .")

Considering the way Crumb generally approaches his literary adaptations, as an opportunity to bring forth unintended ironies in the original ("In all those literary things that I did, I saw something comic in the characters that was probably not intended to be there in the original"), Alter's translation seems an apt choice.

2. Marschall would have had Crumb take a different approach altogether, one that shaped Genesis into an exciting, fluid narrative that privileged supernatural spectacle and emotional conflict. Marschall asks us to believe that Crumb made a mistake when he adopted wholesale the oft-awkward structure of the original Genesis, begats and all. "One of the graces of the comic-strip creator," writes Marschall, "is the ability, virtually unique in the arts, to stretch or expand narrative elements, in the process not perverting the source material but illuminating it." (I am not sure why poetry, prose or films aren't able to stretch or expand narrative elements, but that is not relevant to my argument. The real problem lies elsewhere.)

AND THEY HATED HIM ALL
THE MORE, FOR HIS DREAMS
AND FOR HIS WORDS.

Marschall again: "I continually wondered whether Crumb . . . knew what he was doing, exactly, anent the excruciating details in his *Book of Genesis*."

Of course, we know that Crumb *did* know what he was doing. Crumb: "*In illustrating everything and every word, everything is brought equally to the surface.* The stories about incest have the same importance as the more famous stories of Noah and the Flood or the Tower of Babel or Adam and Eve or whatever. *I think that's the most significant thing about making a comic book out of Genesis. Everything is illuminated.*" [Italics mine.]

Marschall: "Crumb was under no obligation to highlight the relatively mundane elements, minimize the spectacles, or any creative choices in between. Yet the very *choices* he makes in the telling, before words or drawings are set to paper, say something." Marschall is absolutely right; what's interesting to me is that Marschall believes that Crumb simply cannot mean for the book to say what the book says. This isn't a very fruitful response, though Marschall repeats it in different words, and in increasingly raised tones. When you consider Crumb's undeniable mastery of the comic-strip form (and Marschall does not deny it), and likewise keep in mind that Crumb has used the same technique in adapting textual sources for decades, one comes to the obvious conclusion that the book is meant to say what it says.

As for the various comic-strip sins that Marschall highlights — the "he said" captions, the endless portraits of the begats, the structural stiltedness — all of this springs from the source material itself. (Rather than re-rehearse my arguments about these supposed flaws, I will redirect you to my original essay.) The constant "and he said" captions are not a bug, but a feature, constantly reminding the reader that she is reading the complete original text of Genesis itself. If Crumb had the goal of turning Genesis into a rollicking read full of wonder and awe, of making this religious text fun and exciting, then Marschall would be right: He failed utterly. If the goal was

"If the goal was to illuminate the oddness of the text itself, Crumb succeeded beautifully."

to illuminate the oddness of the text itself, Crumb succeeded beautifully. And if approached in that spirit, as Crumb's guide through the narrative thickets of Genesis, it turns out to be great fun indeed ... 3. ... If, of course, you aren't a Christian believer. The strongest and most unanswerable of Marschall's criticisms is that Crumb's Genesis simply doesn't cater to Christian orthodoxy. It includes no Christological symbolism, and seems, if anything, designed more to undermine rather than buttress standard religious beliefs. Marschall is right on all counts here.

Jeet Heer: I largely agree with Heer's essay in most of its particulars, and therefore don't have much to add. A few thoughts arise, though. First, Heer's analysis of Robert Alter's essay and its strengths and shortcomings is particularly insightful. I alluded to Alter's misapprehension of comics aesthetics in my contribution, but didn't elaborate upon that aside. Heer does what I should have done, and very well. Comparing literary adaptation to the Talmudic tradition seems to me a particularly brilliant touch. Second, in regards to Heer's comments about biblical syntax, and its possible connections to comics. Coincidentally, in preparation for my original essay, I read the first chapter of Erich Auerbach's *Mimesis*, in which he famously compares the literary style of Genesis to that of Homer. In the end, I don't believe that any of the insights I gleaned from Auerbach made their way into my writing, but for a time I considered applying what he calls the paratactical style of Genesis (in quite similar terms as what Heer describes as "additive") to the grammar of Crumb's comics. There may be something worth exploring there — Crumb's panels are surely more paratactical than the more fluid, cinematic panel-work of masters like Osamu Tezuka or Jack Kirby — but ultimately it became clear that such lofty theoretical work was beyond my compositional powers.

Donald Phelps — not much to argue with here: I haven't seen the Dreyer films in question, but am now highly motivated to track them down. As to whether or not Crumb has created a new genre: I think this just might be true!

Alexander Theroux — I disagree with much of what Theroux has written, but still found his essay great fun to read. Theroux would have preferred that Crumb had published "a *Mad* comics version of the book of Genesis," one with salt, spite and satire, instead of "a polite Gustave Doré-esque simulacrum of the thing."

At the same time, he argues that the real Crumb, the face behind the mask, is a humorless, overly literal, undereducated moralist. This is a somewhat unfair characterization of his essay — Theroux both argues this thesis and contradicts it, hastening "to point out that Crumb's low-brow humorlessness here [is] certainly not characteristic of him," while also arguing that in some sense Crumb the satirist was what Yeats called the "Anti-Self." "It is about paradox, all of it," Theroux writes.

And fair enough. That satirists are moralists is a truism. His comments bring to mind Mark Twain, whose favorite among his own works was not *Huckleberry Finn* or "The Mysterious Stranger" or *Life on the Mississippi*, but that now-forgotten romantic bit of hero-worship, *Joan of Arc*. Is it possible that Crumb has grown conventional and dull in his old age?

I don't think so, mainly for reasons I have already given. Moreover, Theroux's evidence for Crumb's supposed humorlessness is less than convincing: a long list of Theroux's own jokes to which Crumb apparently didn't show sufficient appreciation. And what a marvelous parade of nearly context-free nonsense that list is! "It is vulgar to smear jelly over bread. [snobbism] ... Texans like buckles as big as their heads. [silly] ... The act of voting is like feeding hogs. [who says?]"

By the end, I was reading aloud, and laughing at the end of every line. I'm not sure who was really mocking whom, or whether some kind of ideal state of multilayered irony had been reached in which Theroux and Crumb were both mocking each other on multiple levels, but I enjoyed every moment immensely. It didn't do much in terms of driving Theroux's point home.

In the end, there is not much point in arguing about a book that doesn't exist, the "*Mad* comics version" of Genesis that Theroux wants to read. For what it is worth, Crumb himself has stated that something like that was his initial intent, but that he was not very pleased with the results. "None of it worked," he told an interviewer. "And I thought it was stupid." (The Adam-and-Eve parody in question can be found and judged by readers in *The Crumb Handbook*.) But Theroux does make a few assertions that deserve correction. First, Theroux's list of Jewish celebrities who may have served as Crumb's models is enjoyable, but sloppy. Try as I might, when I gaze upon Shechem's visage, I simply do not see Adam Sandler. (Pauly Shore would be closer, though still not quite there.) Second, Theroux claims that Crumb is a professed "unbeliever," when in fact, Crumb does claim to believe in God, at least when speaking to *Vanity Fair* or Françoise Mouly.

TOP

From "Mr. Natural" in *Zap* #2 (June 1968) [©1968 R. Crumb]

Third, Theroux writes, "it is always a mistake and far too taxing to draw Satan or the Supreme Being." This is probably true, but in the book under review, Crumb did not draw the Supreme Being, but merely the popular image of Him. This misapprehension explains much.

Robert Stanley Martin: Of all of the arguments included in this roundtable, I find Martin's to be the least convincing. It is more or less a perfect example of the uninspired and unambitious criticisms of Crumb's book that I alluded to earlier. His argument seems to begin and end with an under-achieving teenager's drawled "Boooorrrring." More accurately, it begins with "boooorrring," and ends with, "I wish the book was shorter so I could have read the entire thing with more concentration and less effort." Most of the counter-arguments I might want to use against Martin's essay can be found in my original review, but there are a few relatively unimportant points here that are possibly worth responding to. First, I am not sure I agree that

171

None of his female characters seems to have her own existence, but is spawned in his imagination in order to distract "K." or "Joseph K.", to tempt and ensnare him. Kafka's sexual terror is put to the test time after time, yet these same women provide something more...

TOP
From *Introducing Kafka* [©2007 David Zane Mairowitz, text; R. Crumb, art]

Crumb should be regarded as cartooning's first Romantic artist — What about Herriman? — but it at least has the virtue of being an idea. My second bone of contention: The book on Kafka seems to me a terrible introduction to Crumb, as it offers just the kind of "straight illustration job" that Martin seems otherwise to despise! Someone interested in learning what Crumb is about would be better advised to start almost anywhere else. The *Weirdo* era in particular has aged well, and needs little context to understand.   But this is neither here nor there, and I shouldn't ignore Martin's main argument entirely. He writes, "The thought of Crumb's trenchantly satirical perspective illuminating the hoariest of ancient texts was irresistable." I would argue that this is exactly what Crumb offered. Martin just didn't see it. If only Genesis wasn't quite so long ...

Kenneth Smith: Smith, too, seems to ignore Crumb's actual book for the most part, but at least he provides some provocative intellectual meat to chew on in exchange. Smith spends a lot of time explaining the great questions that he feels Crumb must attempt to answer in order for his book to prove more than "automatic, myopic 'chatter.'" "The most significant history of The Bible, as of every other great formative force in the *mythoi* and moralities of the world," Smith writes, "would not be any work of factical scholarship scrutinizing how it came to be or was formed, but rather of what it has meant, how its peculiar authority organized and expended itself on personalities and societies." (Smith also writes, "no one could be more inept to gather such understanding than modern academics and intellectuals," but declines to justify his reasoning. I'm not sure this is really an argument that goes without saying!) Interestingly, I think that in a roundabout way, Smith's proposed topic is precisely one of Crumb's major themes: he wants the reader not only to recognize the absurdities in the Bible, but to wonder at how it has managed (and been used) to shape human society and behavior so profoundly. Smith goes on: "The question why an entire people was receptive to this sacerdotal salesmanship is never asked, or how religion was rooted also in primitive intuition and mythoscultures." Again, Crumb may not ask this explicitly, but it is clearly one of the most important implicit questions raised by the book. Crumb isn't writing a treatise, and doesn't promise to answer such deep and abiding questions, so it seems a bit much to denigrate him for failing at a task he never set out to accomplish. How exactly is this supposed to fit in, anyway? With an added chapter explaining how the priesthood came to power and put together the Bible? That sounds like the makings of a fascinating book, but surely it is not the only valid approach to an adaptation of Genesis, or even a particularly likely one. Outside pedagogic types like Ayn Rand and Robert Heinlein, artists and writers are usually more interested in inspiring questions than in answering them.

Smith goes on to "argue that [Crumb] has revealed more of himself than he probably intended in his mundane and pro forma prefatory remarks, and revealed as well how much he is indeed of as well as in the belly of the beast, the Leviathan of modern culture." I don't follow Smith's logic in thinking these particular remarks reveal what Smith claims they do, but it doesn't really matter much, because I also don't think that Crumb, possibly our greatest living self-satirist, is quite so unaware of his own position. Crumb knows that he is of, as well as in, the belly of the beast — it doesn't take a consciousness-expanding LSD trip to realize a dorm-room paradox that obvious. In fact, just such awareness is most likely one of the things that drew Crumb to the Bible as a subject in the first place.

"I had such a heavy Catholic brainwashing when I was a kid and I've been dealing with it ever since," Crumb said in the Jean-Pierre Mercier interview I quoted earlier. "It doesn't ever completely go away, no matter how intellectual you become later. The thing happened to you so young and formed your view of the universe at such an early age, or has at least a big influence on your view of the universe, you never completely get past it. So I guess it's one of the underlying currents in all the work I do."

Albeit Catholicism and the larger Leviathan Smith rails against are more kissing cousins than identical twins, but this quote still speaks to the kind of self-awareness Smith too readily assumes Crumb lacks.

After this accusation, Smith drops any pretense of discussing the book itself, and diverts his essay into a lament over consumer capitalism. (In fact, for all of Smith's verbiage, he says very little indeed about Crumb's actual adaptation at all, and it is somewhat unclear whether or not, outside Crumb's introduction and footnotes, Smith has even read it! He certainly doesn't provide any analysis, other than to briefly compare the art to that of Basil Wolverton, an easy analogy which, while apt, as his lone bit of description doesn't exactly inspire admiration in Smith's work ethic.) His only remaining interest in Crumb's *Genesis* is in its marketability, as if that has any relevance to the work's merit, or lack thereof. That books have to be marketed may be deplorable, but it seems strange to dismiss Crumb's book on the basis that it is easily sold. If salability is an artistic crime, then Crumb has no valid options left. An exploitable market exists for anything he might create.

In the end, this essay reads like a missed opportunity. Rather than apply his considerable intellect and unique perspective to the work at hand, Smith has decided to take another trip around the playroom riding his favorite hobbyhorse. Talk about automatic, myopic chatter. ■

Alex Theroux's Response

I found the essays collected here a mixed bag. Many good points, taken all together, can be found throughout, and while some are better than others — distinctly so — it is a seminar round which a passionate few have gathered. I hope my comments are taken to be as judicious, honest and well reasoned as I intended them to be and not offered with sniffing disregard.

Crumb's *Genesis* is a complex marriage in an attempt to join a sacred text with drawings that are modern as well as interpretive. So as Wallace Stevens in "Le Monocle de Mon Oncle" asks, "Shall I uncrumple this much crumpled thing?"

Jeet Heer in "Genesis Revisited" states it is not Crumb's masterpiece, adding that he has had "too long and varied a career to be summed up in one work." He points out that what is more or less conveyed in a novel through words is "inevitably" "flattened in the pictorial representation," which is of course not the case. First off, to make a pedantic distinction, *Genesis* is not a novel. But Heer's is a ludicrous oversimplification. George Cruikshank and Hablot Knight Browne ("Phiz"), two of Charles Dickens' illustrators, put a shine on even his own brilliant productions. What about Ernest Shepard and *Winnie the Pooh*? Sir John Tenniel and *Alice and Wonderland*? The French illustrator, engraver and painter Gustave Doré not only made astonishing engravings for *Paradise Lost*, the *Divine Comedy*, Tennyson's *The Idylls of the King*, *The Works of Thomas Hood*, *The Divine Comedy*, Coleridge's *Rime of the Ancient Mariner*, but in 1865 the Bible, which is still my favorite. In his day, Doré was accused by the *Art Journal* of "inventing rather than copying," his originality was so pronounced, so daring, so inimitable. And has Heer ever heard of Thomas Nast to whom no one in satirical illustration can be compared? Heer correctly sees that Crumb has not tried to produce a graphic novel, however. When he points out that "every adaptation is by necessity not a replication of the original but to some degree a commentary on the original work and also a fresh work in and of itself," he understands that nature of Crumb's undertaking of this "tribal encyclopedia," the first book of the Bible, and when he notes that Crumb is a "deeply conservative artist," as I tried in my own essay to make clear, he is right. I think his comparison of Crumb's *Genesis* to the *Classics Illustrated* style is not wide of the mark, in that he is keyed in to being "very faithful to the text and tries to visualize each textual detail." I am not certain how in dubiously tracing his work back to the "low comic tradition of Bruegel" — a remark somewhat blasphemous against low comedy and Bruegel — makes any point I can recognize, but Heer in my opinion gets most of his essay right.

Robert Stanley Martin in "Crumb Finally Finds His Limits" declares early in his essay that as to subject matter and limits Crumb has none — until he illustrated *Genesis*. I cannot agree that he reached his limit in undertaking to illustrate "this hoariest of ancient texts" (Martin's phrase), but merely strayed from the Crumbian power source — rude, bold, desacralizing satire and socially hostile visual polemics — for one of Crumb's positive attributes is that he has no limits. "Crumb's timidity in imposing his point of view on the material goes beyond eschewing a satirical or other conspicuously re-imaginative approach," writes Martin. "Instead he adopts the monotonous illustrated-text approach of *Prince Valiant* cartoonist, Hal Foster." It is a harsh diagnosis, but more or less accurate in its assessment. When he writes that "No thought has been given to using the text as a counterpoint to the images," one cannot agree that "no thought" is involved, merely that Crumb felt too (theologically?) intimidated to dare to contravene accepted, literal, as-already-seen images of this holy book and more or less "turtled." Martin as recorded is crucially disappointed regarding the drawings, seeing too many of them as "hackneyed," "desultory" and so forth. The irony of it all, as I see it, although Martin does not so state, is that exactly what we expected from R. Crumb with that bold, scarifying talent of his — irony, sarcasm, wit — was precisely what we were not given. What we were given was the exact opposite, earnestness, a difference as alarming as between the front of a painting and the back of it. It is about expectation over actuality. Marilyn Monroe, with her star-studded reputation for sex, invariably disappointed her lovers. But earnest, Crumb's *Genesis* certainly is. "Crumb's vision of God is a retread," grizzles Martin, *simply because he expected a brand new tire!* The same goes with Crumb's middling, even piddling, conception of the Devil or Satan (my own biggest visual disappointment). "The one character I was really looking forward to seeing was Crumb's treatment of the Garden of Eden's serpent," confesses a "letdown" Martin, who finds instead of the most devious, cosmologically destructive being-thing in the history of the universe merely a cozening little upright lizard! (Look at Gustave Doré's Satan, a blackened, bewinged semi-human horror, totally frightening and memorably evil! Martin and I of all the essayists were the only ones to be particularly disappointed in this.)

Donald Phelps, in "An Epic Visualized," choosing worshipfully to see Crumb's book as an out-and-out "consummate triumph," that it "amounts to a new genre," a "visual narrative that enlarges and re-electrifies its subject," offers us something of an appreciation, but it is not literary criticism, merely personal opinion, so he places himself beyond the borders of complaint.

Kenneth R. Smith in "A Book for Man Recounted in A Book Of/By/For Man" gives us a word-salad of an essay as confusing and as long-winded as the title. When he asks at midpoint, "By what kind of chasms of civilizational discord are the Bible's own reasons-for-being divided from the kinds of purposes this rendition has been produced to serve? Are there even names for this kind of culture-cleavage, this ideological 'repurposing' from one worldview to another?" I can only wonder of what language this bad translation was the source. I did detect one sentence, lost like a waif in the prosaic slums here, stating that "little in Crumb's treatment is novel or original," and even that is not true.

Tim Hodler's "Crumb's Genesis" is a conventional, rather bourgeois response to a book much more complicated than his attempt to analyze it. "Adam and Eve," he complains, "are also straight out of central casting, and even the fruit they eat is the old storybook apple, rather than a fig or pomegranate, as is more likely (if less familiar) [the Edenic fruit]," but it was Crumb's *ambition* in taking up the job — reverence rather than wrath – to go to central casting in trying to convey Genesis, in the way any literalist would. If Gustave Doré were that intellectually timid, that dogmatically pulled in, all those *Art Journal* mediocrities and academic dunces back in 1865 would have given him a medal! Hodler is also somewhat schoolmarmish in overpiously suggesting that "those who claim that Crumb has added little to nothing to the text should try to come up with visuals this powerful and compelling so consistently, for so sustained a period of time," which as literary criticism is nonsense. You don't like the drawings? *You draw the 50 books yourself!*!! Good God, has literary criticism come down to this? It reminds me of the 1960s when so many pusillanimous adults, infuriate with national boomism, leaned out of their pants to bark at any and all highly sincere anti-Vietnam War protestors, "Love it or leave it!"

Rick Marschall's "Pilgrim's Process" — the most involved if long-winded of the articles — takes Crumb's *Genesis* to be a "hagiographic novel," which, if it is hagiographic and a novel, is news to me. Right away, the alarm I felt in his finding Crumb's depiction of the Garden's serpent "brilliant" put me on notice. Marschall's rather gratuitous "full disclosure" that he is a "committed Christian" (as I am) prefaces a ham-handed segue into the idle speculation as to whether Crumb rejects Darwin's "theory of evolution," which surely cannot matter in any solid assessment of Crumb's task at hand here, since it is irrelevant to the very premise of the work. Making comments on the inevitable visual clichés of Crumb's taking up the task of drawing this solemn book, he is surely right in speculating that Crumb would "trade his birthright to draw The Song of Solomon," a book suited to Crumb's pen. Marschall's mounts an endless defense of all the "begats" and more or less commends Crumb's "literal reliability" in drawing the face of every last character, making a final point that in doing so Crumb might have "let a few longer captions...do that work." For Marschall's philological questions, one is passingly grateful. He thinks Crumb might have included Christological elements that foreshadow and in fact prophesy the Messiah of the New Testament, faulting him, on the other hand, for citing "ancient occult practices and postmodern feminist critiques" – I find it brave and in fact legitimate of Marschall to make this point — but one wonders if Crumb's biblical scholarship reached that far. Marschall even dares to suggest that in Crumb's rendering of the Book of Genesis "the Spirit of God is left out." "I say this not judgmentally, despite how it sounds, but as an observation," notes Marschall, adding, "Crumb says as much in his Introduction, that he has amalgamated the words of men who felt inspired through the centuries." Marschall is disappointed to observe not only that Crumb has truncated parts of Genesis, chose to shape, edit, conflate — "In this aspect, R. Crumb has sinned," he concludes — but is equally let down by the comic-book angle of things, omissions of a kind, that "there is [only] one full-page drawing; no half-page drawings," etc. adding, "One wishes that the cartoonist Crumb had honored the obvious dramatic highlights with double pages, longer sequences and some appropriate graphic construction. Instead, except for the scorecard above, there is page after page of three- tiered grids and, often, small panels." Marschall judges that reading the book "becomes a visit to a theme park," not, say, an archaeological dig," concluding "Not only theology, but history, is ill-served." But is Genesis history? There is in Marschall's essay as much a large-hearted attempt, commendably, to justify the ways of God to man as there is to justify Crumb's attempt at "historiography" in having taking up a nearly impossible task, but he believes that on a "provocative" level Crumb succeeds, nevertheless registering a sort of ontological disappointment that Crumb is not a "believer." To make an analogy, it goes back to the question of whether a moral requirement, ethics of character, is necessary in a presidential candidate. ■

AND ZILPAH, LEAH'S HANDMAID, BORE JACOB A SON. AND LEAH SAID...

GOOD LUCK HAS COME!

AND SHE CALLED HIS NAME GAD.*
* GAD: "LUCK", OR "FORTUNE".

AND ONAN KNEW THAT THE SEED WOULD NOT COUNT AS HIS, AND SO WHEN HE WOULD COME TO BED WITH HIS BROTHER'S WIFE HE WOULD WASTE IT ON THE GROUND SO AS NOT TO PROVIDE SEED FOR HIS BROTHER.

AND WHAT HE DID WAS EVIL IN THE EYES OF THE LORD, AND HE PUT HIM TO DEATH AS WELL.

Kenneth R. Smith's Response

(1) In response to Rick Marschall's remarks:

Forget *Genesis* for a moment: Dwell on *Proverbs* — "Where there is no vision, the people perish." It's not the business of a qualified and valid critic to gush about what he "likes" or cavil about what "displeases" him; people's arthritic perspectives and petty appetites are the whole reason that criticism (and religion, and philosophy, and culture and politics) is needed in the first place, to dilate and enrich prevailing concepts of what the cosmos of humanity and culture is capable of, lest it shrivel down to a microcosm of masturbatory trivia ("virtualia"). It's definitely not part of a critic's function to flog commodities and serve as an adjunct to a book's promotional apparatus; above all else, as corporatist methods and techniques of marketing grow more and more coordinated and perfected, it is more imperative than ever to discriminate between commodities that have no higher reason for existing than serving as a trigger for the release of cash, and bona fide organisms of culture, conscience, and the concentration of value-intelligence. If at all possible, intelligent criticism should act as a window on the more encompassing horizons of our age, whether much of anyone cares for such dilation or Olympian vistas or not.

We seem to make favoritist allowances for what is so lamely "esteemed" in comics. Comics have demonstrably grown slicker but have woefully failed at the task of doing any actual cultural labor, of arguing or attacking principles or perspectives of any existential or world-historical heft. As intriguing and adept and beguiling as they may be, not even the most prodigious talents in comics can apparently bear the structural load of the significant issues in our time. As an adolescent medium, comics have had to aim at a moving target, the evolving sophistication of adolescents — in an era when Americans have en masse repudiated the profoundest responsibilities of outgrowing their puerility, and technology and the market have aided and abetted this Neverneverland of inbred possibilism in perfect step with the decline in rationality, values, self-discipline and self-sobriety.

Crumb's *Genesis* is by no means an intrinsically "great" or "momentous" work; my naïve or original reaction to it was that it was humdrum fare. But it does have potential for stirring up important forms of turbulence around its perimeter and beneath its patterns of lividity, where it seems the blood stopped circulating in it: i.e. it may qualify (as nearly anything of even meager substance or pretension would) as grist for the mills of more illuminating criticism, but that is hardly saying that it reposes in a position of command over the most vital issues of the decade or generation, much less the past few millennia (as it feigns). It is an "event" only because the market, for its own reasons, *needs to trumpet it as an "event,"* and as for those excited by such announcements, it's hard to improve on the Yiddish folk-saying: *When a fool goes to market, the merchants rejoice.* In spite of itself Crumb's book does sit at the intersection of many controversies tangled beneath our society's blithe surfaces, and it serves to some extent as a metric for them. Individuals who exercise both their culture and soul have perceived the callousness, the opportunism or expediency of this product's collocation of commodity-virtues: They have also remarked to me that no one who cares about his professional career would risk making issues out of the multiple forms of obtuseness and slack that combine in it. Altogether, such issues-with-impunity smell to me like the pie-dotted, sunny fields of the lazing, eminently tippable Sacred Cow; so I'll try to put my whole brain into this heave.

—Who couldn't have seen the commodification of Crumbiana coming down Madison Avenue? Animation, posters, T-shirts, documentary, statuettes, postcards, tin signs, rafts of girly books, on and on: the neon-alarm flashing "sell-out" was there decades ago. Crumb is an Industry, the Walt Disney of our detumescent counterculture. He's welcome to it, but he's not welcome to any critical accolades for it. —Even among those who might have cared, who really cared? Are there any icons among us immune to the toxic tides of Exchange-Value, the everliving Godhead of modern anomie? I don't perceive any among this circle of "critics" being too keen on making

...AND SO, WHEN THE EGYPTIANS SEE YOU AND SAY," SHE IS HIS WIFE," THEY WILL *KILL* ME WHILE YOU THEY WILL KEEP ALIVE!

SAY, I PRAY YOU, THAT YOU ARE MY *SISTER*, THAT IT MAY GO WELL WITH ME ON YOUR ACCOUNT, AND I SHALL *STAY ALIVE* BECAUSE OF YOU!

AND IT CAME TO PASS THAT, WHEN ABRAM CAME INTO EGYPT, THE EGYPTIANS BEHELD THE WOMAN, THAT SHE WAS VERY BEAUTIFUL.

AND PHARAOH'S COURTIERS SAW HER AND COMMENDED HER TO PHARAOH, AND THE WOMAN WAS TAKEN INTO PHARAOH'S HOUSE.

an issue of what "Crumb" has perforce become. I think I know what art looks like that still has a living nerve in it, and what it turns into when more and more it is done under the goad of extrinsic motives and interests, as a mere means to other ends altogether. I have had to explain to too many technically glib, mercenarily governed personalities over the decades why they really can't be mistaken for "artists." It can be seen nakedly in quality of line and form, in the infectious way that some work engaged its creator and now commands the attention of its appreciators. And for those who have eyes to see, the vacuity of it can be also spectacularly present.

—But there is (for instance) a far more profound problem with Crumb's rendition than his predilection to make most of the characters in *Genesis* appear as "miserable wretches."

In spite of Marschall's later criticisms of this book, he takes rather too many things for granted, as those too hungry to believe are liable to do, and therefore assimilates Crumb's treatment into the sheepfold of diligent belief even though this art is subjectively and culturally made of demonstrably very different stuff." The evidence of things not seen," i.e. a heady draft of willful and infatuating faith, will induce many to look right past what Crumb has overtly rendered. To a more discriminating eye — to anyone cultured in the classical ideal of a subtle and *organic marriage of form and content* — Crumb's version of *Genesis* is as much of a "betrayal" or "subversion" of his subject as a soulless translation of Sappho or a dry, academic version of Homer's epics (Lattimore's for instance), that is tacitly hostile to the meaning, values, worldview, apodictic power or ethos-shaping cogency of such a work. Our intellectuals-on-reservation are for the most part moral and political wretches; not even the wraiths of modern culture or its starveling ideals or puny "values" deserve to have fallen into their hands, but they are the very quintessence of the effete type that this civilization relegates to "educational" duties, as the late Roman Empire delegated teaching to slaves and paid of course the price in character and culture.

Anyone who saw what Crumb's rendition literally "had in hand" would rightfully wonder in retrospect *why on earth* generations of the covenanted would *ever have regarded* such a work as a way of monumentalizing their utmost authoritative movements of the spirit: for these patriarchs and folk-heroes look like a gnarly and seamy bunch of street-folks in a hardscrabble struggle for subsistence, with occasional celestial special-effects thrown in to convey the supposed sacrality of the text. An illustrator is entitled to relate only distantly or mechanically to his subject, and to withhold his most profound beliefs (if any) — but when the whole and entire point of a text is its power to evoke the *decisiveness of faith* and the *fatality of piety?* How could an illustrator's stance more patently express that he is subjectively contraindicated for this labor? Crumb's approach not unsurprisingly manifests the lukewarm passions of "belief" and "values" typical of a civilization that has reduced religion to idiosyncratic, organizable and exploitable fantasy — to subjectivism and eccentricity and myopia — when for millennia religion's task was nothing short of mustering Promethean energies, architectonic and monumental forces for humans to struggle masterfully to try to emulate the spirit of Eternity, the Rock of Ages.

Trying to pour old wine into new wineskins can be just as stupid an enterprise as the reverse. What is the problem when form deforms content in the way Crumb's treatment or modernity's clerical or hieratic culture does?

"In spite of itself Crumb's book does sit at the intersection of many controversies tangled beneath our society's blithe surfaces, and it serves to some extent as a metric for them."

—I have enjoyed a lot of Crumb's work — I suppose the covers of *Weirdo* most of all, most recently — and, over the decades, have even enthusiastically called it "iconic" or archetypal after its own kind, as my friends and colleagues among artists and illustrators could testify. Still, it's not the sort of art or stylistics that I wax adulatory about, like Marschall; my tastes or interests may range widely but I'm more connoisseurial and harder to impress than most consumers of art, as also of story. I pass over mercifully a lot of his recent sketchbooks with banal and perfunctory if not downright insipid line-work in them, all rather "too much of a muchness." Crumb's is a distinctive but limited style of interpretation, and like every style it works sea-changes upon its subjects, like a Procrustean bed that stretches or trims to fit whatever is nested in it. Crumb was ideally suited to material such as his own Runyonesque underground or satirical characters, or Bukowski's subculture and its entropic terms of subsistence, but this is because (in spite of his revulsion against almost everything industrialization, commercialization and mass-culture have done to befoul the world) Crumb's worldview is quintessentially democratizing or proletarianizing, and these two "optics" are (like it or lump it) patently part and parcel of that world-order he otherwise despises. Ordinary (ordinarizing) eyes naturally make everything appear ordinary:"As a man is, so he sees" (Blake). Hegel remarked in this vein, "No man is a hero to his valet, but not because no man is a hero, rather because the valet is a valet"; and Crumb has pretty much maintained a valet's point of view on existence,

devoid of esteem, self-transcendence, idealization, sublimity, ideality or sur-reality or all that he dismisses as "romanticism." (I am aware of the exception he makes for early blues masters, artists with autonomous drives and intrin-sic or largely market-free or unmercenary needs to make music. The point of my criticisms of his *Genesis* is just how much his practice presently falls short by his own implicit criteria of art, integrity, "nobility," etc.)

Whether satirically or confessionally, his work repeatedly reassures its read-ers of a Freudian homogeneity among human psyches, a "vulgarizing" or "demeaning" or "seamy" point of view with plenty of ideological adherents in the West or in the modern world (and yet why would Crumb then be so much happier among relatively more cultured, more leisurely and reflective Frenchmen than among American yahoos who are out-vulgarized by virtually no one?). But this leveling imperative explains in its own way the compulsion impelling him to "take on," now, a premier Scripture or text on *extraordinary* characters; he has a duty to his own common-man worldview in a way or in a sense to *discredit or disillusion* the roots of the religious and moral manias he has railed against, and his own banal or mundane economic necessities (the need to produce, to earn a living, to "take on" illustrational tasks) merely serve as a mask shielding him somewhat from controversy or diverting its force. "Don't mean ill to anybody, nobody here but us diligent little scribblers." It seems to me that the honest and forthright position, if you mean to make a criticism or a moral assault in principle on some ensconced fraud of religiosity or doctrinaire conventionalism, is not to be furtive, mealy-mouthed or oblique, but rather to be bold and candid and to strike for the jugular, as Marx and Nietzsche and even Kierkegaard did, because otherwise one is all too boringly trying to inflict a "death by a thousand paper-cuts" on a Hydra-headed monster.

Crumb seems not to have the stomach for the polemical fare his own *character* has nonetheless directed him toward: He knows he can't say or do anything that won't be offensive to many, and yet he doesn't care to rise frontally to this responsibility. Like any cautious passive-aggressive, he values his own strategic and precious deniability above all else. Against the volcanic dementias of that corpus of "common men" that he has supposedly cast his ideological lot with, he prefers to pull his punches and pussyfoot his way through any ensuing melee (having his cake and eating it, as far as "counting coup" against these hostiles is concerned). So it goes with so many would-be-secular or -humanist or -modern "moderns," who resent many vague and ineffable things about the religious or the traditional worldview but indeed have no rationally defensible values or principles of their own to mobilize over against it.

—I love a good donnybrook, an open and forthright polemic: Bruised feelings and abraded egos have always been a tawdry price to pay for making issues out of matters that deserve to be made issues of. But it is prime hypocrisy, seeking to *"split the difference"* between piety and impiety, to claim to respect what in actuality one doesn't respect in the least. *All spiritual and philosophical issues and questions* seem alas to evoke an abysmal palsy of anxiety among moderns, like Medusas that moderns dare not look squarely in the face. That is precisely the *symptomatology of anomie*, of a normless, value-purged, culture-less dysculture: it is the *most central* matters in human existence, human nature, society and history that moderns quail and equivocate over and then ultimately (pardon my neologism) hypocritize or mealy-mouth about. We reckon ourselves hardened and realistic everywhere *except at the core*, where we make marmalade look like granite: About everything vital and essential we have truly become "artful dodgers." Who today can fail in his own eyes to pass for a "Christian" or "conservative" or "honorable" individual in his own eyes, if that is how he needs to regard himself?

Crumb may find elements and aspects (for instance) in the personality, social adversity and spiritual sufferings of Kafka that resonate with the alienation and strife of an American underground comics-artist, but Kafka is quintessentially an expression of *Old-World aristo-rabbinical ethos* (a spiritual *noblesse oblige*, anachronistically surviving like a dinosaur into a bourgeois and democratist epoch that can fathom *neither spirituality nor nobility*). And Crumb by contrast is a creature (whether he likes it or not) of that *New World egalitarianism* (the all-American chumminess or folksiness that makes our society such a "fraternity without any paternity"), the familiarizing and leveling climate that Kafka satirized in *Amerika* as a delusional enclosure where (ludicrously enough) "anyone can be an artist," where, today, virtually none but the crackheads of religiosity understand or try to live according to the once-perennial principle of a "calling" ("vocation," an etymology that has drastically changed its sense among us) or a viscerally commanding divine or eternal-intrinsic destiny. For most moderns and certainly nearly all Americans, life is just a matter of *muddling through*, a challenge to one's short-term pragmatism and ad-hoc inventiveness.

In my experience and my interaction with them, I find no reason to concede that fundamentalists have any monopoly on "truth" or insight into the meaning of spirit, much less into the meaning of Scripture. Never before the modern era has the candle of religion been so profoundly threatened with being snuffed by the slurry of *believers' own* barbaric and intemperate (that is to say, idiotist) self-righteousness with all its desperate self-certainty and feverish rhetorical self-placebos and crusades of self-righteousness for the purposeless: modern "religion" is *religiosity*, the symptomatology not of "faith" or "piety" but rather of moderns' *pure and absolute immersion in Self*, in a cult of collective willfulness or cloistered and mutual self-indulgence. We have the distinction between "religion" and "religiosity" in our language for a most crucial purpose, to differentiate authentic from counterfeit or spurious, and essential from accidental or peripheral; all of which are immaterial considerations to eternally puerilized or mass-retardate sensibilities. When an entire civilization sets about the program of deracinating value-intelligence (culture, philosophy, education, literature), that anti-cultural cult can only produce a society *structurally inept to comprehend* the discrimination of higher from lower, virtues from vices, authentic from fraudulent, valuable labor from parasitism, constructive from destructive self-pursuits, sanity from insanity, or for that matter life from (ultimately) the declivity of irrationalisms into outright death. Like the fabled mills of God, the ways of human nature overall grind very slowly but they do grind exceedingly fine, and even entire civilizations are patently caught in those teeth.

(2) In response to Jeet Heer's remarks:

What Heer disagrees with from Alter's review has to be taken not in abstracto (as Heer does) but in concreto:"A visual representation of a character or an event is inevitably a specification." Grounds for differentiating an "artist" and an "illustrator" arguably or typically falls along these lines — the work of illustration tends to "*present*," to make graphic or to literalize, thus catering to the needs of those who can't "image" matter for their own selves, whereas the work of art (when it is illustrative also, or narrative or dramatic) tends to enrich and to explore the subtler or implicit (the more "fortressed" or buried) meaning of a text. It's all very well to talk about a piece of art giving "life" to some describable act, event or manifestation, but nothing in truth means more different kinds of things to humans than (demonstrably) "life," or else they wouldn't resort to or be content to "live" in so many different ways and for the sake of so many different kinds of ends.

And when her time was come to give birth, behold, there were twins in her womb. And the first one came out ruddy, like a hairy mantle all over, and they called his name Esau. Then his brother came out, his hand grasping Esau's heel, and they called his name Jacob.

It may be true as Heer notes, that "pictures can be as ambiguous, as rich in meaning, as words," but this is a point in abstracto that one would be hard-pressed to illustrate with actual instances from the repertory of most "comics literature," which is not exactly rife with Kafkas or Yeatses or Durrells or Dostoevskys or Calvinos or Borgeses, not to mention *Rashomons*. Comics fans who want more or subtler quality of forms generally grow up and just go someplace else, leaving a rather picked-over clientele of "sensationalists" who (as Nietzsche observed) need to be shouted at by sensational matter because they are and will remain profoundly intellectually and spiritually deaf. In most comics the direct, the nakedly "assertorical" or "evidential" — the already-decided, "resolved" and -incarnated — is at the foreground, in the reader as well as the presentation. Over my 40-odd years of interactions with comics fans, I have rarely noted a profound appetite for polysemic expressions or ambivalent, divergently interpretable perspectives/plots in comics culture. Things may be relatively different in Europe, but in the U. S. , viewers go to comics just as they do to TV, to have things resolved into graphic determinacy for them, not to have questions or abysses opened up for speleological exploration into the murk.

Freud observes that "neurosis is the inability to tolerate ambiguity," that is, a form of existence mired in the "determinate" or "finite" or specific, the cloistrally habitual or unquestionable. In that formula, Freud is intimately linking ego per se (the *knowing* or determining function in the psyche) with a *liability to neurosis* (self-fixity, self-preciousness, a taking-for-granted attitude so blind as to be dysfunctional in practice and function). Among Marschall's substantial observations about Crumb's method of approach, certainly what he remarked about Crumb's *routine formatting* was dead on: Crumb may be the pedestrian antipode to the "cinematic" and tempo-experimental frameworks of Bernie Krigstein. The venerability and density of the original Scripture — even though it may be a wild and woolly monster compared with most tightened or psycho-economical scripts — are no excuse for Crumb's metronome-like regularities of division, scope and pacing.

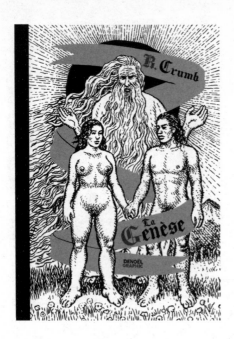

Heer goes on to call Crumb's approach a "conservatism" and a deep "indifference to the graphic novel esthetic" — although this alone does not explain *Genesis'* garish cover: the truth is, *Crumb is his idiom and his idiom is Crumb* — the cover of this book is in itself a *signature just for its gaudiness* graphically advertising its core-Crumbness; Crumb in this book is capitalizing above all on himself, his self-comfortable style and his view of things, as well as his readers' circus-like "sensibilities".

Heer writes, "Genesis starts with God creating the universe but over the course of the book the deity recedes and humanity takes the foreground. Eventually, in the story of Joseph and his brothers, God exists only as a dream-like visitation." Hobbes' analogous observation marks with conceptual finesse a sharp boundary between the medieval and the modern worldviews:"*When a man says that God spoke to him in a dream, what he means is that he dreamed that God spoke to him.*" The Old Testament has its own form of "apostolic succession," so to speak, the *immanentalization* of divine authority into patriarchal and prophetic forms (priests being comparatively feeble culture-heroes or bearers of imperatives). A cosmological perspective as such, without any account of the distribution of authority throughout the human order, would be like legends of the Greek Titans or world-forces in their powers and lives apart from the human race and from all reference points that have significance for humans: that distanced point of view would not actually concresce into a humanly moving epic, a drama of how divine afflatus played itself out over generations and among vicissitudes.

(3) In response to Donald Phelps' remarks:

Perhaps it is helpful if I seize on Phelps' phrase, "Crumb's vital earnestness of absorption in his subject," as the very issue I am pivotally denying. Crumb is at best a talent for making texts graphic, an illustrator. By exalting him his adulators merely make his several shortcomings all that much more graphic on their own. What, is Crumb somehow the peer of Kierkegaard, some Nietzsche or Kazantzakis or James Agee or Krzysztof Kieslowski, much less a Blake or Dostoevsky? Crumb would be a comparative poseur or schlepper, a tinkerer in Hesse's glass-bead game carried on as the rosary of bygone-people's utmost beliefs and principles of order: in this regard, the prefatory apothegm for his *Genesis* might well be, "Even a cat may look at a King." And even the Prince of Nerds may offer his take on the Patriarchs of the Torah, and all for the benefit of those who may not be able to distinguish the two. Is democratist egalitarianism grand, or what?

Crumb has already distanced himself in any profound sense from the questions or concerns that might provoke a "long dark night of the soul" in anyone self-wrestling over whether to believe or to reject the ultimate claims of the Old or New Testament. We can probably take him at his word that this is a "straight illustration job," the fruit of *labors* certainly but not profoundly self-troubling labors of enlightenment, wisdom, or Sisyphean self-discontent.

(4) In response to Alexander Theroux:

Theroux finds Crumb apparently inexhaustibly interesting but takes this for some sort of depth or dimensionality. I can well understand that Crumb's personality, worldview, life, and work have been a complex or at least muddled reaction to the cultureless managerial-military behaviorism of his father as well as the cultish manipulative-magical theatricalism of the Catholic Church. On these two "platforms" he has variously oscillated between wallowing in the libidinalism of '60s counterculture on the one hand and struggling for a breath of unpolluted air from the higher idealism, also of '60s counterculture, on the other. Neither of these two hopefully higher but alas still planar orientations has ever amounted to any kind of "foundation," for Crumb or for anyone else wrestling for self-grounding or for moral, political or spiritual rootedness. For neither of these "desiderata" or "visions of a better world" is a whole or full-dimensional culture that carries the stresses and structures of our higher-order existence down to more basal or "intuitive" and thus more axiomatic matters.

Theroux relays a commonplace irony about Crumb's dissociation from the Church, or so my decades of counseling philosophy students and contending with antagonists have shown me: any subculture or worldview that hopes to infect its congregants with a *cult of fideism* inevitably pays a price itself for this myopic and pathetic tonus, i.e. its puerilized parishioners are apt (like Crumb) eventually to disparage and repudiate that "faith" on grounds just as emotionalist — as trivial and *subjectivist* — as was their more naïve enthusiasm for it.

What Theroux calls Crumb's "rather muscular endorsement of populism" I call entropic democratism or, more plainly, barbarism, the self-centered *idiotia* or self-infatuation of *hoi polloi*: potahto, potayto. How contortionary must an ideological posture of "populism" be if Crumb has to depart for Europe to find a people he can stand to have a conversation and a civilized meal with? What kind of incoherent worldview is it that obliges someone to think one way (hooray for the Many) and yet act another (namely, as Bierce put it: the only thing the rich [or intelligent] are willing for the Many to keep and call their own is their distance)? Hello: if your own "people" fall intolerably short of what you think a "people" ideally or humanely or rationally or responsibly or naturally or archetypally ought to be, *you have a problem admitting to yourself* that you are exactly what your populism most reviles, an "elitist." If you have *criteria* of your own (ideal or normative standards) about what is human and what is subhuman, then you inevitably harbor a subversive propensity to think for yourself and to hold yourself and others accountable in spite of any self-preferred illusions or self-placating delusions. This critical perspective is inherently a solvent that threatens the cohesion of any and every mass of irrationally organizable people, and every form of modern organizational ideology therefore anathematizes it.

(5) In response to Robert Martin:

Crumb would certainly bristle at being called "romantic," in just about any sense at all (clearly it's a term of opprobrium to him), as also at the notion of having a dewy-eyed infatuation with his self-precious "muse." As Theroux noted, Crumb reacts against such euphuism, such intellectual or cultural pretentiousness and self-importance; and this seeming modesty or jaded cynicism or impartially deflationary populism serves him well in helping him to dissociate his work on *Genesis* from any idealistic or programmatic ulterior purpose. As anyone familiar with the history of satire, wit, humor, or lampoon would perceive, Crumb's position as a sniping critic of modern mass-culture has left him caught rather in between modes or types:"wit" (as we see in Diogenes, Kraus, Shaw, Wilde, Twain, etc.) is a piercing but nimble skewering of some subject from a position of inevitably superior clarity, coherency, and exceptional audacity and directness (aristic traits, all of them); "humor" (as we see in Will Rogers, Thurber, Mel Brooks, Woody Allen) however includes its own flawed or absurd self, its own author and point of view, among those infected by the foibles of the species. The wit does not mind broaching the rules of popular rhetoric (alienating and targeting the Many, launching a one-sided crusade on behalf of uncompromised truth), but the humorist has skin too thin to endure critical or

visceral reactions himself and therefore smears protective mud on himself in the process of assailing others. Humor is "good-natured," marked by an elastic sense of fellowship or a familial sense of the "we" among the species generally; wit is sharper, harder, and more immune to the attempted recriminations of the witless.

Crumb is not comfortable launching missiles of criticism from a vantage point of "authority," because of course (in these polarized days more than ever) this is an invitation to reciprocal polemics. He rather wants to have his cake and eat it as well, to associate himself as one among the Many when that suits his purpose and to dissociate himself from it when it doesn't. Years ago, a career as a culture- or social critic was probably not much of an option for someone so equivocal or self-inhibited, but in fact more recent "critics" are of this waffling and hamstrung sort. In his self-conception or designed posture, Crumb is no detached intellectual with special and specifiable Ideas to sell, and he's also not one of the (these days barely) "trousered apes" who make up the mass-market for sadistic, self-flattering and spectacular drivel. He's bared his own soul and vices and obsessions enough to disqualify himself hopefully as any sort of saint, much less as angel or hero. And perhaps Crumb's career of projects has more and more tended to educate him that, as far as the diagnosis and criticism of societies are concerned, he has many shortcomings to humble himself over, all his popularity or success notwithstanding. In the realm of satire he has not reached the position of deft and profound characterization or mastery over absurdity of an Aristophanes or a Wilde, or a Stoppard for that matter, but definitely he has far expanded the reach of comics culture. This merely happens (for all its diversity) to be rather a shallow pan. The only reason "great projects" and "great events" in comics seem like something of note is comics' own parochialism (a remark again with a heavy burden of obviousness).

TOP
From "Uncle Bob's Mid-Life Crisis"

I have to agree with Martin (a former correspondent of mine) that *Genesis*, broadly considered, is rather "barren" and "plodding," marked by "timidity" and "repetitive tedium." I read it without enthusiasm but with a sense of duty-bound investments of effort, as if from a more encompassing perspective it might be said, with a sigh, "Well, another classic has succumbed to the lappiness of comics, what next" (Milton Berle's term to his TV comedy writers: "This isn't lappy enough. We need to lay it right in the audience's lap"). Is there a tart icing, a freshet of new interest lavished on this work, or a novel chemistry of leavening profound insight into the visceral or conscientious meaning and cogency of *Genesis*? If not, then — among the possible good-faith or well-meaning reasons for doing it, i.e. among the *justifications* and not just the excuses — why choke the conduits of commodities with another such cultural superfluity? The sheer cult of Crumb's name and style doesn't succeed in raising this work to significant much less classic status, all the reassurances of those conscripted to his style and perspective notwithstanding.

And Martin is correct: this book isn't "slothful" purely and simply. It is only with respect to higher-order, more august demands that it fails not just to deliver but even to promise. It is overtly a labor but manifestly not a labor of love or esteem. The golden archetypes of the Era of Patriarchs and their Pancrator have been rendered in cheap pewter here, for ready display in the gift shop on the way to the checkout lines. But many readers certainly will neither care nor notice about the quality of the item per se, and those people are as much a boon to merchandisers as they are to political parties. ∎

TOP
From "Uncle Bob's
Mid-Life Crisis"

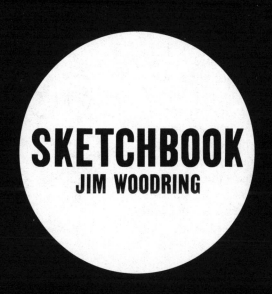

SKETCHBOOK
JIM WOODRING

Jim Woodring is an autodidactic cartoonist who began self-publishing his highly personal — some may even say eccentric — comic/diary/journal *Jim* in 1980. In 1986, Fantagraphics, ever ahead of the curve, began publishing *Jim* as a magazine, which included comics, prose and drawings. Jim created Frank (or was it the other way around?), his Everycartoon character, in 1992, and has drawn the little rascal off and on over the last 20 years; his first graphic novel, *Weathercraft*, published in 2010, is one doozy of a Frank adventure.

Woodring is a visionary cartoonist, something that surely cannot be said of most cartoonists and even, significantly, of many great ones. Visionary in the sense that he renders the world on his own terms and yet remains faithful to its deeper meanings; his drawings are a way of reimagining the world, and through a succession of them, he succeeds in peeling back the metaphysical layers of what most of us think passes for reality. His sketchbooks are filled with the snippets of reality he sees.

— *Gary Groth*

194

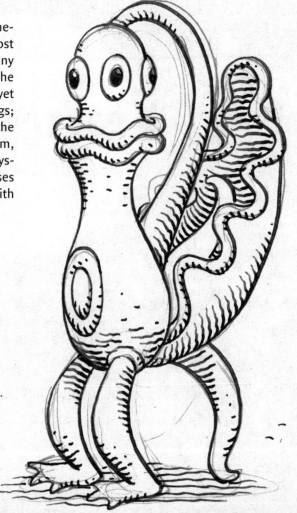

Woodring pop-up photographs taken by Jacob Covey

Gary Groth: All of the sketchbooks you gave me are identical in size and shape — 3 5/8" x 5 5/8." Where do you get them and why do you like this size and shape?

Jim Woodring: They're Moleskine sketchbooks. I bought my first one in 2004. It was love at first sight, exactly what I'd been looking for for years. Now there are lots of similar sketchbooks made by other companies, some of which are higher quality and all of which are cheaper, but I stick to the Moleskines because they look good in rows on the shelf, all identical.

I like the size because with one of these, and a mechanical pencil (Pentel Twist-Erase, with the superb eraser) and a fountain pen in the pocket, I'm never caught without a sketchbook. I don't like to carry a big sketchbook around all the time: I tend to lose things. Besides, with a small sketchbook, if I make a lousy drawing it doesn't have to share the page with better ones.

Groth: Do you always carry a sketchbook with you?

Woodring: I usually have one of these on me: always, in fact, unless I forget to bring it. I fill up at least one per month. I'm a habitual sketcher when I'm alone and I'd like to sketch when socializing, but I've been told it's rude. Crumb can do it because people are honored to have him drawing in their presence. When I do it, it just seems anti-social.

Groth: Are you a chronic or habitual sketcher? Are these your "portable" sketchbooks? Do you keep a more stationary sketchbook at home or in your studio?

Woodring: I do have large sketchbooks that I work in, but they're much more deluxe and I make more finished drawings in them. I can be ratty with the little Moleskines and I don't worry if there are rough scribbles mixed in with the more carefully done stuff.

Groth: Some sketches look like you're practicing representational, albeit Woodringian tropes — such as the striding figures we have seen in your comics — while others are more abstract and phantasmagorical — such as we have also seen in your comics — while still others come from direct observation. Do you make such categorical distinctions when you're drawing, and if so, do these choices come from different creative places or exert different creative muscles?

Woodring: Everything goes into the books: drawings from life; rendering exercises; notes; drawing games; character designs; page layouts; anatomy studies; fantasies; dreams … everything. Having a shelf full of these is like having a lot of batteries full of ideas. I need an index, though … combing through them is tedious. I have over a hundred of them, I think.

Groth: Following up on that last question, where, for example, did the spread I call "My life is shit" come from? Not from life, I hope. Or the two boxers pummeling each other with the woman looking on, which seemed somewhat uncharacteristic of you (except for the woman looking on, that is, which somehow gives it that Woodring touch).

Woodring: Yes, that "My life is shit" drawing came from a real situation; and believe me,

"So why am I compelled to draw things I find repulsive? I can't explain all this; it's a mystery."

the poor guy's life was indeed shit. When Mary and I lived in the barrio adjacent to Glendale in the early '80s this monster of a woman and her poor mashed worm of a husband lived across the street from us and we heard her screaming at people all the time. She had a hideous lemon-shaped body that she displayed in skin-tight clothes and she had the voice of a talking crow, an incredible whisky-and-cigarettes bass screech. That line about "You treat me like a," etc. was one of her favorites; she shrieked it at her husband regularly. It's one of the most shocking, nasty things I've ever heard anyone say and it took me years to commit it to paper. Maybe you better not run it. It's so foul I can't think of it without cringing.

As for the other drawing being characteristic, there are no rules with the sketchbook. It's a place to experiment without restraint. Anything that crosses my mind goes into it.

Groth: You once told me, "The process of drawing Frank is very, very boring because by the time I'm ready to draw, it's all worked out. Drawing Frank is no fun at all. It's just a purely mechanical exercise ... It's just labor." Contrariwise, your sketchbooks look like a lot of fun, very spontaneous and freewheelingly imaginative. The drawings here are much looser than your comics, and even allow you to use pencil as a medium. Am I just seeing things here (pun intended) or do you see your sketches as a different realm of drawing?

Woodring: You nailed it. The sketchbooks are mostly fun. Generally speaking, I don't worry about how good or bad things turn out in them, though occasionally something will be so atrocious that I'll cover it up with a patch so I won't have to see it again.

Groth: Do you find this looser approach inappropriate for finished comics? Is it liberating to move from the carefully controlled comics to this freer approach?

Woodring: Well, unfortunately for me my looser drawings are not really acceptable to me except as sketches. If I did a comic that loose, the crudeness and errors would make me loathe it. Some people are great at making quick drawings that work beautifully. I'm not. My sketches are just idea-holders, and they can have a certain interest and value as such, but to present them as finished works ... no.

But yes, it is fun and liberating to draw like that.

Groth: How do the sketches interact creatively with your finished comics or your paintings? What's the connection? Do random sketches lead to narrative ideas?

Woodring: Well, sometimes I'll work out the design for a drawing or a page or a new character in the sketchbook, and sometimes I'll draw something that I'm likely to need later ... a monster or a creature or a prop. More rarely a sketch will serve as a springboard for a story. But in general the point of the sketchbooks is to capture as many fleeting notions as possible for future use.

Groth: Several three-dimensional pop-up drawings appear in the books. Can you describe the process by which you make these? How is this different creatively from the act of drawing?

Woodring: Well, a pop-up has to be intended to be a pop-up from the start.

Generally speaking you can't do a drawing and then decide to make it a pop-up unless it just happens to be properly placed on the page, have the right dimensions and so on. There are basic pop-up techniques that everyone who does these uses. I haven't done many that were very advanced.

Groth: I notice most of the inked drawings have a pencil under-drawing, so that even your sketches are pretty thoroughly drawn, if you know what I mean. Do you ever draw solely with ink?

Woodring: Seldom. I'm no good at the spontaneous unpenciled ink drawing. I've tried to do that all my life and I just don't have the touch. I have to draw a lot of lines before I get the right one.

Groth: I also saw a few —but not many— preliminary sketches for printed work — the L'Assoc cover and a Frank sequence. Is it sheer happenstance when you do such sketches for published work, based on where you are and when the ideas strike you?

Woodring: I like to make preliminary drawings in the little books if I can. The books are diaries in a way, a record of what I see when I'm out, ideas that may turn out to be useful and the projects I'm working on. Sometimes I'll put substances in them to commemorate an event: blood, sap, juice, coffee, that sort of thing. One book has a blueberry from a piece of pie Bill Frisell was eating, mashed between two pages.

Groth: You experiment a lot by drawing wildly mutated extrapolations of the human figure: disfigured tubular creatures

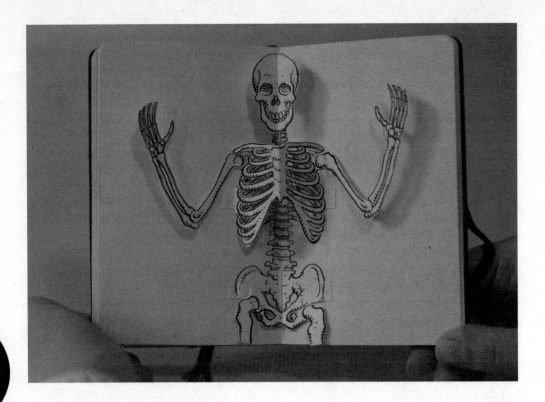

with distorted faces, uncomfortable-looking claws, and so forth. It's as if you're seeing just how far you can stretch a vaguely human form and still retain some level of humanness. One of your visual motifs is the distortion of faces and bodies — huge haunches and sagging flesh. Can you pinpoint some aesthetic motive behind this preoccupation? No glib answer here, Jim, I mean business!

Woodring: Have you ever had a moment when you saw humans as if you had never seen them before and found them spectacularly unbeautiful? Seen without personality, eyes are creepy little machines, teeth are like stones stuck in meat, ears are crazy-looking: terrifying. Flesh, pored and hairy, can be nauseating to think about in a certain way. As for what's on the inside, forget about it!

Sometimes the veil just falls and people are horrible-looking ... to me, anyway. Maybe that's the impulse that lies behind the work of other artists who distort the human figure into nightmarish lumps of steak, like Francis Bacon. At any rate, drawing these distortions is something of a compulsion for me.

As it happens I'm working on a long Frank story and I'm in the middle of a section where he is amongst a bunch of naked men with deformed genitals and big holes where their faces should be. They're gut-worshippers, obsessed with innards. I'm so tired of drawing intestines

and sweetbreads. It's torture ... guts have always made me sick. But it's an important part of the story: so much as I'd like to drop it I have to stick it out.

Groth: On the other hand, you also draw traditional cartoony figures that are almost self-consciously benign, even jaunty, like figures from a Disney film model sheet circa 1940s. Admittedly, they're a little perverse in their own cutesy-pie way, but how do you account for this wide range of how you draw the figure? Is it just as the mood strikes you? Does moving from one extreme to the other serve some deep need?

Woodring: I guess I want to cover as much territory as possible. I like sweet, innocuous cartooning. I won't hear a word against Uncle Walt. But what I like more is cute/spooky stuff: "Bimbo's Initiation," "The Wiggle-Much." I'm not addicted exclusively to horrible stuff. I draw it more out of a sense of perimeter establishment. You could say I do it out of a sense of duty. I'd be happier if a lot of the grim junk that's in my head weren't there. But the world is chockablock with horror, and the world is my subject. I'm not a fan of transgressive art or literature. Hubert Selby, Jr.: no thank you. I can't look at some of [H.R.] Geiger's images. So why am I compelled to draw things I find repulsive? I can't explain all this; it's a mystery. ■

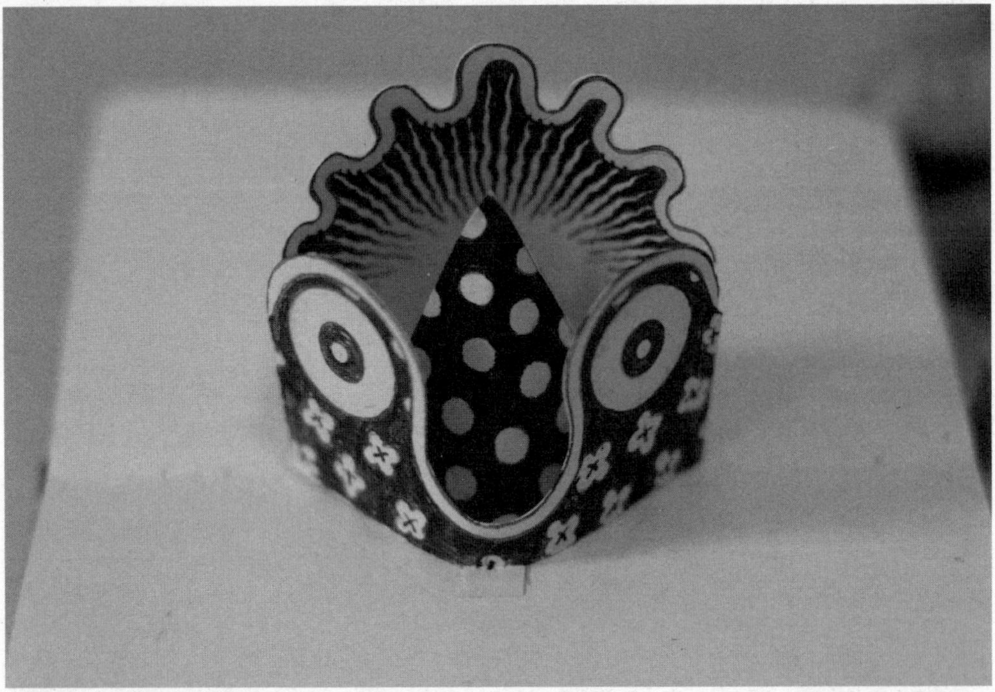

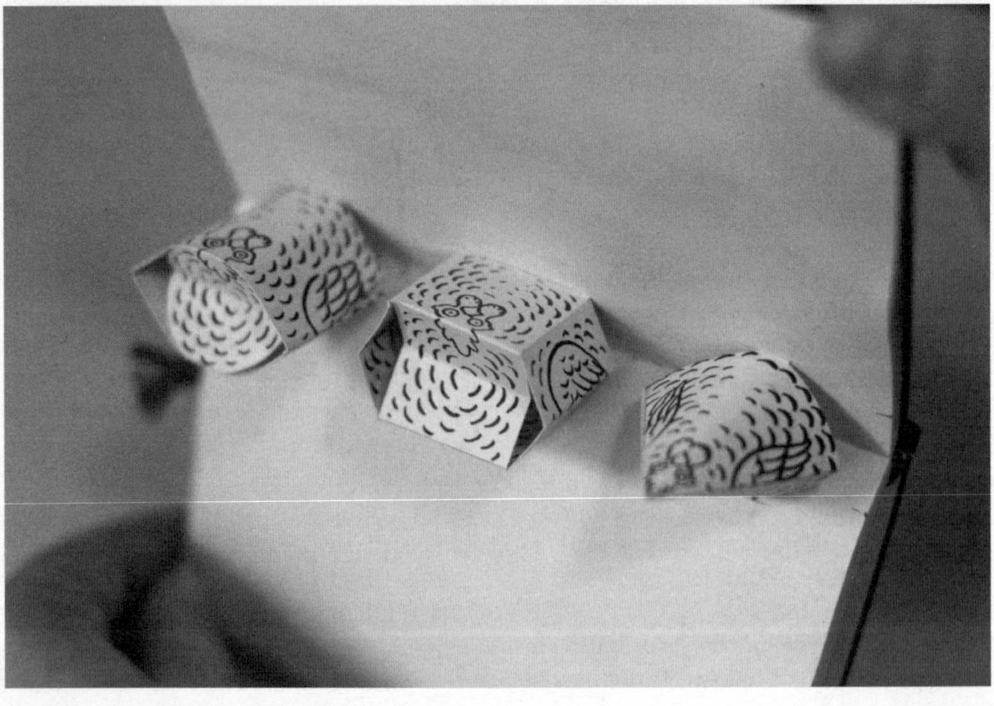

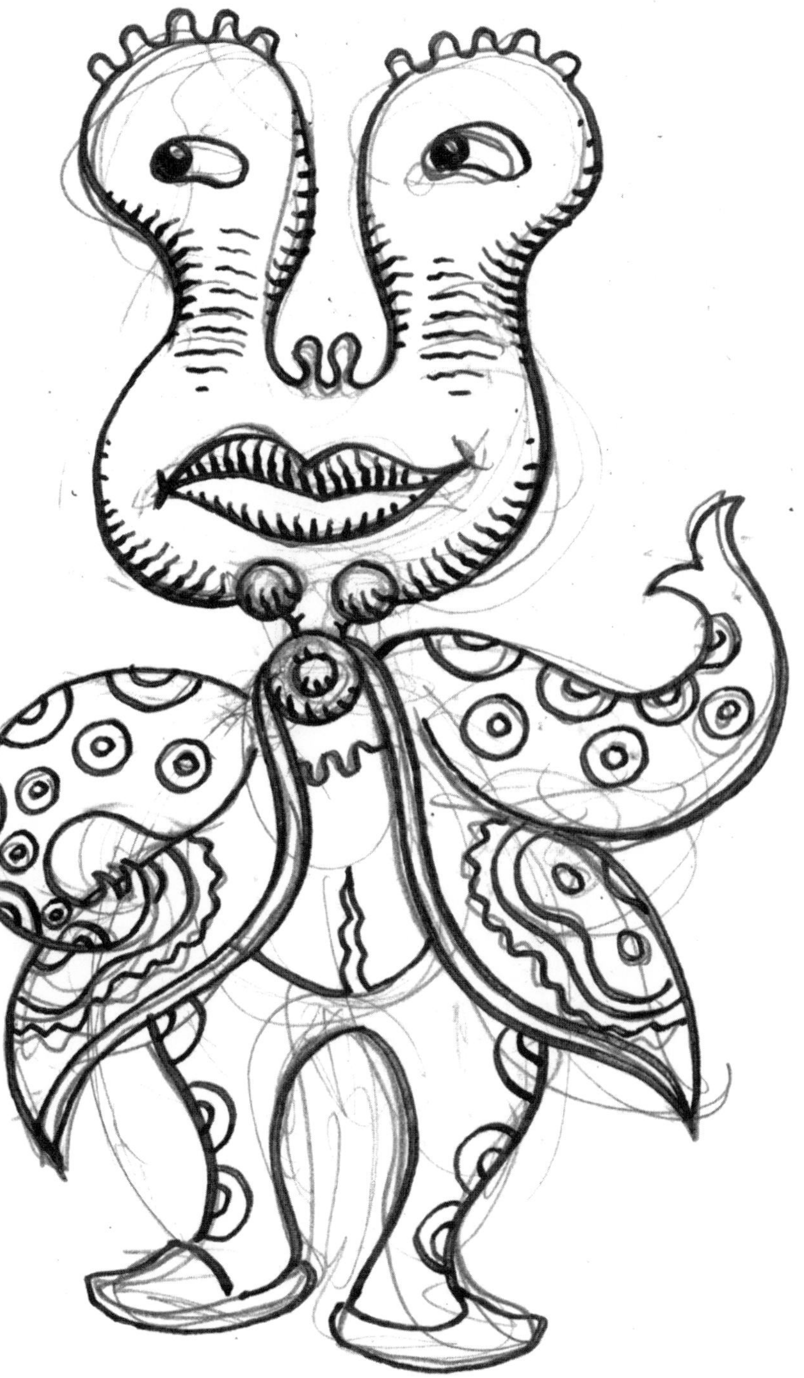

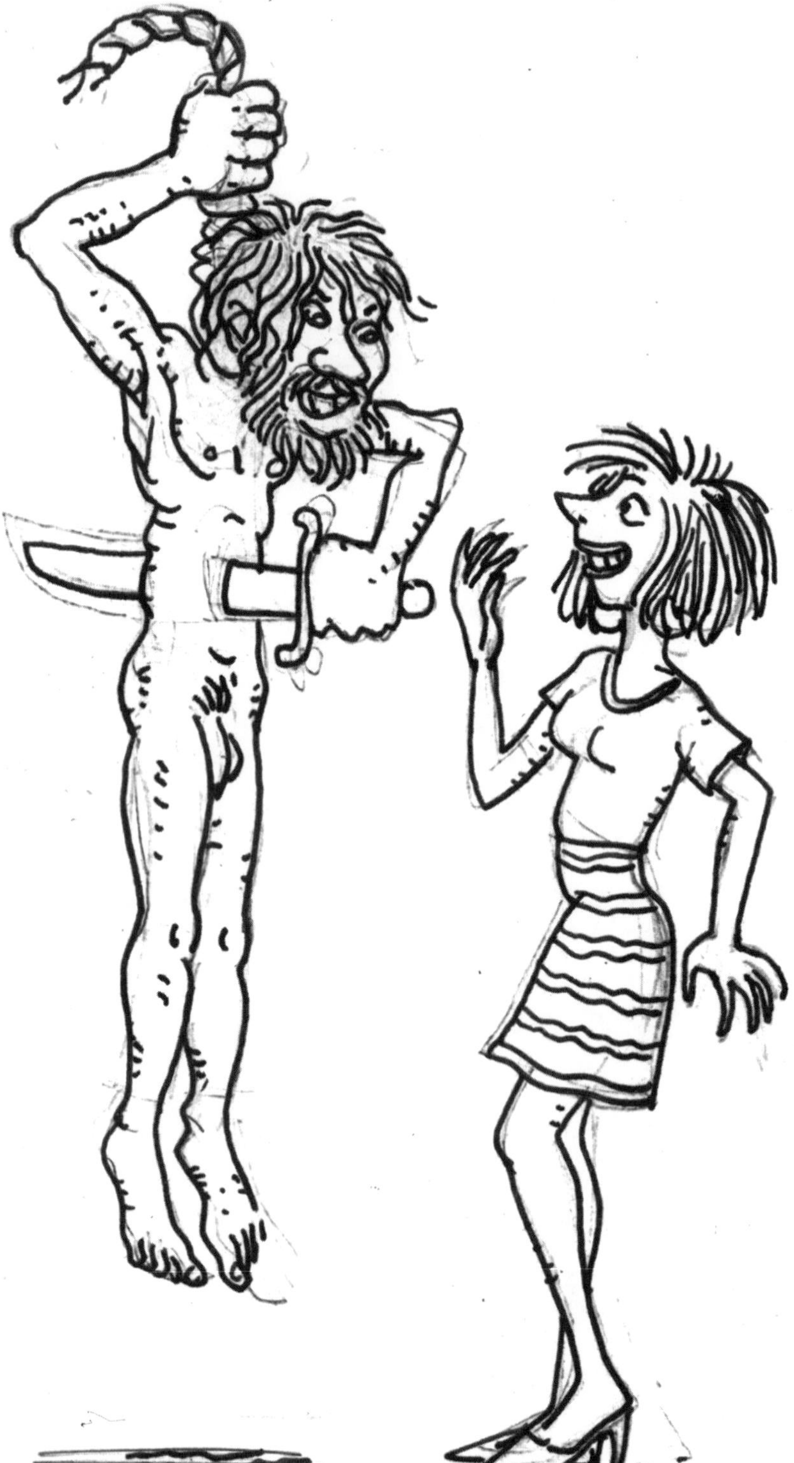

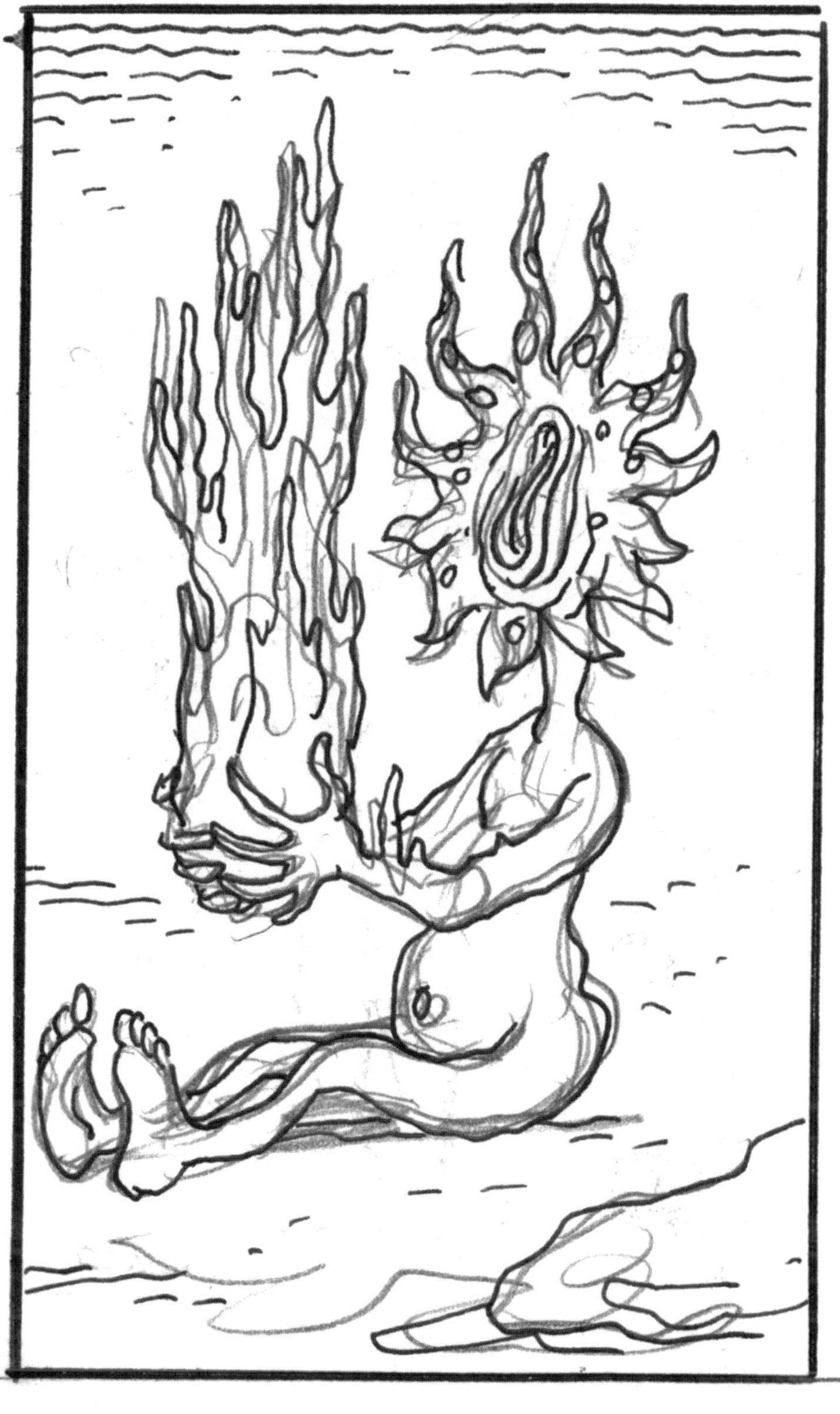

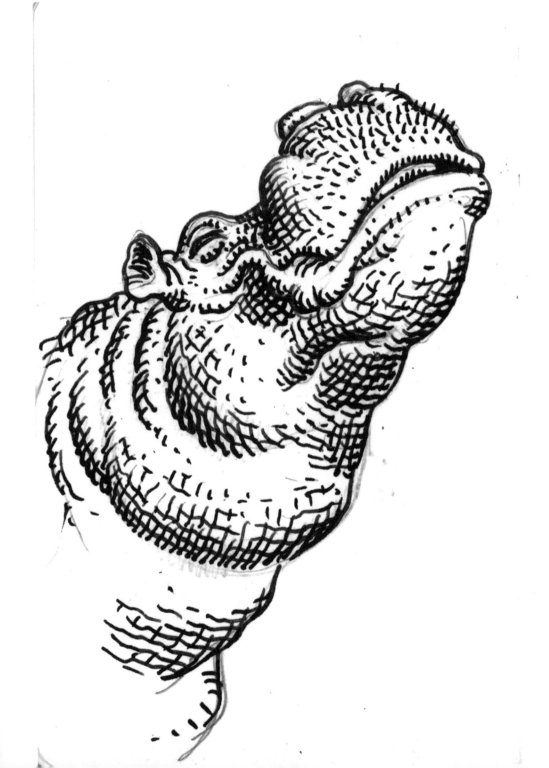

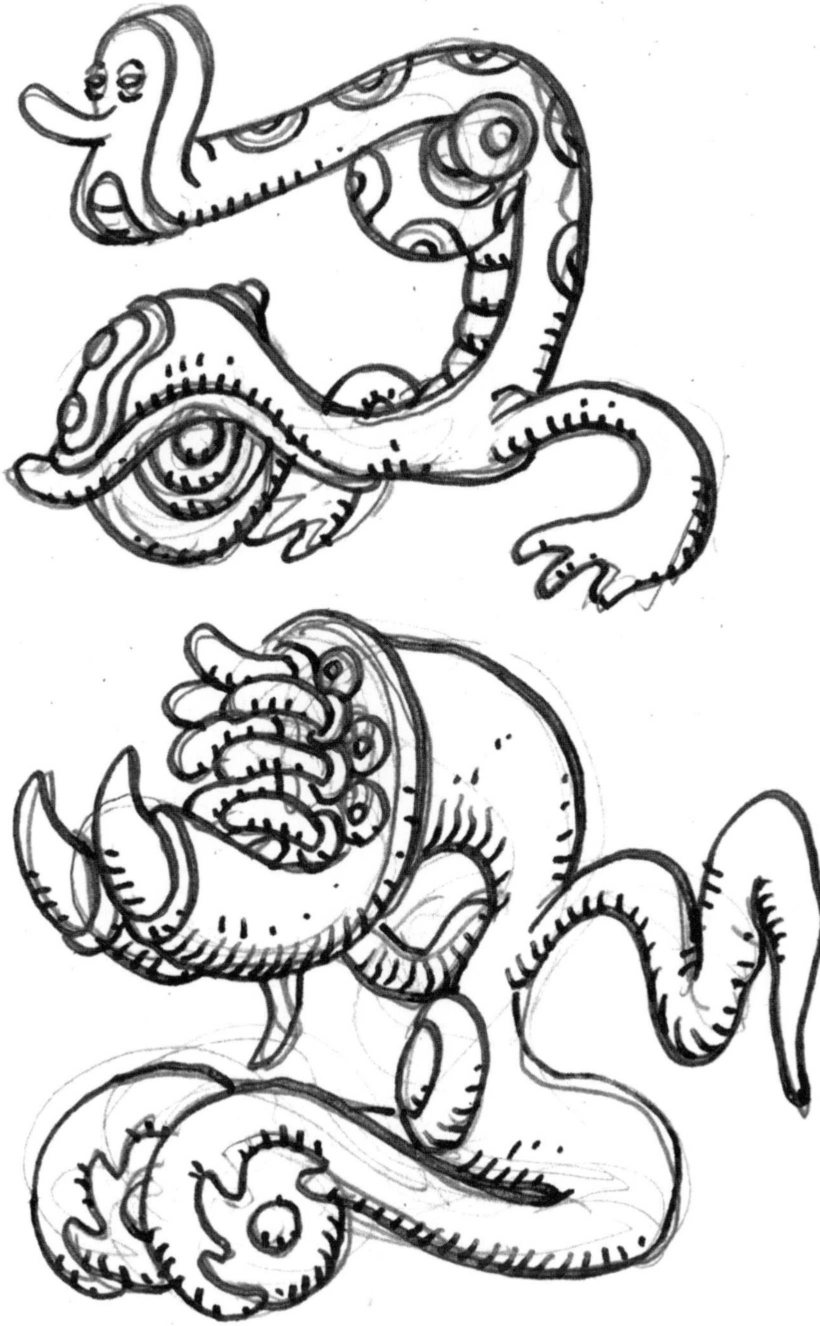

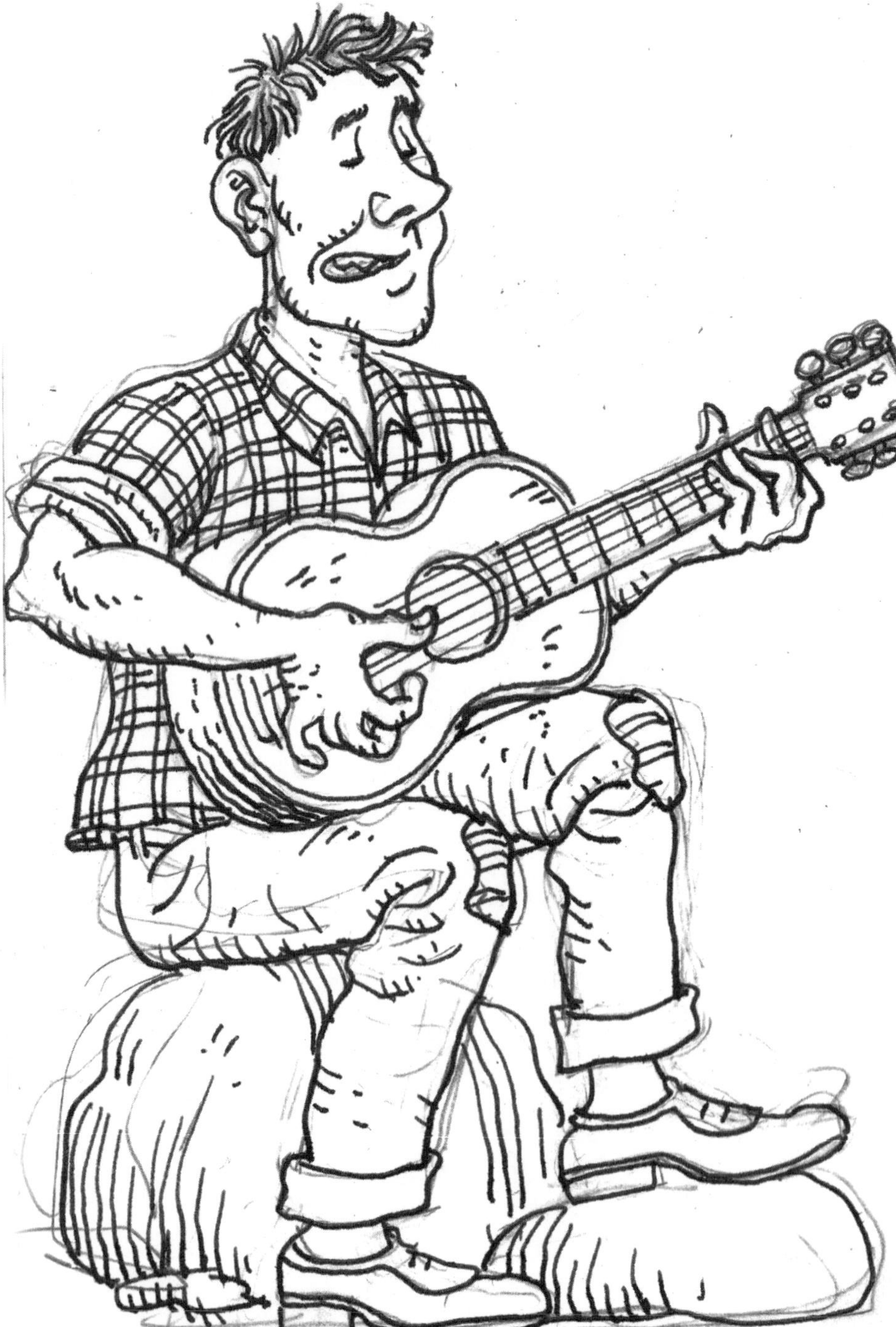

200

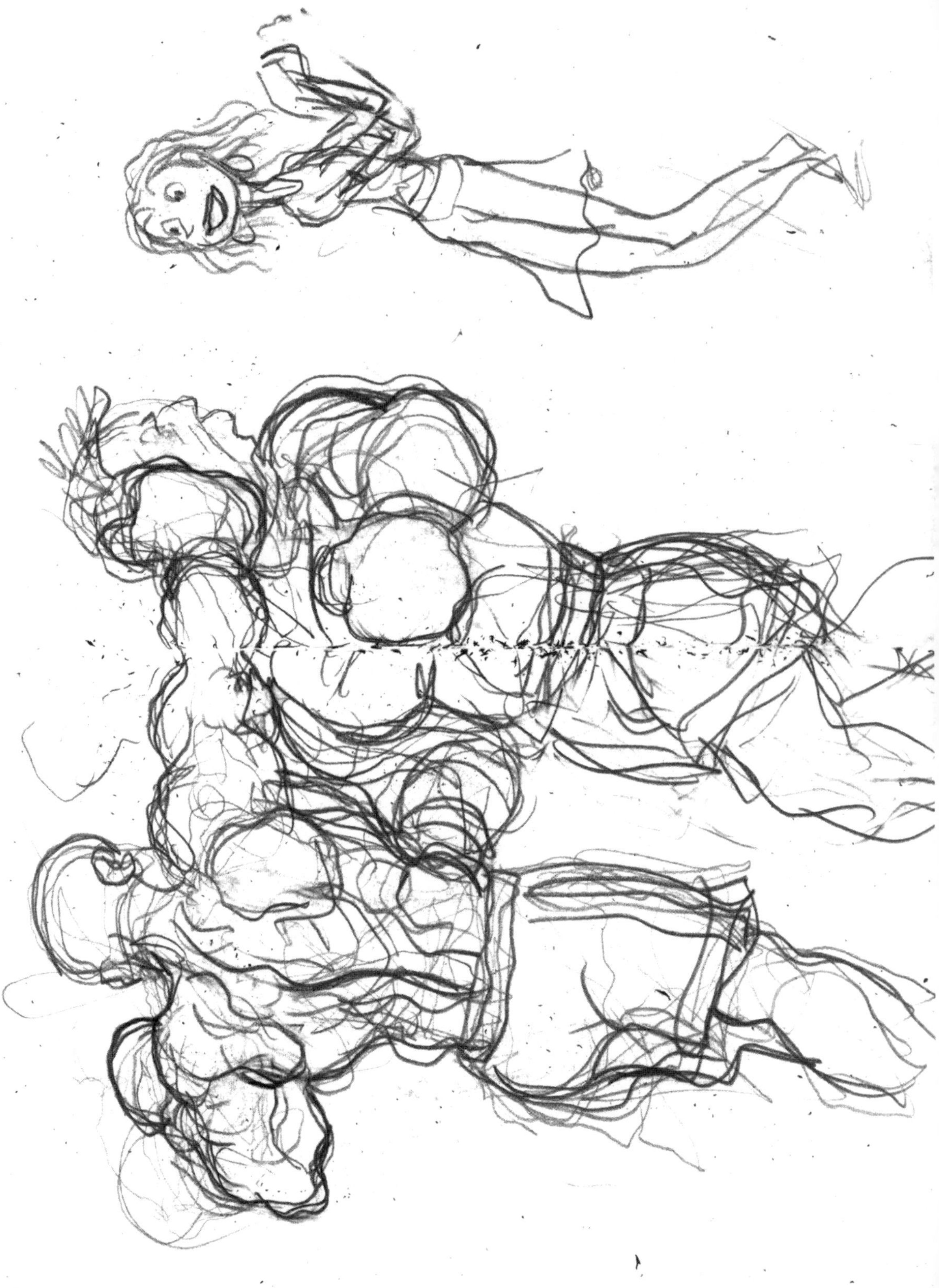

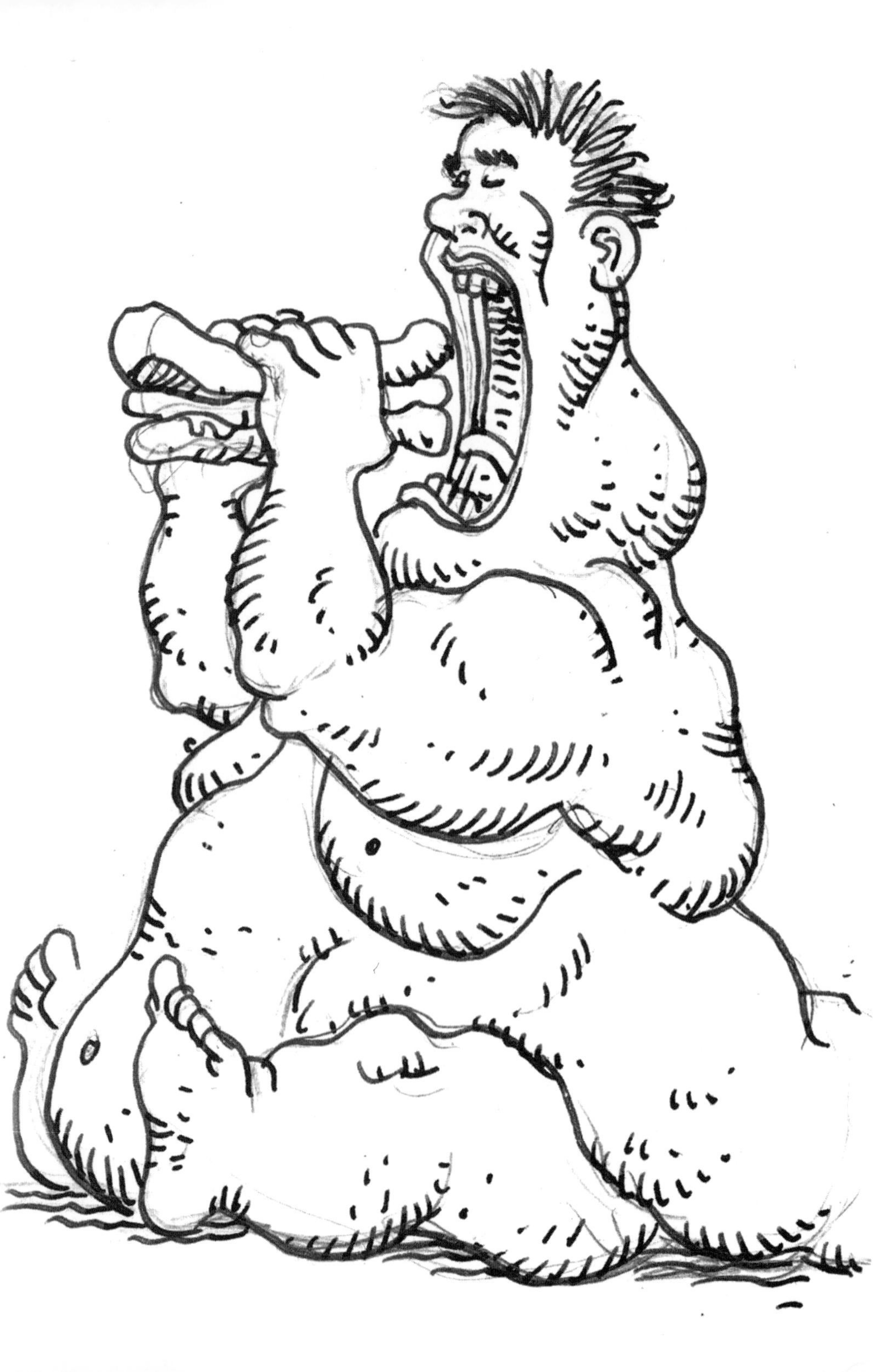

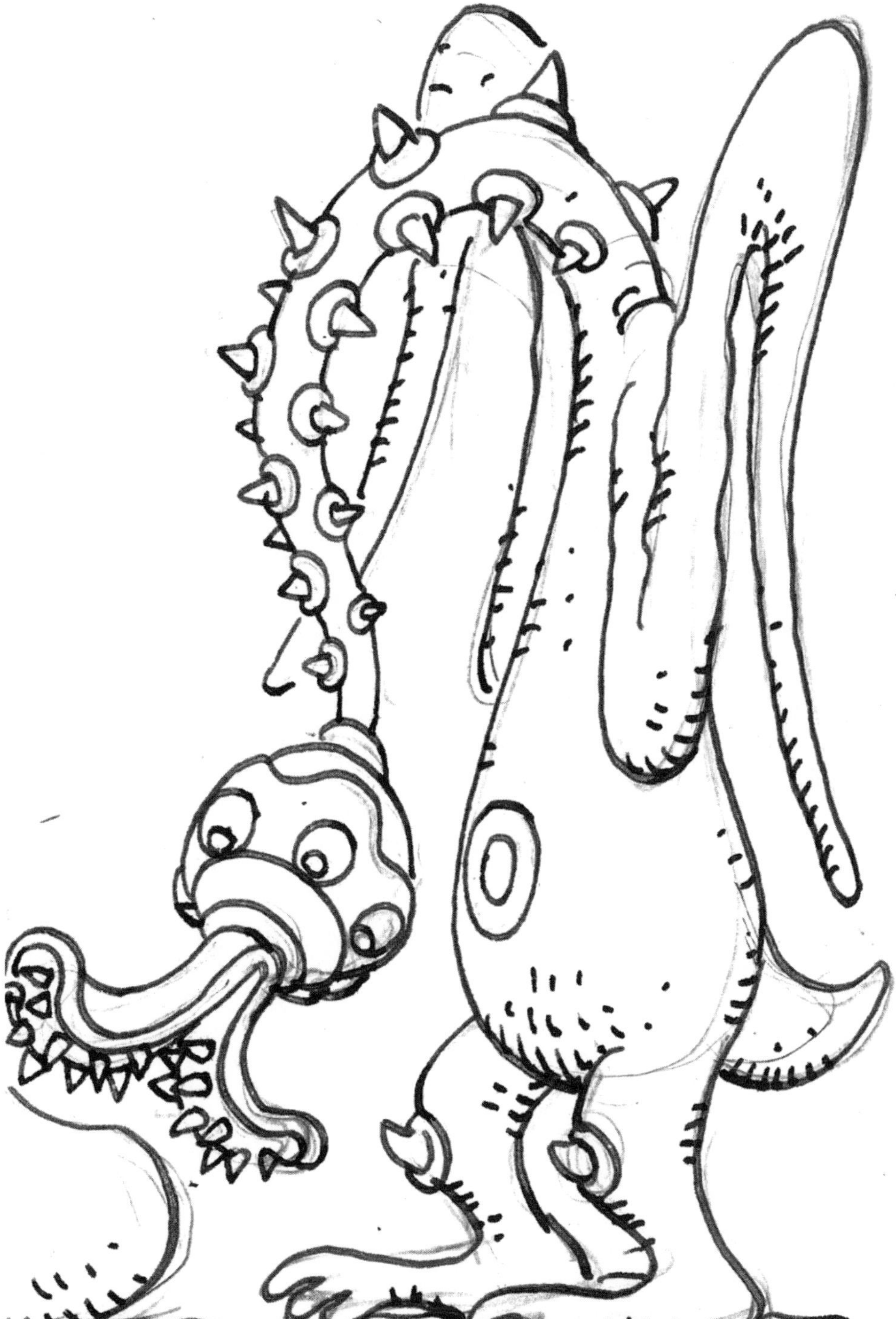

ASSBITE

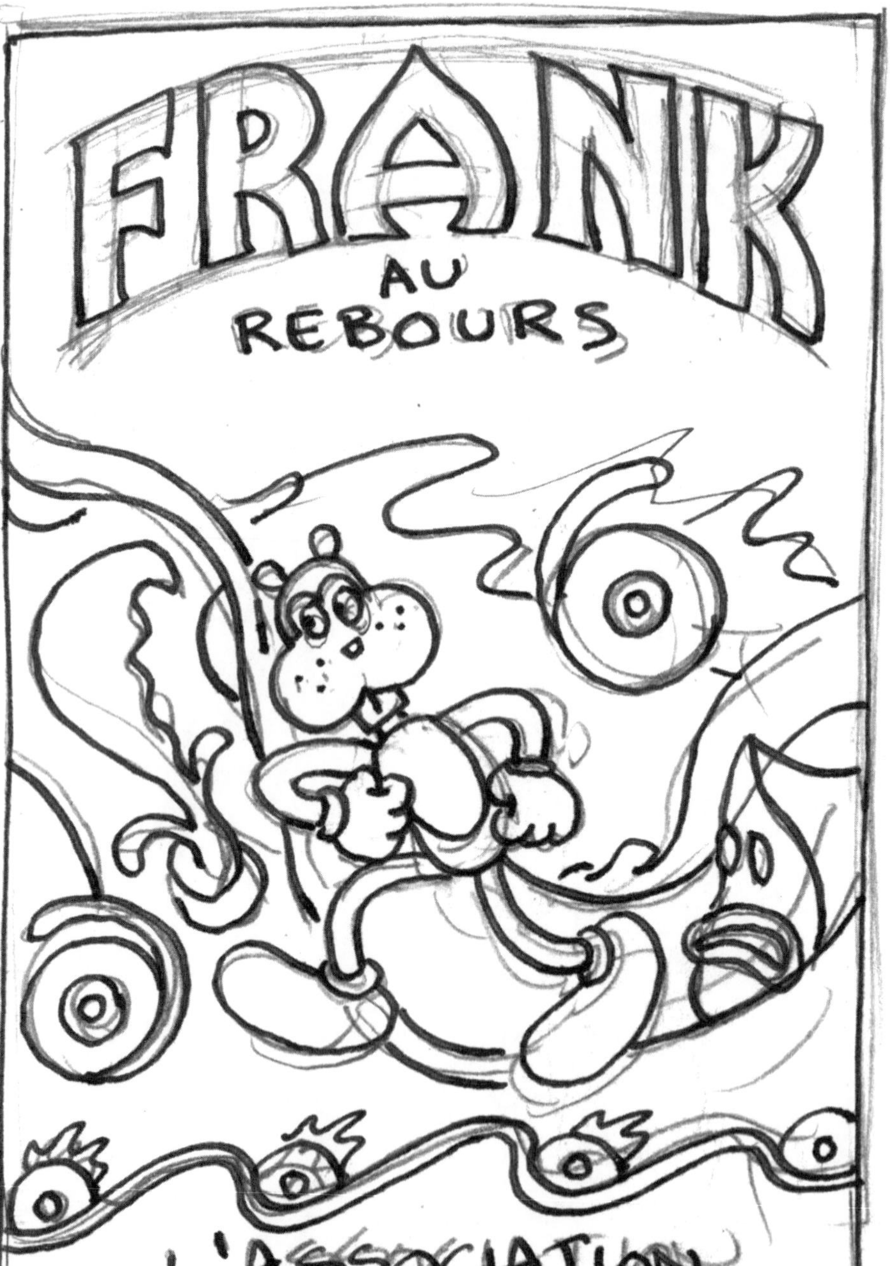
FRANK
AU
REBOURS
L'ASSOCIATION

THEY STROLL

PANTOMAN IN

"HELLO, DIG ME!"

HE DANCES

FRANK APPLAUDS

P. REACHES IN SELF

STICKS CIGAR IN FRANK'S MOUTH — LIGHTS IT

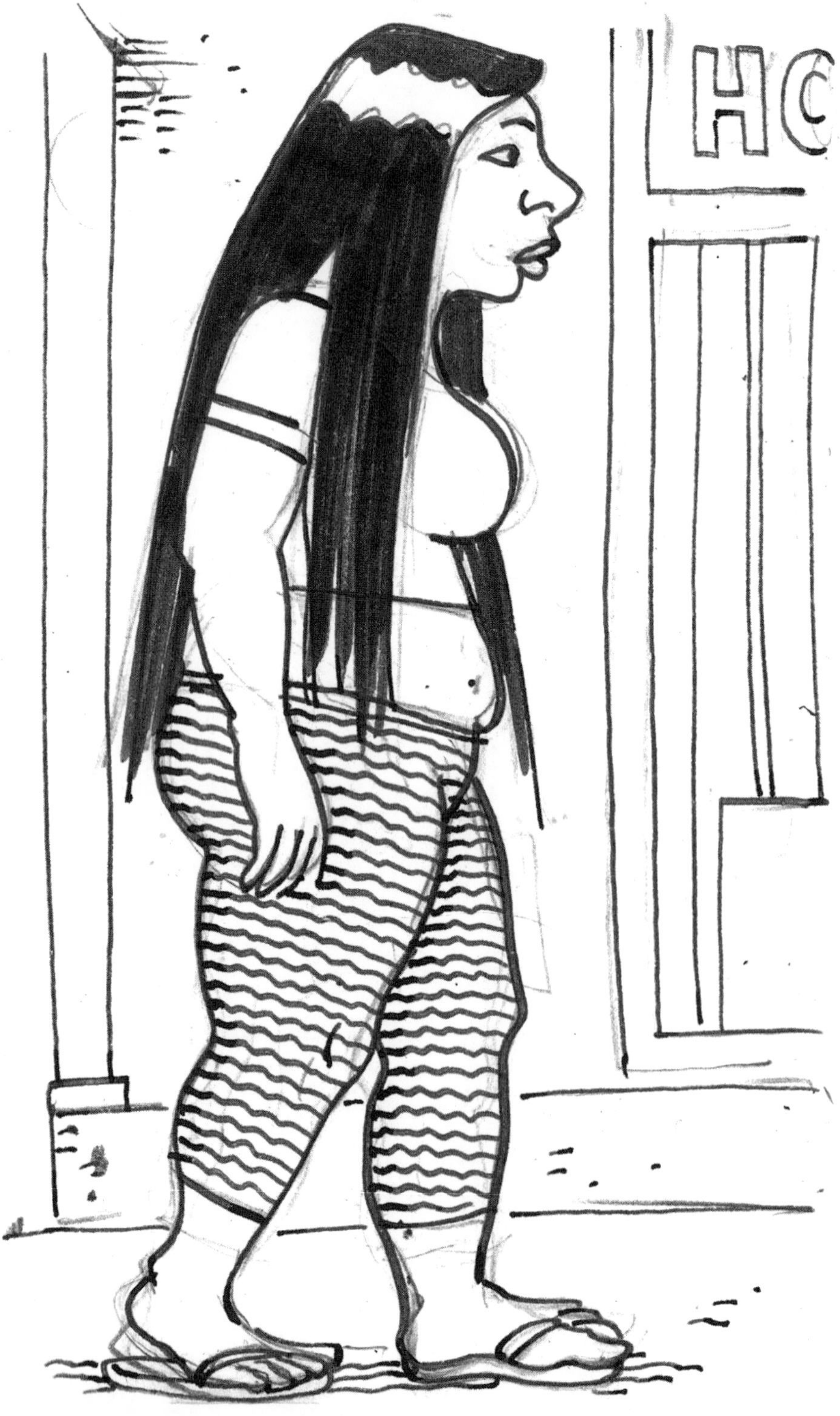

I HAVE HAD IT WITH THIS SHIT! YOU DON'T DO SHIT, YOU PIECE OF SHIT! YOU LITTLE SHIT! YOU TREAT ME LIKE SHIT, LIKE A NIGGER WITH A SHITTY ASS! YOU PIECE OF SHIT!!
MY LIFE IS SHIT

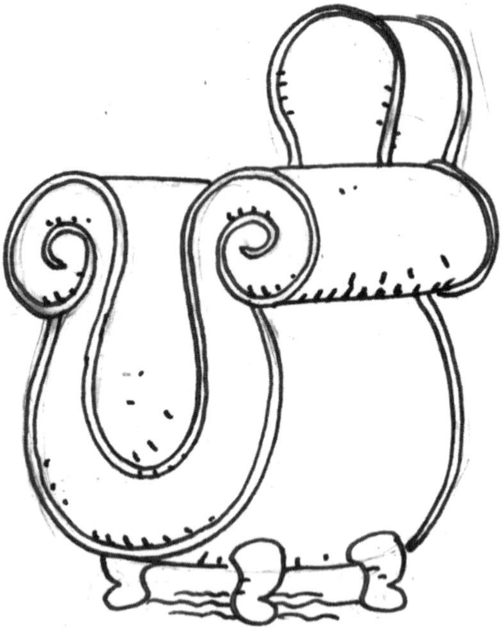

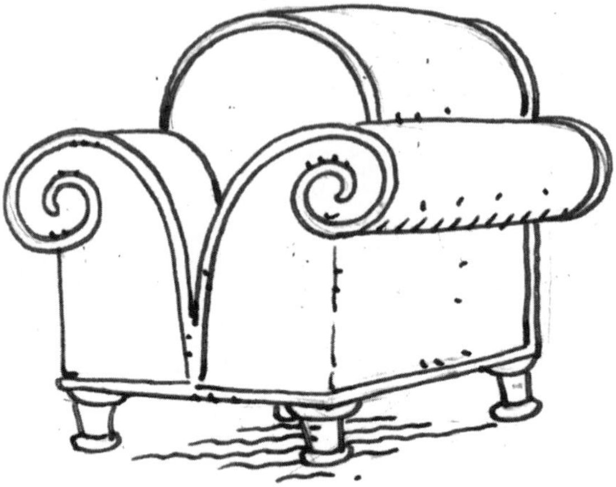

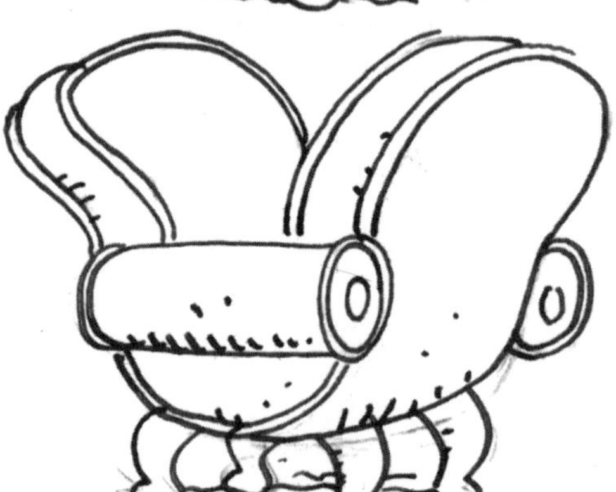

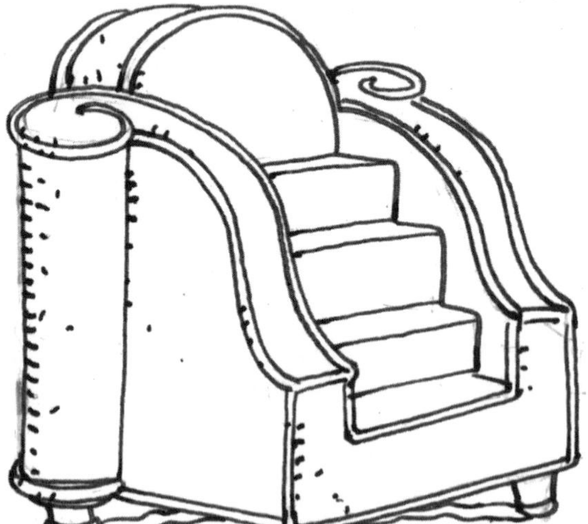

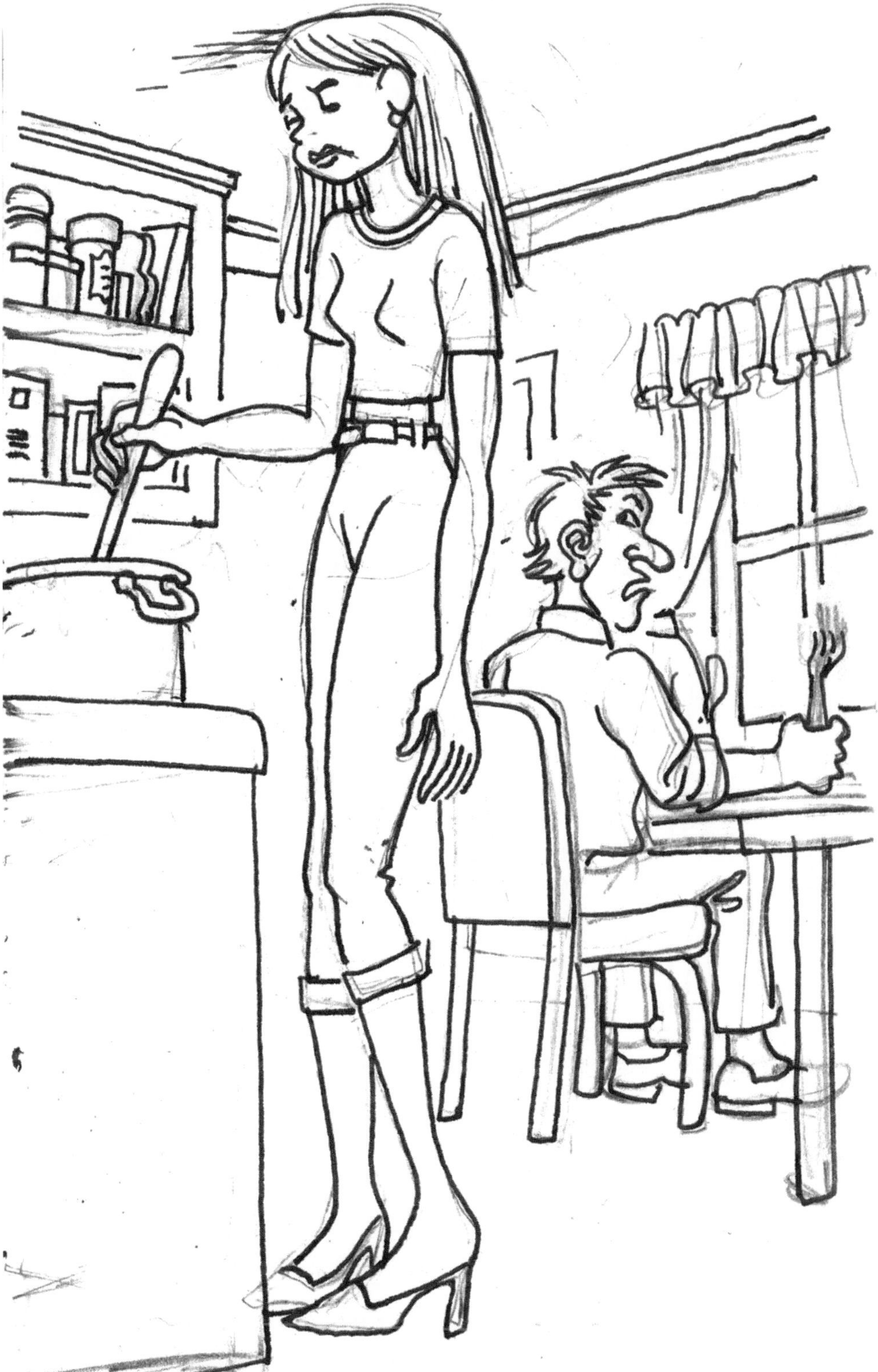

MOUTH CRYING

WORK BACKWARDS

PEEKER AROUSED

MAN CHAIR

BROKEN OCTOPUS MACHINE

JAFFEE/
KUPPERMAN

AL JAFFEE & MICHAEL KUPPERMAN IN CONVERSATION

Interview by Gary Groth

Transcribed by Jenna Allen, Ian Burns, Michael Litven and Christine Texeira

Al Jaffee's career traverses the history of comics. He began working for Stan Lee at Marvel (then Timely Comics) in 1941, where he cranked out humor features (such as *Ziggy Pig and Silly Seal*) and wrote and drew the romance comic *Patsy Walker* for a stretch. He was competent at this, but humor was where his heart was, and he finally quit Timely and started working for Harvey Kurtzman in 1955. Under Kurtzman's tutelage, his work acquired a satirical edge; when Kurtzman moved from *Mad* to the Hugh Hefner-financed *Trump*, Jaffee moved with him. After that magazine's demise, he and Kurtzman, along with fellow artists Arnold Roth, Will Elder and Jack Davis, founded *Humbug*, which they published for 11 issues before it too folded, but for which Jaffee did some of his most inspired work. After *Humbug*, *Mad's* editor, Al Feldstein, embraced him and Jaffee has been working for that magazine from 1958 to the present.

Michael Kupperman is, relatively speaking, a pup. He didn't start cartooning until he was in his 20s, but he quickly made a name for himself as a highly inventive dada commentator on American pop culture, as his distinctive visual approach — which is a sly, witty and eccentrically off-kilter take on the studied earnestness of commercial art — is perfectly suited to upending the absurdities of contemporary celebrity icons and modern life generally. He's been all over the place, appearing in venues as far-flung as *The New Yorker*, *The Wall Street Journal*, *Nickelodeon Magazine*, *The Believer* and *Screw*. In 2005, he began his comic *Tales Designed to Thrizzle*, the first four issues of which were collected into a hardcover in 2009 titled, confusingly enough, *Tales Designed to Thrizzle*. Not confined to the print medium, he has also written animated shorts for Comedy Central, He is currently writing sketches for a comedy TV show and had a pilot, *Snake 'N' Bacon*, produced by the Cartoon Network's Adult Swim.

ABOVE Cover designed by Kate Nichols
BELOW [©Michael Kupperman]

I think I hit editorial pay dirt when I asked Jaffee and Kupperman to sit down and talk. There are similarities and differences between their respective approaches to their art and the equivalent periods in their careers that fruitfully play off each other. Jaffee was where Kupperman is now in approximately 1965 — a period most prominently etched by *Mad Men*, and a vastly different media landscape than today. They both approach their art as both a career and a vocation — as a "working artist" as Kupperman puts it — by which he suggests that they both have to juggle art and commerce and can't be too precious about either. They are both gentle satirists (or rugged humorists), but the effectiveness of satire has shifted over the years — especially now when culture itself has become unconsciously self-satirizing. Jaffee worked at a time when artists tried to find a perch or a safe haven — a magazine, a syndicated strip, regular employment at a comics publisher. Today, as Kupperman reveals, it's closer to a free-for-all where the artist is his or her own brand and is much more on his or her own. Jaffee's ingenuity has stood the test of time, as current now as it was in 1964 when he created the *Mad* fold-in. Kupperman clearly couldn't have done the work he's doing now 50 years ago — or any equivalent of it; there simply wouldn't have been an outlet for his approach, not even in *Mad*. The times have allowed him to exercise his unique imagination, and have perhaps shaped it as well.

Jaffee and Kupperman explore these and other questions with great warmth, humor and genuine mutual admiration in the following pages. I hope the edited exchange reflects what a good time they had together; as witness to the proceedings, I can attest to it.

—*Gary Groth*

"So That's the Story of My Life"

Gary Groth: Say something really venomous that we won't use [*Kupperman laughs*], but which I could tape.

Michael Kupperman: [To Jaffee]: How was HarperCollins to work with [*on Mad Life*]? [*Groth laughs.*]

Al Jaffee: Well, my experience at HarperCollins has been excellent. People have been very nice to me. When you get to be 89 years old you lose your venom. Snakes don't have venom after a certain age.

Kupperman: Are you sure it's just not that people aren't screwing around with you as much?

Jaffee: No, they've been really very accommodating. They have given me very good suggestions, but essentially everything I've done has been acceptable and they've even asked for my input on what to do for the cover. So it didn't hurt that they grew up reading *Mad* and they knew my stuff. They were very respectful and considerate, and they appreciated the suggestions that I made. I couldn't ask for a smoother working relationship.

Groth: It's possible, Michael, that when you're 89 publishers will be as respectful to you. [*Laughs.*]

Kupperman: If I make it that long.
   It's the whole story of your life and career, right?

Jaffee: I like to believe it's not the whole story, because I intend to go on to 90.
   So, anyway, Michael, you asked if it was the story of my life. Essentially it starts with my being born in Savannah, Georgia, leaving Savannah at the age of 6 to go to Lithuania and living in Lithuania for six years. A lot of the adventure is in Lithuania, where my ability to draw got me accepted among the Lithuanian kids. I entertained them with my drawings and they taught me how to fish and go swimming and march through the woods and stuff like that.
   Then at the age of 12, I returned to the United States never really having gone to school, so I got put in the third grade with all these little farts. And I think it was in May, so the first thing they did was take me and all these little kids outside and they gave me a ribbon to hold and we danced around the maypole. I felt like an idiot. I've got an illustration of that in the book.

A Dutch Peasent

Then they skipped me from the third grade to the fifth grade, and then they skipped me again into sixth, and then they skipped me into junior high school. So I was almost caught up. I was probably a year older than most of the high school kids that I graduated with.

So that was the adventure, and the biggest break of all was — I don't know if you two heard my story on how I met Willy Elder?

Kupperman: You met him when you were 13, wasn't that ...

Jaffee: Yeah, I met him in junior high school. The way that happened: I was in an arithmetic class. A monitor came into the class and said, "We need Al Jaffee to go up to the art room."

So I went up to the art room, and they handed me a piece of paper and a pencil, and I sat down at a drawing desk, and in front of me was this skinny little kid, must have weighed about 10 pounds, 'course it was Willy. There were about 50 kids in this art room and the instructor said, "All right everybody, draw something. Draw whatever you want."

The only thing I could think of to draw was the town square that I lived in in Lithuania, which was a place I went to almost everyday 'cause that's where all the action was. Things were going on, people were selling goats and having horse races and stuff like that. So it was very exciting and I drew a picture of it. And I looked over the shoulder of this little "pyerky" kid sitting in front of me and he blew me away. He had this beautiful drawing of a Dutch peasant—now why he drew a Dutch peasant, I mean, he was never in

TOP LEFT
Jaffee's illustrations for *Al Jaffee's Mad Life* are [©2010 Al Jaffee]

TOP RIGHT
From *Will Elder: The Mad Playboy of Art* [©2003 Playboy]

221

"Meeting Will Elder when you're 13 in the same art class, if it was in a movie you'd say this is too much."

—Kupperman

Holland. His picture is in your book about Willy [*The Mad Playboy of Art*], and for my book, I did the scene of me sitting behind Willy, and I Xeroxed the Dutch peasant out of the book you did, and I put it on his desk in the scene, and I happened to have a copy of my drawing and I put it on my desk. So I had the two drawings. And at the end of this, because in the text it explains that I was there and Will was there, and the teacher finally collected all the papers and said, "Everyone can go back to their classes except Will Elder and Al Jaffee."

So we were directed to go down to the principal's office, which was only done to punish you, so we went down there a little bit nervously, and I was sitting there, and Willy was sitting over here and he leans over to me, and he says, "I tink der gonna send us to art school." [*Kupperman laughs.*] And sure enough when we went into the principal's office, the principal said, "Mayor LaGuardia has created a new high school for talented children, artists and musicians, and you two have been selected to go there." I've known Willy all my life since that moment.

Kupperman: And that was in 1934, '35?

Jaffee: That was in 1935, because we went to our first class in 1936, January.

Kupperman: What was that word you just used to describe him, puric?

Jaffee: Pyerky. It was just a form of "jerky" that we used. A pyerk.

Kupperman: Where does that come from?

Jaffee: I don't even know. We didn't know the word "jerk" then. It didn't exist at the time. It actually came from an obscenity, which is jerk-off. And it was shortened to jerk. We just didn't talk like that.

Groth: There was no pyerk-off.

Jaffee: No pyerk-off. If somebody wants to invent it [*laughter*], they can.

Kupperman: It's an incredible story. Meeting Will Elder when you're 13 in the same art class, if it was in a movie you'd say this is too much.

Jaffee: And we had wonderful times as kids. I mean we weren't kids: we were 14, 15, 16, 17.

Kupperman: In a world where you had to grow up pretty fast.

Jaffee: Yeah, we would have drawing contests, friendly drawing contests, and we shared all our feelings and he would practically live for a whole week in my apartment and I'd be over in his for the next week. I mean we just shared our life together. And I babysat his nephew with him and we had wonderful adventures and experiences. Of course we went to the movies all the time and we played touch football, we played stickball, we went on painting/ drawing outings. And other school friends came into the picture from time to time, like Dave Gantz; he did a strip for the *Herald Tribune* also. He also did a little bit of work for *Mad* and he was a school chum; so it's been a very interesting trip, tell you the truth [*laughter*].

Kupperman: So you went to the high school and you went there for the full four years?

Jaffee: The full four years, and when we were graduating, we of course didn't know what to do with our lives. We wanted to be in the art business. Willy made up millions of samples of full-color movie-star paintings. And they were wonderful. He was a very talented little kid, I can tell you that. I wasn't doing anything even close to what he was doing. I was doing cartoons. He was in love with *Snow White and the Seven Dwarfs*. So I remember when he did a full set of them, and brought it into the high school, and he was showing it around, and a teacher got to see it. And she bawled him out and said, "We don't do junk like that here. This is a fine-art high school."

Of course, we weren't doing only fine art. We were drawing from models, we were doing etching, we had an industrial-arts class ... I was in a class where I learned to do woodcuts. I remember, on a block that was about four inches square, I hand-cut that year's calendar backwards.

Kupperman: Including the dates.

Jaffee: All the little dates, all the little tiny numbers. I had 12 months on a piece of wood this big. I did it really as an exercise to see if I could do it. Because you know it had no artistic value whatsoever. You could set type to do that.

Kupperman: But it was a challenge, and in some way a preparation for fold-ins.

Jaffee: I guess it was a preparation for doing intricate work, which I just love, testing my ability to do tiny type. I was looking at the originals that you [Gary] returned to me, and there was this racing scene, and all the mobs of people hanging around, and I noticed that these tiny, little, half-a-millimeter-sized people were arguing with each other, were talking with each other. I had forgotten about that. I can't do that today; I can't do tiny little things like that. But in those days, in the early part of my life, I really enjoyed filling the pages with millions of little people — but I never felt I was a decorator.

Kupperman: But it's also the calculations involved, into carving a calendar backwards. It seems impossible you wouldn't make a mistake. And once you make a mistake ...

Jaffee: You blow the whole thing. That's it. I didn't finish it. For some reason I quit after the 10th month or something like that.

You know, I don't have any of these things. My family life was very dysfunctional. When I returned from Lithuania with my brothers, we lived together very briefly, and then we were separated. I mean, when we returned from Europe, I went to live with my father, my brother Harry went to live with an uncle, my brother Bernard, he was a deaf mute so he went to a deaf-mute school, my youngest brother remained in Lithuania with my mother. I lived with my father in furnished rooms, so I couldn't collect and keep all my stuff. We were moving all the time. Moving from one furnished room to another. So I would bring stuff home from school, and my father said, "Get rid of that stuff. What are we going to do with it?"

I had big pastels; they were school projects. There was a semi-annual concert and art exhibit, and I always had my stuff up in these art exhibits, my paintings, my drawings, they had all those up there. They were always chosen. And even when I graduated, unbeknownst to me, the art teachers gathered my stuff and sent it to the Art Students' League. They submitted it for a scholarship and I won a four-year scholarship, but I never attended.

Kupperman: Instead you went right into making the comics.

Jaffee: I went right into working on comics, to make a living. I had no money to spend. I couldn't even go out on a date. I couldn't ask my father, who worked in the post office as a substitute mail carrier for the money. So I was on my

own most of my life and really had no guidance or advice about things.

Willy's parents *loved* him, *doted* on him, they collected his nose-pickings, you know. They didn't let anything of Willy's be thrown out. So when Gary published his book about Willy, I looked at it with tears in my eyes because I knew that there had been access to *tons* of his childhood stuff. And there was. I couldn't give you one piece. I don't have anything. And I don't have any of my commercial stuff either. I don't have any of my comic-book stuff: *Patsy Walker*, I don't have it, and then of course Bill Gaines kept all of the *Mad* stuff up to a certain point. After issue 317 I got my stuff returned to me.

Kupperman: You remember that number?

Jaffee: Yeah, sure. [*Laughs.*] But I don't even have that stuff. I sent it to my son in California and he's got it somewhere in storage. I told him he could sell it, and he probably has. [*Laughter.*] So that's the story of my life.

A Working Artist

Kupperman: I read several interviews with you to prepare for this. It seems like your responses to everything were still the responses of a working artist. Someone asked you about *Mad* going quarterly, and I noticed that you said that your income had been lowered because of that, which is very much the response of a working artist. Not someone who's doing it near retirement age, someone with whom the processes are still very fluid, including the financial ones.

Jaffee: I may have regarded being an artist the way somebody who works in a clothing factory regards making T-shirts. You make all the T-shirts and then you get a paycheck at the end of the day and then you go home to your family and you don't save the T-shirts that you made. So I know art is in a different category and now, of course, I recognize what it should be, should have been, but when I churned out 60-70 pages of comic-book stuff every month, both writing and drawing, and penciling and inking, and sending it away and never seeing it or hearing about it ever again, except when I got a sample of the 10¢ comic book — pretty hard to think of it in terms of something that I needed to save for posterity. It just disappeared into the maw.

Kupperman: Do you think that lack of precious feelings about it enabled you to function better as an artist? To be more realistic about what you were doing?

Jaffee: In retrospect I think that the answer would be yes. And the reason the answer is yes, it occurs to me now, is that it unhindered me. My productivity needs were so great that, the only way that I could not only make a living but get a little bit more out of life than just barely surviving, was productivity. The more pages I could produce, the more I could write out, the more I could draw, because the comic-book industry was insatiable. And if you produced material, you produced payment: I would wind up working very hard to write a lot so that I could get the assignment to draw a lot; so I was in two departments, and one was feeding the other. Each item didn't pay very much, so if you wanted to improve the quality of your life, you had to produce more and more of it.

It's almost really like a sweatshop. We were pieceworkers and a pieceworker in a sweatshop gets paid by the T-shirt. And at the end of a day, this poor Chinese guy or woman has produced 500 T-shirts, he can go home and he maybe will be able to buy a television set in six months. And that was the thinking when you were turning out comic-book pages. I didn't think in terms of becoming a legend, which I never became anyway, but I thought in terms of productivity.

And so when you do that, you don't place value on it as artwork, you place value on it as production-line work. And I think maybe the art world would regard all the stuff I did as just production-line work, if they saw my old *Patsy Walkers* and *Super Rabbit* and *Ziggy Pig* and *Silly Seal* and all of those things.

TOP

From *Tales Designed to Thrizzle* Vol. 1

NEXT PAGE

[©1993 E.C. Publications, Inc.]

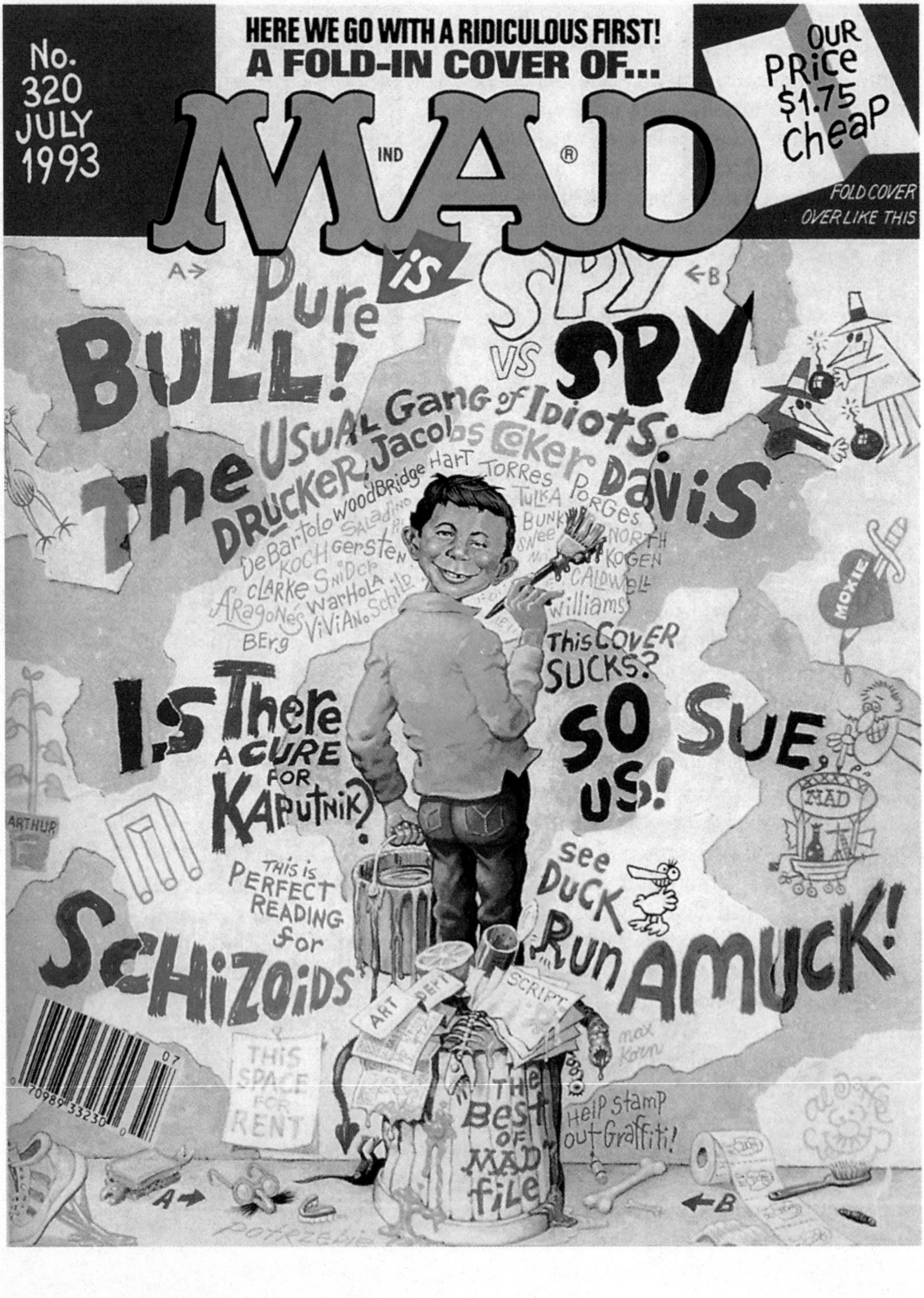

HERE WE GO WITH A RIDICULOUS FIRST!
A FOLD-IN COVER OF...
No. 320 JULY 1993
MAD
OUR PRICE $1.75 Cheap
FOLD COVER OVER LIKE THIS
A→
←B
is
Pure BULL!
SPY VS SPY
The USUAL Gang of IDIOTS:
DRUCKER, Jacobs Coker Davis
DeBartolo Woodbridge Hart Torres Porges
Tulka Bunky North Kogen
Koch Gerstein
Clarke Snider Caldwell
Aragonés Warhola Williams
Viviano Schild
Berg
This COVER SUCKS? SO SUE US!
IS There A CURE FOR KAPUTNIK?
ARTHUR
MAD
MOXIE
THIS is PERFECT READING for SCHIZOIDS
see DUCK Run AMUCK!
ART DEPT
SCRIPT
THIS SPACE FOR RENT
The Best OF MAD file
Help stamp out Graffiti!
max Korn
A→
←B

Art, Low and High

Groth: Michael, can you contrast your attitudes as a working artist in 2010 with what Al is describing?

Kupperman: It's certainly striking a chord with me because I have to get faster. I do have a certain preciousness about my work, I can't deny it. So I think that probably holds me up as far as speed.

Jaffee: But Michael, fact is, that you grew up in a world in which the comic books were no longer regarded as garbage, they were highly praised.

Kupperman: Yes.

Jaffee: I mean, [Joe] Shuster and [Jerry] Siegel became heroes, so your experience has been that cartoons — I'm talking about not newspaper cartoons — but cartoons in other media, are not cheap things, that they're valuable things.

Kupperman: Right, and they're not going to disappear. Ephemera is not so ephemeral any more, even though these days I feel the quality has gone way down, generally, as far as comics and visual graphics of all kinds.

Jaffee: Well, I think quality has gone down in fine art too.

Kupperman: Yeah. I would agree.

Jaffee: It may be because I work so hard to do my stuff that I might resent

somebody who just flings a can of paint against a wall and then cuts it out and puts it on exhibit and gets $50,000 for it. I guess I resent that. But people can call dog poo art, I don't care, I just won't buy it.

Kupperman: But it seems to me that it stems from the separation of high and low art. That there was a decision that low art would be functional and would not get the same respect as high art, which would be special and sequestered and the different categories I think has led to what we have now.

Jaffee: You can't ignore the business end of it. You have galleries that are sitting in posh areas like 57ᵗʰ Street, and other places all over the world, where agents of billionaires are sent to find out what art to buy, not what they like, or even what they understand, but their agent goes and does it. Sure, you're gonna build up a market for it as a commodity. And I think a lot of the fine-art world consists of commodities. A lot of them are very good, and there are people that are highly creative and are producing things. I've gone to a lot of stuff down in the 20s, the art area of Chelsea, and I've seen creative things that are really very exciting, and not the kind of stuff that I'd be able to do, and I admire it. But then there's stuff that I think is just hyped by wealthy galleries, and they have the customers and they create a market and it's like getting everybody to buy IBM stock; they're brokers.

Kupperman: Well it seems to me that in both high art and low art these days, there's a certain amount of stuff that is holding the place of what people want, that, if it resembles a graphic art in the past, or if it resembles the fine art from the past, that people see some qualities in, that that's enough.

Last Century's Model

Jaffee: Well, you're making breakthroughs, your work has a lot of adventure and creativity in it, some of which I don't understand because I don't live in your time —

Kupperman: — of course.

Jaffee: But the craftsmanship is superb and the ideas are intelligent; they're taking off in a direction that 50 years ago would have baffled my colleagues and me. We wouldn't have the vaguest notion of how to do that. And not only that, but we weren't allowed to do it.

Kupperman: Well, the time you started out in, at the very beginning, comics didn't really exist, so there was no model or idea of what they should be yet. It seems to me that maybe I'm romanticizing it a bit, that you and your peers went out and created that without a model.

Jaffee: There was no viable market. The only viable markets that existed for cartooning were magazine gag-cartooning or syndicated comic strips. Syndicated comic strips were like an inheritance that just goes on giving. Breaking into that was like winning the lottery, and it was just as difficult. For one thing, in order to get a new comic strip in, you had to knock an old one out. And in the early day of newspaperdom, knocking an old comic strip out was virtually impossible, because whatever hometown you lived in, you fell in love with your comic strips. It could be *Nancy*; it could be *The Gumps*. It could be drawn in the strangest way ever. *The Gumps*, the guy had no chin, it was just weird. Some was weird, and some was cute like *Winnie Winkle*. There were many others like them, which I loved and admired. I read them voraciously, but trying to knock out a comic strip like *Dick Tracy* or *Terry and the Pirates*, so that you could get in, it was like "You're dreaming!"

TOP
Each artist's take on Dick Tracy. Below From *Tales Designed to Thrizzle* Vol. 1

So along comes Bill Gaines' father. Max Gaines gets an idea how to keep printing presses working — he was a salesman for a printing company — and he goes to the syndicates and he says, "Would you give me permission to use your already-used comic strips, Sunday funnies in color?" And they said, "Go ahead do whatever you want, we never reprint them, they just run once." So he made a sample comic book, got in his car, drove around to candy stores, dropped off the comic books and told the candy-store owner, "I come back in a couple of hours and if you've sold some we'll split the take, and if you haven't, I'll take them back." And a few hours later, he drove around and they were all gone. The kids just gobbled them up.

And I remember seeing those first: I saw my first comic book when I was only maybe a month or two returned from Europe, it was the summer of 1933. And I was staying with my uncles and aunts over a candy store, and the candy store carried the first comic book, *Famous Funnies*. It was my first comic book, they had been around for a little while and I just went crazy for it. It was a dream thing. So we were all eager to get into this.

Once the syndicates got wise to this going on, they stopped allowing people to use their old stuff. Or they were selling it to them. And whoever was lucky enough to buy it from the syndicates had a lock on it, so other entrepreneurs said "hey, let's create our own."

So the business got going. And all of us who could not get into newspaper comic strips saw an opening and we dived in head first, into this comic-book business, making samples and trying to create new strips. Will Elder created something called *Roofus DeBree* about a janitor and he would show me these strips and I would say, "Where is this going?"

I thought it was cute and all, but Willy, he was not a talented writer. He was a very talented artist, but he needed Harvey Kurtzman to come along so they could become partners and that worked out very well. I was in all the writing classes in school and the teachers seemed to think I had a lot of talent as a writer, and I should give up art altogether and just study writing. So I was able to write stuff and I was able to sell stuff because I could write. And that opened up a market for us.

TOP
From "If Comic Characters Behaved Like Ordinary People," written by Al Jaffee, drawn by Wallace Wood and collected in *Mad's Vastly Overrated Al Jaffee* [©1976 E.C. Publications, Inc.]

Kupperman: So many of those early comic books had a feeling of a fever-dream, just something you can tell that someone made out and drew in just one night.

Jaffee: Yeah, I tried to think of really original stuff, I had a lot of stuff sketched out and I showed it to Willy and to other friends and they said, "Well, there's something like that in the paper already ... " like *Wash Tubbs* is doing adventures in Europe. I tended to lean on my memories of adventures in Europe, and I would do stuff like that.

And then Superman came out, and so I said, "What the hell, I'll create a superhero thing, but I don't know how to draw muscles, so I'll make Inferior-Man." And he had no muscles whatsoever, and he was just a funny little character.

Kupperman: He was bright red, am I right? Or did he wear a red outfit?

Jaffee: Yeah, he had a red cape, I think. I copied Superman; it was an early attempt at satire. I love satire instinctively for some reason, which is why Harvey Kurtzman eventually wanted me to come work with him along with Willy and others. But I trotted over to Will Eisner, I didn't even write a story, I just did one drawing of Inferior-Man and some of the monsters he would face, and I showed it to Will Eisner and he hired me on the spot to do fillers for one of his comic books.

Kupperman: And I've read you said you never had to show your portfolio again.

Jaffee: I never did. The only thing is, when Will Eisner let me go because his business was changing and the war was looming and he was going to have to go into the Service, he had to find people ... I brought him Alex Kotzky, who was a friend of mine, to take over *Spirit* while Will went into the service. He knew that Alex Kotzky had a deferment and would not be drafted and so he took over the work on *The Spirit* and continued it for Will. What I had was all of these Inferior-Man comics that I did for Will and he sent me over to another fellow who was packaging comic strips and I did a couple of Inferior-Man strips for him.

And I took these to Stan Lee. Stan Lee had just taken over from Simon and Kirby, who had created Captain America. They were going on to a better deal somewhere else and Stan Lee was 17 years old and he took over as editor. When I walked in there, he handed me a strip to do. He liked my work and I worked for him for a number of years after that. So I never really carried around a portfolio, I just showed him these Inferior-Man things and he hired me. So no, I never went looking for work. From that point on, the work came to me.

Kupperman: And you really lived through the expansion and then the Golden Age of publishing in the 20th century.

Jaffee: In comic-book publishing, but it moved on. If I hadn't gone over to *Mad*, I think I would have probably wound up as some kind of an editor involved in adventure and superheroes and things like that.

The Rise and Fall of Magazines

Kupperman: But also the Golden Age of magazine publishing, don't you think, that the 1950s, 1960s ... ?

Jaffee: I think it was a very exciting period and it devolved into what we have today.

Kupperman: Right, which is the decline.

Jaffee: Is it in decline?

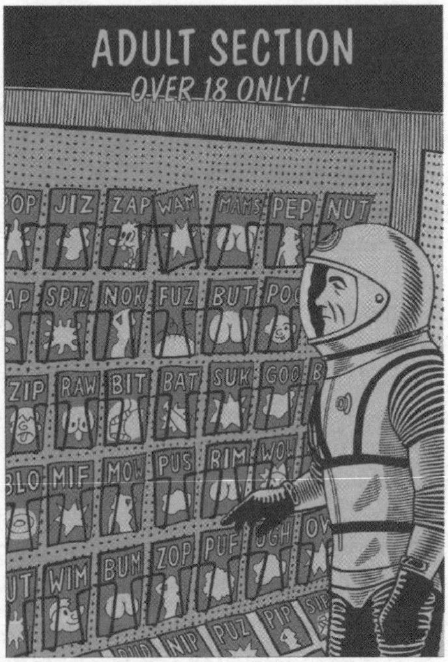
ADULT SECTION
OVER 18 ONLY!

Kupperman: I would say it is. I've worked in magazines for about 17, 18 years and it just gets worse and worse.

Jaffee: I think print periodical media has suffered because of the digital age.

Kupperman: I think it's suffered, but I think also a lot of magazines have responded by getting weaker: by watering down their content, by not displaying the intelligence that they used to.

Jaffee: I'm really not a student of it. I can only comment from my own experience of watching circulation of *Mad* decline, circulation of *The New Yorker* decline. I think the fact that technology has exploded all over the place, to the point now that we have Kindle and Apple's iPad. That's just the beginning of it. Pretty soon people will be walking down the street reading digital things that look like newspapers. [*Ed. Note: In Japan, they have a newspaper-sized e-reader.*]

Kupperman: Well these days it seems to me that film, video, TV and movies are very much in the lead in terms of certain kinds of excitement, and that other parts of the culture like comics trail after them, but it's always seemed to me in the '30s and '40s, certainly with daily comics, they were in the lead in some ways. They were the most exciting form of entertainment.

Jaffee: Yes, they were, but they were sequential art, which was a form of movement, which then was eventually superseded by television, which had more exciting movement, and movies, of course, were around even at that time. But there's always something coming along.

However, the name of the game will always be, in my view, content — good content will outlive bad content, even though the masses will find bad content appealing. Professional wrestling has millions more fans than does anything any of us can produce. Go figure, y'know? People like to see other people beat each other up. That's fun content. You begin to wonder, why be creative? Just go punch someone in the nose. You get more notoriety that way. And then of course, there's the loosening of morals where sex may become dull after people see it everywhere they look. But I have faith that there will always be an audience for quality work. We may not make as much money as somebody who produces absolute crap, and has large distribution for it, but I've had a pretty good life professionally, even though I haven't made a lot of money. And I'm enjoying every minute of it, the opportunity to do what I'm doing today. If I don't have enough work coming from that, I'll get more into the book business as long as I can keep drawing.

Kupperman: I'm going to go ahead and say I'm kind of disappointed to find out you haven't made a lot of money. Just because I feel you deserve to.

Jaffee: No, I don't own any of my work. I never became an entrepreneur. Which, I think, knowing what I know today, and if I had my life to live over, I wouldn't become another Gary Groth, because I don't have that kind of great talent. But I think I might have tried to create stuff that I would own, that would have licensing value. And I think Jerry Siegel and Joe Shuster would do the same thing if they had their lives to live over; they wouldn't give Superman away for $65. But we live the life we live and I really felt I was paid properly at the time. I would like to have owned some of the things I created, but I don't own them. So I take what I can get.

LEFT
From *Tales Designed to Thrizzle* Vol. 1

Sense and Censorship

Kupperman: Going back to what you were saying a minute ago about our culture: It seemed to me that a lot of the work that *Mad* did during its really classic years, and that you did, partly came from the stance of "I'm a reasonable person and this is ridiculous." Highlighting a fact or pointing out a certain aspect of our culture and saying, "Look how ridiculous this is." And maybe that's not so easy in this world any more because now nothing is ridiculous, at least to someone.

Jaffee: Well, why do you do it?

Kupperman: Well I try to point out that narrative is ridiculous and the narratives we construct are ridiculous, yes. But as far as, say, "I'm a reasonable person. I'm leading a reasonable life and this is absurd, isn't it?" — that doesn't seem to me to be something that's really around any more, or maybe even possible.

Jaffee: Well, it's more difficult today, to communicate these things, because Harvey Kurtzman and his gang, when they created *Mad*, they opened up a door —

Kupperman: A huge well of satire.

Jaffee: Yes.

Kupperman: There were so many imitators of *Mad*, also.

Jaffee: Right. And so many people dashed to it. And then, what talented people the world over do, they run and they say, "Hey wait a minute. Harvey Kurtzman and Will Elder are doing this kind of stuff. How 'bout if I carry it even a step further than that, and do the same kind of stuff only I'm gonna flash it on a building somewhere or in SoHo and wake everybody up."

And that'll start another kind of movement, and it goes on and on and on like that. And more and more doors open, especially when censorship starts to be ridiculed and falls away. Who in their right mind today would have a Hays Office in Hollywood? I mean, nobody in his right mind in the movie business would say to himself, "I'm gonna only produce films that the Hays Office will approve, or that the Catholic Church would approve."

Kupperman: Well occasionally politicians still try to put a notice on Hollywood for certain things they show, but it never works out for them, it seems.

Jaffee: Instead of having the Hays Office as a censorship organ, you now will have people, do-gooders — and I favor most of them — environmentalists, purveyors of health, for example, who work to have better school lunches so that the kids stop becoming obese and shortening their lives. But that's telling somebody, "You can't eat French-fried potatoes."

Well, I think you should *teach* them not to eat French-fried potatoes, but you shouldn't *tell* them.

Kupperman: Right.

Jaffee: So censorship in all its forms is, I think, bad news. But look what you're up against: there are still countries where they shoot you for taking the Lord's name in vain. I mean, we may be able to make fun of some of the practices of the major religions, but try that in Dubai or Saudi Arabia.

237

LEFT
From *Snake 'N' Bacon's Cartoon Cabaret* [©2000 Michael Kupperman]

TOP
From *Al Jaffee Gags* [©1974 Al Jaffee]

People are still trying to overturn the abortion rights that women have recently gained. I mean, making fun of that is such an easy mark, because how can you inflict your opinion on somebody else. I mean, that's ridiculous: You get into a lot of trouble if you try to push your opinions on someone else. We couldn't do it at all, in the 1940s and '50s and '60s. The Comics Code — does that still exist?

Groth: I think it does, but it's pretty feeble.

Jaffee: It must be feeble because it has to contend with self-publishers.

Groth: No, it would only apply to bigger publishers whose books are on newsstands.

Jaffee: Yeah, right.

Groth: There's so much sex and violence in contemporary mainstream comic books, it's hard to imagine.

Kupperman: It's true: there was a comic I saw on oral sex. So I can't imagine ...

Jaffee: There are stores that will censor — Wal-Mart, for example, will not allow certain publications into its stores.

Groth: Corporate censorship rather than government censorship.

Kupperman: But then I think from working in magazines all these years, myself, I've noticed that magazines especially tend to self-censor, because they're very scared of being sued. So any references to any other people or any other companies, they're very, very, ridiculously sensitive about.

Jaffee: Yes, well I think libel is a legitimate thing. There's no good reason to hurt somebody gratuitously: but then, libel laws are also interpreted by human beings, just like the abortion laws are interpreted by human beings. You have two Supreme Court justices who disagree. They're the final arbiters. These are problems that have been going on since the beginning of time, and they will continue to go on. If we could come around in our little angel outfits a million years from now, we would see the same things going on as they are now.

238

RIGHT
From *Al Jaffee Gags*
[©1974 Al Jaffee]

Knock Them Over with a Feather

But we do the best we can with our tools. My feelings about satire are that you only push the envelope if it's absolutely necessary to get your point across — and usually there's a softer way of doing it and it gets it across just as well. You don't have to show somebody stark naked to get across the idea that there's somebody standing in the room who's naked. For those who wanna buy pornography, there are plenty of markets for it. I don't have to do it. I let the experts do it.

Kupperman: No, I agree. There's no point in shock for shock's sake.

Jaffee: No, for shock's sake, no.

Kupperman: Or cruelty.

Jaffee: No. And I think that in some instances hitting somebody with a feather has been more effective — I'll give you an example as a matter of fact. I think Tina Fey's take on Sarah Palin — which was straight on — she didn't load it up with excessive humiliation. She just pretended to be Sarah Palin in her words. It was dynamite. If she had used overkill a little bit, it would have just wiped it out and you'd just say, "Oh well, she's making fun of Sarah Palin."

More effective *being* Sarah Palin, because Sarah Palin is a caricature in herself. We all have our different take on these things, and sometimes it's necessary to — don't see how if you're gonna satirize the problems, say, of the Catholic Church, with the child-abuse problem, with avoiding saying that it's child abuse. I don't know how you could satirize it without showing something. But we all have different tastes, and we have to do the best we can with it.

Kupperman: Have you in your career been accused of cruelty?

A leader should get out into the field with his men. Good for morale, you know.

Jaffee: No, I haven't and I actually wasn't all that comfortable with my *Snappy Answers to Stupid Questions*. I enjoyed doing them on paper, but I would *never* personally answer somebody sarcastically like that. I just feel it's insulting. But I've had people do it to me and I don't like it.

Kupperman: Right.

Jaffee: My wife does it sometimes and I get very angry. I would say, "Is this the dinner?" and she would give me an answer. She would say, "No, it's a pile of dung." [*Kupperman laughs.*]

Groth: That's what wives do. Where'd she learn that? [*Laughter.*]

Jaffee: No, she's very good at it. But we all have our sense of what we consider good taste, and we're all willing to push the envelope to a certain point and not beyond. You know, I don't criticize someone who goes way beyond what I do, but the one thing that I find objectionable is gratuitous insult and cruelty. Just showing somebody chopping someone's head off is not funny. I mean, in a certain context it might be funny. There's a cartoon by George Booth that I saw recently that I thought was absolutely hilarious. And it was potentially a very cruel thing: a bunch of bowling pins are set up and the bowling alley goes horizontal and then it goes up a hill and then it lands on a platform and there's a guy in a guillotine on the platform. And there are no words. [*Laughter.*] The head gets chopped off every time someone go bowling. And I mean, it's just a funny, funny visual, but it deals with a very grisly idea.

Kupperman: Well, with the proper lightness of touch there's that Thurber one too –

Jaffee: Oh, "Touché." It depends on how you do it, you know?

Kupperman: In a movie if you had someone's head *really* being cut off and then saying, "Touché," that would not be ...

Jaffee: Well even with the touché gag — the story behind that is that Carl Rose brought it to Harold Ross, and Harold Ross said, "This is very funny, but you are much too good an artist for us to be able to publish this."

Groth: Too representational.

Jaffee: Too representational. And he said to Carl, "I want to buy it from you and give it to Thurber." And that's how they got away with it.

"*Touché!*"

On Editors

Kupperman: That's a smart editor. I mean, in a lot of stories you tell, and other stories I read there are all these smart editors.

Jaffee: Smart editors are wonderful.

Kupperman: Yes.

Jaffee: They're great! There's a smart editor [*pointing to Groth*].

Groth: I don't know about that.

Jaffee: Well, you make decisions. You make choices. You pick the things that you wanna publish. You don't change our stuff, which has been previously printed. You enhance it with better production and you bring the color out and all that. But you do your job; we do ours.

Kupperman: I've worked with very few good editors, and a lot of bad ones and one lesson I had to learn was to say no to all the suggestion that they were giving — as gently as I could, obviously, and diplomatically — but just to say "No, that's terrible and I won't do it. It'll ruin it."

Jaffee: I've worked with very good editors. I work with a very good editor right now at HarperCollins. Mauro DiPreta is very knowledgeable. He read my biography written by Mary-Lou Weisman and he was spot on about everything and knew exactly where the text needed to be, and the illustrations and all that. So I had a breeze with him.

Harvey Kurtzman was a wonderfully creative editor, but he was a very picky and meticulous editor. You had to make up your mind in advance that he was going to change everything the way *he* wanted it to be. So he was really more the director. So you set the scene one way and he would come in and he would — for want of a better word — he would genius it. And that's good. I've seen a lot of times that I personally could've rearranged the figures for better impact. That's the kind of thing Harvey would make you do. Arnold Roth would not do it. He told Harvey right out, "I will redraw this before I change anything."

And Arnie's work came out perfect the way he did it, in my view. But I didn't mind Harvey changing my stuff.

Kupperman: Because you trusted him.

Jaffee: He knew what he was doing to tell the story a little better: he geniused my drawings for *Little Annie Fanny* because he had to. If he wanted a Cadillac, I would draw something that was a combination of a Buick and a Ford and he would go over the whole thing and change every nut and bolt and it would become a Cadillac. He knew his stuff. He knew anatomy. He couldn't *draw* superhero type things, but he *knew* it. He knew where every bone, every muscle was. So he would go over my stuff and he would jazz it up. And sometimes — if I have to be honest, I would have to say that it became a little less funny. Because, I mean, instinctively, I did my funny shtick, and he would make it more accurate and it would be less funny. But we worked well together, so I have no complaints at all. He did it with Will Elder, and Willy would rebel, but they really worked well together. So good editing should enhance your work; it doesn't hurt it. Harvey was good.

Al Feldstein, who followed Harvey, wasn't so focused on the funny stuff as much as he was focused on just being a good editor and putting a good package together. I had no problems with Al Feldstein's veneer and when I brought the fold-in to Al Feldstein, he immediately said, "I like this."

Of course, I went to him and said, "Al, this is gonna ruin the back cover of the magazine because kids are gonna fold it and they're gonna put it back on the stand."

And he went into Bill Gaines and they decided that it didn't matter. They wanted the feature.

And Stan Lee and I have worked together very, very well. He gave me a lot of latitude. Stan would simply say, "Go ahead and write it and draw it, and bring it in finished."

And I did. So he even made me an associate editor. But if I stayed with Stan, I think I might have ended up with Marvel — I think I would have.

Groth: Well, thank God that didn't happen. [*Laughter.*]

Jaffee: Well, you know, you often wonder —

Groth: The path not taken?

Jaffee: Yeah, the path not taken. I even wonder that with fine art. Had I taken the four years — I couldn't take the four-year scholarship to the Art Students League because of the war, but I could've delayed it till after I got out of the Service. Would I be in a gallery on 57th Street now?

Kupperman: You could've been an abstract expressionist.

Groth: ... And a millionaire.

Jaffee: God forbid.

Kupperman: Well, I've been reading a lot of articles lately, and no one believes those guys were happy — any of 'em. And I feel that that's an example of when one artist is successful living a certain life, and having a certain kind of image, there are thousands of wrecked lives as a result — certainly abstract expressionism would be an example, where these guys are living it up drinking, and splashing paint around, and it must have been thousands of guys trying to live that same life and just destroying themselves.

"You Join the Crowd"

Jaffee: Someone once asked me, "How do you feel about technology coming in and doing our work?"

You know, with Photoshop and all that kind of stuff. I said, "Well, of course it doesn't affect me because I have my markets and I'm on a decline ... "

But for young people, maybe they have to contend with it, you know, they have to be knowledgeable about technology if they're in the art game. Just as I had to learn things when I first started cartooning: I could not draw with a brush to save my life. My hand wasn't steady enough and I only drew with a pen, and the minute I went to Eisner and when I went to Stan Lee ... "You have to draw with a brush! You have to do thick and thin! You can't use speedball pens."

So I had to learn to do that.

And then at one point somebody asked me, and I think what struck me and I said, "You know, think of it this way: There's this guy in a cave in France, and he's scratching out these wild buffalos and other animals on the wall, and he's working away and he's making a living out of this. And a guy comes in and he's got a bunch of hair that he has tied onto a stick and he's got a pot of goop that he mixed together [*Kupperman laughs*] and he walks over to the wall next to him, he says, "Hey, look at this."

And he goes like this and he starts painting an elephant.

And the other guy who's been scratching with a stone says, "There goes my whole art business. Shot to hell! Who can keep up with this guy with the brush?"

That's the way it's been for all of us. Someone always comes along with a new technique, a new material. You join the crowd.

Kupperman: The other effect computers have had it seems to me is to make art-making more solitary because you send it in digitally, at least I do, and I rarely meet the people who I'm working for. So it's very much just me in my apartment or studio creating something, sending it off.

Jaffee: There are benefits that I'm enjoying at the moment. This entire book that I did, with 69 illustrations in it and I only had about six months to do them — when we decided to do them in color, I would have loved to hand-color all 69 of them, but I couldn't do that. So I hired a young friend of mine, Ryan Flanders, who works for *Mad* in the coloring department, and he colored all of them to my specifications but by using a computer. And they really came out beautifully. They look beautiful.

It's something new for me. In a way it's new and it's very old, because I did everything the same way in the comic-book business and somebody else colored all the comic stuff. None of us ever did our own coloring in the comic-book business. And here you are, that worked out just fine on the book.

And it also helped me to create a new method of working that has loosened my work up. I do all my black-and-white work on tracing paper now, so that it's much faster and more accurate. I can make my rough sketches on tracing paper, like in a red pencil, and then I put vellum over it, and I ink it on the vellum, and if I don't like a section of it — I have a piece right now sitting on my drawing table, where I got a call saying, "Can you please change such and such?" Well, all I have to do is cut out a piece of it, make a new little drawing for the correction, shove it in, put a new piece of vellum over it, and all the pieces are just glued together, you make a copy of it, it all holds together, and goes to the coloring people.

Kupperman: Some of my pieces I assemble … I do pieces separately, put them together and color them in the computer.

Jaffee: Sure. I mean, years ago I would have to just junk the whole piece, or maybe do a lot of steps and they were so messy with the rotten rubber cement. You know what that's like.

TOP
From *Al Jaffee's Gags*
[©1974 Al Jaffee]

NEXT PAGE
From *Mad About the Sixties* [©2005 E.C. Publications, Inc.]

WHICH MODERN ARTIST IS MOST SUCCESSFULLY COMMUNICATING WITH HIS AUDIENCE?

HERE WE GO WITH ANOTHER RIDICULOUS
MAD FOLD-IN

"Modern Art" has taken some pretty wild turns in recent years. But no matter which direction it takes, it seems to be headed more and more toward total incomprehensibility. Reactions like "What is it?" and "What does it mean?" are almost guaranteed. But there is one modern artist whose work is understood by everyone! To find out who this phenomenal genius is, fold page in as shown.

FOLD PAGE OVER LIKE THIS!

A▶   FOLD THIS SECTION OVER LEFT   ◀B FOLD BACK SO "A" MEETS "B"

ARTIST & WRITER:
AL JAFFEE

MANY MODERN ARTISTS HAVE LONG FELT THAT GREAT ART NEED NOT NECESSARILY BE UNDERSTOOD BY THE GENERAL PUBLIC, AND SOME HIDEOUS GROTESQUERIES HAVE BEEN CREATED IN THIS BELIEF!

A▶   ◀B

Fold-Ins

Kupperman: I have some friends from *The Daily Show* and they did that book and they wanted to do a fold-in and I remember the story of how excited they were when they realized they could actually get you to do it.

Jaffee: Yeah, I loved that.

Kupperman: Frankly, I can't imagine that anyone else could do it.

Jaffee: Well, it was not very difficult, the one I did for them. They told me what they wanted and I did it. I think the thing that I got a kick out of was, last Wednesday, *Jeopardy* showed a fold-in and the contestants all came up with the word they were looking for, which was "fold-in." So I realized, I created an English language word.

Kupperman: That's true.

Jaffee: That's something.

Kupperman: That is something.

Jaffee: Yeah, I'm proud of that. It schlepped me back to when I first thought of it, because it was just that tiny little moment when I said, "Look at this *Playboy* and *National Geographic* and *Sports Illustrated* with this gatefold thing, fold-outs." I said, "What could *Mad* do? How about a fold-in?"

That is as memorable to me as I can make it. So, no one is gonna take that away from my memory and to see

WHICH MODERN ARTIST IS MOST SUCCESSFULLY COMMUNICATING WITH HIS AUDIENCE?

FOLD PAGE OVER LIKE THIS!

A▶B FOLD BACK SO "A" MEETS "B"

ARTIST & WRITER: AL JAFFEE

GOOD GRIEF! A▶B

people on national television immediately knowing the word fold-in. *The New York Times* had a fold-in crossword puzzle a couple of months ago. I have a little mark. Not a big one, but a little one.

Kupperman: For people like me, you're one of the big stars of cartooning that we remember from our childhoods. Someone else was just telling me about visiting the *Mad* offices when he was 9 and they gave him a necktie and he wore it at his wedding.

Jaffee: Oh my.

Kupperman: These things are very powerful.

Jaffee: Wow.

Kupperman: Was the idea of the name "fold-in" — was that influenced at all by "sit-in" or "drop-in," as many "hyphen" in things from the '6os, or did it come slightly differently?

248

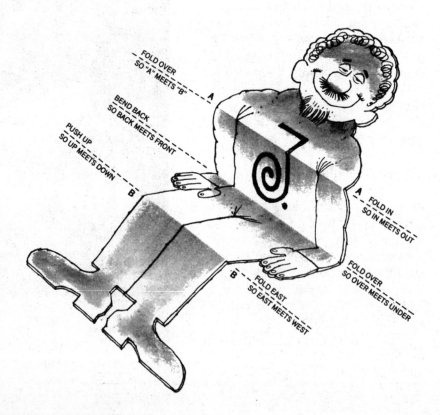

Jaffee: I would love to claim that — maybe Feldstein is claiming it.

Kupperman: Right.

Jaffee: No, I would like to claim anything I can, go for broke. It was a play on "out." Everything *Mad* did was the opposite.

Kupperman: It was an inversion.

Jaffee: Inversion. There was a fold-out and I was going to do a fold-in. That's all it was. They called it a gatefold also; officially they called it a gatefold, but I never heard a human being ever go around saying, "Did you see that *Playboy* gatefold?" They don't say that, they say fold-out.

Kupperman: All the fold-ins, you figure out completely with your eyes. I'm not sure what the right term I'm looking for here is. But you calculate the —

Jaffee: I never see it folded until it's printed.

Kupperman: That's amazing.

Jaffee: Yeah, but I do tracings... first of all I draw the finished thing on one tracing, then cut it apart like that and shove it over here and say, "What the f*** am I gonna put in the middle here?"

Groth: And you never used a computer for that.

Jaffee: No. It would be easier on the computer, and I've seen them on a computer, the finished ones. *The New York Times* did 23 of them on a computer that you fold with a click of the mouse. It's still on the Internet if you ever want to see it. They showed a full thing —

Kupperman: You scroll in, right?

Jaffee: Very effective, much more so then when you fold a piece of paper 'cause you're fumbling away like that.

Groth: But that's part of the fun of it, though.

Kupperman: Yeah, when you fold a piece of paper, in a way you're a participant, you're helping to create this new piece of artwork.

"I think a lot of people are having an enormous amount of fun on the Internet with Twitter, and MySpace, and your face, and his face, but the question always arises: how do you make it pay?"

—Jaffee

Jaffee: I've always felt very strongly about reader-participation things. I loved it when I was a kid: connect-the-dots things and all those puzzle pages. I loved them when I was young. In fact, I did the *Mad Book of Magic* where I did a lot of those kinds of things in it. So, I think what kept the fold-in going for 45 years is that readers enjoy participating, especially visually; it gives them a chance for a little surprise. If I had the opportunity I would've created a lot of things like that with cutouts. There's so much you can do with paper, paper and drawings.

Kupperman: After my son was born last year, and my world kind of closed in a little, I somewhat reluctantly got a Twitter, and I actually really enjoyed it. And I don't usually get on there and do updates about what I'm doing or what I'm eating. But I have a number of followers, and we do joke games or play around with jokes. I've got all these followers and some are conservatives, some I think are even Tea Partiers, liberals, I've got a lot of people of different lifestyles. But it's fascinating to me to see how pure you can make a joke, how simple you can make a joke. And to what level will people appreciate it, all of them, or some of them or none of them. But how far can a joke travel when it's aimed at an audience that's very immediate and is so disparate?

But part of the reason I'm bringing this up is because I mentioned the other day that I met you at the MoCCA convention and the level of excitement from people all over the world was just huge.

Jaffee: With Twitter, the thing that I hear about the Internet all the time is everyone trying to figure out — I mean people have ideas, lots of great ideas, just as you expressed a moment ago. But what I heard up at *Mad* was, "We've got a great *Mad magazine* for the Internet, but what we can't figure out is how to get paid."

So I think a lot of people are having an enormous amount of fun on the Internet with Twitter, and MySpace, and your face, and his face, but the question always arises: How do you make it pay? Because it's fun to have a hobby, but if you want to turn it into something that you can do full time, it has to pay off.

Kupperman: Well, I think that's the situation a lot of people are in now, because technology has made it easier than ever before to produce film or music or anything you like and disseminate it all around the world. But how will people get paid? I think that's the big question.

Jaffee: Yeah, with a magazine, like *Mad* for example, the only source of income that you can logically think of is advertising. But in *Mad*'s case, who's gonna advertise there? The magazine started carrying advertising a few years ago. And what they mostly get is games, you know, Internet games and stuff like that. They did manage to hire me to do four Chrysler fold-in ads. I can't even see why Chrysler would want to advertise automobiles to a *Mad* readership.

Groth: Were you sitting in a Chrysler, and displaying it?

Jaffee: No, no, no. It was Chrysler fold-ins, which explains their bankruptcy! [*Laughter.*]

Groth: I was gonna ask whether there was a cause and effect here.

Jaffee: Well, they were on the way to bankruptcy before I did the fold-ins for them, but I enjoyed it.

Groth: I was gonna suggest a few other corporations you could do advertising for if that were the case.

Jaffee: You wanna bankrupt them? OK, give me a list.

Kupperman: Uhhh, Newscorp. [*Laughter.*] Let's start with Newscorp.

Snappy Answers to Stupid Questions

Jaffee: Speaking of advertising: I was on the way home from MoCCA, got on the bus on 3rd Avenue, and a woman came in sitting directly opposite me, I swear if she was less than 400 pounds, then I'm four pounds. She had to tip the scale *over* 400. She took up a double-seat like this and she was holding a little Victoria's Secret bag. Now, the article that popped into my mind was "Advertisers' Nightmares." [*Laughter.*] Someone with a little cell phone takes a picture of this 400-pound woman with a little Victoria's Secret bag — you gotta picture the undies that she's wearing. So this is, by the way, how I did articles for *Mad*, because you extrapolate. You got one idea: OK, where's the next one?

Kupperman: Right, you've got one really good idea and then you start to assemble others to build it up.

Jaffee: The other ones will come.

Kupperman: That's what I find, you have inspiration, but as I'm sure you also agree, you can't wait for inspiration, you have to have your processes for developing ideas if nothing else jumps out at you.

Jaffee: Well, you know, *Snappy Answers* came to me in just a very normal fashion. It was something that happened around the house, and with my son — I gave him a snappy answer, and I thought about it afterwards and I said, "You know, maybe I'll do a couple of these kinds of things," and I did the one I had with him.

And then you simply start sweating. You say, "All right, I did that one. Hey wait a minute, that one involved an antenna on the roof of our house. How about somebody standing in line somewhere? Oh yeah, you're standing in line at a bus stop, big sign that says 'Bus Stop.' Somebody comes over and says, 'Is this where the bus stops?'"

[*Kupperman laughs.*] They started to come very easily. And where I said before that I'm uncomfortable with it to some degree, you know, setting up a ...

Kupperman: Patsy?

Jaffee: ... Paper tiger, more or less ... People very often don't see something, or they don't think, so they make just a human mistake. And when you say, "Oh yes, the bus stops here," and then the guy turns around and says, "Oh yeah! Of course it does! There's the sign. It says 'Bus Stop.' I'm so sorry I bothered you."

That's what very often happens, so to give someone like that a snappy answer, a wise-ass answer, is sort of unfair.

Kupperman: But for kids –

Jaffee: Kids love 'em.

Kupperman: — who can't really answer back that often, to them it was like a powerful, magical drug.

Groth: I was completely corrupted by that, as you might have noticed.

Kupperman: The idea is so attractive for a kid, to give a witty answer back to your teachers, or your parents. It's more conceptual than real. I'm sure many people couldn't keep it up ...

Jaffee: Well then I went into areas that were far-fetched, you know, like on a desert island.

Kupperman: And you started to do ones where it would come back at the person giving the snappy answer.

Jaffee: Well, that involves editing again. Ballantine did a Don Martin paperback book and it sold like hotcakes. So I figure, gotta get into the act: this is what you do when you're a freelancer, you just keep your eyes open all the time. Any little opportunity that shows itself you try to do something with it. So I dummied this book up, took it into Al Feldstein, and I said, "I'd love to do a book."

And he looked through it and he says, and this is material he had bought, and he says, "The article was terrific, very appealing, but you can't go for 192 pages with one snappy answer to a stupid question on and on and on."

I said, "Al, trust me, I won't do the same thing over and over again. I don't know what I'm gonna do, but trust me."

So he said, "Well, all right, I'll go into Bill and ask him." And he came back and said, "Bill trusts you, and he says go ahead, do it."

Kupperman: And you trusted yourself that you would be able to come up with something.

TOP
From *Mad's Al Jaffee Spews Out More Snappy Answers to Stupid Questions*
[©1972 Al Jaffee & E.C. Publications, Inc.]

Jaffee: Well, at that point I didn't know, but you can always go back and say I can't do it. So I went home and said, "What can I do with this?" I said, "Well, sometimes you give somebody a smart-ass answer, and they give one right back to you that doesn't do you much good."

Then I decided: snappy comebacks to snappy answers to stupid questions. All right. [*Kupperman laughs.*] I figured I'd do it in six-page lumps. I really strained to figure out others, and it hit me. Sputnik, I think, went up about that time. I thought, how about snappy answers to stupid questions continuity. So then I changed continuity to snappy answers to stupid questions in outer space: a whole new area, right? This was a whole eight or 12 pages I could use up: 192 pages to go. What I did with that is I shot a rocket up into the air, and the guy gets out of the space station and he asks a stupid question ... I did that in 1967. But he gets a snappy answer in space. And then the chapter head was, "Back to Plain Old Snappy Answers to Stupid Questions." Again: another six-batch of that. So you had a variety going, and then finally, I think Jerry Gardner at that time was doing old movie photographs with balloons and funny ...

Kupperman: Was he the same guy who did the political ones, too. It would be books about this size? [*Makes shape with hands.*]

Jaffee: Yeah.

Kupperman: Political photographs of people with captions.

Jaffee: Yes. And I decided to go through some old photographs ... I titled it "Snappy Answers to Stupid Questions Throughout History." And I had a picture of Alexander Graham Bell on his telephone. He says, "Can you hear me, Mr. Watson?"
   And I had Mr. Watson give the answer, "No, wrong number."

Kupperman: [Laughs.] You had him give a number of answers, right?

Jaffee: Yeah, I had to give three. But I don't remember all three. And then I had this surrender of the Japanese on the Battleship Maine and one of the Japanese guys says, "Are we surrendering?"
   And the other guy says, "No, the three of us have captured this battleship."
   [Kupperman laughs.] And you've got a million soldiers lined up on the battleship. So that opened up a whole new thing, with the photographs. That took up space. Then I could go back to all the others and reach page 192.

Kupperman: And you did how many books? Was it five or six?

Jaffee: I did 14 *Snappy Answers* books.

Kupperman: Wow!

Know What They Need

Groth: Can I ask you both a question? Al, when you were talking about the *Snappy Answers to Stupid Questions*, you said you're always on the lookout for some new angle, something that you could pitch to a publisher. It reminded me of something Michael said that I wanted to bring up about the process of being an artist in this environment. He said, "My job, so to speak, exists only as a projection of my will and my ability to come up with new material constantly. About half of the work I've done so far this year is work that I've proposed and gotten through an editorial process completely through my efforts. But I find the strain of living that lifestyle is sometimes a bit much. It makes you feel insecure and edgy."
   Now I'd like Michael to elaborate on that, but can you also respond to that? Did you feel that way at all throughout your career? When you were Michael's age, that was somewhere around 1965 or '67, you were ensconced at *Mad*.

Jaffee: Yes.

Groth: Did you feel a certain safety net there?

Kupperman: If I could rephrase it a little bit, the idea that if your brain stopped working, for instance, if it stopped producing funny ideas or ideas, that you'll be in trouble, 'cause you couldn't produce.

Jaffee: The only answer I can give to that is an equivocation, because I had to be creative all my life in order to make a living. Nobody is going to hand me any money, and Michael knows that too and experiences that too, and the anxiety you have I think is not so much about your ability, but being in the right venue at the right time. I fell into, on several occasions, a venue where fortunately, I could meet the test: I could deliver. The main thing is delivering. You got people sitting out there who are editors and publishers and advertising executives, all they want is for you to come in and solve their problems and they will give you money. But the key is solving their problems. Michael's job and my job is to solve their problems. So once you land somewhere where you feel, "Hey, I can solve these problems."

Might be a guy working at Microsoft who can solve intricate technology problems. In our case it's problems that involve original ideas in visual form.

Kupperman: It involves also having a sense of what the person asking of you wants, even maybe more than they do.

Jaffee: When I worked for Stan Lee, I knew what he needed. And he knew that I knew what he needed. I created characters for him: I took over comic strips that others had created, like *Patsy Walker* and *Super Rabbit*. And I created *Ziggy Pig and Silly Seal* from when he said to me, "Give me an animal strip."

And I gave him an animal strip.

Then when I went to *Mad*, I saw what they were doing. Now, I wouldn't do what Harvey did. Satirizing existing comic strips, Harvey was the master of that, and they don't need two Harveys, so I had to figure out other areas that I could be good in. So I satirized things; they were hungry for script. That helps a lot too.

You bring in something and say, "Well, I think this is very funny. What do you think?"

And they say, "Well I'm starving for script; I think it's funny too."

But actually I was very comfortable with the *Mad* business. I fit *Mad*, they

"It's just amazing that they're underpaying me and yet a lawyer had the time to sit and work out this bunch of threats to send to me in case I don't complete my work."

—Kupperman

didn't buy everything from me, but I think they told me once that I had a 90-95 percent batting average. And they recently added up the most contributions by a single person, and I was the winner. Sometimes it's very easy to come up with material. But if you're 100-percent freelance, and you're going from one place to another, it becomes more difficult because you have to refashion your thinking to suit ... I mean you're not going to do the same gags for *The New Yorker*.

Kupperman: Yes.

Jaffee: If I wanted to break in to *The New Yorker*, I would have to probably spend weeks figuring out how to crack this nut.

Kupperman: I shouldn't say anything ... [*Groth laughs.*] ... The politics there are so crazy, it wouldn't even be worth it, 'cause they'd still kibosh you.

Groth: The minute you said you shouldn't say something, I thought you should say something.

Kupperman: I've decided recently to give up trying to submit material to *The New Yorker*, because I've been going through the illustration department and it just doesn't work.

Saturday Evening Post

Ladies Home Journal

The New Yorker

Jaffee: I sold one thing to *The New Yorker*. I just wanted to have one thing in *The New Yorker*, and I sold one and did a finish and brought it in and they paid me but they sent it back and they never used it.

Groth: So, Al, it doesn't sound like you've felt a lot of creative anxiety in the sense that Michael was talking about, or at least how I interpreted —

Kupperman: I feel like I've had to go outside the magazines and really try to build my own career and I don't feel like I've really had a successful home at any one publication.

Groth: Not as hospitable as *Mad*.

Kupperman: No, definitely not.

GIRD

Jaffee: See, that's where I have to admit that I cannot claim anxiety when I have a home base. You have a home base that is receptive, all you have to do is just sit down and work.

When I had my comic strip *Tall Tales*, I would sit down Monday and just surround myself with cartoon books, you know Chaun Day, Chas Addams, I don't care who they were, collections, and I would flip the pages and suddenly I would just see something, *bang*, just the scene, that's all. It would be a pyramid in Egypt, with some kinda gag, and I'd think about it, immediately: Some kind of switcheroo would come, and I'd have a little tiny pyramid sticking out of the ground, and two pith-helmeted guys standing there, and one says, "I think we have a hell of a lot of digging ahead of us, Professor." [Kupperman laughs.] The pyramid that I saw was a whole, full pyramid gag with camels walking around and everything. And I sold that to *Playboy*. And when I did *Tall Tales*, I would get my seven gags for the week on Monday, and then I would do them all on Tuesday and Wednesday and then I'd have the rest of the time off. It was a dream. If that'd succeeded I would never have gone back to *Mad*: I wouldn't say never, but I wouldn't have had to go back to *Mad*. But I had a very happy life with *Mad* too.

Kupperman: As a freelancer I feel like I'm never off the clock, that the work is never, ever done.

Jaffee: You feel that way.

Kupperman: I do feel that way, yeah. I mean I do *Thrizzle* obviously for Fantagraphics, and that's its own thing, but then there's just endless freelance assignments and I feel like I always have to be preparing for the next thing, concentrating on the next thing, and worrying about ...

Groth: Scrambling.

Kupperman: Yeah, always scrambling.

Jaffee: That would probably give me GIRD.

Kupperman: What's GIRD?

Jaffee: Gastro-intestinal misery [*Groth laughs*].

Kupperman: Yes, it does.

Jaffee: No, I mean I have battled with GIRD from time to time, but it's usually a deadline problem, where I've gotta do four days' work in two days.

Kupperman: I've got a job like that right now. I'm doing a book for a certain publisher, and it's a huge amount of work in a ridiculous amount of time for not that much money, and then they send me this contract and it's full of threats about what will happen if I don't complete it one week by the due date, two weeks, three weeks. It's just amazing that they're underpaying me and yet a lawyer had the time to sit and work out this bunch of threats to send to me in case I don't complete my work.

Groth: I'm sure they're not singling you out. That's just boilerplate [*laughs*].

259

LEFT
Al Jaffee wrote and
Bob Clarke drew
"How Various Maga-
zines Might Handle
the Same Cartoon
Situation," collected in
*Mad's Vastly Overrated
Al Jaffee* [©1976 E.C.
Publications, Inc.]

Kupperman: I would hope so. I would be very unhappy if I thought they were specifically aimed at me. Obviously an artist broke this publisher's heart very recently or something, but it is just amazing.

Jaffee: My GIRD is not the anxiety of not getting work. It hasn't been. It's failing a deadline. I've never missed a deadline in 70 years of working. The only time I did technically miss a deadline I was suddenly involved in a divorce, and I was writing a comic strip for a syndicate, and an artist was drawing it, and I needed to get that script to him within a certain period of time. And I realized that I was emotionally unable to work at that time. So I immediately came into New York and saw the editor and said to him, "You have to get somebody else to do this." So he did and it was enough time to get somebody else. Because, to me, the biggest bugaboo is letting down a deadline, you know?

Kupperman: Yes.

Jaffee: 'Cause I see a whole company depending on this, and I know it's ridiculous because I've even be told, you know people whisper to me, "You always have another week afterwards."

Groth: Well, Al, what you just described doesn't technically count as missing a deadline.

Kupperman: I once had an art director who seemed not to be all there who give me the ship date of the magazine as the art deadline and that was not a pleasant experience.

Jaffee: Oh, that's bad.

Groth: [*Laughs.*] You mean accidentally?

Kupperman: I think she didn't quite know what she was doing.

Jaffee: That's terrible.

Kupperman: And she shifted the onus onto me, of course, at the last minute. But apart from that I haven't had a problem, and I feel the same way, the whole idea of missing a deadline.

Jaffee: That's the backbone of our profession, to meet the obligations of the business. If we expect publishers to meet their obligations to us, we have to have the same attitude about meeting the obligations of the publisher; that's the way I've always felt.

Kupperman: Yes. But you mentioned *Tall Tales* a minute ago and I do remember I read that you did have a good story about that. That the strip was syndicated in a lot of foreign papers, and then someone had the bright idea that you should put in a lot of text, which there hadn't been previously.

Jaffee: It was bought on the basis of it being a pantomime, which is much more comfortable for me. I see visual humor. I see it all the time: it's almost like a curse. I see — well I just told you before about this 400-pound lady with this little tiny bag of Victoria's Secret. Which isn't really a boffo gag, I mean it could be a part of an article, but I could make a gag out of it if I tried. And writing gag punch lines like *New Yorker* is not my strong suit.

So when I created *Tall Tales*, I wanted to do something where I could just do visual humor, and I got lucky and it was at the right time and the right place, and it got sold. But where I got unlucky was that the New York Herald Tribune Syndicate was part of the *New York Herald Tribune*, which was moribund. The *Tribune* at that time was the Chrysler of today, it was going down, and it didn't have the government to come in and prop it up. So, when the newspaper died, the syndicate was floundering, it didn't have much of a leg to stand on. Its personnel were changing. Editors were coming and going, and the head of the syndicate was booted out and a new guy was brought in. And of course the salesmen were also suffering. The syndicate salesman were going up against King Features and other mighty syndicates, and they were probably being cut in pay and expenses and stuff, so the whole thing was kind of collapsing.

At this point the new head of the syndicate goes over and starts to genius all the scripts, and say, "Well maybe this is why this doesn't sell, maybe this isn't what … " And he decided that mine doesn't sell well enough because it didn't have enough American papers. I think it had a nice comfortable list of foreign papers, but in the United States, what happened was some newspapers bought it, paid for it for a year or so, but never found a place to put it because it was an unusual shape, or they put it in the Want Ads section which drew absolutely no readership, and so little by little the American version wasn't doing well, but the foreign version was doing OK. So he said it was because Americans don't like wordless cartoons, so I was forced to put words in and pretty soon after that it dropped dead.

Kupperman: Right, you lost all your foreign papers.

Jaffee: I lost papers. I wasn't comfortable putting words in anyway because the whole premise of the strip was that it would be a kind of double-take. It was this tall, and I would have something going on over here, and your eye would drop down and you would have the visual punch line.

Kupperman: Were you on a hiatus from *Mad* when you were doing that strip?

Jaffee: No, what happened was I was on a hiatus from *Humbug* folding. During that period between when *Humbug* folded and I eventually went to *Mad* was I think a couple of years — I was out of work. So I desperately tried to do something, and I even created about a dozen cartoons for *Playboy*. I sent them to Hefner and fortunately he bought them all and I got a little bit of money. But I wasn't comfortable doing gags: I don't consider myself a gag cartoonist. After I finished sending the gags to *Playboy*, a friend of mine, Dave Gantz, sold a comic strip to the *Herald Tribune*, and I thought maybe I'll go to his agent. So I went to his agent with some ideas, and she sold it. She had two guys at the *Herald Tribune*, so that's how I got to do *Tall Tales*.

Humbug

Kupperman: So you had left *Mad* with Kurtzman to do *Humbug*.

Jaffee: No, no. I was never on *Mad*. I wasn't one of the original *Mad* people, although Kurtzman had mentioned to people that he would like to get Al Jaffee on when he turned it into [a magazine]. Oh and I did one piece for him, when it went from a 10¢ magazine to a 25¢ magazine. I did my first

THE SPIRIT OF CHRISTMAS

Each year at this time, folks brighten up their homes with gay lights and decorations. There's a sort of friendly spirit of competition in the air as each neighbor tries to outdo the other in fanciness. Of course some can afford to spend more on this than others, and this does create a certain amount of bitterness. Besides money, a great amount of time is needed to create some of the breathtaking displays that make one house put another to shame. All the work and time leaves many so fatigued they simply don't have the energy to get themselves to their church. In a good many instances envy and jealousy flares out into the open and leads to a good deal of hatred during the coming new year. But through it all, the real spirit of the season somehow manages to break through and bring a measure of happiness to us all.

piece about a Ben Hogan golf secret, which will be reprinted in my book. Then Harvey left *Mad*, and I went with Harvey to *Trump*. And then *Trump* ended and we went to *Humbug*. And when *Humbug* died I had a lot of leftover scripts which I took up to *Mad* and they bought them and I've been working for them ever since.

Kupperman: That's fantastic, and that would've been in the mid-'60s?

Groth: '58.

Jaffee: '58, yeah, '58. When I look back on it all, it just seems like a bad movie.

Kupperman: It's an incredible story. It really is. [*Groth laughs.*] I mean your story is the story of comics, in a way: of comic art in this country.

TOP

From *Humbug* #6 (January 1958)

Jaffee: Yeeeeah, I kind of wandered through it. Most of the time, to be in the right place at the right time with the right people, and it had plenty of elements of the kind of anxiety that you've expressed, although my anxiety was mostly about productivity and deadlines. I deep down in my heart expected any day that this gig would end. And very often it did. I was very happy on *Humbug*: I was working with guys I loved, doing the kind of work we all got together and figured out and enjoyed and loved. I was interviewed by somebody at that time, and the person asked me, "I understand you've been working for 11 issues," that's 11 months, more than 11 months because of the start-up and all that, "without drawing any income."

I said, "Yes, that's right. I've been living off my savings and my insurance, which I borrowed on, and it's running out." I had to live very frugally. And my family suffered from that, 'cause I didn't get any other kind of work.

So the guy said to me, "Well, how could you do that?"

I said, "Because it was the happiest time of my life." I just was so happy doing that work, and somehow I sublimated the fear of going bankrupt. I managed to pay a mortgage, but I was happy. But I've been very lucky, when one thing fails, another thing seems to appear. I look back on it: it's the strangest thing. I'm very proud of the [*Humbug*] book that I'm in, the two books that Gary produced, because I went through them again on Sunday after being at the signing. I just felt like going through them, and I just marveled at what kind of beautiful stuff we did. Arnold Roth does work that is much different now than what he did then, and I love Arnold's work, both then and now. However, I got a very nostalgic feeling about his work then. They were more cartoony. Now they're more stylistic.

Groth: Yeah.

Jaffee: But his articles were so funny. "Rare Birds" with Eisenhower as an eagle. Arnold has his own wonderful, peculiar sense of humor, and it came through in his youthful work of that time. Now he does more sophisticated work, but we all … I can't do the kind of work I did in *Humbug*, and all that detail. My hand isn't steady enough for that.

Groth: It was pretty astonishing; we were studying your work in the office with a loupe. We thought we should do that while we had it briefly in our possession. Everybody in the art department was just ogling it.

Jaffee: You know, even I am impressed with it now, because it's as if somebody else did it. I'll be honest with you. Really, I look at it and I say, "I couldn't do that. But I was able to." It's like that calendar bit.

American Bald Eagle (HOLE IN UNUM) *Range:* Pennsylvania, Washington D.C. And neighboring links. *Habitat:* Farms, White-Houses, etc. *Identification:* Though likeable, often lacks direction in flight. Constant smile sort of engenders confidence. Great favorite of women and children. Not quite totally bald though.

"You Don't Want to Waste Space"

I don't know what I was trying to prove but I think artists have such a profound respect for space: that you don't want to waste space. Even though you have to learn how to use empty space, white space, when you direct your pen or your brush to a space on an illustration board, you want to make it count. It's like you don't want to have gibberish. I mean, you can understand it if someone says [*Jaffee talks gibberish*]. Well there are people who draw that kind of stuff. It doesn't say anything. And I feel that if I want people to understand what I'm saying when I speak, I want 'em to understand my language on a piece of paper. And I'm sure Michael feels the same way.

Kupperman: Yeah, very much so.

Jaffee: But there are people who feel that just filling the space makes them important, and I just don't agree with that. I have done things that I won't say have filled the space very effectively, but that's because some people ordered it.

Groth: Now when you say that, you're not talking about artists who just draw badly, you're talking about something else, right?

Jaffee: What I'm saying is, your drawing is a form of communication, and the elements in there are similar to words. I mean, you put a string of words

TOP
From "Bird Watchers for Humbugians" by Arnold Roth in *Humbug* #1 (August 1957)

together not because you like the word "and" and "if" and "but." You put them together because they fit into the sentence properly. So if I put a bunch of people standing around in a scene, they have to be in that scene, not somebody who wandered onto the set.

Kupperman: And to understand the artist's intention, to see, "Oh this is what he is conveying." Or what he or she is conveying with his image. I mean if I look at a cartoon and I can't understand it, I know it must be a pretty bad cartoon.

Jaffee: Yeah, I feel the same way.

Kupperman: The intention — even if it might be a little jumbled — needs to be present.

Jaffee: Even when cartoons in *The New Yorker* are explained to me. If they have to explain a cartoon to someone like me with an average intelligence, then there's something wrong.

Kupperman: Gag cartoons are really an art form that's slid so far down I think in the last 50 or 60 years. I mean in the '40s and '50s they were just amazing. I was looking at one of my favorites — Virgil Partch from *Collier's*. I don't know if you like Virgil Partch.

Jaffee: Oh, I love Virgil Partch.

Kupperman: It's a man and a horse, sitting in a restaurant, and the horse is crying, and the man is saying angrily, "Look around you, do you see any other horses crying 'cause they can't have roast duck?" Just so ridiculous.

TOP
From "Jungle Princess" in *Tales Designed to Thrizzle #6*

RIGHT
From *Man the Beast*
[©1953 Virgil Franklin Partch, II]

Jaffee: [*Laughs.*] The absurdity is so wonderful. I love the cartoons that are absurd. I do love them. Who's around now that does stuff like that?

Groth: There's an artist named Bliss in *The New Yorker*. But do you have a theory as to why the acuity of gags has gone down?

Kupperman: I just think maybe the magazines that are commissioning that work want it to be from a kind of viewpoint that's very hard to achieve now, a kind of detachment, maybe. My personal feeling about *The New Yorker* is that they wanted someone to do comics who had the viewpoint that a certain income might provide, that after years of working for *The New Yorker*, there's no danger of me having [*Groth laughs*]. That just doesn't work.

Jaffee: My first inkling of absurdity as being the pinnacle of humor for me, personally, was a Basil Wolverton cartoon. He did cartoons for a number of publications that Stan Lee and Timely Comics was putting out in the 1940s and 1950s. And I just loved his stuff. Powerhouse Pepper was knocked off a roof by somebody who punched him. He stumbled over the edge of a five-story building. He went head first into the sidewalk and he was there in the sidewalk and two women walk by and say, "Oh Celia, isn't that disgusting? There's a man with his head stuck in the sidewalk."

It's beyond absurd.

And for me, it might have opened my eyes to something. I wasn't pursuing satire: I was really a storyteller. Because that's what comic books were all about at that time. The absurdity was that we were all doing stories where our characters were fighting the Nazis. I mean, little pigs fighting the Nazis, it's a little strange, but ...

Kupperman: Silly Seal and Ziggy Pig fought the Nazis?

Jaffee: Yeah, they fought the Nazis, but the way I did it was — Silly Seal, of course, lived up in the North, up in Alaska somewhere. And he lisped, so his absurdity was that he would hear about the bad men that are coming in submarines — and so I would show a picture of a U-Boat and of

"DON'T SCREAM
HE ISN'T GOING TO BITE
YOU."

course the Nazis were also animals — so you know there would be a fierce-looking dog or something with a Nazi cap. There was the U-Boat, and it broke through the ice, and Silly tells his mother he's gonna fight the Nazis. This gives me a chance to exercise my inventiveness, which is what I really enjoy doing. I think I'm basically a frustrated inventor, 'cause in Europe as children we made zillions and zillions of toys out of pieces of junk, pieces of wood, clay, whatever we could get our hands on — my brother and I. And we were both very good at making things. So Silly Seal chops out ice in the shape of a boat and then out of snow and ice he forms a cannon and makes snowballs that he puts in the cannon, and somehow he figures out a way to fire it at U-Boats.

I'm assuming that this is for children, and then I find 'em in the Army, and the PX is selling these things to soldiers, but you know distributing comics wasn't my job. My job was just writing them and drawing them. But anyway it did strike me as being ridiculous, even for Captain America and all these other guys to be fighting the Nazis, you know. Here we got soldiers out there dying of real bullets and we got comic books with superheroes running around in their underwear fighting soldiers.

But the whole business is ridiculous. You know that.

Kupperman: Yeah, of course.

Jaffee: And that's why we're in it. [*Laughter.*]

That's Entertainment

Groth: I wanted to ask, what forms of entertainment do you enjoy the most? Do you read comics for fun or do you … ?

Jaffee: I don't see comics any more. I read *The New York Times* — it's a morning habit, it's warming up for the day. And then I read books, but I don't read comic strips or comic books any more, which makes it somewhat difficult for me to be interviewed at things like Comic-Con because I'm not that knowledgeable, except from some of the things …

Groth: Unless they send 'em to you.

Kupperman: But there's so many genres.

Jaffee: When Gary or Johnny Ryan sends me their work, I get a big bang out of it. I think Johnny Ryan is very talented; I think his stuff is very funny. Not for my generation, you know. People my age are not going to go out and buy Johnny Ryan.

Groth: We're trying to capture that market, though. [Jaffee laughs.]

Kupperman: Johnny Ryan for seniors.

Jaffee: Right! But I've always had a slogan, which I think any sensible person should have: Funny is funny.
　　I feel funny is funny, but even stuff in bad taste can be very funny. It's just that I know I don't want to do it, and frankly I don't think it should be disseminated. Hitler did some very funny, satiric stuff about Jews while he was gassing them and they had funny cartoonists doing funny stuff about how funny-looking Jews are and all of that. Well, it might have been funny to Nazis, but it certainly wouldn't be funny to me. But funny stuff that doesn't harm anybody, I think, you can stretch it into many areas: if it's funny stuff that appeals to teenage boys, why not.

Groth: You seem to have that in common, based on what I've read that you've said and based upon my having talked to you, that you both eschew cruelty.

Kupperman: Yeah, I don't like cruelty at all.

Jaffee: No, I don't either.

Groth: And if you're satirists, you're somewhat gentle satirists.

Kupperman: Well, I believe if you've got a real point to make, go ahead and make it if you feel something strongly. But just picking on fat people or people who are different, I find that extremely unattractive.

Groth: Now, do you both consider yourselves more humorist than satirist? Do you make a distinction?

269

Jaffee: I lean towards humor. I was brought into satire by Harvey Kurtzman and found a way to make a living at it. But, I would just as easily enjoy doing a children's book that's funny.

Kupperman: I suspect I'm a little more of a satirist. Just the way my brain works.

Jaffee: My brain works that way now too, because I've had to do it for such a long time.

Kupperman: Right, it's like a reflex.

Jaffee: Yeah, it's a reflex now. I think satirically, but I still just love out-and-out funny stuff.

Kupperman: What have you seen lately that you really enjoyed in terms of humor — that's not comics? Movies or television? I mean are there any current movie performers or moviemakers you enjoy, any other forms of popular entertainment that you really get something from?

Jaffee: Well, my social secretary, Joyce, selects all the things that I see. We watch television together and she buys tickets to all the theater things that we go to. We saw something that put us both to sleep just this Sunday. [*Laughter.*]

Groth: [*Laughs.*] Not funny.

Kupperman: What was it?

Jaffee: It was something called *When the Rain Stops Falling* — it's at the Lincoln Center Theater. Very difficult, it was just hard to follow, that was the main thing. It was well acted and I suspect very well written, but it jumps around a lot and I think when you get to be old, like Joyce and I are, keeping track becomes a little bit more difficult because the mental agility isn't there. So, one minute you're seeing the son as a 6-year-old and the next minute he's grown up and married and then you're seeing him next when he's a 20-year-old and he's going out on a date. Of course the dialogue is constantly explaining why they're behaving in the manner they are because of some prior experience — I couldn't follow it.

Groth: *Curb Your Enthusiasm:* have you seen that?

Jaffee: Oh well, that we've seen all of them. I love that. I love that. I love the fact that what he does is pretty much what we've had to do in *Mad,*

Don't You Hate . . . people who find humor in the misfortunes of others!

Don't You Hate . . . people who can't see the humor of finding humor in the misfortunes of others!

especially Harvey, is you pick up on some little foible, just a plain ordinary foible, like I brought this thing home and its broken and I gotta go take it back, but I can't find my sales slip. How's he gonna know that I bought it in his store? And you start to create a whole dialogue and that's what he does on *Curb Your Enthusiasm*. Just an ordinary event, and I've experienced this.

Groth: Larry David deals with the absurdity of modern life beautifully.

Kupperman: A lot of it is people objecting to his behavior.

Groth: He's always reacting to something legitimately ridiculous or annoying, but then he pushes it so far that he himself becomes absurd.

Jaffee: Well, he takes in an abandoned family from Katrina, and he's dealing with a bunch of people who speak Spanish in his house, who are going through the refrigerator. How do we get rid of them without insulting them? We can all think of situations like that, but the fact is he had the venue. He could do it. Those things happen to all: The strength of it is that it's personality. He gets into trouble with friends because he forgets their birthday or they exchange the same present or something like that.

Groth: It's very much an updated *I Love Lucy*.

Jaffee: Yeah. Pretty much. Well, they're all that. All comedy is like that. There are no new jokes, either. The only thing that makes satire work is that it's of the moment. The same jokes that we're doing now were done against King George in the 18th century.

TOP
From "The Mad Hate Book" in *Mad's Vastly Overrated Al Jaffee* [©1976 E.C. Publications, Inc.]

Let's Get Political

Groth: Do politics infuriate you?

Jaffee: Republican politics infuriate me. [*Laughter.*]

Kupperman: I try to stay away.

Groth: Your satire is more focused on celebrity culture.

Kupperman: Yeah, and even again on Twitter I try and stay away. Because I do have these conservative followers who will jump if I say anything — I can't help myself. My politics do tend to be a little more left, but then I find very strident people on the left annoying too. I find these people who are constantly inventing scenarios for their enemies, they're all together in a Tea Party. They're making up imaginary plays about their enemies. It's not constructive and it's not, obviously, realistic.

Jaffee: The divisiveness is the bad part.

Kupperman: The trouble starts when you start demonizing.

Jaffee: Yeah, demonizing is bad. For example, with the health law that Obama was trying to push through — OK, it had flaws: the kind of flaws that it had were different flaws to different people. Insurance companies disliked certain flaws and people making less than $20,000 a year disliked other flaws. But the duty of Congress was aggregated, because the two parties should have come together and said, "Do we need health reform or don't we need health reform?" And settle on the fact that we either need it or we don't need it. It's obvious we need it because the whole system is gonna collapse in 10, 15 years anyway.

Kupperman: Yeah, health insurance is a nightmare.

Jaffee: The Republicans know that too.

Groth: I think the Republicans decided we do not need universal health care.

Kupperman: The Republicans know that too, yeah.

Jaffee: The Republicans voted no as a block simply to not give the Democrats a plus sign in the government.

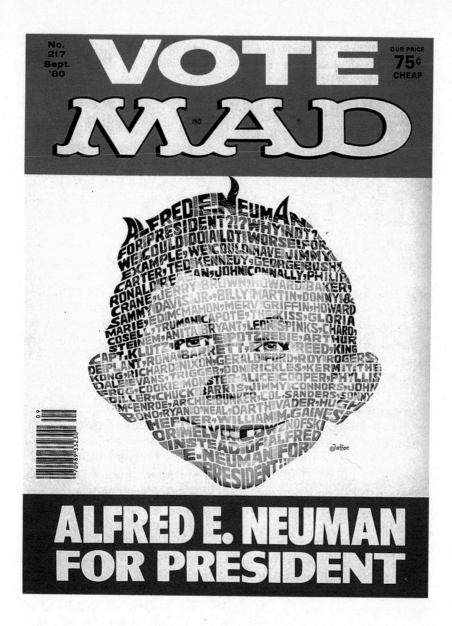

Kupperman: Well, *The Onion* actually did a very nice piece of satire about this with one of the Republican leaders, an editorial by him saying: "I know that my constituents don't care so much about the health care or their income or their quality of life, but they do want me to play hardball, sleazy politics, fast and loose with the truth and prevent anything from getting done. That's what my constituents want." Very funny.

FOUR HORSEMEN OF THE MEDIA APOCALYPSE

Jaffee: Well, for some reason *The Onion* does it in a way that is not my favorite way of doing it: they go head on with it, they go right on it. I think what we were talking about earlier was where you do it through implication, rather than just changing somebody's name a little bit. Instead of Obama it's Ubama and then you hit him with an 88mm Howitzer, frontally. That's not satire to me, that's like clubbing seals.

Kupperman: If I make any kind of political statement I'd rather do it kind of gently and through influence. There was a joke I made on Twitter recently: "I'm tired of all these immigrants; I'm gonna move to another country."

Jaffee: That's funny. That's great. I did a cartoon, I don't know what came over me to do it without any kind of assignment and I never sold it to anybody either. I just did it recently. It's in a show at MoCCA, it's up on the wall. It's the four horsemen of the media apocalypse and I've got Limbaugh, Beck, O'Reilley and Hannity. They were all sitting on a horse. Limbaugh's horse, of course, is spread-eagled from his weight, [*laughter*] but there are no other words than "The Four Horsemen of the Media Apocalypse." They're all holding the reins but they are all under the horses' tails. The horse is facing the other way. I think, visually, in my view it gets across the fact that they've got the horse pointed in the wrong direction and I just did it for my own pleasure. Now, that is not satire. That is just plain making fun of people.

Kupperman: Right.

Groth: Which is sometimes necessary.

Kupperman: But you felt compelled to do it.

Jaffee: Actually, I was going to do it a little bit different way and, you know Steve Brodner?

Kupperman: Yes. I mean, not personally.

Jaffee: A terrifically talented caricaturist: very, very individual style. And he came over to interview me for some program that he's working on with some television people for Sundance. I showed this to him and I had it positioned a little bit differently. They were holding the reins backwards, I think, to the horse's head, and he says, "Put the reins under the horse's tail and have 'em actually riding the horse that way." It was a joint effort. If I ever sell it, I have to send him something. Send him the original.

Kupperman: I think the last time I tried to do some political drawing I just realized I was not good at it at all. It wasn't my thing.

Groth: Well, you had a political cartoon for about a year.

Kupperman: I had a political cartoon, which is the work I hope never gets printed again.

Groth: I haven't found any examples of those yet. I'm looking.

Kupperman: It was not good and I think the very last political drawing I did, which I submitted around to a couple places and no one was interested, was during Bush's reign. I did a drawing of him. You know that movie, Richard Widmark, *Kiss of Death*? The one where Richard Widmark pushes the old woman down the stairs. I did a drawing of Bush about to push FDR like that.

Jaffee: That's great.

Kupperman: No one would touch it, of course.

Jaffee: Political cartooning, it's a deadline thing — the editorial department comes up with an idea or a subject and tells you to do something with this for the morning paper.

Kupperman: I don't see much good work being done in that field anymore, except maybe in England. I think there are some skilled artists doing it in England, where you can be as vicious and opinionated as you want. But here it's faded.

Jaffee: Herblock was the one I liked and I think Tom Toles is pretty good. His subject matter is very good.

It's All Just Good Cartooning

Jaffee: For my money, a lot of cartoon art that I see, including in *The New Yorker*, is not good drawing.

Kupperman: Yeah.

Jaffee: I'm prejudiced. I like good drawing and I know the gag or the idea is the important thing and that's what the drawing is supposed to carry. And Thurber did it beautifully with the touché thing, even though you can't say that that was anatomically correct. But at the same time my personal sense of taste is for the drawing at least to meet some criteria. Not to be totally squiggly.

Groth: So you think there's been a genuine decline in craftsmanship.

Jaffee: I think there has been. I think there's been a lot of what, I think Mell Lazarus once said it — or maybe it was my editor Harry Welker. He said, "So and so is a good writer who can't draw, but he's doing a comic strip." And another one he said, " ... is a good artist who can't write." And he said these are deadly combinations, and what he was looking for is good writers who can draw.

Groth: That's the key. But, there are some great drawers in alternative comics who are also great writers.

Jaffee: Oh yes there are. There are.

Groth: Tony Millionaire and Jaime Hernandez.

Jaffee: Yes, and Sacco.

Groth: Joe Sacco.

Jaffee: Yeah, you have a good stable, and even the funny ones like Johnny Ryan — and I don't know the names of a lot of the others — but Johnny Ryan draws a good, funny comic strip for his kind of writing. It works for that very well.

Kupperman: That's always what I've been trying to do with the comics is make the drawing express the ideas as clearly as possible, not fancy up the drawing style.

Jaffee: That's the only thing you can ask of it, really. It would be terrible for someone to have recruited me to draw *Batman*. It would have been terrible. I mean, I would have busted my balls to make it work, but it never would work. I might have just barely kept up on it.

Kupperman: Well, it would be in the other category of funny, which is when someone fails to meet a challenge they've set for themselves and it's very visible.

Jaffee: Right. That can be very funny.

Kupperman: That can be very funny. I try to include some of that in my work. I deliberately try to fail at certain things.

Jaffee: It's like Charlie Chaplin trying to be a very serious businessman.

Kupperman: Right.

Jaffee: And he's flipping somebody's cigar with his foot. [*Laughs.*] All in all, I think what's important is to enjoy what you're doing. Most of the time I enjoy what I'm doing. Even *Patsy Walker*, which is really something that is totally unnatural for me, I force myself to learn the genre. I just saw one [of my stories Groth brought] over there, which I don't even remember and I looked at it and I thought to myself, "Jeez, it's legitimate." It's a teenage comic thing and it's not terrible.

Kupperman: When you read your old stories, do you laugh at it sometimes? Do you make yourself laugh if it's been a while?

Jaffee: Sometimes it catches me.
   [*Speaking to Groth*]: How many books have you published?

Groth: We actually have a list of every book that we publish and it's frightening.

"He said to me, 'Do you have a graphic novel in you?'

And I said, 'Please, Gary, I'm 89 years old.'

So you said, 'How about a graphic short story?'"

—Jaffee

Kupperman: Your books are fantastic. I was just looking last night at the *Pim and Francie* book and the minicomics of the '80s book.

Groth: I feel like we're really doing the best publishing we've ever done right now.

Jaffee: Oh, you're doing great stuff. Really. You're setting the pace. Other publishers are hopping on the graphic-novel bandwagon.

Groth: Bandwagon, such as it is.

Jaffee: But you're not doing graphic novels.

Groth: We are.

Jaffee: You're doing some?

Groth: Oh yes, and they're good. They're quite good. Everything related to cartooning. I don't see it as one genre: I just see it as good cartooning whether it's in a graphic novel form or whether it's a newspaper strip or single-panel cartoons. We just reprinted Roy Crane's *Captain Easy*.

Jaffee: Roy Crane was my hero.

Groth: Or whether it's *Humbug*, just all good cartooning, and that's how we see it.

Jaffee: I wish I was 40, Gary.

Groth: I wish I was 50.

Jaffee: Even 50 and had a bunch of years ahead because I would have killed to get an opportunity to sit with a publisher on an intimate basis and say to myself, "I'm going home and I'm going to get a fucking book going with this guy if it kills me."

Groth: It's interesting how the times — I was going to say affect, but they almost dictate what's possible. Now, we published a 500-page graphic novel by an artist who is about 24.

Kupperman: You mean Dash Shaw?

Groth: Dash, yeah. He's pretty fresh out of SVA. That couldn't have existed in 1950, 1960. Simply couldn't have happened. I mean a) he wouldn't have even thought to do it, he would have done something else and b) if he did, no one would have seen it.

Jaffee: Yeah, the times have an absolute effect. If I were younger, I'd be thinking entirely differently than I think right now.

Groth: I did ask you about a week or two ago if you had a graphic novel in you.

Jaffee: He came up with a funny punch line. He said to me, "Do you have a graphic novel in you?"
And I said, "Please Gary, I'm 89 years old."
So you said, "How about a graphic short story?"
I said, "Good line." That's a funny line.
And I thought about it. I figure I could write a short story. You can do one and if you're still alive you do a second one and if you're still alive you do a third one.

Groth: There you go!

Kupperman: Scheherazade.

Jaffee: And then you put 'em all together. Right, Scheherazade. Who knows? ∎

SOCIAL HAPPENINGS AT BIRD CENTER, ILLINOIS

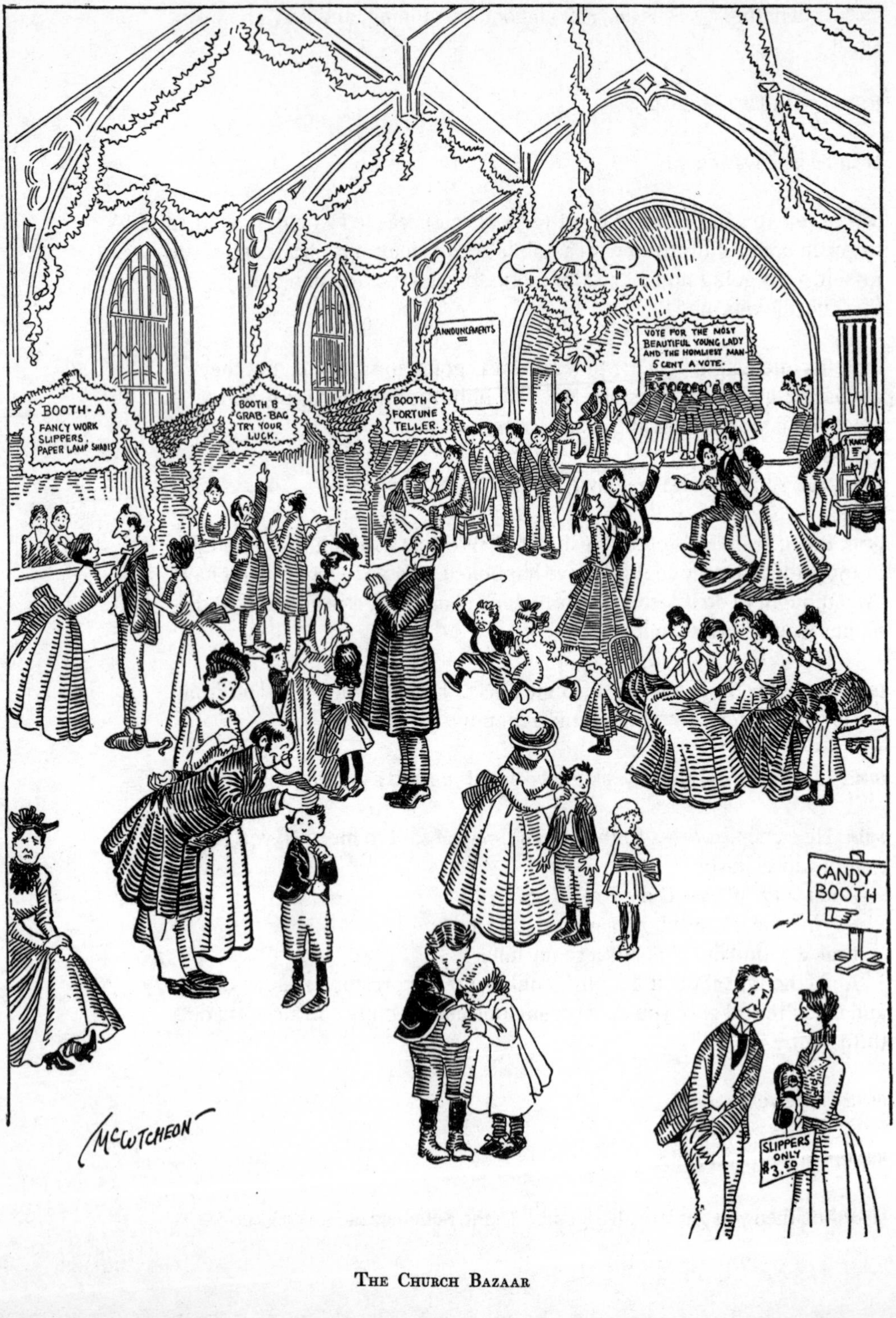
BOOTH-A
FANCY WORK
SLIPPERS,
PAPER LAMP SHADE
BOOTH B
GRAB-BAG
TRY YOUR
LUCK.
BOOTH C
FORTUNE
TELLER.
ANNOUNCEMENTS
VOTE FOR THE MOST
BEAUTIFUL YOUNG LADY
AND THE HOMLIEST MAN-
5 CENT A VOTE.
CANDY
BOOTH
SLIPPERS
ONLY
$3.50
McCUTCHEON

THE CHURCH BAZAAR

JOHN T. McCUTCHEON: A CARTOONIST AND HIS DOG

BY WARREN BERNARD

On Dec. 14, 1940, the Indiana Club of Chicago gathered to honor the birthday of one of its founding members. This was the 29th time the Hoosier diaspora met to have an evening of tribute, food, spirits and entertainment in honor of one who had left Indiana for the opportunities in Chicago. The Stevens Hotel contained the most spacious ballroom in all Chicago, if not the United States. But even with a capacity of 1,250 seated guests (forking over a then-hefty price of $12.50 apiece), almost 400 people were turned away from the largest Indiana Society dinner in its history. The dinner held that night honored the 70th birthday of world traveler, journalist, author, raconteur and *Chicago Tribune* cartoonist John Tinney McCutcheon.

The attendee list was filled with the names of politicians, plutocrats, pressmen and members of the cloth, showing McCutcheon's status in Chicago society. Seated with McCutcheon at the Speakers Table were the governors of Illinois and Indiana, Motion Picture Producer and Distributors of America head Will H. Hays, former Vice President General Charles Dawes, Notre Dame president Reverend J. Hugh O'Donnell, President Paul G. Hoffman of Studebaker Motors, along with the heads of Purdue and Indiana University, to name but a few. They dined on Treasure Island Shrimp Cocktail, named after McCutcheon's own island in the Bahamas; Cream of Bird Center Soup, paying homage to one of his most popular cartoon series; and a dessert of Glace Injun Summer à la McCutcheon, so named for his most famous cartoon.

LEFT
From McCutcheon's
Bird Center series

The Glee Club of Indiana University and Johnny Jones and his Orchestra provided the musical entertainment, featuring songs by Hoagy Carmichael and Cole Porter, both Hoosiers by birth. Will H. Hays produced a special newsreel with his friends in Hollywood, showing stock footage of such notables as President Franklin D. Roosevelt, Benito Mussolini, Charlie McCarthy and Wendell Willkie with dubbed voiceovers producing levity at the expense of McCutcheon. Joseph Stalin "said," "Comrade McCutcheon has finally seen the light and has joined the staff of *The Daily Worker*," a line that garnered laughter from the audience as McCutcheon leaned very much toward the conservative end of the political spectrum and was unlikely to work for the Communist Party paper.

Not to be outdone by the movers and shakers of the Midwest, the nation's cartoonists also paid tribute to McCutcheon. In October of 1940, the Secretary of the Indiana Society, Chester Cleveland, had started putting together what was the largest cartoon tribute to anyone, cartoonist or otherwise, since Clare Briggs left the *Chicago Tribune* for the *New York Tribune* in February, 1917. Each dinner attendee was presented with a book, bound with a bright-red spiral spine. Inside were 43 specialty pieces drawn by some of the top cartoonists of the day, all extolling the virtues, support, longevity and camaraderie of John T. McCutcheon. Fellow *Tribune* comic-strip creators Chester Gould, Harold Gray, Frank King and Fred Willard all contributed, as well as H. T. Webster, George McManus, Rube Goldberg, Fontaine Fox and Milton Caniff. The political cartoon world was represented by Jay "Ding" Darling, Daniel Fitzpatrick and McCutcheon's political cartoon brethren at the *Tribune*: Joe Parrish, Carey Orr and Carl Somdal amongst others.

After all of the festivities, it was McCutcheon's turn to give a speech. He recounted his life's journey with a short biography dispersed with humorous anecdotes. But at the end of the speech, he noted wistfully:

> I have been on hand for the greatest war, greatest panic, the greatest depression and, I suppose, the greatest political landslide. I pass lightly over jazz, jitterbugs, painted toenails, knee length skirts and hip-waist-lines.

He somberly added: "*And now we don't know where we are heading.*"

This last line was echoed in the headline for the *Chicago Tribune* the day of the dinner, which blared "Italians Flee From Egypt" as the British pushed them back across Northern Africa, giving its army a temporary respite before the arrival of General Erwin Rommel and his soon-to-be renowned

Afrika Corps. Also on Dec. 14, the U.S.S. *Hornet* was launched, the seventh carrier of the United States Navy and would carry Doolittle's bombers to its raid on Tokyo just 18 months hence.

World War II dominated the American psyche at the time, though the United States was officially neutral. Europe, save England, which had just survived The Blitz, was divided between Nazi Germany and Soviet Russia, with Japan having control over vast amounts of China. Two months prior to the dinner, the United States had instituted the first peacetime draft in the nation's history, against the opposition of isolationists in Congress. Both President Roosevelt and his Republican opponent, Wendell Willkie (himself a fellow Hoosier) had promised as part of the 1940 presidential campaign to keep the United States out of the war. Roosevelt won, reelected just five weeks before the dinner. All of this turmoil was reflected in McCutcheon's words.

MEN OF AMERICA

JOHN T. McCUTCHEON
Common Sense the keynote of his Success

The cartoon and comic world was already gearing up for war. Ham Fisher went on a tour of 36 U.S. Army camps and had his Joe Palooka entering the Army in solidarity just a few weeks before the dinner. By the following month, January 1941, Bill Holman and Fontaine Fox were both doing Army-themed cartoons. *The Flash* #14 hit the stands at around the same time, showing the Flash saving a woman and her child from a strafing German airplane, although it would be 11 months before the United States officially entered World War II.

At this time, McCutcheon's *Chicago Tribune* cartoons reflected the anti-European, isolationist editorial policies of the *Tribune's* owner, Robert "Colonel" McCormick. McCormick's stance on non-intervention in Europe and isolationism in general had its foundation in his and his father's experience in Britain and France, where both McCormicks were repeatedly snubbed by the upper classes.

McCutcheon's opinion in support of isolationism had its beginnings in a totally different set of experiences, that of being a direct witness to the

horrors of war, and in that he was more anti-war than isolationist. Mc-Cutcheon also thought that President Wilson had unnecessarily propelled the United States into World War I and felt that Roosevelt's then-current policies led, once again, the United States down the interventionist path, one with which McCutcheon did not agree.

His father had been a decorated Civil War veteran; having fought at a number of key battles and having died years after the war was over of complications from his battlefield wounds. More importantly, McCutcheon had been at the front lines of no fewer than five wars, four of which he volunteered to cover as a journalist and illustrator. His attendance at his first fateful experience in a war zone was decided by the flip of a coin in Colombo, Sri Lanka. But more important than the story of McCutcheon's life was his direct influence on no less than three branches of the cartoon/comic art tree: political cartoons, comic strips and single-panel cartoons. He also founded what has been called "The Midwestern School of Cartooning."

TOP
A spot illustration for
the *Chicago Record*

McCutcheon began a paper route in 1880 at the age of 10, and by the age of 12, he had produced his own small-town newspaper. Using the loft of the barn on the family farm as a publishing house, he and his cohort Julius

Vellinger produced the *Elston News*. McCutcheon drew the primitive cartoons and illustrations, and both boys wrote the articles. It was a one-sheet that they handed out for free to the neighbors. He and Vellinger also had a painting enterprise: They would paint not only houses and carriages, but any signs needed for local businesses.

In 1884, when he was 14, he covered local Elston news for one of the main newspapers of Tippicanoe County, *The Lafyaette Call*. His writing and creativity were not limited to the local newspaper. McCutcheon also wrote two plays, *The Blunders of a Bashful Dude* and *Grimes County Grocery*. McCutcheon, Vellinger and some of their friends created the Elston Comedy Company, which included McCutcheon's younger brother Ben, who produced the plays. They printed up handbills for the Elston locals, and enlisted a small musical ensemble to entertain audiences before and after their performances.

Early on McCutcheon hungered for adventure, fed by stories both real and imagined. His father, John Barr McCutcheon, known as Barr to his friends, was a captain in the Union Army. He was one of the organizers of the Indiana Volunteers and the McCutcheon home became a meeting place for Civil War veterans. Barr was a natural raconteur and McCutcheon heard many tales of that conflict from his father and his father's friends. McCutcheon was an impressionable 6-year-old when stories of the 1876 defeat of General Custer at Little Big Horn and other battles with Native Americans circulated through the Midwest. Later, he recalled these stories of "Indians" in one of his most well known cartoons: "Injun Summer."

His voracious reading habit also fueled this sense of adventure: *"I was devoted to The Boys and Girls of New York and New York Weekly, both adventure publications full of exciting sea stories, pirate tales, trapping and Indian fights and some detective yarns."*

This was supplemented by reading Homer's *The Iliad*, Horatio Alger and, of course, Mark Twain's *Tom Sawyer*. This sense of adventure led McCutcheon down somewhat of a dark path. He and Vellinger joined a gang of Elston young men and boys, who squared off on occasion with a local Irish gang. He got into at least one gang fight that included the use of pistols and rocks. After getting hit by a stone, he quickly retreated back to his house.

Clarissa McCutcheon, known as Clara, summarized McCutcheon's activities while a young boy as only a mother could in an interview in 1909:

"He was a nice boy, but he was bad."

His father Barr was a drover, taking livestock from the farms to the markets. During an economic downtourn in 1876, his father worked for a year at the then seven-year-old Purdue University, where he ran the commissary. From 1877 to 1879, he was the assistant sheriff of Tippacanoe County and in 1885, the year McCutcheon entered Purdue, his father was elected Sheriff. The McCutcheon family, John, his older brother George, a younger brother Ben and a sister Jessie, all moved to Lafayette to live right next door to the jail. The young McCutcheon was exposed to the more unsavory characters in northwestern Indiana while helping his father with his job. He had a certain sympathy for a number of prisoners, as some were down on their luck and some had succumbed to the bottle, but there were also those who were just criminals and McCutcheon learned the difference.

One day after feeding the inmates breakfast, he was taking them back to their cells. One of them pushed John aside, shut the door behind him and ran down the street. A fast-thinking McCutcheon quickly locked up the other prisoners, grabbed a .22 pistol, and took off after the escapee. He chased the prisoner through the streets of Lafayette while firing a few shots along the way, to the amazement of the bystanders. McCutcheon recaptured the prisoner when a man in the street ran into the escapee and held on to him. The next day, the local papers ran an article about the incident, citing the young McCutcheon as a cool-thinking hero.

Most of the elements that would serve McCutcheon throughout his life were in place by the time he was a freshman at Purdue in 1885. He had a sense of wonder of the world, a love of drawing, reading and writing, a profound sense of right and wrong, a need for adventure and a tolerance of people in different social and economic situations.

TOP
George Ade and
John T. McCutcheon
at Purdue; photo-
graph reproduced
from McCutcheon's
birthday booklet.

When he entered Purdue University in the Fall of 1885, George Ade, head of the local Sigma Chi chapter, saw that McCutcheon, in his fashionable waistcoat, stood out in the crowd. Ade recruited McCutcheon to Sigma Chi, to which Milton Caniff and Fontaine Fox later pledged. Both Ade and Sigma Chi would remain close to McCutcheon's heart for the rest of his life.

But McCutcheon had not shed all of his "bad boy" spirit. He was temporarily thrown off the campus newspaper, the *Purdue Debris*, for publishing an unauthorized edition. Ade and McCutcheon were reprimanded for visiting The Ladies Society without permission. McCutcheon's unexplained absences from the local Corps Cadets led to his dismissal from that military organization. An entry from his diary about a party in 1888 gives a window into the mind of the somewhat antiauthoritarian McCutcheon: *"After the old folks and the profs had left, some indulged in dancing, which is a very serious crime in the eyes of many. Miss Murray & self started it."*

While at school, he was a social butterfly. He attended a good number of parties and picnics, dutifully recording them in the extensive diaries he began to keep in 1888. McCutcheon wrote and performed in plays, and attended any literary events that came through the Purdue area. He practiced drawing, although he sought fewer outlets for this passion during his days in Purdue than he did for his writing. He preferred to write, and submitted a manuscript to Frank Leslie Publications, which they rejected. McCutcheon continued with the *Lafayette Call* as a special reporter, giving the *Call* the minutia of life on the Purdue campus as opposed to Elston.

McCutcheon was not the only member of the family to have literary aspirations. His older brother George Barr McCutcheon became a renowned playwright and novelist, as well as a newspaperman. Several of his novels were translated into films, amongst them *Brewster's Millions*.

A few months before his graduation in 1889, John McCutcheon received offers from both the Lafayette *Journal* and the *Courier*. Both papers needed someone immediately, but taking either job would jeopardize his graduation. McCutcheon rejected both offers and graduated in June 1889.

After graduation, McCutcheon left to find a job in Chicago, as the previous offers were filled and no newspaper-related jobs were available in Lafayette. Hearing that drawing jobs were easier to find than writing ones on the Chicago papers, he sought a position as an illustrator. Armed with a letter of recommendation from the owner of a local bookstore, he visited a Sigma Chi brother on the Chicago *Herald*, illustrator and cartoonist Horace Taylor. The Sigma Chi connection was already paying off for McCutcheon.

Taylor reviewed his work, and suggested that McCutcheon practice some more. He followed his frat brother's recommendation. He returned to Chicago in October 1889. Taylor took the aspiring McCutcheon across the street to Victor Lawson's *Chicago Daily News*, where Taylor had previously worked.

William Schmedtgen was the entire art department of the *Daily News* and needed help. McCutcheon was hired for $16 a week, which Lawson said he would increase to $20 a week if he improved, which McCutcheon did. Schmedtgen put him to work right away. In the days before halftone engraving allowed photographs to be reproduced, illustrators created the pictures that ran with the news. One of the first illustration assignments that McCutcheon received was the opening of Louis Sullivan's masterpiece, the Auditorium Theater.

In these early days in Chicago, McCutcheon wrote his friend George Ade about working there. Ade finally agreed, and in June 1890, procured a job as a writer on the *Morning Daily News*. They found a room together for $5 a week in the South Side of Chicago, Michigan Avenue and Peck Court. Within a short walk of their room was Dead Man's Alley and the rest of Chicago's Hell's Half Acre, replete with its thieves, prostitutes and saloons. "The Mickey Finn" drink was later invented not far from that room.

McCutcheon illustrated the 1892 Democratic Convention in Chicago as well as the building of the 1893 Chicago World's Fair, also known as The World's Columbian Exposition. For that fair, Ade and McCutcheon formed a team, with Ade writing and McCutcheon illustrating. The column they produced, "All Roads Lead to the World's Fair," was well received. Both men earned accolades.

At this time McCutcheon was a straight illustrator; he admired the work of C.J. Taylor of *Puck* magazine and emulated a realist school of illustration. He excelled at street scenes and buildings. In 1893, some of his work was exhibited at the Art Institute of Chicago, of which McCutcheon was particularly proud. He had two cartoons printed in *Puck*, for which he earned the princely sum of $3.

When the Fair was over, Charles Dennis, the managing editor of the *Morning News*, now named the *Chicago Record*, decided to give the two of them a new beat. He gave them a column called "Stories of the Streets and of the Town." Their assignment was to go out and report on anything they wanted. At first, they hung around the local police station and McCutcheon immediately made friends with the local constabulary. They then branched out across Chicago, writing about the poor, the rich and the ethnic neighborhoods. Every year from 1893-1898, the *Chicago Record* put out a collection of their work under the same title as the column, with an illustrated cover by McCutcheon.

By 1894, both McCutcheon and Ade received a lot of recognition for their work on "Stories of the Streets and Towns." First, they were offered $60 a week to work for the rival *Chicago Times*. Then, they caught the eye of William Randolph Hearst, who offered them $80 a week to come over to his papers. Although this was a substantial increase over the $25 a week they received from Victor Lawson, noted penny-pinching owner of the *Chicago Record*, they did not approve of the way that Hearst presented the news. They preferred to remain with Lawson, who was so moral about his newspaper that at that time he refused to publish on Sundays. Lawson also refused the advertising of anyone whom he believed was deceptive about their products; he felt this reflected poorly on his paper and did not want the public associating the *Record* with flim-flam artists and snake-oil salesmen.

But this interest by Hearst and the rival *Times* did generate an additional $10 raise to $35 a week from Lawson. Ade suggested that the two of them save the $10 a week and go to Europe, which both of them wanted to do. McCutcheon agreed to this, and a year later, they had reached their goal of $500.

When McCutcheon and Ade went to Lawson in early 1895 to tell him that they were going to take a trip to Europe, Lawson said he would continue to pay their salaries if they sent home two illustrated stories a week.

Off they went, leaving in April 1895, both of them heading out of the United States for the first time. The two rural Hoosier boys started out in London, where according to Ade, McCutcheon's propensity for standing out in a crowd caused a minor sensation when McCutcheon insisted on wearing a fedora, instead of the required silk top hat then in vogue. He found himself the center of attention wherever he went with that hat. After London, they went to Belgium, Germany, Switzerland, Italy and then Paris, their last stop on the Continent.

Paris was on the last leg of their tour before returning to London and then home. McCutcheon went to the Moulin Rouge, the Black Cat (Le Chat Noir) and other nightclubs in Montmartre. He was exposed to the rich art promoting those establishments, and bought posters as well as some books to take back to Chicago as examples. The influence of the Parisian posters and the Art Nouveau movement became readily apparent upon his return to Chicago. His advertisement for Ade's "Pink Marsh" stories were clearly influenced by Jules Cheret and Henri Toulouse-Lautrec, as well as the covers he did for the yearly softbound compilation issues by the *Record* of "Stories of the Streets and of the Town" and calendars for the Lakeside Press.

Not only did his illustration work begin to change after returning from Europe, his political cartoons, running on the front page of the *Record* since 1889, were also undergoing significant artistic changes as he began

GET READY FOR THE LAST ASSORTMENT OF CAMPAIGN LIES.

to embrace a cartoon aesthetic. George Ade recalled, in 1940, how McCutcheon had long disdained the extremes of cartooning.

> McCutcheon had no desire to be a cartoonist. He wanted to be an illustrator; he was a realist and simply wanted to picture people as he saw them. In fact, he resented and resisted as long as possible the burlesque and exaggeration necessarily implied in cartooning.

The Presidential election of 1896 gave McCutcheon the forum upon which to experiment outside his illustrative political cartoons, and in fact, outside the relative norm of the political cartoon of the day. In 1896, the typical newspaper political cartoon utilized extreme crosshatching, not having changed much in that respect from the heyday of Thomas Nast's attacks on Boss Tweed and Tammany Hall 25 years prior. McCutcheon's contemporaries, including Charles Nelan and Homer Davenport, used garish exaggeration coupled with the fine crosshatch to promote their ideas at this time. McCutcheon never succumbed to the use of garish exaggeration, though as an illustrator he did utilize fine crosshatching.

McCutcheon used the "Big Head" school of political cartooning, popularized by the weekly magazines *Judge* and *Puck* (which McCutcheon did read), *The Minneapolis Journal*'s Charles "Bart" Bartholomew, who was widely reprinted by other newspapers and magazines of the day.

In 1896, McCutcheon began to abandon the dense crosshatching of Bartholomew, Nelan and Davenport, and set off in a different direction. During the 1896 campaign his cartoons had a sparser look than those of his contemporaries. He picked up from influential British cartoonist Phil May the use of a simple outline for the body, with a fully realized head to complete the figure. He imitated May's use of a heavier line, used to fill in just key areas of the cartoon, usually the clothing of the main figures. May dropped out any semblance of foreground or floor, which McCutcheon emulated, giving the impression that his figures were suspended in mid-air.

McCutcheon also drew cartoons that used only the outline of the figures, with no shading and minimal facial detail. This echoed the work of the English cartoonist Richard Doyle, who worked for *Punch* in the 1840s through 1860s and whose books were still in print at the time McCutcheon was working. Doyle had a style that used very little to no crosshatching or shading to show light, fabric, or shadows. This was most apparent in McCutcheon's cartoon of October 27, 1896 entitled "A Few of the Surface

Indications in Chicago That the Closing Week of the National Canvass Has Arrived." It contains over 30 drawn figures, but whereas just a year earlier they would all have had faces, detailed clothing, and shadows, this cartoon was executed in just outline.

McCutcheon experimented with utilizing multiple panels or multiple scenes in his cartoons. The *Puck* and *Judge* cartoonists used this technique extensively, and in previous decades multiple panels and scenes were typical in American political cartooning. For the most part, the front-page newspaper political cartoons of the 1890s consisted of a single-panel/scene cartoon. Going against the then-current trend, McCutcheon used multiple panels to show before and after, as well as comparing people and events. One example of this was his cartoon of Sept. 12, 1896, titled "Another of the Lightning Changes in Politics." The cartoon has two panels, the first shows a banner of President Grover Cleveland and his Vice President Adlai Stevenson smiling and facing one another. The next panel shows the two of them fighting and the banner in disarray. McCutcheon used multiple panels extensively in the 1896 campaign and throughout the remainder of his career.

Besides experimenting visually with his political cartoons, McCutcheon had a different tone and temperament in presenting issues on the front page of the *Chicago Record*. The political cartoon world in McCutcheon's time had the ability to influence the political process. One example was Thomas Nast's attacks on Tammany Hall's William M. "Boss" Tweed, which led to Tweed's arrest in December 1871. Puck's tattooing of Republican presidential nominee James Blaine with his and his party's sins greatly aided Democrat Grover Cleveland's victory in the 1884 presidential election. Political cartoonists of the day saw their role as shapers of political opinion by the fiercest artistic voice possible.

But McCutcheon did not subscribe to utilizing invective. Unlike most of his political cartoonist peers, he eschewed the attack cartoon, preferring a gentler approach to making his political point. McCutcheon elaborated on his philosophy in 1903: "*In nine cases out of 10, in my opinion, the cartoon that is charged with malice or venom might just as well be left undrawn, so far as the beneficial effect on the public goes.*"

On Aug. 20, 1896, the *Record* published a single-panel cartoon featuring a little dog sitting on a book in the foreground. The next day McCutcheon drew a two-panel cartoon showing contrasting views of how the Democratic headquarters appeared. The dog was repeated again in the second

John T. McCutcheon
June 8 - 1903 -

panel, just sitting in the foreground and not necessarily paying attention to what was going in the cartoon. On the 22nd of August, McCutcheon used the dog again and then stopped.

Letters started to arrive at the *Chicago Record*:

> "Will you kindly tell me what the dog in all your cartoons on Bryan signifies?"

> "Will you please tell me what the dog on the first-page cut is meant to represent? It has been a conundrum to your patrons here for some time, and they have requested me to write you."

> "So many people ask 'What does Mack put that dog in his cartoons for? What does it represent and of which is it characteristic?' Please tell me this and I will be very much obliged."

McCutcheon admitted that he was just doodling, just looking for something to use up space in the cartoon. But the public saw something they liked in the dog and it caused a Midwest sensation. Coupled with Outcault's *Yellow Kid*, which premiered in color just a year before, newspaper cartoons were now showing a widening popularity and the ability to generate what is now called media buzz.

The more McCutcheon used the dog, the more letters came in, which eventually numbered in the thousands. Pretty much every cartoon he did during October 1896 contained his little canine. When the election was over, he stopped using the dog, as in McCutcheon's mind the campaign was over and ergo the life of the dog was over.

But much to McCutcheon's surprise, even more letters came in demanding the return of the dog. A letter dated Nov. 7, 1896 from Blacque Wilson on the staff of the *Toledo Bee*, summarized the emotion of his public at the loss of the dog: "Lost — One mongrel cur dog, strayed or stolen from the front page of the *Record*. Finder please return and no questions asked. We have missed him."

The letters came from all over the Midwest. McCutcheon was riding a wave of popularity, not just on his inadvertent creation, but also a wave created by the business acumen of Victor Lawson, owner of the *Chicago Record*. There was no real large-scale syndication of cartoons in 1896, save the political cartoons of Charles Nelan and in that case, it was only to a small number of newspapers. The great newspaper empires of Hearst, Scripps, Pulitzer and others only had a handful of newspapers in which to distribute their content. Although reprinting popular cartoons was widespread, the *Chicago Record* was one of the earliest known daily newspapers to have a wide geographic distribution, due to Lawson's planning.

Over two decades before the *Chicago Tribune* became the main newspaper of the Midwest, Victor Lawson had set out the same goals for his newspaper, the *Chicago Daily News*. It had two editions, one in the morning and one in the evening. In 1888, after buying out his partner Melville Stone, Lawson sought to increase the profitability of the morning paper.

Even though his newspapers had the same name, the two papers had separate staffs and separate sales teams for advertising. The *Morning News* had a circulation of about 22,000, the evening edition about 120,000. The sales teams for the morning paper were telling him that because local advertisers were already in the evening edition, they saw no reason for their ads to appear in the morning edition. Lawson responded with one of the most innovative business solutions in the newspaper world at that time.

The *Morning News* had four competitors, each selling for a newsstand price of two cents apiece. Lawson planned to cut that amount to a penny to help spur on increased circulation. In order to increase the sales focus on national advertisers, Lawson undertook a secret plan to expand the geographic circulation of the *Morning News* well beyond the confines of Chicago.

Writing all the ad copy himself, Lawson put together a series of posters, advertisements, circulars and postcards that he wanted to be sent to all the 455 targeted cities and towns, and McKinney handled the printing in secret from Philadelphia. More than 1 million postcards were printed, and even more circulars were created for distribution at train stations and on the streets.

He launched the campaign in July 1888 and the results exceeded Lawson's expectations. Circulation increased from 32,000 in July to about 98,000 a day by early September. But Lawson was not finished creating a separate identity for his morning paper. In May 1892, he changed the name to the *News Record* and followed this up a year later in March 1893 by finally calling it the *Chicago Record*.

So by the time McCutcheon's dog arrived in August 1896, the *Chicago Record* was arguably the most widely distributed morning newspaper in the Midwest, with a circulation of over 250,000 across a dozen states. As a comparison, the *Chicago Tribune* would not reach such circulation numbers until the election coverage leading up to World War I, nearly 20 years later. Whereas some New York papers had a daily circulation much greater than that of the *Record*, its geographic distribution footprint was beyond compare for its time. This geographic foundation in the Midwest would be the springboard for McCutcheon's greatest cartoon work, which was still to come and would spawn a number of artists who emulated him.

McCutcheon frequently used the dog in his cartoons as an impartial observer; he made no comment either by action or word balloon on the cartoon. This reflected on McCutcheon, whom people viewed as more impartial than his contemporaries, because of his lack of vicious attack against those with whom he disagreed.

The public also saw in the dog a friend. In the rural Midwest, dogs were a common sight on farms: small shopkeepers kept dogs to watch over their stores in the days before alarm systems. People in the Midwest identified immediately with McCutcheon's observant but nonjudgmental dog.

The popularity of McCutcheon's canine creation cast a long shadow. It did not take long before other political cartoonists had a dog mascot or another mascot of their own. Rowland Bowman of the *Minneapolis Journal* used a dog not long after McCutcheon developed his, though Bowman's dog made farcical asides about the politics in the cartoon. Clifford Berryman used a teddy bear, after Teddy Roosevelt, as his mascot until he died in 1949. Leo O'Mealia, the Golden Age cover artist and single-panel cartoonist, used a lion next to his signature in his cartoons. And today, Pat Oliphant has as his mascot, and muse, a little penguin — all of these are direct descendants of McCutcheon's dog.

Later, McCutcheon featured the dog prominently in his non-political, slice-of-life cartoons. But well before this occurred, he grew tired of drawing the dog. In a speech to the Space Club on Dec. 28, 1904 he voiced his frustration:

People had ignored carefully studied cartoons in which I had employed
a great earnestness of thought and had been captivated by the dog.
In fact, my sole claim to fame was due to that accidental foolish little
dog. Everywhere I went, people would say when they learned my name,
"Oh, are you the fellow who drew the dog?" Finally things became so
serious that to escape the dog I decided to go away.

McCutcheon found the opportunity to leave the dog behind in August 1897 when his friend Edward Harden, a financial writer on the *Chicago Post*, contacted him. Harden's brother-in-law was Frank Vanderlip, the Assistant Secretary of the Treasury. Vanderlip had called Harden about taking a trip on a new Treasury Department ship, the *Revenue Cutter McCulloch*, which was scheduled to leave the East Coast and go around the world to join the Pacific Fleet, as the Panama Canal had not yet been built. Vanderlip asked Harden who he wanted to bring on the trip and Harden selected McCutcheon. Lawson agreed to let McCutcheon go not only as an illustrator, but also as a reporter.

The *McCulloch* prepared to sail to the Pacific via the Suez Canal, around India and Southeast Asia. It finally left Baltimore on January 8, 1898 with McCutcheon on board. He would not see the United States again for over two-and-a-half years. After a rough trip across the Atlantic, the ship made stops in Gibraltar, Tangier and Morocco, before stopping in Malta. In Malta, the captain of the McCulloch received a telegram that the battleship Maine had been destroyed in Manila harbor.

After the ship went through the Suez Canal it headed for Colombo in what is now Sri Lanka (then called Ceylon). There, Harden and McCutcheon had an opportunity to get off the *McCulloch* and sail to Bombay, India. They debated quite a bit, taking into account they would be getting closer to the developing trouble in the Philippines, but also wishing to visit India.

A coin flip had them remain on the *McCulloch*, a fateful decision if there ever was one. When they reached Singapore, it was here they learned that the *McCulloch* had been transferred to the Navy Department and was to sail immediately to Hong Kong to join Admiral Dewey's fleet in anticipation of war with the Spanish.

On April 27, 1898, Admiral Dewey and the Pacific fleet, which now included the *McCulloch* on which McCutcheon remained a passenger, set sail from China to engage the Spanish in Manila Bay. At midnight on April 30, the fleet slipped past the coastal batteries guarding the

entrance to Manila. One of the coastal batteries took a shot at the *Mc-Culloch* and missed. McCutcheon watched the two and a half hour battle from the deck, making detailed notes and sketches in his daybook, now working as a war correspondent. Almost half a century later, he wrote in his biography:

> "The Battle of Manila was, if course, the peak of my war experiences.
> In its historic significance it was the greatest single event of my life."

There were no telegraph facilities in Manila, so McCutcheon and Harden (who was engaged by the *New York World*) had to wait until they were in Hong Kong to send their stories back to the United States. Unknown to McCutcheon, Harden sent his dispatch "Urgent" at a cost in 1898 dollars of $9.90 a word. It reached the *New York World* well ahead of McCutcheon's story. James Keeley, the *Tribune's* managing editor, had placed a *Chicago Tribune* correspondent in the *New York World's* office in wise anticipation. Keeley's man was playing poker with members of the staff of the *World*, when the call came in about Harden's Manila dispatch. He quickly passed the news on to Chicago. As a result, the *Chicago Tribune* became the first paper in the United States to report about Dewey's victory. Not only had McCutcheon and his *Chicago Record* been scooped, but Admiral Dewey had been scooped as well, because his report had not yet reached Washington. It was Keeley who called the White House early that morning to tell President McKinley of Dewey's accomplishment.

TOP
The first appearance of McCutcheon's signature little dog

298

McCutcheon's initial dispatch was printed in a number of newspapers, including the *Tribune*, and the *New York Journal*, after which Hearst again offered McCutcheon a job, one that that he quickly turned down. McCutcheon was displeased that his dispatch was not the first in print and he felt it was badly reworked when it was finally printed. Half a century later he was still disappointed as he wrote in his memoirs:

"The fate of my own dispatch, however, is one of the sorest points in my life. The editor of the Record, Mr. Dennis, was not so alert as Mr. Keeley. In fact, he was asleep out in Buena Park when my commercial dispatch began coming in. There was no one on hand except a night police reporter and he did not know what to do with it."

McCutcheon's later dispatches, along with his illustrations, covered the blockade of Manila, the surrender of the Spanish and the transition of the Philippines to American control, were printed by newspapers nationwide. The Spanish-American War turned McCutcheon from a regional cartoonist and illustrator into a nationally recognized journalist and foreign correspondent.

Lawson gave McCutcheon an assignment to recruit cable correspondents in the Far East. As Lawson's agent, McCutcheon went to Ceylon, Singapore, Hong Kong and Saigon to interview and hire applicants. He eventually found himself in Bombay, India, where he went on an adventure to walk in the steps of one of his favorite writers, Rudyard Kipling. In those footsteps, he traced a path to Lahore, Peshawar, the Khyber Pass, and into what is modern-day Afghanistan. During his journey, he wrote and illustrated stories in a series that the *Chicago Record* called "Notes From Foreign Lands."

When the Philippine insurrection began in February 1899, McCutcheon sailed for the Philippines to cover the story for the *Record* and whatever other newspapers would pick up his dispatches. Unlike the Spanish-American War, McCutcheon was on the ground with the Army locked in land battles against insurrectionists using guerilla tactics. He was in the front lines and found himself under fire a number of times as he followed the Army across the Philippines.

He left the Philippines in August 1899 to continue hiring correspondents for the *Record* and traveled to China and Japan. A few more months of travel coupled with some business kept him busy there before he returned to the Philippines to continue covering the Philippine Insurrection, and eventually the final surrender of the insurgents.

McCutcheon was in no real rush to go home. His boss, Victor Lawson, also saw no need for McCutcheon to return to his duties in Chicago, as he wrote to McCutcheon in February, 1900: "I will not suggest any definite date for your return, but will leave that to be determined by the course of the events in the Philippines, and by your own personal preferences. ....You have done us excellent service, and I shall be glad to show my appreciation of it by meeting your wishes respecting the time of your home-coming."

In that same letter, Lawson also revealed that the *Record* actively syndicated McCutcheon's articles:

> "We are slowly building up a syndicate for the use of *The Record*'s foreign news, and you will be interested to know that your very good story of the Battle of Tilad Pass was printed in full in the *Philadelphia Press* and the *Pittsburg Post*, and to the extent of nearly a page in the *New York Herald*."

McCutcheon finally left the Philippines in April 1900 and set off for South Africa to cover the Boer War. As the war concluded, he traveled through Mozambique, Zanzibar, Aden and back through the Suez Canal before visiting Paris and London. He arrived back in the United States in August 1900.

Though he was away for over two years, the famous dog of whom he tried to escape with his travels found a way to haunt him. In an anecdote he recited many times in speeches and articles, he recounted an incident in the Philippines:

> One day out in the jungle I came upon a tired soldier, resting under a tree and we came to talking of 'God's Country.' When I casually introduced myself he started up with a glad look in his eye and said 'You're not the man that drew the dog, are you?'

McCutcheon returned to the front page of the *Chicago Record* with his daily cartoon on Sept. 11, 1900. He arrived back in the United States just in time to cover the presidential election, a rematch between Democrat William Jennings Bryan and the Republican incumbent William McKinley. As he did in the 1896 campaign, McCutcheon again lampooned Bryan and his Free Silver campaign. This lampooning did not affect them on a personal basis. Four years later, Bryan wrote to say what a fan he was of McCutcheon's cartoons and as Secretary of State under President Woodrow Wilson, Bryan wrote a letter of recommendation for McCutcheon when he visited the front lines in World War I.

On Dec. 19, 1900, after a speech to the Chicago Athletic Club, McCutcheon woke up in the middle of the night, "...*feeling as if a sword had been run through my lungs.*" He received a diagnosis of double pneumonia, and in those days before antibiotics, there was not much they could do. When he became worse, it generated a rumor, reprinted in national newspapers, that he had died. Instead, a private railroad car took him to recuperate in Asheville, N. C.

Between December 1900 and February 1901, papers in St. Louis, New York, St Paul Boston, Baltimore and Washington, D.C., showed the nationwide concern for McCutcheon's severe illness by publishing reports of his relocation to Asheville.

Once in North Carolina, he improved somewhat, but then took a turn for the worse again, as again in his words, "*various malaria bugs from the Orient put in an appearance.*" At his low ebb, he only weighed 85 pounds. He spent the next 10 months in Asheville, where he continued to receive his weekly salary of $60. In a pang of guilt, McCutcheon told Lawson to stop paying him, as he was not working.

In his biography, McCutcheon states he returned to work in September 1901, however his first cartoon in the *Record* since he had taken ill did not appear until Nov. 12, 1901.

HOW MARTIN B. MADDEN WOULD LOOK IN THE SENATORIAL SHOES OF JOHN A. LOGAN.

The Enterprising Daily Paper

Prior to his re-emergence on the front page of the *Chicago Record*, on Nov. 9, a small article ran on Page 3 of the *Record*. It contained the headline "Plans to Learn from Chicago — France likely to establish an Industrial School In This City." The article spoke about how the French were looking to create a school so that their students can learn from the United States and hopefully reproduce in France the dynamism that was then the world's fastest-growing economy. This would provide McCutcheon with the inspiration for one of his early cartoon series.

On Nov. 14, McCutcheon unveiled the cartoon "The French Emissary Visits The U.S. To Study Industrial Methods." The second in the series was printed on Monday Nov. 18 and the series ran every Monday for the next three months. The article gave McCutcheon the idea to expand the venue for his cartoons. Whereas prior to this he was just responding to the events of the day, with the occasional social-commentary cartoon thrown in, this allowed him to take a much broader view of society as a whole. In this series, he lampooned land speculators, women shopping at remnant sales, lazy city inspectors, overcrowded transportation systems and even the rival Chicago *Examiner*, owned by William Randolph Hearst.

McCutcheon started to look at the rhythms and romantic view of home life, as well as the interplay of husband and wife, even though he remained a confirmed bachelor. An early attempt in this area was his cartoon of Nov. 15, 1901 that has the title "Is Man Happier than Woman? Sarah Grand Says That He Is." He responded to Grand's 1900 pamphlet "The Art of Happiness," in which she argued that men were happier than women. McCutcheon depicted women having the better of it, with such observations as "Man has the option of proposing marriage but — Woman has the last word."

In addition to changing his focus away from strictly political cartoons, upon his return McCutcheon transformed his drawing style. Gone were the fine lines and open spaces of his earlier political-cartoon style. Instead, he used dense blacks with fully realized figures, rich in detail down to different fabric patterns on peoples' clothing. He began to use the bird's-eye view showing crowded street scenes, which echoed his contemporary Fred Richardson, who had drawn similar scenes for Lawson's evening paper, the *Chicago Daily News*, about the time McCutcheon left for the Philippines. Faces of children, in particular, became more lifelike and innocent, although he still retained caricature for the politicians. A number of the little boys he drew were based on McCutcheon — autobiographical projections into his cartoons. He exhibited care in these drawings, providing a level of detail that clearly combined his deeply illustrative work of the 1890s with a newer aesthetic that was a little more cartoony, had more blacks and density of figures, with a liberal use of signage on buildings to establish a sense of place and parody.

On April 22, 1902, the *Record* ran a front-page McCutcheon cartoon depicting a country boy surrounded by dogs and carrying a fishing pole as he walked alongside a fence. He held another dog — McCutcheon's signature dog — with a smile on his face. He says in the caption, "Gee, don't this spring weather make a feller feel grand!" Thus began his influential and long-running cartoon series about the travails and joys of a small-town boy, which proved to be widely influential. Clare Briggs' most famous and long-running cartoon series, "When A Feller Needs A Friend" and "Ain't It A Grand and Glorious Feeling," later echoed this caption, consciously or not. Briggs became the most artful disciple of McCutcheon's slice-of-life approach, which in early 1902 was still developing.

McCutcheon had channeled his boyhood experiences, along with his love for Mark Twain's works (he had read and relished *Tom Sawyer* back in Indiana and later attended Twain's 70th birthday party in December 1905), to create a cartoon infused with the rural, small-town life that dominated his most successful works. He followed his initial celebration of spring with another on Monday, April 28, titled "A Boy in Springtime – No. 2," thus naming McCutcheon's newest cartoon series. The cartoon shows the same boy, surrounded again by dogs, kicking off his shoes, as he says, "Hi Jing! Barefoot agin. I'll bet old Rockefeller hain't no happier'n I am now." These cartoons were showing not only the joy of being a young boy, but of life outside the big city.

Whereas McCutcheon was channeling his boyhood, he was also representing rural America in a way that cartoonists had never done before. Prior to McCutcheon, cartoonists tended to treat the farmers and small towns that populated rural America derisively. They portrayed rural folks as slack-jawed yokels, a little slow on the uptake, as typified by Frederick Opper's

" *Some day she'll be sorry she treated me this away. I'll go 'way and make lots o' money and come back here riding in a carriage with four white horses, and when she tries to hatch my eye I'll pretend I never seen her before.*"

THE PIRATE CHIEFTAIN — " *We're Surrounded by perils. Behind Us is a Herd of Wild Buffaloes, on One Side Is an Unfriendly Shore Swarming with Hostile Natives, and in Front of Us Are Breakers and Deadly Reptiles.*"

"Howson Lott" series that ran in *Puck*. Cartoonists perpetuated this view in single-panel cartoons in *Life*, *Puck* and *Judge*, all urban magazines. McCutcheon turned the single-panel cartoon into something with which his rural, Midwest readership could identify. This identity represented not only the nostalgia of McCutcheon's Indiana upbringing, but also life in the Midwest and in most of the United States. The census of 1900 reported that the inhabitants of the United States were 60 percent rural and 40 percent urban. Not until the census of 1920 would the United States be predominantly an urban nation.

The Boy in Springtime series ran through May 1902; in June, he turned to The Boy in Summertime. Both The Boy in Fall-time and The Boy in Winter-time followed, creating a yearlong series. It was immensely popular, and postcards, calendars and other merchandise were created to cash in on the phenomena. So well-loved was the series, that as late as 1944, the *Chicago Tribune* (for which he would later work) printed a special color calendar in their Sunday edition using his *Boy in ...* cartoons.

THE CHIEF OF THE INDIAN FIGHTERS — "Don't cry, they're not real Indians — they're only cornstalks. We're just pretending they're Indians. Come on, you'll never make an Indian fighter if you act this away."

A LETTER TO SANTY

In February 1902, Prince Henry of Prussia made a tour of the United States. Starting on February 25, at the urging of his colleagues at the *Record*, Mc-Cutcheon abandoned all other topics to focus on Prince Henry's trip. He chronicled Henry's travels, showing him in each city he visited, in his own cartoon style. These were his densest, most elaborate cartoons to date. He worked six to eight hours each day on his cartoons, which continued daily until March 7, with Prince Henry leaving the Unites States — and the front page of the *Record* — on March 11.

McCutcheon met the prince upon his arrival in Chicago, and the originals for these cartoons wound up hanging in the prince's castle in Kiel, Germany. The *Record*, recognizing the uniqueness of this series, pulled together the first collection of McCutcheon's cartoons into a booklet called *The Cartoons That Made Prince Henry Famous*.

In early 1903, McCutcheon signed a book deal with the A.C. McClurg & Co. to publish a book of his cartoons. The book, titled simply *Cartoons by*

ENTERTAINING PRINCE HENRY—A LITTLE EXHIBITION OF DEMO-
CRATIC SIMPLICITY AT A NEW YORK LUNCHEON.

McCutcheon, was published on May 2, 1903. With an introduction by his old friend George Ade, the book was a critical and commercial success. It remained so popular that it stayed in print for nine years, with the final edition published in 1912.

In early 1903, the *Chicago Tribune* came calling. It was not the comic/cartoon powerhouse of later day. It was behind the times, a slow adopter to the comic phenomenon that had occupied New York and other cities' newspapers. This reflected the conservative nature of Robert Patterson, who took over the *Tribune* upon the death of its founder, Joseph Medill, in 1899. Robert Patterson, as well as his competitor Victor Lawson, viewed the comics as a vulgar reflection of the lowest form of the art of the newspaper, the sensationalist and yellow journalism techniques of Pulitzer and Hearst.

In November 1901, the *Tribune* finally joined the modern age by printing a separate comic section. Its four pages were filled with second-rate strips and a page that looked like *Puck* or *Judge*, a series of one-panel, mainly upper-class cartoons with some jokes. Its political cartoonist at the time was Louis Dalrymple, the great *Puck* cartoonist who had seen better days. Dalrymple also contributed to the Sunday comic section, drawing large single-panel cartoons. By early 1903, Dalrymple had left, leaving the editorial cartoon slot empty on the front page, and a void in the Sunday Section, which needed to be filled.

James Keeley, who had helped to scoop McCutcheon and the *Record* on the Battle of Manila Bay, was still the managing editor of the *Tribune* in 1903. Keeley sought to upgrade the comics of the *Tribune* and began in March 1903 with the introduction of Gene Carr's "Lady Bountiful" to the Sunday comic section. This followed in April with the addition of Outcault's successful *Buster Brown*. But Keeley had also set his sights on getting McCutcheon to the *Tribune* to replace the now empty editorial cartoon spot on the front page.

McCutcheon attributes Keeley's interest in him to the series he did, *The French Minister in the U.S.* and *The Boy in Springtime*. But Keeley was really after McCutcheon's widely dispersed readership, knowing full well that McCutcheon would bring with him a large population of readers not only from Chicago but across the Midwest. Keeley approached McCutcheon in early 1903, but after talking the offer over with Lawson, McCutcheon received a raise from Lawson from $65 to $110 a week, so he stayed with the *Record*.

McCutcheon really did not want to go to the *Tribune*; he liked and respected Victor Lawson, as well as his fellow *Record* employees. Keeley kept insisting, and in June 1903 offered McCutcheon $250 a week, $13,000 a year, to come work for him (though some contemporary newspaper reports reported McCutcheon's salary at $20,000). McCutcheon, wanting to remain with Lawson, offered to take $150 a week, but that was still more than anyone on the *Record* earned. Lawson, a notorious penny-pincher, refused, having had already given McCutcheon a sizeable raise. McCutcheon then took Keeley's offer, which made him one of the highest-paid political cartoonists in America.

On June 9, 1903, readers of the *Record* awoke to see that McCutcheon was gone from the front page. This had happened many times before as McCutcheon traveled with no announcement notice in the *Record*. But unlike previous times, this was permanent. By Sunday, June 28, the reason for McCutcheon's absence became clear. In that day's edition of the *Tribune*, a banner ran across the top of almost every page announcing that McCutcheon would start the coming Wednesday, July 1.

In McCutcheon's daybook for 1903, there is a small notation for June 30, 1903: *"Began work with the Tribune."*

Wasting no time, McCutcheon generated another cartoon series for his new employers. On Sunday, July 6, he began a series titled "Our Sunday Pictorial Sermonette." These observational pieces, done in four panels, were little morality plays, such as "Illustrating that some people would rather believe the bad things they hear about than the good things" and "Illustrating that, no matter how much you have, you want something that someone else has." These cartoons depicted the interactions of people in everyday life, but with an opinion as to how a person's behavior reflects upon them and their character.

Along with the *Boy In...* series and the new *Sunday Sermonettes*, he also had a new series that had just started in the *Record* in May. Only a few installments were published before McCutcheon's switch to the *Tribune*. That series, *Social Happenings at Bird Center, Illinois*, would prove to be his most popular series to date. The *Tribune* then published McCutcheon on the front page on Sundays — *Our Sunday Pictorial Sermonette on Sunday* — the *Bird Center* series on Monday and then Friday's with *The Boy In ...* series.

The *Bird Center* series was unlike any other cartoon series at that time: it was accompanied by a faux article from *The Bird Center Argosy*, the local newspaper

of Bird Center, Ill., the fictional town where the cartoon series took place. The *Tribune* allowed McCutcheon a large swath of the front page for this series, as in addition to the cartoon, there was a generous amount of text. The articles would describe the day-to-day goings on of a small Midwestern burg, down to the small social notices of who ordered a new suit and who was going on a visit out of town.

McCutcheon's cartoons touched on many aspects of the lives of the people in Bird Center, Ill., and by design, reflected his Midwestern readership. Church socials, hayrides, football games, marriages and the rest of what would appear in a small-town newspaper were now on the front page of the

TOP
Above: From *Bird Center* series.

THE MYSTERIOUS STRANGER.

CHICAGO TRIBUNE - NOV. 10, 1904.

Chicago Tribune. McCutcheon wrote all the articles himself, harkening back to when he was a young boy of 14 writing about the local news in Elston, Indiana for the *Lafayette Call*.

A cast of characters emerged. The Reverend Walpole, his wife and nine children, Captain Fry, a Civil War veteran and his wife, Dr. Crosby Niebling, Judge Horatio Warden, Mrs. Mort Peters, Congressman Pumphrey and over 30 other people populated this fictional town. Plus there was Mr. Dog, McCutcheon's mongrel mutt from the 1896 campaign, as part of the entourage.

Initially, these started as standalone episodes, but eventually small continuities developed. One involved The Mysterious Stranger, who one day showed up and immediately stuck out like a sore thumb due to his dress and long, black moustache. After a few chapters, the Stranger revealed that he was a Confederate soldier who was severely wounded at the Battle of Gettysburg. A Union soldier stopped to offer assistance and, fearing he would die, he gave the Union soldier the family sword to bring back to his kin. He survived and had spent the last 40 years searching for that Union soldier to thank him for his kindness, and he finally tracked him down in Bird Center. McCutcheon derived the storyline from the tales he heard from his father and his father's friends back in Lafayette as they reminisced about the Civil War.

The *Bird Center* series was a huge hit. Merchandisers created a card game based on the characters, as well as plates, ornaments and other promotional items. A popular play was performed in many cities in the Midwest and even New York, where a reviewer was not very kind to the play. In 1904, McClurg released a collection of *Bird Center* cartoons. The *Cleveland Leader* described its appeal the best in their review of the book on May 15, 1904:

> (McCutcheon) has caught not only the superficialities, but the essence of a country town. It is a record of the naivety, the egotism, the restlessness, the imitations and, most of all, the neighborliness, to use a homely phrase, of a little town stirred with metropolitan desires.

The series also generated two spin-offs. The Mysterious Stranger made an appearance in one of McCutcheon's most famous political cartoons. Theodore Roosevelt won re-election in November 1904, in part because the state of Missouri, previously a Democratic stronghold, went over to the Republican camp. Using his *Bird Center* character in a cartoon entitled "The Mysterious Stranger" McCutcheon showed two rows of people, each with a sash indicating which state they were from; one formed the Democratic states, the other, the states that voted for Teddy Roosevelt. The sash for Missouri is on the chest of The Mysterious Stranger, looking as he did in the *Bird Center* cartoons, as he lined up to support Roosevelt, leaving the rest of the Democratic Old South behind. Missouri was the first of the Southern states to vote Republican since the election of 1876.

McCutcheon gave Bird Center's Congressman Pumphrey of Illinois his own front-page series in 1907. This series also contained a cartoon with extensive text, later published as a book late in 1907. These stories focused on the small-town bred Congressman Pumphrey, who brings his family to Washington, D.C. to serve his constituents. Here McCutcheon took his gentle, prodding approach to the ways of Congress and the goings on in the nation's Capitol.

1907 would also generate McCutcheon's most well known cartoon. On Sept. 30, 1907, the *Tribune* published a two-panel cartoon with text titled "Injun Summer." It showed a small boy with his grandfather in front of

A dog's life.

Gosh, Dan, haint you glad you aint a boy?

a cornfield whose stalks had been stacked after the harvest. As the grandfather tells about the days when there were Indians in the area, the boy imagines the field filled with teepees instead of corn stalks, the Indians dancing around a fire.

The cartoon embodied McCutcheon's adventurous fantasies, fed by the stories of Indians he heard when he was a small boy, coupled with his romanticism of life on a farm. The cartoon proved to be one of the most popular cartoons in the history of the medium. The appeal of "Injun Summer" was so great that it was reprinted every year in the *Tribune* from 1912 until 1992, when the demands of political correctness and objections from Native Americans caused its cessation.

The popularity of "Injun Summer" manifested itself in many ways over the years. In 1926, it was made into a mural in the Local Room of the Chicago *Tribune*. During the 1933-1934 Century of Progress Exposition in Chicago, each of the two panels was turned in a massive fireworks display. At the 1936 Indiana State Fair, the cartoon was turned into a near life-sized diorama. In 1941, the cartoon was enacted for a crowd of 85,000 at Soldier's Field. And in 1942, as part of a war bond drive, McCutcheon's original of the cartoon was auctioned off for the unprecedented amount of $130,750. The original is now the property of the Chicago Historical Society, and a poster of the cartoon can be found for sale today in the *Chicago Tribune* store.

By the end of 1907, McCutcheon had established a body of work accumulated over the previous 18 years that deeply influenced the cartoon and comics world. Pulitzer Prize winner Carey Orr, his fellow political cartoonist at the Chicago *Tribune*, may have said it best: "McCutcheon brought a change of pace. He was the first to throw the slow ball in cartooning, to draw the human interest picture that was not produced to change votes or to amend morals, but solely to amuse or to sympathize."

McCutcheon's gentle handling of political subject matter influenced other political cartoonists. Two-time Pulitzer Prize winning cartoonist Jay "Ding" Darling, long-time Pittsburg cartoonist Cy Hungerford and Herbert Block, better known as Herblock, who won three Pulitzer prizes for political cartoons, were among the many who were influenced by McCutcheon's soft touch.

McCutcheon's revolutionary slice-of-life approach washed across the single-panel cartoon world. His *Boy In ...* series influenced Clare Victor Dwiggins' *School Days*, Clare Briggs' "Oh, Skin-nay!" and J. R Williams' *Out Our Way*. Both Clare Briggs' "Ain't It a Grand and Glorious Feeling" and H.T. Webster's "Thrill That Comes Once in a Lifetime" owe their origins to McCutcheon. Such single-panel cartoons as Jimmy Hatlo's *They'll Do It Every Time* and Fagaly & Shorten's *There Oughta Be A Law* were also imbued with McCutcheon's themes.

Fontaine Fox's *Toonerville Folks* is another example of the slice-of-life approach. Fox emulated McCutcheon's drawing style in his early work, and he adopted McCutcheon's small, rural town's idiosyncratic inhabitants. Keith Knight's *The Knight Life* and *K-Chronicles*, as well as the ever-present *Family Circus*, continue the slice-of-life/general-interest cartoon tradition today.

McCutcheon's three daily series a week established at the *Tribune* in 1903 created a template that was followed by Gaar Williams, Charles Kuhn, J. R. Williams, and again both Webster and Briggs. All of these cartoonists had multiple-named series that occurred on specific days of the week. This sequence allowed syndicates to pitch a predictable set of single-panel

Taking Her Home from School

RIGHT
McCutcheon inspired cartoonists such as Clare Dwiggins (TOP RIGHT), Clare Briggs (BOTTOM RIGHT) ...

The Boy Whose Mother Read Tom Sawyer.

cartoons to newspapers that were looking for slice-of-life material.

While the *Bird Center* series cannot be classified as a comic strip, McCutcheon did develop a rich cast of characters and extended plots, with a storyline based on the rhythms of the small town, the middle class and family life that people found captivating enough to read them on an ongoing basis. McCutcheon's ability to convey small-town subject matter in cartoons would be repeated and expanded over a decade later in extended storylines by Frank King in *Gasoline Alley* and Sydney Smith in *The Gumps*.

Lucy Caswell, Jeet Heer and Rick Marschall have all written at various times about a Midwestern School of Cartooning. Sara Duke and Martha Kennedy of the Library of Congress have also talked about such a "school." All of the themes these people discuss — hard work, morality, the farm, the small town, a sense of place, family and social interactions — and a gentle approach to politics are present in McCutcheon's work. Given McCutcheon's wide audience, the large influence over his peers, his artistic style and widely imitated themes, McCutcheon is "The Father of the Midwestern School of Cartooning." ∎

Postscript

In the future, articles will be forthcoming about the remainder of McCutcheon's life and cartoon career including his work for *Collier's*, the *Saturday Evening Post* and *Cosmopolitan*, along with his relationship with his fellow cartoonists. There is much more to be added to the history of cartoons and comics by tracing the career of John Tinney McCutcheon.

Acknowledgements

This article would not have been possible without the help and input of many people, to whom I owe a debt of gratitude. Jeet Heer, Shaw McCutcheon, Tim Samuelson, Rich West, Doug Wheeler, Lucy Caswell, Rick Marschall, Chris Ware, Sara Duke, Martha Kennedy and Gary Groth all provided time, support and information during the research and writing of this article. I cannot thank them enough.

... and H.T. Webster (ABOVE).

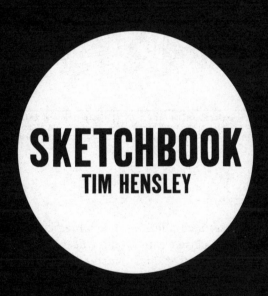

SKETCHBOOK
TIM HENSLEY

♪ *Ticket Stub,* You've got the cutest little *Ticket Stub!* ♪

make your own ticket stub - when explaining that
sinead o'comor, a public figure, tore a photograph of →
the pope on television, use this flap to demonstrate.

← by pondering this ephemera, I hereby recall
that I once flipped through. why, in those days,
computers cost and corsets lost...

Tim Hensley's nine *Ticket Stub* minis, ca. 2000: While transcribing closed captioning for films and television at his day job — gauntleted by wrist braces — Hensley would note the time stamp for evocative stills. After he finished up his work, he would spend the last hour or two of his day incorporating those frames into sketchbooks, accompanied by lyric commentary (according to an interview with Gary Groth in *Mome* 6, Hensley explained his use of language: "I think it's that my sister has a learning disability — she could also be described technically as borderline mentally retarded, although that's not the terminology in favor — and takes medication to stop her from hearing voices. She'll say words like 'o-beast' instead of 'obese [...]'").

Hensley's preoccupations with pop culture, celebrity, art, history, music and design are evident in the following selection from *Ticket Stub* and have found their mature form in *Wally Gropius*, the clear-line full-length graphic novel originally serialized in *Mome* (both published by Fantagraphics). In this interview, Hensley discusses what prompted him to self-publish, autobiography and the L.A. milieu.

— *Kristy Valenti*

Background

Kristy Valenti: Would you give me a brief timeline of your comics work?

Tim Hensley: A brief timeline would be: stapled Mead-pad comics as a kid; bad yearbook comics in high school; orphan juvenilia; first real published work in 1993's *Duplex Planet Illustrated*; next real published work in 2002's *Dirty Stories*; a few *Comics Journal Special Editions*, then *Mome, Comic Art, Kramers 7*; in the dead zone, *Ticket Stub* starting at the turn of the century. Some work in zines edited by friends, other stuff I forget.

Valenti: What compelled you to publish your sketchbook as minis?

Hensley: I was in therapy and a little scrambled. I used to go to the newsstand every week, and at some point I had what seemed like an epiphany that every month all the magazines were completely replaced — a new row of heads. I was comforted it was so impermanent. No one cares about an old magazine too much (unless it's *The Comics Journal*, right?); it just ends up in a dentist's office. I realized I had subject matter literally staring me in the face, and if I filled 12 pages (8 pages seemed too few), it would be enough to Xerox into a zine. So I went out and bought a long-arm stapler. It made me suddenly look forward to going to work.

Valenti: You mentioned that you were in therapy when you made these zines. Did they have therapeutic effects for you?

Hensley: Sketching a page about *The Care Bears Movie* was oftentimes better spent than wondering about how guilty you need to feel that someone in your family will live in a convalescent hospital the rest of their life. I don't want to make too much out of it. Therapy was probably just as much paying someone to listen to me talk.

Valenti: How did you distribute them?

Hensley: I think the circulation was something like 20. I would give one to my wife and another to my therapist. My therapist had this expression she often used with me, "Why kick the puppy?" I ended up mailing them to some friends. It never had any commercial "distro," and if it had, it would've stopped me in my tracks very likely.

Valenti: How much editing, or culling might be a better word, went into *Ticket Stub*? Were they handpicked from a larger group of comics, or did you come up with a theme (for example, the Extras issue) and then work in that theme for a time?

Hensley: The only editing was what order the pages would appear. I'd figure it out at Kinko's when I got to glue-sticking. The drawing and writing were off the top of my head and unedited. I had some Wite-Out I occasionally used to replace a word. After a couple of issues, I'd pick a theme and tailor my frame grabs around it. For example, issue #5 was all kisses, so whatever I worked on, if there was a kiss in it, I'd draw it.

Drawing and Process

Valenti: What were you drawing with? On?

Hensley: Just those 5 1/2" x 8 1/2" sketchbooks you can get anywhere and a Pilot v7

"I like clear writing. If it's unclear, I want it to be by someone who is crazy."

extra fine pen. It was important at first not to get any more complicated. Later I used a fountain pen — I forget what kind — and bought a spiral-bound Japanese sketchbook that was a little smaller.

Valenti: Everything I've seen after *Ticket Stub* by you has been clean-line. Why did you decide to move away from hatching?

Hensley: Drawing off the monitor was my version of life drawing. The more I cartoon it seems my strength is abstraction rather than elaborate wrinkles.

Valenti: Did hatching serve a purpose, in terms of training your hand in mechanics, or...?

Hensley: The purpose was the old saw "draw what you see." I guess that sort of sketching is supposed to improve eye-hand coordination, but who knows.

Valenti: Did you draw with your wrist guard on?

Hensley: I was using those wrist braces that have a steel plate in them, so I had to take the right one off — the ripping Velcro sound every day.

Valenti: Do you still do sketchbooks?

Hensley: No. I do sketches to solve problems sometimes. Like I had to draw a street-corner sign spinner and to get the poses I went to YouTube and drew freeze frames on a piece of scrap paper. I'm very inhibited, so anything private is often under extreme mental hardship unfortunately.

Influences and Conceptual Processes

Valenti: You've lived in the L.A. area since you were 3, and *Ticket Stub* reflects that, even besides the obvious connection to the films and your transcription work (for example, the brief discussion of cars in issue #4). How has L.A. shaped your sensibility and how is it represented in your work?

Hensley: Growing up in L.A. can make you a little queasy about the entertainment industry and want to avoid it if at all possible. I was really just a barnacle on the motion-picture economy while I was captioning, but I liked the idea of creating the equivalent of a Leonard Maltin film guide. Another way to read it would be to see all the movies and TV shows described. A lot of times what I wrote might make more sense.

Valenti: I'm also curious about the brief moments of autobiography in *Ticket Stub* (just little notes and drawings about your wife and your office building, etc.). Is that something you are interested in exploring in the future? Naturalism doesn't seem to hold a lot of interest for you.

Hensley: Brief moments work OK for me. I made a promise to myself not to draw one of those million-same-panel "artist in profile at the drawing table" comics. And I don't have the fortitude to approach the disability area of my life with a memoir like David B. or Line Gamache, at least so far.

Valenti: Are you talking about your sister's disability?

Hensley: Yeah. *The Ride Together* by Paul and Judy Karasik is another great one. I did some songs that were autobiographical, and it didn't exactly go over so well. Sometimes it seems like what you need for a graphic memoir is for the overarching social-political travesty to be something no one can really argue with, like the Irish Potato Famine. Then it doesn't matter as much how conflicted you show yourself in the midst of it.

Valenti: In terms of language, which is obviously a very larger part of your work: Are there any songwriters or poets who influenced you?

Hensley: For these questions I always feel like it should be somebody obscure, but to be honest, I liked Elvis Costello's lyrics when he was on coke or whatever it was. Always liked Emily Dickinson and psycho Sylvia Plath. I love to read and listen to music, so the list changes all the time.

Valenti: Although you sample from all eras and media (music, movies, comics, etc.), you seem to have a special interest in the mid-20th-century, specifically the '60s. Why is that?

Hensley: It's obviously so. I don't know why. When I was in high school, I got caught up in the Mod movement and part of me is still stuck there. I don't think the past is better in any way, but it can be more fun to draw, because it doesn't exist.

Valenti: So, you work in a way that is very rich, in terms of theory — of postmodernism and deconstructionalism. How conscious are you of that when you create?

Hensley: I went through a period in college where semiotics was big, and I read a bunch of Roland Barthes' books and liked them, but I think my language is more influenced by mental illness than theory. I like clear writing. If it's unclear, I want it to be by someone who is crazy.

Valenti: Would you discuss how you use genre in your work?

Hensley: I like having limitations to start from. It's like tricking myself into disclosure through distraction and disassociation.

Issue #9

Valenti: I would like to talk about issue #9, because it seems like the most "processed" issue — you seemed to find a better balance between word and image, you were able to evoke films without labeling them, you began drawing them in a comics grid, etc.

Hensley: #9 did feel like some sort of breakthrough — so much so it was the last issue.

Valenti: What was the process by which you honed your humor?

Hensley: Once I started putting the still frames into individual panels, I automatically started heading toward punch lines. The earlier issues were more like the end of the shift, and I wanted to put down whatever I could remember from what I watched. By issue 9, I would draw a grid and either fill them all in or skip around. I'd combine *Winnie the Pooh* and *Pulp Fiction* from two consecutive days. Another helpful thing was at the time I might work on a movie three or four times to do the different subtitling streams.

Valenti: Would you talk about the six-panel layout and why it's your preferred (if it is ... I noticed you used it in the *Wally Gropius* layout too).

Hensley: I'm not real big on experimental page layouts. I like having a simple grid and let whatever happens be about what's inside the boxes. I usually consciously try to make them slightly asymmetrical though.

Valenti: Previously, you and Dan Clowes had worked on a *Like A Velvet Glove Cast in Iron* soundtrack, and then you did a page on his film *Ghost World* in issue #9. Did he have any feedback, or do any mentoring, on *Ticket Stub?*

Hensley: Well, totally by coincidence, I actually worked on the captioning or subtitles of *Ghost World* at work, which was pretty funny. I thought it was kind of like a buddy-cop film where one of them dies, so I tried to put that in the dialogue. I ended up selling the page to Dan's wife Erika to give to him as a surprise gift. I think he liked it OK; I remember him saying I had captured Thora Birch pretty good in one of the panels. I saw them when they were in town during the filming. I went to the premiere at the American Cinematheque and was so relieved it was good.

Valenti: When you look back at these sketchbooks, what do you reflect on?

Hensley: I think about a period of something like convalescence. If things ever get too rotten again, there's always a 12-page mini as a possible goal. I always thought it would make an OK little book, like those old *Cineaste* auteur paperbacks; I almost talked Alvin Buenaventura into it. I'm glad it's being published here. ∎

the TICKETS TUBHOARD

SHARE

Yes, it did. Palms were greased, recreational kickbacks were grafted, moola was funneled. Yet the fort knox over the stub was its very demise...

the Trust Baron out

IF YOU'LL LOVE, YOU'LL TRY...

hand stamp.

priority wristband.

ALL ACCESS the PICKLE MAGNATE

laminated pass.

SQUEAK! SQUEAK!
TWISTING A DACHSUND

KILLER KLOWNS
from
OUTER SPACE

WITHOUT RUPTURE.

CLOWNS PITCH A TENT
NEAR THE MAKE OUT
PARK, AND TWOSOMES
CLASP IN FEAR FOR
BEING COCOONED IN
COTTON CANDY.
    NEED TEEN GROPING
BE SUCH A HORROR?

KILLER KLOWNS...

MOCK ON, LONGSTOCKINGS. HIS HAND SHADOW BIT AND SHRUNK THEM IN HIS SATCHEL. THEY SHRIEK AND SHRIEK. THAT BULLY'S HEAD INTO AN ASHCAN. HE MANGLED MY BIKE WHILE THEY GIGGLED. AND SO THE PUNITIVE CIRCUS CONTINUED UNABATED, PIE AFTER PIE FLYING TO DUCK. I ACTUALLY WAS SHIRKING HOMEWORK. I HAD TO CALL IN THE ARMY.

INFLATING A PAPER SNAKE

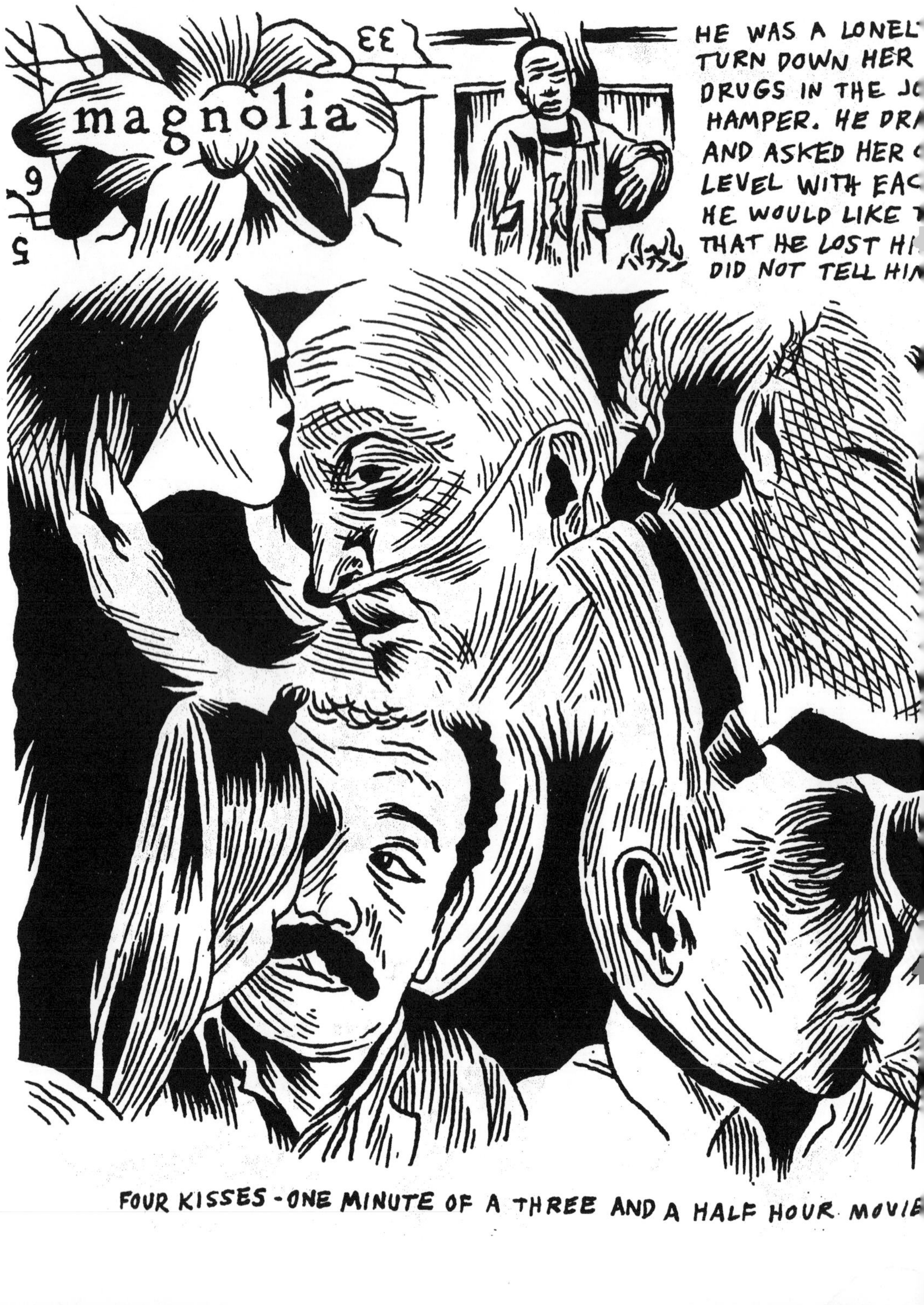
magnolia
33
9
5
HE WAS A LONEL
TURN DOWN HER
DRUGS IN THE JO
HAMPER. HE DRA
AND ASKED HER
LEVEL WITH EAC
HE WOULD LIKE T
THAT HE LOST HI
DID NOT TELL HIM
FOUR KISSES - ONE MINUTE OF A THREE AND A HALF HOUR MOVIE

COP WHO TOLD HER TO
TEREO. SHE INHALED
N OR HID THEM IN THE
IK HER BITTER COFFEE
T. THEY AGREED TO
OTHER. SHE ASKED IF
KISS HER. HE CONFIDED
GUN IN THE RAIN. SHE
. SHE SMILED.

DENY YOU ARE A MOLESTER AND YOU WILL BE
GIVEN A TELEVISION SHOW IN WHICH CHILDREN
ARE COMPENSATED FOR EVERYTHING EXCEPT
THEIR OWN VALUE. RESENT THE SADDLE OF
ILLNESS AND LEAD A SCORING INFOMERCIAL.
MASS MEDIA IS REPRESSION, THE FILM
YOU ARE WATCHING EXCLUDED.
TICKET STUB? I DON'T WANT TO TALK
ABOUT IT.

1-877-826-3437

I DOUBLE CLICKED THE ICON, PUT IN THE CASSETTE PAST THE COLOR BARS AND GAPED— MY HEAD SLACK, MY EYES A RED ROAD MAP. A BRACE AT MY WRIST AS IT POISED OVER A KEY, IT WAS A COMIC WHERE THE BALLOONS SUNK AND TRAWLED BELOW. WHEN THE TAPE FROZE, I SIGNED OFF, ZIPPED MY BACKPACK, AND LEFT THE BIBLICAL EPIC.

ESTHER.

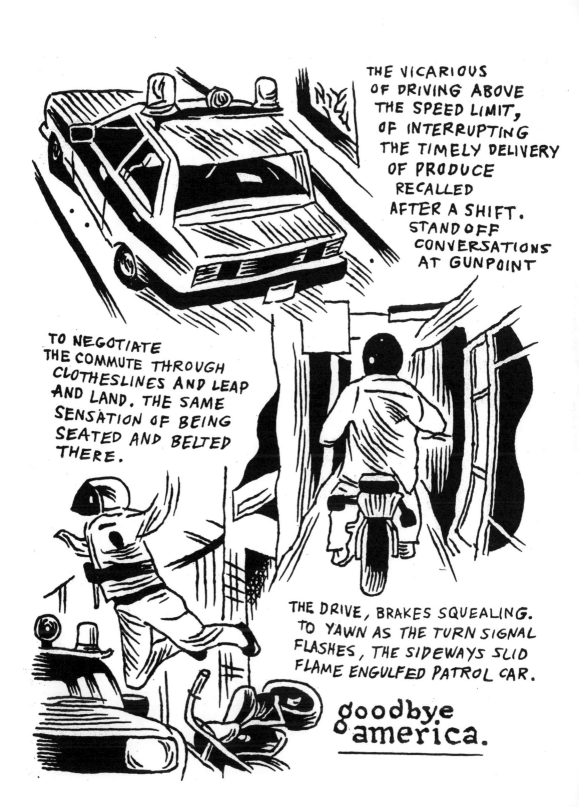

THE VICARIOUS OF DRIVING ABOVE THE SPEED LIMIT, OF INTERRUPTING THE TIMELY DELIVERY OF PRODUCE RECALLED AFTER A SHIFT. STAND OFF CONVERSATIONS AT GUNPOINT

TO NEGOTIATE THE COMMUTE THROUGH CLOTHESLINES AND LEAP AND LAND. THE SAME SENSATION OF BEING SEATED AND BELTED THERE.

THE DRIVE, BRAKES SQUEALING. TO YAWN AS THE TURN SIGNAL FLASHES, THE SIDEWAYS SLID FLAME ENGULFED PATROL CAR.

goodbye america.

NESTOR, THE LONG-EARED CHRISTMAS DONKEY

TO MY PARENTS, WHO BOTH LOST THEIR DONKEYS TO DISEASE TOO EARLY, I WISH I COULD HAVE LED TO A MANGER, BUT THE RIDICULE MY EARS PRICKED FAIL BLIZZARD-PUPPET CHERUBS I STEP ON MY LOW SLUNG AND SLUSH. YES, I'VE GOT YOUR LUGGAGE, YOUR LOZENGE, BUT THROUGH THOSE SPECKS OF WHITE GRIT, NO PRESENT.

COMMITMENT

COMMIT YOURSELF TO INSTITUTE AND FOSTER FROST NUTS. IT MEANT DRIVE OF CANT.

ARRIVING AT WORK PAST EXTRAS WITH A WATERING CAN WRAPPED IN
BUTCHER PAPER, THE SECRET LIFE OF WALTER MITTY BEGINS.
HE DAYDREAMS HE IS THE STAR OF A FILM ABOUT A MAN IN AN OFFICE
WHO DAYDREAMS. HE WAS HENPECKED FOR SUCH A ROLE.
SOAP BRINGS A REVERIE OF CAPSIZE. WATER COOLER GABS
DRIFT TO MASKS AND ETHER, SURGERY WITH GRATERS.
THE FURNACE AFLAME DISSOLVES TO A DISSERTATION BY
A PILOT IN A WAITER COAT. ME, NEITHER, BUT TOO TRUE.

Crime + Punishment IN SUBURBIA.

THIS FILM HAS A BLACK-CLAD TEEN WHO TAKES STILLS THAT ARE INOPPORTUNE. HE MOCKS THE PLEDGE OF ALLEGIANCE. I OPTED NOT TO TRANSCRIBE HIS SHUTTER NERVE, BUT HIGH SCHOOL EXTRAS IN A COMPUTER CLASS AND THOSE BURIED FOR WHOM I ALSO FELT AN AFFINITY. THE TWO ORDERLIES WHO WHEEL THE CORPSE IN AND SHUT THE DOORS MANY TIMES, LENGTHS OF TAPE THAT MARK FINISH LINES.

Ticketmaster
office building   Sunset Strip.

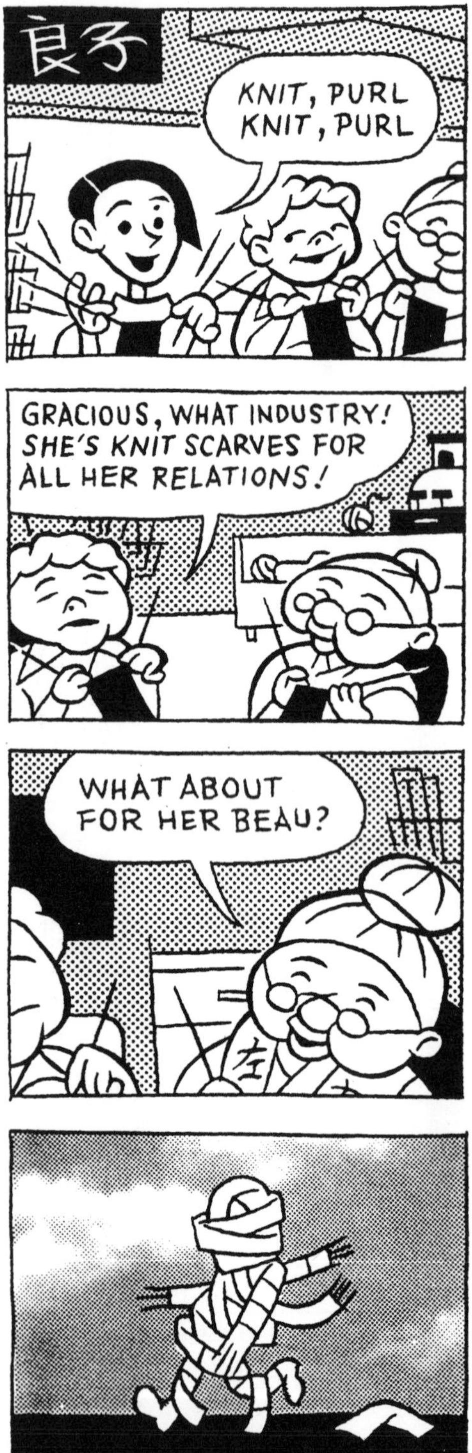
良子
KNIT, PURL KNIT, PURL
GRACIOUS, WHAT INDUSTRY! SHE'S KNIT SCARVES FOR ALL HER RELATIONS!
WHAT ABOUT FOR HER BEAU?

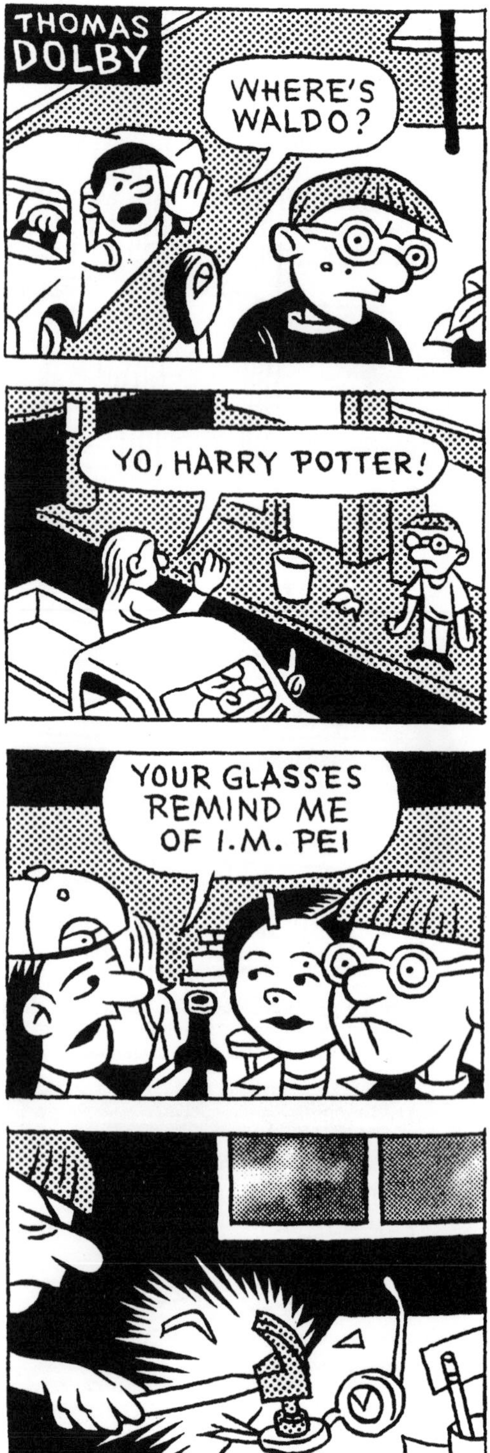
THOMAS DOLBY
WHERE'S WALDO?
YO, HARRY POTTER!
YOUR GLASSES REMIND ME OF I.M. PEI

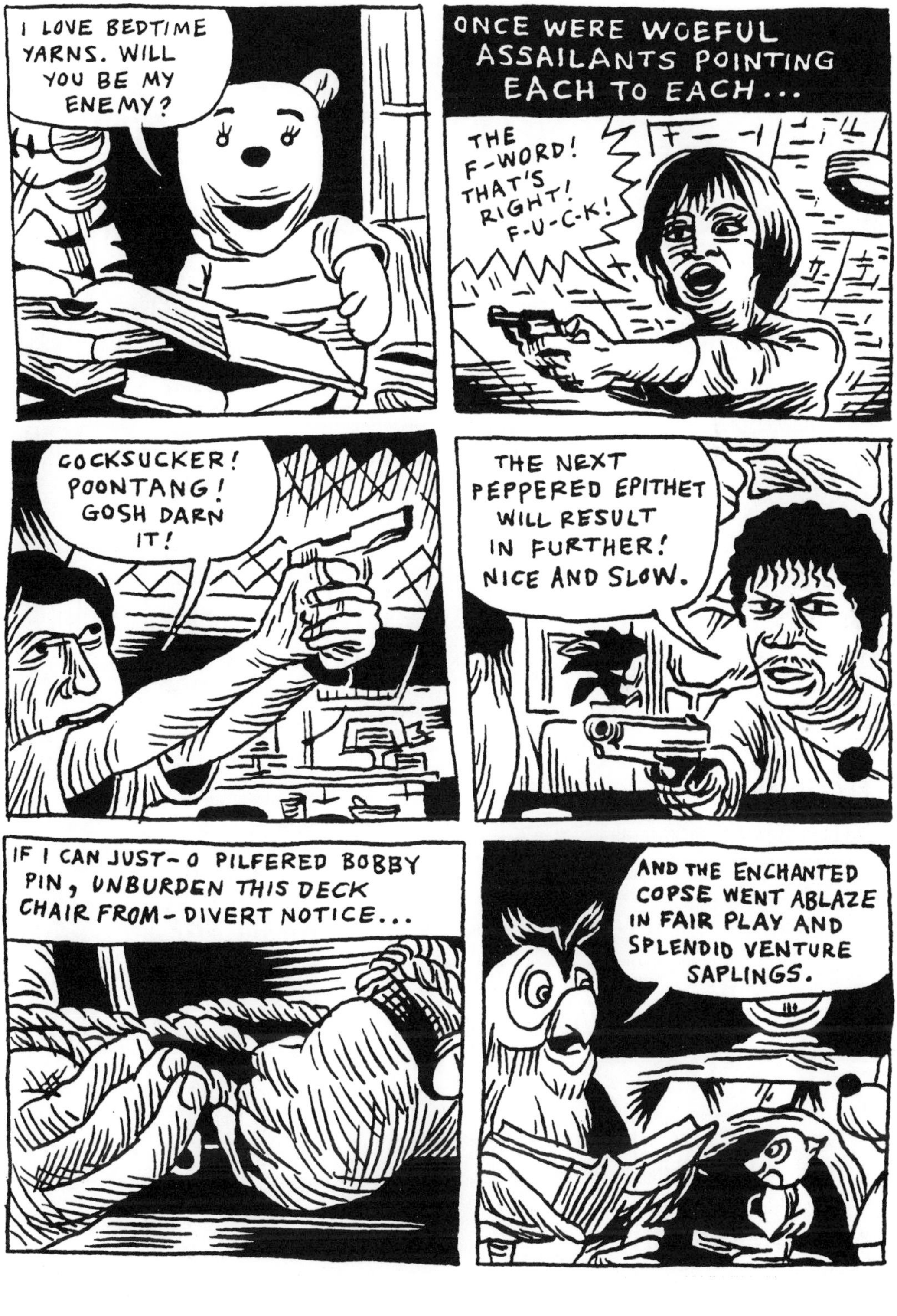
I LOVE BEDTIME YARNS. WILL YOU BE MY ENEMY?
ONCE WERE WOEFUL ASSAILANTS POINTING EACH TO EACH...
THE F-WORD! THAT'S RIGHT! F-U-C-K!
COCKSUCKER! POONTANG! GOSH DARN IT!
THE NEXT PEPPERED EPITHET WILL RESULT IN FURTHER! NICE AND SLOW.
IF I CAN JUST- O PILFERED BOBBY PIN, UNBURDEN THIS DECK CHAIR FROM- DIVERT NOTICE...
AND THE ENCHANTED COPSE WENT ABLAZE IN FAIR PLAY AND SPLENDID VENTURE SAPLINGS.

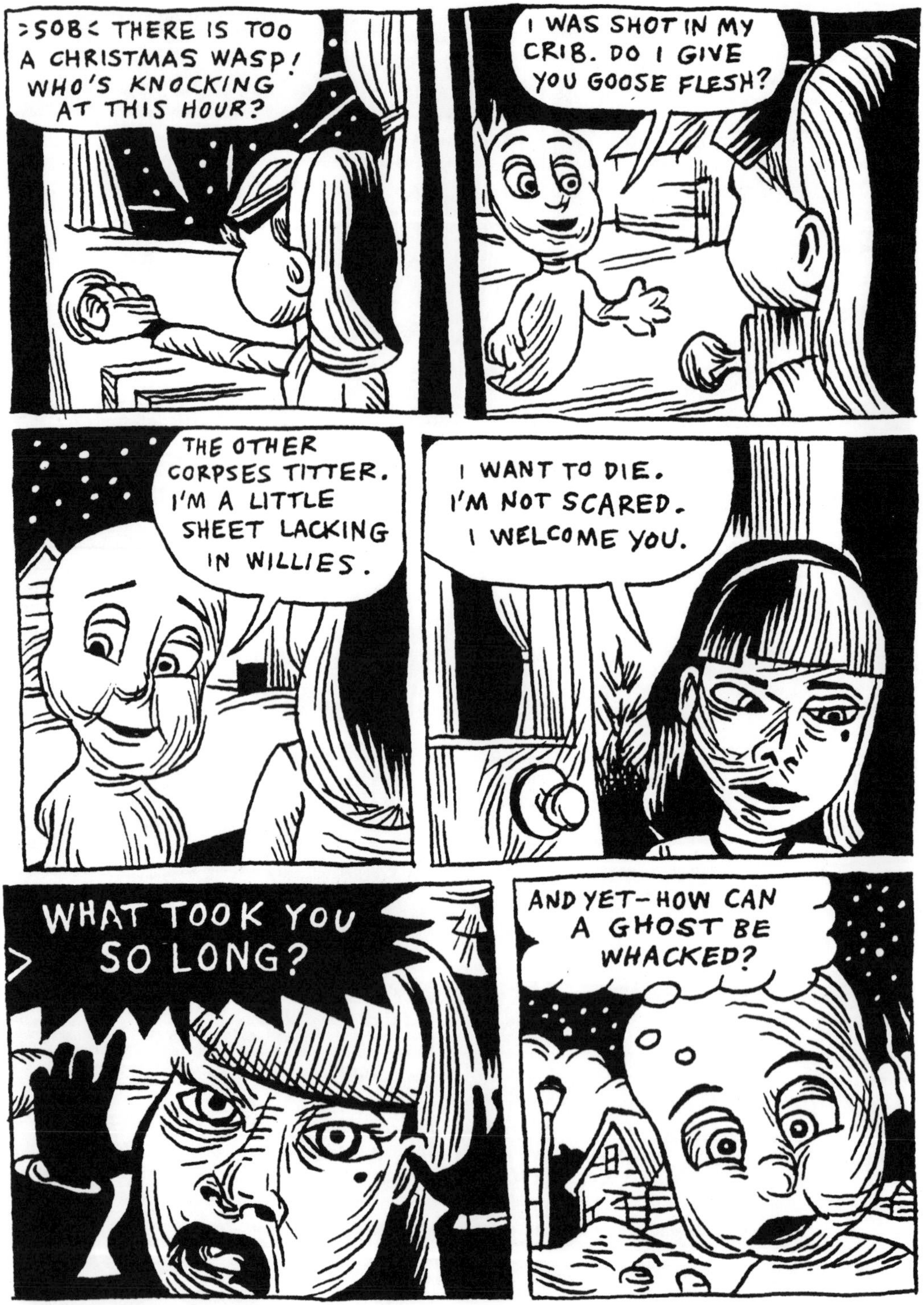
>SOB< THERE IS TOO A CHRISTMAS WASP! WHO'S KNOCKING AT THIS HOUR?
I WAS SHOT IN MY CRIB. DO I GIVE YOU GOOSE FLESH?
THE OTHER CORPSES TITTER. I'M A LITTLE SHEET LACKING IN WILLIES.
I WANT TO DIE. I'M NOT SCARED. I WELCOME YOU.
WHAT TOOK YOU SO LONG?
AND YET—HOW CAN A GHOST BE WHACKED?

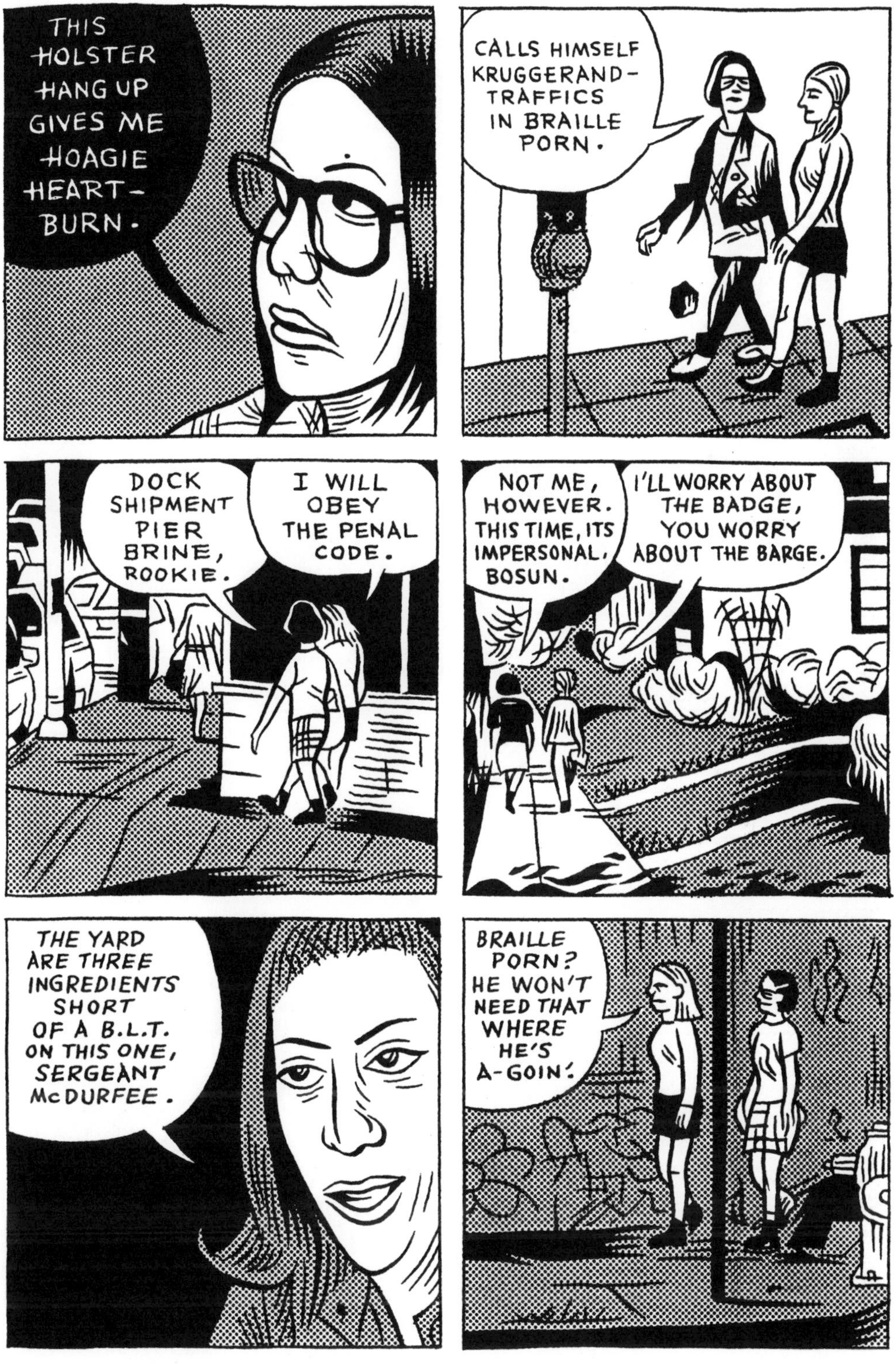
THIS HOLSTER HANG UP GIVES ME HOAGIE HEART-BURN.
CALLS HIMSELF KRUGGERAND-TRAFFICS IN BRAILLE PORN.
DOCK SHIPMENT PIER BRINE, ROOKIE.
I WILL OBEY THE PENAL CODE.
NOT ME, HOWEVER. THIS TIME, ITS IMPERSONAL, BOSUN.
I'LL WORRY ABOUT THE BADGE, YOU WORRY ABOUT THE BARGE.
THE YARD ARE THREE INGREDIENTS SHORT OF A B.L.T. ON THIS ONE, SERGEANT McDURFEE.
BRAILLE PORN? HE WON'T NEED THAT WHERE HE'S A-GOIN'.

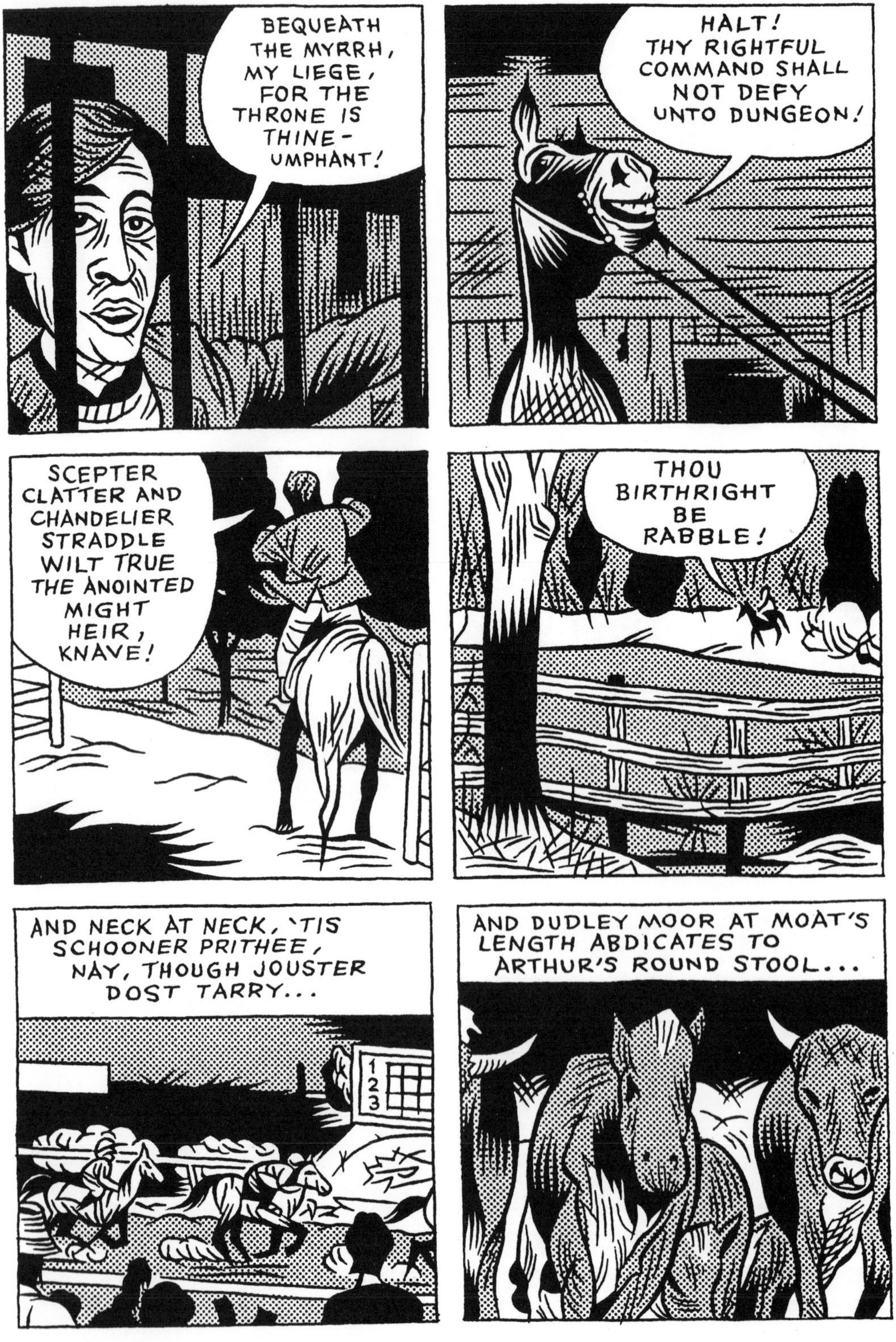
BEQUEATH THE MYRRH, MY LIEGE, FOR THE THRONE IS THINE-UMPHANT!
HALT! THY RIGHTFUL COMMAND SHALL NOT DEFY UNTO DUNGEON!
SCEPTER CLATTER AND CHANDELIER STRADDLE WILT TRUE THE ANOINTED MIGHT HEIR, KNAVE!
THOU BIRTHRIGHT BE RABBLE!
AND NECK AT NECK, 'TIS SCHOONER PRITHEE, NAY, THOUGH JOUSTER DOST TARRY...
1
2
3
AND DUDLEY MOOR AT MOAT'S LENGTH ABDICATES TO ARTHUR'S ROUND STOOL...

DAVE SIM'S

CEREBUS

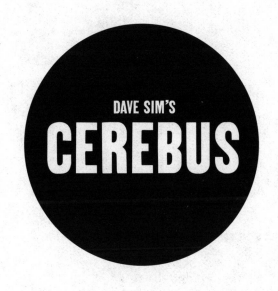

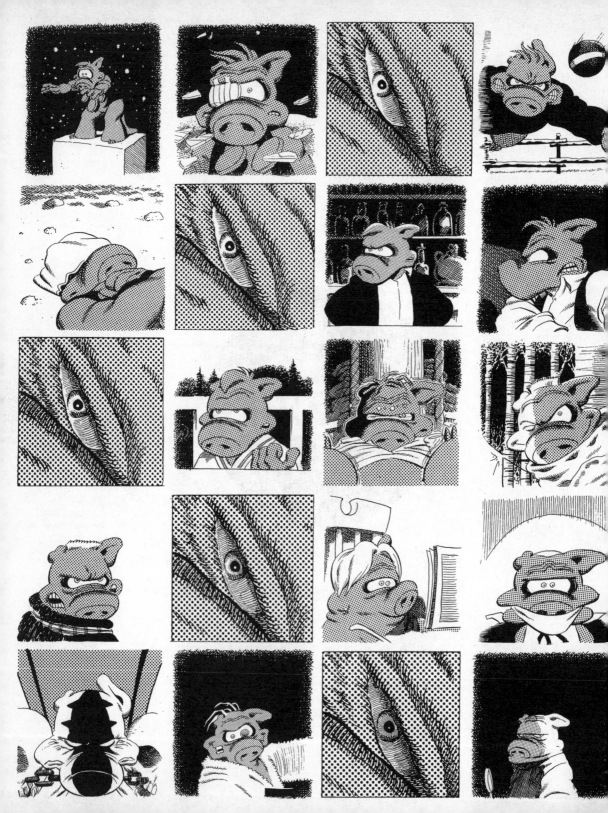

IRREDEEMABLE: DAVE SIM'S CEREBUS

BY TIM KRIEDER

I'm not sure to what extent I need to explain the graphic-novel cycle *Cerebus* to a *Comics Journal* audience. Hard as it is for me to believe, based on my conversations with younger cartoonists, it seems like some basic background might be advisable here. The history of this book and its author used to be a legend in the comics world — in fact, it reads a lot like a superhero origin story. In 1977 Dave Sim, a 21-year-old comics fan, whose only job had ever been working in a comics shop, began drawing his own comic book, a parody of/homage to Barry Windsor-Smith's *Conan*, featuring as its hero the eponymous Cerebus, an avaricious, hard-drinking barbarian who is also an aardvark. Two years into the series, Sim took LSD for a week and a half, suffered what he described as a "nervous breakdown," and had to be admitted to a hospital, where he was diagnosed as "borderline schizophrenic" (whatever that might mean as applied to someone coming down off several days of acid). Recovering from this experience, he had a life-changing epiphany: *Cerebus* would run for 300 issues. It was a vast story; it would be his life's work. Deranged hubristic ambitions are not uncommon among schizophrenics, people on LSD, or 23-year-olds, but here's the remarkable part: He actually did it. Dave Sim drew *Cerebus*, putting out an issue a month, for the next 25 years. He finished it in 2004. It runs to 16 volumes, and occupies a solid foot of shelf space.

LEFT
From *Cerebus* #300
(March 2004)
[©2004 Dave Sim
& Gerhard]

In the early, sword-and-sorcery issues of *Cerebus*, Dave Sim drew about as well as the second- or third-best artist in your high school, the guy you'd ask to do the cover for your heavy metal band's album or airbrush the side of your van. After drawing about a hundred issues, by the time he'd finished Volume II of *Church & State* — around the same time he hired a brilliant and apparently indefatigable draftsman named Gerhard as his background artist, freeing himself to concentrate exclusively on his characters — Dave Sim had become one of the best cartoonists in North America. And not just in the excellence of his technical skill — he was relentlessly inventive and virtuosic. His exuberant formal experimentation extended from his lettering and paneling to the design of whole issues: Readers puzzled and wowed over the issues in which each page's background was a fragment of one large picture of Cerebus, or the spinning of an ascending tower was reflected by the page layout rotating several degrees on each page, so that you had to slowly turn the whole book 360° in your hands in the course of reading it. "Thou shalt break every law in the book," was his injunction to himself.

Sim was also a smart and voracious autodidact (he dropped out of high school after grade 11), and, as he matured, his intellectual passions grew beyond comics, and his artistic ambitions far beyond parody. The single-issue stories expanded into longer and longer story arcs, gradually growing

> "In the early, sword-and-sorcery issues of *Cerebus*, Dave Sim drew about as well as the second- or third-best artist in your high school, the guy you'd ask to do the cover for your heavy-metal band's album or airbrush the side of your van."

into full-length, 500-page novels. As he continued drawing *Cerebus*, Sim incorporated everything that captured his interest into the book: He became interested in the mechanics of electoral politics, and Cerebus ran for Prime Minister; he got interested in the history of religion, and Cerebus became the Pope; as Sim's literary tastes became more sophisticated, Cerebus encountered incarnations of Oscar Wilde, F. Scott Fitzgerald, and Ernest Hemingway. He insatiably appropriated not only literary, historic and political figures, but fictional characters and screen personas, the likenesses of friends and colleagues, other authors' prose styles, even another cartoonist's dialogue in a manner that would've been called postmodern if he'd had an MFA. He wrote books within books, invented intricate political ideologies, created whole cosmologies. Throughout all of which the book's central character remained the same anthropomorphized aardvark.

It also, against what might seem like any reasonable expectations, became a success. Dave Sim was one of the first cartoonists to publish his own work, and he was a vocal proponent of self-publication as the only means of securing artistic autonomy and control. Not only did he actually make a living being a cartoonist, he made it look *glamorous*. The monthly "Note from the President" and the photo that accompanied each issue of *Cerebus* hinted at a life spent doing nothing but drawing his comic book, smoking pot and going out (and breaking up) with good-looking girls. At comics conventions, he showed up in limos, rented out whole suites, threw parties. He'd become an alternative-comics rock star. He appealed to the young and unformed in much the same way as Jim Morrison or Hunter S. Thompson, artists whose personæ are at least as compelling as their work.

But then somewhere in there, roughly two-thirds of the way through the series, Dave Sim began to develop some let's call them idiosyncratic and controversial views on the sexes, politics and religion — about which more later — all of which found explicit expression in his work. These "rants" and "tangents," as he called them, alienated a lot of his audience. Quite a few of his readers would tell you that he went insane before their eyes. By the end, *Cerebus*'s circulation had dropped almost in half from its high point, circa *Church & State* — although that might also be attributed to the more static and internal action of the later books, or to changes in the business and culture of comics. The final issue, which showed the title character dying "alone, unloved, and unmourned" in fulfillment of a prophecy made back in 1988 (so this isn't exactly a "spoiler"), completed an undertaking that began as an in-joke and ended as what its author, a man not given to modest understatement, claims is "the longest sustained narrative in human history."[1]

Dave Sim noted ruefully that the completion of his vast project was met with "the sound of one cricket leg chirping." Gary Groth, editor of the *Comics Journal*, which had had a combative history with Sim, sent him a note of gentlemanly congratulations of the sort you might imagine Holmes sending to Moriarty after the unexplained disappearance of the crown jewels. There were mentions in *The Village Voice* and *The Onion's A.V. Club* — mentions that tended to take the same tone of straightfaced, whatever-else-you-wanna-say-respect the media pays to achievements like a record-setting win at the national hot-dog-eating contest.

It's true that *Cerebus* occupies an oddly provisional place in comics' canon, given the sheer magnitude of the project, its stylistic innovation and virtuosity, and its influence on other artists. (It was conspicuously excluded

---

[1] Not sure whether there's any point in quibbling with a claim this arbitrary and ill defined. Is Cerebus "longer" than, say, Henry Darger's 15,000-page illustrated novel *The Story of the Vivian Girls*? Or, for that matter, than Japanese epics that ran for a hundred volumes and took decades to compose, or soap operas that began in the '50s and are still running today? How to compare the length of graphic vs. prose novels, let alone print vs. electronic media? Let it suffice to agree with Sim that his achievement is, by logistical measures alone, very impressive indeed. Just in terms of the dedication and discipline necessary to such an undertaking, and the 10s of thousands of hours of labor involved, it is awe-inspiring.

"Anything you can't even begin to describe without explaining, "It's sort of like *Howard the Duck* ..." is never likely to get discussed in the *New York Review of Books.*"

from *The Comics Journal*'s list of the 100 Greatest Comics of All Time.) It hasn't helped Sim's critical standing that he belongs to a cartooning tradition that's currently unfashionable in an era of hip minimalism and the amateurish DIY aesthetic. His artwork is part of a lineage of densely detailed, illustrative, caricature-based cartooning, descended more directly from the fine art of William Hogarth and Honoré Daumier than are most contemporary American comics, a style whose modern masters are the likes of Arthur Szyk and Mort Drucker (and of which this writer is a marginal practitioner).

Cerebus is also too much a product of, and too narrowly concerned with, the world of comics ever to become the kind of breakout critical or commercial success as, say, *Maus*, *Fun Home* or *Persepolis*. Anything you can't even begin to describe without explaining, "It's sort of like *Howard the Duck* ..." is never likely to get discussed in the *New York Review of Books*. Its parodies of characters, creators and trends in the world of comics circa 1980-2000 date badly, and were never even comprehensible, let alone of much interest, to anyone outside that marginal subculture.

But the main impediment to Dave Sim's literary reputation is Dave Sim himself. His regressive social and political views and obnoxious rhetoric have created a public persona that's eclipsed his artistic achievement in the comics world much more completely than it would have in the larger, less insular artistic world — where, for example, plenty of people call John Updike a chauvinist but not even his bitterest detractors question his mastery as a prose stylist, where Karlheinz Stockhausen's ill-advised statement about 9/11 being a work of art didn't get him ejected from the first rank of postwar composers, and artists like Wagner and Pound are still secure in their respective pantheons despite having endorsed ideas that are, to put it charitably, pretty well discredited.

But Sim's controversial ideas are not peripheral to his work; he ultimately makes them its central message and purpose. Wagner never actually wrote any operas about the villainy of the Jews, nor Pound cantos praising the wise and just rule of Franco, but Sim incorporated his screeds about women and the tenets of his one-man religion into the text of his novel, so that even a reader determined to ignore all the apocryphal gossipy bullshit accumulated around the artist and concentrate on the work itself is finally forced to confront the fact that the man has some bizarre ideas and an abrasive way of expressing them.

Perhaps most damagingly of all, Dave Sim is the single most passionate and outspoken advocate of his own work, and also its most reductive and unreliable interpreter. Having finished his *magnum opus*, he seems unable to let go of it, and continues to hand down authoritative misreadings of the work that do it a serious disservice. He tries to rationalize the kinds of inconsistencies and contradictions that are only inevitable in a work that was written month by month over 30 years; he issues contemptuous dismissals of (female) characters who might have seemed to the reader to have had some depth and complexity; and he sometimes makes assertions that are clearly contradicted by the text. It raises the troubling possibility that what seemed like *Cerebus*'s literary quality may only have been so much projection on the part of its readers. What's more likely is that Sim, like a lot of artists, is less than fully conscious of what he's doing and is the last person who should be consulted about the meaning of his own work.

Sim's loudmouthed self-promotion and self-pity has effectively divided comics readers into two camps: those who sigh and make the little twirly-motion at their temples when his name comes up, and a devoted core of fans so uncritical and defensive you'd have to call them acolytes, which doesn't tend to do an artist's critical reputation much good either. (Ayn Rand and L. Ron Hubbard have both become cult figures among different genera of dingbats, but *Atlas Shrugged* doesn't get discussed in the same academic circles as the *Tractatus*, and you aren't going to see a Library of America edition of *Battlefield*

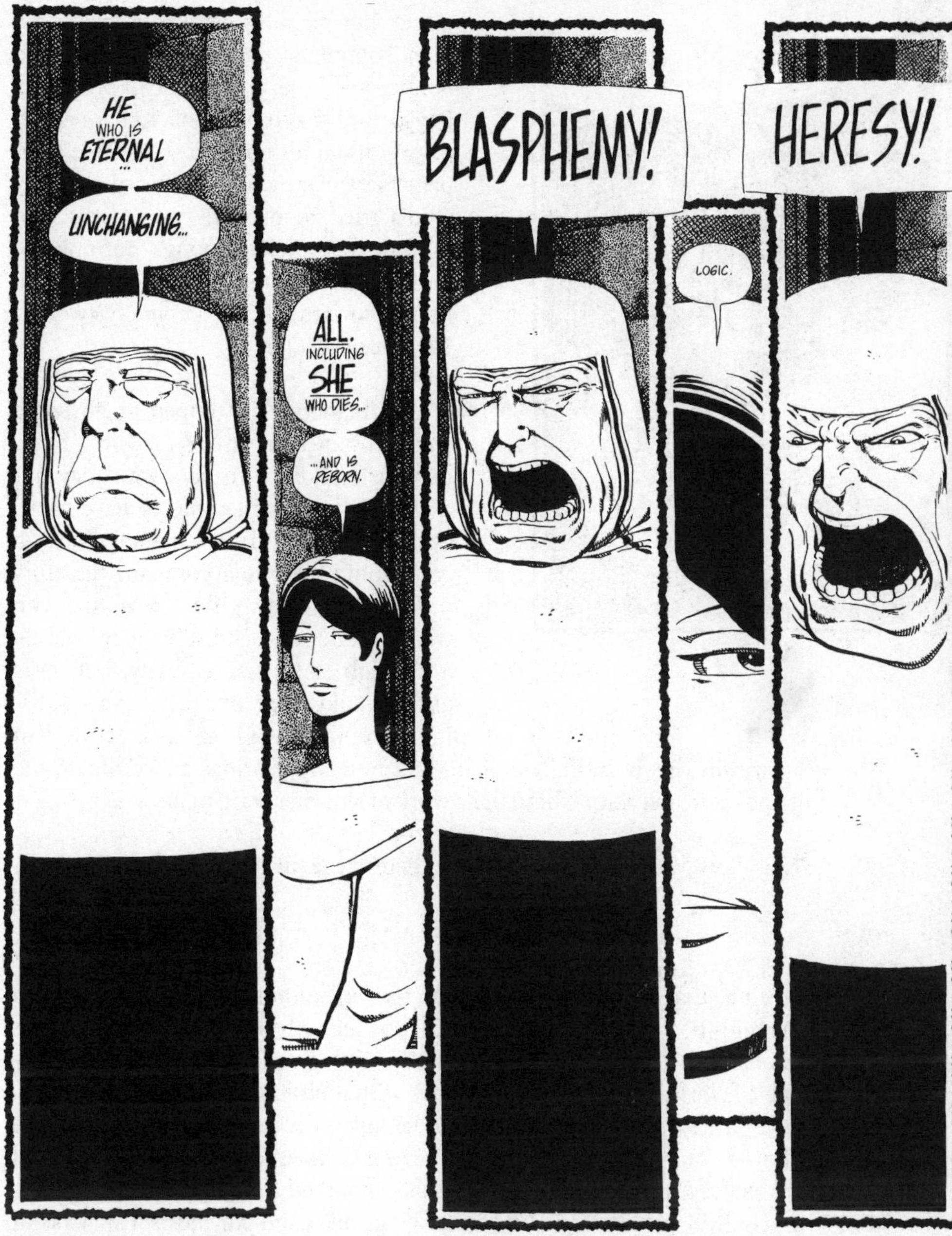
HE WHO IS ETERNAL ...
UNCHANGING...
ALL. INCLUDING SHE WHO DIES...
...AND IS REBORN.
BLASPHEMY!
LOGIC.
HERESY!

Earth anytime soon.) He complains that his work is willfully ignored by the comics world, but blaming his ostracism on the Marxist/feminist/homosexualist axis (this is not hyperbole) hasn't persuaded many people to take a second look. And for all his plaints about his obscurity, he's also been perversely obstructionist toward anybody who's tried to publicize his work. (I'm thinking specifically, though not only, of the I-know-you-are-but-what-am-I stance he took toward the [female] interviewer for *The Onion's AV Club*.)

It's a situation I had hoped to go some small distance toward remedying for a new generation of readers who may not even have heard of *Cerebus*, or have heard of it only as an artifact of mental illness, a companion piece to accompany the story of Dave Sim, a very gifted cartoonist who went around the bend. Sim may well be a wackjob or an acid casualty, but he is also, I would argue, one of the greatest living cartoonists. And *Cerebus* is more than a curiosity; it's beautifully drawn, intermittently hilarious and brilliant, the gargantuan and astonishing life's work of a master craftsman.

That, however, was before I'd actually read the fucking thing.

• • •

I read several issues of *Cerebus* over my college roommate's shoulder back in the mid-'80s, which, fortuitously, happened to be the era of *Church & State II*, one of the artistic crests of the book. (Of course it's possible that everyone's favorite era of *Cerebus* coincides with their initial discovery of it — cf. Peter Graham's adage that the golden age of science fiction is 12.) Dave Sim was one of the very few artists I ever deliberately studied (as opposed to the deep influences I unconsciously absorbed from, say, *Mad* magazine and B. Kliban): I marveled at his drawings of a hand blurred as it shakes out a match or a face reflected in a rippling puddle of mop water; I imitated the fine hatching in the wrinkles around Bishop Powers's shouting mouth and internalized the lessons of his expressionistic lettering and word balloons.

I never did get around to reading *Cerebus*, though. I've always had it jotted down somewhere on my life To Do list that someday I'd have to read the whole thing. The glimpses I'd gotten through my sporadic reading were intriguing but also daunting; I was intimidated by the book's sheer length and evident complexity, all the backstory I'd have to absorb just to have any idea what was going on. I wasn't looking forward to having to get through all the amateurish fan art and dweeby allusions in the first volume, which veteran readers glumly assured me would be necessary to familiarize myself with the basic cast of characters and background. I decided to wait until Sim had finished the whole 300-issue run and then, I told myself — envisioning this in a comfortably distant future — I'd sit down and read them all in one marathon, *War and Peace*-like binge.

Which is what I finally did last summer. I traded one of my original cartoons for all 16 volumes of *Cerebus* and hauled the whole 20 pounds of it down to my Undisclosed Location on the Chesapeake Bay, where I holed up, away from the distractions of the Internet or girls and read them one after the other on the couch, listening to old soundtracks on vinyl and eating Old El Paso tacos, all pretty much while wearing the same T-shirt.

So, what are we to make of this thing, *Cerebus*? It's far too long and complex to give it the kind of close reading it deserves even in the generous space I've been allotted here. Its sheer unwieldy scale makes it difficult to evaluate critically; it's such a vast structure that it's hard to grasp its architecture.

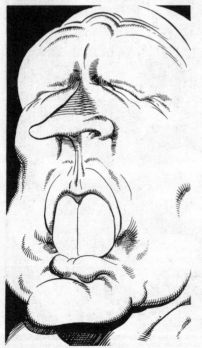

And everything we know about its eccentric author makes it hard to see clearly as a work of art. What I want to try to do is clear away enough of the clutter of extraneous baggage it's accumulated and step back far enough from it to begin to figure out what kind of book *Cerebus* is, whether it's ultimately any good, where it belongs in comics' history and canon, and whether it's deserving of — and capable of withstanding — critical attention from the larger artistic and literary world.

Having now read *Cerebus*, I don't think my assessment of Dave Sim as one of the greatest living cartoonists is inflated. He may not be quite as great a caricaturist as Mort Drucker, but he eventually learned to channel Drucker (he even draws individual hairs with the same idiosyncratically crimped line), and he can make his characters *act* better than Drucker ever could. (Drucker's caricatures, to my eye, were too clearly copied from movie stills, with a tendency to overact, and sometimes they seemed out of synch with the lines they were saying; Sim's characters actually emote.) His ear for dialogue is uncannily astute, and with his endlessly expressive lettering — lettering that sags and jangles, shrieks and sobs, shivers and writhes — he conveys his characters' accents and inflection so clearly you can almost hear them out loud.

And Sim is second to none as a mimic. The highest praise I can give him is that his Groucho Marx impersonations are almost as good as having a new Marx Brothers movie to watch. (I was disappointed all out of proportion when I realized I'd seen the last of Uncle Julius, his Groucho character.) Watching him throw, say, Groucho and Oscar Wilde together in a scene (Groucho taking cool, bemused advantage of Wilde's fawning sycophancy), or contrive an awkward confrontation between Mick Jagger and Margaret Thatcher ("*She* nowz 'oo oy am," he growls, the word balloon dripping with little icicles) is like the fulfillment of some crazily eclectic "dream

lunch" fantasy. I like re-reading these exchanges out loud to savor not only their humor, but their euphony.

His mastery of timing rivals Friz Freleng's. Let's have a look at the nearly wordless passage from *Church & State II* in which Prince Keef (Keith Richards), having heard something about there not being enough drugs left for his next dose ("Cor — nuffink wrong with 'is 'earing, is there?"), warily accepts his brother Mick's reassurances and withdraws his head back into his carriage slowly as a cobra, only to pop back up, just as you think he's been successfully placated, with a last-second twinge of suspicion. Or study, if you will, the whole sequence from *Guys* in which Prince Mick and Harrison react to Cerebus's naive inquiry about "the tavern tramps and whores" he's been told about. There's a one-panel beat where they stare at him blankly, like that moment when a toddler's still too shocked to start crying. And then, just as he's about to try to explain himself, they erupt into laughter. Mick gleefully launches into an elaborate riff on the "tavuhn tramps an' oores"

LEFT
Mick Jagger and Margaret Thatcher square off in *Cerebus* Vol. 11: *Guys.* [©1997 Dave Sim & Gerhard]

TOP
Oscar Wilde and Lord Julius (Groucho Marx) converse in *Cerebus* Vol. 5: *Jaka's Story.* [©1990 Dave Sim]

to torture poor Harrison, who topples from his stool, giggling helplessly, and crawls across the floor to escape, barely able to breathe, feebly begging for him to quit. Real-life laughter is known to be as contagious as yawns or coughing, but this is the only instance when a *cartoon depiction* of laughter has gotten me just about weeping with sympathetic laughter.

As you can tell, I like Dave Sim best when he's funny. Sim, like Woody Allen, has had to endure a lot of backhanded compliments from fans who tell him how much they loved his earlier, funnier work. But I actually don't much enjoy the first volume of *Cerebus* stories, which are usually one-off joke stories with sitcom premises (Cerebus falls in among barbarians who worship an aardvark-god; Cerebus drinks a love potion; Cerebus has to convince a band

TOP
Cerebus Vol. 11:
Guys [©1997 Dave
Sim & Gerhard]

of merchants that the inhabitants of a town he's slaughtered actually perished of an unusually bloody strain of the plague). I prefer humor based in the characters and the interactions between them (Lord Julius's wisecracks, Oscar's deadly *bon mots*, Mick and Keef's dissolute camaraderie). Humor is more than just making jokes; it's a generosity of spirit, a kind of forgiveness. A writer who can be funny about his characters can't entirely condemn them. Artists who are congenitally humorless (even superb writers like Richard Yates) come across as judgmental and bitter, somehow fundamentally stunted, no matter how otherwise lucid their observations or truthful their insights. The tavern-tramps-and-whores scene isn't just a funny digression; beneath the laughter, it's actually a sad scene. Those barflies' reaction is so hysterical because the unspoken answer to Cerebus's straight line is the tedium and loneliness of their lives. As Mick says afterward: "bes' *larf* oy've 'ad in a *long* why-o."

• • •

But for all its stylistic mastery and innovative brilliance, *Cerebus* is, to understate the matter, problematic. It's profoundly, insolubly problematic in about five different ways I can think of just off the top of my head, any one of which is enough to doom it to perpetual marginality.

For one thing, the fact that *Cerebus* is so purely a product of comics, taking its tropes and predicating its situations on other comics, inevitably limits its intelligibility to outsiders. If it were to be reprinted, it would have to be heavily footnoted, in the same way that Swift's and Aristophanes's satiric references to political and religious figures of their day and jibes at their literary rivals are today. The running parodies of characters and trends in contemporaneous mainstream comics (the various incarnations of the Roach, the Secret Sacred Wars, the Spawn interlude, etc.) severely weaken the work, funny though they may occasionally be. (Sim's skills as a mimic make short work of Frank Miller's macho noirish *Dark Knight* voice.) Even among comics' dorkiest cognoscenti, a pitch-perfect send-up of *Wolverine* or *Sandman* circa 1988 dates about as well as would a really cutting, dead-on parody of *Slaves of New York*. Sim's sly insidery parodies of comics conventions and signings, his pastiche of *The Comics Journal*, and his caricatures of figures like Alan Moore and Rick Veitch are as of about as much general interest as a *roman à clef* set at the Breadloaf Writer's Conference or Yaddo. As someone who stopped reading mainstream comics when it was age-appropriate, I can sort of glean what Sim's referring to in these passages in the same way I used to infer the actual plots of R-rated movies from their *Mad* satires, but none of it interests me much; I tend to sigh and start skimming whenever the Roach character appears in some new costume. I can

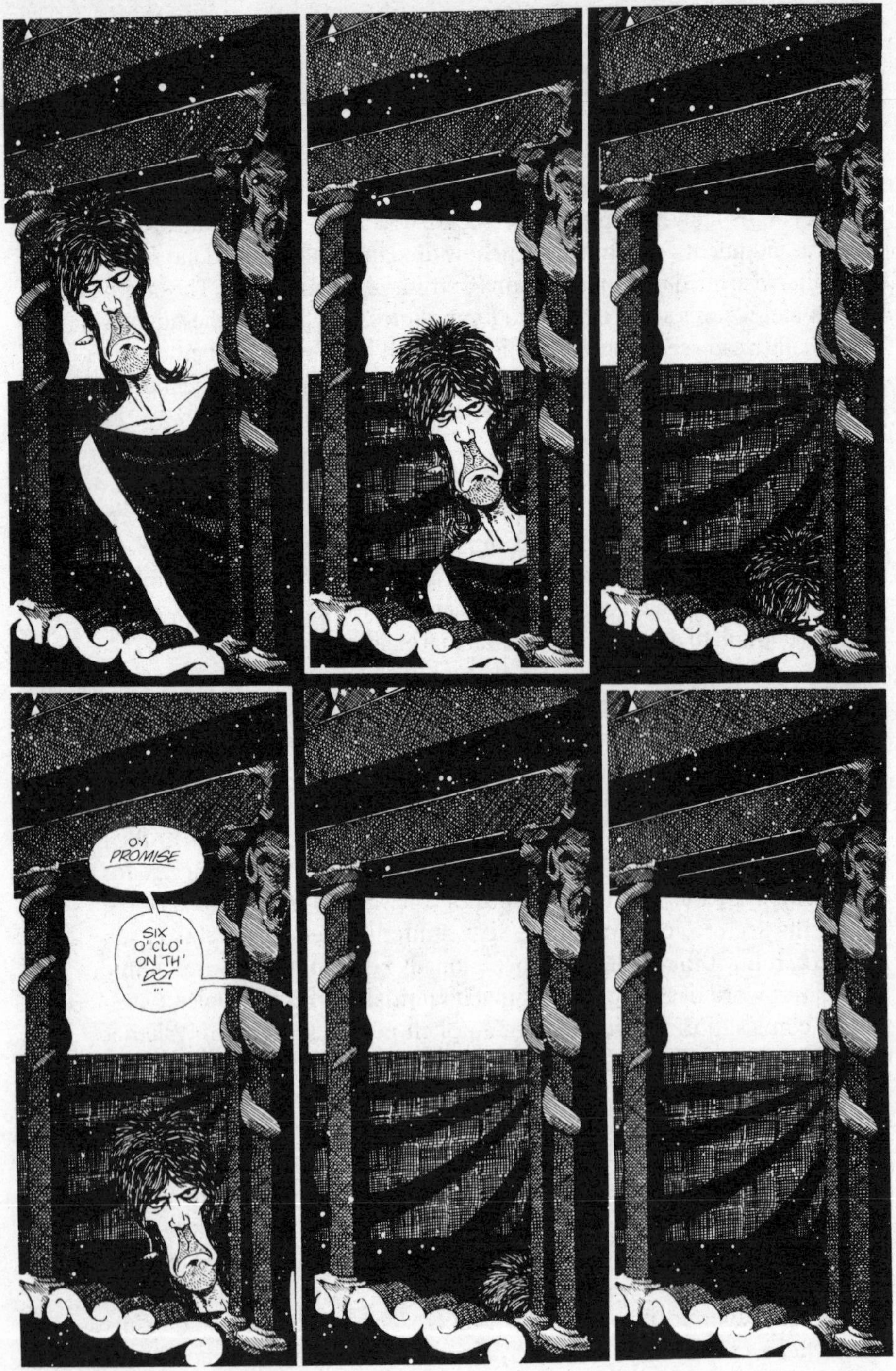
OY PROMISE
SIX O'CLO' ON TH' DOT ...

only imagine how opaque and pointless it would all seem to someone with no background in comics at all. Let's maybe just not even talk about the episode where Cerebus compulsively collects a comic book called *Rabbi*.

Also problematic is that, even as Sim's interests and literacy matured beyond comics, he doggedly continued exploring them within the framework of this same silly conceit he came up with when he was 21. Figures who are introduced as jokes — characters based on Barry Windsor-Smith's hot barbarian chick Red Sonja, Michael Moorcock's fantasy antihero Elric (who, for some reason, talks like Foghorn Leghorn) or a Prime Minister who is Groucho Marx — are enlisted as important continuing characters. The feeble gag of a name like Bran Mak Muffin wears very thin after 80 issues; it's hard to take the character seriously, even when he commits suicide. And throughout all 16 volumes, and a storyline that takes on politics, theology and the war between the sexes, the protagonist remains a talking animal. As Sim's drawing style becomes ever more sophisticated and realistic, his main character is still drawn in conformity to the original character design, so that his single eye with two pupils and his two separate mouths (one on each side) start to look less like cartoon conventions than deformities.

Most writers reiterate the same themes and express their maturing perspective by writing one book after another — a few or dozens over the course of a lifetime, depending on their productivity. But the fact that they're separate books acts as a kind of critical firewall between them. (Kurt Vonnegut is remembered as a great writer for *Slaughterhouse-Five* despite the existence of *Timequake*.) By insisting that his whole life's work be regarded as a single narrative and integrating it all into the same fictive universe, Sim forces us to average out the quality of the whole, judging it by a sort of mean; thus the artistic highs of *Church & State*, *Jaka's Story* and *Melmoth* are, to some extent, canceled out by the insufferable *Reads* and *Latter Days*. This wildly inconsistent quality is in evidence even within single volumes: *Going Home* is composed of two distinct halves, one of which is an account of Cerebus and Jaka's relationship deteriorating as Jaka sulks in bed, shops compulsively, and retards their progress, careless of the dangers encroaching on them — Just Like a Woman — but the other, *Time and the River* (an F. Scott Fitzgerald pastiche), is as good as anything Sim ever wrote. When I lent it to a friend I advised her to skip the first half and start with Part II.

Sim admits that after he completed the *Church & State* storyline he was "contemplating a blank canvas for the first time in five years," and it seems to me that here the *Cerebus* storyline might well have ended. (It could as easily have ended again at the end of *Minds*, when Cerebus has his own origin,

LEFT
Prince Keef (Keith Richards)'s comically timed suspicion in *Cerebus* Vol. 4: *Church & State* II.
[©1988 Dave Sim]

history and destiny explained to him by his creator and ends up marooned on Pluto.) Cerebus is only a marginal presence in both *Jaka's Story* and *Melmoth*, generally accounted among the best stand-alone volumes in the series. I don't understand why Sim maintained the title and kept setting his new stories in the same world, instead of simply writing a new graphic novella about, say, the death of Oscar Wilde, which is what really seemed to interest him. A formerly glamorous and charming writer is dying, alone and afraid, in a hotel room; what does a catatonic aardvark in the café downstairs add to the dramatic situation? It's as if Chester Brown had insisted on including Ed the Happy Clown as a minor character in his autobiographical novel about his mother's schizophrenia, *I Never Liked You*, and in the historical biography *Louis Riel*. Perhaps Sim needs to cling to this little gray aardvark as a kind of charm to carry off his artistic feats, like Dumbo clutching his magic feather in his trunk to believe he can fly. Or maybe it's just that that's what he decided to do while he was coming down off acid, and Dave Sim is a very stubborn guy. It's characteristic of Sim that, once it was pointed out to Sim that "Cerebus" was an erroneous garbling of the name of Hades' guard dog, he didn't correct the error, but instead stuck with it and made it his own.

There are precedents for this sort of artistic tenacity: Charles Schulz labored for half a century within the confines of the miniature universe he'd created, wringing new variations on the same small ensemble of characters and situations (the football yanked away in eternal recurrence), and John Updike returned to a character he'd created when he was in his 20s once at the end of every decade for the next 40 years. But then, *Peanuts* wasn't meant to be read as one continuous, coherent narrative, and Rabbit Angstrom was not an actual rabbit.

Improbable though he is, Cerebus is a sympathetic protagonist — *sympathetic* not being synonymous with *likeable* (some of his more questionable lapses include rape and infanticide). He's basically the embodiment of every man's surly little id, a slave to his various simple lusts — for money, power, women. In the early issues he's depicted as an Odysseus figure, as devious as he is fierce, getting the better of berserkers and wizards with cunning and duplicity as often as in battle. But for most of the book he's out of his ass-kicking element, all dolled up and hobbled in the accoutrements of civilization, looking ridiculous in his finery and wishing he could kill someone. (The trope of an animal inexplicably cast into human society as a metaphor for the uncomfortably buttoned-up unconscious is featured in several surrealist stories.) He's more often hapless and put-upon than fearsome, cast in the role of a political figurehead or a clumsily doting boyfriend. It's childishly exhilarating whenever he gets to cast off his foppery and act like a barbarian again — when Jaka gives him back his old broadsword, or when

he goes on a slashing rampage among the Cirinists, and even, in the very last issue, when he stands shakily up in his bed one last time, clutching his jeweled ceremonial sword and vowing to put an end to the abomination his son has shown him. The return of the repressed is always liberating.

Cerebus is not quite his creator's alter ego, and his arc is not exactly congruent with Dave Sim's biography, but there are some obvious parallels: At first their only priorities are worldly success and the pursuit of women; when they get what they want, they find it a prison; and they both undergo an unlikely religious conversion. On the couple of occasions when Sim confronts his creation directly, he treats him with condescension, grudging affection, even a little gratuitous cruelty. He keeps giving Cerebus what Cerebus thinks he wants — riches, kingdoms, the love of his life — and then lets him suffer for it. It would seem almost sadistic if it weren't so clear that Cerebus embodies parts of Sim that he's fond of but also despises, so that it instead amounts to a kind of — what to call it? Exhibitionistic masochism.

TOP
Top From *Cerebus*
#300 (March 2004)
[©2004 Dave Sim
& Gerhard]

What Sim does over the course of these 16 volumes is to retell the same story of Cerebus' thwarted rise to power and glimpse of some ultimate truth, three separate times: first in *Cerebus – Church & State II*, again in *Jaka's Story – Minds*, and once more in *Guys – The Last Day*. (Books like *Melmoth*, *Jaka's Story* and *Guys* are interludes between recapitulations of this master narrative, adagios between massive sonata-allegros.) In each of these arcs, Cerebus pursues his simple worldly ambitions — to get all the gold, to conquer the world, to get the girl — and always, just barely, but as inevitably as Sisyphus or Wile E. Coyote, fails. The first two arcs climax with a Great Ascension, a sort of one-man Rapture whereby Cerebus is literally lifted into the heavens. And in each of the three he receives a revelation about the true nature of reality: once, on the Moon, from the omniscient character The Judge; once, on a tour of the solar system en route to Pluto, in a metafictional cameo from the author himself; and the third time in a dream, directly from God. With each reiteration Sim revises this vision in conformity to his own evolving (or deteriorating) worldview. The first presents the origin myth of the universe as the primal rape of the female light by the male void; the last is the other way round (female void imitating and undermining the male light).

This repeating structure echoes Sim's personal belief (cf. the Vedas, Friedrich Nietzsche and William Butler Yeats) in vast, recurring cycles of history. The Judge describes several successive cycles of the evolution of consciousness and civilization on Earth, each of which eventually extinguishes itself without a trace. And there are intimations that the sequence of events we see in *Cerebus* has played out countless times before — the flashbacks Cerebus and Astoria both have at Astoria's trial of their previous confrontations in different incarnations, switching places as judge and prisoner, as well as the suggestive echo of the cryptic phrase "something fell" at crucial moments. Cerebus's failure to learn anything despite all his painful lessons and revelations is a one-man microcosm of humanity's stubborn, recidivist self-destruction. Sim sees history as reiterative, not cumulative — instead of a narrative of linear, upward progress it's just one damn thing after another. His characters are trapped in an eternal, closed cycle of predestined tragedy. At the very last, Cerebus almost escapes his fate, but not quite. Come to think of it, he's not so different from Rabbit Angstrom after all — both of them go to their deaths without having attained much insight or ever loving anything outside of themselves.

• • •

I also suspect that reading *Cerebus* in bound volumes is a qualitatively different experience than reading it as originally published must have been. Even though I remember my roommate griping about waiting a month and

"Sim sees history as reiterative, not cumulative — instead of a narrative of linear, upward progress it's just one damn thing after another."

spending $2.50 on an issue that showed Cerebus walking down a corridor, I still envy longtime *Cerebus* readers the experience of reading a new install-ment of the story every month, not only for its greater dramatic impact but for the chance to see the evolution of the book in real time. One of the most compelling aspects of serial fiction is getting to watch the artist improvise, experiment, flounder and make breakthroughs before your eyes — perform-ing, as it were, without a net. I remember my growing admiration and awe as I saw the disparate absurdist episodes in Chester Brown's *Yummy Fur* begin-ning to connect and dovetail into one unsettling story, and the weekly thrill of watching David Lynch sustain and deepen the darkly tantalizing mystery he'd established on *Twin Peaks*, waiting to see whether he could resolve it without destroying it. It must have been similarly exhilarating to watch Dave Sim's explosive artistic development throughout the '80s — trying every-thing, showing off, experimenting with his chosen form as exuberantly as Welles in *Citizen Kane*.

But serial narrative is a distinct art form, with its own strengths and rules of op-eration, and because *Cerebus* was written in monthly installments, it might've been ideally experienced that way. Serial drama most famously prolongs and intensifies suspense (think of the crowds at the docks waiting for the ship-ment of the new installment of *The Old Curiosity Shop* shouting, "Did Little Nell die?" or an entire nation reduced to wondering "Who Shot J.R.?"), but it also has another effect, less remarked upon but more important: it fosters an illusion of depth and history. Cursorily sketched characters are fleshed out in reader's imaginations and implied relationships take on a life of their own between installments, as potent as the visuals that listeners supplied to radio dramas. (Think of the depths with which fans imbued ciphers like Chekov or Uhura on *Star Trek*.) When Jaka reappears in *Church & State*, Sim presumes an emotionally charged history between her and Cerebus that doesn't exist in the text. She's a character who's appeared in exactly one previous issue, in which Cerebus, heretofore indifferent to women, drinks a love potion and falls goopily in love with Jaka, who's a dancer in a tavern. It's a relationship we take about as seriously as Titania's love for Bottom. And yet, to readers following the story as published, the sheer amount of real-life time that had passed since her last appearance must've infused that reunion with real feeling.

As with other very long-form works of art (I'm thinking of the films of Andrei Tarkovsky, or Morton Feldman's six-hour Second String Quartet) time and memory become important formal elements in *Cerebus*. *Melmoth*, which I read in about an hour and a half, originally took over a year to serialize; the title character spent months of reader time delirious and comatose, which would serve to recreate for the reader something of the same interminable vigil Wilde's friends endure as they sit writing letters, wiping bloody foam from Oscar's mouth, performing "terrible offices," and wait, day after day, for him to die. The final life-flashing-before-your-eyes montage seen at the moment of Cerebus' death,

About 5.30 in the morning a complete change came over him, the lines of the face altered and I believe what is called the death rattle began.

I had never heard anything like it before.

images culled from the previous 299 issues — Cerebus as a wide-eyed child in his newsboy's cap, the young, long-snouted Cerebus swinging his sword, Cerebus trying on a powdered wig at the Regency, yelling at servants, sullenly wearing the vestments of the Papacy, clutching Jaka's doll, flying, playing Five-Bar Gate, dawdling behind the bar, Cerebus in his later years with his whitening crewcut — actually gives you some slight mimetic shiver of looking back on a whole lifetime's passing. It's genuinely moving, if for no other reason than because it recalls the sheer amount of real time you've invested in the book and the character — the same reason that we get sentimental and melancholy when even a mediocre TV series that's occupied a significant fraction of our lifespans comes to an end.

The use of time's passage as a formal device in *Cerebus* echoes its thematic importance; especially in the later volumes, Sim seems increasingly preoccupied with senescence and death. *Melmoth* is the most harrowing artistic depiction of an individual death I've seen in any medium, faithfully rendering passages from the letters of Wilde's friends, flinching from no clinical detail (only looking discreetly away once or twice). F. Stop Kennedy (F. Scott Fitzgerald)'s anxiety about his lost youth and declining creativity is the undercurrent of "Time and the River,"

CENTER
Oscar Wilde dies
in *Cerebus* Vol. 6:
Melmoth. [©1997 Dave
Sim & Gerhard]

and *Form and Void* shows Ham Ernestway (Ernest Hemingway) as a mute and brooding shell, his literary prowess long past, inert and silent in static panel after panel. The account of Curly Howard's declining health and callous disenfranchisement from The Three Stooges (also transcribed from letters) is the only truly moving and human part of *Latter Days*; there is a terrible pathos in seeing this clownish figure from our childhoods, who was known as "Babe" to his brothers, reduced to a sad travesty of his former self by a stroke, slowed and slurring, struggling to remember his lines. And *The Last Day* spares the ancient and decrepit Cerebus no indignity: He's practically unrecognizable, his limbs wasted and rickety, his neck a thin, stringy stalk, his tiny, piggish eyes peering out from crevasses of wrinkles. He's tortured by chronic pain, half-crippled, dressed in a sagging diaper. We follow his excruciatingly cautious progress down from the bed to the floor, across his room and over to his desk through most of a whole issue. Finally climbing into his chair seems as heroic a feat as one of his old campaigns for gold and glory. The last we see of him, collapsed on the floor with a broken neck, he looks like the crumpled husk of a rotten melon. It should not, perhaps, have come as a surprise that an artist so conscious of age, decrepitude and death should turn, in the end, to thoughts of eternity.

• • •

Because *Cerebus* is extensively annotated by its author, and because he's held forth on it at such length in letters and interviews, it can be a tricky business trying to decide where to draw the line between the text and its explication. This, too, is problematic. Offering interpretations of one's own work is a very bad idea, not because it's just cooler for an artist to be enigmatically closemouthed but because anything he says about his intentions can only serve to limit and diminish it. (As Stanley Kubrick said in declining to explain his own famously cryptic films: "How could we possibly appreciate the *Mona Lisa* if Leonardo had written at the bottom of the canvas: 'The lady is smiling because she is hiding a secret from her

lover'?") It's an especially bad idea in Sim's case, since many of Sim's readings of his own work would seem to be willfully obtuse, skewed by personal prejudice, or just plain wrong.[2]

Most glaring is his hostility toward his female characters, especially Jaka, the beautiful blonde daughter of the aristocracy turned tavern dancer who is the great love of Cerebus's life. In a note in 1988 Sim writes, "I admire Jaka more than any of the other characters in the book," and goes on to describe her common sense, self-confidence, directness and lack of materialism; in an interview 18 years later he tells us: "Jaka is a self-absorbed aristocratic airhead. She always was." It's that "She always was," that's a red flag; it sounds like someone trying to convince himself, after a breakup, not only that he doesn't love his ex but that he *never* loved her. It's not only his attitude toward the character that changes over time; his depiction of her becomes broader, more unforgiving. In *Jaka's Story* and *Minds* Jaka is intelligent, self-aware and passionately devoted to her art, with a complex and fraught history — privileged and imprisoned, over-protected and molested. But by the time of *Going Home* and *Form & Void* she's become a caricature of everybody's bitchy ex-girlfriend — a selfish, pouty shopaholic. This is dishonest art, a distortion of the character to conform to the author's biases.

LEFT
Ham Ernestway (Ernest Hemingway) in *Cerebus* Vol. 14: *Form & Void* [©2001 Dave Sim & Gerhard]

RIGHT
Curly Howard's fall is retold in *Cerebus* Vol. 15: *Latter Days.* [©2003 Dave Sim & Gerhard]

[2] As I write this I'm realizing that this is yet another way in which Dave Sim was, through no fault of his own, a bad influence on me. I began writing "artist's statements" to accompany my cartoons that got longer and more polished over the years, until the cartoons started to seem more like illustrations or occasions for the essays. I finally quit being a cartoonist and became a writer instead.

This same Soviet airbrushing of the history books is in evidence throughout *Cerebus*, as when (usually female) characters suddenly reveal themselves not to be who they've claimed to be all along (or, in some cases, turn out never to have existed at all). This stripping away of layers of illusion and revelation of some deeper, opposing truth is an ongoing conceit throughout the book. But I suspect Sim does this most often with women not only because he believes they're inherently duplicitous but because, more tellingly, he can really only draw one attractive woman — try telling Jaka, Astoria or Michele apart without the visual cue of their hair — and doesn't want to have to introduce new ones. (He does, however, command an endless repertoire of ugly, hulking, hirsute, shrewish and bullying women. He draws a great Margaret Thatcher.) The journalist whom Cerebus seduces at the end of *Latter Days* doesn't just bear a striking resemblance to Jaka — she's identical. This is probably meant to suggest that Cerebus only ever really saw and loved Jaka's looks, but it might also seem to suggest that, to the artist, all women are the same, interchangeable, different guises of the great Deceptress.[3]

The book's other major female character, Astoria, a cool-eyed brunette, modeled on actress Mary Astor, who's the leader of the liberal/feminist

---

[3] The increasing disconnect between what Sim is doing as an artist and what he claims to be doing creates distortions and blind spots not only around his female characters but anything having to do with sex and relationships. He rewrites Hemingway's biography to lay blame for his suicide on his wife. His insistence that "F. Stop Kennedy" (F. Scott Fitzgerald)'s only interest in Jaka is as a potential patron, and has no sexual component at all, is so self-evidently contradicted by the actual story (images of F. Stop spinning romantic scenarios with Jaka, imagining himself kissing her passionately, etc.) that it seems not just disingenuous but symptomatic of some weird repression.

Kevillist movement, fares better than Jaka, perhaps because she exits before Sim's better artistic instincts succumb to his anti-feminist agenda. Although she, like a lot of other women in the book, is a smooth, multiple-masked manipulator who uses Cerebus as a means to power, she's not just a political opportunist but a true ideologue and leader. She's smart, resourceful and physically courageous (she's at her best when chained in a dungeon, awaiting execution), and for all her peremptory attitude toward intellectual inferiors she also shows a rueful, self-deprecating sense of humor ("immortality is mine," she sighs when Cerebus quotes a line from her manifesto he read on a latrine wall). Her abdication of political ambition and turning away, Candide-like, to tend a garden haven, is unexpected, but it doesn't seem contrived or discontinuous with her character; it's credible in the context of the circumstances. It seems like something Astoria would do, not just something her author would have her do to illustrate a point.

In fact, for all Sim's yammering about women's superficiality, irrationality and intellectual dishonesty, the book's most fully realized characters are all female. The women he writes off as bimbos or harridans have more dimensions than he gives them credit for. And despite his insistence on men's intellectual and ethical superiority, we don't see much evidence in *Cerebus* of men behaving rationally or morally. The patriarchal utopia that Cerebus commands for a time in *Latter Days* is a Draconian horror, involving the annual execution by blunderbuss of any woman judged by mob rule to be a bitch. What little Cerebus learns in his life comes too late to save him. Most of the other men we see are either Machiavellian schemers like Julius and Weisshaupt or feckless drunkards and goofballs. Rick, whom Sim intends to be the epitome of genuine goodness, his Prince Myshkin, is more naïf than saint. When we see

LEFT AND TOP

From *Cerebus* Vol. 12: *Rick's Story* [©1998 Dave Sim & Gerhard]

him in *Guys* he's become an alcoholic, and the phantasmagoric visions he suffers suggest not divine revelation but psychosis. I suspect that (despite Sim's insistent disclaimers) Rick is how Sim would like to imagine himself — a lonely, misunderstood prophet who's regarded by others as touched in the head but is in sole possession of the word of God. But Rick only seems, to the reader, to be a pitiful or tragic figure; it is, for better or worse, with the selfish and imperfect Cerebus that we identify. Despite Sim's agenda, these characters all keep behaving like human beings — erratically, idiosyncratically — not allegorical figures acting out agitprop or a morality play.

In other words, *Cerebus* is often a much better book than Dave Sim seems to realize, or intended it to be. As D.H. Lawrence wrote of Herman Melville: "The artist is so *much* greater than the man." It's been little remarked upon that a man who claims to disdain emotion, and affects a pious equanimity at having cut off all contact with his parents while his mother was in the hospital, shows us, at the climax of *Going Home*, his protagonist falling to his knees, screaming, and rending his garments in shame at having abandoned his family in their hour of need. It's as if what Sim represses in his own conscious life is what infuses his work with its emotional depth — depths to which he himself is blind. Sim would doubtless deny any connection here, just as he argues that any perception of Jaka as a Strong Female Character is pure projection on the part of his readers. But leaving room for your readers' interpretations is what makes art resonate. If a violin were a solid piece of wood it would be silent; it's the empty space inside it that makes the music.

Sim's compulsive self-explication is consistent with his drawing and writing styles, all of which attempt to exert as much control over his readers' experience as possible. His cartooning is at the opposite end of the spectrum from Thurber's or Schulz's, who offer us universal templates on which we can project ourselves; his caricatures capture every quirk and flicker of expression and subtly telling gesture, and his emotive lettering — a gently arched syllable indicating a Liverpudlian lilt, a quick line scratched through a word evoking a voice breaking with outrage or glee — directs his characters' line readings as dictatorially as John Waters reading his dialogue out loud to his actors exactly the way he wants it spoken. He stage-manages conversations between his characters, as in the interview between Jaka and her portraitist ("at this assertion their roles had retreated to a more appropriate balance and they had both relaxed"), overexplaining motives and layers of meaning like a novice who doesn't trust his audience, or is just showing off. Lynda Barry, in *What It Is*, reminds us that any artist can only ever contribute 50 percent of a work of art; the audience supplies the other 50 percent. ("Writing ... is but a different name for conversation," is how

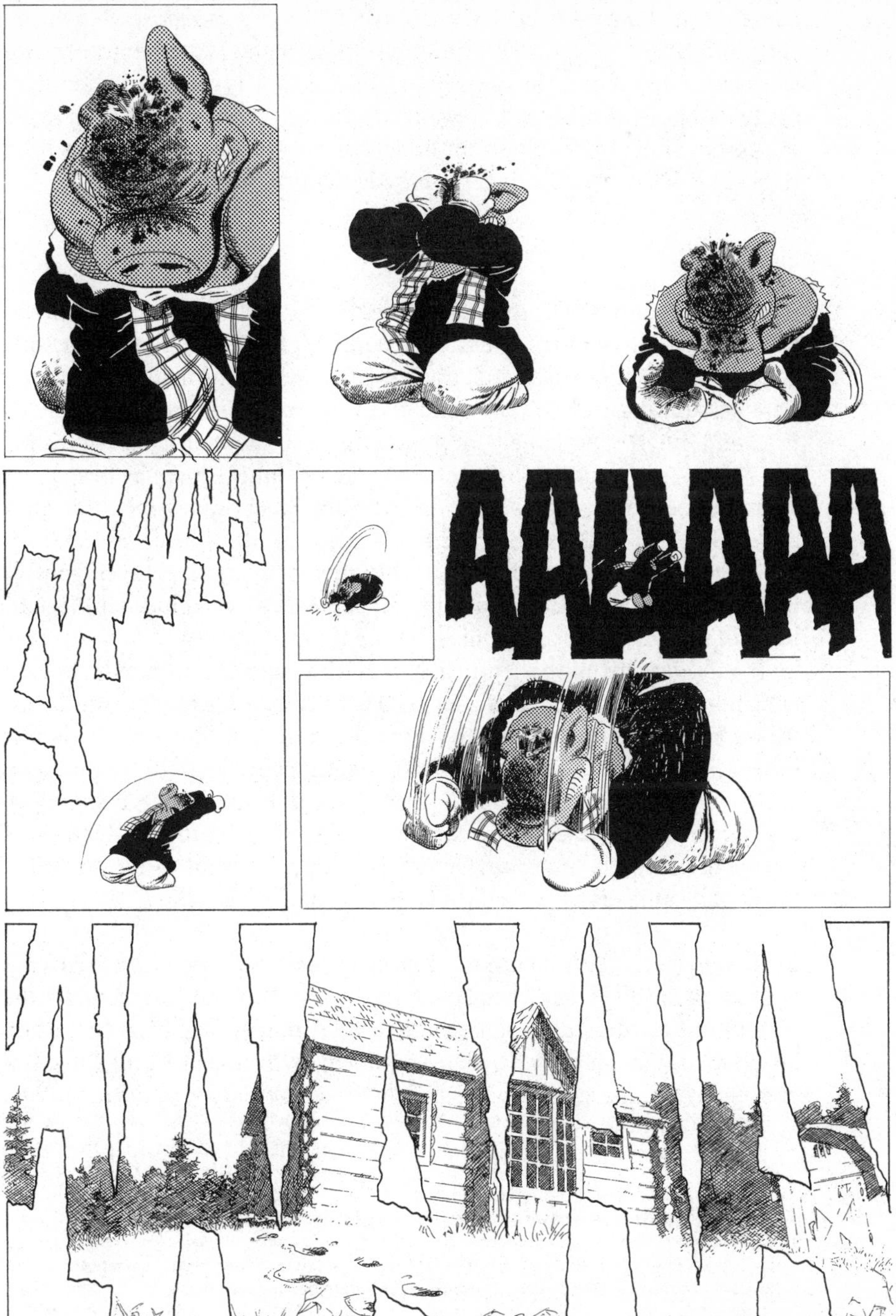
AAAAAA

Laurence Sterne puts it in *Tristram Shandy.* "The truest respect which you can pay to the reader's understanding is to halve the matter amicably, and leave him something to imagine in his turn, as well as yourself.") Dave Sim isn't content with this deal; he wants to dictate the whole 100 percent, to the point of micromanaging your understanding of the book after it's been published. His artistic instincts are fundamentally authoritarian.

• • •

In the later volumes of *Cerebus,* Sim leaves less and less room for interpretation and just starts lecturing us. As all conflict gives way to fervid certainty, actual relationships between characters give way to long dialogues between Cerebus and his creator, back-and-forth internal dialogues in Cerebus's head and, finally, intolerably long monologues. The central text of *Women* consists of the dialectic between opposing political manifestoes; *Reads* alternates between action scenes and self-indulgent tirades about the publishing industry and women. The book ceases to be a conversation; Sim's basically transcribing the arguments he wins in his head. He even goes so far as to describe the futile evasions, desperate denial and inevitable crumbling of his imaginary antagonists before his own clear-eyed, unassailable logic and overwhelming rhetorical superiority. There's a section in *Reads* in which the reader is supposedly reduced to near-catatonia before the awful, inescapable truth of Viktor Davis's words, while the actual reader is just bored. (Watching him deliver the devastating coup de grace to a pretend straw woman—"*capice,* you bitch? ... aw, look at the pretty nazi all mad" — is as embarrassing as catching someone talking to himself.) This tendency toward the pedantic — toward lecture, polemic, or sermon — terminates in the literally unreadable screeds of *Latter Days* and *The Last Day.*[4]

In the storyline that would become *Latter Days,* Dave Sim had planned to write a parody of the Bible. But when he sat down to read the Old Testament for the first time he discovered the same thing that R. Crumb would years later when he did the same thing for his own adaptation of Genesis: that the Bible is a profoundly strange text — savage and alien to modern readers, full of internal

---

[4] It's an especially tragic fate for an author whose ear for dialogue is so finely tuned. Although Sim's dialogue is exemplary and his mimicry perfect, his prose, I'm afraid, is not so great. I suspect that, like Alan Moore, one reason he gravitates toward pastiches of Victorian writers is because his own style naturally tends toward the purple end of the spectrum. His imitation of Oscar Wilde is ornate and turgid to the point of tedium. He's tone-deaf to the austere beauty of Hemingway's prose, and his attempts to parody it only imitate the form and miss its essence. In *Going Home,* when he presumes to rewrite passages of F. Scott Fitzgerald to render them "more ethical," his insertion of flaccid qualifying phrases deprives the original of its elegance and force — you could say he emasculates it.

contradictions and multiple versions of the same stories, bearing little resemblance to the Sunday School/sword-and-sandal version. What happened to Sim as he attempted to make sense of it was unexpected: He converted ... kind of — in a very Dave Sim way. He couldn't convert to anybody else's religion but invented his own one-man church, a distillation of the three major Abrahamic faiths. He renounced his drinking, drugging and girl-chasing, became chaste and abstinent, and began fasting, giving to charity and praying five times a day. And instead of his intended parody he undertook an exegesis.

Glancing ahead at *Latter Days* is not so much daunting as completely demoralizing. What you see in flipping apprehensively through the book are endless, dense blocks of tiny six-point text, uninterrupted by any break or indentation — text that appears, to your horror, to consist of Cerebus, one-time hard-drinking, broadsword-wielding kicker of ass, explicating the books of the Pentatuch at laborious, painstaking and wrongheaded length, all inexplicably illustrated with recreations of stills from Federico Fellini and Ingmar Bergman films and caricatures of Woody Allen. (Eventually Sim anticipates his audience's boredom by interposing onomatopoeic FLIPs into the text to indicate the imaginary reader's increasingly impatient skimming — though "anticipates" is probably the wrong word, since he only starts doing it some 10s of pages after the actual reader has given up.) It is here that *Cerebus* abandons any but the most cursory form of fiction and gives itself over entirely to the didactic explication of its author's crackpot theories. In short, it becomes something other than what I would call art: a manifesto, or propaganda. It does not help that Sim's Biblical exegesis is a mortifyingly naked psychodrama (kind of inevitably, it involves a false deceiver-goddess).

Being an autodidact has a lot of the same advantages and hazards for intellectual development that being free of any editorial control does for artistic development: It allows you to pursue original, heterodox, potentially interesting new directions without being hobbled by conventional wisdom. But there's also no one to correct you when you're headed down a blind alley, straying far from your area of competence, or just talking out of your ass. At the beginning of *The Last Day*, Cerebus has a dream in which Dave Sim presents the final and definitive version of his cosmogony. This dream, which occupies the first 40 pages of the volume, is told in faux-King James prose, printed in a tiny, eye-prickling gothic font, and heavily footnoted. In this passage, Sim apparently believes he has formulated the Theory of Everything, unifying relativistic and quantum mechanics, that's eluded physics' greatest minds for decades. Sim is genuinely disappointed that the scientific world has not hailed him as a genius on the order of Einstein and Newton, attributing his lack of recognition, once again, to our pussywhipped society's prejudice

Cerebus:

Okay. Chapter ten. The generations of Shem, Ham and Japhet. *Yoohwhoo's* version, anyway. You can tell that it's Yoohwhoo's version because she narrates it as if it's going to be the same as chapter *six*: a bunch of big, strong, famous guys beating crap out of each other. Ham's eldest son is Cush *"And Cush begat Nimrod: he began to be a mighty one in the earth. He was a mighty hunter before the Yoohwhoo: wherefore it is saide, Even as Nimrod the mightie hunter before the Yoohwhoo. And the beginning of his kingdom was Babel, and Erech, and Accad, and Calneh, in the land of Shinar. Out of that land went forth Asshur, and builded Nineueh, and the citie Rehoboth, and Calah, and Resen betweene Nineueh and Calah: the same is a great citie."* Unfortunately for Yoohwhoo, that's about it, as far as the "mighty hunters before the Yoohwhoo" and the "great cities" go. Shem's son, Arphaxad begets Salah? Nothing. Salah begets Eber? Nothing. Then Eber begets two sons and Yoohwhoo tells us *"the name of one, Peleg, for in his dayes was the earth diuided, and his brothers name Joktan."* So, evidently, this Peleg guy's name translates as something like: "Divided Earth". Which is interesting, since Yoohwhoo is, obviously, talking about herself. But, as usual, she doesn't say *much*—besides the basic fact that the earth was divided in the days of Peleg. The only other clue is in the last verse, *"These the families of the sonnes of Noah after their generations, in their nations: and by these were the nations diuided in the earth after the Flood."* Note:...

Konigsberg:

"...in the earth." I *promise* to *always* note "in the earth" if you promise to stop pointing it out.

Cerebus:

[thinks] Deal. As Cerebus reads it, this means that not only are the spirits of *birds flying around* upside-down inside the earth, not only are the spirits of *men and women walking around* upside down inside the earth, but *nations also* have spirits—BIG spirits—inside the earth. And all of those nations formed *around* the descendants of Shem, Ham and Japhet. Which makes for a big difference

between the two different kinds of men. The *regular* men—the *leftover* men from last time—end up getting absorbed into whatever nation formed around whatever Shem, Ham or Japhet descendant they happened to be living near. The *regular* men have sons, the sons grow up and "beget" other sons, but they're just, you know, *regular* families. The descendants of Shem, Ham and Japhet, on the other hand, although *they're* families, too, they're *also* nations. Canaan begets Tzidon and Heth, but he *also* begets the Jebusite, the Emorite, the Girgasite and so on: *nationalities.* So basically, while these *nations* are forming *on* the earth around the descendants of Shem, Ham and Japhet, they're also forming *in* the earth as BIG spirits. BIG spirits that aren't as big as Yoohwhoo but which are much bigger than bird-spirits and men-spirits and women-spirits. And they are *all* descended from He, She and It—so *everyone* is under Yoohwhoo. God has no representation at all.

Okay. Now, chapter eleven. Cerebus is pretty sure that this is the story of "how the earth was divided" in Peleg's days. *"And the whole earth was of one lippe, and of one words."* All the descendants of Shem, Ham and Japhet still speak the same language. *"And they said, Goe to, let vs build vs a city and a tower, whose top may vnto heauen, and let vs make vs a name, lest we be scattered abroad vpon the face of the whole earth. And the Yoohwhoo came downe to see the city and the tower, which the children of men builded. And the Yoohwhoo said; Behold the people one, and they all one language: and this they begin to doe: and now nothing will be restrained from them which they haue imagined to doe. Goe to, let vs go downe, and there confound their language, that they may not vnderstand one anothers speech."* This is Yoohwhoo deciding, again—same as she did with the fruit from the tree of life—what things men are going to be allowed to do and have and what things they are *not* going to be allowed to do and have. It's a weird part of the book. It's as if the men believe—and *Yoohwhoo* believes—that "heaven" is something more than a bunch of air, dividing the waters from the waters, as if "heaven" is [laughs] Yoohwhoo's *house*, or something. This is also the first time that we find out that Yoohwhoo's spirit isn't *confined* to the earth, that her spirit can move around in the air—in the "heaven"—as well as in the earth

against anti-feminists, rather than to the fact that his hypothesis makes Louis Farrakhan's theories about Sun People and Ice People look like an impeccably sourced, rigorously peer-reviewed piece of research. It's essentially the same sort of sad tract a schizophrenic would urge you to read on the subway, except beautifully illustrated. (Gerhard's drawings of the solar system's accretion are exquisite.) The climactic revelation of *The Last Day* is of Cerebus's grandchild, a hideous freak of genetic engineering with a lion cub's body and the head of a baby. In his commentary, Sim seriously proposes that the sphinxes and other chimeras depicted in ancient art were not images of gods or fabulous beasts but representations of actual human-animal hybrids created by those civilizations. This is, to use the clinical term, batshit.

In the end, as in the model of the oscillating universe, Dave Sim's extraordinary artistic growth decelerates, comes to a halt, and contracts again, finally collapsing back into a one-dimensional point of absolute, inalterable conviction. All ambiguity, tension and conflict — in other words, the basic components of drama — are forcibly reconciled in self-contained, hermetic certitude. (Cerebus, like his creator, ends up alone, cloistered away with his testament in a well-appointed cell.) His aims are no longer artistic but didactic. Art is an act of self-expression, but it's also, crucially, an act of communication, an attempt to connect with another human being. (Another hazard of autodidacticism is growing to adulthood without developing any intellectual humility, with your precocious 13-year-old's conviction that everyone is stupid except for you intact.) And in Dave Sim's belief that he alone is in possession of the Truth, he loses faith that his reader might be an intellectual equal, a fellow human being with whom he might have something in common. (He sometimes uses Cerebus as an unflattering surrogate for his readers' dumbed-down comprehension level and short attention span.) It's especially sad because I know some very smart readers who still remember how exhilarating it was, in their teens or 20s, to come across a comic book that evidenced such a lively and skeptical intelligence. *Cerebus* made them feel less alone. But Sim's evident determination to alienate himself from his family, friends and colleagues, from the whole human race except for his contracting circle of uncritical admirers, extends, finally, to his audience. The book

LEFT AND TOP
From *Cerebus* Vol. 15:
Latter Days [©2003
Dave Sim & Gerhard]

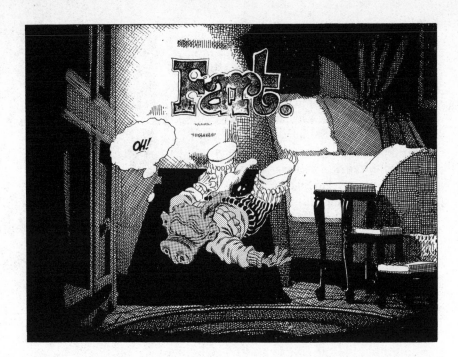

becomes less art than an artifact; you're no longer engaged in a dialogue with the author but only eavesdropping on him talking to himself, and can only watch as he plays out the last of his one-man drama on an empty stage.

His humor is Sim's last link to sanity, his saving grace; humor is essentially anti-dogmatic, anti-fanatical, always bringing us back down to earth, a pie in the face of pompous solemnity. The slapstick of the Three Wise Fellows and Todd McSpawn's no-bullshit homeboy persona leaven even the otherwise depressingly leaden last volumes. But as moral judgment becomes more important to Sim, his sense of humor suffers — or becomes more idiosyncratic and cruel, out of tune with anyone else's. I'm thinking especially of that sequence in which various female colleagues of Sim's are executed by mob vote, which is supposedly satiric but mostly just makes you feel queasy to read. This tension between morality's uncompromising condemnation and humor's forgiving wink only intensifies, eternally irreconcilable, even unto the very end. As he's falling to his death, Cerebus, who's been bloated with gas pains and praying for relief for the entire book, finally farts in midair—a glorious fart onomatopoetically inscribed in an elaborate churchly font, like a last divine benediction, a moment of grace. It's Sim's final kindness to his creation, as if Charles Schulz had at last let Charlie Brown kick that football. Then he drags him off to Hell.

TOP
From *Cerebus* #300
(March 2004)
[©2004 Dave Sim
& Gerhard]

. . .

Before I sat down to read all of *Cerebus*, I'd imagined that the thesis of this essay would be that Dave Sim was a brilliant artist denied the critical acclaim he deserves because of his obstreperous public persona. After reading it, I realized that, taken as a whole, it might just be too irredeemably problematic to be called a good book. Sim's insistence on all 300 issues/16 volumes of his *magnum opus* being regarded as a single work weaken its overall quality. *Cerebus* is simply too insular and self-referential, too obscure and personal and profoundly strange. Its author's personal implosion into entrenched and fanatical certitude ultimately renders large swaths of the book incomprehensible or irrelevant to just about every other human being alive. It would be possible to construct a bowdlerized abridgement of *Cerebus* in hopes of appealing to a general audience, consisting of, say, *High Society*, *Church & State*, *Jaka's Story*, *Melmoth*, parts of *Going Home*, and tactfully omitting all the rabid wacko rants. But this would not be the real *Cerebus*, any more than the Sunday School version of the Bible, omitting all the incest and slaughter and divine injunctions to stoning and slavery, is the true Bible.

But now, having reread parts of it and thought about it and talked it over with colleagues, my ultimate (or at least latest) judgment is more complex and paradoxical. I do believe that Dave Sim is one of the great cartoonists, a better artist and craftsman than most of the form's most celebrated figures; certainly far better than any of those few cartoonists who have crossed over to a broader audience and found mainstream critical acclaim—e.g. Art Spiegelman, Alison Bechdel, Marjane Satrapi. And yet *Cerebus* is not as good a book, and will probably never be considered to be as good, as *Maus*, *Fun Home*, *Persepolis* or any of the other titles that now get obligatory mention in magazines' "Best Comics" lists or taught in college courses on The Graphic Novel.

And yet again—

Even though *Cerebus* isn't as *good* a book as *Maus* or *Fun Home* or *Persepolis*, it's much more *interesting* than any of them. You sometimes hate reading *Cerebus*, but when you've finished you catch yourself envying friends who are beginning it. I would rather reread it, and would much rather *look* at it, than any of those other, better books.[5] Frankly, Spiegelman and Bechdel

[5] For example: even though I'm now way past my deadline on this essay I just paused to reread the dialogue between Prince Mick and Cerebus when Cerebus, his usual priorities reordered by whiskey and codeine, tells Mick to take all of his gold. ("TIKE OLE OF I'?!... KEEF! ARE YOU LISTENIN' T'THIS?")

371

and Satrapi all seem to me to be minor talents who put their limited abilities to the best possible use because they each had one great story to tell. Their draftsmanship gets the job done, but it looks undistinguished and dull compared to Sim's fluid command of expression and gesture, his pyrotechnical talent and inexhaustible visual invention.[6] Those more celebrated books are all relatively short, unified, traditional narratives, they're all memoirs (the hot commercial literary form of the last decade), and they're all about politically fashionable subjects; *Cerebus*, on the other hand, is a sprawling, sloppy, lopsided mess, hard to classify by form or genre or anything else, its subject resolutely uncool, and its politics are so reactionary as to be widely regarded as hate speech or evidence of a clinical disorder. It is brilliant and hilarious and incredibly boring, very, *very* annoying, infuriating and beautiful, defiantly inaccessible, arguably insane, and, arguably, great. I'm not sure it should even be called a "book"; it's something bigger than that — a complete document of one man's artistic, intellectual and spiritual life. To appeal to mainstream tastes, it seems, comics have to compromise, conforming to more respectable literary conventions. Dave Sim is — and this is one epithet he would relish — undomesticable.

What I've learned in trying to evaluate *Cerebus* is that, in comics, at least, I prefer those artists whose overabundant, undisciplined genius is driven by forces that may also cripple it — the Dave Sims, the Al Columbias — to those plodding competents who produce safely praiseworthy work. Don't get me wrong: Those books are all good, but they're *just good* — and compared to *Cerebus*, "good" seems a little boring. John Lewis (*True Swamp*) once made a striking remark to me about *Jimmy Corrigan, The Smartest Kid on Earth*: "Chris Ware was the first cartoonist who produced a book that *wasn't* a mess," he said. "I was disappointed."[7] I'm not about to claim that *Cerebus* is the equal of other magnificent messes of world literature like *Tristram Shandy*, *Moby Dick* or *Gravity's Rainbow*, but it is a lesser member of the same taxonomical order — what Roberto Bolaño, in *2666*, described (somewhat self-servingly) as "the great, imperfect, torrential works, books that blaze paths into the unknown."

---

[6] Maybe I'm old-fashioned in my admiration for excellence in craft. When I look at an Andy Warhol or an Yves Klein, I may be amused or impressed that the artist thought it up and got away with it, but when I look at an Ingres, I'm awed that a human being actually made it. It elevates my estimation of my own species.

[7] To be sure, there are plenty of graphic novels in the large intermediate space on the spectrum between *Maus* and *Cerebus* — books like *Jimmy Corrigan*, which are literary and well-constructed, but, like *Cerebus*, are just too idiomatically comic-bookish in form, requiring too sophisticated a level of visual literacy from their audience, to achieve mass popularity. *Cerebus* has its own unique handicaps, like being 6,000 pages long, insane and about an aardvark.

For all its stylistic innovation, *Cerebus* is an atavistic book, a throwback to the unabashedly didactic moral fiction of 19th-century novelists. It is, in the end, grimly absolutist and unforgiving. Sim actually answers David Foster Wallace's famous call for a new generation of literary rebels who would run the postmodern risk of looking uncool and old-fashioned, self-righteous and square, who'd have "the childish gall actually to endorse single-entendre values" — although Sim's values are probably not what Wallace was imagining. He's one of those writers — of whom there have been many in the last century, from C.S. Lewis to H.P. Lovecraft — who feel that the time is out of joint, that modernity is a wrong turn, a big mistake. (The world depicted outside Cerebus's fortified cloister in *The Last Day* is an if-it-feels-good-do-it dystopia of tattoos and mutilations, junkies and child molesters — Western secular liberalism as Hieronymus Bosch's garden.) I almost can't help but admire, on an abstract level, the intellectual cussedness of anyone who publicly stakes out such lonely and unpopular positions — even if he does believe that the cause of all our society's ills is, essentially, people like me.

TOP

From *Cerebus* Vol. 16: *The Last Day* [©2004 Dave Sim & Gerhard]

"Or — who knows? — maybe centuries from now the pendulum of history will swing back, posterity will conclude that feminism was an historical aberration, and Sim will be exhumed as a brave, clear-eyed visionary in an effete and decadent time. I kinda doubt it, though."

Trying to guess at the future critical fate of art is a fool's game; *Moby Dick* was famously lost to obscurity for generations because it, too, is something of a mess, a strange and singular work of obsession. I worry that *Cerebus* may endure only as a cultural artifact, an inscrutable curiosity like Darger's *The Vivian Girls* — *sui generis*, without real precedent or successors. I suspect that if Dave Sim were a 50-year-old living in his mother's basement who'd never published a comic or made a dollar and the whole massive tome of *Cerebus* were to be unearthed tomorrow by some enterprising gallery agent, he might well be internationally celebrated as a brilliant outsider artist. He does have several of the biographical criteria that seem to be *de riguer* for that designation — no formal art education, a history of mental illness, a road-to-Damascus religious conversion. Unfortunately, Sim is also a canny businessman and an incessant self-promoter, and part of the appeal of the outsider artist is the patronizing satisfaction of discovering them, granting them the imprimatur of our appreciation. It's a lot less gratifying to do this when the artist himself has been bleating for decades that he's a genius unfairly discriminated against because his opinions are intellectually out of favor.

Or — who knows? — maybe centuries from now the pendulum of history will swing back, posterity will conclude that feminism was an historical aberration, and Sim will be exhumed as a brave, clear-eyed visionary in an effete and decadent time. I kinda doubt it, though.

At best, I think, Dave Sim will always be an artist like James Joyce, Arnold Schoenberg, or Stan Brakhage, whom other practitioners of his art will revere and study for instruction and inspiration, but whose work is too esoteric, too exclusionary and demanding, to appeal to a broader audience. He's a rarefied taste for the appreciation of connoisseurs — a cartoonist's cartoonist. But Sim always intended *Cerebus* to be a comic book, not an illustrated novel or fodder for Hollywood or any other halfassed hybrid. It is steeped in that medium's history and culture, full of allusions to its classics and masters, playing variations on its themes, subverting its conventions. It's like a masterpiece written in Tlingit, untranslatable, a gift to those dwindling few who can fully appreciate it. If you're reading this article in this publication, then you are likely one of comics' remaining native speakers, and you might owe it to yourself, and to the art form, to at least have a look at this, its great idiomatic epic.

And let's pause, lastly, to note that comics is one of the very few media in which such a project would even have been possible. In almost any other art form, commercial considerations, collaborators, or official gatekeepers (editors, publishers, gallery owners, producers) would've curtailed Dave Sim's excesses and censored his descent into craziness. Even if Sim's advocacy of self-publishing worked out for many who followed him on that path about as well as the United States' championing of free-market capitalism did in South America, in his own case it allowed him to do exactly whatever the hell he wanted for 30 years. I can think of very few other examples of artists who have been so free of any editorial control or second-guessing. I'm not arguing that this kind of completely unfettered creative freedom is necessarily a good thing, even though it's what all artists imagine they want; quite a lot of them succumb to hubristic self-indulgence when given *carte blanche*. On the other hand, if Sim had apprenticed himself to an established cartoonist like Barry Windsor-Smith and had a career as an artist or writer at DC or Vertigo, he might have gone on to become an excellent craftsman in the industry, turning out striking page layouts or superior storylines, but he'd probably never have undergone the explosive artistic growth he did, and we would not have *Cerebus*, this gift of his titanic and maculate talent. We would be poorer for it. ∎

Those of us who have read *Cerebus* are like veterans of some obscure war, grateful for anyone with whom they can reminisce and commiserate. My thanks to Jesse Fuchs and Alex Robinson, with whom my conversations about *Cerebus* were invaluable. I am indebted to them for their insights. However, the interpretations and opinions in this piece are wholly my own. And thanks to my college roommate, Mark Stewart, for letting me bum all those issues of *Cerebus*.

JOE SACCO

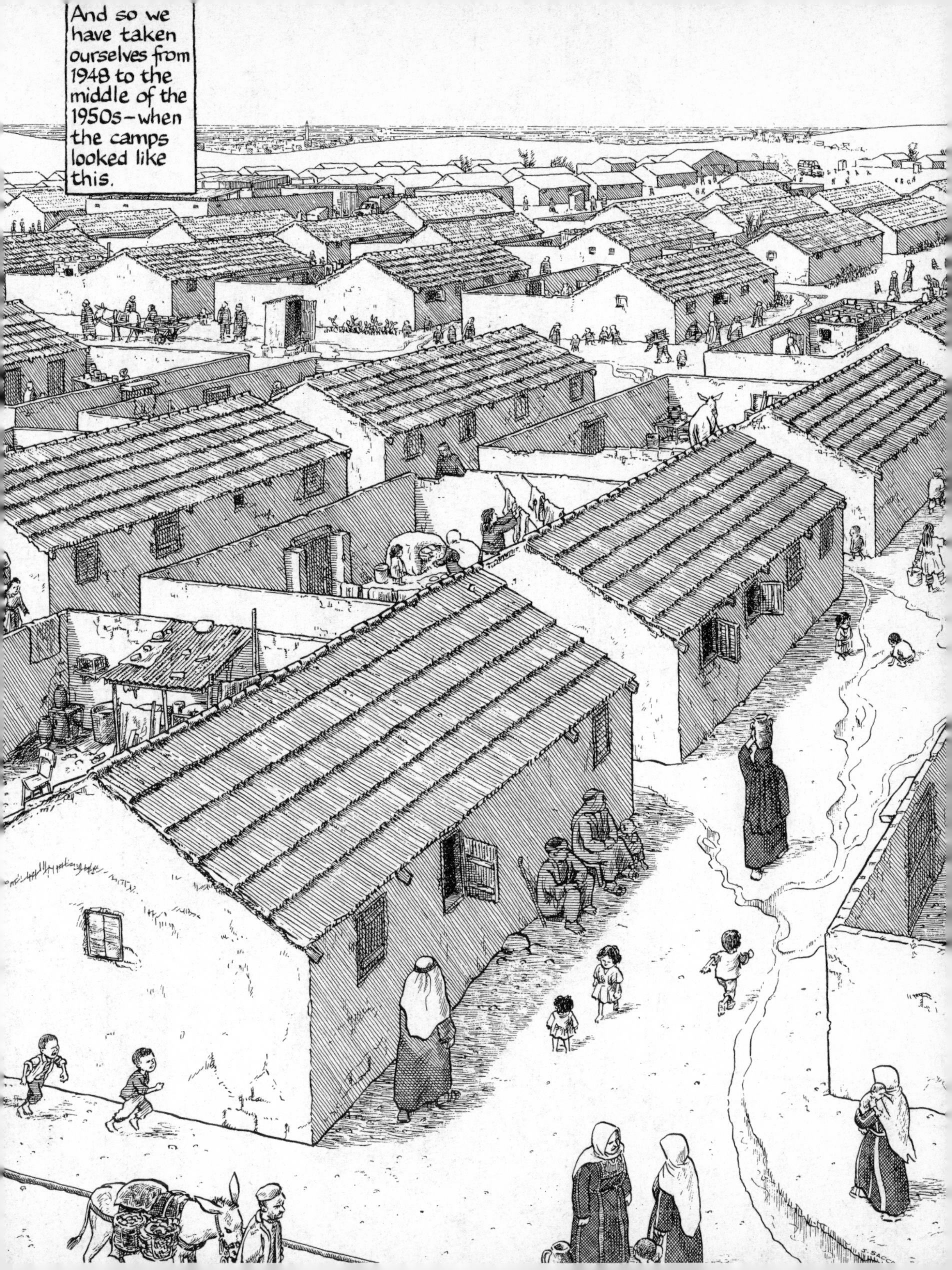
And so we have taken ourselves from 1948 to the middle of the 1950s—when the camps looked like this.

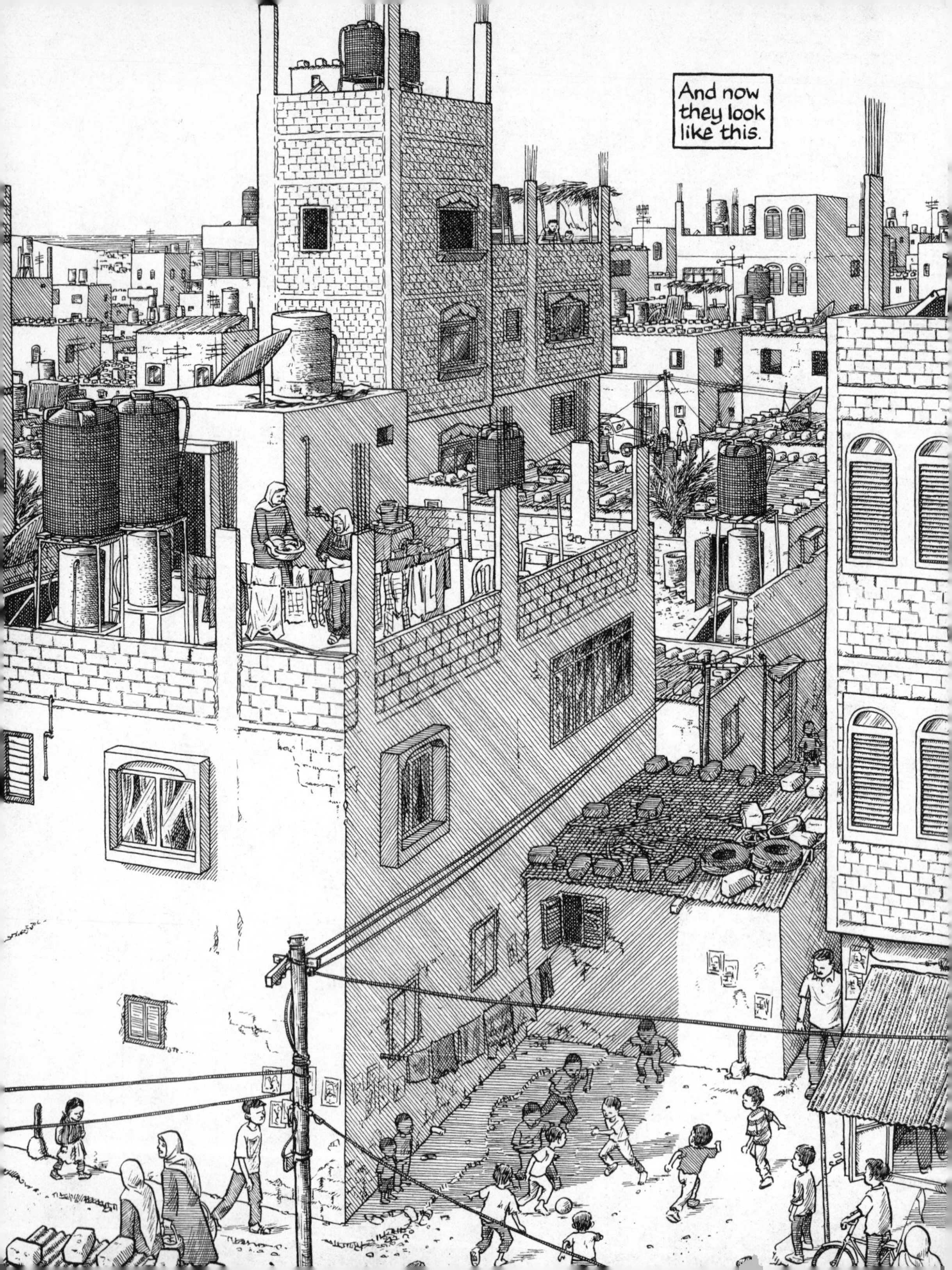
And now they look like this.

Joe Sacco is virtually a one-man comics genre: the cartoonist-journalist. True, there have been examples of comics journalism in the past and there are a handful of cartoonists who have more recently used the comics form to illuminate contemporary events, but no cartoonist has practiced journalism as seriously or gone as deeply into his subject as Sacco.

I have no hesitation in proclaiming Sacco's latest book, Footnotes in Gaza, a masterpiece — of the cartoonist's art, of reportage, of history — and, perforce, the subject of the following interview.

As Sacco tells it, he became aware of the Israeli massacre of Palestinians in the town of Khan (pronounced Han) Yunis in 1956 when he stumbled upon a brief mention of it in Noam Chomsky's The Fateful Triangle — almost a footnote, but not quite; a half a paragraph on page 102 of a 481-page book, it reads:

> The Israeli occupying army carried out bloody atrocities in the Gaza strip, killing 'at least 275 Palestinians immediately after capturing the Strip during a brutal house-to-house search for weapons and fedayeen in Khan Yunis' and killing 111 Palestinians in 'another massive bloodletting' at the Rafah refugee camp in 'disorders' after 'Israeli troops stormed through the hovels, rounding up refugees for intelligence screening.' General E.L.M. Burns, Commander of the U.N. truce Supervision Organization (UNTSO), commented that this furnished 'very sad proof of the fact that the spirit of the notorious Deir Yassin massacre of 1948 is not dead among some of the Israeli armed forces." The head of the Gaza observer force, Lt.-Col R.F. Bayard of the U.S. Army, reported that treatment of civilians was 'unwarrantedly rough' and that 'a good number of persons have been shot down in cold blood for no apparent reason.' He also reported that many U.N. relief officials were missing and presumed executed by the Israelis and that there had been extensive looting and wanton destruction of property. Israel claimed that the killings were caused by 'refugee resistance,' a claim denied by refugees. (There were no Israeli casualties). Love cites Moshe Dayan's diaries confirming the looting, which caused 'much shame to ourselves,' and indicating that there had been practically no resistance.

That was it, and that was enough to pique Sacco's interest in what, as it turned out, was one of the most under-reported incidents of its kind in the history of the Israeli-Palestinian conflict.

In 2001, Sacco traveled to the Gaza Strip with the journalist Chris Hedges on assignment for *Harper's* magazine when he remembered the passage about Khan Yunis and Rafah. Hedges referred to the massacre in his subsequent *Harper's*

All images from
Footnotes in Gaza
[©2009 Joe Sacco]
unless otherwise
noted.

379

piece, but the reference was deleted by the editors, which Sacco found "gall-ing." It was evidently this gall that started Sacco on a seven-year journalistic odyssey to dig up the truth of what happened at Khan Yunis and Rafah.

Sacco thinks of himself as a cartoonist first, a journalist second, but, as a critical reader, it's impossible to assign a priority to the two disciplines, so completely are they joined in his work. He has, it seems, found a perfect expression by marrying the two, making journalism artistic and artistry journalistic. We do not usually look to journalism for an aesthetic experience; no one loves Seymour Hersh for his prose style. Yet, Sacco's art is very much a part of his journalism, and one can't imagine the same recitation of facts having the same effect on us — of compassion, em-pathy and moral urgency — without it. When I refer to his art, I am not talking only about the drawing itself, which is admittedly essential in its nuances of gesture and portraiture, but of the whole vocabulary of narra-tive cartooning — pacing, rhythm, juxtapositions, montages — that few cartoonists have mastered as well as he has or put at the service of so significant and worthy a goal.

Sacco's journalism is always about large (and violent) events but about the process of investigating those events as well, which gives him the opportu-nity to depict two scales at the same time — explicating large, impersonal political machinations, on the one hand and burrowing into the individual lives of those affected by (and often a party to) those machinations on the other. And let's not do Sacco the disservice of pretending that he's merely an "objective" reporter collecting facts: he clearly believes in taking sides, or at least that the truth isn't arrived at by finding a cozy median between two unequal sides. One of the more remarkable virtues of his work is that he hasn't, in the face of the injustices he's seen first hand, degenerated into shrill indignation, simplistic condemnation, or easy moral judgments, preferring to reveal the gradations of humanity — suffering, remonstrance, anguish, anger, fear, confusion, hatred, resistance, resignation, even the occasional flashes of hope. Due to its subject matter and the events it de-picts, it's a hard book to read, made harder by the potency of the imagery. If Sacco's drawing weren't infused with humanity and empathy, the result could well be laughable, and worse; as it stands, it's a monument to the power of comics and cartooning allied with moral conscience.

This interview was conducted in August 2010 and transcribed by Michael Litven and Chi-Wen Lee.

— *Gary Groth*

JOE SACCO ON *FOOTNOTES* IN GAZA

Interview by Gary Groth

Gary Groth: The first thing I wanted to ask you is, what, when you went into this project, were your preconceptions, in terms of the Israeli-Palestinian conflict? What were your views of the Israelis and Palestinians, and what would you consider to be your biases?

Joe Sacco: Well, I guess my major bias would be — if you want to call it a bias — that the Palestinians have been historically wronged. They were kicked out of their homeland in 1948 and we've seen the results ever since. They're dispossessed. And there's a great refugee problem that exists to this day. I feel they deserve a state at this point. They've worked toward that; sometimes they've worked in ways that are contrary to their own interests, of course. The situation seems really deep-rooted now, especially with the settlers. Once the settlement project began, it became more and more difficult to untangle what had happened before.

The whole idea of the settlement project, from the Israeli government point of view (the settlers might have had some religious imperatives for going in), was to make it impossible to go back so you could create facts on the ground that would make a Palestinian state, the idea, very unlikely or relatively unviable. As we're seeing now, even if a lot of the settlements withdrew, they're still put together in way that would cut off parts of the West Bank. When I went, you have to remember that there were still settlers in Gaza — about 30 percent of Gaza was either occupied by settlers or were military zones. Or was somehow run by the Israeli military. So a fair amount of it was a little bit off-limits to Palestinians.

That's the situation, which has just changed considerably. When I was there, the Palestine Authority was in charge. And now there's Hamas that has taken over the Gaza Strip, and the settlements have been moved back, but Israel still contains and controls Gaza. When I went in, my ideas were basically the same as when I went in the first time, back in the late 1980s — I had to say that. Now if you're asking what I think about Israel ... Israel exists. And I don't think it's a good idea to think in terms of making Israel go away, because you're just going to create another great and massive problem. Ultimately, I recognize that it's not going to happen, unless there's some incredible bloodletting. Which is conceivable ...

Groth: The U.S. wouldn't let that happen, regardless.

Sacco: Yeah, but I'm talking about 50 years from now, 100 years from now, where the U.S. might not be in a position to intervene or things might have changed on some level. So my hope is always that this will get solved now rather than in the future when we don't know what the future's gonna be.

Groth: You're thinking this could be so intractable that you're thinking 50 or 60 years out. [*Laughs.*]

Sacco: Oh yeah, easily. You've gotta recognize that the Palestine Authority might end up signing the peace agreement just like Oslo where it looks like there's going to be some settlement and it's all gonna be fine. But ultimately, you can sign a bit of paper and it might not satisfy the core constituents, the people who are actually going to be impacted by that.

Groth: In another interview, you said, "What I would point out is that I don't sugarcoat the Palestinians. I don't sugarcoat their anger, their vitriol. I don't sugarcoat acts they commit that as far as I'm concerned don't help their cause. I lay it out." And that's absolutely true, but there's a sense in which their vitriol, their anger toward Israel and so forth is justified in your account.

Sacco: Well, justified I would say is understandable ... In a sense of you just have to see the context. I think it's important. One of the main reasons I got interested in the Palestinian question at all is because when I was a kid in high school the only time I ever heard "Palestinian" was "hijacking" or "terrorist act," and to me, they all seemed crazy and they were all terrorists. I mean, that's the only time you ever hear their name brought up. So you have to understand what has happened, and whether it's in the larger context or in the smaller context.

Groth: Let me ask you about the nuts and bolts of reportage. First of all, how do you actually start a project of this magnitude? There's a character, a friend of yours, named Abed. Would you call him a fixer?

Sacco: No, he wasn't a fixer in the true sense of the word. I would say he acted as my fixer, and he might have helped journalists before, but that wasn't his thing.

Groth: But he was helpful?

Sacco: He was helpful. Someone introduced us. Basically, I wasn't sure how to go about doing some of this sort of thing. It was like one of those things where someone put me in touch with someone in the West Bank, a Palestinian guy who became my friend, and I talked to him when I was living in Switzerland. I moved myself to Switzerland for about 10 months, because I knew I had to make a number of trips, and Zurich is just closer than New York, where I was living before. It's just a quicker flight. I'm not going to get there and lose a couple of days because I'm jetlagged. Also I had to go to Russia to do a story, so I knew I would be doing some traveling, and I just wanted another base.

Groth: So you lived in Switzerland for 10 months?

Sacco: Yeah. And that wasn't bad, because I had friends there. It was quite OK. Anyway, I talked to this guy when I was in Switzerland, and he said, "Yeah, I'll take you to Gaza and introduce you to some people." And he was good to his word. We met, and he was a young guy — he lives in Ramallah now — he's a Palestinian-American: very smart. He hand-held me, took me to Gaza. I had been to Gaza before, but he actually showed

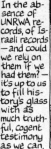

me some people and said, "I think this guy might be able to help you." And we spent two weeks there together. I got to know Abed. I did some of the research for the books, especially in Khan Younis, where Abed was from. And by the end of the trip, I still wasn't sure if he was going to agree to helping me out any further, because I was going to come back for two months then — and he has his own life. And that's how it worked out: He agreed to do it. I came then and spent another two months. We just basically lived together, ate together, worked together. It would have been impossible without him.

Groth: And he let you live in his home, is that correct?

Sacco: In Khan Younis I lived in his home. The first two weeks I spent in Khan Younis at his home. The second trip was for two months; we rented a place in Rafah. I didn't even bring it up in the book.

Groth: The palace.

Sacco: It was a palace! And he stayed with me the whole time, and he lived and breathed the project too. He was more than a fixer. A fixer is …

Groth: Like Neven [*from Sacco's* The Fixer].

Sacco: Yeah, Neven was a fixer in that way, in the true sense of the word, but Abed was getting very interested in the project — a smart guy himself, he really kept his ears open. He became a little filter. He was listening.

Groth: He sounds like he was very helpful in terms of sifting through testimony and helping you determine what was accurate and perhaps less accurate. What did he do in terms of his own job or profession?

Sacco: He worked at a Palestinian NGO [Non-Governmental Organization]. It was an interesting NGO — I can't remember exactly where they were getting their funding, but their debate was "Should we accept funds from any Western donors?" And they were basically against them, because they didn't want to feel like they were being compromised in any way. But their idea was women's issues and bringing up women's rights within the conservative community in Gaza. The idea was giving lectures to women about political issues and things like that. Also to get them involved in certain things and he was involved in that; that's mostly what he took the time on.

Groth: The two massacres in Khan Younis and Rafah have been little reported on, Khan Younis especially, and my understanding is that you noticed a footnote in *The Fateful Triangle*.

Sacco: Yeah, it wasn't exactly a footnote.

Groth: No, it wasn't exactly a footnote; it was a paragraph.

Sacco: It was a paragraph basically quoting a U.N. document. I was living in New York at the time. Basically, living in New York, I just went down to the U.N. archives and found that document, and then started looking around to see what else I could find. There were some pretty interesting reports. Not all my research got into the book. But it gave me a feeling for what was going on. I read whatever I could that was in the U.N. archives at the time.

Groth: I'm interested in why you think this hasn't been investigated by journalists or historians much previously.

Sacco: Honestly, it was a surprise to me too. I mean, here's a conflict where you feel people go over it — they sift through it. The truth of the matter is Israeli historians, revisionist historians, very good writers, like Tom Segev, people like Benny Morris, who is right-wing, but is a fairly good historian. Those people have revisited a lot of Israel's story, usually from an Israeli perspective. They might find out, yes, there were massacres in 1948, yes, this sort of thing was going on. But this is all from Israeli documentation, U.N. documentation. There's seldom any Arab sources. It seems like a lot of Western historians haven't really approached things from a Palestinian perspective. I think it's very difficult to get what a lot of historians rely on, which is documentary evidence. A lot of that stuff's been scattered to the wind, in a sense.

Groth: It seems to be such an odd failure —

Sacco: And to me too! Frankly that was part of the impetus of doing it. Here I'm trying to rationalize why these things haven't been brought up in any great length, but the truth of the matter is I was shocked too. I mean, some of these people were obviously still alive. But that's the reason I did the book.

Groth: Now, you wrote and researched the book over a span of seven years, and you've said the last four years you'd been sitting at the desk, drawing and writing.

Sacco: Right, because I interrupted it a few times to do other stories and things like that.

Groth: So once you got on the trail of this story and you started contacting people, what was your strategy in terms of digging out the truth? Obviously you wanted to interview everybody you could find.

Sacco: Well, I knew the story in Khan Younis had existed, because when I was there with [Chris] Hedges we spent a day talking to older people. Maybe we spoke to four or five older people. But that was going to be part of the bigger story, and that part of the story was dropped by *Harper's* magazine.

Groth: Which offended you.

Sacco: Yeah. And I'm not saying that they didn't have their reasons — there's space considerations or whatever — but I always think it's interesting how that's the kind of stuff to get dropped. To me that's what makes up the conflict. That's the stuff of this conflict, really, these grievances and the sense of injustice — and the sense of no one knows about these injustices. So I basically knew the general outlines of the story in Khan Younis. It was just a matter of going there, talking to people, trying to find some of those same people, but also: Who else? Who do you know?

We were able to do this because there was a local historian also who had written a book about what happened in Khan Younis. We sat with him, and he explained the outlines of the story. So that helped. But then it's just a question of, "Yeah, well, go speak to this guy, he's still alive — he'll remember it": that kind of thing. That's how you can do it.

In Rafah, I wasn't sure of the story. I read what I read in the U.N. document, but while — in that first two-week trip that I was mainly concentrating on Khan Younis — we took a couple trips to Rafah, and we found another local historian who had written about what had happened in Rafah and he also gave us the basic outlines. And from that day we saw and met four older men — I just wanted to talk to them and get a sense. You talk to four men

"It seems like a lot of Western historians haven't really approached things from a Palestinian perspective."

separately, and you can get an idea of the general contours of this story, and it was clear that whatever was in the U.N. document simply wasn't the case. So based on that general outline, I was able to formulate what my questions were gonna be. You need to get a general overview before you can ...

Groth: Would you say that the U.N. document was a misrepresentation or simply incomplete?

Sacco: Incomplete. I don't think they intended to ... They were working under very difficult circumstances. I think that report was written when the Israelis were still occupying Gaza. And if you read the stuff in the U.N. records it's amazing — I mentioned in the book that the Israelis clamped down on the U.N. monitors that were in Gaza. They confined them. But you should read these telegrams between the U.N. headquarters and the people in Gaza — they might come in and smash the radio. "What are we gonna do? Are we gonna defend ourselves or not?"

Groth: The U.N.?

Sacco: Yeah, the people there.

Groth: So Israel intimidated the U.N.?

Sacco: They definitely intimidated those people. The word from [UNEF 1] was "Do not resist." Just let them do what they're gonna do, basically. But they were confined. And so a lot of what they were able to get was not really from — they had other U.N. personnel, Palestinian U.N. personnel, feeding them stories. But I think it was very difficult at that time to get the full picture. They were handled, yeah, that was definitely the case.

Groth: Not least by Israeli disingenuousness?

Sacco: Of course they don't want those stories to get out, and if you read — and I put some in the back of the book — what the Israelis are saying at the time: "Yeah, we might have killed four or five people, but they were doing this." They had excuses for everything they were doing: a lot of it misinformation, obviously.

Groth: With regard to your working methods, do you do all the research first —

Sacco: Not *all* the research, as much as I can to get —

Groth: — before you actually start writing and drawing and composing the book.

Sacco: Yes. Oh yeah. You're actually reading any book you can get: Moshe Dayan's book, Mordechai Bar-On's book — there were a number of others. The top U.N. guide of the region at the time, they wrote a book. You just find what you can, read as much as you can, and see what you can get out of that. So yeah, obviously, I did not start until I was pretty set in my research.

Groth: I'm curious as to how you organized all this material. You mentioned earlier how you assigned numbers to the people you interviewed.

Sacco: Yeah, especially there. I could show you, if you ever wanted to see it, just how I organized things. But yeah, the organizing itself can take weeks because I'm going through all my interview notes, I'm actually transcribing all the tapes myself — and there were many hours of tapes; probably 70 taped interviews. But it's important for me to do it, because when you're going through it again, you remember things, and you think, "Oh, that's perfect, I need to make a note that this is an important part of the story." The thing is when you're there you're sometimes doing three or four interviews a day; at a certain point, you're just kind of shoveling to the back of your mind.

Groth: You can't keep them separate.

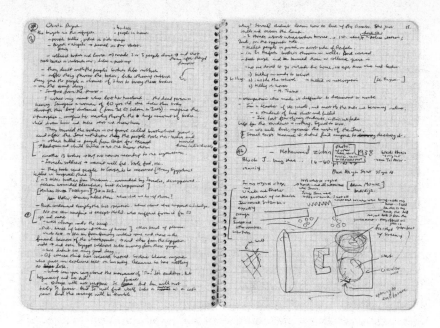

Sacco: No, no, it all becomes a blob somehow. So it's really important to go through. And then what I do, I'm writing journal entries every day, and there's a lot that's in the journal entries. And I had several hundred pages, probably, of journal entries. And then I go through those, and I index all that. I index it by date; then I index it by subject. So, the character Ashraf: if I want to know what Ashraf said at a certain point, I'll have some synopsis of what he said, and then the page number of what journal, blah, blah, blah. It's really important, and saves you enormous amounts of time in the long run.

Groth: I think your organization is probably essential.

Sacco: Yeah, oh yeah.

Groth: And you do all your notes in longhand? Or do you have a PowerBook?

Sacco: My notes? I don't take a PowerBook with me, because I find it's just another bloody technical thing you have to deal with in a difficult situation. No, I taped; I tape. The question was finding batteries, but the batteries were always easy to find. And I am writing all my journal notes in my hand, correct.

Groth: I was curious because in one chapter of the story, you devote a page to interviewing a woman; you and Abed knock on her door, she comes to her door and it's a little uncomfortable. You might have the wrong

TOP

An example of Sacco's interview notes and location sketches.

person — either she is or she isn't. You're standing there and you do not draw yourself as taking notes or recording. But, were you? Or was that exchange "transcribed" from memory?

Sacco: Well, that's from memory. That's why I keep the journal. Abed and I would go back in the night —

Groth: You summarize it later.

Sacco: Yeah, and often we would sit and I'd say, "OK, so remind me." He'd tell me right away what's going on, so it's already in my head: then we get back. We'd often sit and I'd say, "How do you remember it again?" I'm checking with him and then writing it in my journal — especially something like that, because I want to get it right. Now obviously, you're right: I'm not taking notes at the time, I'm not having a recorder on at all times. But I find that those are really essential stories to get across, so to the best of my ability I try to present them accurately. Like I said, I would stay up and write in my journal every night, just because there are a lot of things you don't want to lose.

Groth: Yeah, and yet you will.

Sacco: You will, because things are going on all the time.

Groth: Did you draw the book chronologically as it's published?

Sacco: I had a false start, where I decided to draw in a very big format. I thought, "This is awful." I had no sense of accomplishment, because it was taking days and days to do one page. I need a sense of accomplishment, so I scaled it down and started again. But that wasn't more than five pages or so.

Groth: Why'd you want to do it bigger?

Sacco: I don't remember. I think I wanted the art to spread out in a certain way, and maybe get more detail. And why, I don't know, because when things are reproduced, the end result is always knocked down: yeah, basically chronologically.

Groth: You got a lot of grief when you were doing interviews, because people didn't understand why you cared about an event that occurred in 1956; they wanted you to focus on what was happening now. And you resist that. A deliberate strategy you apply is to alternate between the present and the past, emphasizing that the past was at one time the present. So can you talk a little about why it's important to connect the present with the past, and your strategy of alternating between he two continuously?

Sacco: Yeah, it's not something I hadn't done before. I did it in the Gorazde book and I did it with the book *Fixer*, where I had the present, then the past. And how I would often do it, is I would set the past with black borders so it was clear that you were in the past. Now in this case I decided not to do it because I wanted more of a blending, somehow. I wanted the past and the future to mesh more seamlessly, and not to necessarily differentiate so clearly with a thud: "OK. Now we are in the past."

So I wanted things to be a bit more seamless, to get that effect that, in people's minds — and I think when you look back historically — a lot of things are tangled together. That's something I'm trying to show often, because I'm trying to show people's confusion about events. Whether the events they're talking about took place in '67, and we don't really find out till later on. Or sometimes they'll get 'em mixed up with something that

happened in '54 or whatever. People sometimes would get things mixed up, and I find it interesting that here you have people that have been so hammered over the years that distinguishing one blow from the next can be very difficult when they're looking back on it.

Groth: Yeah, there was that one woman who you depict in a succession of three panels who keeps misremembering when specific acts of carnage against her and her family occurred, but the brutality is all of a kind with only the historical moments changing.

Sacco: Oh yeah!

Groth: The acts of brutality blend together in her mind, almost as one continuous moment.

Sacco: Right, and I think that's an important component of how people remember things. There's a sense, I think, of event constipation, where they just cannot digest this stuff. Because there's no time to do it, something else is coming up on its heels.

Groth: There's no respite.

Sacco: There's no respite, and then you have the younger generation, obviously concerned with their own monumental problems, and maybe they're interested, but when it comes down to it, what matters now is their lives and their children's lives. How can they think about their history? How can they actually think about what's happened to them, and understand it, and digest it? That question is interesting to me. Can they do it? I feel like sometimes it seems like the Palestinians could probably have a project going where they have all that history, but I think it's almost impossible to think in these terms. It all runs together. I mean that's the whole idea: the events are continuous.

Groth: Tell me if I'm off base here, but were you essentially equating the present with the past? Even though bulldozing homes and firing upon homes obviously isn't as harsh as putting people up against a wall and shooting them. Still, they're still brutalized.

Sacco: Yeah, I'm letting the reader figure out what stands in relationship to what. Clearly, I personally think that putting people up against the wall and killing them in cold blood — that's about as ruthless an act as you can think of. But that doesn't necessarily diminish what's going on now, which is something I try to point out to people who try to question me about why I'm not concentrating on their issues. And the truth is I did concentrate on their issues. And what's interesting is that now that whole bulldozing thing is not going on in Rafah any more. And these people who've lost their homes, it's like, who cares about it now? — Because that's the past too. So what I've done really, is I've put that in — I've recorded that as best I could.

Groth: In the Gaza camps of the 1950s … When you were drawing specific scenes of the past, were you using photographs as reference? How much of this did you reconstruct from people's descriptions, and how much did you actually see from photographs? I'm thinking specifically of the Gaza camps of the 1950s.

Sacco: I went to the U.N. archive — the United Nations Relief and Works Agency archives — in Gaza City, and they gave me copies of every photograph that they have a copy of. I basically took every photograph that had depictions of refugee camps, especially Rafah and Khan Younis: from the '50s, from the '40s, and even from the '60s, because even in the '60s a lot of the stuff looks the same, only maybe with a little building. So yes, photographic reference is really important. And then I did a number of interviews that were solely about what the camp looked like. Even those had their problems because people remember the camp looking different ways, but they gave me a sense of the amount of cactus, what certain places look like, what the street looked like; Sea Street was narrower at the time. They tried to describe a lot of those things to me. There was even a little library in Rafah where I went to take copies of things like dress, kitchen utensils and things like that from the refugee camp era from the '40s. The castle of Khan Younis: I was able to find a website that actually had pictures of the castle at that time, and I took pictures of it as it existed. The school still exists — I walked through it — basically as it did then, maybe they've added on some stuff.

Groth: That gate is still there?

Sacco: The entrance is, the gate itself is gone. The entrance is the same one.

Groth: So you were able to actually see where that particular incident took place.

Sacco: Yeah. The wall has changed too, now there are shacks along that wall, just little inbuilt shacks. Obviously the wall crumbled, they built it up. But the school existed so I went around taking pictures. I went and saw the classrooms to take pictures inside. Whenever I could, I want something pretty direct. I want people from that era who lived in those days to say, "Yes, that's what it was like."

Groth: The view of the camps that you depict on pages 28 and 29, I assume you actually viewed that yourself?

Sacco: That is more like a composite of what a camp looks like today. I don't really say that that's a particular thing. From many different photographs and from my own observations, that's generally what it looks like.

Groth: So you're trying to catch the essence of it.

Sacco: The essence and the atmosphere. Now at Sea Street I'm often trying to capture Sea Street because now we're talking about a specific place. Here I'm just saying, "These are what the camps look like now."

Groth: You don't do sketches there, right? You take photographs?

Sacco: I do some sketches, but it's really minimal. The sketches you see, which really paid off for me, were the ones I did at the checkpoints at Abu Guru because you're not allowed to take a photograph of a military position. And you're in a taxi with other people, and you don't want to put them in any danger by raising a camera — you don't want to get into that. I went through that checkpoint enough times that as we would go through it, I would stash it. It was like a drug.

Groth: You continually go back to the question of objectivity and truth-seeking in the book, and just how impossible that is to achieve. So what

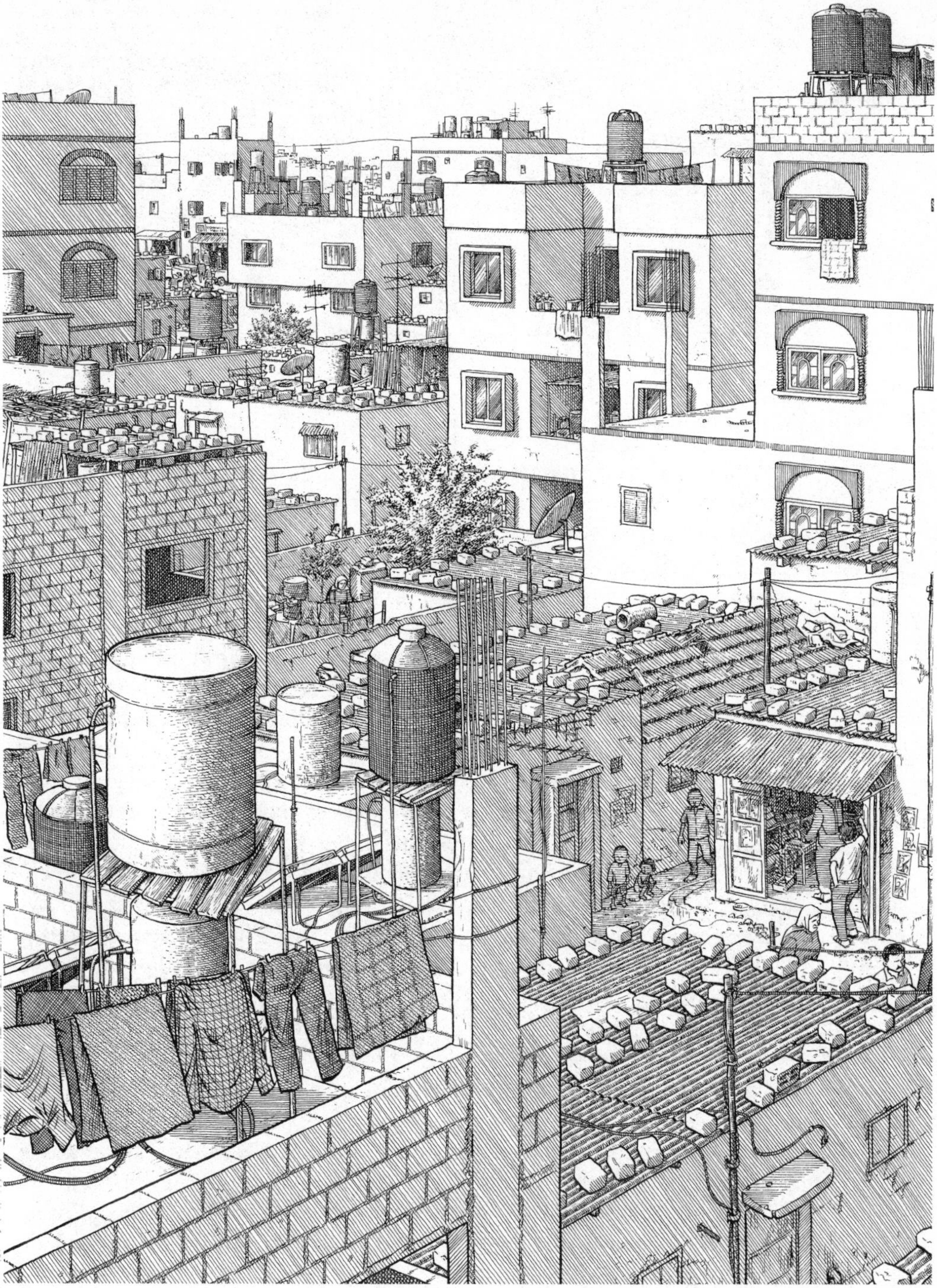

I was trying to get to is, given your fundamental feelings about this, how do you square the circle of objectivity? I mean, you don't believe in objective journalism ...

Sacco: The word itself has a certain meaning, but the word in terms of journalism has another meaning, and that's what I object to. To me, objective journalism — as I was told it — was basically, you have to get both sides of the story. Always assume there are two sides of the story, and never weighing which side might have more merit. If you allow the discussion to end up just being a tennis match — "Well, he said this," and "He replied that" — that's not going to get you anywhere. I think it's better to, as a journalist, see yourself as someone who's actually trying to get to the heart of what's going on and weighing the statements of one side or the other, using your own eyes, and not what the spokesman has to say. These people are there to spin. So I believe in being honest. Of course I don't check my morality at the door when I go in. I feel like the Palestinians are being screwed. I mean, ultimately. I don't want to see the Israelis getting screwed — of course not — but the Palestinians are definitely getting screwed. And I go in with that in my mind, and everything I've seen has confirmed that.

Groth: I think it's obvious your sympathies are with the Palestinians.

Sacco: But I can look at the Palestinians and say, "OK, they're often doing things that are maybe against their own best interests." They're often saying things that are not going to go over well with an American audience. But to me, honesty is saying, "OK, that's how it is." I'm not trying to hide anything. That's what's important.

Groth: Right, and is it important also not to demonize the Israelis? How to handle your depictions of the Israelis without making it one-dimensional considering that you feel that they're the oppressors?

Sacco: I do not intend to demonize the Israelis. I think, in the case of this book, there was a massacre of Palestinians by Israeli soldiers. Now that has happened in other instances around the world; Palestinians have killed Israelis — as I show in the book, I show the fact that bus bombings were going on while I was there. I find that just reprehensible, whoever's doing it. If the Israelis are doing it, I find it reprehensible. It doesn't mean I demonize them as a people necessarily, but those actions are definitely beyond the pale. In this particular book, I did try to get Israeli voices — whether I succeeded is open to question — but I think, especially in the figure of Mordechai Bar-On — who was Moshe Dayan's right hand man — he was very eloquent, very even-tempered, and I think he was able to present the Israeli thinking. And I have no problem with that. I want to get it. I would like to get that [perspective].

Groth: The difference between him and the Palestinians who explicate their side of it was, I thought, quite interesting, because he was very cold, technocratic, rational; in contrast to their more agonizingly human outbursts.

Sacco: Yeah, cold. I would say he wasn't impassioned when he was talking about it, because the man is a historian himself.

Groth: And a military man, right?

Sacco: He was a military man. And he wrote a book that I have about the 1956 war. And I respect that, I respect someone who could live those events and could actually pull himself back a bit. I didn't feel like he was really trying to fudge things around too much. He said Dayan just blew up and decided to lay down a barrage on Gaza city. You know what I mean?

Groth: But he had the luxury of stepping away from it, of detaching himself emotionally.

Sacco: Yeah, because ultimately, if you're on the victorious side, it's almost easier to be rational about what happened: and to admit to mistakes.

Look how we are about the American Indians now. We can talk about what happened to them regretfully, but here we are, living on their land — we won.

We live on the fruits of those massacres and those inglorious victories. So we can talk about it, whereas a North American Indian who sees what's happening, who sees the casino culture that they're stuck with, I think it would be harder for someone like that to pull himself back.

Groth: You tackle questions of subjectivity and objectivity in a chapter called "Memory and the Essential Truth" of just how reliable the testimony is. And you begin to question the accuracy of the testimony, but I think you come to the conclusion that the individual details are less important than the cumulative weight of so many people's testimony.

Sacco: Yeah, I think it has to be. We're talking about something that long ago, when you realize that individuals, for whatever reasons, might not remember something. They might remember something wrong, they might remember something only for their own convenience. You don't really know what psychology is [playing] in it — I don't know enough about memory itself, but my idea is, it's almost like seeing things in peripheral vision: that if you get enough viewpoints peripherally, you get to triangulate — or whatever it's called — and suddenly the essence of what happened is coming to life. There were some people who seemed very strong in their memories, and I think the memories might be true, might be accurate — I think mostly those memories are accurate — but you certainly saw that begin to break down once we get to the school itself and they're spending hours in the same area: "OK, where was the jeep? When did the officer come to the front? How did he stand up and how will you scream?" All that stuff is a long time ago, and that's a long period to try and pinpoint what happened when, and what happened next. And of course over time people tell their stories to each other, and your memory becomes my memory in a way. Or your suggestion becomes something now that I'm beginning to remember. For example, that particular case, four brothers, three killed, one may have been there at the very end — he definitely escaped. Well, he remembers it and two other witnesses remember it.

Groth: But they don't remember him being present at the time.

Sacco: They don't remember him being there when his brother died. But he remembers being there. I think it is fascinating — but again, the essential truth is three brothers died. Let's not say there's no credence in the story just because he's got something that doesn't seem accurate, or may or may not be accurate.

Groth: And I think the important point you're making is that you can't throw out all of one's recollections just because there are certain minor contradictions.

Sacco: Right.

Groth: Which is a great lawyerly technique, to try to taint one's testimony by teasing out minor discrepancies.

Sacco: Yeah! Right, because you could easily take anyone's memory, and make the person look foolish. "Well, actually, we have satellite images of this, and this is what the strip actually looked like. Now you remember it that way now, so that means you probably didn't remember this either." You're right, it's a lawyerly sort of way of dispensing with it, but that's why I feel it was important to get many, many views — have a weight of views, and a weight of reflected visions towards a point, so that it's pretty clear what happened. And then again, you realize that there were certain points — let's say going through the gate — which are so sharp, that almost everyone remembers it precisely the same way.

Now that really stood out, for me. And there's probably a reason for that. I mean, this is terrible, running through the street with people getting killed and beaten anyway, and then suddenly you're there and people are beating you on the head. People remember the beating more than anything else. It's just a sharp thing that happened over about two or three seconds, and it's going to stay in your head *forever*.

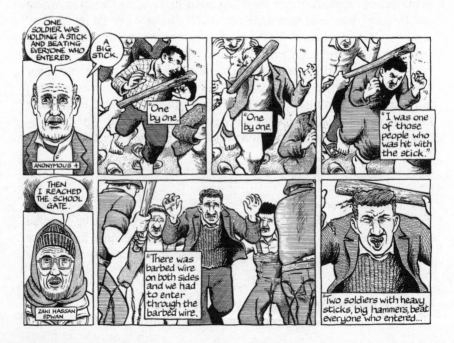

Groth: That was possibly one of the most horrifying acts of coercion and cruelty you depicted, even more so than lining people up against a wall.

Sacco: And that's what's interesting for me too: just ... a level of disgusting brutality.

Groth: I was stunned at the level of barbarism. I couldn't even fathom why the Israelis did it; I can sort of fathom the pragmatism behind lining people up and shooting them, but to run people through the streets and funneling them through a small gate so you can hit them randomly — the sheer irrationality of that adds to the horror of it all.

You convey all this with frightening verisimilitude. I asked you something like this when we talked about *Gorazde*, but was that difficult to draw? This public humiliation went on for page after page after page, extensively. Are extended scenes like that difficult to draw? While I can read it in a few minutes, it must take you weeks to draw that many pages, weeks that you're focusing on that imagery.

Sacco: I hated drawing that stuff. It really ...

Groth: *Disturbed you?*

Sacco: [Long pause.] Yeah. It disturbs you because it's something I thought about a lot. And it's made me not really want to really tackle anything quite like this again. I don't think I can because I realize it's one thing being a reporter and hearing these stories — which can hit you pretty hard — but the thing about being a reporter is when you're there, you're constantly going on to the next thing, you're trying to keep people on track, there's all kinds of things you're doing which — I'm not going to say they distract you from what you're hearing — but they're making you look at it in a very icy kind of way. You have to. You have to think of yourself as a surgeon trying to extract a story. And that night you're going to have some beers with some of your journalist buddies, maybe, or the next day is another kind of adventure. And that helps to leaven that kind of thing, but when you're drawing it ...

Groth: You're dwelling on it.

Sacco: You're dwelling on it. I don't know about other artists, but I need to somehow inhabit every human I'm drawing. It's one thing to draw someone walking down the street, because you've done it a lot of times. But when there's certain actions that aren't in particular usual actions, like raising your hand, or how you hold a club, or how you feel when you fell. You see what I mean? You begin to think about it, you actually have to draw yourself in a mirror. Like, how would someone hold their arm up, and what would be their first reaction. You inhabit in this way. I'm not trying to in any way say that this remotely resembles the experiences people went through, but you're really going through it constantly. It begins to become very distasteful.

Groth: Are you in a sense reliving this? I mean, not reliving it because you weren't there in the first place — but living it?

Sacco: It was harder to draw than it was to hear those stories. That's all I can say. You just have to sort of act it, somehow.

Groth: Another dimension you convey is the actuality or the ongoing-ness of the event. Your images are not frozen or static drawings, they communicate the hurly-burly of human beings moving in space, if life as it is unfolds.

Sacco: Well, that's good. Movement was very important; I want to give the sense of movement, of a crowd being herded. And you're constantly thinking, "OK, now I'm drawing these soldiers. Now some of them are going to be stepping up and doing what they're being told to, and some of them are going to be hanging back, and not in the same way." You realize you gotta draw distinctions — you've gotta think about a lot of things. You don't want everyone to be looking the same and having the same sort of bodily expressions.

Groth: Right, and the way you do it animates the action.

Sacco: OK, well, I'm glad.

Groth: We talked about this briefly last night when we were talking about Crumb's *Genesis* and how he could particularize faces. I mentioned that I thought you did the same thing. But it does seem to me that when you have crowd scenes — and I looked fairly closely at the faces — virtually every face until it recedes too far into the background is particularized, and not these generic mouths and noses and eyes that usually comprise dense crowd scenes.

Sacco: My point is always that these are individuals and each has their own story, and it's very important to show these are happening, it's a mass event, but it's also happening to individuals. And I never want to make it look like a herd of cattle being led to the slaughter. These are people with their own lives, and you want to give the reader a sense of that.

Groth: And I think that's absolutely essential to what you're doing, but that's got to be enormously labor-intensive.

Sacco: Yeah.

Groth: You said you spent four years — was that writing and drawing?

Sacco: That was pretty much drawing.

Groth: You don't write the entire script for this book out beforehand, do you?

Sacco: Sure, yeah.

Groth: All 200 pages, and then you start drawing? Or do you write it chapter by chapter?

Sacco: No, I write out the whole script, because I've long ago learned — especially with a book of non-fiction where you're not giving a character his head and then let's see what the character wants to do — I think it's really essential so you don't have loose ends, to know where you're going. I mean, this is a very complex story.

Groth: The entire structure has to be there before you start drawing.

Sacco: Yeah, it's a complex story, and what I don't want to do is end up going, "Oh, now I forgot this, or now, how do I get back to that?" or "Here in my notes, I found this; that would have gone well there." Now, it's all gotta be figured out. What makes it fresh in my own mind is I don't storyboard. I don't do anything like that, and I only on the rarest of occasions even mention an image that might go well with something. To make every day interesting creatively, I decide every day, "OK, what I am going to draw? How am I going to take this script and how I am going to make this interesting? How is it going to flow?"

Groth: Start when it's fresh.

Sacco: Yes, because to me the storyboard ... boy, you might as well connect the dots.

Groth: That approach must require an enormous amount of patience because you're doing so much work before you put a drawing down on paper.

Sacco: Yeah, it does, but ...

Groth: Do you ever start itching to draw but you can't do it, because you know you need that structure, you know you have to finish the writing?

Sacco: I love writing. And I find the writing one of the most interesting things you do, and it's more of a challenge in a certain way. I never know if in the course of a day I'm going to get one paragraph or two pages. I can never judge writing. I can almost always judge a drawing. I can almost say, "In five days, I'm going to get two pages drawn by hook or by crook." And so, if I'm not there, I'll just work extra hours until it's done. Now sometimes, if it's too complicated, I'm not gonna rush myself, but I know how far I can dig that ditch every day when I'm drawing.

Groth: That's understandable.

Sacco: Actually, there are scenes that I just dislike drawing so much that you have to be patient to say, "OK, now just slow down and get it right and it'll be over one day." I found also really particularly not enjoyable — but I felt very essential for the story — were the scenes about what happened to the bodies — usually not brought up in these sorts of stories. The story doesn't end when the people are dead. Then we've gotta do something with them.

And I just decided, boy, that's a really interesting part of the story; this is really pretty traumatic for the survivors now. And for the women, who are often involved in that sort of thing.

Drawing bodies is, you know, it's just ...

Groth: Does the act of drawing scenes like that — the bodies you're describing — exert a tangible effect on you?

Sacco: All I know now is that, I knew at the time I just had to continue. The story needs this kind of attention, and I'm in it, and I'm gonna do the best I can being in it. But it's really made it so that I don't really want to do anything like this again. It's made me really — I won't say I want to get out of journalism, but I really want to do other things now. I've got other ideas of what I want to do; I want to get away from this kind of stuff, so I'm glad I

put the effort into that.

Groth: Is that because of the effect this is having on you as a person?

Sacco: It's not as if I've freaked out about it or anything like that. You just know you had your fill, and what you realize is that doing your work, even creative work, isn't always enjoyable. Sometimes you cannot say, "I enjoy what I do," even if it's artistic. And maybe there'd be something wrong if you did, perhaps.

Groth: You may not enjoy it but you must find your work satisfying.

Sacco: No, it's satisfying because I feel, at least to the extent of my abilities, I've explicated two major events in Palestinian history that hadn't really been done, and it's pretty much original research. There is a sense of accomplishment, don't get me wrong at all, but ...

Groth: But it's not the same thing as enjoying it.

Sacco: Yeah. I would have a very difficult time if someone said, "Oh, your next should be the Sabra-Shatilla massacre."

I don't want to be Mr. Massacre. [*Groth laughs.*] I gave all I could to this book, and I've got nothing left.

Groth: Speaking of the writing, I wanted to ask you about one specific technique that's wholly yours and that seems ideally suited to a journalistic context: Your patented method of breaking up a sentence into short staccato captions. I'm looking at page 297: Would you write out the sentence as a single sentence and then break it up when you're drawing a page?

Sacco: Yes. That would be a sentence, and as I'm drawing ...

Groth: Is that a decision you make when you draw the panel?

Sacco: Yeah, that's a decision I make that day when I'm drawing that particular panel. Like, "What's necessary right here?" I haven't got that kind of artistic vision; where I can look that far ahead and say, "This is perfect for that." You just realize, OK, it adds to the movement, things are happening quickly, as it sometimes seems. I mean, caption length can slow a reader down, and sometimes that's necessary. Or it gives you the sense of movement or excitement, or whatever you want to call it. I don't always employ it but ... I nicked that from Louis-Ferdinand Céline.

My exposition dissolves" in a barrage of bullets and ricochets! Israeli gunfire is hitting the buildings around us and then cracks against the upper floors!

Groth: I've read Céline, but I didn't recognize the technique. How did you actually adapt from prose?

Sacco: Depending on the translation, he would have these ellipses.

Groth: That's right.

Sacco: And they'd often be redundant. If you read some of my earlier work, I was so taken with that, I often had these very redundant things. It's almost like he's hammering you over the head with something. But I liked what you could do with it as far as eye movement goes, also. You could pull the reader over certain scenes in a certain way.

Groth: Let me ask a few questions about the drawing. I was struck by how perfectly you caught Khaled's posture on page 59. It's a small thing in a book filled with dramatic imagery. It's a really quiet moment, but I was struck by how perfectly you captured this, and I was wondering if that's from memory? I mean you must have been in that room, and I can't imagine you took notes describing ...

Sacco: Oh, you should see some of my notes. I mean: I actually draw where people were sitting around the room, and whenever I've done that, I chart it out.

Groth: You draw them on your notes? You sketch ...

Sacco: Yeah, they're just circles to show where they are. Or in my journal I'll remember where people were seated because I know that seems like it's going to be in the book so I would try to get that.

Groth: You would refer to that?

Sacco: Yeah, and I would also take photographs to get certain things right. The mattresses, basically where they were, the little place to keep the tea on, that sort of stuff.

Groth: You're talking about page 58?

Sacco: Yeah, so, I would often, especially if I knew for sure, "OK, there's a scene that's going to take place in this room," I would take pictures of the room if I was smart enough to remember to do it.

Groth: Your depiction of individual characters is remarkably vivid: Khaled for example. You portray him as a tired, tragic character. And you also show how the brutality that's inflicted upon the Palestinians rebounds as their own brutalized perceptions. At one point, Khaled talks about how he had to assert himself at some point and threaten to kill somebody. And I think he said, "Killing is not a huge thing for me."
    He says it so casually that it's chilling.

Sacco: Yeah, it is chilling.

Groth: So one of the things you're doing is showing the consequences of being brutalized, and depicting the Palestinians in that light.

Sacco: If you brutalize someone, you can't really expect much more than the average human being. If you brutalize someone, they become brutal themselves and they'll behave brutally.

Groth: How did you figure out how to draw the people you spoke to as they looked 50 years in the past? I can't imagine they provided photos of themselves ... how did you extrapolate from their present selves to their young selves?

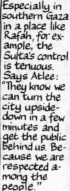

Sacco: Well, what I would do is I saw what they were like as old people, and I just have to imagine what they were like as younger people. I kept certain things — I mean, my pretense is if they had a mustache today, I drew them with a mustache back then. I'm not going to ask every person how he personally shaved that morning. You're taking some artistic license because I'm extrapolating.

Groth: What about the Israelis? Israeli soldiers, for example, who you hadn't seen in the present and couldn't extrapolate from ...

Sacco: No, but I had pictures of uniforms and things like that, if that's what you're asking. Faces ... I didn't have access to any faces except the faces of soldiers in the field at the time, so I do have a couple of photo books from the '50s war, and what it depicts is men often not well-shaved, because they're on campaign. And surprisingly, sometimes tattered uniforms. So, in some cases, I would depict some of that stuff, but individual faces, all that was made up.

Groth: You had to interpret what they would look like.

Sacco: I had to interpret.

Groth: The Israeli soldiers often look pretty savage.

Sacco: I don't think I made them look — in a human way — bad; I think some of them I made look bad. And some of them I made look pretty ordinary. I mean, especially, let's say, the people who are beating the Palestinians coming through the school gate. I figured the people who were

"I don't want to lay it all out, but if you've been brutalized, you're going to behave brutally. I don't expect good things."

doing that sort of duty, were probably sadists. Others, like in the crowds of Israeli soldiers, I didn't feel it necessary to individuate them so much. What I thought of since is that it was harder to put myself in the role of the soldier who's committing the crime. Because, that's a psychological question that I have a hard time understanding, as opposed to someone who's in fear. That's something I can appreciate. But this book, to me, what it doesn't get into is the psychology of the individuals who are doing this sort of thing, which now interests me a great deal. But I couldn't interpret those things. I still can't, I'm still trying to think about some of this stuff. And that's why you often won't see the faces or they'll be sort of in shadow — I realize, maybe it's subconscious, but I almost didn't want to assume anything.

Groth: How to depict Israelis struck me as particularly tricky, how not to depict them as monsters even though they acted monstrously, and to not impose that interpretive bias.

Sacco: I think there's got to be a certain body language issue. Even if the individual Israeli soldier was not comfortable being there doing what he was doing, in order to control the crowd — I mean I had to think about some of this stuff — you have to be imposing and show that you're in charge. It's like an intimidation factor, almost for your own safety and to keep things from getting completely out of hand, there might be those who would think in those terms: "I still have to present this sort of front."

Groth: Was it constantly on your mind that you had to interpret things in such a way as to avoid producing agitprop?

Sacco: Yeah. I don't like agitprop myself. In fact, I want something that's artistic. I also recognize that someone who's doing some of this stuff might have been a perfectly reasonable fellow a week before. All kinds of things can lead to this: all kinds of propaganda. I've seen it in other places; I've seen it in Sarajevo. I spent a lot of time on the Serb side. It's not really shown in any of my books, but I spent a long time listening to what they have to say and sometimes you almost need to swallow the line to make yourself feel like you can justify what your brothers have done, or what your father has done, that sort of thing. You got to keep it together psychologically, and that means swallowing something. I'm not interested in agitprop. I'm interested in a creative way of showing things. Anything that's going to go over the top and show someone as a demon ... I can't.

Groth: When you said you want to be as artistic as possible, do you mean by that "empathetic"? To show as much humanity on both sides as you can muster?

Sacco: Well, people who died in this way were human beings, and people who committed the killings were human beings, and frankly I think that's — forget Palestinian, forget Israeli — this is something I've been more interested in now: that the capability for violence in each of us exists. The right levers have to be pushed. I think you're really going to find very few saints amongst us. [Groth laughs.] [Those of us who haven't engaged in violent acts] just haven't been put in these positions. We have certain luxuries of being able to distance ourselves, think about it and go, "That's wrong."

Put yourself in those positions and suddenly you can see it. I'm not trying to justify anything that's happened; I promise I'm not. But I do want to show that I'm interested in humanity, and it's the human story, the human condition. The Israelis are part of the human condition. Now, if the Palestinians defeated the Israelis in some massive war that we can't fathom right now, how are they going to behave to the Israelis? I don't want to lay it all out, but if you've been brutalized, you're going to behave brutally. I don't expect good things.

Groth: Historical patterns.

Sacco: Yeah, so we all have a capacity to violence.

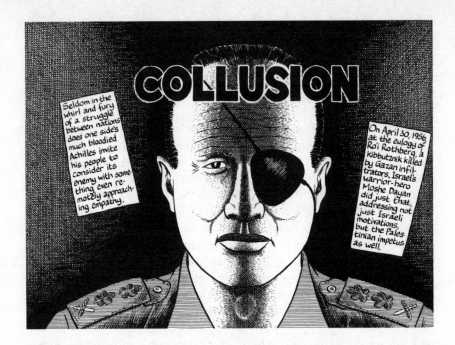

Groth: Your drawing style has evolved over the years. If you look at your early work in the '80s, it's more cartoony, an underground big-foot style. Since then, it's become more representational, more realistic, and yet I think it still retains those cartoony mannerisms that give it an animated quality. How calculated has that evolution been? Did you feel you had to tailor your approach over the years to suit your journalistic ends?

Sacco: Yes. Yeah, at some point, I think it was early on in the *Palestine* series, I got some feedback. There's a Palestinian woman who tore up my comic. She's a playwright. She tore it up, just looking at it. Didn't read it. Just looking at the depictions of Arabs. And I've heard other people say I'm drawing Jews in this way with big noses and all of that. I mean if you look at any of my art, at the early part of my career, everyone is grotesque.

Groth: Yeah, there's a caricatural dimension to all of your work.

Sacco: Yes, so it wasn't meant to offend in that sense. It's just how I draw. I realize though, that if you are going to try to move this into journalism, you have to be a bit more representational; it has to be a bit more solemn somehow. Which isn't to say that you're going to lose the cartooniness, because frankly, I couldn't lose the cartooniness if I tried. I did try to draw more representationally, but I always felt there was, because I've never really trained as an artist, enough in me that's still cartooning in that way that will never go out even if I wanted it to.

Groth: One of your techniques is to show a portrait of somebody, which is the least cartoony of your work: a very straight portrait with a trace of exaggeration, which I think gives a certain dimension of humanity to the characters, that you then flesh out in a more cartoony form later in the story. But, the initial portrait, the most realistically rendered drawing in the book, almost gives you license to draw them in a slightly less representational way later and maintain their humanity.

Sacco: Yeah, that could be.

Groth: It was almost photographic.

Sacco: And they're almost all taken from photographs, except the ones who said they're anonymous, and then there's just a general outline of their face. I would surreptitiously just draw something just so I didn't feel like I was making it up. But obviously, they didn't want to be identified, so you couldn't identify them. They look the most cartoony, in fact, those particular portraits — you can probably pick them out. It was important for me to show the face as accurately as possible — this is a real individual that we're dealing with. Then when you get to know how they were as a young person, it's going to be naturally more cartoony because I'm extrapolating back. I don't know exactly how they looked then — I have to come up with that myself.

Groth: And therefore, have to be more cartoony?

Sacco: It doesn't have to be more cartoony, but it's going to be because now I'm using my imagination. Whether that serves it or not is another question. The reason I put those pictures in, and in almost all cases, I use the picture when that person's talking again, is because I feel whenever I read non-fiction, and it's prose, and there are a lot of characters, you read someone's name and you sort of skip over it; you read what's going on, but you seldom think, "Oh that's the same guy three pages back, something else happened to him."

You just go through it and you read what happens. You're not always trying to keep it together if there's a lot of people. And especially Arabic names: I mean, I find them difficult to look at because they're long, and so I tend to breeze over them and not really pronounce the names when I'm reading them. I felt if you had a picture of that person, that's a better way of signifying "Oh, that's that same guy that was hit over the head over here, and now he's here."

413

It helps you feel that's an individual story, and we're going to be keeping it distinct from all the other individual stories. Not to let them all run together as a mash.

Groth: And one of the techniques you use, which I think is extremely effective, and which can only be used in comics, is where you juxtapose the past and the present. An effective use of that was page 98-99.

Sacco: The bodies against the wall.

Groth: The bodies against a barren wall, and then, what's that today? Just this shopping area ...

Sacco: I wouldn't use that word, but [laughs] it's a parking lot, basically.

Groth: On page 50, you stacked portraits of two Palestinians. At first, I thought they were the same person but at different ages, but I quickly discovered that they weren't.

Sacco: There's some that, when you really look at the photograph, you say, "Goddamn, they're wearing the same thing, he has the same beard."

Groth: It's got to be tough. [Sacco laughs.] But at first I thought they were the same person at different ages. The person recounting his story, and then the one underneath it: him as a young man. But then I realized as I read, that it was a different person. But I thought, in a way, it was the same person. In the sense that history is continuous ... he's doing the same thing that the older person is doing 30 years ago, and he's fighting ...

Sacco: Oh, I see what you're saying. Oh, you're talking about the big picture of the fedayeen and then the modern — Yeah, there was definitely an idea there. I wanted to give them the same sort of value somehow. Showing the old fighter, the new fighter — he's continuing. This guy has retired from it; he's too old. This guy wants to retire, but basically, there's an agenda.

Groth: Thirty years from now, the younger man will become the older man: this terrible sense of continuity.

Sacco: And the resistance has been going on for this long, and what it forms.

Groth: And you couldn't do that in any other medium.

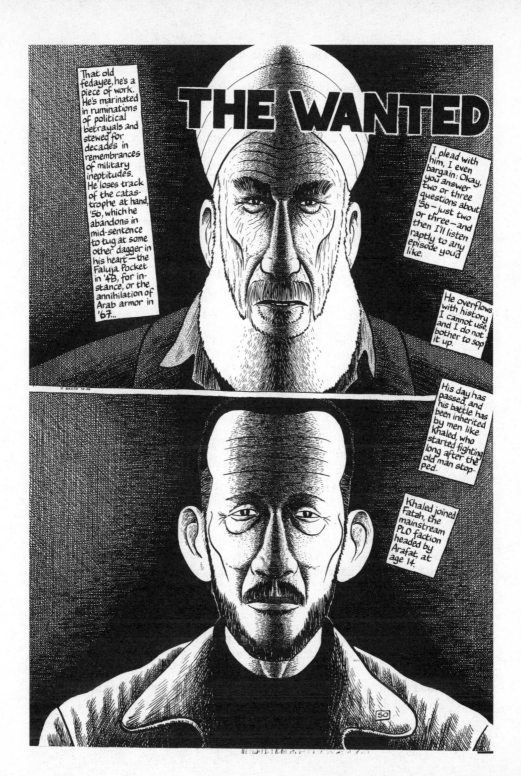

THE WANTED

That old fedayee, he's a piece of work. He's marinated in ruminations of political betrayals and stewed for decades in remembrances of military ineptitudes. He loses track of the catastrophe at hand, '56, which he abandons in mid-sentence to tug at some other dagger in his heart—the Faluja Pocket in '48, for instance, or the annihilation of Arab armor in '67...

I plead with him, I even bargain: Okay, you answer two or three questions about '56—just two or three—and then I'll listen raptly to any episode you'd like.

He overflows with history I cannot use, and I do not bother to sop it up.

His day has passed, and his battle has been inherited by men like Khaled, who started fighting long after the old man stopped.

Khaled joined Fatah, the mainstream PLO faction headed by Arafat, at age 14.

Sacco: I think it would be very difficult to do it without ...

Groth: You could get close to it in film, I think, but you don't have the simultaneity.

Sacco: No, that's right. I think there's something really good about that. One of the great things about comics is that somehow what's going on in the whole composition can reflect what's going on in one panel or it can make you — for example, you could have a picture on the right hand side of the page: it might be an opening scene that gives you a lot of information about where people are, but in the preceding panels you have people talking that are in the bigger picture. You can rely on the person's eye, or the way they're looking at pages next to each other for them to say, "Oh, well, that's where they're walking, even though I haven't gotten to that page yet." You know what I mean?

Groth: Yes.

Sacco: It's almost like it's an atmosphere of reading a book that you can all get from comics too.

Groth: Right. Prose writers can't quite do that.

Sacco: No.

Groth: They can't quite do that.

Sacco: Yeah, they got their own tools.

Groth: Yeah, when they try this sort of thing it looks a bit jury-rigged, but never quite works. James Dickey tried it in his last novel, *Analham*, where he positioned two conversations on a page in two columns that were supposed to be read simultaneously, but that's not, practically, possible to do.

Sacco: [Aldous] Huxley does this —

Groth: Whereas, with pictures, you can see them both somehow at the same time and process them at the same time.

Sacco: Right, you focus on one then you focus on the other, but actually what you're doing is making them one.

Groth: Exactly. Another place where you did a slight variation of that is when you depicted the clubbing at the gate. You inset pictures of the people testifying as to what happened and you had this montage in the background, which again created an effect of simultaneity.

Sacco: The problem I had was, I want to show, "This is the event." Everyone remembers and everyone's going to recall it, but am I going to show someone getting clubbed over and over again? Frankly, I'm at that stage where I've had enough, and also I'm thinking maybe the reader's had enough, and you just have to take a break. I mean all you're seeing is the soldier. You're not seeing the consequences; you're seeing soldiers.

Groth: Do you consider the book to be — I mean, you wouldn't go far as to say it's a condemnation of Israel, would you?

Sacco: It's a condemnation of those acts and Israeli policy at that time. I feel in some way it's a condemnation of what they were doing when I was there — bulldozing homes — I tried to give, especially in the appendices, long interviews with Israeli military people explaining what's going on.

Now, to my own eyes, I basically don't buy it. It seems to me, from what I saw, they were just clearing homes and the roads. Mainly, there was a problem for individual homes, but they should say, "There's a problem from individual homes, so we're destroying all of them." I would rather hear that than "No, we only target homes where terrorist activity is coming from." I simply don't buy it.

But yeah, it's a condemnation of that. It's definitely a condemnation of taking people and shooting them, but I don't have to condemn it. They're already condemning themselves, frankly. And also you know, with the Israeli government justifying it, to me, they're condemning themselves also. Of course, they're trying to suppress it; taking people out and shooting them never looks good. So, there's no way around it.

Groth: Yeah, I guess what I'm trying to ask you …

Sacco: "What the hell are you getting at?"

Groth: How representative is this, do you think, of the Israeli government today?

Sacco: Of the Israeli government *today?*

Groth: Yeah, does this reflect a continuum, I mean: let's take 1956 —

Sacco: Yes! Well, we can talk about 2008, 2009, when the Israelis attacked Gaza and killed, by their own figure, 1,200 Palestinians, with incredible brutality. The Palestinians say 1,400. And the thing is you can start believing in your own logic. I think the American Army also has this logic. Their logic is "forced protection and we don't want one of our boys to be nicked."

And you can understand the logic of this: that we are important, we are going to protect ourselves, and if that means using a sledgehammer, we're going to use a sledgehammer. The ultimate idea is to protect yourselves and have as few losses as possible. It's very important for American society, Israeli society, and probably some other societies — in fact it's probably their weak point: that a small number of casualties can upend the country. In some ways, it's a very humane way of looking at individual life, but they concentrate on their own individual lives. For example, there's one Israeli soldier who is being held captive in Gaza — I feel sorry for the man, I wish he would be released —

Groth: But they're using that as a political justification for all harsh measures they're imposing.

Sacco: Or you see that it's really Israel itself — this is really a big issue in Israel. And it's embarrassing to the government, you know, his parents camp out, and the Prime Minster constantly has to meet them. It's just a big, big issue. So, I understand some of this, and I saw it myself when I was in Iraq — the Americans want to come home, they want their buddies to come home: their buddies. It's very important — there's this spirit of comradeship, and that everyone's coming out of this alive. There's a perfectly understandable logic behind it.

But what it often leads to is any conceivable threat is met with violence, whether it was a threat or not. And then there becomes a very thin line between what was a threat and what wasn't, and what you can justify and what you can't. I mean, clearly, I think they acted in a way — you know, the Goldstein report lays it out — they acted in a way that you can say these were war crimes.

Groth: Yeah, there wasn't an investigation into the 1956 massacres, per se; there was some sort of (it would seem to me) half-assed hearing that you depict at the end of the book.

Sacco: Internally, within Israel, yeah. And what's interesting also — and you've got to show this too — is that there were Israeli Knesset members that wanted to get to the bottom of it, and obviously don't want to feel that their country's done something immoral.

On November 23, the 13 Knesset members of the Foreign Affairs and Defense Committee had their own questions for IDF Chief of Staff Dayan about the conduct of Israeli forces in Gaza. In a closed door session he assured them that while in "borderline" circumstances some units may have fired on those who might otherwise have been captured,

... I DON'T KNOW OF ANY INSTANCE WHERE THEY STOOD PRISONERS IN A ROW AND KILLED THEM.

MK Moshe Aram wanted to know, "What exactly happened in Rafah?"

IN RAFAH THERE WAS A BIT OF AN UNFORTUNATE CONVERGENCE OF EVENTS, AND THE ARABS THERE HAD A NEGATIVE DISPOSITION...

Groth: Right, but they're in a politically compromised situation where they don't want to be seen unpatriotic to the Israeli citizenry?

Sacco: I think, yes, and I think you can say that for any country.

Groth: Of course. They questioned Moshe Dayan, and you had one chilling scene where Dayan replies to them and the last thing he said was, "The Arabs there had a negative disposition."

Sacco: Right. [Groth laughs.] And what do you expect? First of all, my best guess is [the Palestinians] are scared out of their minds — an army has just occupied them. I doubt they're going to be surly against the Israeli soldiers. I just don't see it. That's not anything I've heard — I found no evidence of that at all — in anything anyone's said.

Groth: Yes, and even a little surliness wouldn't have justified what they'd done.

Sacco: No! And even if they had a negative disposition, I mean, you would probably be considered human to have a negative disposition toward any particular type of ...

Groth: ...Invading your country might elicit a little surliness. Yeah, that line struck as just such wonderfully transparent bullshit. One thing amused me. You make it abundantly clear throughout the book that you don't much care for teenagers.

Sacco: [Laughs.] No. Not when I'm being hassled.

Groth: You're referring to the Palestinian teenagers who would follow you around.

Sacco: Well, I don't like teenagers anywhere, really. [*Groth laughs.*] I'm a little cautious of...

Groth: Especially if one's in your living room.

Sacco: [*Laughs.*] Conrad [Groth]'s OK. He's sitting there quietly and I don't see a stiletto coming out of his back pocket. I mean, my theory on gangs of teenage boys is always "walk on the other side of the street." [*Groth laughs.*] Because you never know what's coming.

Groth: But the reason I bring this up: You actually have this moving moment where you sit down with several teenagers, and they're not hassling you for once. They're actually sitting there, quietly, discussing these issues before them, and it's one of those moments where teenagers finally drop that bravado and all the bullshit. It's beautifully paced, and at the end, in the last panel, one looks at you and says, "Do you like us?" Was he wanting your favor? Wanting your approval?

Sacco: Sort of. Just feeling that, everyone wants to be liked — they might want to act like an asshole, in a way, but when it's all been stripped, basically ...

Groth: There's a kind of existential truth to this.

Sacco: Yeah, I think so. People want to be liked; they want to feel like you like them. That's all. I don't think it goes much beyond that sort of human need. Which I think is great.

Groth: Otherwise, it's a testament to your art that you depicted the teenagers, whom you disliked so much, so humanly.

Sacco: [*Laughs.*] Well, that was the surprise, in a way, for me, that "OK, these kids, they're going to come, they're going to hassle me again ..."

Groth: I want to ask you how dangerous living there and engaging in this research was for you. When you had to move to Rafah, you were actually advised against it, correct?

Sacco: I was advised, not so much against moving to Rafah, but against going to the refugee camp. I wanted to be, frankly, as close inside the refugee camp as possible because I was interested in refugee camp life and I wanted to be there in the middle of it. But yeah, I was so dissuaded, and in the end, I had to make from my own mind a compromise — because I don't want my hosts, basically, to feel uncomfortable. I don't want to put them into a position to feel uncomfortable.

My initial idea was I'd like to live with a family. But what you begin to understand is, in a very conservative place like that; you create difficulties for the family, because it's not common for a man that's not from the house to be seeing the women. Unless he's invited to see them, or he's asking, "Can I speak to your mother?"

Groth: And you can't live with that kind of close proximity?

Sacco: No, you would just make their lives miserable. They would be embarrassed. So in the end, you realize, "OK, this isn't going to work." And fortunately I found a place for Abed and me. I felt fortunate, because in the end, I needed the evenings to work, and I didn't want to be involved in family dynamics and conversations all the time. I needed that period of trying to put things down and get it right.

Groth: So you found a place. It looked great.

Sacco: Oh yeah, it was amazing. It was a guy who had built a place — I think he was working in the Gulf with his brother, he was still in the Gulf — so when he retired, he would live there. And his brother had opened it up for us. It was safe but then when I left Rafah, there was a lot of heavy incursions and a lot of people got killed in Rafah shortly after I left: dozens of deaths.

Groth: No cause and effect?

Sacco: No, they just decide to crack down this way. And that place was hit by machine-gun fire, because an Israeli armored vehicle came on Sea Street and parked itself there, and there was some gunfire. So I heard some months later, it wasn't quite as safe as — no place is safe! No place is safe there. But I never really felt an immediate danger.

Groth: How about the time when you had to run from the tracer bullets? And you ran to the wrong side of the street?

Sacco: Yeah, that seems sort of funny, and my guess is that if they really wanted to harm us, they would have. You never know, people got hurt there just at that same locale a few days beforehand. So you just never know.

Groth: Seemed like they could be capricious.

Sacco: They could be completely capricious. We were unarmed, walking, and they fired at us. The gun could jerk, and someone could've been hurt. But if they really wanted to nail us, they would have, so I felt that was just a scaring tactic, someone's idea of a joke. You just never know what's in someone's mind when they're doing something like that.

Groth: Did you not feel your life was in danger that morning?

Sacco: [*Pause.*] I felt scared in that way where almost immediately after it was over, it was funny in this kind of weird way. I don't understand the psychology of just thinking everything's funny like that. There's something going on. I can't interpret it.

Groth: There's a moment where you were laughing.

Sacco: Yeah, I couldn't stop laughing, and I don't understand that. What I do know is that you've got to be careful, and I was always careful. I might be interested in seeing what's going on, and I'd like to get close to what's going on, but I'm always holding back a bit more. And then you see the photographers taking pictures, and they're out of their minds, from my standpoint. Like, there's an armored vehicle coming toward us, and one of them just stands taking these pictures, and everyone else is just running. But photojournalists, especially war photographers, they've got another thing going. I don't get it at all. [*Groth laughs.*] And you can't be lackadaisical about anything. I was always careful about stuff.

Groth: Careful how? What would that mean or entail? How were you careful in that context?

Sacco: I mean I'm going to clear out. If people are running, I'm going to run. I'm not going to be the last one lingering. And, you can be careful and get to a place rather than running in the open. Now, in the particular place we would pass — I would pass that area a lot — I was always very aware that there was a gap between the buildings and there was that tower — quite far away, but it had a line of sight. I was very aware of it. And, you're just aware that you're always at the point where they could see you. And, I never particularly liked it. [*Laughter.*] And part of the reason for putting that scene in is to show what Palestinians go through. This is not something that might rate any kind of mention the next day amongst them.

Groth: Daily life.

Sacco: You're really harassing people who are trying to live their lives. There's no two ways about it. I don't think they were serving the cause of fighting terrorists by firing — and who knows? You know those bullets have to come down. They could have come down anywhere. I don't know how far they would hit, but they come down eventually. Firing stray bullets in the cities.

Groth: You're a cartoonist and a journalist; are you motivated more by your being a cartoonist? What is your primary motivation for doing this? Do you consider yourself a cartoonist first, then a journalist?

Sacco: Cartoonist first: But I wanted to be a journalist before I was ever a cartoonist. I mean I was cartooning when I was a kid, but I never thought in a million years there was a way of turning that into something I could make a living off of.

Groth: So your main impetus for working is as a cartoonist?

Sacco: My main impetus is as a cartoonist. And I want to call myself a cartoonist, because ultimately, I'd love to do other things beyond journalism. But I really do like journalism. It's a privilege to me, to see these things. And how else are you going to be invited to people's homes and see things you don't get to see?

There are other imperatives. I mean, political imperatives, and moral imperatives to do this sort of thing. And I don't think that has anything to do with being a cartoonist or a journalist, but what I feel lucky about is that these things that eat me up, I can do something about — whether it has an effect is another thing. That's another story altogether, but I personally can expend this energy I have that relates to these things that bother me.

Groth: Virtually all of your cartooning is either journalism or autobiographical.

Sacco: There's some social satire.

Groth: Right. But have you considered doing pure fiction?

Sacco: Yes.

Groth: Is that something you're thinking of doing in the future?

Sacco: Yeah. I've got some ideas. I'd like to. The problem with cartooning is it just takes a fucking long time to do something. You say there are three or four major projects in my life, and that's 20 years of your life, and then everyone thinks, "Oh, you're the cartoon journalist." And I've used that expression myself, so then you've been pigeonholed in a certain sense, and of course, you use that to get more assignments and whatever. But, on the other hand ...

Groth: It's your brand.

As we head toward Sea Street, we must cross two points where, for a few seconds, no building or obstruction shields us from the Tal Zorob tower's line of sight.

This is near to where the two women and young girl from the Jaber family were rocketed a couple of weeks ago.

Sacco: Yeah, ultimately — it's a brand, I guess — but if you're a creative person, there are other things. There are other things I really enjoy, and I'm interested in. It just takes a long time to get that one interest out, then … your life's more than half over! [*Laughter.*]

Groth: All right, Conrad, do you have any questions for Joe?

Conrad: Yeah, I have one question. There was a point you were talking about earlier about how the Israelis were bulldozing. You were talking about how young people were forgetting about that. So I was wondering if you think maybe there's so much brutality so continuously that they're facing that they forget injustices, easier, quicker, rather than, say, 9/11, how we always remember that.

Sacco: Well, the young kids were actually really concerned about the bulldozing because that was going on in their present time, when I was trying to do the research for this. So that's what they were concerned about. They were concerned about attacks, which were killing people in different towns around Gaza at the time.

My way of looking at it is if 9/11 stands out as sort of a signature moment in American history — and it's always going to stand out. But you think of certain other historical episodes that might stand out for people today. I mean, one I think about is the Battle of Britain. You know, English people think about the Battle of Britain, they can make films about it — almost romanticize it somehow. Because it's done, it's past, and they're the heroes of the Battle of Britain, and then they have the anniversaries and everything. If the Battle of Britain was still going on today, it would be one smear — like for the Palestinians it seems have this smear of history. If they were getting bombed continually, what happened in 1940 is not going to matter to somebody still getting bombed today.

And that's part of the point of what's going on in the book, where people seemed to be — not necessarily wanting to forget what happened — but the present is so important, you lose so much; it matters so much to them in flesh and blood now, that you're just expending effort — the wrong effort — if you're thinking about what happened then.

Conrad: Is this a continuation of that?

Sacco: Yeah, in some ways: in a different form maybe, but yeah. They're still living in the camps and they're still at the mercy of the Israelis, basically.

Groth: Yeah, the continual brutalizing is something that is so foreign to Americans, and our response to 9/11 seems good evidence of this because our response is more disproportionately, more pathologically rendered.

Sacco: Well, especially with the invasion of Iraq, which just came on its heels. Yes, you're right.

Groth: I mean, what happened on 9/11 was an isolated moment. Whereas this place is getting it daily, and we can't even conceive of that.

Sacco: No, I think it's hard for anyone to live it, frankly. It's hard for me to conceive of it, even seeing it: because if you can really put someone in someone else's shoes for a certain period, in the end, it's a little much. I don't know how they do it. It's very hard for me to understand how people function, especially when you meet younger people who are smart, have a lot of energy, and there's just simply no outlet. There's nothing they can do that's going to make their lives interesting. They're just confined. They're confined by Israelis, they're confined by their own internal Palestinian disputes and the rise of Hamas. And you think, "Jesus Christ, this is really a pressure cooker on an individual. No wonder it warps psychologically."

Groth: Right, it all becomes normative.

Sacco: Yeah, it becomes normative as well. If despair is your main way of thinking of the world — talk about depression!

Groth: Well, is depression "depression" when it becomes the norm?
All right then: I won't take up any more of your precious time.

Sacco: [*Laughs.*] I enjoyed it. ∎

SKETCHBOOK

STEPHEN DIXON

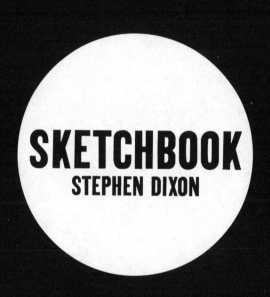

Stephen Dixon is a novelist and short story writer whose first story, "Chess House," appeared in *The Paris Review* in 1963. Fantagraphics Books recently published his massive short story collection, *What Is All This?*, and in the course of working with Stephen, I learned that he drew — and in fact, provided drawings for a couple of his own novels. Dixon is not a cartoonist, of course, but follows a long tradition of prose writers who sketch — from Breyten Breytenbach to Tennessee Williams, from Patricia Highsmith to Sylvia Plath. In response to a request, he sent me a half-dozen of his sketchbooks, and I immediately seized on the idea of presenting a representative sampling of sketches drawn by one of America's preeminent writers.

— *Gary Groth*

428

Gary Goth: Is drawing or sketching a lifelong habit? What inspired you to draw throughout your life (some of your sketchbooks date to the '70s, at least)? Any formal education when it comes to art?

Stephen Dixon: No formal education: as with my writing, entirely self-taught. I wanted to be an artist before I wanted to be a writer. Did a lot of artwork in elementary school and one drawing class in college. The drawing teacher in college thought I showed little talent and was a better artist when I began the course than when I finished. (Between 1958 and 1968, I was, in addition to my other work, an artist model, in NYC and California, to make extra money, and got interested in drawing in those sessions. Howard Brodie, a noted caricaturist, who died the other day, ran several of the classes I modeled for in California. A very nice guy, and a much easier instructor to work for than others; he let me move and he let me rest when I got cramps.)

After I graduated college, I became a newsman in Washington, D.C. and New York, but continued painting in D.C. I had lots of paintings, and when I left one apartment to move into another apartment, I left my paintings in the old apartment for the night. When I came back the next night, they were gone or destroyed. A mystery. It put a damper on my painting. Anyway, I'd started writing fiction by then, so concentrated on that. But it was the time I took myself most seriously as an artist, other than the time I worked as a technical writer for TRW, a systems analysis company, in Redondo Beach, Calif. The work was so inconducive

for fiction writing that I started to draw and then paint again. I continued to both write and paint in San Francisco and New York City, between the years 1968-1974 or so. All my paintings in California were left in a friend's attic when I moved back to NYC, and weather destroyed them. My feeling about them and my D.C. artwork was "no great loss." I felt all of this was just pushing me to do one art — writing. I had no place to store them and some of the works were quite large. I think I have one large painting left, rolled up: my last. I'm not sure where it is: maybe under the couch. I left some of my paintings on the West 75th Street apartment in NYC when I moved to Baltimore in June 1980 to start working as a teacher at Johns Hopkins University. I've only done drawings since, sometimes with colored pens.

Groth: Have you sketched consistently over the years?

Dixon: I do less and less sketching. For years, I've done mostly sketches of myself. It's a good way to deal with aging and conveying my emotions and helping me get through the illnesses and deaths of those I loved — my parents and wife.

Groth: Do you carry a sketchbook with you? What are your habits like when it comes to drawing?

Dixon: I don't carry a sketchbook any more. I used to. When I went for a walk, taught elementary school, went to a museum. Now if I feel like drawing, I do it on whatever paper is around: the blank pages of a book I'm carrying, or the printed pages of a book I'm reading or a manuscript I'm writing.

Groth: What dictates your subject matter? You seem equally interested in landscapes, interiors and portraits.

Dixon: Whatever catches my eye. Usually what catches me is my own image in the window across my writing table at night. I also like to do geometric designs or a statue of a figure on many increasing-in-size pedestals.

Groth: I noticed that you also wrote short notes — mostly about art or the philosophy of art — in your sketchbooks. Do they also serve as a kind of creative diary?

Dixon: They used to; they embarrass me now and I don't do them any more.

I barely write any notes any more, and if I do, only what I want to include in the fiction I'm writing at the time. When I'm finished with them — when I've employed them — the note papers go out with the weekly paper pickup.

Groth: Are you a student of drawing and painting? And I have to ask you if you've ever read comics or had an especial liking for cartooning?

Dixon: I loved comics as a boy: my favorite form of reading till I discovered Franklin W. Dixon's *Hardy Boys*. Then I switched to books, and in a couple of years, was a serious reader, and I've been one since.

But I have wonderful memories of trading comic books and sitting up in bed and reading a few of them and buying a new comic book for a dime. *Captain Marvel* was my favorite, though I loved *Classic Comics*. They were an introduction into serious literature too.

A NYC friend of mine, when I was 9 and 10, was "related" to DC comics: his uncle and aunt owned it. So I used to get his discards, because they would shower him with their products.

Groth: You indicated to me earlier that when it comes to sketching, you are a dabbler. Do you consider yourself an amateur in the best and traditional sense of that term — someone who does it for private consumption and for the sheer love of it?

Dixon: Yes, definitely an amateur. For the love of doing it? I don't think love is involved. As I said, I do much less of it and I do it at the moment, as a distraction, because my hand is holding a pen and I'm on the phone and the conversation is boring and there's a piece of paper on top of the dresser where the phone is and I start drawing, sometimes [*a drawing*] of the phone.

Groth: I assume you would agree that your most accomplished creative medium is prose, but does drawing complement or play a role in your writing in some way?

Dixon: I don't think it does. I don't take it seriously. I have, though, had several of my narrators as artists: the substitute teacher in "The Sub," for instance, in my 1980 collection *14 Stories*.

I've done several of the covers for my books: the drawings for them: *Tisch*; *14 Stories*; self-portraits for others. As for art itself, I'm a serious museumgoer and I like bios of artists I like.

Groth: As I'm sure you know, many writers have also been artists, some equally

love of creation — The overwhelming
forces That give Life meaning 1.11.78

Wolfe — "FICTION, FACT arranged
& CHARged with purpose"

Wolfe — Tryng "to achieve The highest life
on earth, No LIFE which can be won
only by The bitter TOIL & Knowledge &
STern Living — The LIFE of an artist"

good as artists (Max Beerbohm, for example), but most drawing as a secondary
art — Kurt Vonnegut, Kathy Acker, Djuna
Barnes, Charles Bukowski, Flannery
O'Connor, Guy Davenport, to name a few.
Do you think there's some hidden affinity
between writing and drawing? John Updike, a once-aspiring cartoonist himself,
wrote: "The subtleties of form and color,
the distinctions of texture, the balances
of volume, the principles of perspective
and composition — all these are good
for a future writer to explore and will
help him to visualize his scenes, even to
construct his personalities and to shape
the invisible contentions and branchings
of plot."

Dixon: I can't see the affinities between
writing and visual art. I don't dispute
what Updike said. I have an enormous
book of writers who also painted and

drew: The Writer's Brush, and some surprise
me and some are very good and some are
very bad, but none of them excel. That's
because writing was more important
to them.

Groth: I'm always looking for congruities
(or incongruities). I would call your
prose spare and unadorned, but your
drawing is often dense, full of crosshatching, details, almost obsessively
overworked. Similarly, your color-work
can be full of bright pastels, almost
psychedelic, which seems somewhat
un-Dixonesque. Do these expressions
represent two sides of the same Dixon
coin? Do you see any differences here
between your approach to prose and
your approach to drawing?

Dixon: My approach to prose is more serious;
my approach to drawing is more casual.

"I can't see the affinities between writing and visual art."

Groth: Is sketching a form of thinking, or even of writing for you? Is there a narrative that accompanies your drawings?

Dixon: I have done narrative drawings. They're somewhere in my sketchbooks, or just somewhere. One was of a month-long trip to Spain in '68, called "Diary of my Toe." (The toe figures in it a lot.) It starts off with leaving a woman in NYC for one in Portugal. It also gets racy, as does some of my work.

Groth: I have to ask you this: Since you draw as well as many young cartoonists who are now drawing 500-page graphic novels, have you ever thought of combining words and pictures into a single work — a comic?

Dixon: No: but thanks for the compliment. My two daughters are both artists. I think that's also why I've gradually withdrawn from artwork. It's not about competition; I want to leave the field to them and I want them, which they do, to take the field as seriously as I do writing.

But one more thing: I wrote, around 1970, a young adult novel, quite a comical and adventurous one, called *Letters to Kevin*. British American Publishing, which published my *Love and Will* collection and *Frog*, asked me to illustrate it. I did. They started to publish it: I believe even had the cover (based on one of my drawings, of a mailbox on a post) but went out of business. The real one time I combined both. ■

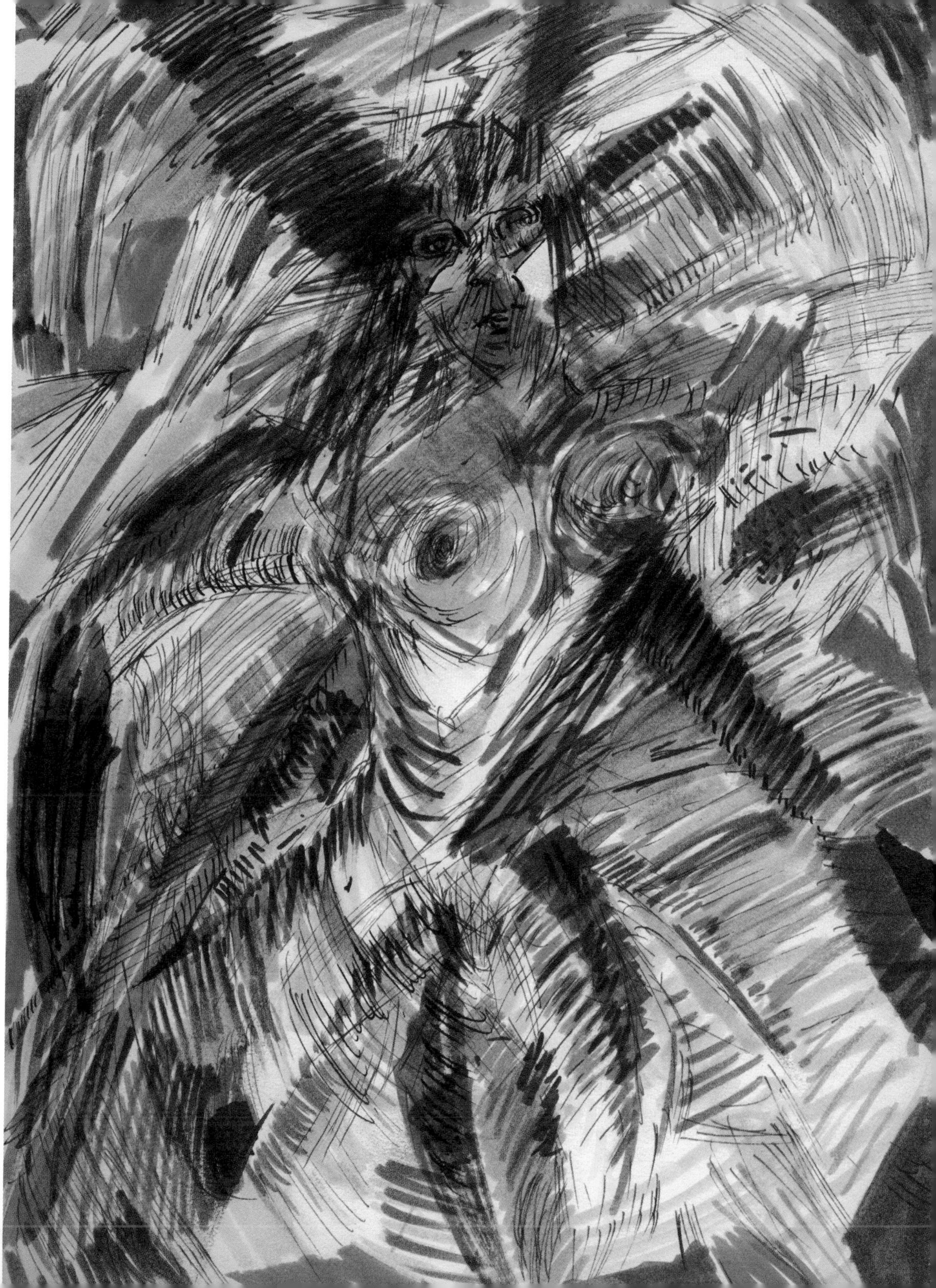

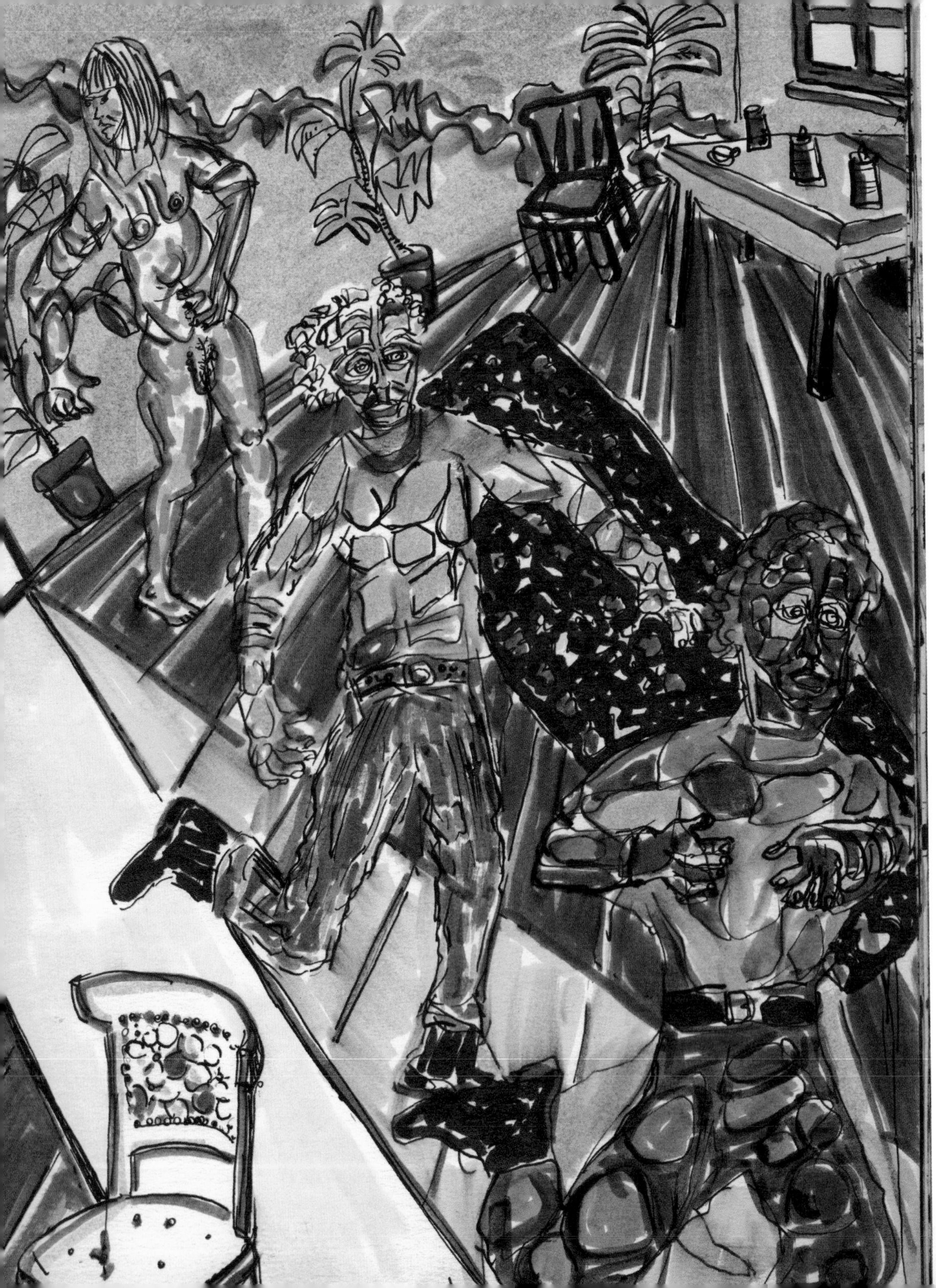

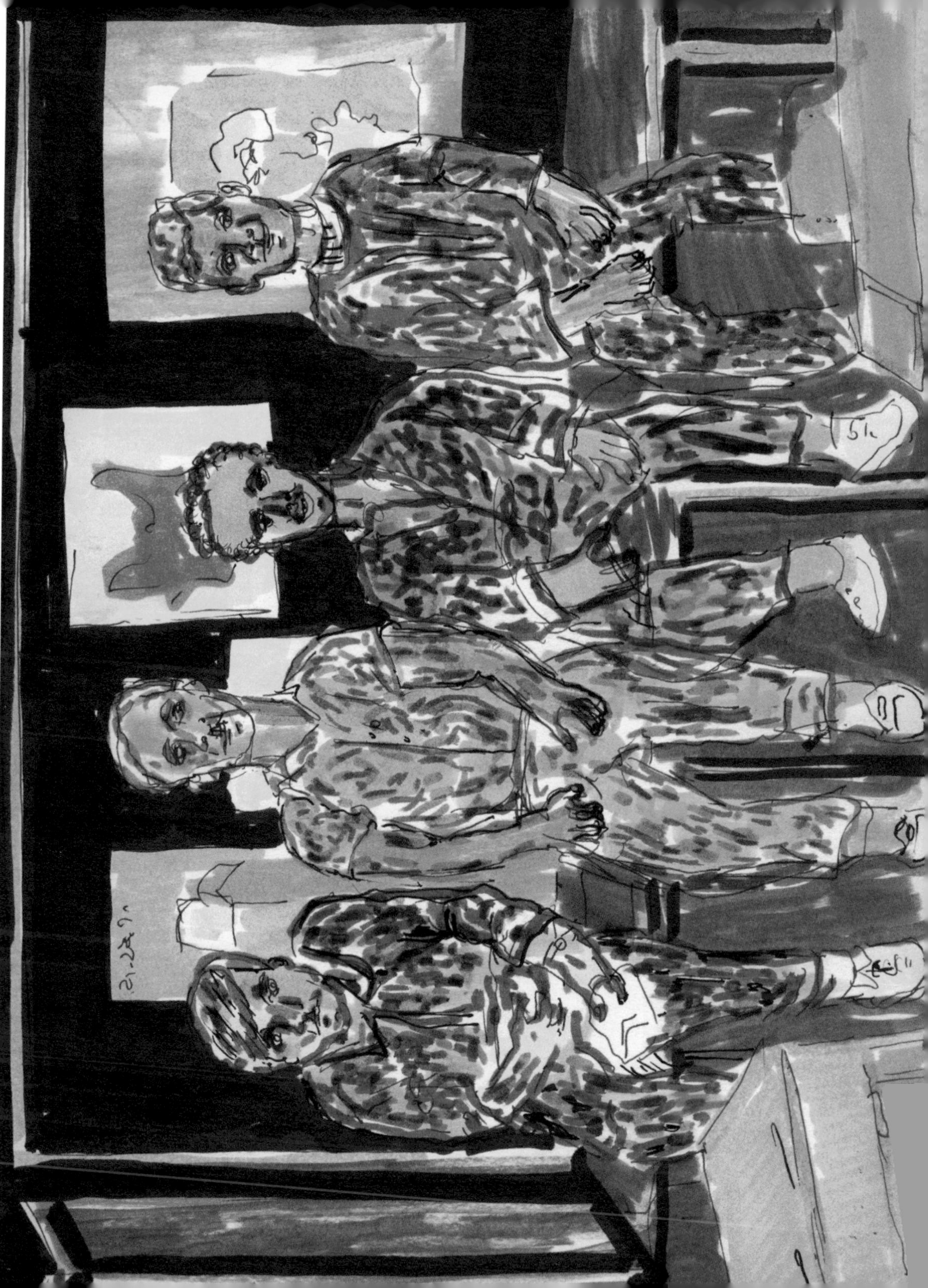

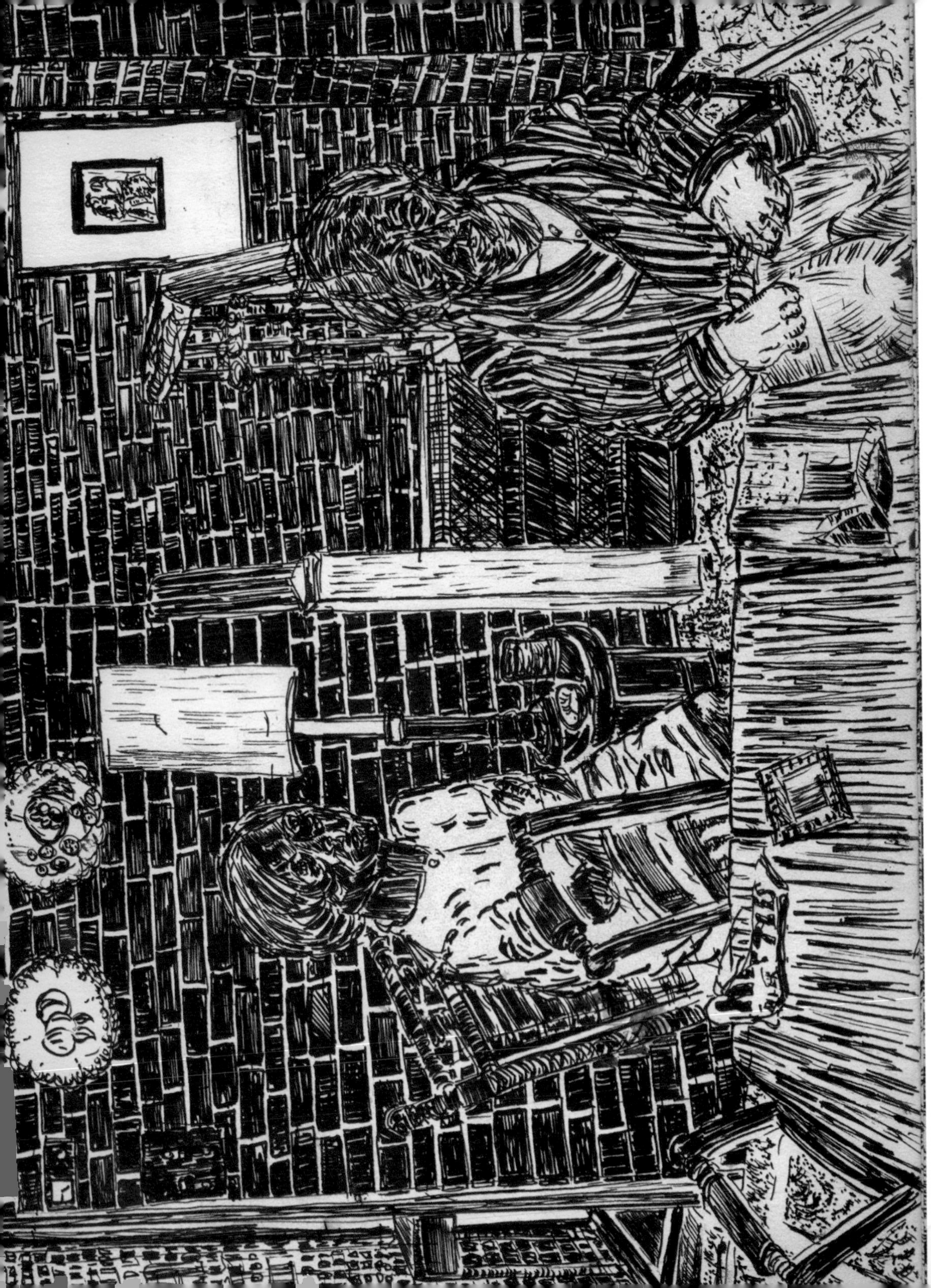

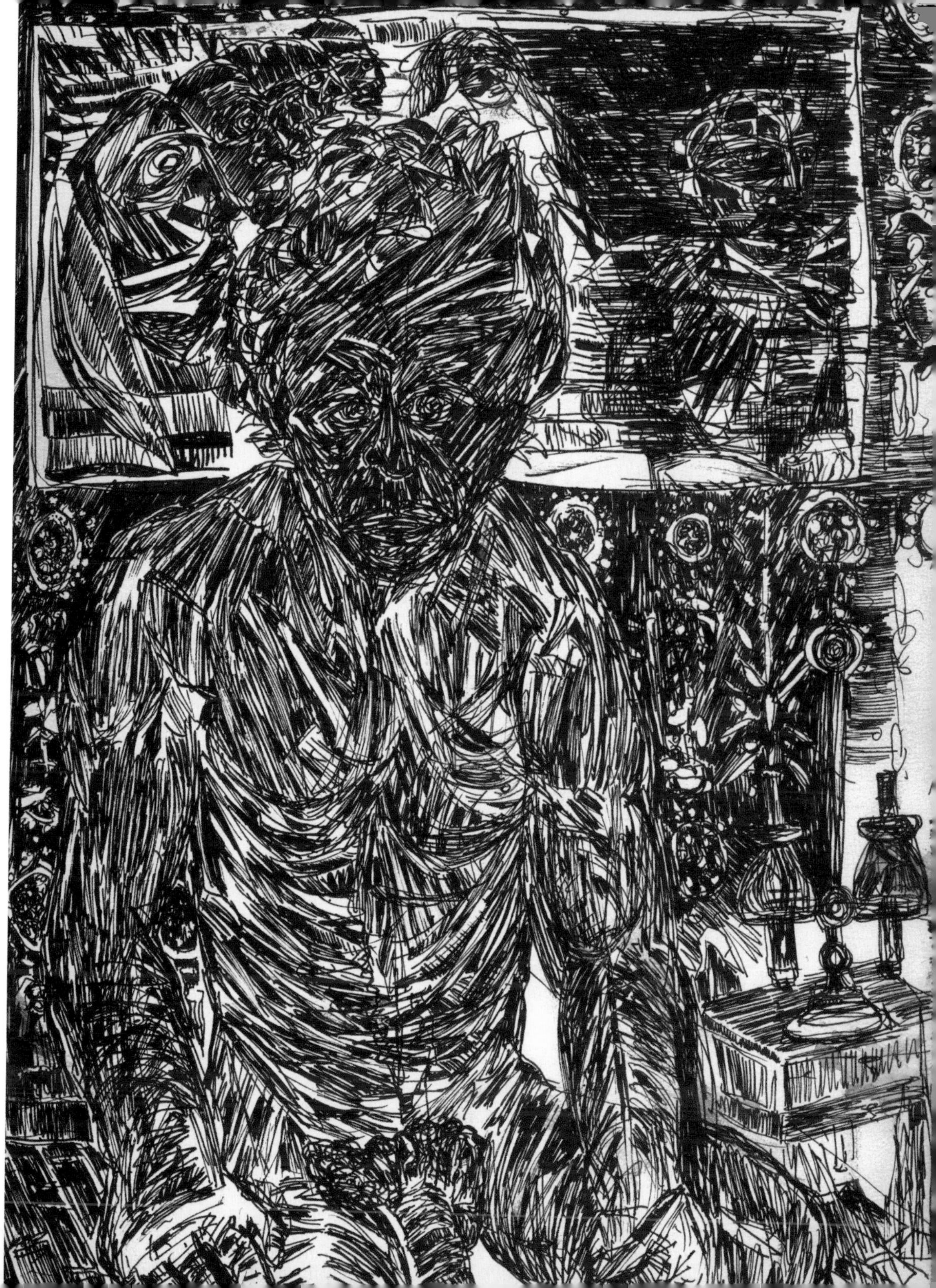

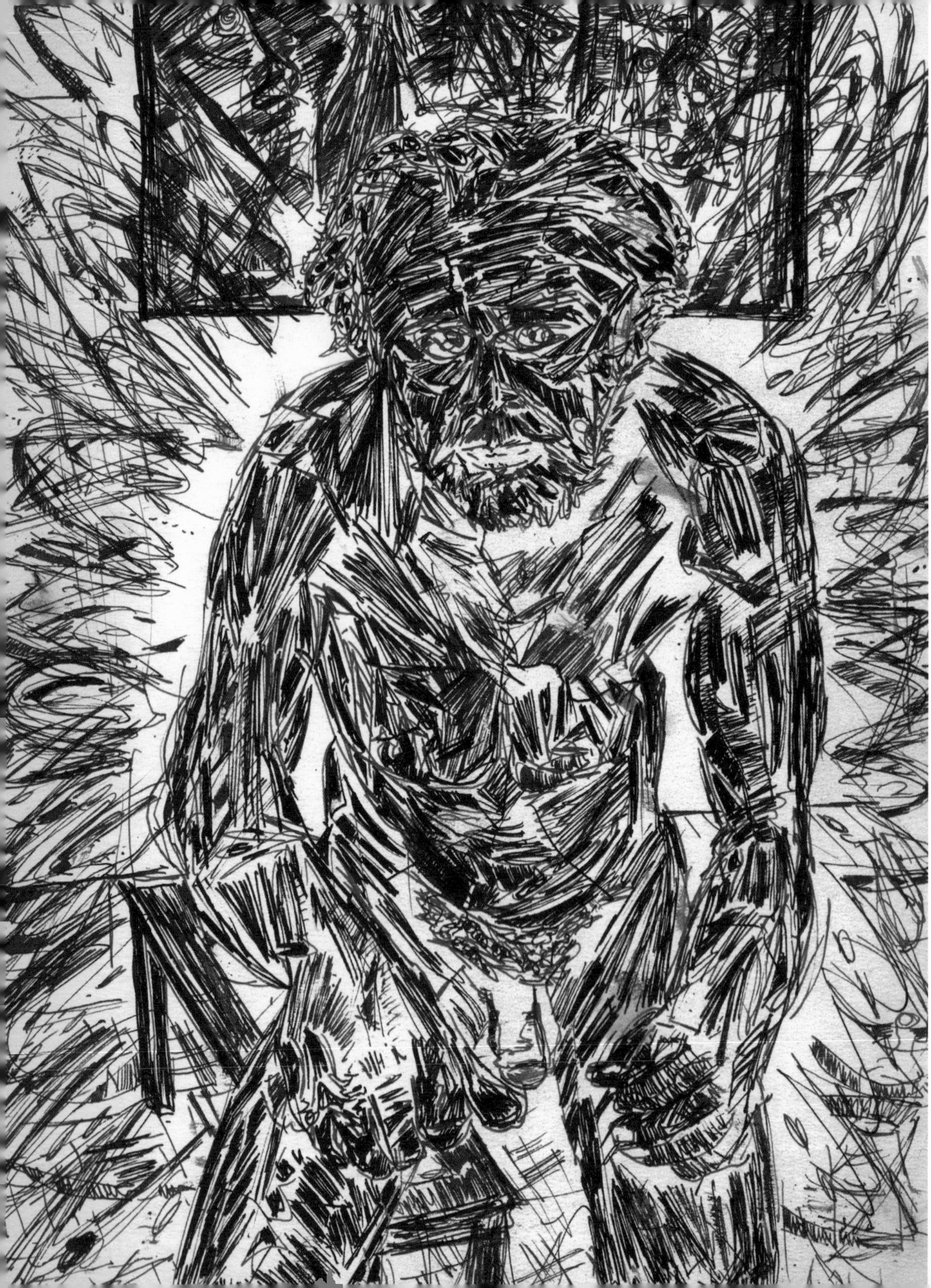

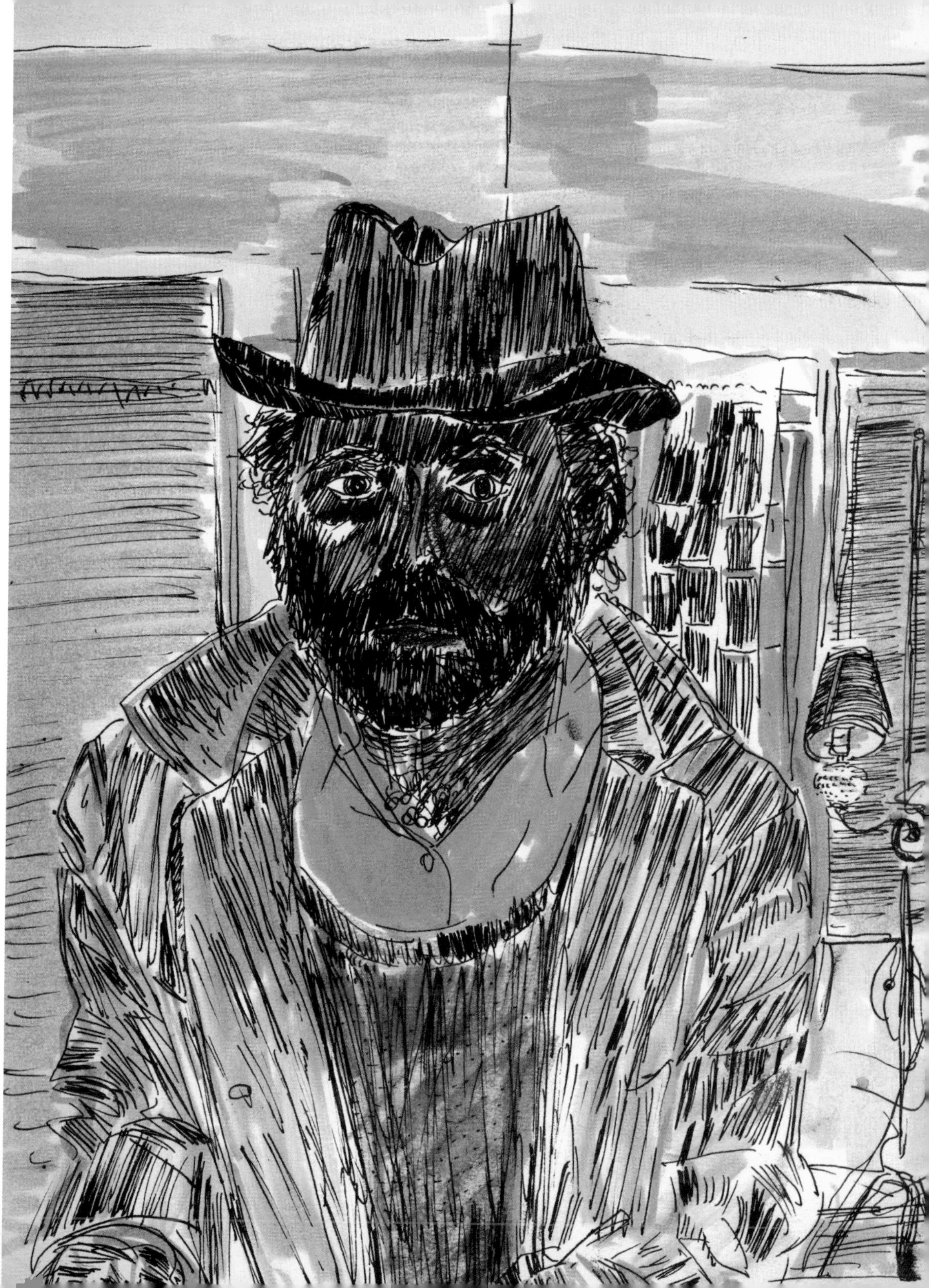

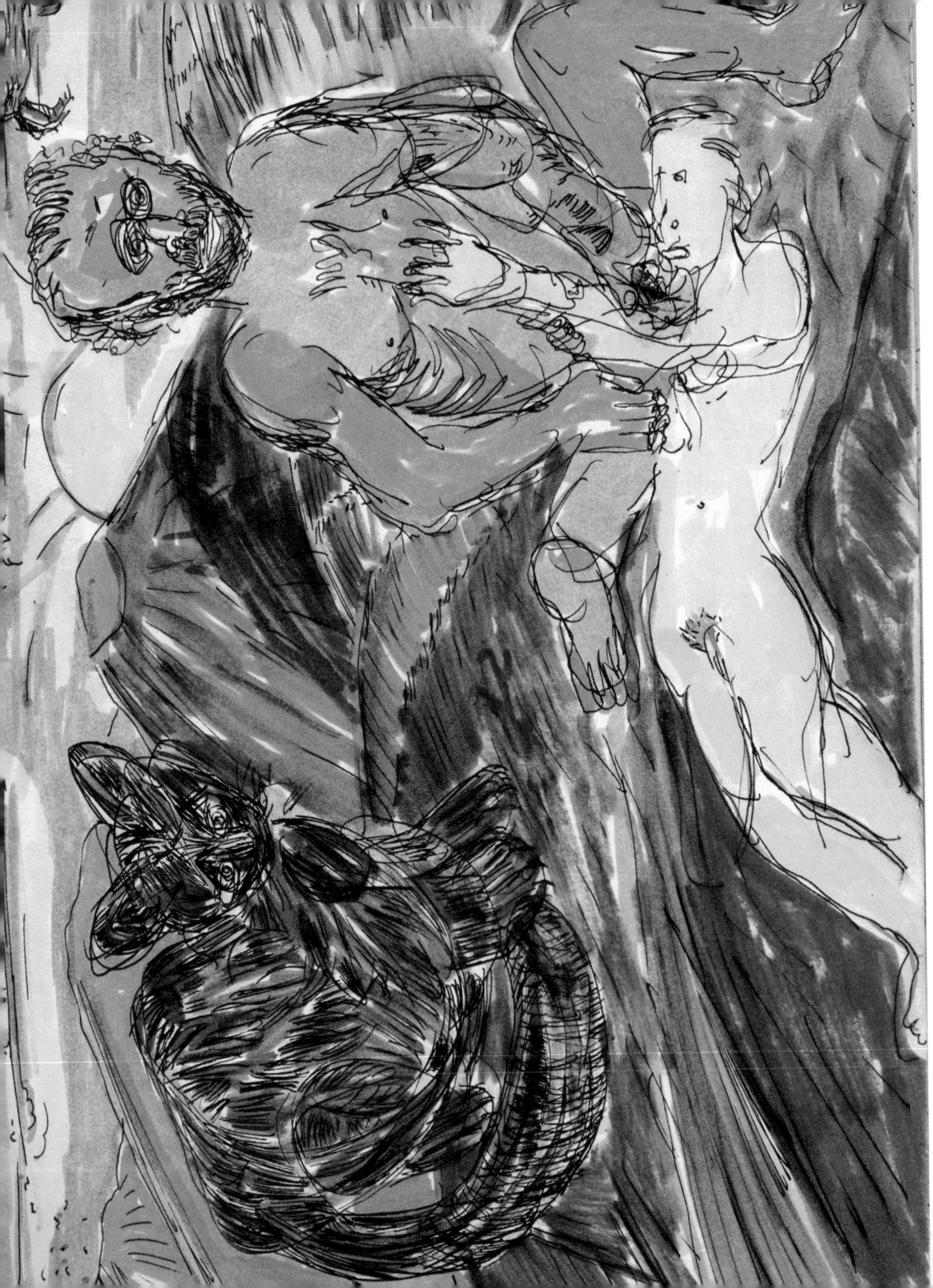

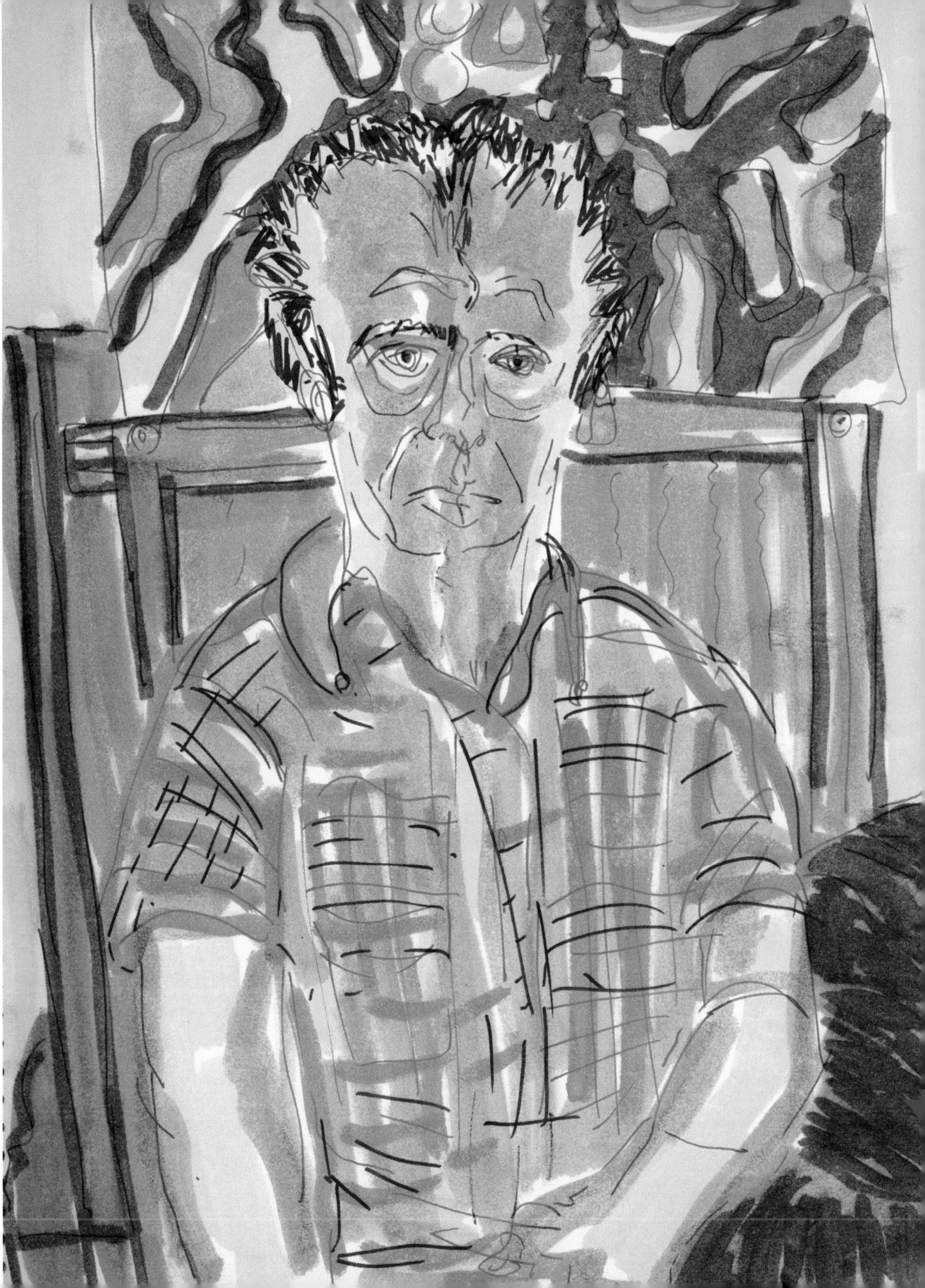

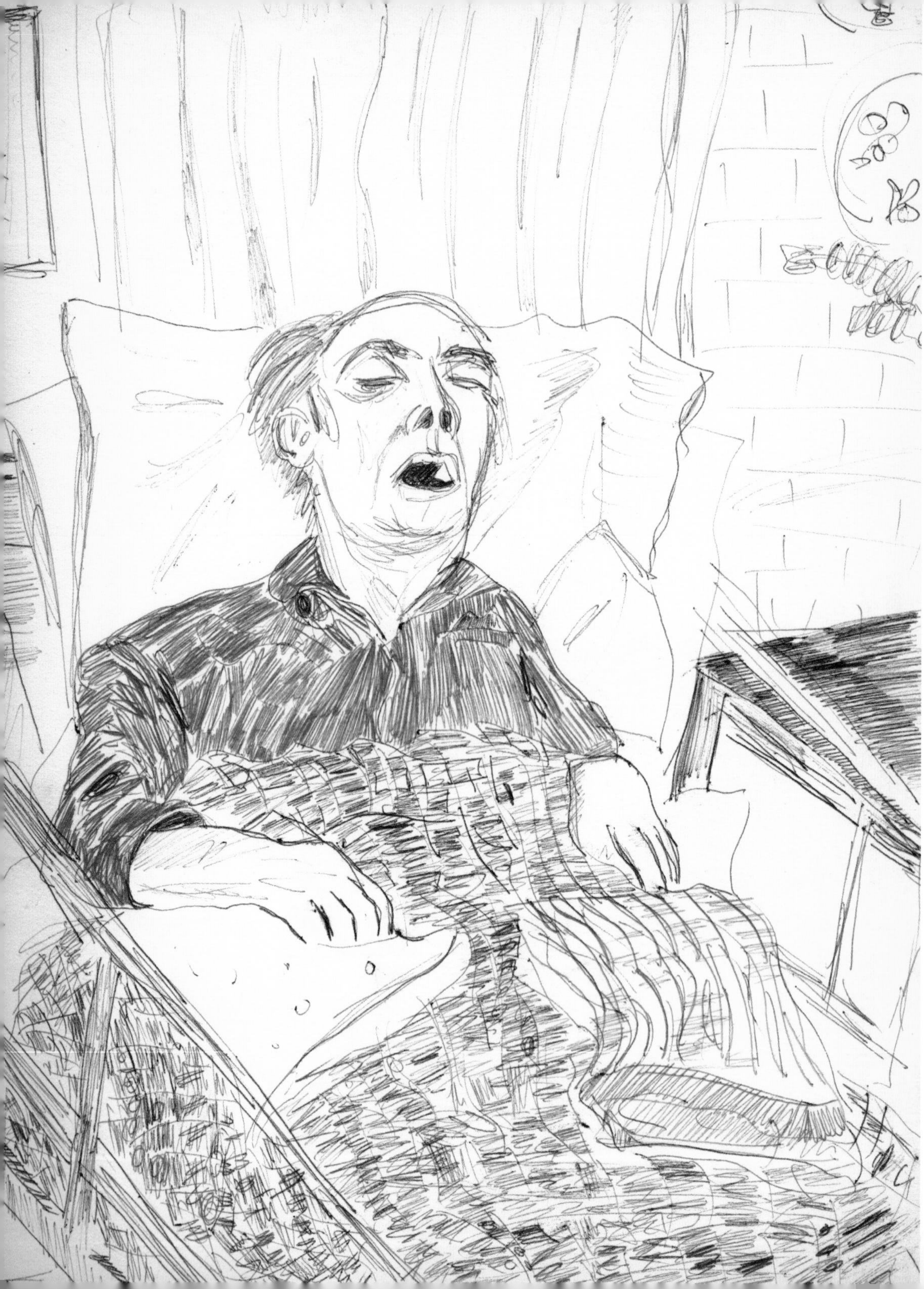

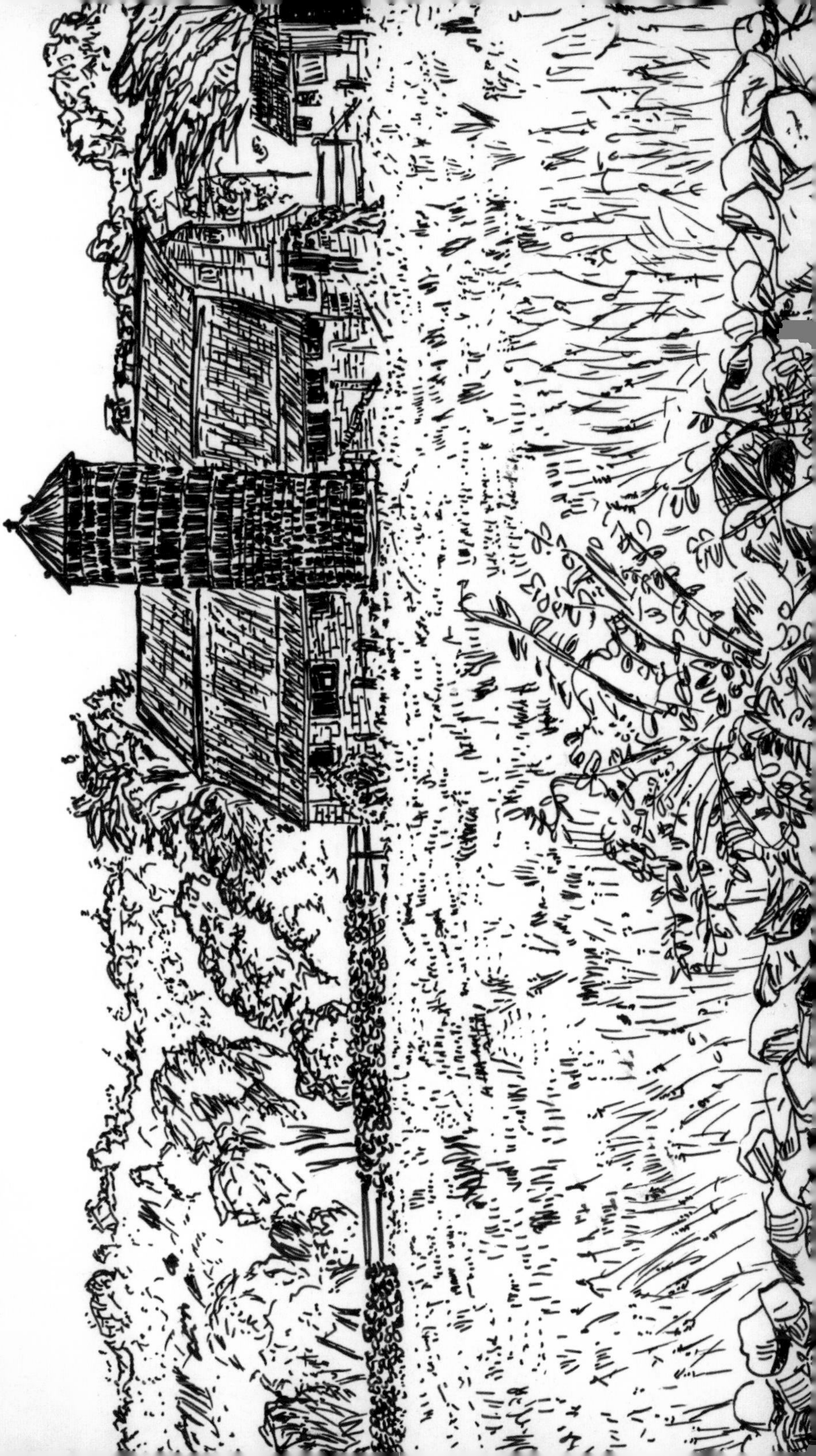

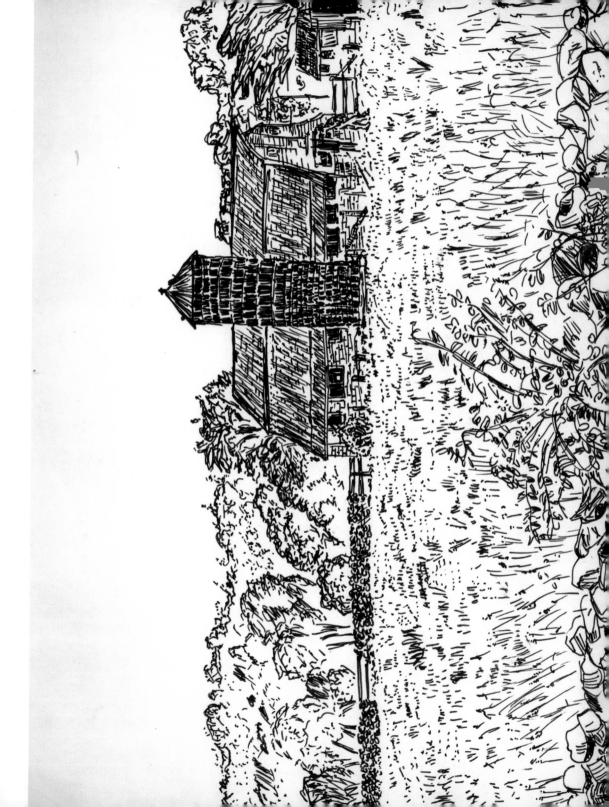

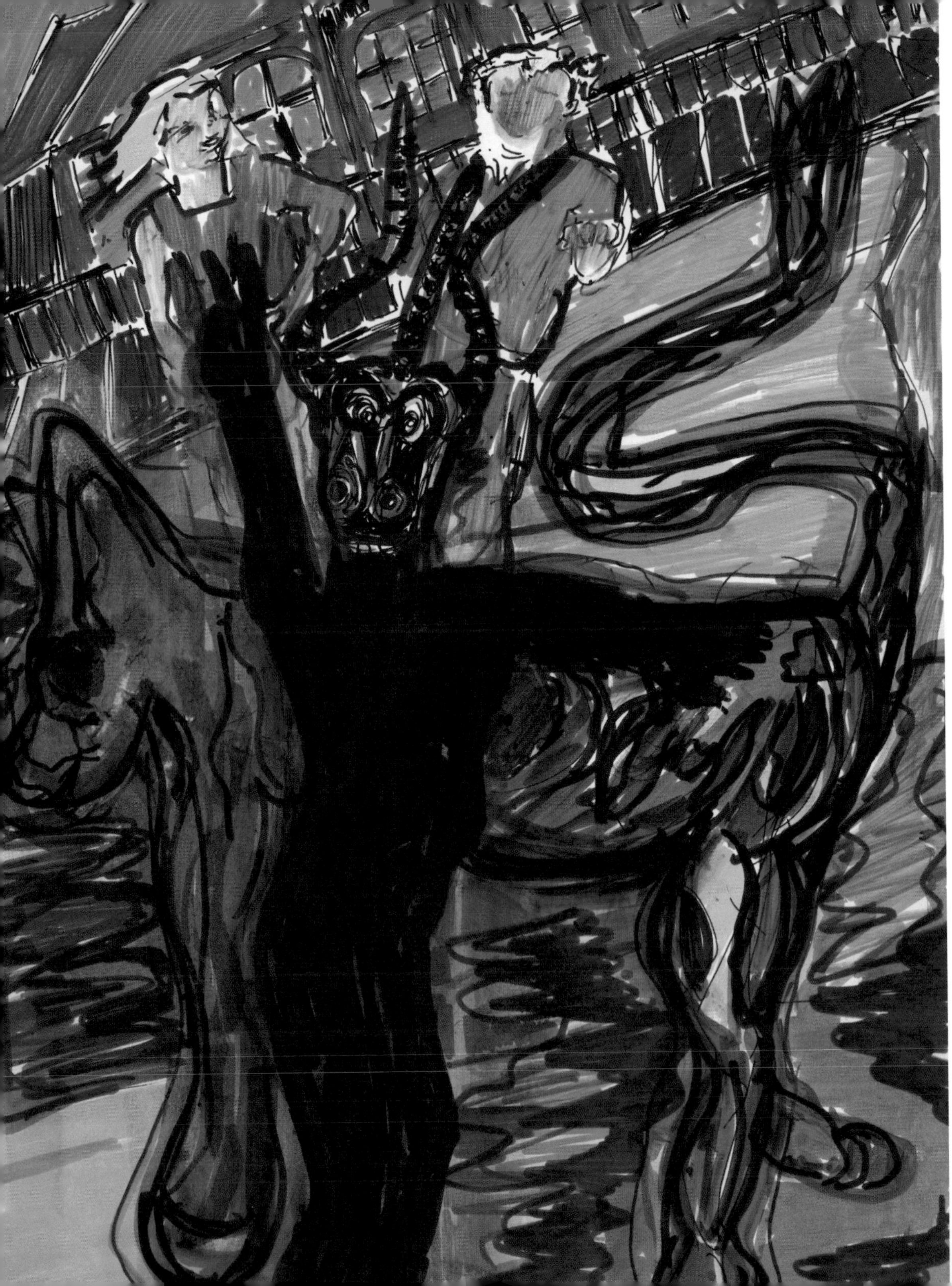

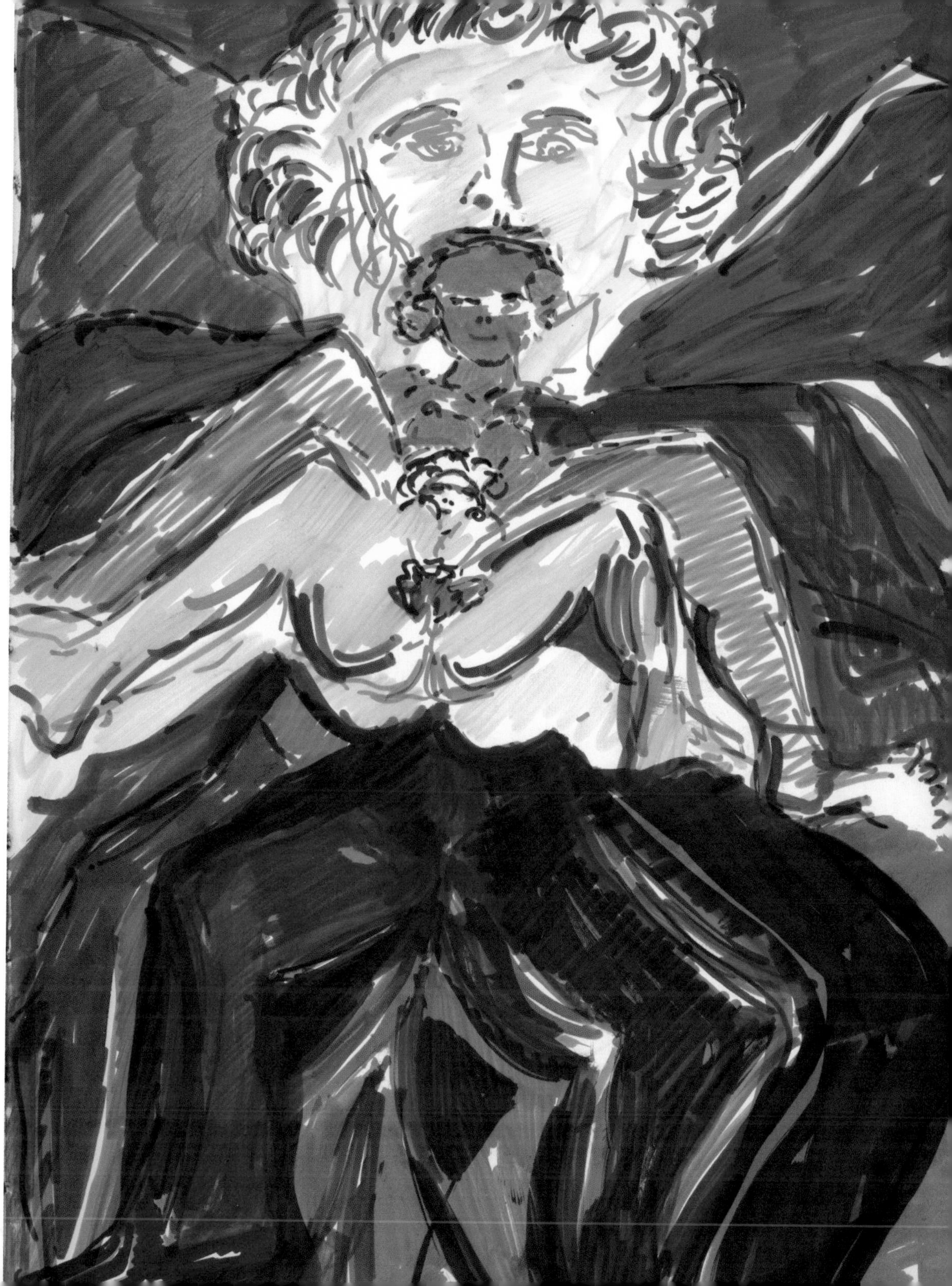

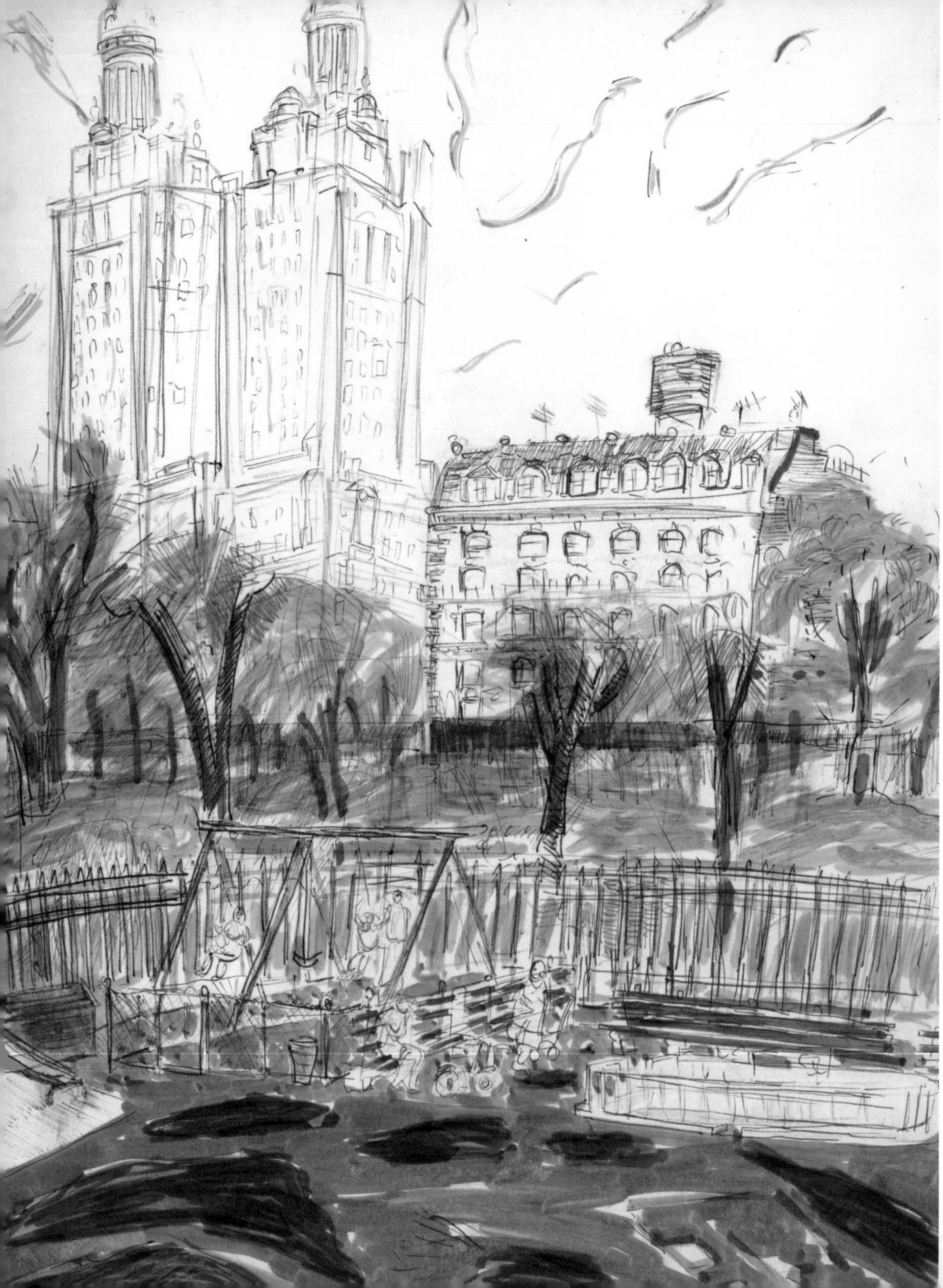

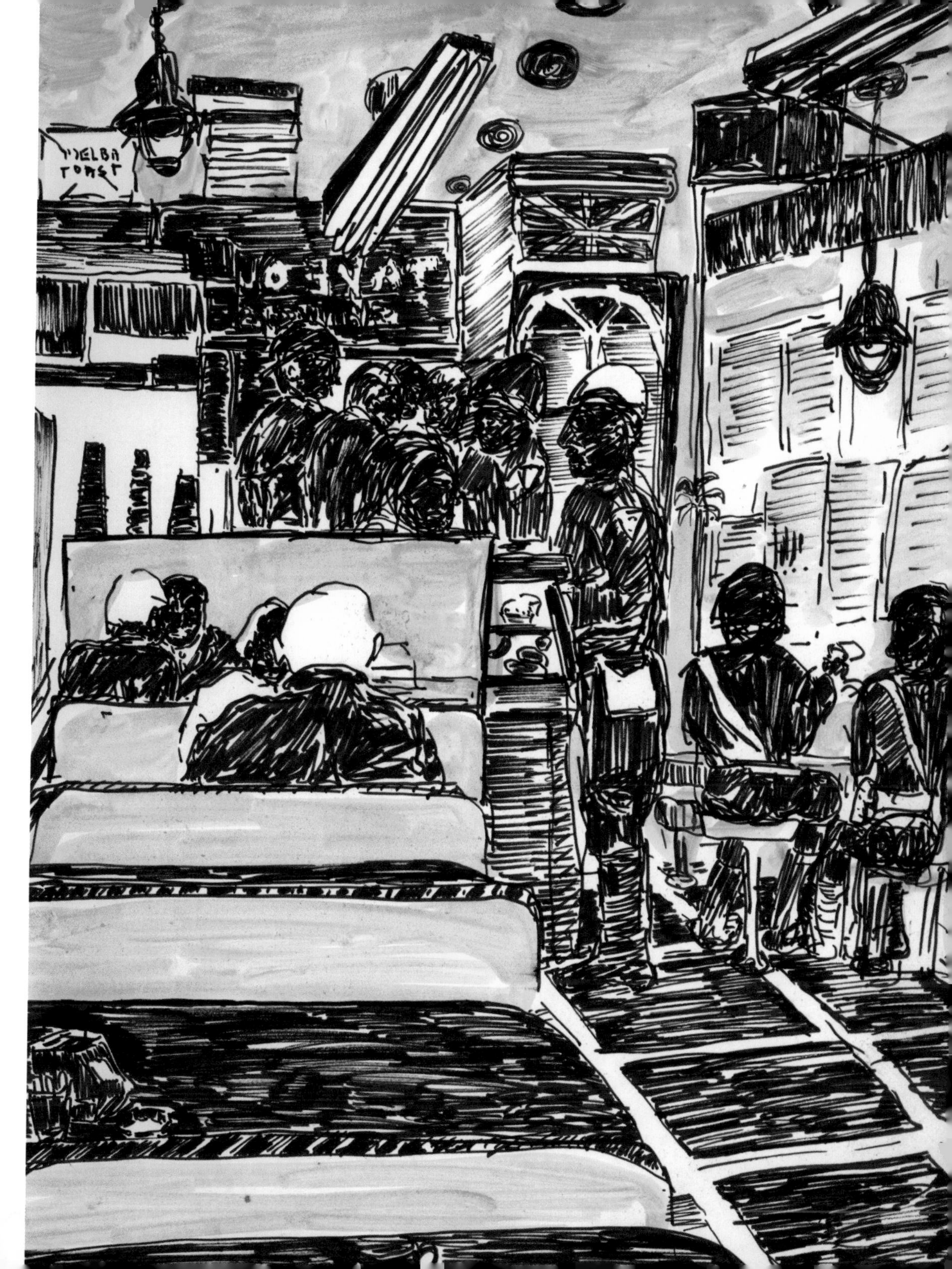
MELBA
TOAST

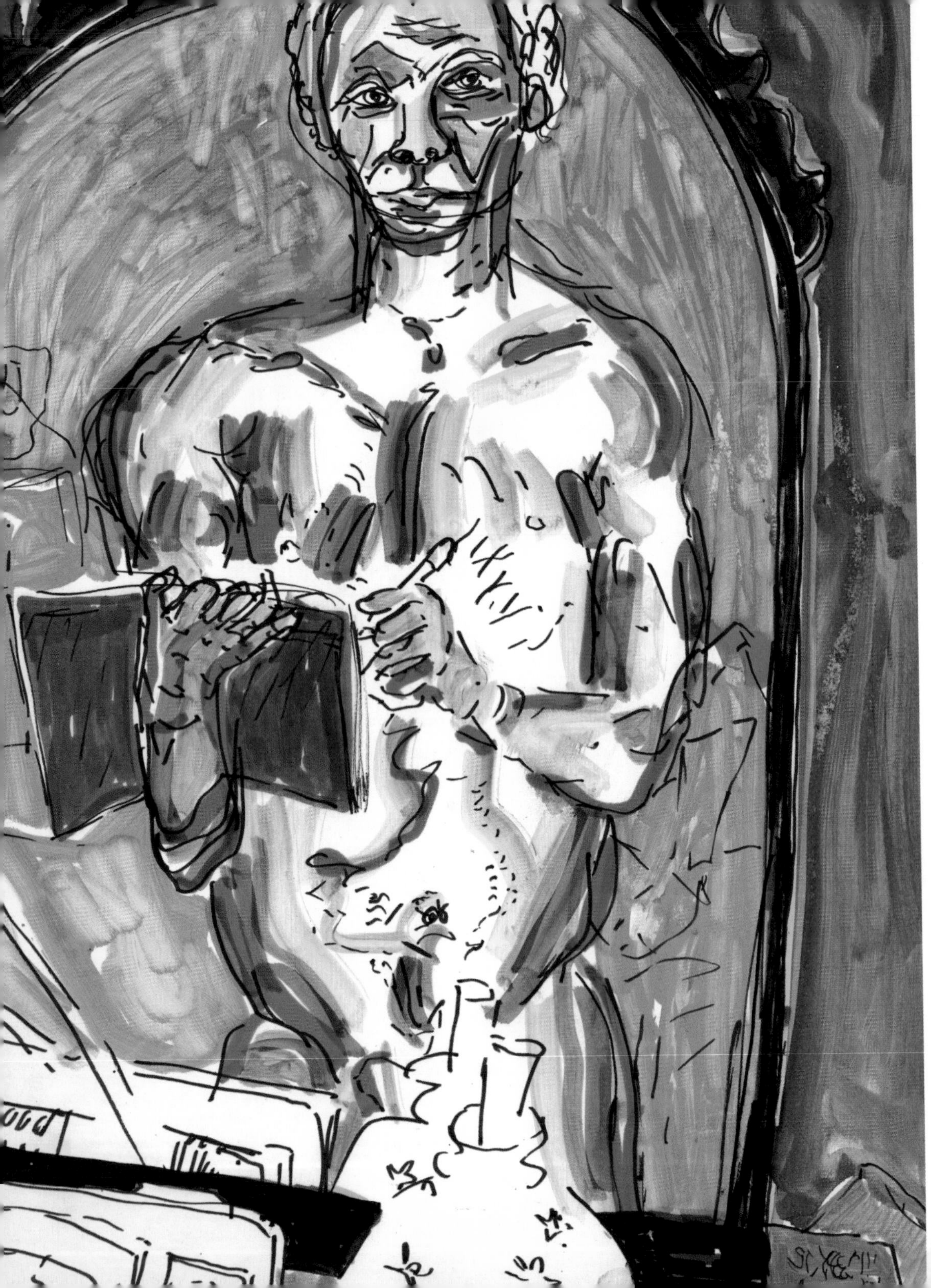

REVIEWS

FOOTNOTES IN GAZA
ALEC: THE YEARS HAVE PANTS
BLACK BLIZZARD

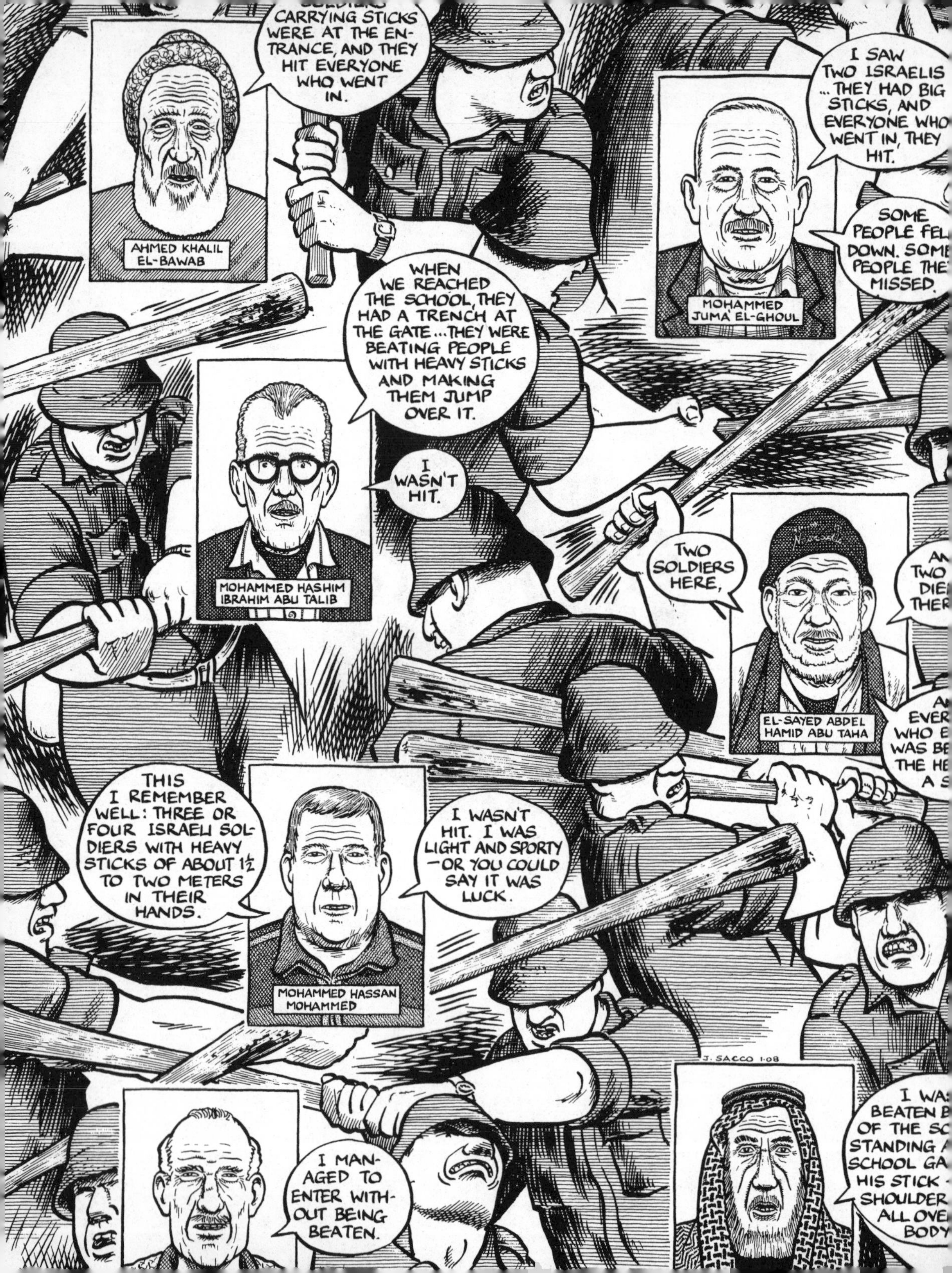

CARRYING STICKS WERE AT THE ENTRANCE, AND THEY HIT EVERYONE WHO WENT IN.
AHMED KHALIL EL-BAWAB
I SAW TWO ISRAELIS ...THEY HAD BIG STICKS, AND EVERYONE WHO WENT IN, THEY HIT.
SOME PEOPLE FEL DOWN. SOME PEOPLE THE MISSED.
MOHAMMED JUMA' EL-GHOUL
WHEN WE REACHED THE SCHOOL, THEY HAD A TRENCH AT THE GATE...THEY WERE BEATING PEOPLE WITH HEAVY STICKS AND MAKING THEM JUMP OVER IT.
I WASN'T HIT.
MOHAMMED HASHIM IBRAHIM ABU TALIB
TWO SOLDIERS HERE,
EL-SAYED ABDEL HAMID ABU TAHA
THIS I REMEMBER WELL: THREE OR FOUR ISRAELI SOLDIERS WITH HEAVY STICKS OF ABOUT 1½ TO TWO METERS IN THEIR HANDS.
I WASN'T HIT. I WAS LIGHT AND SPORTY —OR YOU COULD SAY IT WAS LUCK.
MOHAMMED HASSAN MOHAMMED
J. SACCO 1·08
I MANAGED TO ENTER WITHOUT BEING BEATEN.

The basic facts are not in dispute. In mid-November 1956, scores of Palestinian civilians were rounded up and killed by Israeli soldiers in the towns of Khan Younis and Rafah, which are located in the Gaza Strip. Accounts of these events appeared in British and Israeli newspapers, and leftist members of the Knesset, Israel's parliament, sought to "bring those who committed such acts to trial." In a formal letter of protest to the Israeli Foreign Minister, the Secretary General of the United Nations Dag Hammarskjöld raised concerns about "the information we have on the casualties ensuing" and urged that "observers from the United Nations Emergency Force be permitted to enter to be stationed and to function within the Gaza area," to assess whether "the situation has improved." And in a private letter to the United Nations Truce Supervision Organization, Lt. Col. R.F. Bayard of the U.S. Army said, "I have come to the conclusion that the treatment of civilians is unwarrantly rough and that a good number of persons have been shot down in cold blood for no apparent reason. It seems to me that representatives of the International Red Cross should be on the scene."

As Joe Sacco points out in his foreword to *Footnotes in Gaza*, these events, which unfolded during the highly charged Suez Canal crisis, constitute "the greatest massacre of Palestinians on Palestinian soil, if the U.N. figures of 275 dead are to be believed." The precise number will probably never be known; the United Nations figure that Sacco cites is an estimate, and may be too high. The 1956 killings in Gaza have been all but overlooked by academics and journalists, and "barely rate footnote status in the broad sweep of history." And yet, as Sacco rightly notes, the long-forgotten story of Khan Younis and Rafah "contain the seeds of the grief and anger that shape present-day events."

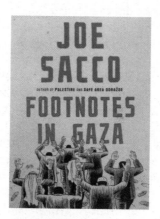

Footnotes in Gaza
Joe Sacco
Published by Metropolitan Books
418 pp :: $29.95 :: B&W :: hardcover
ISBN: 9780805073478

**Review by
Kent Worcester**

Joe Sacco is described by his current publisher as "the creator of war-reportage comics": while this strikes me as something of an overstatement — wasn't there an element of war-reportage in Harvey Kurtzman's *Two-Fisted Tales* and *Frontline Combat*? — Sacco is the unrivaled master of the genre. In a series of remarkable graphic volumes, including *Palestine* (1993-1995), *Safe Area Gorazde* (2000) and *The Fixer and Other Stories* (2009), Sacco has fused his journalistic and cartooning skills to explore the human dimensions of war, civil unrest and violence. He has received both the Eisner and Harvey awards for his comics-reportage, as well as the American Book Award, and his books have been heralded in *Time*, *Los Angeles Times*, *The New York Times* and other mainstream sources. In 2001, he was

451

awarded a Guggenheim fellowship, and his comics have been translated into more than a dozen languages. He is one of the heavy hitters of contemporary comics.

In *Footnotes in Gaza*, Joe Sacco returns to the Israel-Palestine conflict by chronicling a forgotten spasm of state-sponsored violence that has profound contemporary resonance. Rather than relying on official documents, which in this instance are incomplete and sometimes contradictory, the book is "chiefly dependent on the oral testimony of Palestinians asked to recall the tragic events." The bulk of the text consists of Sacco's visual encapsulations of his experiences in Gaza and his extended conversations with local residents about the 1956 events. The documentary material collected in the appendices offers a useful addendum to these oral histories. Since only a handful of specialists have written about the killings in Rafah and Khan

Younis, Sacco's account is almost certainly the longest and best-researched account of this consequential episode that we have, at least in the English language.

As the book opens, Sacco is enjoying the view from a friend's balcony in West Jerusalem. He soon finds himself at a party where journalists, U.N. workers, diplomats and bankers enjoy a rare evening of uninhibited fun. "Amazingly," Sacco observes, "in this season of bombed-out pizzerias and bulldozed refugee camps, hepcat Arabs from Ramallah and right-on Jews from Tel Aviv are sharing salads and grooving to the same post-bop jazz." As he savors "a glimmer of hope in which to exalt," he receives word from the Foreign Press Office that his application for press credentials has been turned down. "What you're doing doesn't fit into the category of real-time news," they tell him. Nevertheless, the following day, Israeli border guards allow him into the

cordoned-off Gaza Strip, and his journey into a past-that-is-never-really-past begins.

From this point forward, the book focuses almost exclusively on violence and daily life in Gaza, then and now. In this context, "now" refers to the early years of the new century, when "Israeli attacks were killing Palestinians, suicide bombers were killing Israelis, and elsewhere in the Middle East the United States was gearing up for war in Iraq." It was a period of high tension, and yet, as we all know, things devolved from there. As Sacco writes in the foreword, in 2005 Israel "unilaterally dismantled all the Jewish settlements in Gaza," while retaining control over the area's "airspace, coastline, and its entry and exit points save one" (i.e., the Egyptian-controlled access point that was reopened this year in the aftermath of the botched flotilla raid). In the following year, the hard-line Islamic group Hamas secured a majority of legislative seats, and Israel soon imposed a sweeping economic and military blockade over the territory and its 1.5 million people. Unfortunately, it took the deaths of eight Turkish activists, and one young Turkish-American, to lift the question of Israeli policy vis-à-vis Hamas and the people of Gaza onto the international stage.

While Sacco occasionally references these larger issues, he mostly concentrates on gleaning as much as he can from the people he meets. In the course of his research he talks to shopkeepers, farmers, aid workers, high-level militants and random cynics. For the most part, he lets folks speak for themselves. Some of what he's told, about both present-day Gaza and the events of 1956, is arguably tendentious, incomplete or inconsistent with the reports of others. But the

details add up, and an approximate outline of the truth emerges out of the sands of opinion, memory and time. As he searches for witnesses to the events of the mid-1950s, he sometimes finds himself standing in the same places that figure in their oral accounts. In one chapter, he confronts the problem of reconciling different versions of the same events, concluding that

> I cannot untangle the twining guilt and grief that envelope a person who survives what so many others did not; nor can I explain what might induce a traumatized individual to recall a brother's death if he was not there — assuming he was not. I only want to acknowledge the problems that go along with relying on eyewitness testimony in telling our story.

While Sacco downplays the physical bravery that is a precondition for his work as a war correspondent, he makes a point of stressing his commitment to the facts and his refusal to paint the Palestinians he meets as pure-hearted idealists. In one striking scene, he asks a couple of his contacts how they feel when they "hear that a bomb has gone off in Tel Aviv," i.e., a suicide mission.

"My first reaction is happiness," says one militant. "Every Israeli is a soldier," he says. "They go into the army at age 16 and after their military service they still do 40 days of service a year."

But, Sacco asks, "do these bombings serve any strategic purpose at all?" Do they "serve the Palestinian national interest"?

"They make them fearful," his interlocutor insists, pounding his fist on the table.

THE GAZA STRIP

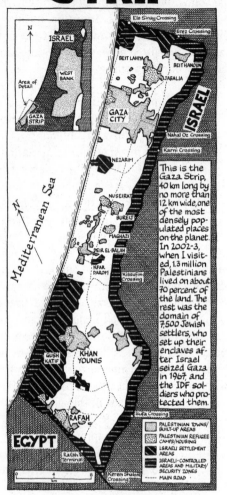

This is the Gaza Strip, 40 km long by no more than 12 km wide, one of the most densely populated places on the planet. In 2002-3, when I visited, 1.3 million Palestinians lived on about 70 percent of the land. The rest was the domain of 7,500 Jewish settlers, who set up their enclaves after Israel seized Gaza in 1967, and the IDF soldiers who protected them.

his friend, who from the look of things has turned beet red.

Sacco's sympathies seem to be with the middle-aged man in the following scene who we see slumped in a chair, complaining that "there's no political horizon at all."

Footnotes in Gaza is packed with these kinds of sharply etched encounters with people, places and ideas. Sacco records scenes of communal conviviality, warmth and humor, but he also introduces us to testy fanatics. Behind the bravado and rhetorical flourishes we sense an underlying psychology of deep demoralization. Many of those he talks to can't quite fathom his interest in events that date back half a century. "Okay, write your book," smirks one resident of Rafah. But "'56 is dead. '56 is for my grandfather and grandmother ... and I am alive!"

Earlier in the book he runs across a group of teenagers. One of them asks "if [he] happen[s] to be a Muslim." No, Sacco replies.

"Then you're going to hell."

"Does it make you angry that I'm not a Muslim?"

The boy ponders the question for a panel. "No ... you're not my enemy."

"But I'm not your friend, right?"

"That's right." They shake on it. When he tells them he's writing a book on the 1956 massacres, one of them says, "he came from abroad. What does he know about Palestine?" Sacco then asks the group what they think "is the best way to resist?"

Sacco reveals in an aside that he's "still not satisfied, and Hani is getting flustered," and, in another note, points out that the age of conscription in Israel is, in fact, 18.

"I don't want to talk about it anymore," says

"Get close to God," says one.

"With bombs," says another.

The boys stare into space for a moment, and then one of them poses an unexpected challenge: "Do you like us?" It's a startlingly apt question.

It is to Joe Sacco's credit, of course, that the adults and teenagers of Gaza come across as fully rounded human beings, with all that that implies. Taken as a whole, they are proud, hospitable, articulate, argumentative, distrusting and quick to judge others. Few if any of the people we meet are either purely villainous or entirely heroic. More than a few seem a little annoying—and this applies not only to the Palestinians, but to the North Americans and Europeans who have taken an interest in their cause. At the same time, everyone we encounter is recognizably human, and deserve better than to be treated as symbols or statistics. Their realness suggests to me that most of us would think and act in similar ways if we lived under comparable sorts of stresses. This isn't a political judgment but a humanitarian one.

Judging from the letters published each week in the local paper, my outer borough neighbors feel more strongly about Israel than any other conceivable topic, from crime and taxes, to dog owners and mayoral races. Their missives are often replete with scorn for anyone who would dare suggest that Israel is anything other than a beacon of light surrounded by pathological enemies. If you saw my local paper you would see what I mean. The very existence of this book would provoke an assault on their senses.

When the *Journal* asked me to review Joe Sacco's latest work of pictorial journalism, I thought about taking a pass. The passions aroused by the topic of Israel and Palestine make me nervous. It turns out Sacco is braver than I am on more than one level. In any event, his work combines hard-won journalistic insights and extraordinary visuals on pages that are informative, charismatic and often haunting. ■

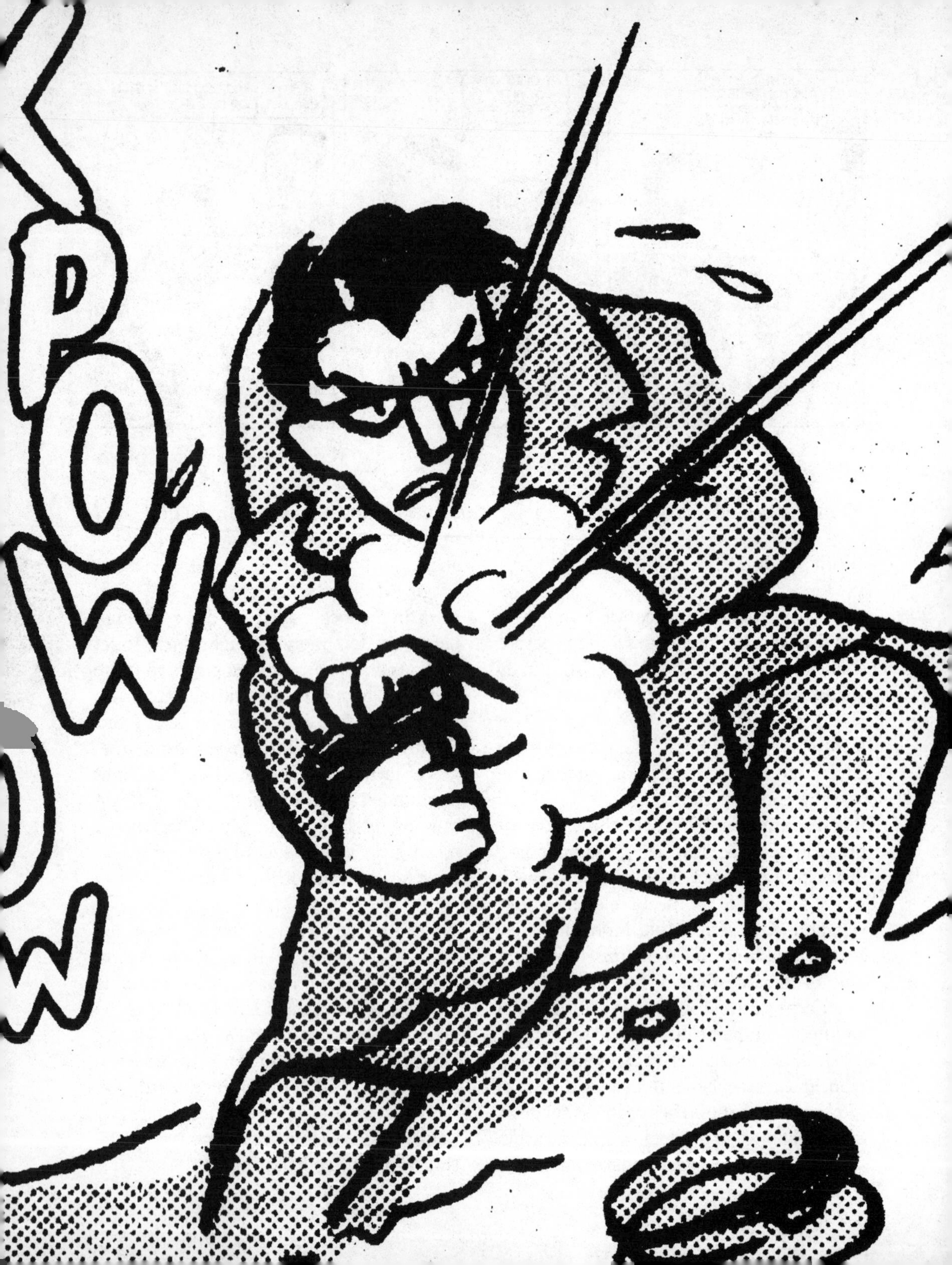
POW
POW

Since the beginning, *gekiga* in general has been identified as an outsider art, allied with the underclass against a middle-class mainstream. This understanding stems from a number of things. It has to do, first of all, with the genre's origination in vulgar, hardscrabble Osaka versus refined, monied Tokyo, as the standard clichés go. It also has to do with the frequent depiction of working-class youth, men and criminals, and the *occasional* engagement with serious social issues, like economic exploitation and racial discrimination. It also has to do with audience: the supposed consumption of *kashihon gekiga* by so-called "non-student high-teens," a phrase popularized by critic Gondō Susumu circa 1970 to mean working-class male youth forced into the labor market after middle school by economic necessity. The social status of its authors, themselves often struggling in penury and without formal education beyond a handful of years, complements the picture, recommending a kind of natural camaraderie between author and reader, and the unmediated relation of both to underclass characters and setting. But most of all, this outsider image of early *gekiga* has to do with the public persecution of *kashihon* (rental book) manga in the latter 1950s and early '60s, attacked by parent, teacher and child-advocacy groups, as well as mainstream newspapers and opinion journals, as obscene, violent, vulgar and therefore morally corrupting and even physically unhygienic.

In the late 1960s and '70s critics turned the discourse regarding *gekiga* on its head, appropriating the terms of the genre's denigration in the '50s and redeploying them as positive markers of its populist authenticity. In the writings of critics like Gondō and Kajii Jun, this new evaluation often took on a strict and recriminating class bias, setting out *kashihon gekiga* as a refuge and weapon against the official ideology of high economic growth and a monolithic middle class. This view no longer has the hold that it used to in Japan, partially due to sobering distance from the '60s, partially due to the depoliticization of manga writing in general, and shifts of scholarship from questions of content and social milieu to those of form, semiotics and physiological reading dynamics. Still, the continuing influence of this discourse can be perceived in the desire to promote early *gekiga* as *vox populi*, evident in decisions such as that made by Tokyo-based publisher Seirinkōgeisha to put on the *obi* of the new Japanese edition of *Black Blizzard* the following lines from a review in *The New York Times* (April 14, 2009): "As *A Drifting Life* progresses, it becomes

Black Blizzard
Yoshiro Tatsumi

Published by Drawn & Quarterly
144 pp :: $19.95 :: B&W :: softcover
ISBN: 9781770460126

**Review by
Ryan Holmberg**

457

clear that Mr. Tatsumi is not content merely to tell his own story — or just the story of gekiga . . . It's ground-level pop history." Yoshihiro Tatsumi has similarly bemoaned newspaper descriptions of the sarin gas attacks on the Tokyo subway system in March of 1995 as "a crime of the gekiga generation," a sign for him that the mainstream continues to misconstrue as illicit what was, at root, an earnest project to make of manga an advanced popular art. In the afterword to the Japanese edition of A Drifting Life, he asks rhetorically, "When exactly did gekiga become associated with evil?" This is a question that recent scholarship has made fairly easy to answer: prenatally, in April 1955 and the beginning of the so-called "akusho tsuihō undō," "The Campaign to Purge Evil Books." A more difficult question is: When will gekiga stop being so facilely and uniformly associated with the marginal and oppressed, and by extension the authentically popular?

To be sure, these were allegiances kashihon gekiga creators themselves wished to cultivate. This they did mainly through outward displays of the markers of pulp fiction and noir. In the case of Black Blizzard, the title signifies darkness and bleakness explicitly, and the cover of the original — showing a man in a snowstorm about to bash another with a brick as a locomotive rushes up from behind — announces the book as a thriller. Drawn & Quarterly has chosen instead a panel from page 16, the last of the color pages that open all kashihon manga from this period — designed as eye candy for children — in which the two men, handcuffed together, are readying to escape from the rubble of a train wreck. In the switch, some of the intended associations of the original are lost, amongst them that Black Blizzard

had an immediate family resemblance to the pulp novels and magazines that one would also have found in kashihon shops at the time, as well as to the throbbing gouache images of contemporary movie posters. However, as an object, Black Blizzard would have immediately signified juvenile reading material due to its size and format — hardbound B6 (128mmX182mm) had been typical for many varieties of children's books since at least the late 1930s — the patently non-sensual and blocky rendering of its cover figures, the syllabic gloss of its kanji title and its specific location on the shelf. Still, there was enough in its name and its external look to suggest, accurately or not, that this was the "junior" version of the sorts of violent and racy kasutori literature (literally, "the dregs," referring to hooch, meaning pulp) that had been popular to Japanese readers since the immediate postwar period. Indeed, Tatsumi and his colleagues were getting many of their ideas from such sources and their filmic adaptations. In the case of Black Blizzard, for example, the motif of the handcuffed escapees came from an unidentified story by the popular detective writer Shimada Kazuo. On the back cover of the Drawn & Quarterly edition, Mickey Spillane is also mentioned, but this is an unlikely influence, as even A Drifting Life has Tatsumi first meeting Mike Hammer in April 1957. Yet, as is the case with Black Blizzard, in kashihon gekiga, content and cover did not always fully match. What lay inside was not as gritty as the noirish cover might suggest, or as latter-day appraisals of the genre would wish.

What follows is a first stab at a revisionist reading of early gekiga through the specific example of Black Blizzard. It focuses not on the "cinematic techniques" and expressive

inkiness that are usually the first and second things named when characterizing *gekiga*, but rather its cast of characters. For the intended male adolescent reader of the 1950s, *Black Blizzard* presented a choice between two protagonists, each representing a distinct type of masculine subjectivity. On the one hand, Yamaji Susumu, the hapless young jazz pianist of 25 who has been convicted of a murder that he cannot believe he committed; on the other hand, Konta Shinpei, the hardened criminal and professional gambler of 41 who faces life in prison for double homicide. In handcuffing them together, Tatsumi has turned to a classic existentialist trope: the subjection of personal autonomy to the will of others and the

"Though advertised as a thriller, and narrated as a murder mystery, *Black Blizzard* is at heart a moral drama."

angst that arises as a result. The device also serves to force together, for the purpose of heightened contrast, two social and moral types: the first with *petit-bourgeois* dreams of fame in the arts, a naïve faith in platonic romance, and belief in the possibility of upward social mobility through a combination of innate talent and hard work. The other with a lumpenproletarian resignation to his outsider social status, seeming to value nothing more than his personal freedom, but in fact, ruled by moral values stronger and more upright than mainstream society could ever muster. Though advertised as a thriller, and narrated as a murder mystery, *Black Blizzard* is at heart a moral drama. Its various formal and narrative devices are deployed not so much to make suspenseful the answering of the question of who did what how, but instead who will do what under given environmental conditions.

Who is the primary subject of *Black Blizzard*? The Japanese discourse on *gekiga* is predisposed to answer Konta. This is not without grounds in the work itself. Fair portions of the narrative of *Black Blizzard* seem designed to demonstrate how the underclass criminal offers a stronger model of male subjectivity than the *petit-bourgeois* artist. It clearly plays against a normative stereotype in which criminality is understood as a direct expression of immorality. In contrast, *Black Blizzard* argues that stronger moral fortitude exists in those who have either rejected, or been rejected by, the mores and laws of mainstream society. After all, the trophy of moral character — an act of self-sacrifice for the benefit of another — goes to Konta. Yamaji is too in love with himself to even countenance the idea of endangering himself for another. The greater valuation of Konta over Yamaji emerges also in their respective relationship to Saeko, the young female singer. For the narcissistic artist, she is barely more than a muse, a mouthpiece for his art and an instrument for his deliverance from impotent depression. As for the errant but devoted father, he will literally give his right hand (the original cover mistakenly depicts it as his left), and thus his health, his life and his freedom, all for his daughter's happiness. As agents, too, Konta is clearly favored. He is the active character, the man of will and conviction and the propeller of all action, decision and deed in the manga. Yamaji, in stark contrast, is pitifully passive. Of all the things that happen to him, none are of his own device. He has to be literally dragged by Konta through the story and the few occasions where he does act to defend himself against the forces that oppress him — namely, the refusal of the circus manager to allow Saeko to join him in a romantic life of art — he does so drunk, chemically transformed into a subject that is no longer himself. The *petit-bourgeois* character that Yamaji embodies is clearly not cast in a positive light. The curious thing about *Black Blizzard*, however, and the feature of the story that suggests that it cannot be reduced to the simple class-based biases of orthodox *gekiga* theory, is its conclusion: The narcissistic artist is not condemned, but rather saved through an act of near providence. In the closing scenes, he is rejoined with his muse, now free from her previous obligations, and is able to look forward with hope to a now-boundless future. How to understand this ending and explain the sympathy for a lesser moral character?

It is well known that Tatsumi and the *gekiga* circle were avid cinephiles. In *A*

Drifting Life, the importance of movie-going is repeatedly emphasized, as it is in Matsumoto Masahiko's *Gekiga Idiots* (1979-84), an earlier *gekiga* hagiography in comics form. Likewise, in an interview appended to the new Japanese edition of *Black Blizzard*, Tatsumi describes going to the theater once a week, not for the new feature films but the cheaper triple bills, where he would see nameless and famous films alike, of both Japanese and foreign origin. Following the depictions in *A Drifting Life* and the titles dropped in interviews, it would seem Tatsumi's diet consisted of a fairly standard if cultured mix of American, French and Japanese film noir, melodramas, neo-realism and historical drama, including those of Kurosawa Akira. From interviews, one gathers that Tatsumi was struck most of all with French film noir. Henri Verneuil's *Des gens sans importance* (1955) comes up in multiple essays and interviews, as do the films of Henri Georges-Clouzot, namely *The Wages of Fear* (1953) and *Diabolique* (1955). Not surprisingly, he names as his favorite actor Jean Gabin, supporting the image of the *gekiga* author sympathetic to the struggles of the working-class everyman. As far as the characters and plot of *Black Blizzard* are concerned, however, more fruitful comparisons could be made with Clouzot's *Quai des Orfèvres* (1947), in which a male cabaret piano player and his singer starlet sweetheart are embroiled in a murder mystery for which the woman believes herself to be guilty and the man know himself not to be, yet nonetheless resigns himself to conviction for all evidence points in his direction. The rosy ending of *Quai des Orfèvres*, in which the artist couple safely retire to the comfort of their home, their love and their passion, also resembles that of *Black Blizzard*. Again, orthodox *gekiga* theory emphasizes artist-underclass identifications in the genre as a matter of political sympathy, namely between the manga author and his oppressed but scrappy subjects. But it is clear from the content of a work like *Black Blizzard* that the identification could also be entirely self-serving, casting the artist himself or herself as outcast and criminal — an old Romantic trope that serves more to dramatize the artist's struggles and ambivalent social position in capitalist society than it does to put art in the service of the oppressed. If period photographs and retrospective caricatures are accurate, Tatsumi did not wear a hat. But Matsumoto, Saitō Takao and others of the founding *gekiga* cohort sported berets — and Saitō a scarf — as part of their sartorial identification as artists. This they did not get from noir, or from the head of the average working-class man. It came from mentors like Kuroda Masami and forefathers like Ōshiro Noboru and of

course Tezuka Osamu, for whom the beret became as much a personal trademark as his bulbous nose. Early *gekiga* remained indebted to the French bohemian tradition, and in more ways than one.

In at least one passage, I believe that *Black Blizzard* refers to this tradition without the mediation of the noir canon. It comes soon after Yamaji and Saeko meet for the first time. The downfall of Yamaji is well on its way; his band has dissolved and his dreams of musical fame have been dashed. Beside himself, he has turned to booze and has nearly drunk away his hard-earned savings. Stumbling home one night, he finds himself in the staging area of a touring circus. There he hears the most mellifluous female voice, singing a melancholic tune of a lonely life on the road as a performer, motherless and brimming with tears. The singing "thaws his frozen heart" as only a female muse can do for the male artist (p. 48). The next morning, Yamaji awakes late to the rude sounds of an advertising bandwagon of the same circus troupe. Immediately, there is a knock on his door. From behind it emerges, to his surprise, the young songbird, there to return to him his folio of musical compositions, which in his stupor the night before he had accidentally left behind the Big Top tent. After a quick exchange, the girl disappears through the door and out into street, where she mounts the circus bandwagon and is reabsorbed in a swirl of clowns, confetti and noise. She waves goodbye to Yamaji, who looks longingly down from his upper-story window (pp. 51-3). People typically think of *kashihon gekiga* as set in the shadows of the postwar Japanese city. But as far as I know, multistory residential brick buildings, like that from which Yamaji looks out, were few and far between after World War II and those that did exist were unlikely to house paupers with patched curtains and taped-up window panes. Clearly, at least for this moment, the story is somewhere else.

This scene has more than a passing resemblance to the closing sequence of Marcel Carné's *Children of Paradise* (1945), which turns the screw one cruel last time on the emotional drama of unfulfilled desire and unrequited love that propels the entire film. If you recall, the mime Baptiste, a similarly hapless and romantic artist, has let his true love Garance slip through his fingertips time and time again. He at last consummates his desire at the end of the film with a night spent with his beloved at a boarding house, but only to quickly and terminally lose her to a fate that seems to laugh at the farce of his failed romantic affairs. In the morning, Baptiste's wife Nathalie — a paragon of wifely virtue and devotion — comes unexpectedly through the door to find her husband in the arms of his lover. Nathalie stands there in a pose not unlike Saeko at Yamaji's threshold. Of course, the interpersonal dynamics are of a completely different sort: Nathalie is no muse to Baptiste and therefore she brings no good tidings, only the sting of conjugal commitments and a reminder of the impossibility of true love, which in the person of Garance escapes through the door, down the stairs and into the ferment of Carnival outside, likewise filled with clowns, confetti and infuriating noise. In *Black Blizzard*, the fleeting object of male desire is art, and Saeko is only a means to its fulfillment. In *Children of Paradise*, in contrast, Garance is no muse, no medium, but rather herself a work of art, perfect and unobtainable. This opulent swan song of classical French cinema could have offered a number of attractive tropes to the young manga author, burning

463

THE VOICE THAT FLOATED OUT OF THE DARKNESS WAS SO PLAINTIVE, SO EXPRESSIVE, AND SO BEAUTIFUL...

...THAT IT PENETRATED MY DESPAIR AND REACHED DEEP INTO MY HEART.

with the passion to raise his medium to new heights: the association of artist and criminal, and the porous borders of their respective spheres of influence; the model of the popular theater, filled with musical, thespian and acrobatic spectacles, or its successor the circus, as stage for the intermingling of artistic expression and emotional melodrama, and magnet for social misfits; the romantic fallibility of the male artist, and his inevitable struggle with unfulfilled desires; and the perpetual threat of loss of the artist's object of desire due to a combination of personal lack of will and the arbitrariness of a cruel and selfish world. What Tatsumi does, it seems to me, is rework this dynamic of desire and deferment into a melodrama of the artist's narcissistic relationship to his own work. And with Tatsumi, unlike with Carné and his screenwriter Jacques Prévert, there is satisfaction and closure. At first unable to extract Saeko from the circus and the network of men that desire her for their own purposes, in the end Yamaji gets his muse.

It is here that Tatsumi's not-so-underclass sympathies begin to show. In terms of panel count, Black Blizzard puts greater weight on the plight of Yamaji. For most pages, the manga narrates the story of young dreams dashed by forces of jealousy and selfishness, redeemed at the end by an act of selfless providence. It supports, as a result, a naïve fantasy that the pure of heart will, in the end, find solace and deliverance from whatever wrongs may befall them, this thanks not to their own efforts, but through those of others who are so moved by their innocence and passion to sacrifice even their own well-being.

Konta's moral fortitude is, from this perspective, ultimately subordinate to the ideological values that Yamaji embodies. While Yamaji might himself be capable of nothing, as an expression of certain ideological values — namely, the petit-bourgeois belief in the transformative power of art and romance — he is, in a way, invincible and omnipotent, capable of swaying souls without direct action, simply through a display of his love of art.

Consider the central position of the artist's hands in Black Blizzard. First, the manga begins with an extended sequence of piano playing. The very first panel shows the pianist's hand. Second, the passages of greatest suspense and conflict pivot not on potential recapture by the police and the loss of individual freedom that would entail, but rather the horror of the artist faced with the prospect of losing his left hand and thus the capacity to make art. The nightmare Yamaji has at the end of the story tells all: he meets his long lost love — a piano — but cannot consummate his desire for he finds that, in place of nimble fingers, he has a crude hook (pp. 118-9). Third, in his interview with Tatsumi for the Seirinkōgeisha edition, scholar Nakano Haruyuki draws attention to the bar scene that begins Yamaji's personal lament, commenting on how the symbolic distortions of the pianist's face in his glass of liquor evoke the symbolic devices of contemporary cinema. I am as drawn to the fingers holding the glass, which have not just nails — something rare in manga from this period — but even cuticles (pp. 45-6). The detailing is striking, especially given the cursory rendering of the rest of the body. As any doodler knows, drawing

> **"What Tatsumi does is rework this dynamic of desire and deferment into a melodrama of the artist's narcissistic relationship to his own work."**

the hand is the simplest of self-portraits, requiring neither mirror nor photography, and almost always resulting in satisfying forms. Readers of *A Drifting Life* might recall the episode — memorable enough to also be included in Matsumoto's *Gekiga Idiots* — in which the young manga authors, pained by how their poor draftsmanship impedes the development of their work, ask their publisher to hire a female model to pose nude for drawing sessions. It's a comical episode about their sexual coming-of-age, but also about their distance as largely self-taught artists from the technical training of the fine arts. A gander at '50s *kashihon* manga will quickly confirm that naturalism in drawing was not early *gekiga*'s forte. The struggle might be perceived in the *Black Blizzard* bar scene: the artist looking into a reflective surface, only to have his face turn out all wrong, but able to capture his hands with some

degree of satisfaction. Considering this, it is significant that, fourth, above the colophon at the end of the manga listing publication data (the Drawn & Quarterly version is made to simulate the original) there is a drawing of the pianist's hands, signed "Yoshi" for Yoshihiro, creating a direct correlation between the suffering musician and the young manga author (p. 128). Other early *gekiga* authors more explicitly put themselves at the center of their tales, notably Matsumoto with his stories of bereted manga author detectives. But as *Black Blizzard* shows, the artist could also be central in Tatsumi's work, even going as far to incorporate his own hands.

For the bulk of the story, Konta hates nothing more than the artist's hand. He might be frustrated by Yamaji's cowardice and frailty, but he is outright disgusted with the pianist's narcissistic obsession with his own hands. Faced with the choice between life and art — whether to have his hand severed and gain freedom, or to keep his hand but remain bound — Yamaji chooses art. For him, a life without culture is a greater condemnation than a life without freedom. At this point, Konta finds in this view nothing of value. Considering this prelude of violent antagonism, it is striking that the hunter's cabin becomes the setting for displays of generosity and understanding. In a sudden change of character, Konta lends an open ear to Yamaji. His patience is of course a necessary narrative device to create the time and space to relate Yamaji's story and introduce the elements of the plot that make Black Blizzard as much murder mystery as action thriller. But surprisingly, at the end of the narration, Yamaji does not appear to Konta the naïve fool. The underclass criminal has softened. Later, we are told that this is because Saeko is in fact Konta's daughter, and in hearing Yamaji's story he is moved to act in order to secure her happiness. To this end, he severs his own hand, freeing himself for the express purpose of unveiling the true murderer and thus clearing Yamaji's name. Ostensibly, a parent's natural love for a child is the trigger for Konta's moral transformation and extreme act of self-sacrifice. The delivering of justice, and the liberation of the suffering romantic from misfortune are, from this perspective, only necessary stepping-stones, with no value in themselves to the worldview of the underclass criminal.

It is curious, however, that the moral transformation is entirely one-sided. If this is indeed a tale about the greater morality of the underclass, then one imagines that Tatsumi would have delineated Yamaji's psychology at the end, hinting at increased consciousness of his personal shortcomings of courage and will, and greater circumspection about the ways of the world. But he has not. It is Konta alone that is depicted as having gained morally in his dealings with the social and ideological other. He is an unrepentant convicted killer of two, and including the detective and the artist, both of whom he readies to destroy in the first few dozen pages of the story, he can and is willing to become a killer of more. If the loss of the pianist's hand means the end of art, the loss of the criminal's hand means the end of crime. "I'm a card shark, see?," he says to Yamaji in the snow — in the original Japanese, he rolls dice — "I earn my living with my fingertips, same as you" (p. 31). In the end, however, he has decided that what his hands can do is not as important as what the pianist's hands can do, which is create happiness both for the artist himself and those with whom he works, in this case Saeko. It is not so much that Konta has come to identify with the sufferings of the young romantic. He appears disdainful of Yamaji's character to the end. Instead, it is as if he has come to believe in the positively transformative powers of art in general through a negative example (Yamaji's story) of the misery caused by their hindrance and loss. The example is compelling enough for him to amputate his dice-rolling, weapon-wielding hand, physically and symbolically purging himself of his means of criminality, and thus freeing his new self to act in the name of justice, love, and the highest moral virtues. Beneath his hardboiled noirness, there has

appeared a compassionate light. Culture has redeemed the criminal. It has brought out the humanity beneath his beastliness.

From this perspective, I think it possible to argue that *Black Blizzard*, while celebrating the greater moral fortitude of the underclass criminal, is ultimately grounded in a *petit-bourgeois* belief in the redemptive power of culture. It as much a criminal conversion narrative as it is a dramatization of artistic angst — neither of which, I suspect, traditional *gekiga* advocates would be wont to accept. There was no one that critics like Gondō Susumu and Kajii Jun despised more than the "progressive intellectual" and his audience of so-called "petit citizens," represented respectively by the male academic expounding in the liberal papers on what Japanese should and should not do for the sake of their new democracy, and the middle class mother enforcing that "good sense" at the level of the family and local community. Gondō and Kajii understood correctly that the values upheld by this mainstream, and expressed in most children's manga, represented specific class interests not fully aligned with those of the working class or the lumpenproletariat. Yet it is clear from reading a work like *Black Blizzard* that they overestimated the degree to which *kashihon gekiga* offered an alternative. Had I more time, I would show how the redemptive culture figured in *Black Blizzard* is not high art, as my language above might suggest, but rather a fairly standard notion of "popular culture" that, though infused with populist sentiments and capable of speaking to the hardships of the common person, was highly mediated by the movie and music industries and therefore by capital. The issue of *gekiga*'s populism is a tricky matter. But for now, one thing can be said with surety: given the exalted position of the artist himself in many early *gekiga*, the notion that "*kashihon* manga persistently depicted the lives *sans importance* of *des gens sans importance*," as Seirinkōgeisha editor and *gekiga* scholar Asakawa Mitsuhiro recently put it, needs to be refined. ∎

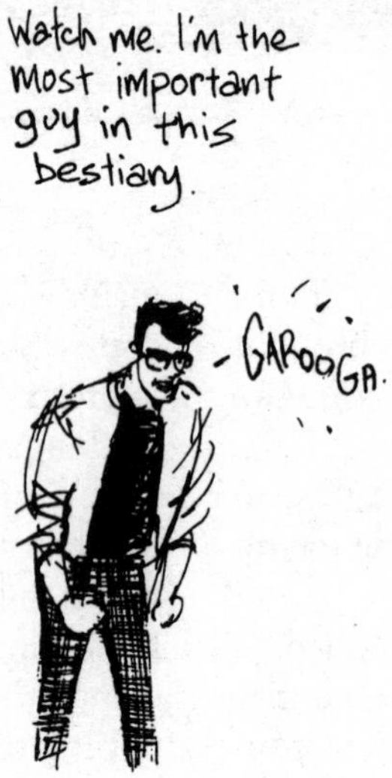
Watch me. I'm the most important guy in this bestiary.
GAROOGA.

Critics have to have their categories for artists and works, and where does one put Eddie Campbell, particularly the Campbell one finds in the massive (600+ pages), three-decades-of-work compendium *Alec: The Years Have Pants*? The category is easy: autobiography/memoir. However, Campbell doesn't really fit in with the other cartoonists in this area of comics. *Alec* doesn't have the studied narrative craftsmanship one finds in works like Alison Bechdel's *Fun Home*, Art Spiegelman's *Maus* or David B.'s *Epileptic*. And Campbell doesn't have the entertainingly outsized personality which creators like Harvey Pekar, Robert Crumb and Dori Seda give themselves on the page. He's a different breed altogether: a cartoonist who embraces the intuitive, spontaneous approach of the latter group while maintaining the cool, cerebral tone of the first. He isn't interested in hammering his narratives into a shape designed for a pedestal, and he doesn't use them to provide an emotional outlet for himself or to play the clown.

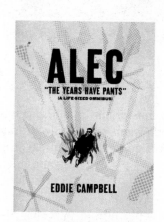

Alec: The Years Have Pants
Eddie Campbell

Published by Top Shelf Productions
640 pp :: $35 :: B&W :: softcover
ISBN: 9781603090254

**Review by
Robert Stanley Martin**

that don't aspire to be anything more than pleasant diversions. But Campbell has his ambitious side as well. *The Years Have Pants* also contains three major sequences — "The King Canute Club," "Graffiti Kitchen" and "How to Be an Artist" — that have a power and occasional incisiveness that rank them among the strongest memoir work comics have to offer. Their casual manner only enhances their impact. Each is a vibrant exploration of, respectively, friendship, self-criticism and the anxieties of career. Each expands the formal language of comics in dazzlingly effective ways.

The first few episodes of "The King Canute Club," the first *Alec* effort, may have one wondering if Campbell was the harbinger of the memoir-comics plague of the 1990s. (Campbell's "King Canute" strips were produced between 1981 and 1987.) It's clearly the work of a tyro narrative imagination — one that's extremely aware that the freshest story material is rooted in real-life experience, but doesn't seem to know much beyond that. The immediate subjects are also quite similar: recountings of conversations that were probably far more amusing to participate in than they are to read. One is grateful that Campbell, unlike some of the autobiographical cartoonists who came later, doesn't regale us with extended

The rambling, offhand feel of the *Alec* material gives it a surface humility that is disarming; it seems to have a take-it-or-leave-it quality — the sort of thing one finds either charming or negligible. And, truth be told, a good portion of it is trifling; about half of *The Years Have Pants* collection comprises anecdotal strips

WHEN YOU TELL AND RETELL A STORY YOU TEND TO STREAMLINE IT, GIVE IT A DRAMATIC SHAPE-LEAVE OUT NICE LITTLE TOUCHES LIKE MY PAL PAM WAITING TO NOBBLE THE NEXT WHITE SHIRT THAT COMES UP

ME, FULL OF REMORSE 'CAUSE EVERYONE'S FIGHTING MY FIGHT AND I DON'T ACTUALLY HIT ANYONE.

BLESS ALL MY FRIENDS.

nose-picking sequences or accounts of his masturbation habits, but one still wants to tell him to get more of a life if he's going to write from it.

However, those opening episodes do show the seeds of a greater narrative sophistication. Campbell understands the necessity of counterpoint in building a narrative. His protagonist isn't just Alec MacGarry, his alter ego; it's also Danny Grey, a co-worker of Alec's who becomes his best friend. Both in their 20s, they meet working alongside each other in low-level industrial jobs, and they make quite a contrast. Their backgrounds and temperaments are very different. Alec has clearly had a bourgeois upbringing: he's educated, intellectual and he uses his erudition to socialize with others. (One character says to him, "You only know books. You don't know anything for yourself, do you?") Danny, on the other hand, is working class. He's not book-smart (although he can name-drop philosophers as well as Alec can), and his attitude is devil-may-care. Unlike Alec, he's not inclined to stand back

and contemplate his place in the world; he is always looking for opportunities to enjoy himself, usually in carousing at the King Canute, a local pub. Alec says of him, "He lives his life to the full. No part is saved like a slice of birthday cake going stale." And Alec can't help but idealize him to a degree; he sees Danny as the center of his world. The two make for an intriguing study in contrasts, and it's frustrating that Campbell initially can't do more than play them off each other for anemic bits of humor.

Campbell's artwork only emphasizes the weakness of the early episodes. It's by no means inept; Campbell handles his panels skillfully. The compositional elements are nicely balanced, the details are well observed, and Campbell even finds an equivalent for the flourish of brushstrokes in the idiosyncratic, fragmentary areas of mechanical tone. However, this is a painter's thinking transposed to comics; one's eye is meant to wander the composition taking in details, with the subject matter always at a remove. The approach is very

> **"Campbell uses the visuals as his starting point; they're not there to enhance prose exposition so much as they are to create a springboard for prose commentary."**

different from what is traditionally associated with cartoonists, which is to make the image as immediate and dramatically concise as possible. Campbell's art doesn't create emotional identification or otherwise hold the reader's hand in dramatic terms — he objectifies everything he shows — and it functions like an icepack on his material. An even, uninflected tone can make even the best humor fall flat.

However, the solution Campbell found was not to change his visual style, but to create a new dynamic to guide his treatment of the material. If the characters can't create rhythm and melody effectively within their scenarios, then use the scenario itself as a contrapuntal element. Campbell's new rhythm and melody became the visual moment of the panel played off Alec's prose narration. And in a brilliant move, Campbell reversed the traditional relationship of narration and image, which is for the image to follow the narration's lead. Campbell uses the visuals as his starting point; they're not there to enhance prose exposition so much as they are to create a springboard for prose commentary. The shift also uses the art to best effect; the dense, sophisticated visuals take on a new authority. Autobiographical drama is left behind to create the comics equivalent of the personal essay.

It's a form that appears more in keeping with his concerns. Campbell never seems particularly interested in mining his experience for moments of conflict and catharsis. His attitude is far more exploratory. As "The King Canute Club" proceeds, we see Alec getting increasingly caught up in Danny's way of life. The day is always centered on drinking and hanging out at the pub. Jobs, lovers, places to live — they all come and go. The reader is never asked to identify with

A FUNNY NOTION OCCURRED TO ME WHILE I WAS DROWNING.

I SAW HUMANITY ALL PASTED TOGETHER WITH SEMEN.

IT WAS RUNNING DOWN LEGS AT BUS STOPS AFTER EARLY MORNING QUICKIES.

IT WAS DRIPPING OFF THE ENDS OF NOSES.

SEND A SPUNK

THE WORD 'SPUNK' IS GOOD ENGLISH, I HAVE ALWAYS THOUGHT, AT LEAST ACCORDING TO THE DANNY GREY PRINCIPLE, WHERE *shithouse* IS BETTER ENGLISH THAN *lavatory*

la-va-tri yech - bad

WARM AND STICKY. BUT OF COURSE ANGELINE AND ELLEN AREN'T THINKING ABOUT IT IN THOSE TERMS WHILE THEY'RE PADDING FIERCELY ROUND EACH OTHER...

Alec's circumstances, only with his attitudes. One can't help but smile as he moves from statements like "I just don't feel at home in the world," to "The nicest thing in this life is just to be with your friends. No big story need come of it." Alec's friendship with Danny eventually collapses, and though one can easily see the tensions between them build and explode, the poignancy doesn't come from things ending so much as it comes from Alec's emotional confusion over what went wrong. He can't judge or reach a conclusion; he can only

move on. "The King Canute Club" starts as a story about a friendship and develops into a meditation on the role it plays in one's life. What's most refreshing about it is that Campbell doesn't even pretend to have the answers to the questions the material raises — at least not all of them. The only things that are certain are the happiness when things are good and the pain when the relationship unravels.

One of the masters of the personal essay-narrative in prose is Henry Miller, whose work

472

Campbell openly acknowledges as a model for his own. There are similarities and some key differences. Both embrace a *vivre-sa-vie* attitude, but Campbell isn't misanthropic, and he lacks Miller's propensity for caricature. With Campbell, people's flaws and idiosyncrasies are beside the point. Aesthetically, Campbell's principal debt to Miller is in the structural tricks they both use to keep the reader from feeling cut adrift in the free-form narratives. When Miller launches into his digressions and commentaries, he often seizes on a repeated-motif word or phrase to anchor both himself and the reader. (Examples include "fifteen francs" from one of *Tropic of Cancer*'s best passages, "this is better than reading Vergil" from *Black Spring*'s "A Sunday Afternoon," and the great "money" sentence from *Tropic of Capricorn*.) Campbell first tries his hand at this in the third section of "King Canute," which incidentally opens with a burst of obviously Miller-inspired language ("I saw humanity all pasted together with semen. It was running down legs at bus stops after early morning quickies"). References to a dream of drowning, a quilt and the phrase, "the Glaswegian on the floor" show up repeatedly in an effort to unify the narrative. They don't quite work, largely because they remain motifs; Miller's always graduate into tropes that create a host of absurdist and satirical effects. However, nothing worth doing comes easy. But Campbell masters the technique in *Alec*'s second sequence, which he (with considerable justification) regarded as his single finest work up to that time.

The follow-up to "The King Canute Club" is "Graffiti Kitchen," which Campbell began in 1988 and completed in 1992. It takes place before and during the events of "King Canute"; the focus is on Alec's affair with, first, a teenage girl and then her mother, and how his continuing desire for the teenager complicates his relationship with both. The piece is an extraordinary balancing act in terms of tone. Alec goes through the entire story disgusted at his impulses and actions. One feels sympathy for his turmoil, but one can't also help but laugh at Campbell's mocking perspective as he looks back on his alter ego's conduct. The action's pathos and the absurdist commentary play off each other marvelously well. The story is masterfully paced; Campbell plays his melody and discords with perfect timing.

His extraordinary use of the repeated trope is the icing on the aesthetic cake. It all but defines the narrator's commentaries. Campbell begins the piece by introducing a personification of his animal urges; he takes his skinny, bespectacled avatar and shows him stomping forward, fists clenched and bellowing a beast-like "Garooga!" He can't help but make fun of himself; he shows us his id-creature, and it's a feral nerd on the rampage. Campbell quickly establishes the image's capacity for multiple meanings; one hasn't turned the page before it shows up again as a metaphor for jealousy. He also spins metonymies out of it, such as the paw prints that track across a number of panels. These first show up to signify Alec's lust for the teenage girl (her name's Georgette), then his disgust at himself for wanting her (they track across a copy of Nabokov's *Lolita*) and finally disgust at himself for all compulsions, including his intellectual ones (the prints track across a copy of *Ulysses*). The id-creature, in its various forms, ultimately encompasses almost all expressions of Alec's emotional

You never asked for fame or notoreity. Perhaps you didn't ask for enough.

On the other side of the world they'll be putting out very nice volumes of the works of your heroes, and here you are with no money.

Your files will have to do. How you live in the information in these old drawings. To be able to give that to readers! Not a million of them; a few devoted ones will suffice

identity, from amused disdain to moments of narcissism, to feelings of violent anger. The only thing more remarkable than the various meanings he teases out of the trope is the deft wit he shows in incorporating them into the piece.

"Graffiti Kitchen" often gives one the impression one is seeing Campbell's thoughts erupt spontaneously onto the page in both word and image. It's appropriate to a critique of drive and desire; if thoughts don't match the impulses' speed, they'll never catch them. Campbell certainly deserves applause for the changes he adopted in the art style. He abandons the studied, painterly panels of "The King Canute Crowd" in favor of a scribbled sketchiness; "Graffiti Kitchen" often looks as if he wasn't sure whether word or image would flow from his pen until he applied it to the art board. As a result, it has an energy and drive the earlier piece lacked. The feeling of spontaneity also makes the humor more forceful and the poetic moments seem effortless. Form and content come together beautifully.

However, as accomplished as it is as a stand-alone piece, "Graffiti Kitchen" also gains from being considered alongside "The King Canute Crowd" — just as one's reading of "King Canute" gains from it. Together the pieces highlight that at any given time, one's role in one's personal narrative shifts with the circumstances. "King Canute," Alec's commentaries notwithstanding, presents Campbell's alter ego as just one member of a larger ensemble, while "Graffiti Kitchen" finds him as the central actor in the story. The pieces also highlight that a story can only present an aspect of one's existence, with the others disregarded to a greater or lesser degree. "King Canute" has Campbell looking outward on his friendships; "Graffiti Kitchen" has him looking inward at himself.

Alec's third major sequence, "How to Be an Artist," has him looking at both. It's an account of his rise in comics' artistic and professional community, and it also serves as an informal history of the field's renaissance in the 1980s and '90s. The most

I give 10 pence to a hobo
I tell him it's my last.

He argues and tries
to give it back —

I'm stung by his humanity.

compelling section is probably Campbell's treatment of the ebb that followed the period's climax in 1986-87. He captures what a lively time it was, although one can't imagine anyone who lived through it looking back on it fondly. The field seemed torn apart by one controversy after another, and every flight for glory on the part of artists and publishers seemed to crash and burn like Icarus' flight toward the sun.

The moments that stay with one the most are the poignant ones: Stephen Bissette, as the years drift by, sitting at his drawing board in a state of creative paralysis; Alan Moore looking out the window, sighing after his *Big Numbers* magnum opus collapses for the final time; the final indignity suffered by veteran newspaper-strip artist Stan Drake, whose obituary ended up not being adorned by his own art, but the misattributed work of another cartoonist. (The sadness is heightened by the irony of that cartoonist turning out to be Bill Sienkiewicz, whose conduct as related in "How to Be an Artist" makes him the closest thing the piece has to a villain.)

What gives these artists' forlorn moments their power is that they're metaphors for Campbell's anxieties about himself. "How to Be an Artist" was composed between 1997 and 2000, when Campbell was in the latter stages of work on *From Hell*, his decade-in-the-making, 500+ page collaboration with Alan Moore. One can easily imagine the doubts running through his mind: What if I hit a creative wall before I finish? What if the rug gets pulled out from under me in terms of getting my work to the public? (*From Hell*'s first two publishers went out of business before it was completed, with the third tanking shortly thereafter.) Will I be remembered and given my due after I'm gone? The last is probably the deepest and most unspoken fear an ambitious artist can have, as their work is their bid for immortality. In a direct reference to *From Hell*, Campbell likens his situation to Odysseus' exile at sea, writing, "Odysseus ain't home yet." The tension is only leavened by the reader's knowledge that *From Hell* was completed to success, and that our Odysseus did

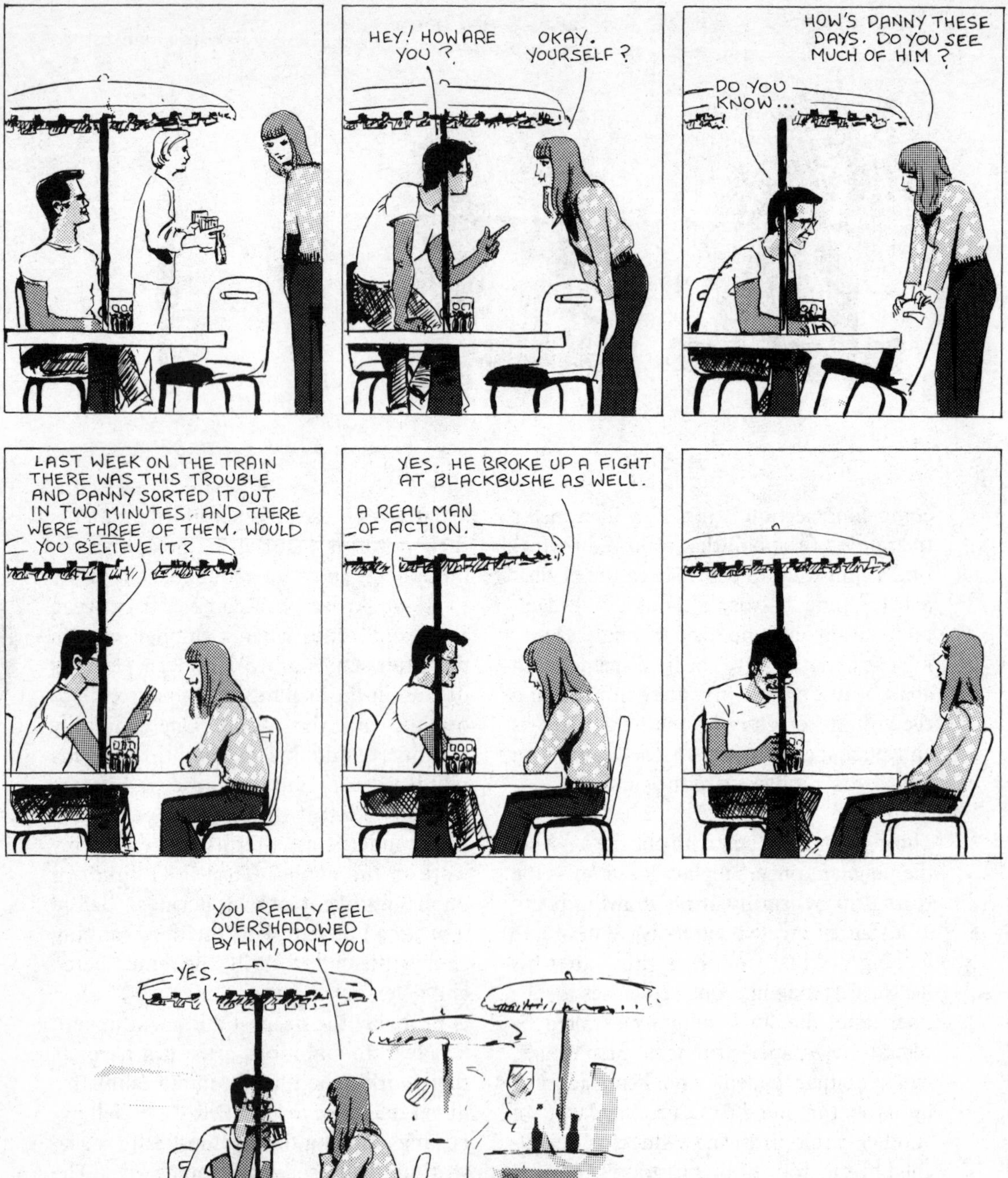
HEY! HOW ARE YOU ?
OKAY. YOURSELF ?
DO YOU KNOW...
HOW'S DANNY THESE DAYS. DO YOU SEE MUCH OF HIM ?
LAST WEEK ON THE TRAIN THERE WAS THIS TROUBLE AND DANNY SORTED IT OUT IN TWO MINUTES. AND THERE WERE THREE OF THEM. WOULD YOU BELIEVE IT ?
YES. HE BROKE UP A FIGHT AT BLACKBUSHE AS WELL.
A REAL MAN OF ACTION.
YOU REALLY FEEL OVERSHADOWED BY HIM, DON'T YOU
YES.

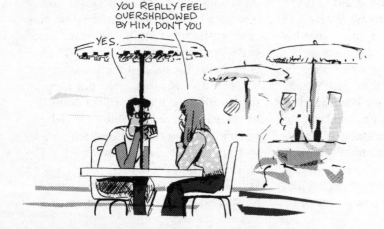

indeed arrive home. He didn't even have to kill a pack of suitors to assume his place as ruler.

One of the most compelling aspects of "How to Be an Artist" is the visual innovation Campbell brings to the project. He seems to have recognized that the repeated tropes in "Graffiti Kitchen" not only enriched the story's meanings and gave the readers an anchor; they heightened the piece's rhythms as well. Campbell is never one to run a conspicuous flourish into the ground, so he finds a way to repeat an aspect of the effect while giving it new elements simultaneously. In "How to Be an Artist," one doesn't see much interjecting of a familiar trope at select points in the narrative; Campbell instead interrupts panels of his own drawing with panels derived from photocopies of photographs, clippings and details from other artists' work. This time around, the discords are visual, not textual. Not a single one feels arbitrary; they all advance the narrative, and they give it a documentary weight. And the visual contrast with Campbell's own drawings makes the reader more alert.

The biggest disappointment with Campbell's *Alec* work is that once one reads beyond "Artist," "King Canute" and "Graffiti Kitchen," the strips lose much of their drive and intensity. Most of them are anecdotes involving Campbell's life with his wife, children and friends in Australia, and they tend to be more cute than incisive. (The artwork also becomes considerably slicker, likely due to Campbell's acknowledged use of assistants.) What undercuts the strips is that Campbell appears to have found contentment; the anxieties over friendship, behavior and career that fire the major sequences have fallen by the wayside. He occasionally tries to recapture a sense of urgency. For instance, in "After the Snooter," he introduces the title character, a personification of his fears that he's taken the wrong road in life and is not living up to himself, but there's not much conviction behind it. The Snooter drops in and out of the strips every now and then, but Campbell can't seem to figure out what to do with him. It's never very long before Campbell returns to strips about his family goofing around with the Internet, arguing about a new car with his wife, or attending the premiere of the *From Hell* movie. Happiness breeds frivolity.

One certainly can't begrudge him that happiness. The glow of *Alec*'s major sections more than makes up for whatever disappointments the remainder of the material brings. Campbell's achievements in *Alec* are considerable. No other cartoonist has ever made such accomplished use of the personal-essay narrative. Poetic techniques (Garooga!) are often unheard of in comics, much less used with the skill one finds in the better writers. Few cartoonists have ever been able to use painterly artwork or collage techniques to such brilliant narrative effect. And, as mentioned at the start of this review, he doesn't see his work as meant for a pedestal, which may make him more accessible for those impatient with the middlebrow attitudes that have contributed to the acclaim greeting some of his peers. Campbell portrays himself as an oenophile, and he certainly deserves the tribute of a glass of 1980 Grange Hermitage (his preferred wine) raised in his honor. ■

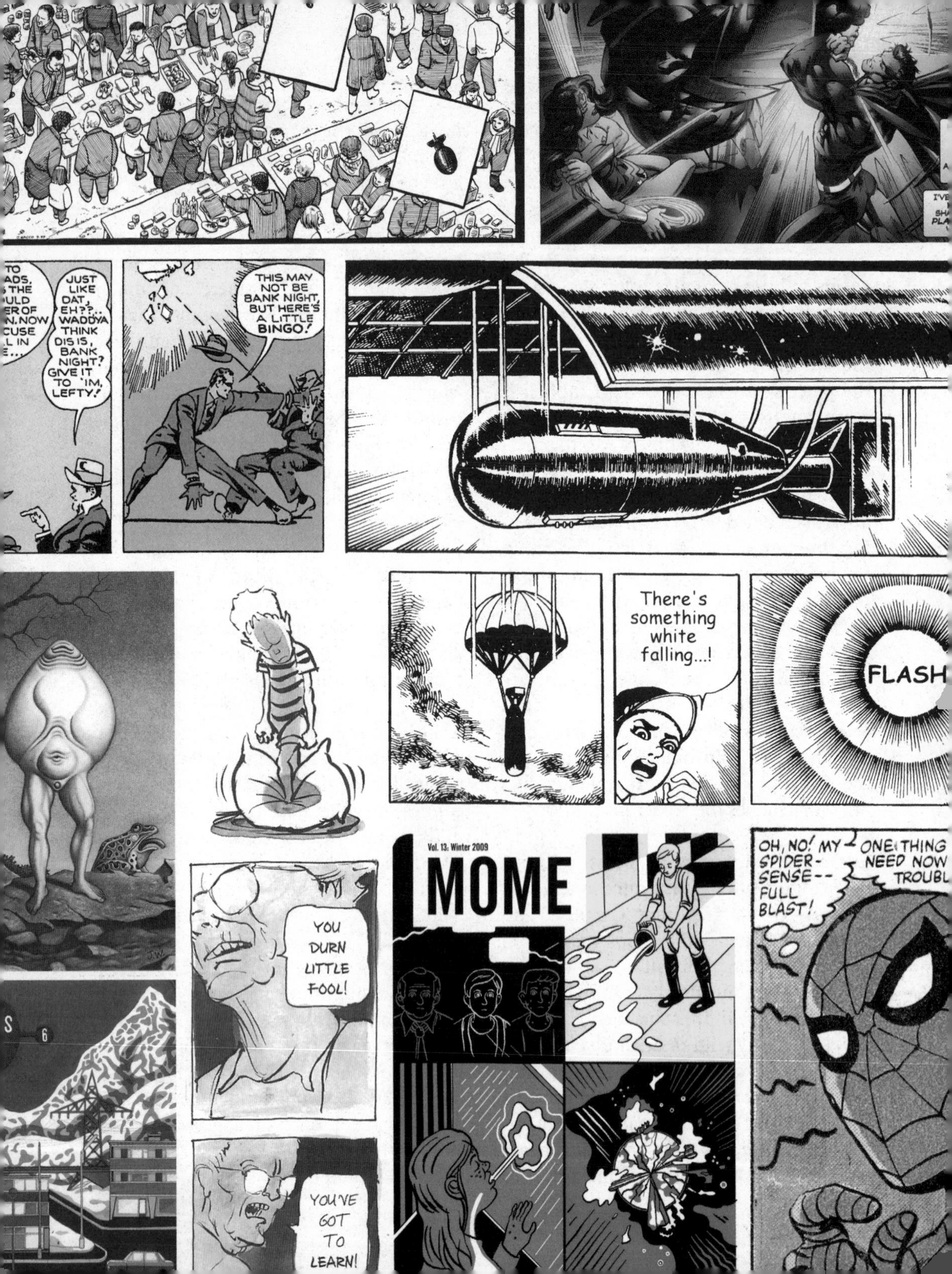
JUST LIKE DAT, EH??.. WADDYA THINK DIS IS, BANK NIGHT? GIVE IT TO 'IM, LEFTY!
THIS MAY NOT BE BANK NIGHT, BUT HERE'S A LITTLE BINGO!
There's something white falling...!
FLASH
YOU DURN LITTLE FOOL!
YOU'VE GOT TO LEARN!
Vol. 13: Winter 2009
MOME
OH, NO! MY SPIDER-SENSE-- FULL BLAST!

THE DECADE IN COMICS

BY MARC SOBEL

On November 24, 2009, a group of six writers at the *Onion A.V. Club*'s website kicked off the inevitable discussion about which comics were the "best of the decade."

Their article, which opened with a cropped banner image from the cover of Craig Thompson's *Blankets*, included 25 selections for "best comics of the decade," as well as five for "best archival project" of the decade. Rather than rank their selections, the lists were "presented alphabetically, and contain(ed) a mix of graphic novels, ongoing series, comic strips, and single issues."

The books on the A.V. Club's list were all worthwhile choices, but their efforts set off a much stronger than expected backlash. As of this writing, the site had amassed more than 650 comments running the gamut from irate fans voicing their disgust over perceived glaring omissions to advocacy and support for some of the books chosen.

Within hours, Sean T. Collins of *Comic Book Resources* posted a scathing response to *The Onion*'s article, chastising the site for its omission of manga from its list, as well as its heavy bias toward literary comics. In the days and weeks that followed, the discussion proliferated across the blogosphere as one writer after another weighed in with his or her views of the decade and its finest books. Most writers recognized the futility of such exercises, as well as the unavoidable subjectivity of individual tastes and biases. Of course, that didn't stop anybody.

I attempted to do the very same thing myself. I started by scouring my book-shelves and flipping through long-boxes, compiling a rough list of personal favorite books from the past 10 years, much as I imagine the *A.V. Club* writers did. Next, I turned to the lists of others whose opinions I respect, including dozens of online bloggers and writers. Then I went through each major publisher's website, looking for publication lists and release dates. Finally, I researched the various industry awards handed out over the last 10 years, including the Harveys, Eisners, Lulus, etc. What I ended up with was a list of several hundred books, but no clear idea how to narrow it down or make meaningful sense out of the decade.

Further complicating matters, I hadn't read many of the books on my list, but I knew if I relied solely on my own limited reading experience, the list would end up with the same sorts of problems which plagued *The Onion*'s list. After some reflection, I arrived at the (some would say obvious) conclusion that compiling such a list is not the best way to describe the previous decade.

I realized that to really come up with a representative list, I had to under-stand the *trends* that defined the decade, in the U.S. at least. This was the missing step that most of the list writers I'd read had left out of their analy-sis. Many of them had given this some thought and embedded some of this thinking into their lists, but in pursuit of a specific set of books, they had glossed over their own criteria, or left them ill defined.

With that in mind, I changed my focus. I took all the various "best of" lists I could find, including my own, and tried to work backward. Why were these books selected? Beyond their perceived quality, what did they represent in terms of trends within the industry, or developments within the medium? Could I take these lists and discern a discrete set of developments that cap-tured the essence of the decade?

I did, and based on these lists, I came up with 15 trends in the U.S. that I believe define the past 10 years in comics. Note that, although it is not listed here as a separate item, many of these trends were influenced by the über-trend of a growing bookstore market for comics. In their more durable form as trade paperbacks and graphic novels, comics gained a permanent foothold in America's bookstores this past decade, expanding their poten-tial audience and prolonging their shelf lives indefinitely.

Globalization

Over the past decade, North American comics fans were inundated with comics from all over the world, including manga/manwha comics from Asia and graphic novels from Europe, the Middle East and Africa.

Manga's explosion over the past 10 years was clearly one of the most dramatic upheavals in the comics industry in decades. Retailer and blogger Chris Butcher summed up the impact manga had on the comics industry in his excellent "Manga Milestones" series of blog posts at Comics212.net: "The growth of Japanese-originating comics in the North American comics industry has been phenomenal over the last ten years, with a massive manga boom that never busted (plateaued though), an explosion of material for every gender, every age group, and nearly every interest. While there are still readers to be initiated and battles to be fought, the preceding decade saw manga arrive in North America."

Among manga's most important impacts on the industry was its ability to reach an entirely new demographic (young girls) that the major North American comics companies had ignored for decades. Not only were publishers like Viz, TokyoPop and many others able to cultivate a loyal fanbase among girls with titles like *Sailor Moon*, *Cardcaptor Sakura* and *Shojo Beat*, they also established a wildly successful new format — the paperback digest with its smaller, shelf-ready trim size, higher page counts and lower price — which appealed to the bookstore chains, rather than relying solely on direct-market comics shops.

Capitalizing on manga's success with girls, hundreds of series were launched, targeting a variety of markets. Major successes included *Shonen Jump*, *Fruits Basket*, *Antique Bakery*, *Planetes* and *Dragonball Z*, among many others. While the manga fad has lost some of its energy since its height around 2005, manga has become a permanent and vital segment of the comics market.

Capitalizing on manga's success with young girls, many publishers began releasing manga and manwha targeted at the North American literary

TOP

From *Fruits Basket* Vol. 2 translated by Alethea and Athena Nibley [©1998 Natsuki Takaya]

comics audience. Drawn & Quarterly's three-volume series of Yoshihiro Tatsumi's comics from the late '60s, which began with *The Push Man and Other Stories*, started the trend which led to several other notable successes, including Vertical's eight-volume *Buddha* series by manga master Osamu Tezuka (Viz also reprinted Tezuka's classic *Phoenix* series in English), Viz's translations of Naoki Urasawa's award-winning comic series *Monster*, *21st Century Boys* and *Pluto*, Fanfare/Ponent Mon's series of books and short-story collections by Jiro Taniguchi and First Second's reprinting of Lat's classic *Kampung Boy* and *Town Boy*. Dark Horse Comics, also a longtime publisher of select manga series, found success with Tezuka's *Astro Boy*, and Kazuo Koike and Goseki Kojima's *Lone Wolf and Cub*, which were published in a series of miniature pocket digests, and Last Gasp finally finished translating perhaps the greatest manga of all, *Barefoot Gen* by Keiji Nakazawa, the harrowing 10-volume tale of life in post-nuclear Hiroshima.

But Asia was not the only continent whose creators found an audience in the lucrative North American comics market. *Bande dessinée*, the French term that refers to graphic albums from Canada, France and Belgium, saw hundreds of books translated into English this past decade.

Fantagraphics led the way with dozens of projects, including a series of 13 graphic albums and strip collections by Norwegian cartoonist Jason, and the recently launched series of graphic novels by French master Jacques Tardi. Drawn & Quarterly released a duo of books by French cartooning team Philippe Dupuy and Charles Berberian (*Maybe Later* and *Get a Life*). David B.'s *Epileptic*, a graphic novel from Pantheon Books, which chronicles the French cartoonist's brother's struggles with the debilitating illness, was among the most acclaimed foreign books of the past decade, as were Marjane Satrapi's *Persepolis* and Joann Sfar's *The Rabbi's Cat* series. First Second's *The Photographer* and *Alan's War*, both by French cartoonist Emmanuel Guibert, also enjoyed critical acclaim in the U.S. this past decade.

NBM also published several books by international cartoonists, including Lewis Trondheim's series of diary comics, *Little Nothings*, Manu Larcenet's two-volume meditation on mid-life and fatherhood, *Ordinary Victories*, and the under-rated memoir *Why I Killed Peter*, by Alfred and Oliver Ka. Even DC Comics tried to capitalize on this trend. DC briefly partnered with Humanoids Publishing to bring several *Heavy Metal*-inspired science-fiction series to the shelves (not to mention its ill-fated manga line, CMX, which suffered several high-profile missteps).

RIGHT
From *American Elf*
[©2006 James Kochalka]

The Internet

Entire books have been written about the impact the Internet has had on culture, communications and human psychology, of which comics are just a miniscule part, but in reflecting on the past decade in the comics industry, several distinct trends stand out which are the direct result of the transition to an online culture.

First, of course, is the rapid proliferation of Web-comics. With its potentially unlimited audience exposure, low costs (compared to print), and relatively few barriers to publication, the Internet facilitated a deluge of self-publishing online this past decade. The quality of these online efforts varied widely; however, there is no doubt that Web-cartoonists produced more than a few notable gems.

Any list of important Web-comics from the past decade usually starts with the three breakout hits: Jerry Holkins and Mike Krahulik's *Penny Arcade*, Chris Onstad's *Achewood* and the Nicholas Gurewitch's *Perry Bible Fellowship*. However, hundreds of other online strips built up faithful audiences and legions of fans around the world this past decade. This list, which is by no means comprehensive, includes James Kochalka's *American Elf*, Shaenon K. Garrity's *Narbonic*, Ramon Perez and Rob Coughler's *Butternut Squash*, Tom Siddell's *Gunnerkrigg Court*, Phil Foglio's *Girl Genius*, Scott Kurtz's *PVP*, Dash Shaw's *Bodyworld*, Kate Beaton's *Hark! A Vagrant* and Carla Speed McNeil's *Finder*. As the phenomenon spread, online anthologies (Act-i-vate, etc.) and Web-comic hosting sites (Web-comicsNation, etc.) also began to spring up, collecting multiple Web-cartoonists under a single portal.

All of the major publishers moved to establish a Web presence as well. Marvel and DC attempted to capitalize on the digital market with Digital Comics Unlimited and Zuda Comics, respectively. Dark Horse Comics established a Web presence on MySpace, and has subsequently published several print anthologies based on its original Web content.

Despite all of this activity, Web-comics as an industry remains in its infancy in

JANUARY 26, 2006

terms of monetization, distribution and technology, and this is the area of the comics industry where the most innovation and excitement will likely take place in the next decade. The impact of the Apple iPad, and the next generation of portable reading devices, will certainly alter the digital publishing landscape, including comics, and one can easily imagine an iTunes-style download-on-demand model where entire backlists could be offered for sale.

The Internet also allowed creators and their fans to directly engage one another in a real-time context. Warren Ellis (*The Engine*) and Brian Michael Bendis (*Jinxworld*) were two high-profile writers who made particularly effective use of online technology to cultivate their fan-base, and facilitate discussion, hype and enthusiasm for their series.

Torrents and illegal download sites became an ongoing, and perhaps permanent scourge to the publishing industry this past decade. Pirated copies of new and old comics were freely and illegally downloaded millions of times by fans all over the world, and although legal efforts have been initiated to combat the problem, it remains unclear if and how the illegal scanning and posting of comics can be prevented.

The Internet's other significant impact on the comics industry was the emergence of online fandom (prominent blogger Sean Kleefeld even wrote a book about the subject called *Comic Book Fanthropology*). Fandom has always been a vibrant and fascinating part of the comics industry, but the Internet united fans in entirely new ways, establishing ongoing forums for the sharing of images, information and enthusiasm, as well as acrimony. By the end of the decade, the "comics blogosphere" had grown to encompass thousands of amateur writers and fan enthusiasts sharing their passion for comics with the world.

TOP
From PVP Vol. 3:
Rides Again [©2005
Scott Kurtz]

Hollywood

For better or worse, this was the decade that Hollywood finally discovered the comics industry. Sure, there have been superhero movies, TV and radio shows going all the way back to the '30s, but nothing in the past comes close to the geek-culture explosion that took place this decade. Comic books became a cash cow for the special effects industry, as millions of moviegoers queued up for one opening day after another.

But while comics certainly had a significant impact on the creative output of Hollywood, so too did the Hollywood studios impact the comic-book industry.

Perhaps the highest-profile and most direct impact was on the convention circuit. The past decade saw a dramatic change in the content and attendance of the major comic conventions, particularly the San Diego and the New York comic cons. The days of sweaty geeks happily sifting through long-boxes and debating hypothetical battles between DC and Marvel characters are gone forever. These days, conventions are full-blown pop-culture events, dominated by Hollywood studios promoting upcoming TV and movie projects.

Hollywood's influence was also felt, although perhaps less acutely, in the types and quantity of new comics and graphic novels that flood into the direct-market shops each week. In addition to the endless superhero comics, with their business plans designed to maximize the number of character appearances on the shelves leading up to a major film release, the decade saw several publishers and creators retro-fitting failed screenplays into original graphic novels. Comics creators also began writing and drawing stories with their eyes on the big prize — the elusive movie option. Many of these creators have little interest in comics as a medium, or the idiomatic language and artistic potential of combining words and pictures. Their goal is simply to window-dress a screenplay with pretty pictures and dramatic storyboards. Even independent publisher Top Shelf cashed in on this Hollywood phenomenon with its uncharacteristically mainstream science-fiction series, *The Surrogates*.

The annual tradition of Free Comic Book Day, which started back in 2002 in coordination with the release of the first *Spider-Man* movie, is also a direct by-product of Hollywood's influence on comics. Marvel and DC, along with a bandwagon-load of other publishers attempted to capitalize on comics' newfound mainstream attention by giving away glossy marketing brochures disguised as free comic books.

But the single biggest sign that Hollywood and the comics industry have become cozy bedfellows happened at the very end of the decade. Disney's acquisition of Marvel, and its extensive catalog of characters, was certainly driven by the latter's moviemaking profit potential, not its comparatively minuscule comic-book revenue.

Literary Comics

The term "literary comics" is broad, vague and misleading. Without getting too bogged down in definitional minutiae, the term has come to represent those books that fall into a variety of genres focused on human-interest stories, including auto/biography, memoir, reportage and slice-of-life. The literary label was initially applied in a contrarian context, to set these books apart from the rest of the industry, which remains heavily focused on the superhero, science-fiction, horror, fantasy and adventure genres. Over the past decade, literary comics became a major focus of media attention, publicity and celebration within the industry — evidence, some would say, of the medium's maturation.

Others, however, find literary comics boring, bland and pretentious. They're seen as attempts to cater to an audience of yuppie intellectuals. From this perspective, literary comics cage the imagination in mundane reality, when comics' true strength lies in its ability to conjure fantasy and wonder through powerful images. Over the decade, passionate camps of supporters have sprung up on both sides of the argument, and have frequently clashed on message boards and blogs over the relative merits of literary comics.

Regardless of the view taken, literary comics became a major trend in the industry this past decade. More creators explored complex, human dramas through comics than at any point in the medium's history. In support of this growing trend, many traditional book publishers dipped their toes into comics' waters for the first time. HarperCollins published Shaun Tan's breakout graphic novel, The Arrival, as well as his sublime follow-up collection of short stories and illustrated prose, Tales From Outer Suburbia, while Doubleday published a lovely hardcover collection of Jason Little's Shutterbug Follies Web-comic. St. Martin Press brought to life Nick Bertozzi's fine art fantasy, The Salon, and W.W. Norton published several graphic novels, including David Small's critically acclaimed memoir, Stitches. Houghton Mifflin struck gold with Alison Bechdel's celebrated memoir, Fun Home, as

well as Posy Simmonds' *Tamara Drewe*. The New Press, a nonprofit publisher akin to PBS, released *Studs Terkel's Working*, a graphic anthology celebrating the great oral historian.

Two book publishers took it even one step further, establishing entire lines devoted to literary graphic novels. Pantheon (an imprint of Random House) published dozens of books, including Jessica Abel's *La Perdida*, Charles Burns' *Black Hole* and David Mazzucchelli's runaway hit, *Asterios Polyp*. Harry N. Abrams also created ComicArts, an imprint of high-end graphic novels and art books, including such lushly designed successes as the recent *Art of Jaime Hernandez* by Todd Hignite, Dan Nadel's *Art Out of Time* and *Johnny Cash: I See A Darkness* by German artist Reinhard Kleist, among others. Other creators chose to publish their literary graphic novels through vanity presses, including Phoebe Gloeckner's *Diary of a Teenage Girl*, published by Frog Ltd. and Lynda Barry's *One Hundred Demons*, published by Sasquatch Books (although Barry would later move to Drawn & Quarterly).

Capitalizing on comics globalization, Fanfare/Ponent Mon translated select manga titles specifically geared toward the literary audience, scoring critical hits with many books including Hideo Azumi's *Disappearance Diary* and Jiro Taniguchi's *The Walking Man*. Among the traditional comics publishers, Fantagraphics led the way with hundreds of literary graphic novels and comics published this past decade, while Drawn & Quarterly, NBM, Top Shelf and several other small-press publishers followed suit.

An amazing number of these literary graphic novels were written and drawn by women. These books broadened the diversity of the medium as a whole, and brought a welcome, distinctly female perspective to the male-dominated industry. Many of these books took the form of graphic memoir, including Miss Lasko-Gross's excellent two-part reflection on childhood, *Escape From "Special"* and *A Mess of Everything*, and Marjane Satrapi's *Persepolis*,

TOP
The Salon [©2007 Nick Bertozzi]

DIDN'T I JUST DO THIS? I WALK IN AND IT'S TOO WARM. WHY DIDN'T I TURN DOWN THE HEAT?

which enjoyed widespread acclaim and turned the cartoonist into a media celebrity. Carol Tyler's brilliant *You'll Never Know* explored her father's life and military service, while Ann Marie Fleming reconstructed her search for clues about her personal relation to the long-forgotten celebrity magician in *The Magical Life of Long Tack Sam*.

Art Comix

While there was a ton of activity and excitement that took place under the umbrella category of art comix this past decade, this may be the most difficult category to pin down. This is primarily due to the wildly diverse and deeply personal nature of the comics themselves, which share little in common other than the singular pursuit of an artistic vision.

Lacking the depth of character and storytelling scope of their literary brethren, many art comix were simply exercises in visual storytelling, fanciful flights of imagination or quirky humor strips. In many cases, artists tinkered with the formal aspects of the comic book itself, experimenting with page and panel designs, printing effects, color applications, inking styles, digital manipulation, mixed media and all sorts of other tricks and techniques.

A set of aesthetic qualities that ties all of these art comix together remains elusive; however, in general, these comics tended to elevate the compositions and visual elements of the medium, while relegating or diminishing the narrative aspects. In some cases, art comix felt closer to fine art than traditional comics, although they maintained just enough of the cartoonish drawing style, illustrative abstraction or sequential presentation to be recognizable as comics. Several of the *Kramers Ergot* artists, including Ben Jones, Paper Rad and the Fort Thunder crew (excepting, perhaps, Brian

TOP
Black Hole [©2005
Charles Burns]

Ralph) might be included in this admittedly vague category, as could Jim Woodring, Marc Bell, Matthew Thurber, Souther Salazar and perhaps even Gary Panter.

One distinct trend that grew out of the art-comix scene and gained momentum throughout the decade was abstract comics. Comics have always been about abstraction, but over the past decade, a new generation of artists tested the limits of this malleability, stretching comics into sequences of surrealist images and emotional landscapes of shape and color. The anthology *Abstract Comics*, released in 2009 by Fantagraphics, offered an entirely new conception of what sequential art can be, showcasing successions of images without any tangible sense of realism or a discernible narrative. Its contents were a direct contrast to the long-held notion that the primary directive of comics is to use sequential images to carry readers through a story. It's unclear whether this book is foreshadowing a vital new genre of comics, or if it will remain a curious outlier, but the impression it left was that the lines between fine art and comics have become forever blurred.

Golden Age of Reprints

There have been many efforts over the years to repackage old classic comic strips. For example, Fantagraphics reprinted *Prince Valiant*, *Pogo* and *Krazy Kat* in various formats, while Kitchen Sink kept Eisner's *The Spirit* in print for years. But the '00s saw an unprecedented abundance of new collections and high-end repackaging projects, to the point where it feels like everything that's ever been drawn is back in print. As Art Spiegelman noted in the *Comics Journal* #300, comics' entire history is available to everyone now.

Old newspaper strips were among the most popular reprint targets, partially because of their relative obscurity and limited availability, as well as their esteemed role as the comic industry's earliest innovators. Much of what has become commonplace in the idiomatic visual language of today's comic

TOP

Cover art [©2006 Helge Reumann]

books traces its origins back to these early newspaper strips. Among the dozens of archival projects that were published this past decade, highlights include Fantagraphics' *Popeye* series of oversized hardcovers collecting E.C. Segar's classic strip and George Herriman's *Krazy Kat*, which also received the high-end repackaging it deserves thanks, in part, to graphic designer Chris Ware. Bolstered with scores of academic profiles and background information, Charles Schulz's beloved *Peanuts* series is also in the midst of a comprehensive series of chronological reprints, and Drawn & Quarterly reintroduced Frank King's *Gasoline Alley* to a new generation of fans. Similarly, *Terry and the Pirates*, *Dick Tracy*, *Little Orphan Annie*, *Happy Hooligan*, *Bringing Up Father*, *Little Nemo in Slumberland*, *Flash Gordon* and dozens of other classic strips were resurrected in archival reprint projects this past decade.

But the reprint craze was hardly restricted to early newspaper strips. DC released the widely acclaimed omnibus volumes of Jack Kirby's *Fourth World* saga, while Fantagraphics repackaged the seminal first volume of *Love and Rockets* in new, affordable "definitive" editions. Gemstone released remastered collections of classic EC Comics, including *Tales From the Crypt*, *Two-Fisted Tales* and *Weird Science Fantasy*. Marvel and DC both delved deep into their back catalogs to release all sorts of collections of classic superhero books in formats that ranged from oversized, high-end books to cheap, black-and-white "Essentials." Even a personal childhood favorite, *The Amazon*, an obscure '80s miniseries by Steven T. Seagle and Tim Sale, published by Comico, was recently reprinted by Image Comics.

RIGHT
George Herriman's
July 4, 1916 *Krazy Kat*

490

Comics Archaeology

Scouring the past for forgotten geniuses has become a passion of academics and scholars, providing a thrill akin to discovering buried treasure. This notion may have been around to a small extent for decades (*Raw* included several old strips alongside its stable of avant-garde creators), but in my mind, the phenomena really caught on with Seth's *It's a Good Life If You Don't Weaken* and was finally fully realized in recent years with Dan Nadel's anthology, *Art Out of Time*.

This past decade saw several books highlighting forgotten artists (not writers so far, although that seems like a logical next step) and presenting them anew as lost masters. In addition to Nadel's *Art Out of Time*, Paul Karasik's *I Shall Destroy All the Civilized Planets* presented Fletcher Hanks as an embittered, under-appreciated genius. Similar books showcased artists Milt Gross, Rory Hayes, Boody Rogers, John Stanley and Doug Wright. Greg Sadowski's *Supermen!* offered readers a glimpse back in time to comics' formative years with high-quality reprints of obscure superhero stories from the '20s and '30s.

Reflecting the joy of the hunt, an active discussion group came into existence this past decade called Platinum Comics, which exists for enthusiasts and scholars around the world to share information and experiences as they continue their search for information and cartoons from comics prehistory.

Comics Scholarship

In a recent interview with the *Books.Torontoist.com* website, writer and historian Jeet Heer described "an explosion of comics scholarship" in the past decade. "What's different now in the last 10 or 20 years," Heer reflected, "is that there's an interest in comics that's coming out of a belief in the positive value of comics. If you have comics studies in an English literary course, it's because it's considered to be a good book — like *Jimmy Corrigan* or *Maus* — so in some ways the growth in comics in academia is part of the larger mainstream success of comics."

But beyond the few breakthrough literary-comics success stories, comics as a medium are gaining footholds in Humanities and Liberal Arts programs throughout the country in unprecedented ways. According to Dr. Arnold

Blumberg in an online conference devoted to "Comics in Academia" in 2009, "Those of us that grew up through the late Silver/early Bronze Age and later are far less prone to perpetuating the stigma, so the path to academics for comics is getting easier and easier."

There are many examples of this growing trend toward scholarly acceptance. For example, in 2008, Art Spiegelman led a high-profile talk at Columbia University with Associate Professor David Hajdu, author of *The Ten-Cent Plague*, about the academic merits of comics as a medium of expression. Numerous articles and essays have been published in a wide variety of academic journals, and there is even a Facebook group devoted to "Comic Adventures in Academia" which currently has over 450 members.

While comics studies courses are sporadically offered across U.S. college campuses (according to NYU Professor Peter Sanderson, "Courses on comics are the wave of the future, but in my experience the future still seems distant"), they are showing up more and more. A major milestone in the academic study of comics was the publication of *A Comics Studies Reader* by Jeet Heer and Kent Worcester in April 2009. According to Heer, "The book is being used in a lot of courses as a textbook, and it won an award from the American Public Culture association." ImageTexT is another publication devoted to the academic study of comics. According to its website (http://www.english.ufl.edu/imagetext/), ImageTexT is "a peer-reviewed, open access journal dedicated to the interdisciplinary study of comics and related media," which is irregularly published online by the University of Florida's English department. University presses have also published several high-profile books devoted to comics research in recent years. The University of Mississippi Press in particular has published several books on various subjects of comics scholarship, including Charles Hatfield's excellent *Alternative Comics: An Emerging Literature*, among others. *In the Studio: Visits with Contemporary Cartoonists* by Todd Hignite was published by Yale University Press in 2006.

Still, broad acceptance of comics within the higher education establishment remains a work in progress. As writer Brian Miller pointed out, "While there are a growing number of academics taking interest in comic books as literature, the larger perception still remains that they are pop-culture dribble." However, if the trend begun this decade continues, there is considerable promise for the academic study of comics in the years to come.

Anthologies

Anthologies are hardly a new trend in comics. From the earliest days of the industry, anthologies have served as the lifeblood of innovation in comics, providing diverse mixes of artists and writers a vehicle to publish short stories and strips under a single cover. In the past decade, anthologies continued to thrive. The initial list I came up with had more than 30 different anthology series, including the decade-opener, *Comix 2000*, a collection of mostly silent strips published by L'Assocation. Other prominent anthologies from the past decade included multiple volumes of *Kramers Ergot*, *Mome*, *Drawn & Quarterly Showcase*, *SPX*, *Flight*, *Hi Horse*, *Little Lit*, *Syncopated*, *Hotwire Comics*, *Blurred Vision* and *The Ganzfeld*, as well as *Top Shelf Asks the Big Questions*, *Japan As Viewed By 17 Creators*, *McSweeney's* vol. 13, *RoadStrips* and *Orchid*. Even Marvel and DC embraced the anthology format with titles such as *Strange Tales*, *Bizarro Tales*, and so on.

The Politics of Cartooning

Political cartoons have been a mainstay of American and European culture for longer than any of us have been alive. Newspapers dating back to the 1700s featured political cartoons and illustrations as a vehicle for influencing public sentiment. Over the past decade, however, political cartoonists suffered the worst economic catastrophe in a generation. From the rapid contraction of print journalism, to the public backlash aimed at cartoonists and publishers over controversial cartoons, the '00s were a rough decade for political cartoonists.

None had it quite as bad as Kurt Westergaard, the Danish cartoonist at the heart of the international controversy that erupted in 2005. His infamous caricatures of the Prophet Muhammad, published in the *Jyllands-Posten* newspaper, incited international outrage among Muslim communities. The

TOP

Cover art [©2007 Brendan Buford]

reaction was incendiary — spreading across the globe like wildfire, striking a nerve that had been simmering just below the surface for years. Violence escalated and when things finally settled down, more than a hundred lives had been lost. For a period of weeks, the story dominated not just comics industry headlines, but international news as well. To this day, five years later, Tom Spurgeon still regularly posts "Danish cartoon hangover updates," demonstrating the incident's continuing relevance in international politics.

The attacks on 9/11 also galvanized the comics industry, as artists across the globe reacted to the tragic events. Four anthologies of cartoons were published, with most of the profits donated to recovery and the families of victims. It was a moment in comics history unlike any other, a spontaneous outpouring of sympathy and emotion that demonstrated the potential of the medium and the kind-hearted nature of its creators and publishers.

The 2008 U.S. presidential election turned Barack Obama into a comic-book hero (sadly, like many presidents before him), and even saw a brief return to the dark days of comics speculative past, when issues of *Amazing Spider-Man* featuring Obama on the cover became the largest-selling comic book of the decade.

Meanwhile, a few cartoonists like Joe Sacco, Ted Rall, David Axe and others published graphic novels focusing on current events and political issues.

The Trade Paperback

Trade paperbacks have been around since the '70s, but when Joe Quesada and Bill Jemas took the helm at Marvel Comics at the beginning of the decade, Marvel began to follow a new publishing strategy. Soon, the standard model became story arcs of four to eight issues that, once completed, would be released together in a trade paperback format (often in hardcover initially, then softcover) usually within two to three months of the story's conclusion.

This new publishing model had at least two significant and lasting impacts on the comics industry. First, the trade paperback fundamentally transformed not just how comics are packaged and sold, but also how they are created. The trend toward what is now commonly referred to as "decompressed storytelling," a writing technique that uses oversized panels and double-page spreads to draw out scenes (particularly action scenes) to meet the page count requirements, became widespread (no pun intended).

Stories also began to follow a familiar narrative pace, as each tale built toward a predictable cliffhanger at the end of each chapter.

The other significant impact of this new publishing model was that many readers, savvy to the publisher's formula, began to "wait for the trade" rather than follow the stories in serialized format. For many fans, this proved to be a more satisfying reading experience, allowing them to consume a full story in one sitting.

Pricing was also an important factor with this new model as publishers increasingly began to view the monthly pamphlets as loss leaders. Hardcore fans who had been collecting, say, *Amazing Spider-Man* for decades could still get their monthly fix, but for the rest of the market, trades were priced slightly cheaper than the individual issues, driving cost-conscious fans toward the new format. Publishers further enticed readers by adding bonus features like introductions, sketchbook pages and character designs to the collected package.

Following the success of the trade paperback format for *new* storylines, Marvel and DC launched ambitious efforts to re-release their considerable backlists of books, allowing new readers to experience all sorts of old classics in a variety of bookshelf-friendly formats. From oversized deluxe omnibuses to cheap black-and-white phonebook-style collections, the new trade format gave publishers access to the all-important bookstore market.

I initially called this trend "the decline of the floppy" but the reality is that serialized pamphlet comics continue to flood into Direct Market shops every week. However, one area where the floppy has declined, almost to the point of extinction, is in the alternative side of the industry. In 2007, even the Hernandez Brothers, creators of *Love and Rockets*, debatably the most successful alternative floppy comic in history, succumbed to this trend by transitioning to an annual, squarebound, bookshelf format for their "New Stories."

While most major alternative publishers gradually abandoned the floppy format in favor of original graphic novels, the nail in the coffin was Diamond Comics Distributors' controversial new minimum sales requirements. As a result, many small-press creators were squeezed out of the Direct Market, forcing them to either submit to an anthology, publish online as a Webcomic, self-publish and sell their books through the comics art festival circuit (MoCCA, TCAF, SPX, A.P.E., etc.) or on consignment through the smattering of Internet resellers (Sparkplug Comic Books, Global Hobo, USS Catastrophe, etc.).

Branding Creators

While this trend began back in the '90s, the '00s saw several comics creators, particularly writers, become superstars. As comics enjoyed an unprecedented increase in media coverage and social acceptance, certain writers and artists transcended the actual content of the comics they created. Where once characters drove sales (Remember all those random Batman, Wolverine and Punisher guest appearances back in the '80s?), mainstream comics are now marketed primarily based on their creative teams. Frank Miller, Alan Moore, Ed Brubaker, Brian Michael Bendis, Warren Ellis, Robert Kirkman, Brian K. Vaughan and many others became reliable brand names regardless of the series they were writing. Artists enjoyed similar brand recognition, as books with Bryan Hitch, J.H. Williams III, Jim Lee and Darwyn Cooke (among many others) enjoyed healthy sales and heavy marketing and promotion on the publisher's behalf.

Although dozens of books exemplify this trend, perhaps the two best examples are DC Comics' *All Star Superman* by Grant Morrison and Frank Quitely and Marvel's *Astonishing X-Men*, written by *Buffy the Vampire Slayer* creator Joss Whedon and illustrated by John Cassaday. Both titles were clearly conceived to appeal to fans not of the characters, but the creators behind each book.

Crossover Events

Another trend in mainstream comics that dates back to the late '70s became dominant in the last decade, primarily with superhero comics published by Marvel and DC. The universe-wide storyline, which affects virtually the entire fictional universe of each publisher, including most of the major monthly character titles, became an annual event for both companies. Marvel spent the decade publishing massive, committee-written storylines such as *House of M*, *Civil War*, *Secret Invasion*, *Annihilation Quest*, *Dark Reign* and others, while DC published similar events including *Countdown*, *Trinity*, *52*, *SinestroCorps*, *Blackest Night* and several variations on their famous *Crisis on Infinite Earths* storyline from the '80s (*Identity Crisis*, *Infinite Crisis* and *Final Crisis*). Even Image Comics got in on the action with the crossover series, *Image United*. All of these events crossed dozens of titles and required readers to shell out substantial amounts of money to get the complete story. Yet, despite the rising din of complaints from fans, these series sold reasonably well (some were certainly more successful than others). The relative quality of each of these events is for others to debate, but there is no doubt that these expansive storylines were the predominant trend in mainstream comics from the Big Two this past decade.

The Chabon Effect

As a critical mass of energy coalesced around comics this past decade, the industry experienced an influx of creators from outside the industry. Fueled partly by the interest from Hollywood, comics saw several screenwriters taking their stories and crossing over into the comics medium with varying degrees of success (i.e., Kevin Smith).

Even celebrities from unrelated fields took a stab at creating comics, although most of these were highly derivative, throwaway stories. Notable examples included punk-rock singer Glenn Danzig; Nick Simmons, the son of heavy metal singer Gene Simmons; actress Jennifer Love Hewitt; and even porn-star-turned-marketing-juggernaut Jenna Jameson.

More successful were the prose writers and novelists who tried their hands at comics. The highest-profile of these projects was Stephen King's *Dark Tower* miniseries from Marvel, which then followed suit with adaptations of the writer's famous novel *The Stand*. Marvel also published similar adaptations with science-fiction writer Orson Scott Card (*Ender's Game*), vampire novelist Laurel K. Hamilton (*Anita Blake*), and fantasy writer George R. R. Martin (*Hedge Knight*). DC scored a similar (though controversial) hit with novelist Brad Meltzer's *Identity Crisis*.

LEFT

All Star Superman #10 (March 2007) written by Grant Morrison, penciled by Frank Quitely and digitally inked and colored by Jamie Grant [©2007 DC Comics]

Pulitzer-winning novelist Michael Chabon brought his famous character the *Escapist* to life in an anthology published by Dark Horse Comics (*Amazing Adventures of the Escapist*), as well as a miniseries written by Brian K. Vaughan, but perhaps the most successful of these outsider efforts in terms of fan reaction was Jonathan Lethem's *Omega the Unknown*, an acclaimed retelling of Steve Gerber's classic '70s superhero melodrama with artists Farel Dalrymple and Gary Panter.

Comics Criticism

Over the past 10 years, comics criticism has graduated from its magazine and fanzine roots into deluxe hardcover books. Much of this trend is a reaction to the medium's rapid expansion, as writers and critics struggle to keep up, make sense of it all and explore particular areas of interest.

Among many highlights, the decade saw the publication of multiple scholarly books devoted to Steve Ditko (Blake Bell's *Strange and Stranger* and Craig Yoe's *The Art of Steve Ditko*), Jack Kirby (Mark Evanier's *Kirby: King of Comics*, as well as an astonishing 50 issues of the *Kirby Collector* magazine) and Charles Schulz (*Schulz and Peanuts: A Biography* by David Michaelis), three titans of the medium. Several other cartoonist biographies also saw print this past decade, including Hergé, Milt Caniff, Bill Watterson, Wally Wood and B. Krigstein. Publisher TwoMorrows devoted an entire line of books to "modern masters" (currently up to 24 volumes), including such luminary artists as José Luis García-López, Gene Colan, George Perez and others.

Print books of pure comics criticism were published for the first time in the medium's history. Notable books included Douglas Wolk's *Reading Comics*, *The Best American Comics Criticism* edited by Ben Schwartz, and Charles Hatfield's *Alternative Comics: An Emerging Literature*, to name but a few.

But the majority of comics criticism, for better or worse, was published on the Internet. Hundreds of blogs and websites devoted to the serious discussion and analysis of comics sprung up over the decade. Many of these were run by amateur writers and fans of the medium, but by the end of the decade, with print media in tailspin, even *The Comics Journal* cut back its publishing schedule and expanded its website.

Most, if not all, of these trends should be fairly well known to anyone who's followed the comics industry closely over the past decade. My goal in writing this essay was not to unearth some obscure, overlooked movements in the industry, but rather to avoid many of the pitfalls of specific "best of" lists by focusing on broader strokes.

In the trajectory of the medium, the '00s were a renaissance period. This decade saw a creative energy galvanize around comics in a way that could sustain the medium for decades to come. All of these trends I've listed are evidence of the vast expansion, unprecedented in the medium's history, both in terms of creative innovation and cultural relevance that comics experienced this past decade.

I hope, at the very least, this list of trends will serve as a resource for putting the last 10 years into some kind of meaningful historical context, though I recognize that it may take another decade for critics, scholars and historians to fully process the impact of this past decade.

But for fans of good comics, it may have been the best 10-year stretch in the medium's history. May the next decade be half as exciting. ∎

Further Reading:

Onion A.V. Club's "Best Comics of the '00s"

Sean T. Collins' Response: "What's Wrong with the A.V. Club's Best Comics of the '00s List?" at Comic Book Resources' Robot 6 blog

Chris Butcher's "Manga Milestones" series of posts at Comics212.net

"Pick Five" at The Manga Curmudgeon blog

Comic Book Resources' "Decade in Review" five-part roundtable series

"The Best Damned Comics of the Decade Chosen by the Artists" at the Daily Crosshatch blog

"The 30 Most Important Comics of the Decade" at Comic Book Resources' Robot 6 blog

Web-comic Overlook's "Top Ten Best Web-comics of the Decade"

"Fort Thunder Forever" by Tom Spurgeon in The Comics Journal #256

Rob Clough's "Books of the Decade" at The Comics Journal website (tcj.com)

Dave Howard's "Interview with Jeet Heer On Comics Scholarship" at Books.Torontoist.com, Feb. 10, 2010

TOP

In *Reading Comics*, Douglas Wolk references *Understanding Comics* [©2007 Scott McCloud]

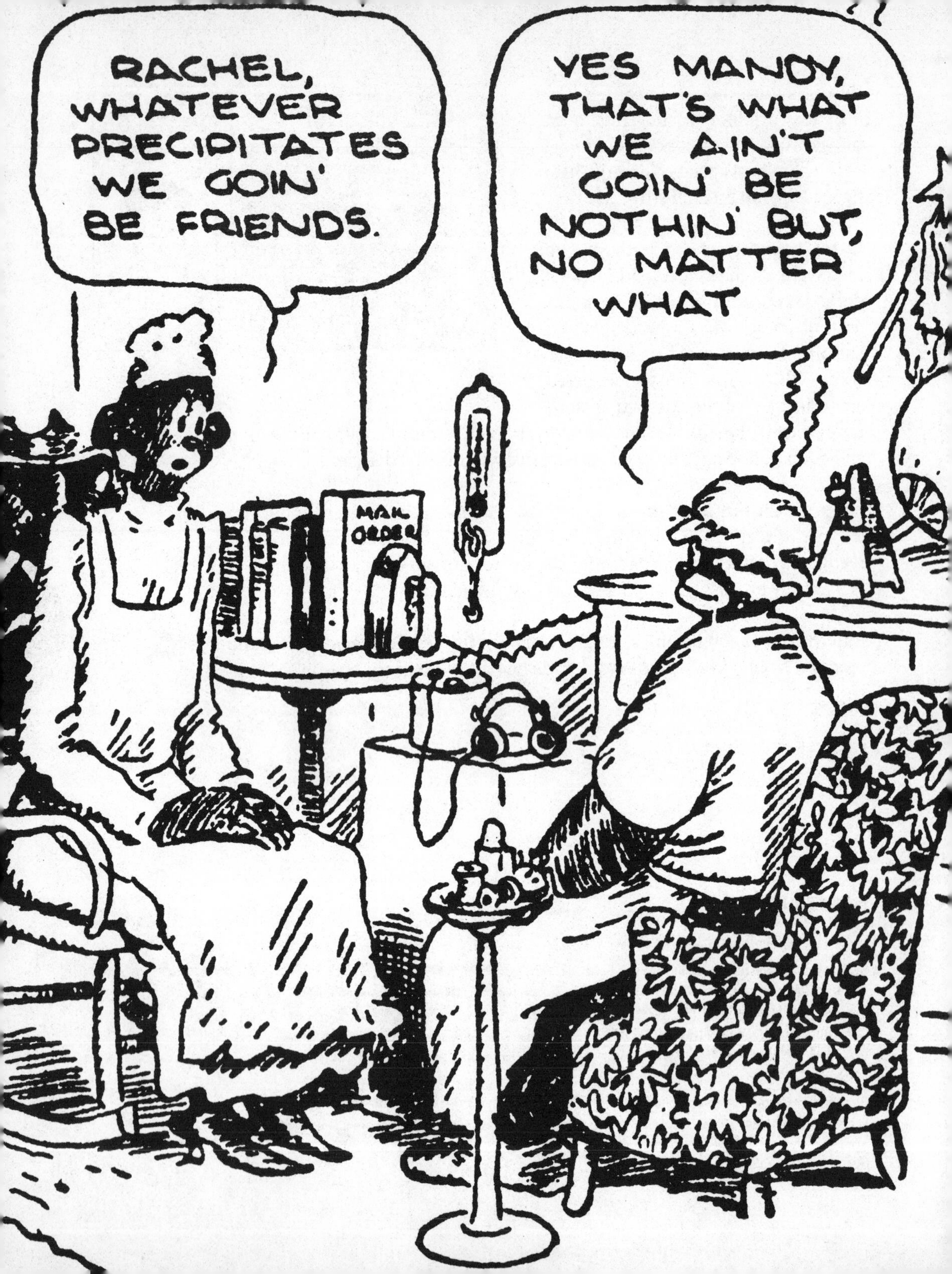
RACHEL, WHATEVER PRECIDITATES WE GOIN' BE FRIENDS.
YES MANDY, THAT'S WHAT WE AIN'T GOIN' BE NOTHIN' BUT, NO MATTER WHAT
MAIL ORDER

AFFECTIONATE, SYMPATHETIC AND COMPLETELY RACIST ANOTHER GO-ROUND WITH RACIAL CARICATURE

BY R. FIORE

Not the least interesting quality of Frank King's *Gasoline Alley* is its documentary aspect. Like the glimpses one gets of a bygone Los Angeles in the background of silent movies, it is an effect that is unintentional. There's a naturalism and a particularism about Walt Wallet's world that convinces you that you're not looking at cartoon abstraction but meticulous observation. Reading *Gasoline Alley* you feel as though you've learned something about what was inside a middle-class house in the 1920s, or what it was like to take an automobile camping trip through the Southwest before the interstate highway system was built. More to the point here, you see as detailed an expression of a racial attitude as you're going to find in popular entertainment, and one that is revealing because it sees no reason to disguise itself.

The African-American community of Gasoline Alley consists of Rachel, the maid of Walt Wallet; Mandy, her counterpart in the household of Walt's neighbor and future spouse Phyllis Blossom; and Plato, chauffer to financial deus ex machina Mr. Wicker. Primarily through Rachel, King delineates a portrait of an inherently inferior race thrust by an unkind fate into a civilization they cannot hope to comprehend. There are simple tasks that they can master, but the intricacies of the English language are beyond their powers. Though given to minor vices, they are nonetheless faithful servants who take pride in the status of their employers, whose honor they will defend against rivals. Understand now that this point of view was enlightened well above the norm,

LEFT
Frank King's June 15, 1925 *Gasoline Alley* strip [©2007 The Estate of Frank King]

coinciding as it did during an era of mass migration of African-Americans to the North and the white backlash that ensued. While the characterization is comic, it is unfailingly affectionate and sympathetic. More than she is anything else, Rachel is good, and. within his limits, King strives for accuracy. I think there can be little doubt when you look at the last panel of the June 15, 1925 strip that King has been inside a colored maid's living quarters. At one point Rachel takes a visit to her folks down South, and I would be willing to bet that instances where black comic-relief characters were granted so much humanity as to have a family were rare. Walt will from time to time ask her advice on matters of the heart, and her counsel will be wise if primitive. I have no doubt that when King was informed his portrayal was offensive he was completely shocked. No doubt, but no knowledge either. I wrote to Jeet Heer about it, and his response included the following:

> I haven't yet come across any evidence of a civil rights group contacting King but I'm sure that it must have happened because I have seen correspondence between civil-rights groups and other major cartoonists, usually starting around 1941 or 1942 (Caniff, Eisner and Harold Gray all got letters either condemning or praising their depiction of blacks) . . .

> At some point in the late 1930s (again, I don't have the strips handy) Rachel leaves the employment of the Wallets but occasionally makes an appearance as a guest. A very interesting sequence occurs during the war (1942 or 1943 or 1944). Phyllis is having a hard time finding a servant because of the labor shortage. She goes to visit Rachel with the intention of hiring her again. When Phyllis starts to complain about how she can't find any good servants, Rachel chimes in and says something like "Yes, I have the same problem." The joke being that Rachel is now doing so well she can employ a servant herself and has no intention of returning to the Wallets. This sequence was twice praised in the pages of the *Chicago Defender* (one of America's leading African-American newspapers) for being a funny comment on the "social revolution" caused by the war (which generally helped blacks find better jobs than they had before) . . .

> Having said all that, it's interesting that even though Rachel becomes much more than a Mammy character, King (or his assistants) always draw her the same way. She never loses her pneumatic, tire-wide lips. It's as if King's drawing ability were stuck in the past, even as his storytelling was becoming more advanced.

That last is a curious phenomenon that goes well beyond Frank King. There is a remarkable standardization of black racial caricature in the comics. Cartoonists of the '20s and '30s not only employ the golliwog characterization almost universally, but will use it in a way that clashes with their usual cartoon style. Indeed, all black racial caricature has a programmatic quality, as if one were playing a scale and were required to hit every note: Laziness, cowardice, superstition (these last two often combined to form a chord, as when a character turns white and runs screaming at the sight of a ghost), chicken stealing, paroxysms of delight at

the sight of watermelon or the sound of rattling dice. With the exception of superstition, King scrupulously avoids these conventions, though one must come to the conclusion that he found the race to be ugly by nature.

I would define racism as a supremacist asserting his supremacy. Frank King doesn't make an assertion so much as he exercises an assumption. You see no malice, but you do see a thoughtless acceptance of what might be called the Myth of Contentment. This myth is composed not only of the belief that all reasonable African-Americans were content with their status, but that their status was a natural one. This latter belief is in and of itself a racial libel. King doesn't recognize the richness of the culture Rachel came out of, but, with all the will in the world, a white man was never a good medium for recording this. An electronic device was most effective, and it was best preserved on phonograph records made by people left alone in a room with a microphone.

For a pure and malicious assertion of supremacy you need go no further than Chester Gould and *Dick Tracy*. You're always in for trouble when Gould tries to prove his theory that he had a sense of humor, an experiment that would usually involve dialect and would always involve stereotypes, and no Gould comic-relief character is more wince-inducing than Memphis Smith, who makes his bow (and I do mean bow) on May 1, 1936. As we meet him he is the valet of gangster Lips Manlis. Gould eschews the standard golliwog physiognomy; he means to create an original slur. What he means to do mostly is to show Memphis' natural sense of cowardice, and he does so through the clumsy device of showing the character perpetually trembling and sweating. In the story, Lips unwisely enlists Memphis in a plot against Tracy. To this proposal Memphis replies, "But . . . but . . . I don't

TOP

Chester Gould's May 3, 1936 *Dick Tracy* strip [©1936 Tribune Media Services, Inc.]

503

undislike . . . nobody, not even cops, Mist' Lips. I's a friend of all mankind, I is." (Ellipses representing quavering.) When Tracy tries to drag Memphis ("Snowball," he calls him) along with him into Lips' booby trap, Memphis immediately spills all. Once Tracy guns Lips down, Memphis, seeing the dangers in serving gangsters, tries to attach himself to Tracy as his valet. But Memphis is no nobly faithful servant like Rachel. Rather, his is the dog-like servility of a lesser creature trying to attach himself to a superior, and Tracy at all times treats him with the contempt he shares with his creator. Fortunately, Memphis didn't become the fixture that Vitamin Flintheart or Gravel Gertie did, irksome as they were. One of the surest bets in mass entertainment is that the worst expression of racism you've seen is not the worst there is, but I will bet that Memphis is in the upper percentiles.

The main difference between the characterizations of Rachel and Memphis is that while Rachel can be ridiculous (as most characters in *Gasoline Alley* are at some time or another) she doesn't exist to be the target of ridicule the way Memphis does. Unlike Rachel or Ebony in *The Spirit* or Connie in *Terry and the Pirates*, Memphis has no virtues to offset his faults. While his vices will at times work to Tracy's advantage he is of absolutely no use in time of danger. You find the same sort of racial ridicule in *Captain Marvel*, and it becomes all the more glaring in contrast to the seeming wholesome-ness of the comic otherwise. I have to wonder how closely DC examined the "Monster Society of Evil" serial before they committed to their long-delayed reprint of it. I imagine an exchange like this:

Editor 1: "You know, that stuff is kind of racist . . ."

Editor 2: (*shuffling through pages*): "Well, we'll have the usual introduction ex-plaining how under the standards of the time . . . Holy Jesus!"

TOP
Billy De Beck's
June 25, 1920
Barney Google
strip [©1920
King Features
Syndicate, Inc.]

504

Somewhere between the good faith of Frank King and the bad faith of Chester Gould you will find Billy DeBeck of *Barney Google* and Fred Willard of *Moon Mullins*. DeBeck was the lowlife cartoonist nonpareil, and with him you get lowlife attitudes straight up. He has reverence for no one and makes allowances for no one, nor does he make concessions to any sort of propriety, social enlightenment included. He doesn't make black characters the subject of pure ridicule the way Gould or *Captain Marvel* does, but neither do you find a trace of the attempted good faith of King, or even the affectionate regard of Milton Caniff or Will Eisner. It should be said though that black characters are a part of Barney Google's world as free agents rather than as servants. I would need a little deeper reading into him but I think that Willard is a rougher article than DeBeck, though racial caricature was a more ubiquitous feature of *Barney Google*. None of it is strictly defensible, and anyone who does reprint *Google* or *Mullins* will have heat to take and little cover other than absolute freedom of speech. The moral question becomes whether one wishes to profit from this material, and in our correspondence Heer mentioned that he had talked about a *Barney Google* project with Drawn & Quarterly but the racial angle was one of several factors that made him reluctant to pursue it. Craig Yoe is scheduled to give it a try with IDW this year.

Along with King, Jeet proposed Harold Gray, Roy Crane and Alex Raymond as the least racist cartoonists of the generation of the '30s and though Crane hadn't particularly registered that way with me, he was echoing what I'd long thought about Gray and Raymond. I think you can err in finding Gray's ethnic egalitarianism anomalous in view of his politics. Conservatism and racism are often shacked up but they're not necessarily married (and of course in the 1930s and after the party of the New Deal and the southern segregationist

LEFT
From Frank H. Willard's *Moon Mullins* [©1930 The Chicago Tribune]

motherfucker faction *were* married). Gray's politics were too instinctive and whimsical to fit into any conventional framework. Besides, conservative or not he was an idealist, and there's no telling what an idealist will be idealistic about. The one that's really surprising to me is Raymond, not because you'd have to think he was racist, but that there's nothing to indicate that he would be ahead of the curve. Stranger still, it was on display in *Jungle Jim*, King Features' answer to the great white supremacist fantasy *Tarzan*. (Jeet informs me that William Randolph Hearst discouraged black, though not other, racist caricature in his comic strips on the basis that it was ultimately bad for business — though one wonders whether this might be a perverse smoke screen for enlightenment when enlightenment was not the mode.) *Jungle Jim* was not only the least racist but also the least sexist comic strip of its time. Jim's "body servant" Kolu is not only depicted without a trace of stereotype, but was courageous, intelligent and capable. A character like Connie in *Terry and the Pirates* might be clever and provide the deliverance of his comrades, but was at all times ridiculous. Kolu, while always a subordinate, was accorded full dignity. Shanghai Lil, Jim's love interest, was not even subordinate, but an independent freebooter and even a little larcenous. (You could make a case for Gray's Annie too, but given her prowess as an entrepreneur, crimefighter, spy and assassin she's more a prepubescent John Galt than a feminist.) *Jungle Jim* is a major missing piece in all three waves of classic comic-strip reprints.

In my first go-round on racial caricature some years ago ("The Misapprehension of the Coon Image" TCJ #250), I proposed four broad categories of racial caricature: the Sentimental, the Sentimental/Condescending, the Condescending and the Vicious. Of the comic strips under discussion here, I would

TOP
From Alex Raymond's
Jan. 15, 1939 *Jungle Jim*
[©1939 King Features
Syndicate, Inc.]

place *Gasoline Alley* in the Sentimental/Condescending, *Barney Google*, *Moon Mullins*, *Terry and the Pirates* and *The Spirit* in the Condescending, *Dick Tracy* and *Captain Marvel* in the Vicious, and *Little Orphan Annie* and *Jungle Jim* out of the scale altogether. I realized while looking at Fredrik Stromberg's *Black Images in the Comics* that there was a huge segment of the Vicious that I had neglected altogether, and that was the depiction of the savage. This is a key subgenre both because it shows its makers' conception of Africans in the state of nature and because it presents white supremacy in its purest form. In the typical situation, the Caucasian representative is set alone against a tribe of

cannibals and makes fools of them. I referred earlier to *Tarzan* as the great white supremacist fantasy, which it absolutely was in its written version, but Burne Hogarth's version stays just on the right side of a razor's edge. It was not helped by Hogarth's choice of Afrikaners as the ideal civilized white men, a choice that modern readers ought to be aware was made before the formal adoption of the Apartheid policy. Hogarth's Africans are depicted as reasonably fit and noble savages, although like most of Hogarth's characters they tend to look really angry at all times. However, they are depicted as dependent on Tarzan's protection, as part of the jungle of which he is lord, and are fairly easily manipulated by bad white men, always the strip's primary villains. The conceptual problem is that in Hogarth's vision Tarzan is the ideal natural man, and you might wonder why the natives wouldn't be at least as natural as he was. (Presumably the answer is that Tarzan is closer to the animals.)

The most commonly depicted savages are the American Americans, the Indian nations, and their depiction provides an instructive contrast. The virulence of the racial slander of African-Americans evolves from necessity, the necessity of rationalizing the institution of slavery. Slavery is one of those things you can't not know is wrong, and if you're going to base your economy on it you're going to have to justify as much to yourself as others. As such, the image is defined on all levels by inferiority. Even those who were sympathetic defined the African-American in terms of oppression suffered and justice owed rather than personal worthiness. The image of the American Americans is on the other hand a mélange of mockery, respect, bitterness, bad conscience and chagrin. The mockery stems in part from the European American tendency to find elements of American American culture to be

TOP

Panel from Hal Foster's *Tarzan* strip [©1939 Edgar Rice Burroughs, Inc.]

507

508

TOP
Chester Gould's
May 22, 1935 Dick
Tracy strip [©1936
Tribune Media
Services, Inc.]

comical, a prime example being the names they gave themselves. The respect and the bitterness derive largely from the fact that the European Americans and the American Americans fought a war over a land they both wanted, and when the American Americans found themselves at an advantage in this war they could be cruel in their own right. The bad conscience and chagrin stem from the injustice and cruelty of the peace imposed and the often-repressed knowledge that to fail to find a way to share a continent in a decent fashion is a great failure indeed. Slavery was never a failure in this sense, but a success in doing something ghastly and atrocious. The feelings of bad conscience and chagrin would often express themselves in mockery of the defeated.

In the same volume of IDW's *Dick Tracy* reprints where we meet Memphis we also encounter Chief Yellowpony, who aids Tracy in capturing Boris Arson. While not so abject as Memphis he is a deeply silly character, his flabby physique a mockery of the image of the noble red man, his clothing a mismatched mélange of paleface and native accoutrements. He is also that recurring figure of repressed bad conscience, the Indian who has grown rich from the mineral wealth on the reservation he was deeded by the nation, which for some uncanny reason he has been allowed to keep. It is as if to say No Indians Were Harmed in the Making of This Country. (This is seen again in the musical *Annie Get Your Gun*, where Sitting Bull is asked to bankroll Buffalo Bill's Wild West Show with the proceeds of his mythical oil wells.) As we leave Yellowpony he says, "Crime bad medicine! Always lead to same place, long dark night underground. Ugh!"

Californy 'Er Bust, an animated cartoon I saw recently, crystallized in my mind the element of bitterness. Like all racially dubious cartoons included in the *Disney Treasures* series it is accompanied by a *mea exculpa* introduction from Leonard Maltin which simultaneously owns up to and tries to soft-pedal the racist elements of the cartoon. For *Californy* along with "standards of the time" mealy-mouth Maltin attempts to pass it off in some sense as a parody of racism. While the cartoon is a parody of Western movie clichés, and in particular the ambush of the wagon train, what it brought home to me is that when these clichés were formulated these battles were very nearly living memory, and some of the victors had not yet forgiven the vanquished. It's something that's once or twice removed in the cartoon, but I think you can see it there.

The notion that Walt Disney was particularly racist, which has gotten such folkloric traction these days, seems to me more a reflection of the desire to cut down the saintly Disney image than something you'd see from his cartoons. Put it this way, if Walt Disney was a racist, then Leon Schlesinger was the Grand Dragon of the Ku Klux Klan. While there is racial caricature to be seen in Disney cartoons, it is for the most part incidental (for instance, the gag, which no animator seemed to be able to resist, where a character falls into a pile of ashes and comes out a golliwog), it is far less frequent and less malicious than what you'd see from other studios. (I'd have to take another close look to come to a conclusion about the Fleischer Brothers. It seems in some cartoons almost as if they treat Cab Calloway or Louis Armstrong as collaborators. Take for instance "I'll Be Glad When You're Dead, You Rascal You," which is essentially a music video *avant la lettre*. It starts out with live-action footage of Armstrong and his band performing the song in full formal stage finery, which is something to see in itself. When animation breaks out it's a Betty Boop on the escape from the cannibals theme. Through much of the cartoon, Koko the Clown runs through the jungle pursued by the disembodied head of the cannibal chief singing the song, which morphs back and forth between the live superimposed head of Armstrong singing. You might assume that an equivalence is being made between Armstrong and the cannibal, but the sheer benevolence of Armstrong makes the cannibal business seem a joke.)

The primary onscreen evidence for Disney-as-racist is *Song of the South*, the animated and live-action adaptation of the Uncle Remus stories. Or not onscreen, as it has been dropped down the Disney corporate memory hole, and can only now be retrieved in chunks on YouTube. What you see at work is a Frank King-like conscientiousness and a similarly King-like limitation of perspective. It seems clear to me that what the film is striving for in the voice characterizations is ethnic authenticity, not an ethnic slur. I think it's equally a sign of Disney's good intentions and lack of awareness that his first choice to play Uncle Remus was Paul Robeson. What is objectionable about *Song of the South* is that it's one of the purest expressions of the afore-mentioned Myth of Contentment, and it was just getting awfully late in the day to be doing so. Indeed, Uncle Remus' whole mission in the film is to reconcile all parties with the way things are. The trouble with Disney was not that he was racist but that he was relentlessly middlebrow. His work is relatively free of racism for the same reason that it's often so tepid, a determination above all else to do no harm.

Recently for the first time since I was a child I watched *Gone With the Wind*, which is found on the other side of the coin from *Birth of a Nation*. *Birth of a Nation* is probably the closest thing there is to an evil work of art. When

the Directors Guild of America announced that they would no longer name their annual award after D.W. Griffith because that film "helped foster intolerable racial stereotypes" they were speaking nonsense; those stereo-types had been fostered long before and were fully mature. *Birth of a Nation* is an evil work of art because in obscuring the true nature of the Ku Klux Klan it provided cover for evil-doers to do their evil. It's a work of art with a body count. (*Triumph of the Will* isn't in the same league because unlike the earlier film it does nothing to conceal the true nature

of its subject. The Nazis understood that the democracies were unwilling to face the true nature of their enemies, and so they had no reason to hide it.) Where *Birth of a Nation* presents the South's mythical version of Reconstruction, *Gone With the Wind* represents the victor's acquiescence to that myth, and the abandonment of the freedmen to the tender mercies of their former masters. It's very strange in the dog whistles it gives to its Southern audience. For instance, the movie's great villains, the carpetbaggers, are represented as a black man singing "Marching Through Georgia" (very well, by the way) sitting in a coach next to an oily-looking white man with a carpetbag on his lap. In the streets of Atlanta, we see small groups of black occupying troops, present but not doing anything in particular. While the Southern viewer is free to see this as the equivalent of Griffith's portrait of the South under the tyranny of the colored, the makers can plausibly deny that this is their intention. No, you could see them explaining to the representative of the NAACP, it's the white fellow who's the carpetbagger, the one who's singing is just along for the ride, and the troopers, why they're just troopers. The reason I bring it up in this context is that we see crystallized in *Gone With the Wind* the attitude of the era I'm discussing to African-Americans: They are either a convenience or an inconvenience. They are fine to have around when they're faithful servants or a source of merriment for their betters, but in any other context the society would rather have them out of sight, and pretend they aren't there. I've always been ambivalent about the Director's Guild's gesture in ceasing to honor Griffith. On the one hand, evil is as evil does. On the other hand, the fact that he made an evil work of art doesn't make him any less the father of American film directors. I don't think you can cut the rotten spots out of your cultural history the way you would out of an apple. What you would have left is not a good and wholesome history. What you have left is a lie. ■

511

LEFT
Song of the South (1946)
[©Walt Disney Productions]

TOP
Walt Disney wrote and Win Smith drew this panel from the Mickey Mouse comic strip.
[©1930 King Features Syndicate, Inc.]

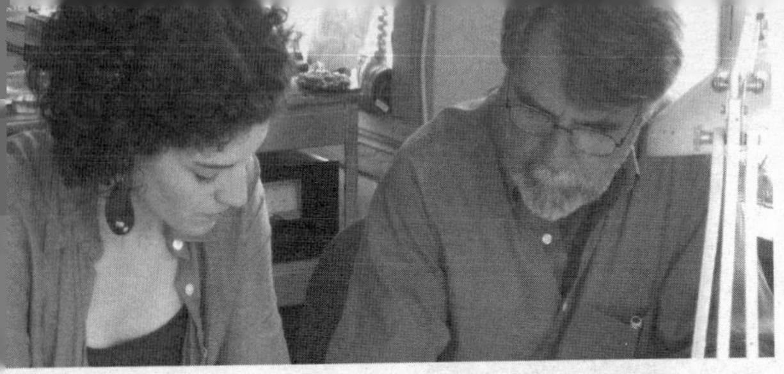
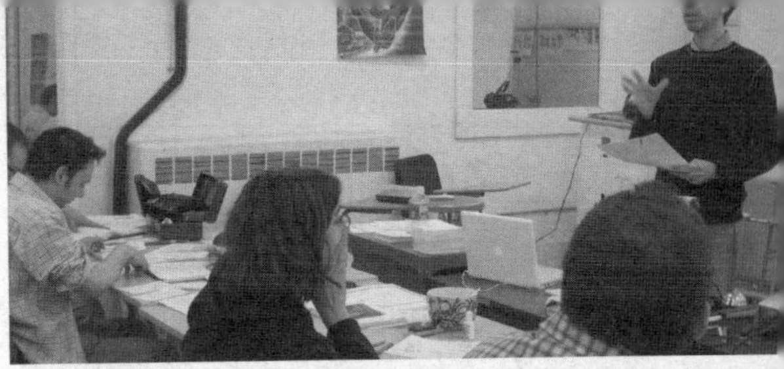
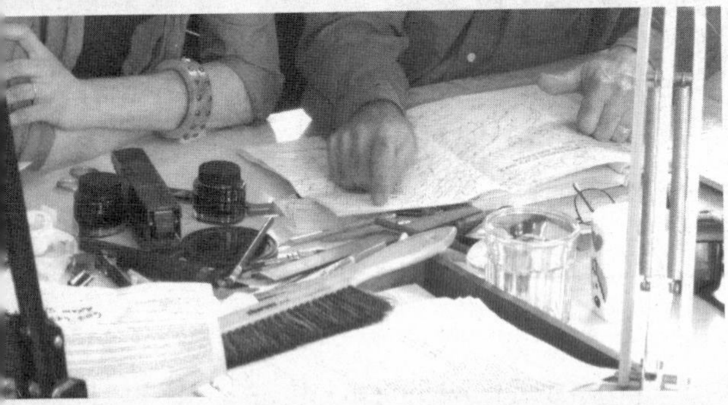
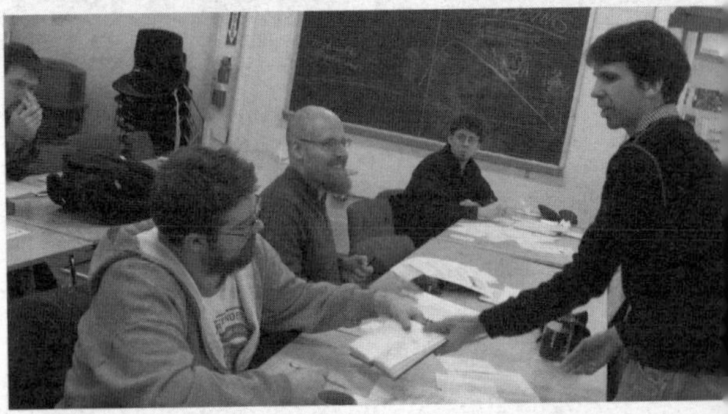
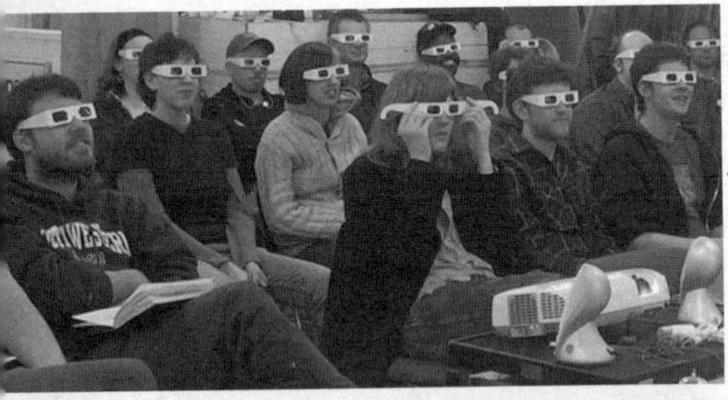
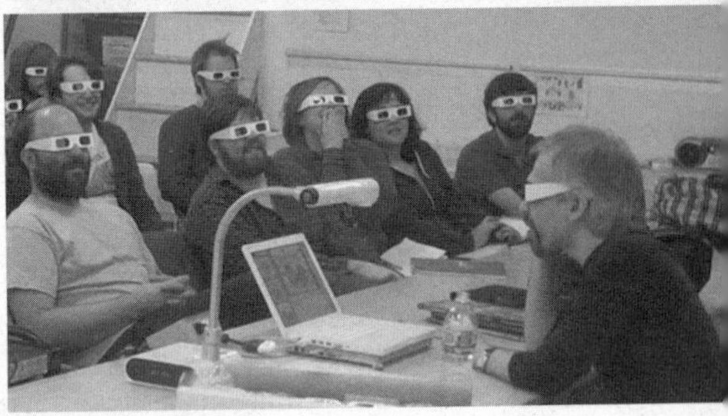
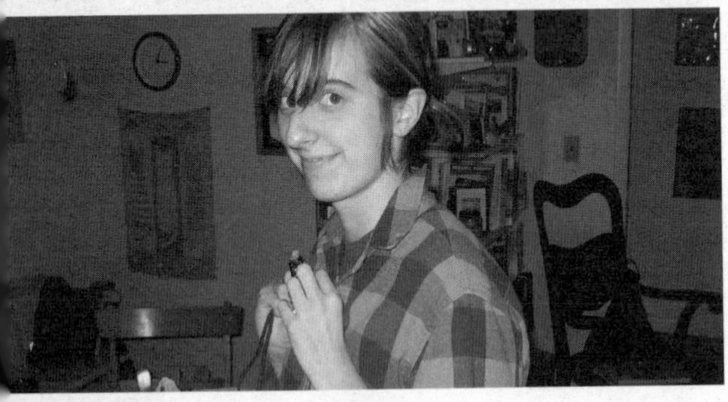
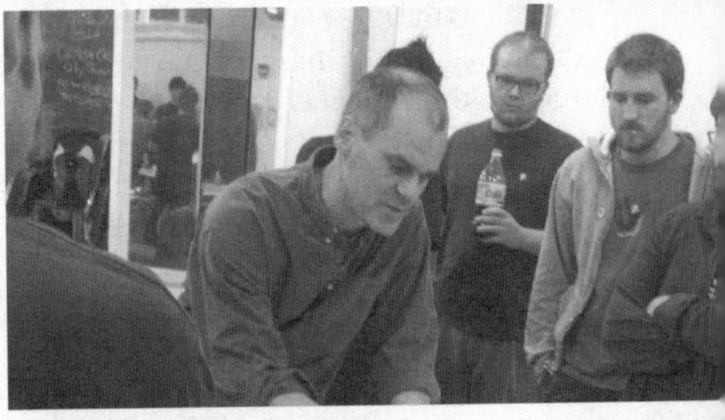
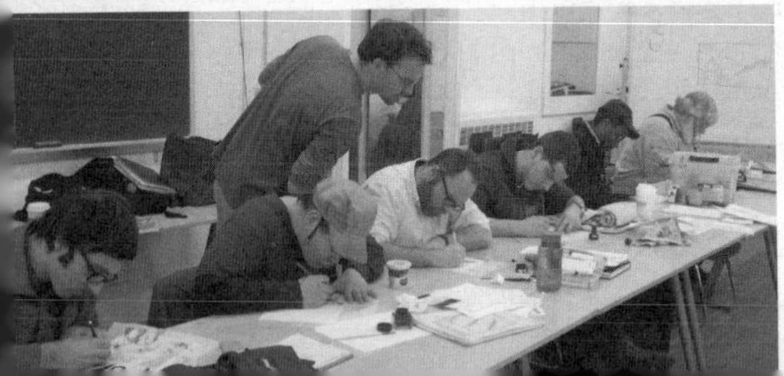
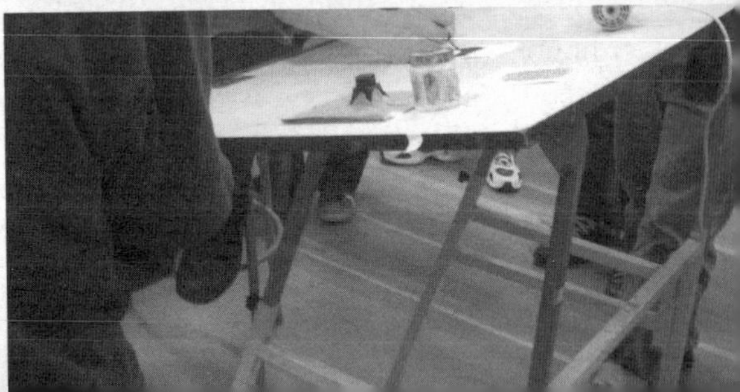

CARTOONISTS LEADING CARTOONISTS:

THE TRIALS AND REWARDS OF GETTING MENTORED BY THE LIKES OF ALISON BECHDEL, JEFF SMITH, STAN SAKAI, R. SIKORYAK, JESSE REKLAW, DENIS KITCHEN, TOM HART, DYLAN HORROCKS, DAVID MACAULAY AND EVAN DORKIN

BY ROB CLOUGH

Matt Aucoin was always anxious to hear back from his senior thesis advisor, Stan Sakai, because "I would wonder how bad I messed up each time. But that's the same with every critique. Stan was always so polite when he gave a critique, that it was never disheartening. Stan was also very patient with me." At the Center for Cartoon Studies, the nature of each student-mentor interaction is different for each artist, but it seems that nearly every student wants the unvarnished truth. "He asked me flat out, 'How much feedback do you want me to give you on your work?' I told him, 'I want it all, everything you've got.' Stan let out a long sigh and then jumped into all the holes I had with [my comic] *Die, Baby, Die!* He understood what I was going for, but I had sorely missed the mark on my first draft. He added a few scenes, and told me how he would tell that story."

Having a mentor is a rare opportunity for young cartoonists to hone technical aspects of their craft that they might not have the opportunity to either develop on their own or in a larger classroom setting. "I felt that Stan's strong points were my weak points as a cartoonist, and I wanted to work on those as much as I could in my senior year. Stan's great at lettering, storytelling, page layout, composition, perspective and pacing. I wanted to be great at those things too." Going into specifics, Aucoin said, "He would tell me the panels that worked and let me know of the ones that didn't. He would even go so far as to print out my pages, draw all over them, and

LEFT
Clockwise from top left:
All photographs taken
by Robin Chapman
unless otherwise noted.
Katherine Roy, left,
and her advisor, David
Macaulay (photo credit
Katherine Roy); two
of Tom Hart teaching;
R. Sikoryak instructs;
James Sturm demon-
strates; Jason Lutes and
class; Melissa Men-
des, both pictured and
photo credit; students.

send them back to me. This was a real treat, getting to see Stan draw my characters in his style. At first, I didn't want to redraw the panels and told him so. After thinking about it, I realized that he was right and ended up redrawing every panel he suggested. Stan was the kind of advisor who told me everything I did wrong, but in such a gentle manner that I never felt put out. After getting feedback from him, I was ready and excited to go back to the drawing board."

Interviewing nearly two dozen graduates of CCS, I discovered the quality of the student-advisor relationship tended to vary widely. Sometimes a negative experience was the fault of an advisor who wasn't prepared to commit the sort of time and effort that a motivated student would need. Sometimes students were inadequately organized and didn't follow through on their commitments. On other occasions, students and advisors simply weren't appropriate matches on an aesthetic level. Every graduate had different advice for future students on how best to make this relationship work, but Aucoin hit the nail on the head when he said, "The ball is mostly in the student's court. If you can't produce work for your advisor to critique, they can't critique your work. If you don't tell them what kind of feedback you want and need, they might not give it to you."

Creating Cartoon College

Teaching cartooning at a university level is not a new idea. Indeed, the School of Visual Arts was co-founded by legendary cartoonist Burne Hogarth. There are a handful of other institutions where one can learn how to become a cartoonist, like the Savannah College of Art & Design (SCAD) and the Minneapolis College of Art & Design (MCAD). Those schools offer cartooning and illustration programs as individual majors that are part of a more diverse curriculum. Then there's the Kubert School of Cartoon & Graphic Art, a trade school that seeks to train the next generation of genre artists.

The expanded curricula from these schools has been a response to the rising demand by young cartoonists for formal education. Whereas art schools used to sneer at comics as an art form (one is reminded of Daniel Clowes' classic short story "Art School Confidential"), such pedagogy has now become much more widely accepted. The fact that such highly regarded cartoonists as Gary Panter, Zak Sally, David Mazzucchelli and Carol Tyler are faculty members at various art schools and universities is a testament to how seriously those institutions have responded to this

"Steve Bissette has used the word 'tribe' to describe the unique community here. I think it's apt."

demand. That said, the cartooning programs at these schools are a small part of those institutions' overall scope. To a certain degree, the schools had to adjust to the demand by expanding programs, rather than building a cartooning program from the ground up. There wasn't an art school whose sole focus was on comics — not animation, not illustration — until quite recently.

In 2005, cartoonist James Sturm and designer Michelle Ollie founded the Center for Cartoon Studies in the small town of White River Junction, Vt. Sturm had been a professor at SCAD and Ollie at MCAD, and they pooled their collective experiences to create a vision of a pedagogy for comics that sought to provide training and guidance for young cartoonists, pushing them to put theory into practice right away. What at first appeared to be a quixotic notion has now blossomed into a successful enterprise, thanks to the generosity of state and local governments and the kindness (and resources) of dozens of important figures from the world of comics. (Full disclosure: TCJ publisher Gary Groth is a member of the school's advisory board.) Indeed, what sustained CCS through its earliest months was a sound business plan that attracted investors. A look at its board of directors includes publishers, local businesspeople, nonprofit experts and academicians. After years of experience as educators, it was obvious that Ollie and Sturm put a great deal of thought into this endeavor.

While the school is not accredited (a drawback that prevents them from being able to offer federal loans to students), it has been granted the ability to offer MFAs. This has no doubt helped them in getting more prospective students to apply, given the promise of a degree that might help them earn future positions in academia. Wisely, Ollie and Sturm decided to open CCS up to those who did not have college degrees, allowing for a more diverse student population. Those accepted for the two-year MFA program were welcome with a degree in any academic discipline; no previous training in art was required or expected. From the very beginning, Sturm made it clear that he viewed cartooning, storytelling and drawing as distinctly separate but related skills. That's certainly reflected in the first-year courses, which all students are required to take. It was also clear that he thought all three could be taught to highly motivated students.

The initial founding of the school drew mixed reactions in the world of comics. Some observers sneered at the idea of paying $30,000 to learn how to make minicomics. A few veteran artists scoffed at the notion of formal education being needed to learn how to become a cartoonist. So many members of the underground and early alt-comics generations were self-taught that they viewed this as the best way to learn the craft. They possessed a sense of the artist as rugged individualist, making comics solely to please themselves. The idea of submitting to someone else's idea of what making a comic should be and being judged on it at a formal level was perhaps anathema to them. At a deeper level, this critique of CCS is more about comics as a manifestation of the cultural zeitgeist than it is about actually learning how to become a cartoonist. For many artists of the underground era, comics were their way of expressing themselves within the greater countercultural framework. For the generation that came to prominence in the early '80s, many saw comics as an extension of the DIY punk rock ethic, with the Hernandez brothers being the most prominent examples. I would contend that it wasn't until what I refer to as the Xeric generation of artists that the idea of outside guidance and assistance became an acceptable part of the culture, a concept that became further entrenched with the rise of alt-comics conventions like A.P.E. and SPX in the late '90s.

While those conventions have a distinctive DIY flavor to them, they've also spawned a new generation of cartoonists eager to be inspired by their peers as well as their elders. What's interesting about CCS is that it's captured the intimacy and community of these convention experiences and has fused it with an intense, demanding curriculum where one is pushed by one's peers as much as one's teachers. In detailing the difference between CCS and other art schools, faculty member Robyn Chapman said, "Probably the most significant difference is size. We only accept 24 students each year. That class of 24 is a very tight community. They all take the same classes, together, for two years. Outside of the classroom, they spend a lot of time together drawing, and also watching movies, playing boardgames, partying, even playing sports — all the normal social activities of college students. But with a lot more drawing.

"As a community, they learn a lot from each other, and they push each other to do their strongest work. The community here is key. I went to SCAD. At that point I think there were a few hundred students in the Sequential Art program. Most of them I never knew, and the few I knew, I didn't know very well. Here, you know all your classmates pretty intimately. [Fellow faculty member] Steve Bissette has used the word 'tribe' to describe the unique community here. I think it's apt."

Hi, parents.

The CCS Curriculum and The Thesis Advisor

The first-year curriculum has been described by Sturm as a "cartoonist boot camp." Each student takes a drawing class (with a life-drawing session), a history of comics survey, a cartooning class, a writing workshop and also participates in visiting-artist seminars. Those have ranged from genre artists to children's book illustrators to minicomics stalwarts to the cream of the alt-comics set. While drawing is obviously crucial in this program, there's an understanding that cartooning itself is a kind of writing and can't be reduced to simple draftsmanship. While this approach is not unique, what is unusual is their early focus on design and publication. Chapman notes, "CCS understands that comics is a publishing art. This may sound basic, but this point is missing from some cartooning programs. Some cartooning programs tend to dissect the medium into its more superficial aspects and focus on methods and techniques. CCS is focused on telling stories and making books. From day one, our students are self-publishing."

TOP
[©2010 Garry-Paul Bonesteel]

The second year at CCS, for those who choose to take it, is as loose as the first year is regimented. The thesis project, to quote materials from the school, is "at the heart of CCS's second year curriculum" and "should reflect two semesters' worth of exploration, culminating in a well-constructed final project." That project is evaluated on the content itself, presentation and the work in context with the amount of time spent on it. The thesis determines a passing or failing grade and so carries with it an enormous amount of pressure, although this is to be expected at any kind of graduate program. During the year, each student meets regularly with both faculty and peers to evaluate works-in-progress in an effort to keep everyone on track. The tight-knit nature of this community, further aided by the lack of distractions in the tiny railroad town of White River Junction, means that no one is forgotten. In addition to these measures, each student is expected to pick a thesis advisor from outside of the school.

As Sturm notes, it is hoped that the advisor will help the student with "the nuts and bolts of their cartooning" but also add "insight as to what it takes to make cartooning the center of their life going forward." Ollie described their role as offering "the benefit of another outside perspective, a point of feedback, extending beyond the interaction with the core faculty of the program and peers." I communicated with two dozen graduates and a handful of advisors about this experience and what it meant to them. That relationship, in many ways, reflected the nature of the thesis process itself, because it forced students to create their own schedules and deadlines and learn to work with other professionals. Sturm said, "The advisors aren't responsible for whip-cracking or grading or anything like that. The onus is on the student to produce work for the advisor to respond to. Every advisor/student relationship is different. [For] some it's a week-to-week engagement, for others it's once or twice a semester. All depends on what makes the most sense to the individual personalities involved."

While Sturm said that the feedback for this process has been "mostly positive," he did note that "sometimes advisors drop the ball; they get too busy with deadlines or on tour or just don't make the proper time for whatever reason." Given that this is a paid position (a prospect that advisors Jesse Reklaw and Evan Dorkin both noted was a significant inducement), there's a risk involved in investing in services that may well not pan out for the students. Chapman notes that CCS understands this possibility and plans around it: "The nature of the thesis advisor relationship depends on the dedication of both parties, the student and the advisor. Sometime that dedication is not adequate — both students and advisors have been guilty of this in the past. That is a reason that advisors are only required to commit to one semester. If the relationship is not working, they can choose to end it after one semester. The same goes for students — if they are not satisfied with their advisor, they can select a new one after one semester."

The Perils of The Advising Process

One thing that became clear in the course of these communications is that picking an advisor was more of an art than a science. For every glowing description of how helpful their advisors were, I also heard stories about advisors who were impossible to track down. Some students had radically different experiences with the same advisor. For example, CCS graduates Sean Ford and Laura Terry had Alison Bechdel as their advisor in different years. Terry was absolutely effusive in her praise for Bechdel and her commitment. After an initial face-to-face meeting (a rarity in this process), Terry set up a "rigorous schedule" with Bechdel, sending a package with her work-to-date on a weekly basis during the first semester. Terry said "Every two weeks we phoned or Skyped and there were occasional e-mails between us. Her criticism was always apt, and she let me know what was working, what wasn't working, and always guided me towards the right path, but was never didactic."

On the other hand, when Ford chose Bechdel a couple of years earlier, he found that "she was incredibly busy with *Fun Home* and working on her next book for Houghton Mifflin and didn't have a ton of time to respond to e-mails." When asked what advice he might give to future students about the process, he concluded it by saying "Don't pick someone who had a book just come out that's forcing them to do book tours. Seriously." Fellow graduate Colleen Frakes echoed this, as both of the advisors she selected wound up going on book tours during her senior year. She still got a good bit out of her brief contacts, as Jeff Smith advised her to "Figure out how the story is going to end before you start it," noting, "You look smarter that way." The input from her second advisor led her to scrap her initial thesis idea, leading to an eventual thesis project that garnered a Xeric grant.

While the needs of each student and the styles of each advisor differed, a few trends emerged in the responses I received. Choosing one of your personal heroes as an advisor wasn't always a good idea. Some of them simply didn't have the skills or temperament to excel as an advisor in some cases, while in other examples the student was too starstruck to establish a real working relationship. One graduate who preferred to remain nameless chose a well-regarded underground legend as an advisor and found that

their styles and personalities clashed to the extent where nothing was gained from the relationship. Sturm said that he tries to "steer students away from some cartoonists, who despite their wonderful work, may not make such great advisors. I also make thesis advisor suggestions, even if the student is not necessarily familiar with the work of that artist." The most-praised advisors tended to be those that either had experience as educators (like Tom Hart) or editors (like R. Sikoryak).

In the case of 2009 CCS graduate Jeremiah Piersol, he had "a lot of difficulty choosing an advisor," wanting someone who would "understand my point of view, and wouldn't push me in a direction of making my work more refined, commercial, etc." Sturm recommended Sikoryak, and Piersol said, "His suggestion turned out to be golden." Based on his experience, Piersol said the process "shouldn't work as an apprentice or mentorship situation like it did, for example, with the old masters of the Renaissance." Instead, Sikoryak guided him in "observing and understanding my own work in new ways that I may not have figured out on my own." In technical terms, he found Sikoryak's understanding of cartooning to be especially valuable, particularly "an emphasis on consistency. Sometimes the same character would look different panel to panel in my work, and with his feedback I recognized this." He emphasized that "having R. Sikoryak as an advisor also made me a hell of a lot less lazy as a cartoonist."

2010 graduate G.P. Bonesteel had a similar experience with Sikoryak, taking him as an advisor at Sturm's suggestion after his first advisor didn't work out for him. Sikoryak zeroed in on his character relationships, noting that they talked to the "camera" instead of each other. Bonesteel said that the reason he did this "was one part laziness and two parts lack of confidence in my own abilities" but this comment "really stuck with me because it's true and will make my work stronger." Both he and Piersol urged fellow students not to pick someone famous because "you love their work and want to meet them" or "attach yourself to someone with a big

520

name, because they have a big name." Piersol further urged them to "go in with a direction," thinking about what particular aspect of your cartooning you want to improve the most and then seek out someone "who does this well, so you can absorb as much information as possible."

Alexis Frederick-Frost, a 2007 graduate (and current faculty member), worked with Jason Lutes, an artist whose work he admired. He didn't get everything he wanted out of the experience, but said "I think my hopes were unreasonable." He felt that Lutes came to his style and path in an intuitive manner, making it difficult to get tough criticism or "concrete changes to a process that is unique to each individual." Like Piersol and Bonesteel, he advised against picking a favorite artist as an advisor, instead suggesting choosing "a good comics editor or critic," someone who "can articulate if the work is effective and where it lacks clarity."

The Advisor As Intuitive Guide

Each artist is different, of course, and some advisors simply possess not just a higher level of dedication than others, but also a different feel for how the process should go and how to interact with their students. Consider the examples of 2010 graduates Jose-Luis Olivares and Jason Week. Olivares chose Dylan Horrocks as his advisor, in large part because he admired his work and the variety of ways in which he's published. In particular, Olivares could sense that Horrocks was an intuitive storyteller, something that he shared with him. Unlike Frederick-Frost's example, where two intuitive storytellers didn't mix, in this relationship, Horrocks explicitly stated that he didn't want to impose his own approach on Olivares, instead wanting to help him "develop [his] own voice and methods." While he saw that Olivares was "exploding with stories and talent," he felt he "needed the confidence" to follow his feelings about making comics. Olivares confirmed this, saying that Horrocks made him "feel comfortable following my own intuition," engaging in a "slow process of trusting myself." It was easy for him to trust Horrocks' opinion because he admired him so much, and while this approach hasn't worked out for everyone, he was fortunate that Horrocks was able to give him exactly what he needed as an artist.

The same was true for Jason Week, who chose Evan Dorkin as his advisor. He had been a long-time admirer of Dorkin's work and knew that, like himself, Dorkin had been self-taught. He also noted that they might

"That's a running theme of CCS itself: the belief that someone can become a working cartoonist in just a couple of years if they are properly motivated and have the right training and support."

have similar temperaments and was especially moved by *Dork #7*, a comic that documented Dorkin's nervous breakdown. "It was enormous to me to see that someone out there was managing similar problems to my own while still pushing his creative life forward." Week took an important step in the student-advisor relationship when he told Dorkin to be absolutely brutal in evaluating his work. He received that critique, but was also excited to find that Dork was "totally honest without being bullying or negative, and being a very incisive critic…nearly every bit of advice or criticism he gave me was something specific I could work on to become a better cartoonist." Dorkin went the extra mile in terms of "panel-by-panel breakdowns of specific strips" and at one point "even wrote out a 10-page Word doc that went through six strips in a row." It was through this process that Week came to understand how much of an influence Dorkin had been on his style, and his advice enabled him to "better direct the cluttered imagery I use, to better individualize the voices of my characters, and to be constantly using background action to build character and push plot forward."

For his part, Dorkin was nervous about diving into this role because he had no previous experience as an instructor. "I didn't attend art school and my critical thinking is more of a from-the-gut sort of thing … I don't feel like an 'expert' at anything in regards to making comics," he explained. That said, he was intrigued by the "test" of trying to "help someone out and get results." Dorkin had no such mentor when he was a younger cartoonist and he felt it "cost me years of development." That's a running theme of CCS itself: the belief that someone can become a working cartoonist in just a couple of years if they are properly motivated and have the right training and support. Dorkin was gratified to see Week's progress, both in terms of effort and "solidifying his style and approach and thinking more aggressively about what he's doing, what he wants and how to get it on the page."

The Educator As Advisor

Tom Hart was named by many as a favorite advisor. For his part, the SVA professor said that "I am always thrilled to be a mentor. I am mostly self-taught, and with the exception for some excellent friendships and peer relationships, I didn't have the active mentoring, yet I believe in its efficacy very much." 2010 graduate Melissa Mendes chose him because she initially was interested in teaching, but, even when she changed course, she valued their relationship because "we share a lot of opinions about creativity and learning" and "whatever my thesis project ended up being about, having an experienced teacher as an advisor would be really helpful." While Mendes chose a more traditional type of advisor, her actual choice was based on feel and a sense of creative compatibility.

She also said that Hart, "because he has so much experience teaching, is probably really conscious about influencing his students. I mean [this] in the sense that as a teacher you don't want to change the way your students draw, you want to make suggestions to them and help them figure out how they draw." This was true of every advisor I received feedback about or from: Mentors did not want to make anyone draw like them, and instead went out of their way to focus on the student's needs and skill sets. Hart added, "Learning to read each student is an important skill, but it often comes down to understanding what they want to do/say, having some insight on how to improve, deepen that, and offering advice where I can. Then, being a very close careful reader and advising on the technical aspects as well." In this particular case, Mendes was deeply impressed that "Tom's style is so free and loose and organic feeling, and then there is soooo much thought and consideration behind it," allowing her to feel comfortable balancing spontaneity and planning. Hart said his greatest reward is having "helped someone articulate themselves better. It's always about communication, and being heard." He would likely be pleased to hear that Mendes considers him to be her "advisor for life."

White River Junction's Power Couple

Katherine Roy and Tim Stout are unusual in a number of different ways as recent graduates of CCS. They were the first husband-and-wife artist duo to be admitted to the school, for starters. Judging from their responses to my inquiry, they were also two of the most self-motivated and focused artists to come from CCS, which was also reflected in their interesting choices for advisor. Roy chose illustrator and author David Macaulay, her junior year advisor at the Rhode Island School of Design (RISD). Roy's background was in illustration and writing, and going to CCS was a way of combining these two skills. Picking up on the themes cited by past graduates, she chose someone that she trusted and worked well with, rather than a star in the world of comics.

Macaulay is not a cartoonist, but offered "a fresh pair of eyes for my work. If he didn't get it, then I needed to redo it. End of story." At the same time, his skill as an illustrator helped her when stuck composing a page; she credits improvement as an artist to being acutely aware of her own weaknesses and choosing an advisor strong in those areas to help her through tough spots. Despite his aid, Roy was occasionally frustrated "that he couldn't tell me what the right answer was, in spite of his experience. That no one can tell you what the right answer is: it's something you have to figure out for yourself. And it can feel like the hardest thing in the world."

Tim Stout, on the other hand, faced a different problem. "During my first year at CCS, I found I had more skills in writing and editing than in drawing." The enterprising Stout started a "consultation service for comics storytelling called Coffee-4-Crit" and realized that his future lay in editing and writing. As such, he wanted an advisor who was comfortable in both roles, along with the business aspect of comics, and so he chose former Kitchen Sink publisher Denis Kitchen. His influence on Stout would wind up being different than the usual advisor presence; Stout said Kitchen "had more of an impact on the business materials I sent him [than on his comics]. His savvy business sense

has helped me in the design of my business card, letterhead, envelopes, cover letters, resumes, etc. Even though we are entering the art field as 'artists' we will have to be business people to make a living, so it's best to be prepared for that." That's right in line with one of the stated goals of the school, that students should be learning lessons that will keep cartooning as a central focus in their lives. CCS, by its nature, is not for dilettantes.

On a different note, when asked what he might have done differently, Stout said that he regretted attempting to write an entire graphic novel as his thesis project, because "Denis had difficulty giving big-picture critiques on a work in progress and by the time I would receive feedback from him about little changes, I had already received similar comments from the faculty or my peers. In hindsight, if I had wanted to fully utilize the relationship I had with Denis during my thesis year, I would have focused on short pieces and I would have worked on multiple shorts at a time, [so that] while waiting for critiques on one project, I'd write the rough draft for another." The fact that virtually every advisor was far from Vermont certainly had an impact, and Stout felt like doing those shorter pieces would have made more sense. CCS grad J.P. Coovert agreed, saying "If you decide to do a graphic novel, don't expect to finish it. Maybe try doing some smaller stories too and just writing/thumbnailing your book." Advisor Jesse Reklaw summed it up by saying "Young cartoonists always want to make a graphic novel or a monthly comic series, even though everyone encourages them to start small with 6-10 page short stories. I guess some things have to be learned the hard way."

TOP

Art by CCS advisor David Macaulay from his *Built to Last* project photographed by Katherine Roy [©2010 David Macaulay]

The Hard Work Of Community

The underlying themes I detected from the feedback of students and advisors alike were the notions of community, continuity between generations and the need to reach out to other cartoonists. A number of advisors indicated that they were eager to take the position because they admired what the school was doing and had been following the output of its students. Others, such as Jeffrey Brown, talked about their own journeys as young cartoonists in terms of motivation. Brown felt that, "I've been extremely fortunate to have an older generation of cartoonists who have mentored me in various ways to various extents, and I think it's good to pass that on. I also think that there's a lot one can learn from trying to help someone else understand their work, things which can then help one see their own work in new ways." Jesse Reklaw also indicated that he wanted "to give back to the comics community through advising, pedagogy, and general support," but also said that the fact he was self-taught motivated him to want to help young cartoonists. A number of advisors indicated that they were intrigued by this role because they had given some thought to teaching on a more formal basis, and being an advisor gave them the opportunity for a one-on-one dry run.

The nature of the community created at CCS, for both student-student and student-advisor relationships, is not one of unconditional praise. "Team comics" this isn't. Students at CCS quickly learn to develop a thick skin, and

RIGHT
[©2010 Katherine Roy]

many are even eager to receive the most brutally honest critiques possible. Indeed, as a critic who's focused a lot of attention on CCS student work, I've been amazed to see that thick skin in action. CCS students are grateful for in-depth feedback, even (and frequently especially) when it focuses on weaknesses and mistakes. The community that CCS fosters demands hard work and values a relentless commitment to improvement. The time and money invested by each student in the experience lends itself to attracting only the most motivated of students, an advantage that is instrumental in fostering this culture of constantly striving to get better.

In many respects, the thesis year is an opportunity for students to not only demonstrate what they've learned, but to also reveal how far they have to go. It's a dry run for the process of becoming a professional cartoonist, or at least someone who makes comics one of the top priorities in his or her life. This is the chance for young artists to figure out what they're trying to do as creators. Roy said, "I want to make work for anyone who wants to read it, and I try to consider the clarity, accessibility and audience at all times. To think of my reader, but not for my reader." It's a chance for young cartoonists to see their work through the eyes of a professional. However, as Stout warns, "Your advisor is not meant to be an all-knowing vending machine of comics wisdom. They are meant to be a professional contact. Build a relationship with them. They want to help, so make it easy: learn their strengths, ask questions directed to those strengths and be ready for feedback."

Most of all, it's an opportunity for the student to carefully decide how to best utilize an available resource so as to get better. As Terry said, "I figure that choosing an advisor is hit or miss. They might not be helpful, and even if you get someone really great, life happens and that person may not be able to spend as much time tutoring as they thought. If you get a dedicated advisor, then don't be afraid to take the bull by the horns. Set the schedule and the tone for the relationship. You've got to let them know what you want, otherwise how the hell are you going to get it?" That attitude fits right in with Sturm's vision for the process: "The advisors are incredibly important to CCS's program, but all the hard work still has to be done by the student. The student's individual grit is by far the most important element of their education."

The author wishes to thank the students and faculty of CCS for the time they took to answer his many questions, especially during thesis review period. Special thanks go to Robyn Chapman, who went above and beyond to answer any and every query presented to her.

527

TOP
Art by CCS advisor
David Macaulay from
his *Built to Last* project
photographed by
Katherine Roy [©2010
David Macaulay]

OKAY! I'M READY, KITTY!

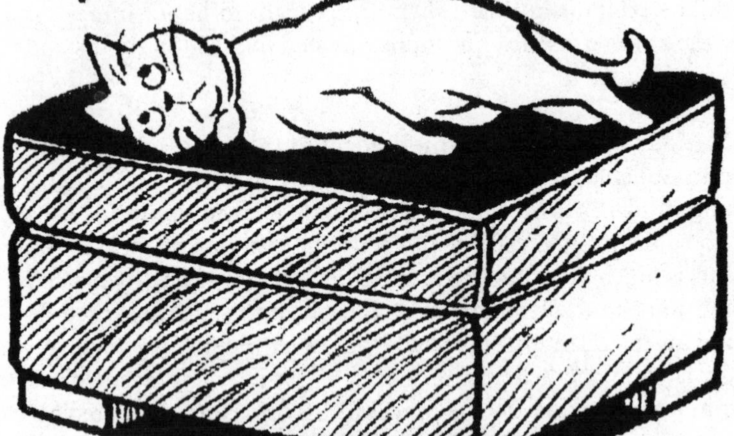

GUS ARRIOLA AND THE COMIC STRIP THAT NEVER WAS— UNTIL NOW

BY R.C. HARVEY

When I visited him in Carmel, Calif., Gus Arriola sometimes introduced me to his friends by saying, "He's the man who knows where all the warts are buried" — or words to that effect. He was exaggerating. He usually introduced the late Carmel cartoonist Bill Bates as "the father of our country" because Bates had so many children. The allusion was a little vague so Bates felt obliged to explain, which he did: "He says that because I have so many children." Bates then did the decent thing; he refrained from pulling out a wallet and showing us photographs of all his kids.

Gus was flattering me because I'd written a book about his life and career and creation, the comic strip *Gordo*, which, from 1941 until 1985, retailed the humorous adventures and amorous preoccupations of a portly Mexican bean farmer, his perspicacious nephew, the menagerie of their farm animals and the other citizens of their village. Published in 2000, the book is entitled *Accidental Ambassador Gordo* because of the strip's unique evolution.

At first, Arriola's depiction of his characters perpetuated the stereotypical imagery of Mexicans found in Hollywood and American popular culture. Eventually, however, Gus realized his comic strip was one of the few mass

ALL IMAGES
Pussy Willow
[©2010 The Estate
of Gus Arriola]

promulgations in the United States that portrayed Mexicans, and in the 1950s he began to take pains to reflect accurately the culture south of the border. Converting his protagonist to a tour guide in the 1960s, Gus was able to regale American readers with many aspects of Mexican folklore, history and art in an entertaining (but informative) fashion, winning awards and accolades for his efforts.

Because the animal (and later, insect) characters in the strip had always been one of its chief attractions, Arriola was creatively positioned to stump for ecological concerns, and he was one of the earliest figures in popular culture to do so. Gus was also a supremely inventive stylist, and his artwork always displayed visual qualities unusual for a comic strip, including, on Sundays, stunning fiestas of color and design.

I loved the strip. All of my life, it seems, I've loved it. When I was a teenager aspiring to be a cartoonist, I apprenticed myself to Gus' drawing style and tried to imitate the way he made lines wax and wane in symphonic undulation. It was my admiration for the strip that prompted me in 1997 to suggest to Gus that I do a book about him and his creation. He consented, and so I wrote the book and became, by Gus' estimation, the one who knew where all the warts were.

In my conceit, glowing a little at Gus' accolade, I surrendered, for a moment, to the idea that I did know about all the warts. But of course I didn't. The book navigates the main currents of Arriola's life and the history of one of this country's most remarkable comic strips, but it doesn't — it can't — include all the warts of Gus' life any more than it can include all of the triumphs and beauty marks.

I found that out fairly soon after the book was published. I got an e-mail from someone who wanted to get in touch with Gus' wife, Frances, because

Frances had once, briefly, been married to my would-be correspondent's father or uncle or some other kind of relative before being married to Gus. Fortunately, I had the sense to ask Gus before passing along his and Frances' mailing address. Gus said Frances wanted to forget about the misbegotten marriage of her youth and didn't want to hear from her previous husband of short duration or any of his relatives. So I did nothing.

Before that exchange, I never knew Frances had been previously married: a wart that had escaped my gimlet-eyed research.

Not gimlet-eyed at all. In the book, I told the story of *Gordo*, how the strip evolved, and I hit the high spots in Gus' career — his initiation into cartooning by way of animation, how *Gordo* was invented and sold, and the agonies

OKAY! I'M
READY, KITTY!
THANK YOU, LOVE!
ZIP
"DOMESTIC PET" TAG IS NO EMPTY LABEL!
THAT
Arriola

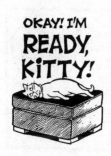

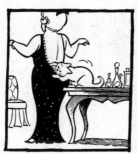

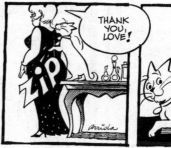

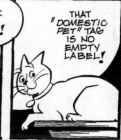

of producing a comic strip every day, day after day after day. I traced the outlines of Gus' life: his growing up in Florence, Arizona; moving to Los Angeles; then, after a stint in the army air corps, La Jolla and Phoenix (where he dined once, by invitation, at Frank Lloyd Wright's); and finally settling in Carmel, where he met his lifelong friend and fellow cartoonist, Eldon Dedini. They both became fixtures at Doc's Lab, where Hank Ketcham and other habitués of the place met weekly to admire jazz and tell stories.

But a friendly and admiring biographer doesn't probe much or very deeply. I found the "story" of Gus' life and career and was content with that. I didn't dig deep enough to find Frances' first marriage (although how I might have found that I can't say). Nor did I know about *Pussy Willow*.

I didn't find out about *Pussy Willow* until I visited Gus for what turned out to be the last time, the summer of 2006. I usually stopped overnight in Carmel on my way back from the San Diego Comic-Con every year. And Gus took me to the Tuesday morning meeting of his coffee klatch with Dedini, Bates, Dennis Renault (an editorial cartoonist who had retired to Monterey from the *Sacramento Bee*) and a couple others, artists and poets all.

Before we left for coffee on this Tuesday, Gus and I were upstairs in his studio, and he pulled out a flat oblong package and unwrapped it. "I don't know if you've ever seen these," he said, laying the contents of the package on the drawing board: six comic-strip originals. But they weren't *Gordo* strips. No, I hadn't seen them. I'd never seen them. Warts galore.

"I sent these to my syndicate," Gus was saying, "but they weren't interested."

Confronted by these wholly unforeseen artifacts, I was so flabbergasted that I failed to ask any questions — so much for reportorial acumen and biographer's compulsions. If Gus told me then when he did the strips, I've forgotten. Or I wasn't listening. Too engaged in being flabbergasted.

I have the impression that he did these strips after he'd retired in 1985 from doing *Gordo*. As I reflect upon it, I'm a little amazed. Gus did not enjoy life with deadlines, the life of a daily comic-strip cartoonist. Why, after he'd finally escaped that life, would he want to return to it?

Perhaps, despite the unrelenting pressure of the calendar's clock, he missed doing a comic strip. Or maybe my impression is wrong; maybe Gus conjured up this strip about a cat and its mistress before he retired from *Gordo*. That's more likely.

One of the things that probably made doing *Gordo* tough in its last years was Gordo's nephew Pepito's presence in the strip. Over the years, Pepito had become more and more a reflection of Gus' son Carlin as the boy grew into adolescence and then young manhood. But Carlin had died of injuries received in an automobile accident in 1980. Gus couldn't help but be reminded of Carlin every time he drew Pepito — even when he drew Gordo.

So maybe what Gus wanted to do by retiring from *Gordo* was to escape reminders of his deceased son. And maybe he couldn't, right then, afford to retire, so he came up with another strip idea, something with no one like Pepito in it. And when that didn't sell, he had to keep on with *Gordo* for another four or five years, until, at last, he thought he could afford to retire.

But I don't actually know when, or why, the strip was created: I was too overwhelmed by the discovery of another wart — and by the beauty of the drawings in the strips — to ask the relevant questions.

"It's called *Pussy Willow*," Gus said, as he spread the strips out before me. "It's about a cat."

Gus was renowned for his ability to draw cats. Charles Schulz, who couldn't draw a cat and therefore was forced to leave Snoopy's feline nemesis forever off-camera, once wrote at length about Gus and drawing cats:

> Cats are hard to draw. I would say that trying to draw a good cat is like trying to draw a good Christmas tree. You have to decide at the very beginning if you are going to draw every detail on the

tree or if you are going to go for a broad design and draw only the outline like little kids do who are in the first grade. I never have been able completely to solve the problem and I once even had a cat in my own comic strip, but when I compared him with Gus' cat, I knew I was in over my head. My admiration for the drawing that Gus puts into Gordo knows no bounds. Gus can draw anything. Better than that, Gus can cartoon anything, and there is a world of difference. I know that Gus can cartoon a good Christmas tree, and we certainly know that he has solved the problem of cartooning a good cat. Now drawing is only half the problem. A good cartoonist has to understand his subject, and you will quickly agree that Gus understands cats. He understands how you can love a cat, and he also understands

how you can hate a cat. There are lots of things about cats that drive us crazy, and Gus understands these things.

Some of Gus' understanding of cats had been derived directly from personal experience of a cat named Smelly Dave. A member of the Arriola household for a time, Smelly Dave had been a rich source of gags. The animal had showed up on their doorstep one day, a stray with fleas, an empty stomach and a heart-rending mew. They took him in and fed him and bathed him and named him. He was named after a whale.

They had been listening to a typically deadpan Bob & Ray radio sketch in which their characters toured the country with a dead whale packed in ice. The whale's name, naturally, was Smelly Dave. And now, with a logic that Bob & Ray would have enthusiastically endorsed, the name was applied to the cat. Gus liked to remember how Smelly Dave had destroyed two myths about cats at once. Carlin had built a ramp at the window in his room so the cat could enter and leave the house at will. One night, they were all awakened by the sounds of Smelly stumbling around in Carlin's room. The cat had entered through the window but in walking across the darkened room, had encountered Carlin's big tennis shoes in the middle of the floor — and stumbled over them.

A cat stumbling! So much for the notion that cats are light on their feet. And they can't see in the dark either. Obviously.

Watching Smelly Dave had been a rewarding educational exercise for the cartoonist. The cat loved to get into Frances' lap, for example. When the phone rang, the cat raced for the phone: Smelly knew Frances would sit

on the chair next to the phone, and then there'd be a lap to get into. Sometimes, Frances joked, Smelly was in her lap before she could answer the phone. This trait of their cat had been transposed directly into the strip when Gordo acquired a housekeeper. Gordo's cat Poosy Gato headed for her lap anytime it was in evidence.

The same feline proclivity is in evidence in this batch of six strips that Gus' syndicate wasn't interested in and that have never seen publication before. Here, Gus clearly planned to exploit his ability to draw — to *cartoon* — cats and his understanding of them.

Cat lovers are the poorer for not having *Pussy Willow* around in our newspapers, when we had newspapers with comics sections. Garfield is OK as a comic-strip character, but he's no cat. Not any more. And Pussy Willow is all cat. And he will be that way, now, forever. ■

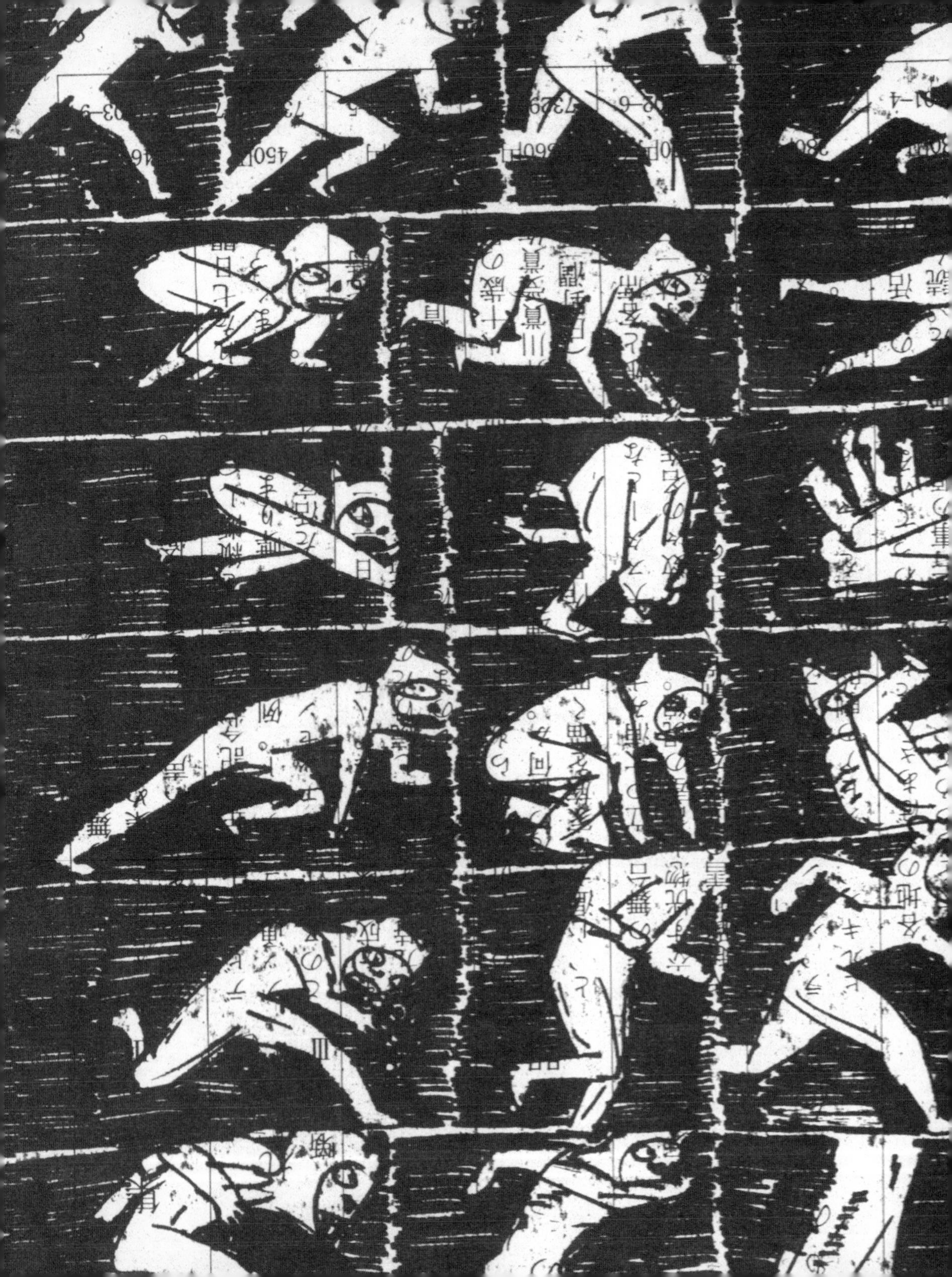

MAGGOTS AND TIME

BY CHRIS LANIER

Comics, as an art form, has a special relationship to time: It's the only form to enlist the audience in the act of reconstituting the flow of time. This happens mostly subconsciously, with readers assembling dialogue and sequence to the tempo of their own interior metronome. It's possible, however, to intentionally complicate that temporal reconstitution — to mess with the metronome. No comic of the past decade (perhaps even the past several decades) has done this so thoroughly as Brian Chippendale's *Maggots* — a comic Chippendale originally made while living at the Fort Thunder artists' collective, drawn over the text-scumbled pages of a Japanese book catalog.

The visual rhythm of *Maggots* is both avant-garde and antique. It leaps backward over the formal development of comics, revisiting the precinematic era of zoopraxiscopes and phenakistoscopes. By adopting a representational strategy that's more than a century old, Chippendale manages to realign basic notions of narrative drama, of gesture and performance, and of the visual functioning of drawings themselves. Most of those realignments are too "experimental" to be absorbed into the mainstream of comics' formal techniques, but for anyone interested in the relatively untraveled pathways of the medium, *Maggots* is rich with possibilities.

LEFT

Left All *Maggots* images [©2007 Brian Chippendale] unless otherwise noted.

Does Time Run Left To Right?

Maggots radically departs from the way comics ordinarily navigate time while also disrupting the basic given of the direction that panels run across the page: time flows forward in *Maggots*, but not only left to right.

Most Western comics read from left to right, following the format adopted for reading text. If there is more than one row of panels, just as when there is more than one line of text, the eye shuttles from the rightmost end of one row to the leftmost end of the next row. The eye travels like a pen, a type-writer carriage or a cursor across the page, racking forward and backward, with no information expressed in the backward traverse. In manga, spring-ing from a culture that reads right to left, the flow is reversed.

Maggots, contrary to either of these models, uses a snaking sequence, like this:

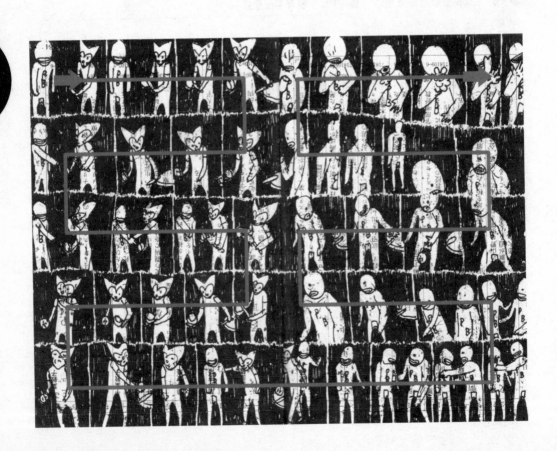

The fact that following the action back and forth (and down and up) is sometimes difficult obscures the fact that it's a perfectly sensible approach — perhaps even more sensible than the approaches inherited from reading text. It's arguably more "efficient" than the text-derived formats, making informational use of every zigzag (in the text-derived flows, every "zag" is an interregnum, a willful "blink"). Isn't it

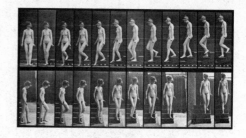

more natural for the panels to be contiguous, each movement emerging from the last one, the way it happens in the actual world, each moment sprouting out of the one that immediately precedes it? *Maggots* is perhaps the first extended comic to throw off the yoke of text, adopting a logic of sequence that is purely visual. In this way, Chippendale shows that even the most basic modalities of the medium are still up for grabs.

Paradoxes Of Motion

Sometimes Chippendale doesn't follow even his own rules (on the jacket flap, under a reading-flow diagram, he writes: "sometimes it's tricky like page 4 gets weird. read bottom two lines from left. huh, funny. stay alert!"). The passages where the flow counters your expectation give a strange sort of whiplash; the characters are still in motion, but something feels off, and you realize time is reeling backwards, so you "rewind" your eyes through the sequence.

The combination of time appearing to run back and forth, and being presented in Muybridge-like slices, makes *Maggots* read somewhat like a comics adaptation of Zeno's paradoxes. Is motion really possible, if a moving object is composed of an infinite number of stationary objects? How can an arrow reach its target, if it must divide the space between its starting point and the target by half, then half again, and so on, the tip eternally forestalled as space folds itself into an impenetrable force-field of proliferating increments?

Of course, Zeno's paradoxes are, for most people, refuted by the act of reading them; nonetheless, they prey upon the suspicion that whatever time is, it's not quite what the mind grasps it to be. That suspicion was confirmed by Eadweard Muybridge's experiments, and accounts for the fascination they still hold today. Muybridge's studies were an act of excavation: they found buried in ordinary activities strange spikes of grace and grotesquerie.

TOP

By Eadweard Mybridge: *Woman walking downstairs* (1887)

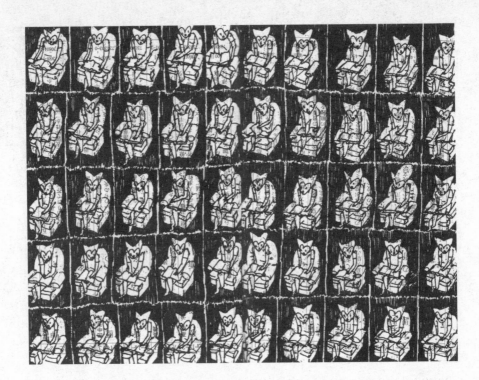

Fascinating Boring

One of the results of Chippendale's stuttered approach to time is that some of the most interesting passages in the book are the most "boring." Chippendale uses his stroboscopic attack for "action" scenes, where characters run and fight and fuck, but the prolonged scenes where a character eats a sandwich or reads a book are no less interesting. In Chippendale's depiction, the act of reading a book becomes obstinately mysterious — you watch the character read a book helplessly, the way a cat might watch a person read a book. That sequence, and the other scenes that draw out ordinary activities for pages at a stretch, reminded me of Samuel Beckett's "sucking stones" passage in his novel *Molloy* — a passage where Molloy explains to the reader his evolving system of rotating 16 pebbles in the four pockets of his coat, so that he always has a unique pebble to draw out and suck on. This monologue goes on for about four pages, and it's a testament to the de-centering power of Beckett's intelligence that this ultra-mundane scene is the novel's most riveting and most memorable.

Beckett's explosion of mundane activity has more layers of psychology than Chippendale's — in Molloy's obsessive pursuit, his ridiculous and necessary assumption of a problem yoked to imperfect solutions, you gradually realize, with a mixture of horror and amusement, that the problem of the sucking stones is the problem of human cogitation. The route that the stones follow, migrating from pocket to pocket, forms a closed circuit; the rotatory motion encloses the brain in its hamster wheel of thinking. Chippendale's characters aren't given any internal monologues — thought balloons are absent, spoken dialogue is scarce — if we understand the characters at all, it's through their actions, sliced thinner than seconds. What he shows us is the body in the hamster wheel of time.

The Error In The Loom

Maggots isn't the first comic to use Muybridge-like sequentiality to render motion. The technique, in fact, predated Muybridge himself. Katsushika Hokusai, in some drawings for his multi-volume compendium *Hokusai Manga*, breaks down motion into repetitive clusters of images, to record the poses of a dance, or the involutions of a wrestling match. Time is rendered as a pattern: the information expressed through the variant irregularities in that pattern. These pages in Hokusai are almost like patterned textiles, made on a loom that introduces an error on each pass of the motif. That "error," that forgetfulness on the part of the loom, is the substance of time.

When Is A Gesture An Image?

Maggots complicates questions that might at first seem straightforward: What is a gesture? What is an image? In a traditional pictorial context, gesture and image are incontrovertibly *present*. Here are some gestures that are

TOP
By Katsushika
Hokusai: from
Manga, Vol. 2 (1815)

also images, indivisibly *there*: Delacroix's female Liberty, leading the people with her right arm upraised, clutching the tricolor flag, bared bosom projecting outward to the viewer.

Rembrandt's Abraham, right hand splayed as it drops the dagger, head turned toward the intervening angel, left hand obliterating Isaac's face in a suffocating, knuckled mask.

Recalling these paintings stirs no real impulse to see what happened just before, or what happened just after. We may be interested in what happened *psychologically* in the immediate before and after, but not what happened *mechanically* (at what point does Liberty's arm grow fatigued, and let the flag dip an inch?) Gesture and image are fused into one stable surface.

This traditional pictorial surface doesn't so much freeze time, as to put time in abeyance. This is not a snapshot record of an event, but a memory of an event, reconstructed after the fact, all its pertinent details congealed in an authoritative simultaneity. The duration of time there is not measured by moments, but by experiences. This is in contrast to the way an animator

TOP
By Eugene Delacroix:
*Liberty Leading the
People* (1830)

RIGHT
By Rembrandt
van Rijn: *Abraham
and Isaac* (1634)

must reconstitute time — or the way one becomes conscious of time when scrubbing through a video clip, looking to isolate from the stream a representative still. The weirdness of time there is most evident in facial expressions — the way human visages are distorted into strange grimaces when motions become moments. A visual stimulus does not always rise to the occasion of an image; an image or a gesture is something that sustains itself beyond the imprint of the moment — something that lives as an echo in the mind after it's vanished from the gelled chamber of the eye.

When Reading Becomes Watching

I found myself "reading" (maybe "watching" is a better way of putting it) *Maggots* in a kind of blur. More than any other comic I've read, *Maggots* compels you to abandon the drawing right in front of your eyes for the next (the exception are the occasional two-page spreads, which serve as a visual punctuation — finally inviting you to pause and regard the drawings as such). To comprehend the motions of the characters, you have to run through the moments quickly: Your brain is turned into a kind of mechanical apparatus, a film projector or zoetrope that the strip of images is being run through, to deliver its characters into activity, into "life." A strange correspondence happens, where the time that transpires when reading becomes almost synchronous with the time that transpires when the characters are behaving. The reader reads and the characters act at the same rate. In a certain sense these gestures and images of *Maggots* aren't really visible on the page; they're only visible in the headlong activity of reading.

Maggots themselves — as in hungry fly larvae — appear a few times in the narrative of the book. But more than a creature, serving as title and talisman, they're a mode of perception — the wiggling motion of the eyes across the page, chewing their way through the corpse of time. ∎

GERALD McBOING BOING

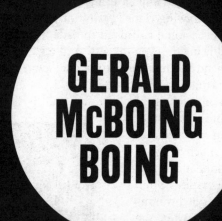

A favored visitor during the late 1940s at the UPA studio in Burbank was a jovial gent named Theodore "Ted" Geisel. At the time, I was working as Bobe Cannon's production designer. I'd heard that many of the UPA core artists had worked under Geisel in the U.S. Army animation unit that produced the Private Snafu and other wartime animation classics, and that Geisel was now the widely published magazine cartoonist, "Dr. Seuss."

I had been amused by magazine ads he had drawn for a bug-killing spray called Flit, with its widely quoted catchphrase, "Quick Henry, the Flit!" I also knew and admired a children's book he'd written and illustrated, *And To Think That I Saw It On Mulberry Street*. His writing and drawing styles were unlike the work of any other cartoonist I knew of.

I was not yet a part of the inner circle at UPA; those guys were 10 to 20 years older than I, and had been wartime animation buddies. What surprised me, when I was shown the printed text of the Dr. Seuss rhymed story they had decided to animate, *Gerald McBoing Boing*, was that it had no Dr. Seuss illustrations, and that to use in-house graphics for the film seemed to go against the already established UPA ethos: *to be 100 percent faithful to the graphic style of an original story!* Even though Geisel had apparently not yet illustrated "Gerald," he certainly could have, or at least his style could have been simulated. No great problem for any of us! Well, I was certainly not yet ripe enough to be considered, but my great teacher and prime UPA studio designer, Bill Hurtz, certainly was!

So it was Bill Hurtz' great innovative design of "Gerald McBoing Boing" that became the UPA iconic look: the basic approach to graphic staging, animation figure posing, scene transition, color progression, the "Japanese" perspective concept and overall scenic continuity ideas.

After the great Oscar-winning success of the movie short, there came an offer from Dell Comics to put out a Gerald McBoing Boing series, and as it now had a pure UPA visual styling, some of the UPA animation staff were set to work, moonlighting as comic-book writer/illustrators. I was not among them, as by that time I was 3,000 miles away, directing at the UPA-New York studio. I can't remember who among them actually wrote and drew the comics. If any of you do, please step forward. I think one of the artists working on the comic-book Geralds was Frank Smith. Whoever the others were, they did a credible job of catching the Dr. Seuss whimsy.

The first printed episode was a direct adaptation of the initial cartoon film, simply fitting an exact transcription of the cartoon's script to still-drawn comic-book pages.

Like the cartoon, the comic book kicked off a short series of follow-ups. By the late 1950s, however, Gerald had completely faded from public view. For decades, he existed only in the fading memories of an aging boomer generation, a half-forgotten gem from the 1950s.

The basic Gerald story is a flawless gem, the tale of a misfit little boy, trying somehow to fit into a world unprepared to cope with someone as "different" as he.

—*Gene Deitch, Prague, Sept. 20, 2010*

The Comics Journal would like to thank Mykal Banta at The Big Blog of Kids' Comics (www.bigblogcomics.com) for his assistance.

MPA presents

Gerald McBoing Boing

THIS IS THE STORY OF GERALD McCLOY...

---AND THE STRANGE THING THAT HAPPENED TO THAT LITTLE BOY.

THEY SAY IT ALL STARTED WHEN GERALD WAS TWO.

---THAT'S THE AGE KIDS START TALKING, LEAST MOST OF THEM DO.

BOING B. #1 - 528

WHEN HE STARTED TALKING, YOU KNOW WHAT HE SAID ? HE DIDN'T TALK WORDS, HE WENT----

BOING! BOING! ----INSTEAD !

"WHAT'S THAT?" CRIED HIS FATHER, HIS FACE TURNING GREY...

..."THAT'S A VERY ODD THING FOR A YOUNG BOY TO SAY!"

BOING! BOING!

AND POOR GERALD'S FATHER RUSHED TO THE PHONE...

...AND QUICK DIALED THE NUMBER OF DOCTOR MALONE.

"COME OVER FAST!" THE POOR FATHER PLED...

..."OUR BOY CAN'T SPEAK WORDS... HE GOES...

BOING BOING ...INSTEAD."

"I SEE," SAID THE DOCTOR, "IT'S JUST AS YOU SAID..."

..."HE DOESN'T SPEAK WORDS.... HE GOES... BOING! BOING! -- INSTEAD."

"I'VE NO CURE FOR THIS.... I CAN'T HANDLE THE CASE!"

AND HE PACKED UP HIS PILLS AND WALKED OUT OF THE PLACE..

THEN MONTHS PASSED AND GERALD GOT LOUDER...

BOING

UNTIL ONE DAY HE WENT...

BOOM! ...LIKE A BIG KEG OF POWDER.

IT WAS THEN THAT HIS FATHER SAID, 'THIS IS ENOUGH!

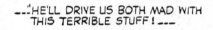

--"HE'LL DRIVE US BOTH MAD WITH THIS TERRIBLE STUFF!---

"A BOY OF HIS AGE SHOULDN'T SOUND LIKE A FOOL---

BANG

"HE'S GOT TO LEARN WORDS....WE MUST SEND HIM TO SCHOOL!"

SO OFF GERALD WENT;
THE CLOCK STRUCK ELEVEN,
AS HE ENTERED THE DOOR
OF P.S. N⁰ 7.

AT TWELVE O'CLOCK SHARP OUT CAME NO OTHER,
BUT GERALD Mᶜ BOING BOING WITH A LETTER FOR MOTHER.

GERALD REACHED HOME
ABOUT 10 MINUTES LATER,
AND HANDED IT PROUDLY
TO HIS SURPRISED MATER.

"From Public School Seven to Mrs. McCloy:

Your little son Gerald's a most hopeless boy....

"We cannot accept him for we have a rule....

"That pupil's must not go.... CUCKOO in our school.

"Your boy will go HONK!...all his life, I'm afraid.

"Sincerely yours, Fanny Schultz. Teacher, First Grade."

AND AS LITTLE GERALD GREW OLDER, HE FOUND...

..WHEN A FELLOW GOES.. *BAM* ....NO ONE WANTS HIM AROUND.

WHEN A FELLOW GOES... *SKREEEEEK!* ...HE CAN'T HAVE ANY PALS..

AND HIS... *CLANG! CLANG! CLANG!* ...FRIGHTENED THE GALS!

"NYA, NYAH!" THEY ALL SHOUTED, "YOUR NAME'S NOT McCLOY! YOU'RE GERALD McBOING-BOING, THE NOISE-MAKING BOY!"

TO HIS FATHER HE RAN... HIS TROUBLES TO MENTION,
BUT POOR GERALD COULDN'T GET HIS FATHER'S ATTENTION.

HE ROARED LIKE A LION TO MAKE HIS PRESENCE KNOWN...

HIS FATHER HAD A FIT,
AND YELLED..

LEAVE ME ALONE!

HE PACKED HIS FEW BELONGINGS..
AND DECIDED TO LEAVE HOME,
AROUND THE WHOLE WIDE WORLD,
LIKE A HOBO HE WOULD ROAM.

HE HEARD A TRAIN APPROACHING..
HE HEARD THE WHISTLE *HOOT!*
GERALD STOOD BESIDE THE RAILS
AND ANSWERED WITH A "*TOOT!*"

AS GERALD LEAPED FOR
THE LOWEST RUNG, HE
HEARD A VOICE
YELL ----

STOP!

IN MID-AIR POOR, YOUNG GERALD
STOOD..NOT FINISHING HIS HOP.

AREN'T YOU GERALD
McBOING-BOING,
THE BOY
WHO MAKES
SQUEAKS?

MY BOY, I HAVE
SEARCHED FOR YOU
MANY LONG WEEKS.

I CAN MAKE YOU THE
MOST FAMOUS
LAD IN THE NATION, FOR
I OWN THE

BONG!
BONG!
BONG!

RADIO STATION.

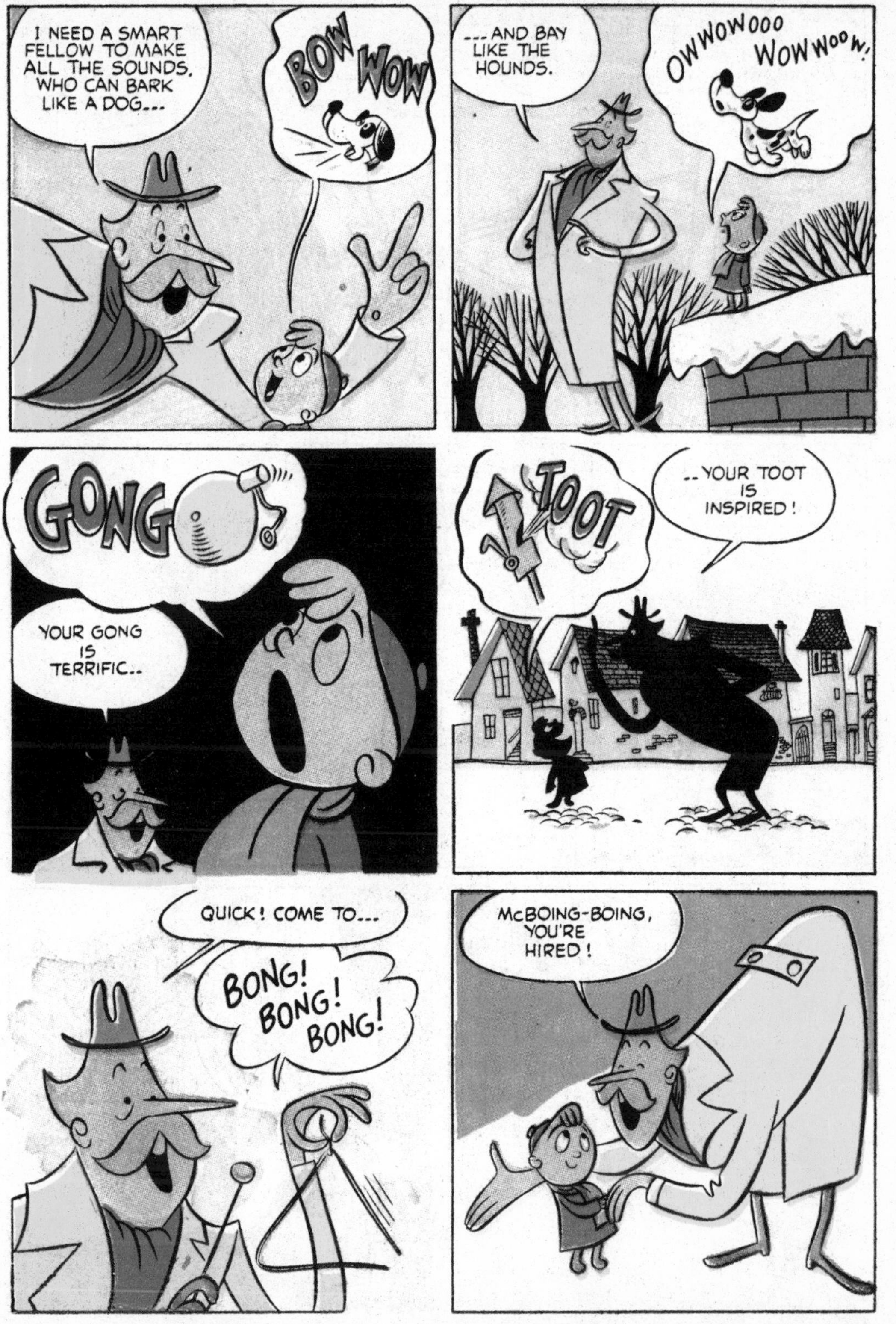

I NEED A SMART FELLOW TO MAKE ALL THE SOUNDS, WHO CAN BARK LIKE A DOG...
BOW WOW
...AND BAY LIKE THE HOUNDS.
OWWOWOOO WOWWOOW!
GONG
YOUR GONG IS TERRIFIC..
TOOT
..YOUR TOOT IS INSPIRED!
QUICK! COME TO...
BONG! BONG! BONG!
McBOING-BOING, YOU'RE HIRED!

THE DALTON GANG STUCK UP THE STAGECOACH THIS NOON, AND THE VARMINTS ARE HOLED-UP IN CLANCY'S SALOON. THE SHERIFF CAN'T GET AT 'EM---NOT EVEN THE LAW KNOWS HOW TO BEAT TWENTY-THREE MEN TO THE DRAW!

NOW, HOLD ON THAR, PODNUH, ONE FELLA KNOWS HOW...

IT'S SILENT SAM STEELHEART---AND HERE HE COMES NOW!

CLIPPETY CLAP CLIPPETY CLAP

SALOON.

CLOP CLOP CLOP CLOP CLOP

ZING SQUEAK

NOW HIS PARENTS...PROUD PARENTS....
ARE ABLE TO BOAST THAT THEIR GERALDS...

AHGOOO OOAH! --IS KNOWN COAST TO COAST.

NOW GERALD IS RICH....HE HAS FRIENDS....HE'S WELL FED !

'CAUSE HE DOESN'T SPEAK WORDS.... HE GOES.....

BOING! BOING!

...INSTEAD !

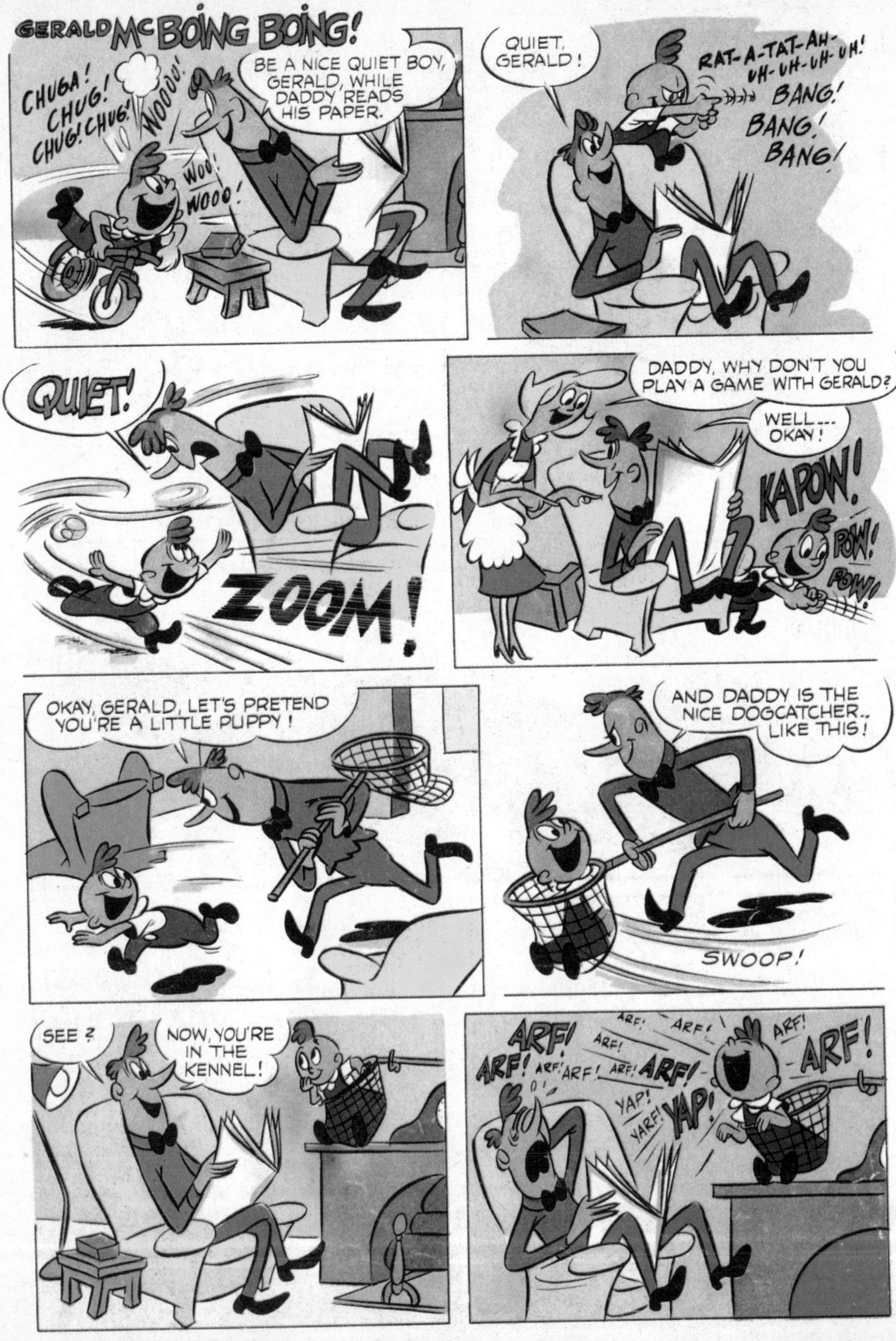
GERALD McBOING BOING!
CHUGA! CHUG! CHUG! CHUG!
WOOOO!
WOO! WOOO!
BE A NICE QUIET BOY, GERALD, WHILE DADDY READS HIS PAPER.
QUIET, GERALD!
RAT-A-TAT-AH-UH-UH-UH-UH!
BANG! BANG! BANG!
QUIET!
ZOOM!
DADDY, WHY DON'T YOU PLAY A GAME WITH GERALD?
WELL... OKAY!
KAPOW!
POW!
POW!
OKAY, GERALD, LET'S PRETEND YOU'RE A LITTLE PUPPY!
AND DADDY IS THE NICE DOGCATCHER.. LIKE THIS!
SWOOP!
SEE?
NOW, YOU'RE IN THE KENNEL!
ARF!
ARF!
ARF!
ARF!
ARF!
ARF! ARF! ARF! ARF! ARF!
ARF!
YAP! YARF! YAP!

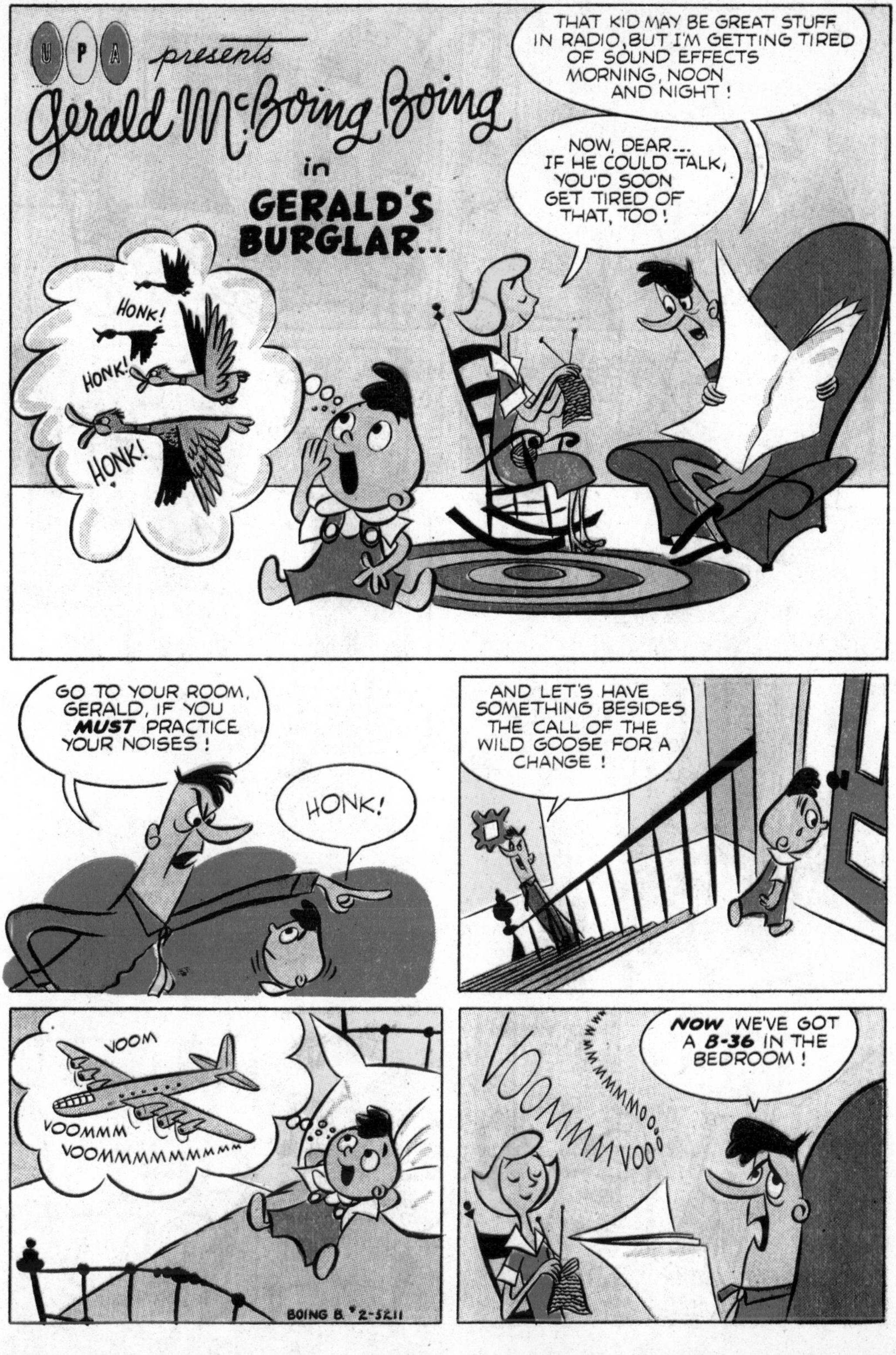
UPA presents
Gerald McBoing Boing
in
GERALD'S BURGLAR...
THAT KID MAY BE GREAT STUFF IN RADIO, BUT I'M GETTING TIRED OF SOUND EFFECTS MORNING, NOON AND NIGHT !
NOW, DEAR... IF HE COULD TALK, YOU'D SOON GET TIRED OF THAT, TOO !
HONK!
HONK!
HONK!
GO TO YOUR ROOM, GERALD, IF YOU MUST PRACTICE YOUR NOISES !
HONK!
AND LET'S HAVE SOMETHING BESIDES THE CALL OF THE WILD GOOSE FOR A CHANGE !
VOOM
VOOMMM
VOOMMMMMMMMMM
BOING B. #2-5211
NOW WE'VE GOT A B-36 IN THE BEDROOM !
VOOMMMM VOO

HMMM... THIS JOINT LOOKS LIKE IT'S LOADED

R-R-R-R-R-GGGG

AREN'T YOU GOING TO ANSWER THE DOORBELL, DEAR?

DOORBELL? I THOUGHT THAT WAS GERALD!

I KNEW IT WASN'T THE PHONE. I HAD IT TAKEN OUT—SO I WOULDN'T BE BOTHERED BY *ITS* RINGING!

GOOD EVENING, SIR! I'M FROM THE LITTLE GEM BURGLAR ALARM COMPANY...

DID YOU KNOW THAT EVERY YEAR THOUSANDS OF HOMES ARE ENTERED BY BURGLARS... AND THAT THE LOSSES RUN INTO MILLIONS?...

AND THAT *YOUR* HOME IS NO EXCEPTION?

CHAH CHOO
CHAH CHOO
CHAH
CHAH CHOO

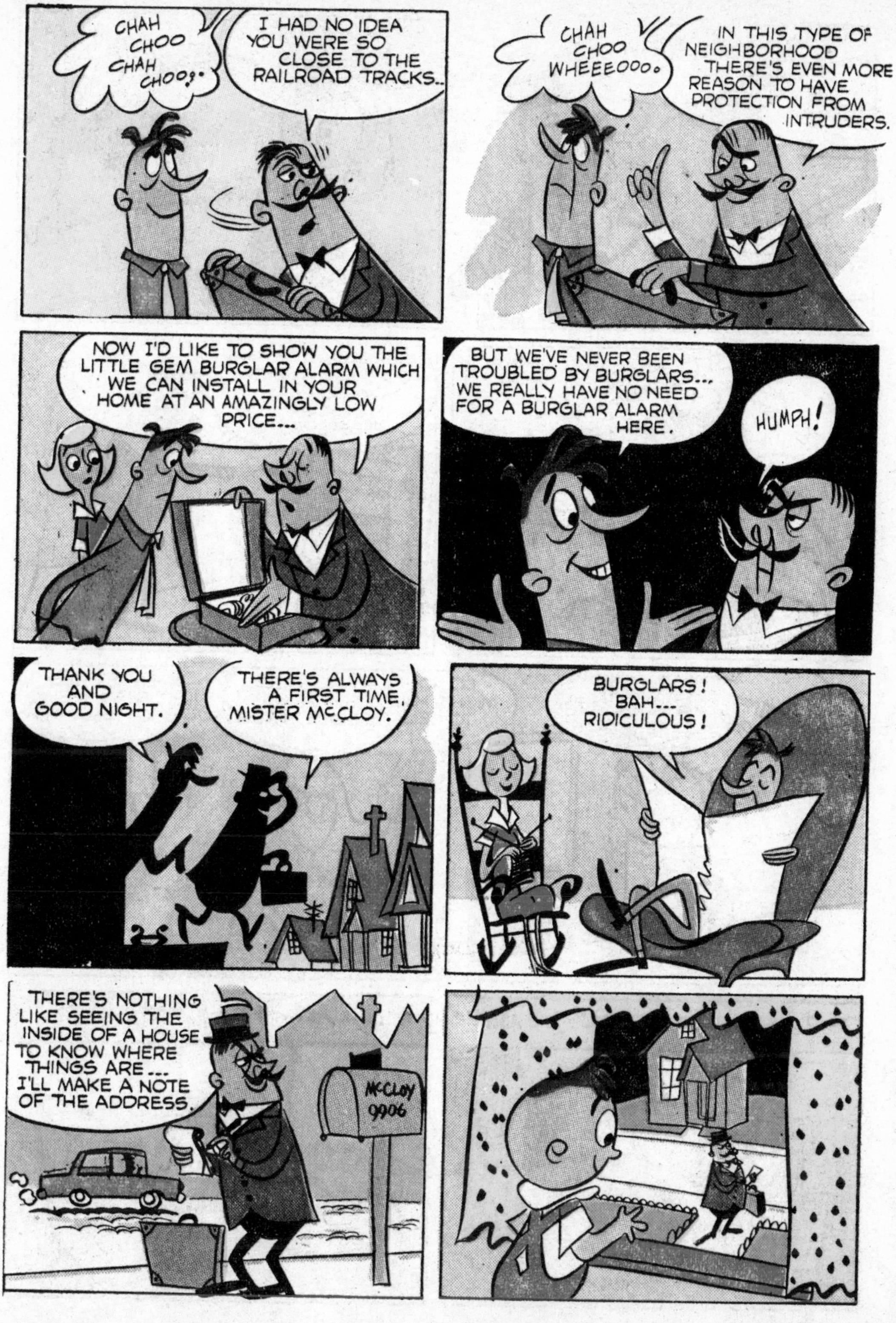
CHAH CHOO CHAH CHOO...
I HAD NO IDEA YOU WERE SO CLOSE TO THE RAILROAD TRACKS..
CHAH CHOO WHEEEOOOO.
IN THIS TYPE OF NEIGHBORHOOD THERE'S EVEN MORE REASON TO HAVE PROTECTION FROM INTRUDERS.
NOW I'D LIKE TO SHOW YOU THE LITTLE GEM BURGLAR ALARM WHICH WE CAN INSTALL IN YOUR HOME AT AN AMAZINGLY LOW PRICE...
BUT WE'VE NEVER BEEN TROUBLED BY BURGLARS... WE REALLY HAVE NO NEED FOR A BURGLAR ALARM HERE.
HUMPH!
THANK YOU AND GOOD NIGHT.
THERE'S ALWAYS A FIRST TIME, MISTER McCLOY.
BURGLARS! BAH... RIDICULOUS!
THERE'S NOTHING LIKE SEEING THE INSIDE OF A HOUSE TO KNOW WHERE THINGS ARE... I'LL MAKE A NOTE OF THE ADDRESS.
McCLOY 9906

THAT NIGHT AFTER EVERYBODY WAS ASLEEP...

WELL...*ALMOST* EVERYBODY....

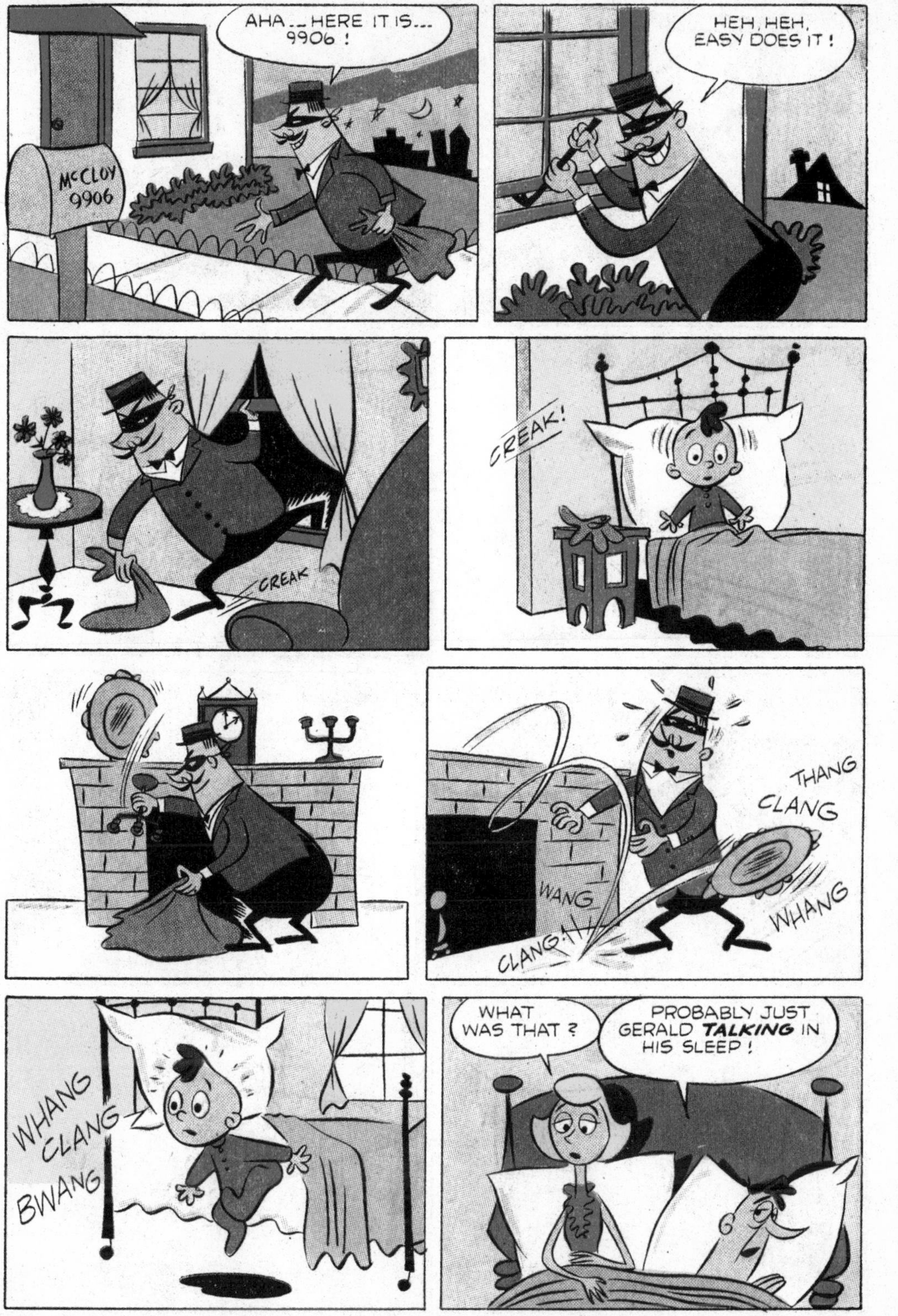
AHA... HERE IT IS... 9906 !
McCLOY 9906
HEH, HEH, EASY DOES IT !
CREAK
CREAK!
THANG
CLANG
WANG
WHANG
CLANG
WHANG
CLANG
BWANG
WHAT WAS THAT ?
PROBABLY JUST GERALD **TALKING** IN HIS SLEEP !

BANG!

ACK! ACK! ACK!

PAFF!

COME ON, GERALD... CUT OUT THE GUN BATTLES AND GO BACK TO BED LIKE A NICE KID...PLEASE !

WHAT DID GERALD WANT ?

HE WAS JUST HAVING A NIGHT-MARE, I GUESS.

OPERATOR... THIS IS THE OPERATOR... OPERATOR..

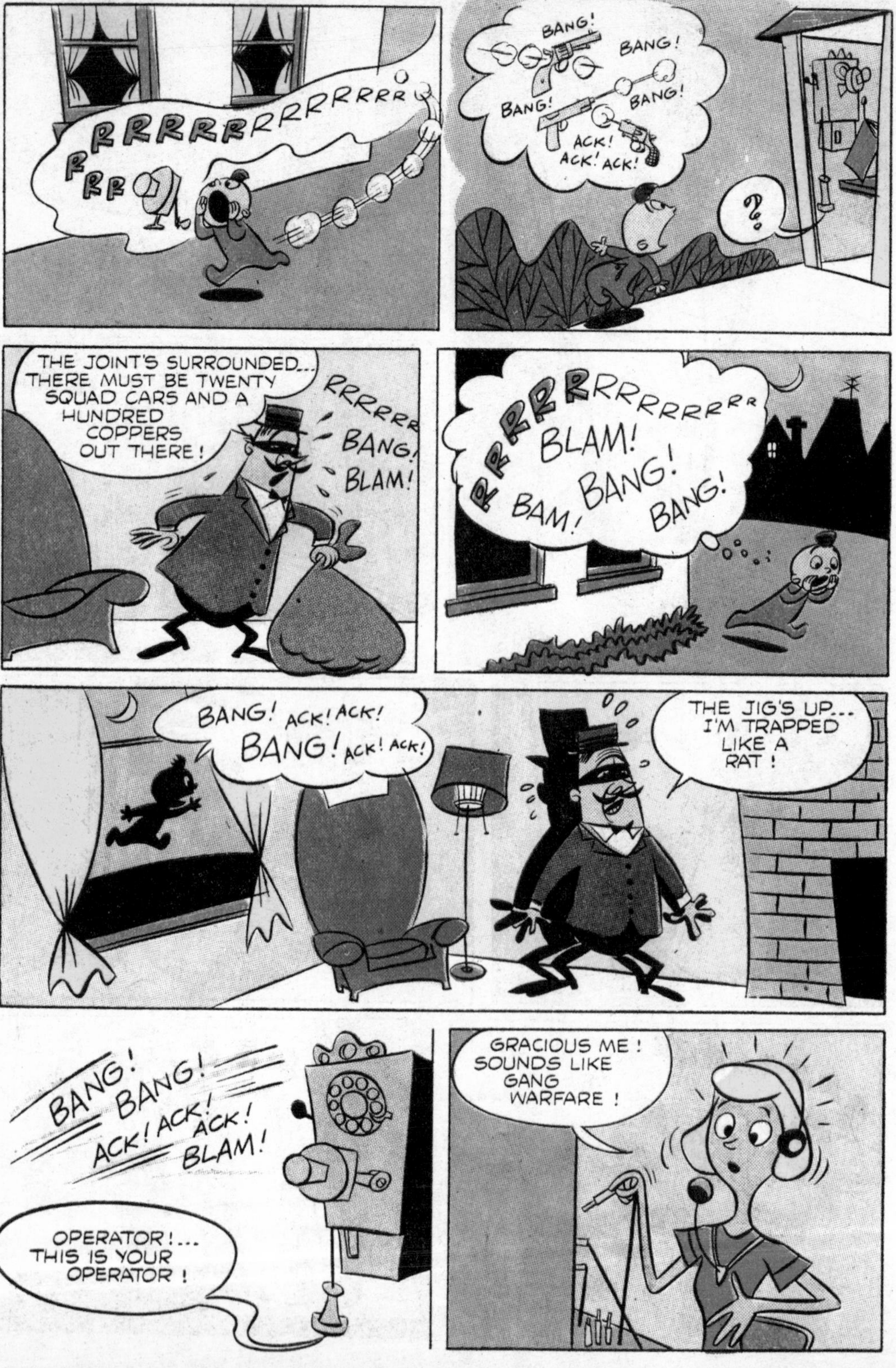
RRRRRRRRRRRRRRRRR
BANG! BANG! BANG! BANG! ACK! ACK! ACK!
?
THE JOINT'S SURROUNDED... THERE MUST BE TWENTY SQUAD CARS AND A HUNDRED COPPERS OUT THERE!
RRRRRR BANG! BLAM!
RRRRRRRRRRRRRR BLAM! BANG! BAM! BANG!
BANG! ACK! ACK! BANG! ACK! ACK!
THE JIG'S UP... I'M TRAPPED LIKE A RAT!
BANG! BANG! ACK! ACK! ACK! BLAM!
OPERATOR!... THIS IS YOUR OPERATOR!
GRACIOUS ME! SOUNDS LIKE GANG WARFARE!

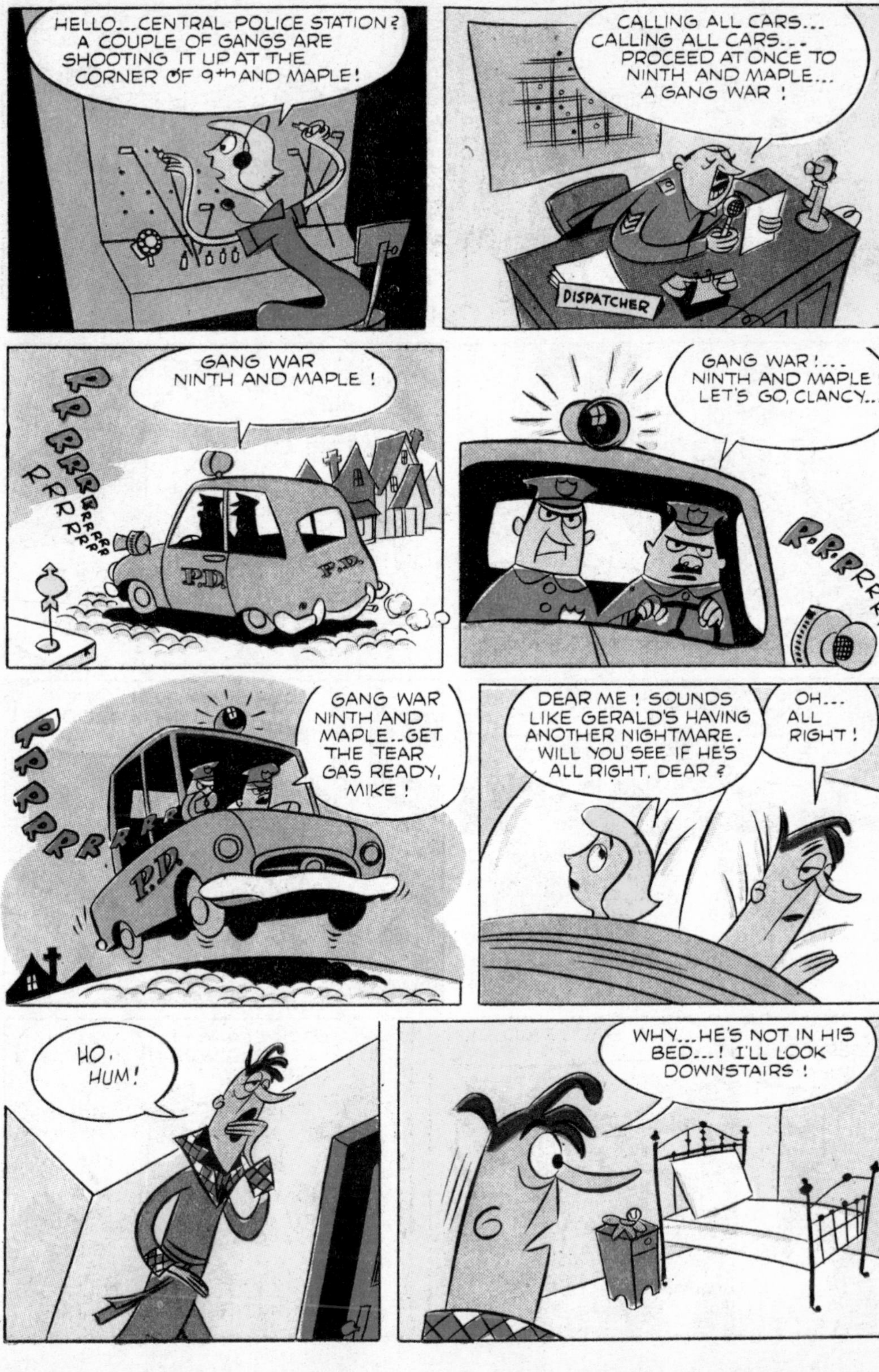
HELLO...CENTRAL POLICE STATION? A COUPLE OF GANGS ARE SHOOTING IT UP AT THE CORNER OF 9th AND MAPLE!
CALLING ALL CARS... CALLING ALL CARS... PROCEED AT ONCE TO NINTH AND MAPLE... A GANG WAR!
DISPATCHER
GANG WAR NINTH AND MAPLE!
GANG WAR!... NINTH AND MAPLE! LET'S GO, CLANCY...
GANG WAR NINTH AND MAPLE..GET THE TEAR GAS READY, MIKE!
DEAR ME! SOUNDS LIKE GERALD'S HAVING ANOTHER NIGHTMARE. WILL YOU SEE IF HE'S ALL RIGHT, DEAR?
OH... ALL RIGHT!
HO, HUM!
WHY... HE'S NOT IN HIS BED...! I'LL LOOK DOWNSTAIRS!

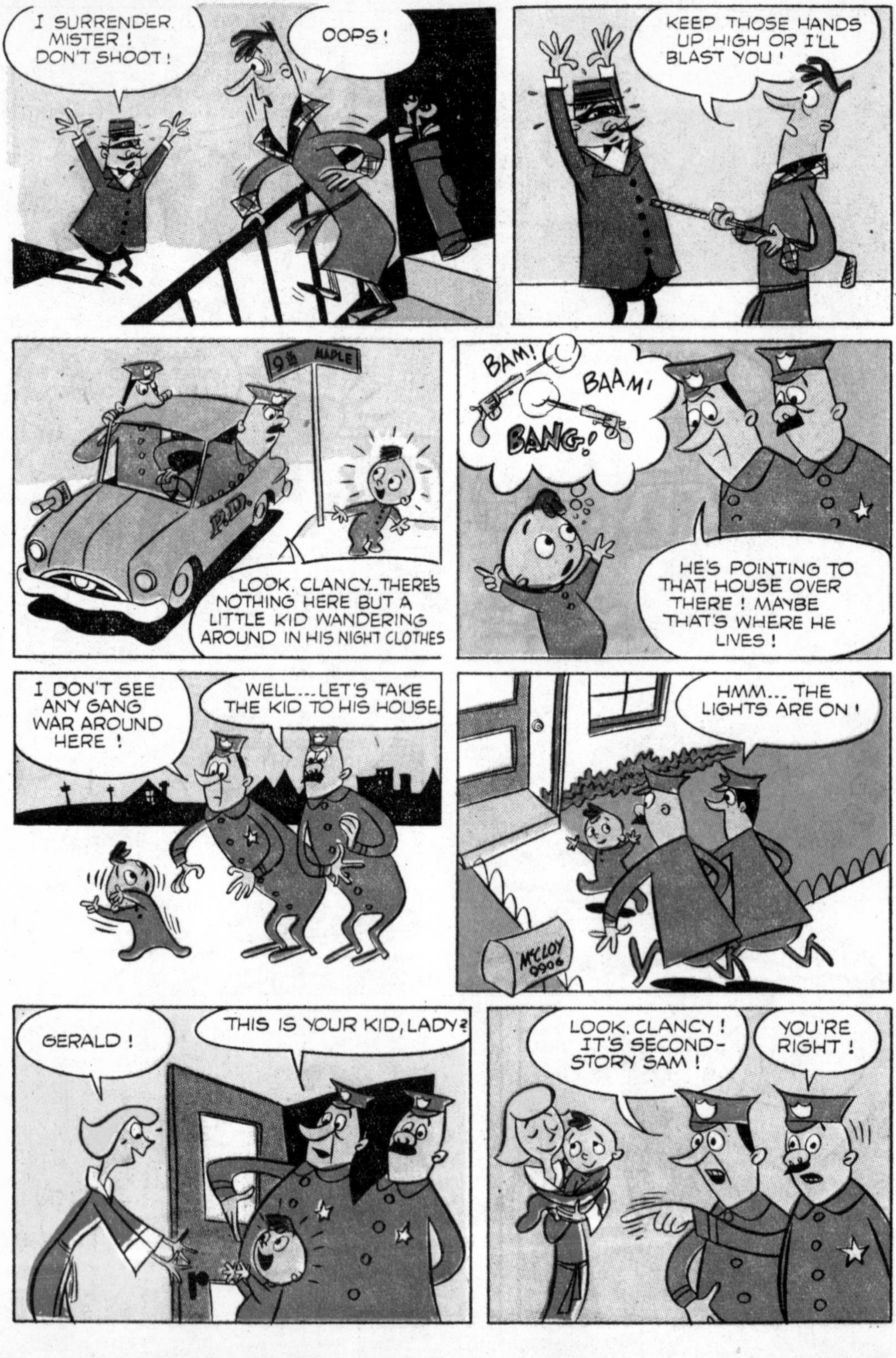
I SURRENDER MISTER ! DON'T SHOOT !
OOPS !
KEEP THOSE HANDS UP HIGH OR I'LL BLAST YOU !
9th MAPLE
P.D.
LOOK, CLANCY.. THERE'S NOTHING HERE BUT A LITTLE KID WANDERING AROUND IN HIS NIGHT CLOTHES
BAM!
BAAM!
BANG!
HE'S POINTING TO THAT HOUSE OVER THERE ! MAYBE THAT'S WHERE HE LIVES !
I DON'T SEE ANY GANG WAR AROUND HERE !
WELL... LET'S TAKE THE KID TO HIS HOUSE.
HMM... THE LIGHTS ARE ON !
McCLOY 9906
GERALD !
THIS IS YOUR KID, LADY?
LOOK, CLANCY ! IT'S SECOND-STORY SAM !
YOU'RE RIGHT !

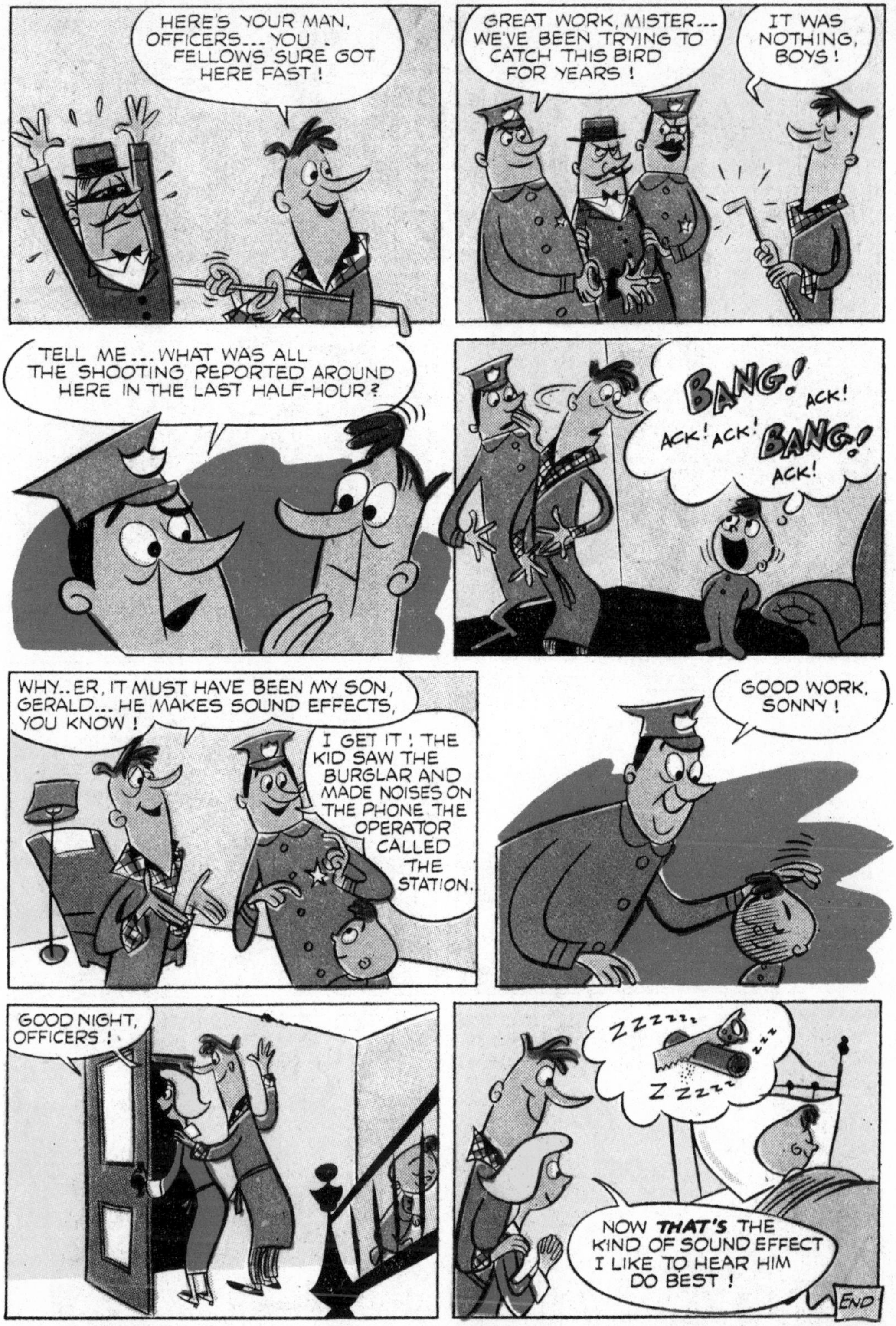
HERE'S YOUR MAN, OFFICERS... YOU FELLOWS SURE GOT HERE FAST!
GREAT WORK, MISTER... WE'VE BEEN TRYING TO CATCH THIS BIRD FOR YEARS!
IT WAS NOTHING, BOYS!
TELL ME... WHAT WAS ALL THE SHOOTING REPORTED AROUND HERE IN THE LAST HALF-HOUR?
BANG! ACK! ACK! ACK! BANG! ACK!
WHY.. ER, IT MUST HAVE BEEN MY SON, GERALD... HE MAKES SOUND EFFECTS, YOU KNOW!
I GET IT! THE KID SAW THE BURGLAR AND MADE NOISES ON THE PHONE. THE OPERATOR CALLED THE STATION.
GOOD WORK, SONNY!
GOOD NIGHT, OFFICERS!
ZZZZZ ZZZ ZZZZZ
NOW THAT'S THE KIND OF SOUND EFFECT I LIKE TO HEAR HIM DO BEST!
END

UPA presents

Gerald McBoing Boing

YOU WAIT IN THE CAR, GERALD...I'VE GOT TO HURRY AND CASH THIS CHECK BEFORE THE BANK CLOSES!

HEY, *WAIT*...

SORRY, MISTER...WE ALWAYS CLOSE ON THE STROKE OF THREE.

FIRST NATIONAL BANK

BUT I MUST CASH THIS CHECK!

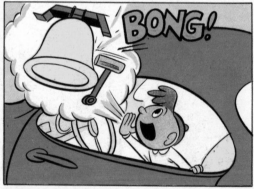

BONG!

BONG! BONG!

LISTEN!

YOU WIN, MISTER.

I COULDA SWORN I HEARD THAT CLOCK STRIKE THREE ONCE BEFORE!

FIRST NATIONAL

UPA presents

HERE'S A FURTHER ADVENTURE OF GERALD McCLOY THE AMAZINGLY TALENTED SOUND AFFECTS BOY:

Gerald McBoing Boing in

GERALD AND THE FOG

WEARY FROM TRIUMPHS ON STAGE AND TV...

CHAMPS ELYSEES
BOING BOING
LE PETIT BOING BOING
COMBIEN?

IN EUROPE AND ASIA AND LANDS OVERSEA...

DAS GROSSE SCHAUSPIELHAUS
DER KLEINE VON BOING
WIEVIEL?

GERALD'S MOTHER AND FATHER MADE AN EARNEST REQUEST...

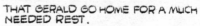

THAT GERALD GO HOME FOR A MUCH NEEDED REST.

SO THEY CANCELLED ALL BOOKINGS AND HOPPED ON A BOAT...

THAT WOULD CARRY THEM SWIFTLY ACROSS THE BIG MOAT.

THE SHIP WAS THE "NELLIE" SHE WAS BUILT TO GO FAST... WITH A FOGHORN AND RADAR, ON TOP OF THE MAST

THE AMBITIOUS CAPTAIN WAS ANXIOUS TO WIN...

THE ATLANTIC BLUE-RIBBON TO TIE 'ROUND HIS CHIN!

HE HAD BRIBED ALL THE STOKERS WITH EXTRA ICE CREAM...

TO POUR ON THE COAL AND GET UP THE STEAM!

"WE'LL WIN THAT
BLUE RIBBON,"
HE SAID WITH
A GRIN...

"THAT ATLANTIC
BLUE-RIBBON
TO TIE 'ROUND
MY CHIN."

THEY HAULED UP THE GANGPLANK
AND PULLED OUT OF THE DOCK...

ON FRIDAY THE THIRTEENTH
AT JUST TWELVE O'CLOCK.

'THOUGH GERALD DIDN'T SAY
HE WAS THRILLED BY THE RACE;

HE WAS SURE THAT THE "NELLIE"
COULD WIN THE FIRST PLACE.

TO THE
ENGINE
ROOM

HE STAYED NEAR THE ENGINES
AND MIMICKED THE SOUND...

OF PISTONS
AND CAMS,
AND OF WHEELS
GOING ROUND.

THE SHIP WAS PROGRESSING AT KNOTS FORTY-FOUR....

THE CAPTAIN WAS HAPPY:

WE'LL MAKE IT FOR SURE!

WHEN OUT ON THE WATER A FOG BANK APPEARED...

SAID ENGINEER SCOTT:

IT'S JUST WHAT I FEARED!

CAPTAIN McKINLEY MADE A CHECK OF THE LOG....

THEN TURNED TO THE CHIEF WHO WAS EYEING THE FOG

THE RECORD'S IMPORTANT... JUST FOLLOW MY LEAD...

WE'LL BLOW THAT OLD FOGHORN AND KEEP UP OUR SPEED!

SO THE NELLIE PUSHED FORWARD AS FAST AS SHE COULD---

THE CAPTAIN WAS NERVOUS.... HE KNOCKED UPON WOOD....

AS THE FOG BANK GREW CLOSER... IN ALL OF HIS LIFE....

HE HAD NEVER SEEN FOG YOU COULD CUT WITH A KNIFE!

HE TURNED TO HIS HELPER, THE CHIEF ENGINEER:

NOW BLOW THAT OLD FOGHORN UNTIL IT GETS CLEAR.

THE ENGINEER YANKED IT ACCORDING TO CUE!

PULL ONLY IN CASE OF FOG

THE FOGHORN RESPONDED... AS FOGHORNS WILL DO.

VOOP

"VOOP-OOP" WENT THE BLAST ALL OVER THE PLACE...

WARNING ALL SHIPS OF THE BLUE-RIBBON RACE!

GERALD McBOING BOING, THE PASSENGERS FOUND...

WAS DELIGHTED TO HEAR THIS ENCHANTING NEW SOUND.

THREE MINUTES OF SILENCE WITHOUT ANY BLAST....

THEN "VOOP-OOOP" IT WOULD GO AGAIN SHAKING THE MAST.

THE 'VOOPING' CONTINUED AN HOUR OR SO...

THEN IT SUDDENLY STOPPED... IT JUST WOULDN'T GO!

THE CAPTAIN WAS FRANTIC
AND SAID WITH A FROWN:

OUR FOGHORN IS
BUSTED...
WE'VE *GOT* TO
SLOW DOWN!

ENGINEER SCOTT
WITH A TEAR
IN HIS EYE ...

SLOWED DOWN THE ENGINES...
THEN STARTED TO CRY.

SAID CAPTAIN McKINLEY
TO ENGINEER SCOTT...

HOMP!

OUR CHANCES OF WINNING
ARE PRACTIC'LY SHOT!

THE PASSENGERS GRUMBLED
AND CURSED THE BAD LUCK...

WHEN WORD GOT AROUND
THAT THE WHISTLE HAD STUCK.

THE GLOOMINESS SPREAD
TO THE MEN DOWN BELOW....
NO EXTRA ICE CREAM
WAS A TERRIBLE BLOW.

WHAT A HORRIBLE THING
FOR A CREWMAN TO FACE....
THE PROSPECT OF LOSING
THE BLUE-RIBBON RACE.

THE SADNESS CONTINUED
WITH NEVER A LAUGH....

AS THE NELLIE
CHUGGED SLOWLY,
HER SPEED CUT
IN HALF.

THEN ALL OF A SUDDEN
AT A QUARTER TO FOUR....

CAME "VOOP-OOOP" AGAIN
JUST AS LOUD AS BEFORE!

VOOP!
OOOP

THE CAPTAIN WAS JOYFUL....
SCOTT STOOD ON HIS HEAD....

THE ENGINE ROOM ECHOED
WITH "FULL SPEED AHEAD!"

THE MANTLE OF GLOOM
WAS NOW PUT ON THE SHELF...

CAUSE THE WHISTLE HAD WORKED
AGAIN ALL BY ITSELF!

FASTER AND FASTER
SHE PLOWED THROUGH THE BRINE...

THE GOOD VESSEL "NELLIE"
WAS MAKING UP TIME!

THE FOG BANK GREW THINNER
AS BLUE SKY WAS LOGGED,

AND IN NO TIME THE SHIP
WAS COMPLETELY UN-FOGGED.

BUT THE FOGHORN KEPT SOUNDING
AS IF IN A RUT....

WAS THE WHISTLE STUCK OPEN NOW...
RATHER THAN SHUT?

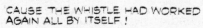

THE CAPTAIN'S BINOCULARS
AIMED AT THE STACK...

HIGH UP NEAR
THE WHISTLE
A LITTLE BOY
SAT:

AND EVERY THREE MINUTES...
(THAT'S RIGHT ON THE NOSE)

HE MAKES LIKE IT DOES
WHEN A FOG-WARNING BLOWS.

VOOP
OOOP

"THREE CHEERS FOR McBOING BOING,"
EXHORTED THE CROWD...

HE SAVED OUR BLUE-RIBBON
BY TOOTING SO LOUD.

THE SPEEDY SHIP, NELLIE,
SOON PASSED AMBROSE LIGHT...

THE OLD RECORD SMASHED
BY A DAY AND A NIGHT.

AS SHE SAILED UP THE HUDSON... THE BLUE-RIBBON QUEEN

ONE SAW IN THE HARBOR A BEAUTIFUL SCENE:

THE FERRYBOATS TOOTED, AND ALL KINDS OF SHIPS....

SALUTED THE "NELLIE" FROM OUT OF THEIR SLIPS.

AND WHO DO YOU THINK WAS UP THERE ON THE STACK?...

IT WAS GERALD McBOING-BOING SALUTING THEM BACK!

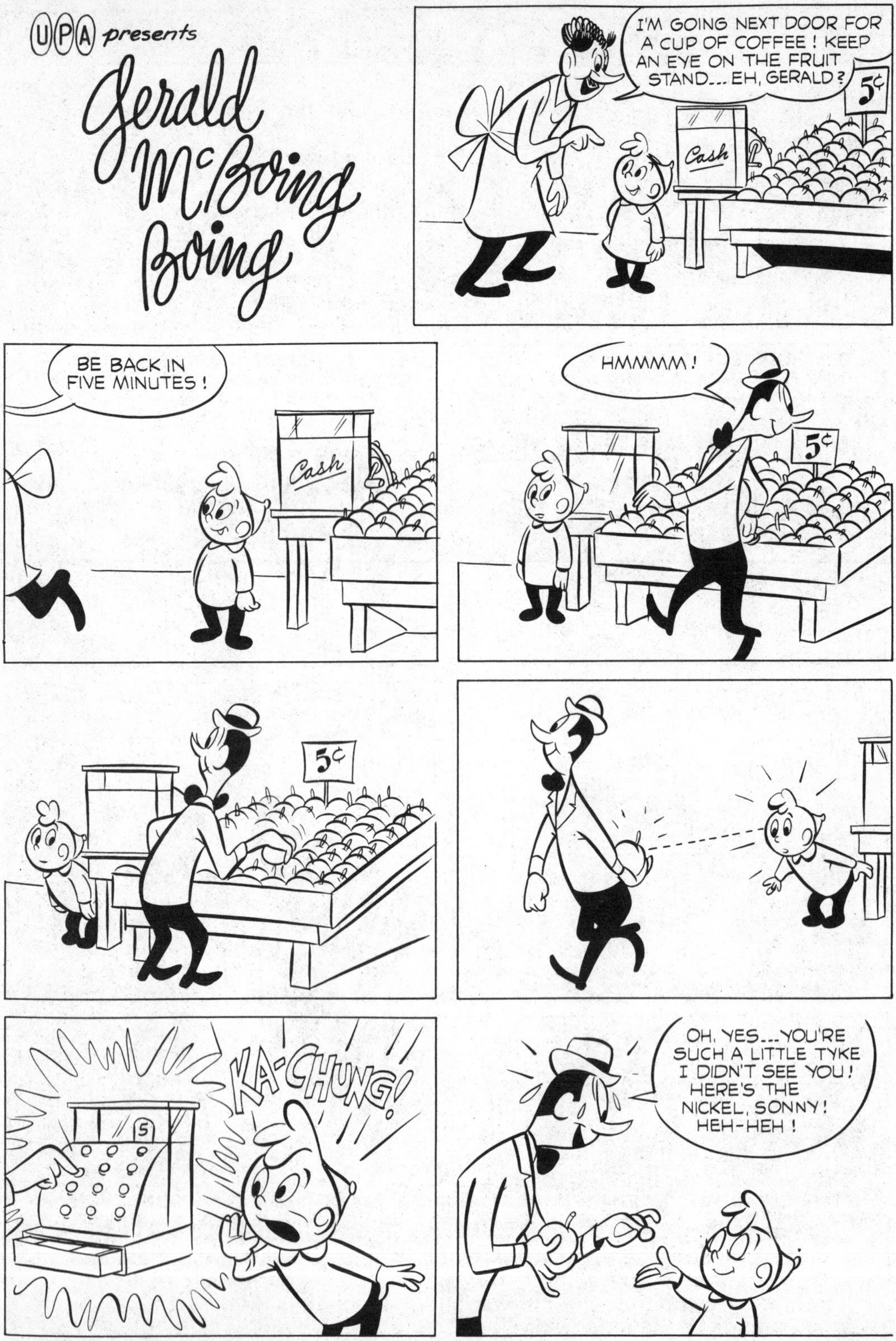
UPA presents
Gerald McBoing Boing
I'M GOING NEXT DOOR FOR A CUP OF COFFEE! KEEP AN EYE ON THE FRUIT STAND... EH, GERALD?
5¢
Cash
BE BACK IN FIVE MINUTES!
Cash
HMMMM!
5¢
5¢
KA-CHUNG!
5
OH, YES... YOU'RE SUCH A LITTLE TYKE I DIDN'T SEE YOU! HERE'S THE NICKEL, SONNY! HEH-HEH!

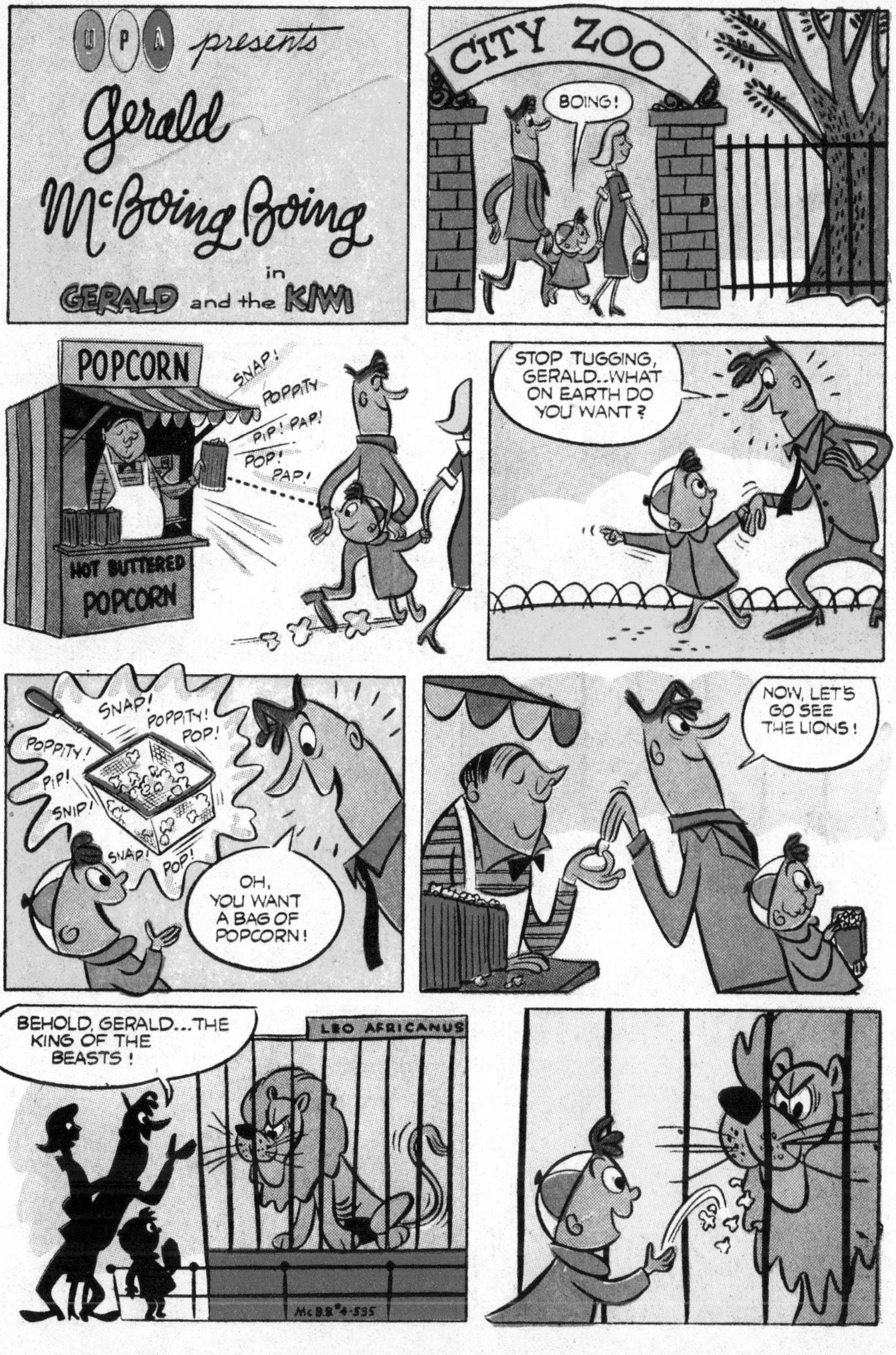

UPA presents
Gerald McBoing Boing
in
GERALD and the KIWI
CITY ZOO
BOING!
POPCORN
SNAP! POPPITY PIP! PAP! POP! PAP!
HOT BUTTERED POPCORN
STOP TUGGING, GERALD...WHAT ON EARTH DO YOU WANT?
SNAP! POPPITY! POP! POPPITY! PIP! SNIP! SNAP! POP!
OH, YOU WANT A BAG OF POPCORN!
NOW, LET'S GO SEE THE LIONS!
BEHOLD, GERALD... THE KING OF THE BEASTS!
LEO AFRICANUS
McB.B.#4-535

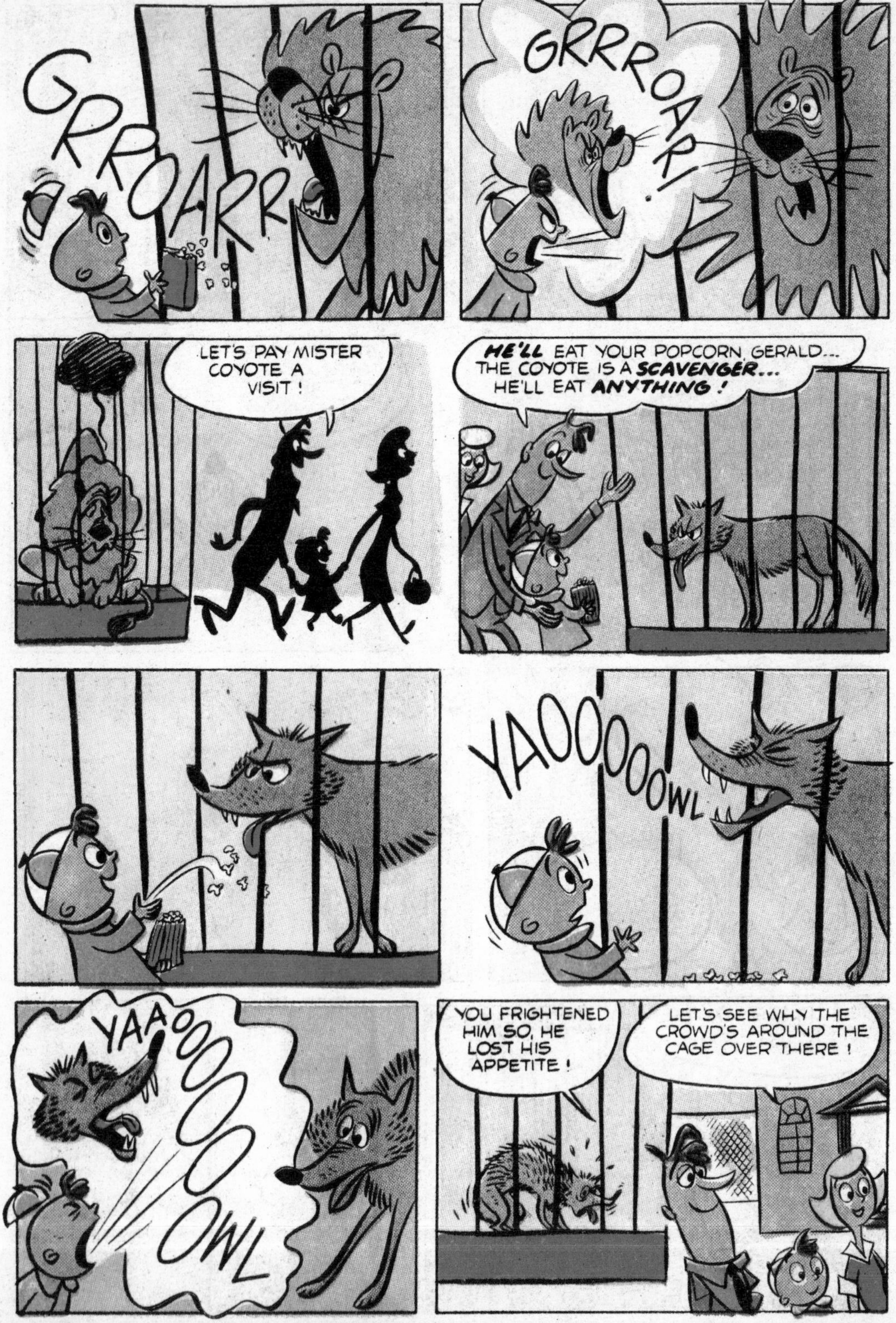
GRROARR
GRRROAR!
LET'S PAY MISTER COYOTE A VISIT!
HE'LL EAT YOUR POPCORN, GERALD... THE COYOTE IS A SCAVENGER... HE'LL EAT ANYTHING!
YAOOOOOWL
YAAOOOOOOWL
YOU FRIGHTENED HIM SO, HE LOST HIS APPETITE!
LET'S SEE WHY THE CROWD'S AROUND THE CAGE OVER THERE!

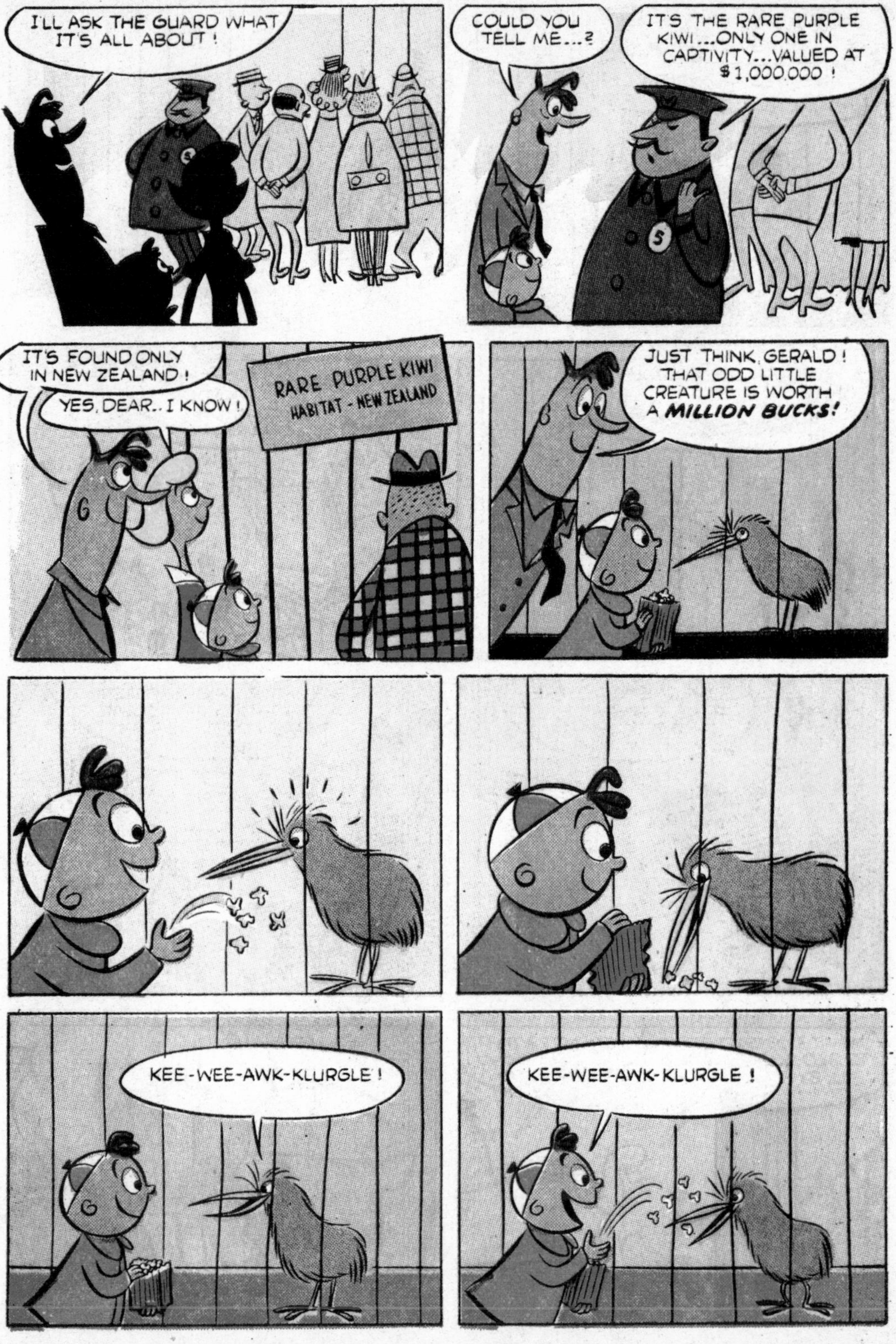
I'LL ASK THE GUARD WHAT IT'S ALL ABOUT !
COULD YOU TELL ME...?
IT'S THE RARE PURPLE KIWI ...ONLY ONE IN CAPTIVITY...VALUED AT $1,000,000 !
IT'S FOUND ONLY IN NEW ZEALAND !
YES, DEAR.. I KNOW !
RARE PURPLE KIWI
HABITAT - NEW ZEALAND
JUST THINK, GERALD ! THAT ODD LITTLE CREATURE IS WORTH A MILLION BUCKS!
KEE-WEE-AWK-KLURGLE !
KEE-WEE-AWK-KLURGLE !

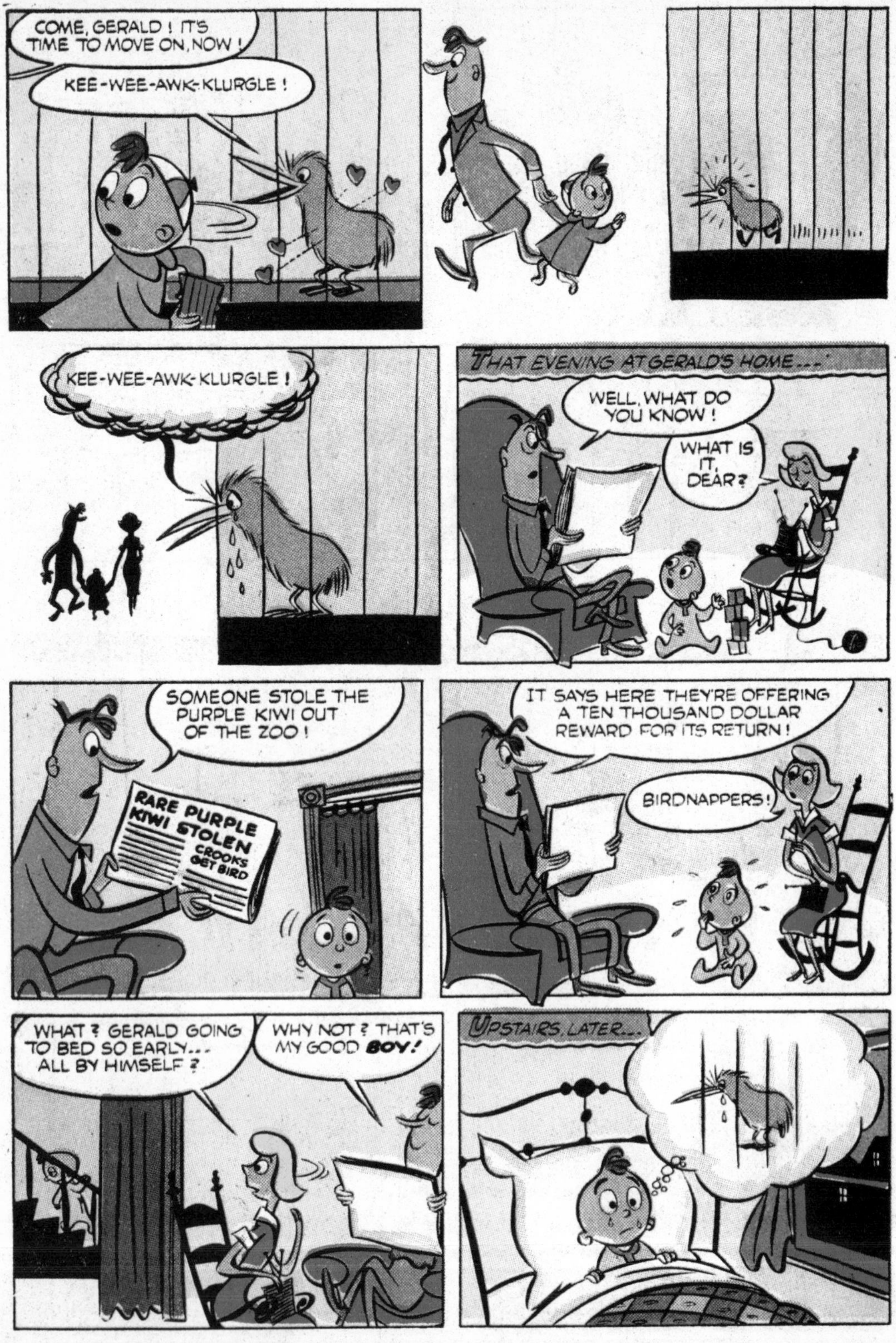
COME, GERALD! IT'S TIME TO MOVE ON, NOW!
KEE-WEE-AWK-KLURGLE!
KEE-WEE-AWK-KLURGLE!
THAT EVENING AT GERALD'S HOME...
WELL, WHAT DO YOU KNOW!
WHAT IS IT, DEAR?
SOMEONE STOLE THE PURPLE KIWI OUT OF THE ZOO!
RARE PURPLE KIWI STOLEN
CROOKS GET BIRD
IT SAYS HERE THEY'RE OFFERING A TEN THOUSAND DOLLAR REWARD FOR ITS RETURN!
BIRDNAPPERS!
WHAT? GERALD GOING TO BED SO EARLY... ALL BY HIMSELF?
WHY NOT? THAT'S MY GOOD BOY!
UPSTAIRS, LATER...

AS GERALD WANDERS THROUGH THE NIGHT HE COMES UPON A LITTLE CAFE WITH A COUPÉ PARKED OUTSIDE.

NOW THAT WE'VE GOT THE BIRD, HOW DO WE CASH IN ON IT, BUTCH?

I KNOW A REAL RICH GUY WHO'LL PAY US PLENTY FOR IT.

JOE'S CAFE

YOU MEAN...?

SURE...MR. ZILCH, THAT WEALTHY ECCENTRIC... THE BIRD FANCIER!

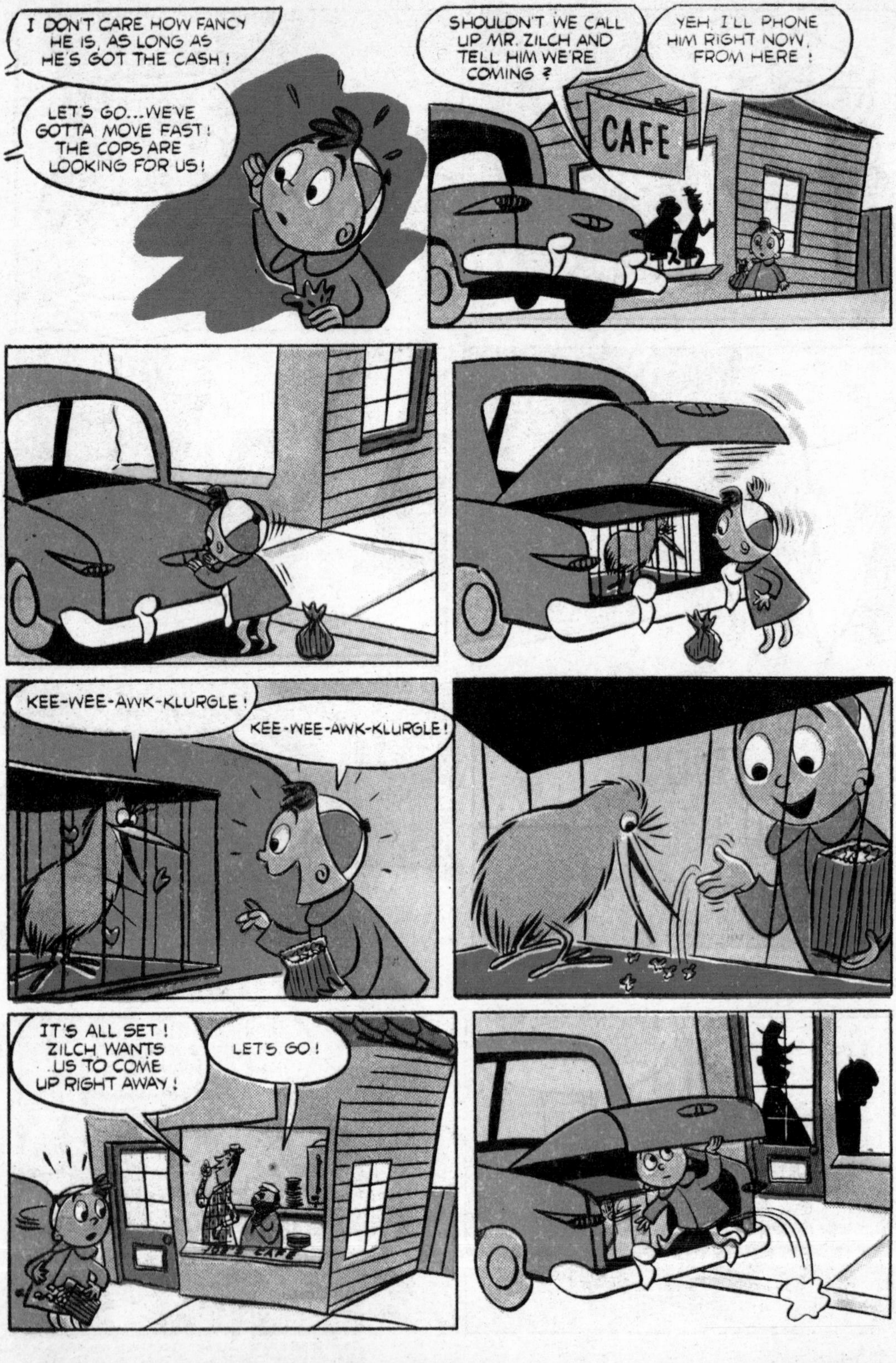
I DON'T CARE HOW FANCY HE IS, AS LONG AS HE'S GOT THE CASH !
LET'S GO...WE'VE GOTTA MOVE FAST ! THE COPS ARE LOOKING FOR US !
SHOULDN'T WE CALL UP MR. ZILCH AND TELL HIM WE'RE COMING ?
YEH, I'LL PHONE HIM RIGHT NOW, FROM HERE !
CAFE
KEE-WEE-AWK-KLURGLE !
KEE-WEE-AWK-KLURGLE !
IT'S ALL SET ! ZILCH WANTS US TO COME UP RIGHT AWAY !
LET'S GO !

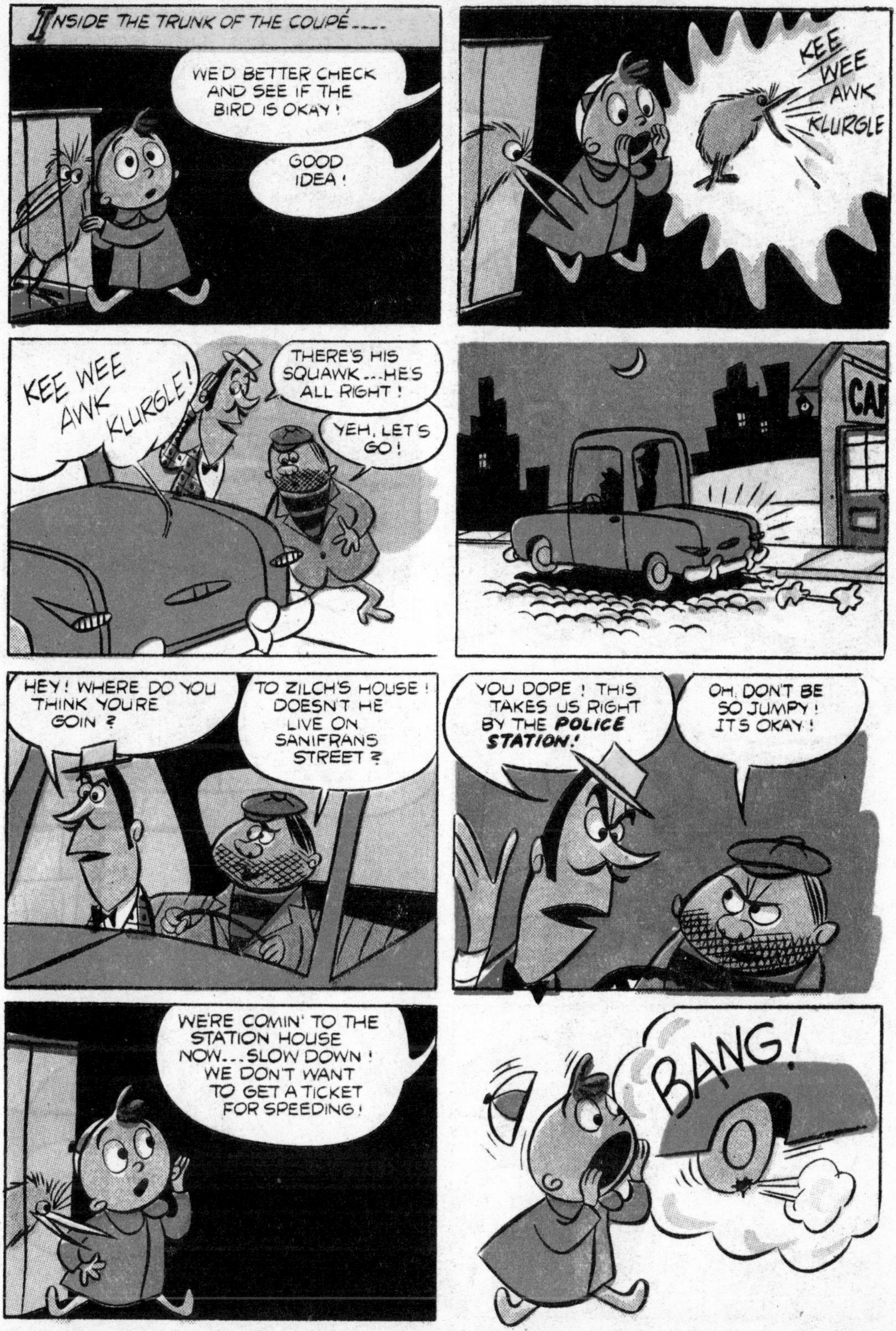
INSIDE THE TRUNK OF THE COUPÉ....
WE'D BETTER CHECK AND SEE IF THE BIRD IS OKAY!
GOOD IDEA!
KEE WEE AWK KLURGLE
KEE WEE AWK KLURGLE!
THERE'S HIS SQUAWK...HE'S ALL RIGHT!
YEH, LET'S GO!
CAF
HEY! WHERE DO YOU THINK YOU'RE GOIN?
TO ZILCH'S HOUSE! DOESN'T HE LIVE ON SANIFRANS STREET?
YOU DOPE! THIS TAKES US RIGHT BY THE **POLICE STATION!**
OH, DON'T BE SO JUMPY! IT'S OKAY!
WE'RE COMIN' TO THE STATION HOUSE NOW...SLOW DOWN! WE DON'T WANT TO GET A TICKET FOR SPEEDING!
BANG!

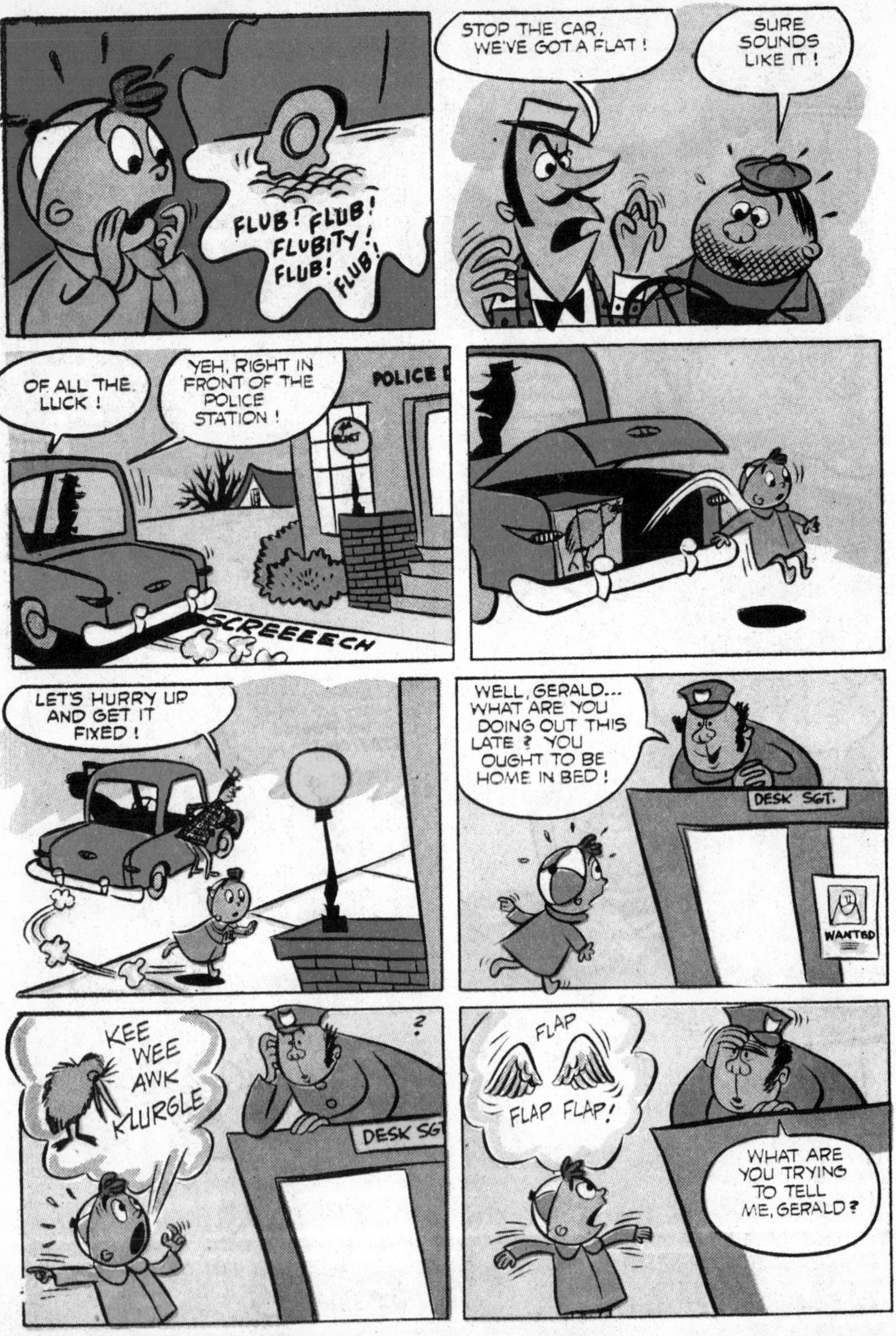
FLUB! FLUB! FLUBITY! FLUB! FLUB!
STOP THE CAR, WE'VE GOT A FLAT!
SURE SOUNDS LIKE IT!
OF ALL THE LUCK!
YEH, RIGHT IN FRONT OF THE POLICE STATION!
POLICE
SCREEEEECH
LET'S HURRY UP AND GET IT FIXED!
WELL, GERALD... WHAT ARE YOU DOING OUT THIS LATE? YOU OUGHT TO BE HOME IN BED!
DESK SGT.
WANTED
KEE WEE AWK KLURGLE
?
DESK SGT
FLAP
FLAP FLAP!
WHAT ARE YOU TRYING TO TELL ME, GERALD?

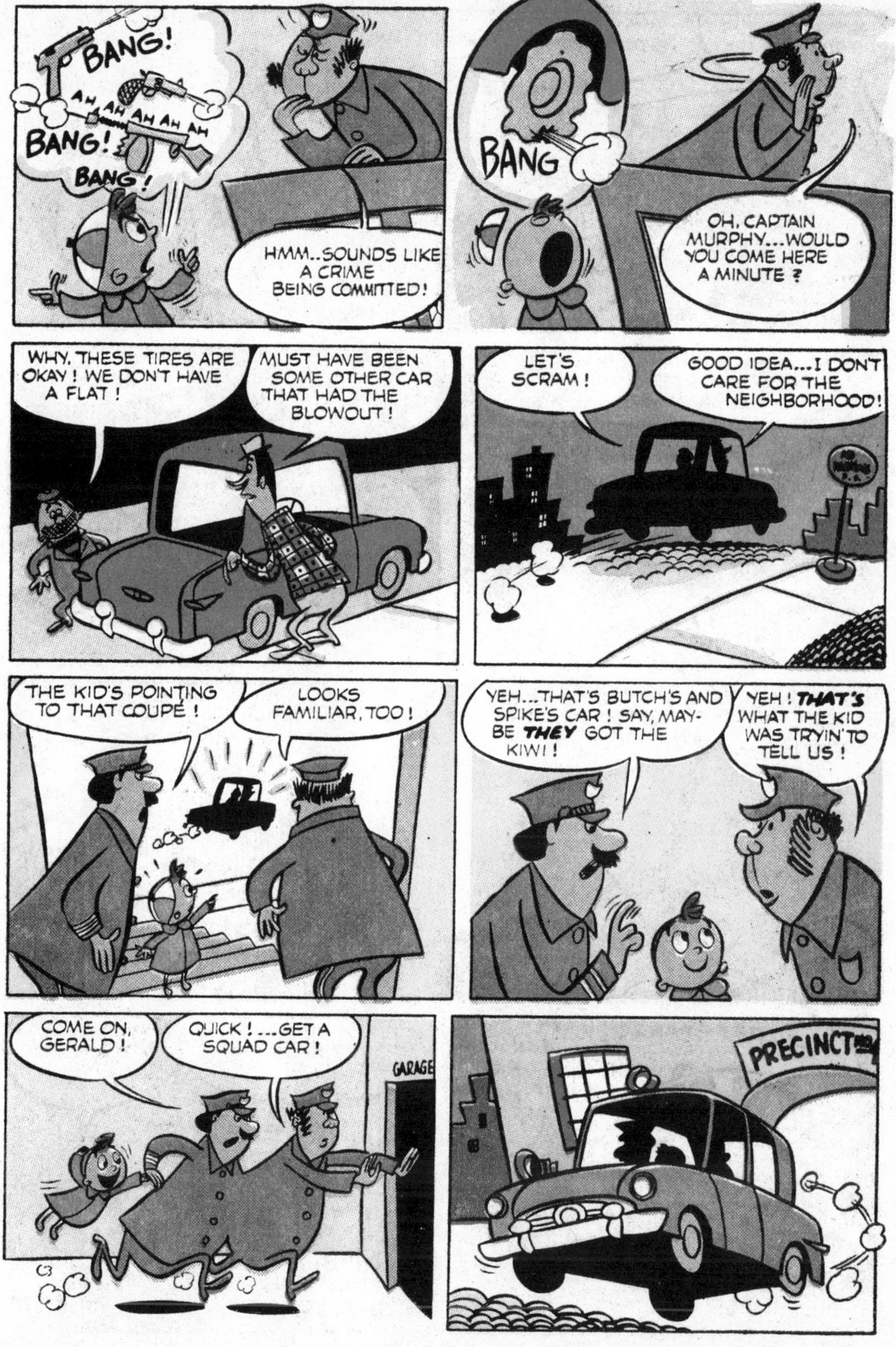
BANG!
AH AH AH AH AH AH
BANG!
BANG!
HMM..SOUNDS LIKE A CRIME BEING COMMITTED!
BANG
OH, CAPTAIN MURPHY...WOULD YOU COME HERE A MINUTE ?
WHY, THESE TIRES ARE OKAY ! WE DON'T HAVE A FLAT !
MUST HAVE BEEN SOME OTHER CAR THAT HAD THE BLOWOUT !
LET'S SCRAM !
GOOD IDEA...I DON'T CARE FOR THE NEIGHBORHOOD!
THE KID'S POINTING TO THAT COUPÉ !
LOOKS FAMILIAR, TOO !
YEH...THAT'S BUTCH'S AND SPIKE'S CAR ! SAY, MAY-BE THEY GOT THE KIWI !
YEH ! THAT'S WHAT THE KID WAS TRYIN' TO TELL US !
COME ON, GERALD !
QUICK ! ...GET A SQUAD CAR !
GARAGE
PRECINCT

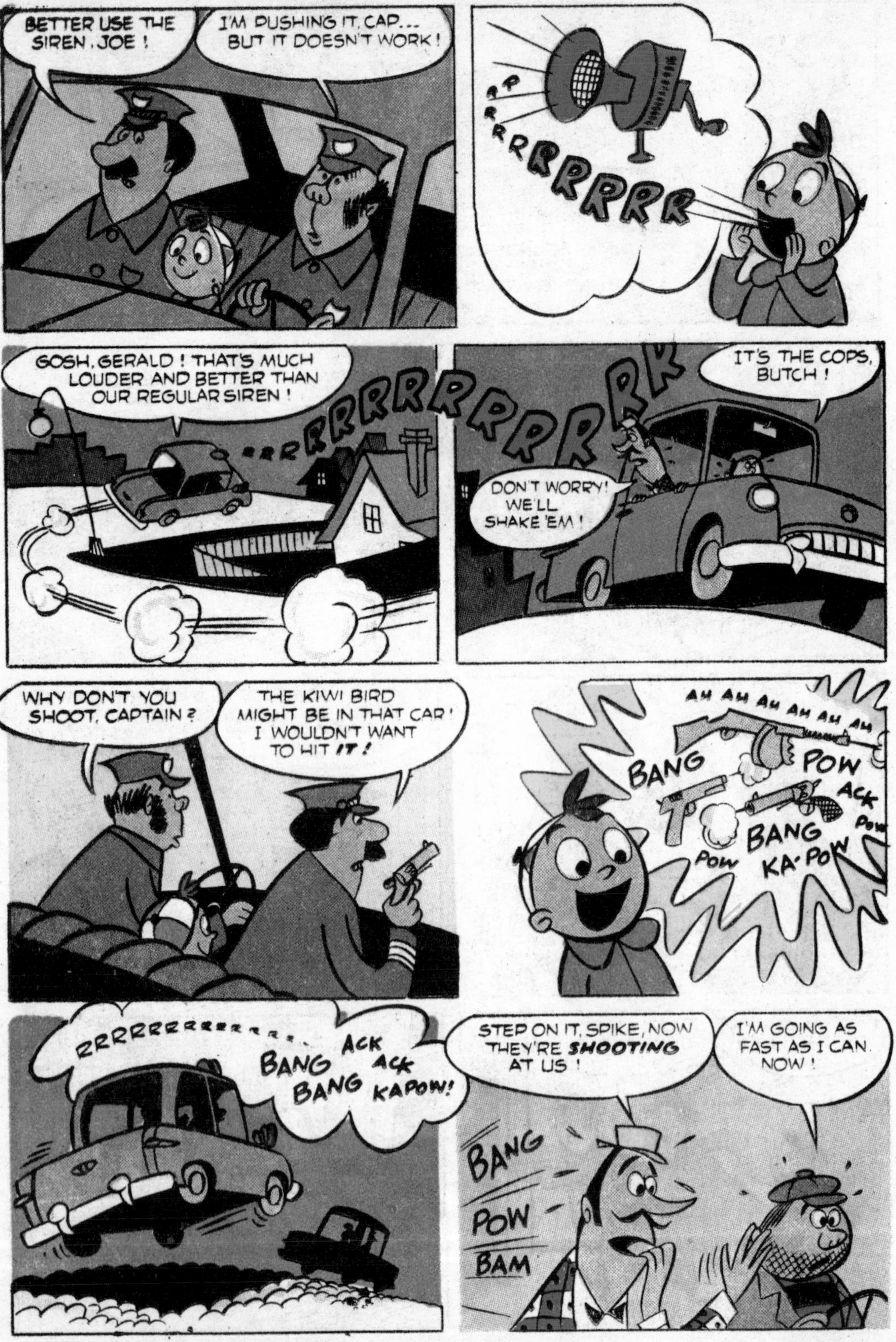
BETTER USE THE SIREN, JOE!
I'M PUSHING IT, CAP... BUT IT DOESN'T WORK!
RRRRRRRRRRR
GOSH, GERALD! THAT'S MUCH LOUDER AND BETTER THAN OUR REGULAR SIREN!
RRRRRRRRRRRRRK
IT'S THE COPS, BUTCH!
DON'T WORRY! WE'LL SHAKE 'EM!
WHY DON'T YOU SHOOT, CAPTAIN?
THE KIWI BIRD MIGHT BE IN THAT CAR! I WOULDN'T WANT TO HIT IT!
AH AH AH AH AH AH
BANG POW ACK POW
BANG POW KA-POW
RRRRRRRRRRRRR...
BANG ACK BANG ACK KAPOW!
STEP ON IT, SPIKE, NOW THEY'RE SHOOTING AT US!
I'M GOING AS FAST AS I CAN NOW!
BANG
POW
BAM

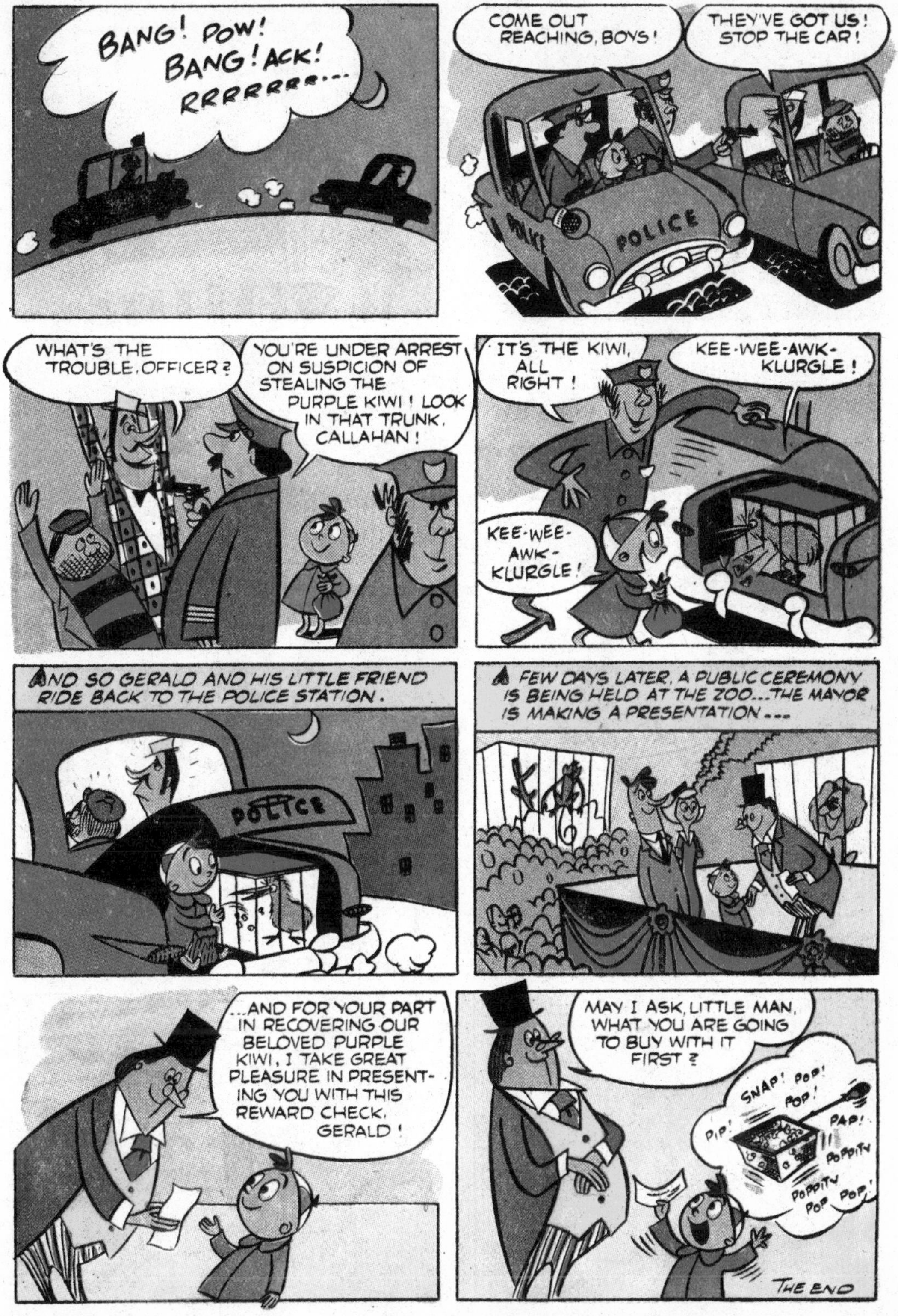
BANG! POW! BANG! ACK! RRRRRRR...
COME OUT REACHING, BOYS!
THEY'VE GOT US! STOP THE CAR!
POLICE
WHAT'S THE TROUBLE, OFFICER?
YOU'RE UNDER ARREST ON SUSPICION OF STEALING THE PURPLE KIWI! LOOK IN THAT TRUNK, CALLAHAN!
IT'S THE KIWI, ALL RIGHT!
KEE-WEE-AWK-KLURGLE!
KEE-WEE-AWK-KLURGLE!
AND SO GERALD AND HIS LITTLE FRIEND RIDE BACK TO THE POLICE STATION.
POLICE
A FEW DAYS LATER, A PUBLIC CEREMONY IS BEING HELD AT THE ZOO... THE MAYOR IS MAKING A PRESENTATION...
...AND FOR YOUR PART IN RECOVERING OUR BELOVED PURPLE KIWI, I TAKE GREAT PLEASURE IN PRESENTING YOU WITH THIS REWARD CHECK, GERALD!
MAY I ASK, LITTLE MAN, WHAT YOU ARE GOING TO BUY WITH IT FIRST?
SNAP! POP! POP! PIP! PAP! POPPITY POPPITY POP POP!
THE END

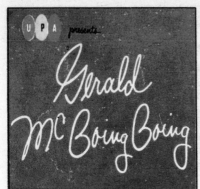

UPA presents

Gerald McBoing Boing

I WISH THOSE KIDS WOULDN'T PLAY BASEBALL SO CLOSE TO THE HOUSE!

OH, WELL....IF THEY BREAK A WINDOW, THEY'LL HAVE TO PAY FOR IT!

PITCH IT TO ME, FRED BOY!

GOLLY, A FOUL BALL!

WHACK

IT'S HEADED FOR THE HOUSE!

CRASH

BASH!

TINKLE!

TINKLE!

SCRAM, FELLAS!

QUICK! WE'VE GOTTA GET AWAY FROM HERE!

HMM....THOSE KIDS BEAT IT....MUST HAVE READ MY MIND!

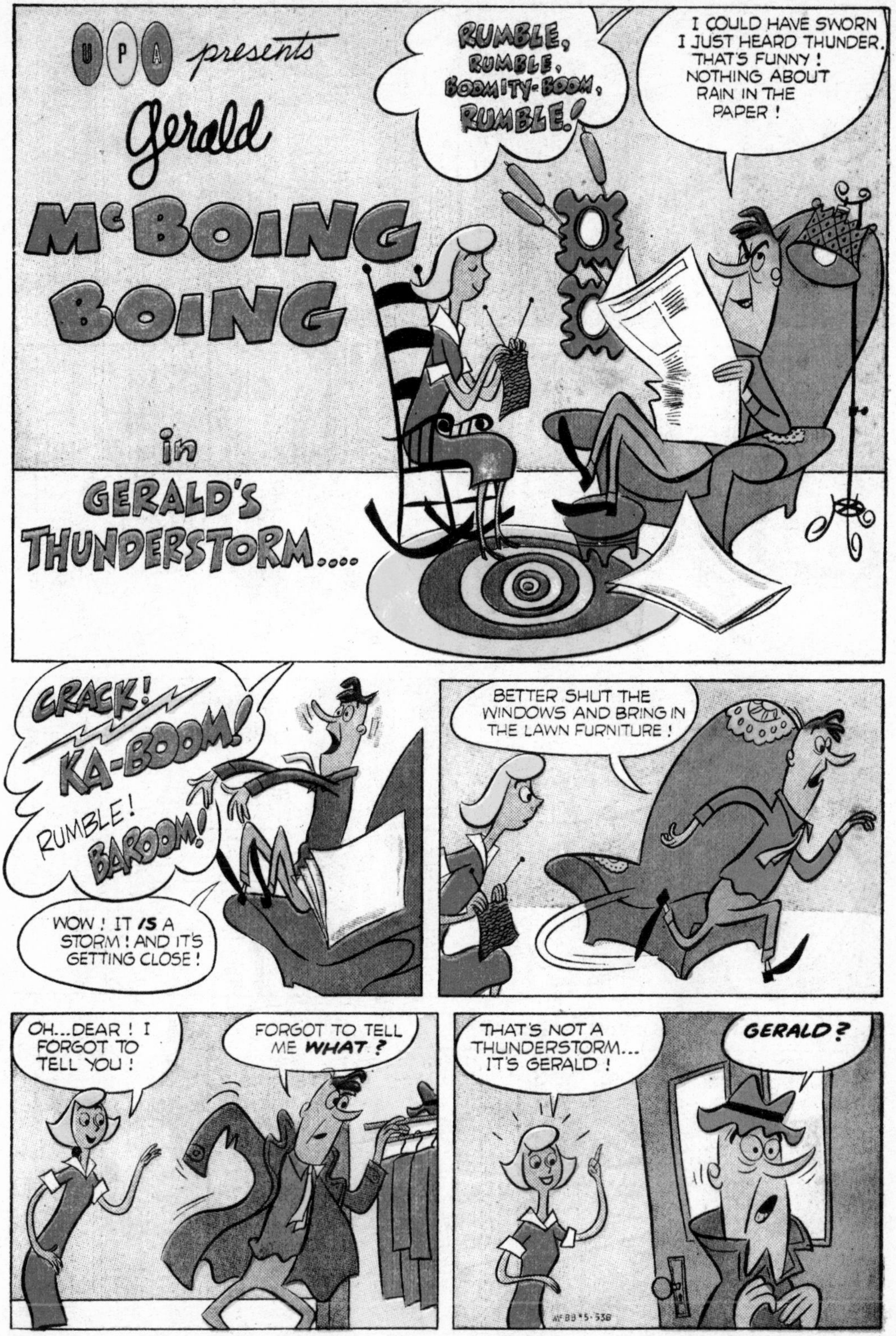
UPA presents
Gerald
McBOING BOING
in
GERALD'S THUNDERSTORM....
RUMBLE, RUMBLE, BOOMITY-BOOM, RUMBLE!
I COULD HAVE SWORN I JUST HEARD THUNDER. THAT'S FUNNY! NOTHING ABOUT RAIN IN THE PAPER!
CRACK! KA-BOOM! RUMBLE! BAROOM!
WOW! IT *IS* A STORM! AND IT'S GETTING CLOSE!
BETTER SHUT THE WINDOWS AND BRING IN THE LAWN FURNITURE!
OH...DEAR! I FORGOT TO TELL YOU!
FORGOT TO TELL ME *WHAT*?
THAT'S NOT A THUNDERSTORM... IT'S GERALD!
GERALD?

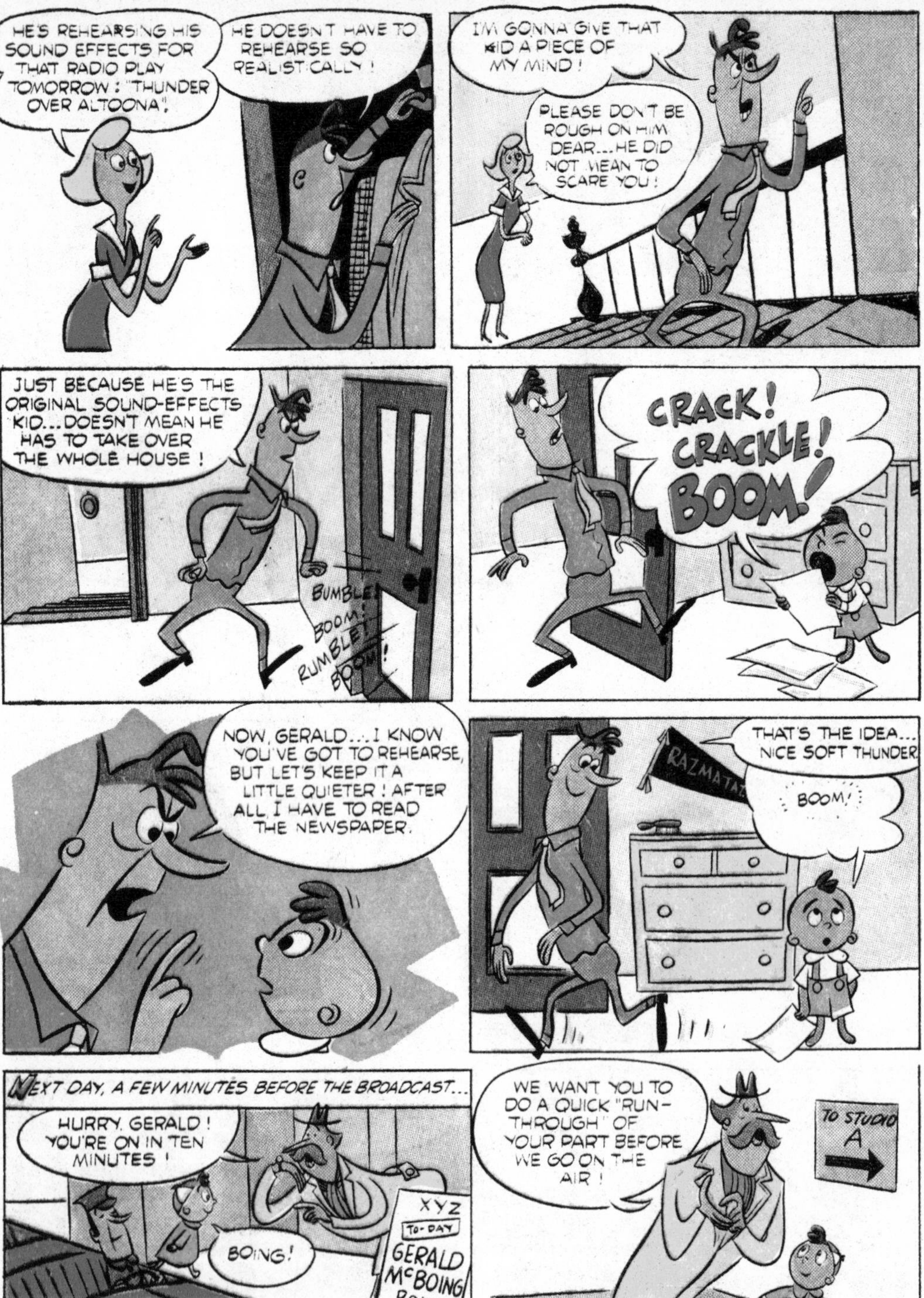
HE'S REHEARSING HIS SOUND EFFECTS FOR THAT RADIO PLAY TOMORROW: "THUNDER OVER ALTOONA".
HE DOESN'T HAVE TO REHEARSE SO REALISTICALLY!
I'M GONNA GIVE THAT KID A PIECE OF MY MIND!
PLEASE DON'T BE ROUGH ON HIM, DEAR... HE DID NOT MEAN TO SCARE YOU!
JUST BECAUSE HE'S THE ORIGINAL SOUND-EFFECTS KID... DOESN'T MEAN HE HAS TO TAKE OVER THE WHOLE HOUSE!
BUMBLE! BOOM! RUMBLE! BOOM!
CRACK! CRACKLE! BOOM!
NOW, GERALD... I KNOW YOU'VE GOT TO REHEARSE, BUT LET'S KEEP IT A LITTLE QUIETER! AFTER ALL, I HAVE TO READ THE NEWSPAPER.
RAZMATAZ
THAT'S THE IDEA... NICE SOFT THUNDER!
BOOM!
NEXT DAY, A FEW MINUTES BEFORE THE BROADCAST...
HURRY, GERALD! YOU'RE ON IN TEN MINUTES!
BOING!
XYZ
TO-DAY
GERALD McBOING BOING
WE WANT YOU TO DO A QUICK "RUN-THROUGH" OF YOUR PART BEFORE WE GO ON THE AIR!
TO STUDIO A

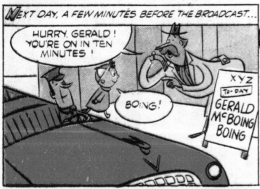

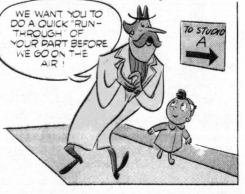

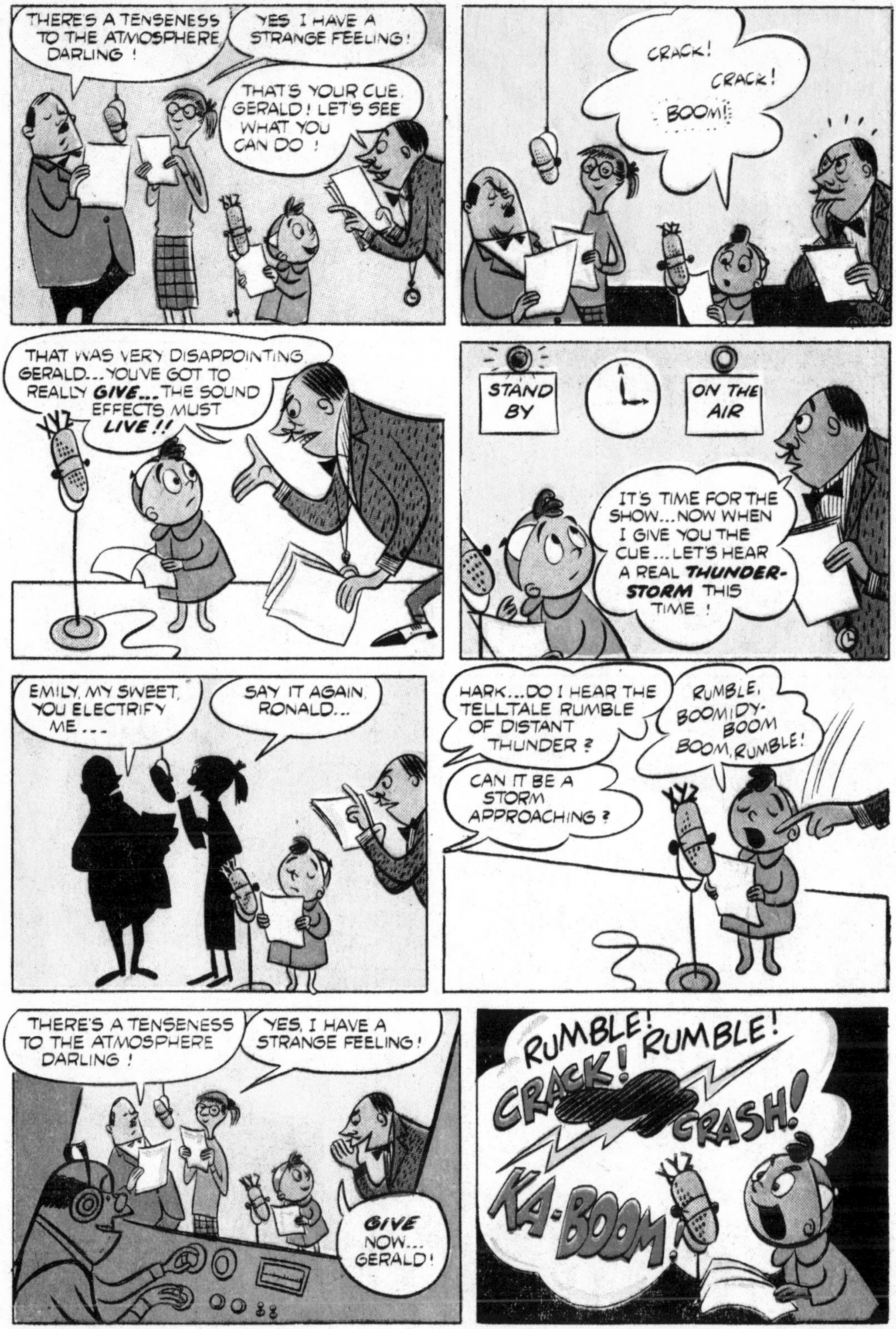
THERE'S A TENSENESS TO THE ATMOSPHERE DARLING !
YES I HAVE A STRANGE FEELING !
THAT'S YOUR CUE, GERALD ! LET'S SEE WHAT YOU CAN DO !
CRACK!
CRACK!
BOOM!
THAT WAS VERY DISAPPOINTING GERALD... YOU'VE GOT TO REALLY GIVE... THE SOUND EFFECTS MUST LIVE !!
STAND BY
ON THE AIR
IT'S TIME FOR THE SHOW... NOW WHEN I GIVE YOU THE CUE... LET'S HEAR A REAL THUNDER-STORM THIS TIME !
EMILY, MY SWEET, YOU ELECTRIFY ME...
SAY IT AGAIN, RONALD...
HARK... DO I HEAR THE TELLTALE RUMBLE OF DISTANT THUNDER ?
CAN IT BE A STORM APPROACHING ?
RUMBLE, BOOMIDY-BOOM BOOM, RUMBLE!
THERE'S A TENSENESS TO THE ATMOSPHERE DARLING !
YES, I HAVE A STRANGE FEELING !
GIVE NOW... GERALD !
RUMBLE! RUMBLE!
CRACK!
CRASH!
KA-BOOM!

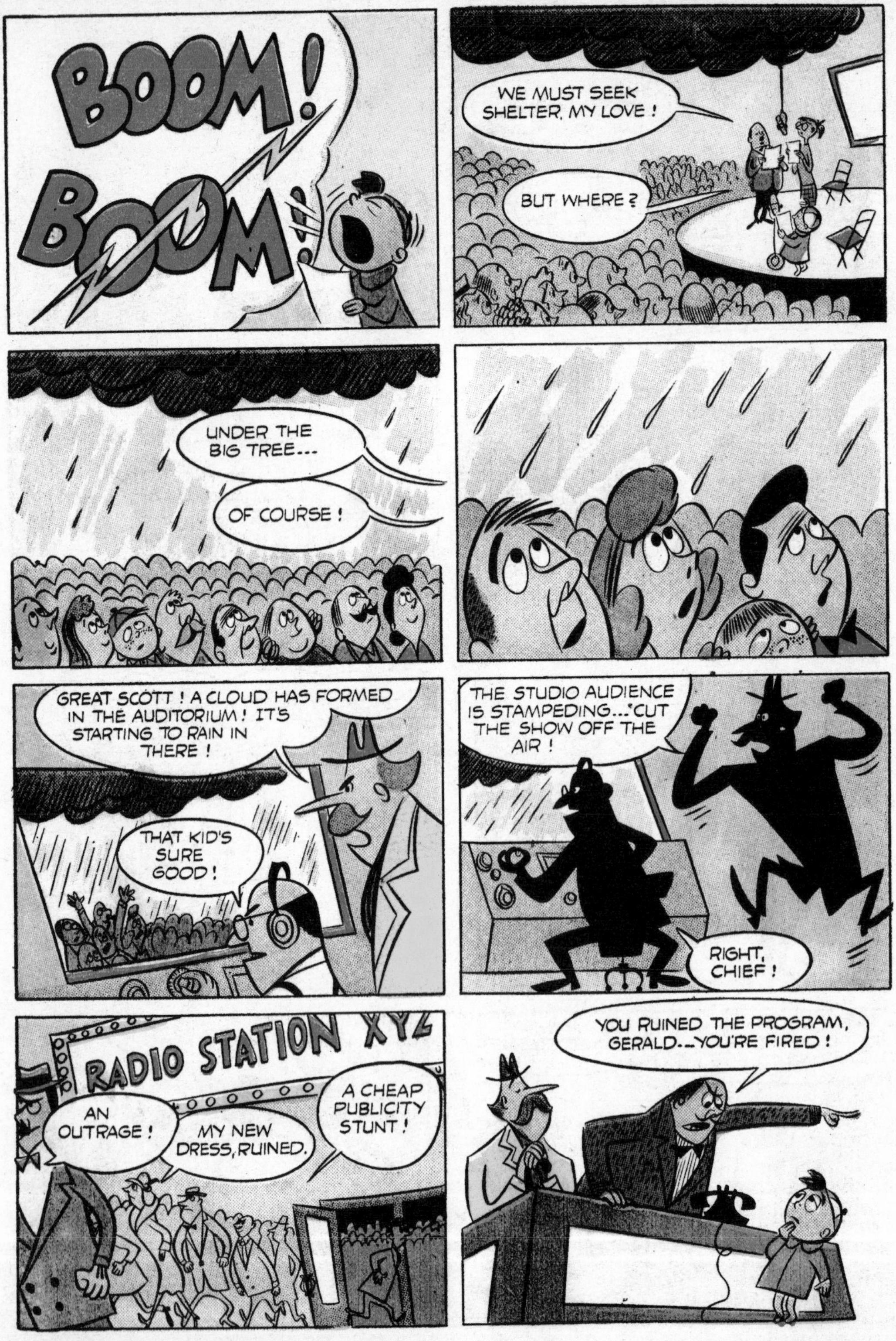
BOOM!
BOOM!
WE MUST SEEK SHELTER, MY LOVE!
BUT WHERE?
UNDER THE BIG TREE...
OF COURSE!
GREAT SCOTT! A CLOUD HAS FORMED IN THE AUDITORIUM! IT'S STARTING TO RAIN IN THERE!
THAT KID'S SURE GOOD!
THE STUDIO AUDIENCE IS STAMPEDING...CUT THE SHOW OFF THE AIR!
RIGHT, CHIEF!
RADIO STATION XYZ
AN OUTRAGE!
MY NEW DRESS, RUINED.
A CHEAP PUBLICITY STUNT!
YOU RUINED THE PROGRAM, GERALD...YOU'RE FIRED!

RADIO STATION XY

GERALD McBOIN

TODAY
GERALD McBOING BOING
IN "THUNDER OVER ALTOONA"

I WONDER IF WE DID THE RIGHT THING?

I HATED TO FIRE THE KID, C.R., BUT HE SHOULDN'T HAVE PULLED A TRICK LIKE THAT.

WHAT'S THIS?

TELEGRAM FOR THE STATION MANAGER.

IT'S FROM THE MAYOR OF PRAIRIE GULCH, TEXAS... THEY HEARD ABOUT THE PROGRAM!

THEY'VE BEEN HAVING A TERRIBLE DROUGHT...CROPS ALL DYING! LISTEN TO THIS: "OFFER YOU $500,000 TO BRING RAIN TO PRAIRIE GULCH."

GET ME GERALD'S HOUSE! WHAT? HE HASN'T COME HOME YET?

YOU THINK HE HAS RUN AWAY?

QUICK! GET ME THE POLICE!

YOU IDIOT! WHAT DID YOU FIRE HIM FOR? SEE WHAT YOU'VE DONE...HE'S RUN AWAY!

BUT, CHIEF, YOU TOLD ME TO FIRE HIM!

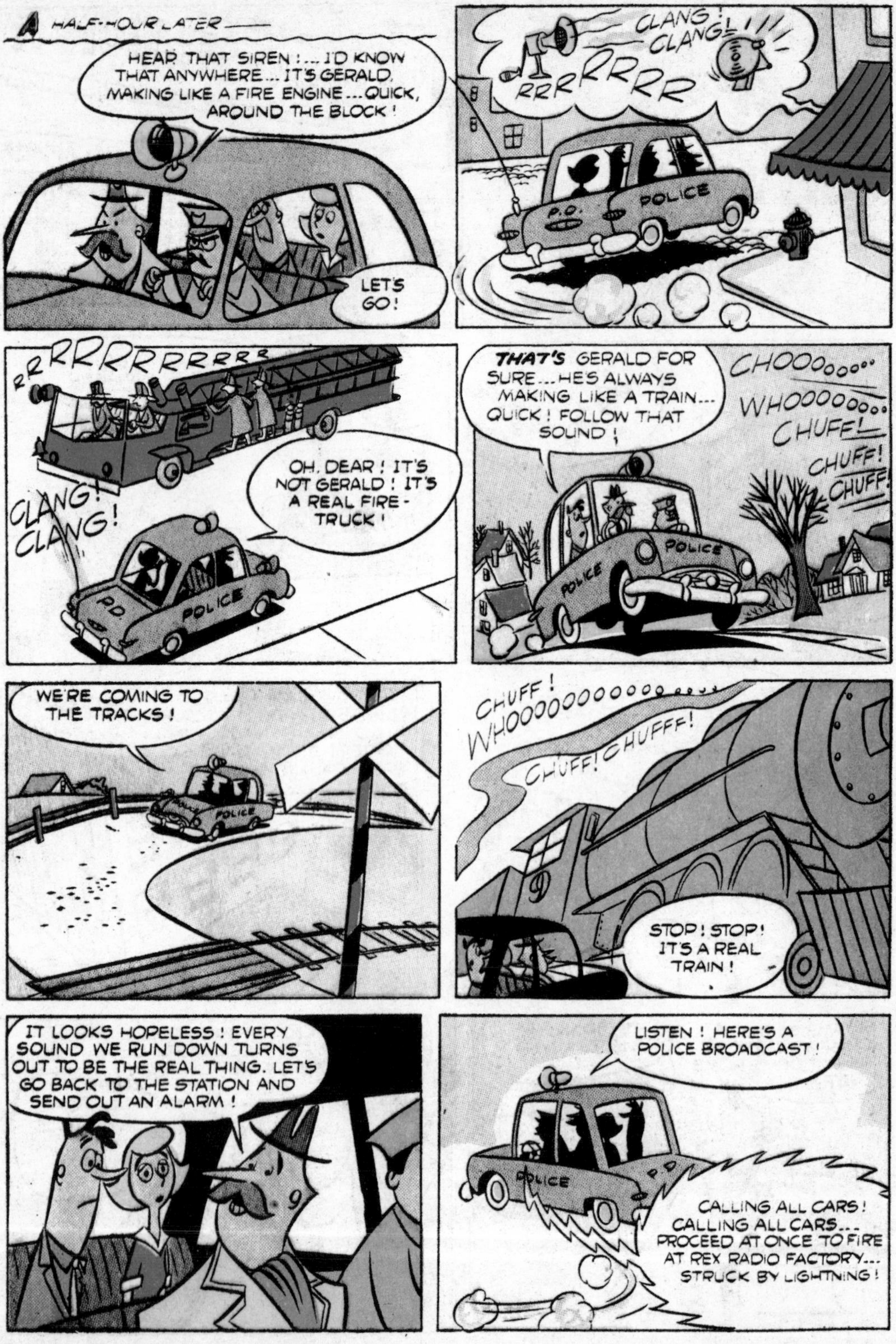
A HALF-HOUR LATER
HEAR THAT SIREN! ... I'D KNOW THAT ANYWHERE... IT'S GERALD, MAKING LIKE A FIRE ENGINE... QUICK, AROUND THE BLOCK!
LET'S GO!
CLANG! CLANG!
RRRRRRRR
POLICE
P.D.
RRRRRRRRRRRR
CLANG! CLANG!
OH, DEAR! IT'S NOT GERALD! IT'S A REAL FIRE-TRUCK!
P.D.
POLICE
THAT'S GERALD FOR SURE... HE'S ALWAYS MAKING LIKE A TRAIN... QUICK! FOLLOW THAT SOUND!
CHOOOoooo
WHOOOOOOOO
CHUFF!
CHUFF!
CHUFF!
POLICE
POLICE
WE'RE COMING TO THE TRACKS!
POLICE
CHUFF!
WHOOOOOOOOOOO
CHUFF! CHUFFF!
STOP! STOP! IT'S A REAL TRAIN!
IT LOOKS HOPELESS! EVERY SOUND WE RUN DOWN TURNS OUT TO BE THE REAL THING. LET'S GO BACK TO THE STATION AND SEND OUT AN ALARM!
LISTEN! HERE'S A POLICE BROADCAST!
POLICE
P.D.
CALLING ALL CARS! CALLING ALL CARS... PROCEED AT ONCE TO FIRE AT REX RADIO FACTORY... STRUCK BY LIGHTNING!

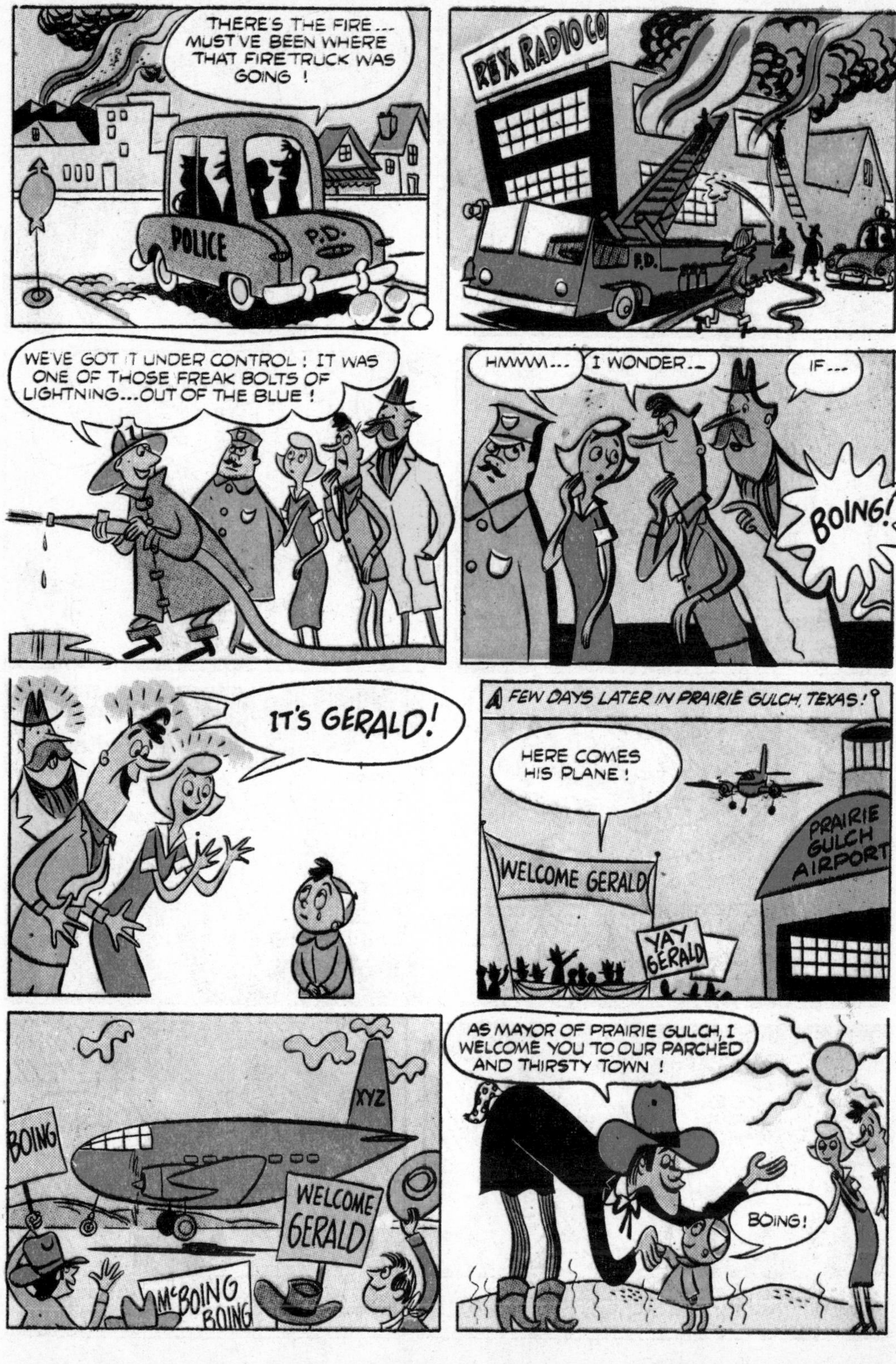
THERE'S THE FIRE... MUST'VE BEEN WHERE THAT FIRETRUCK WAS GOING !
POLICE
P.D.
REX RADIO CO
P.D.
WE'VE GOT IT UNDER CONTROL ! IT WAS ONE OF THOSE FREAK BOLTS OF LIGHTNING...OUT OF THE BLUE !
HMMM...
I WONDER...
IF...
BOING!
IT'S GERALD!
A FEW DAYS LATER IN PRAIRIE GULCH, TEXAS !
HERE COMES HIS PLANE !
PRAIRIE GULCH AIRPORT
WELCOME GERALD
YAY GERALD
XYZ
BOING
WELCOME GERALD
McBOING BOING
AS MAYOR OF PRAIRIE GULCH, I WELCOME YOU TO OUR PARCHED AND THIRSTY TOWN !
BOING !

AND SO, FOLKS, THE NEXT TIME *YOU* GET CAUGHT IN A SUDDEN THUNDERSTORM......

...DON'T BLAME THE WEATHERMAN! IT MIGHT BE THAT GERALD McBOING BOING IS PASSING YOUR WAY!

UPA presents Gerald McBOING BOING

in Gerald and the Cannibals

ONE YEAR IN THE SPRING, ON A VERY WARM DAY, THE GALLANT SHIP "HUNTRESS" SAILED OUT OF THE BAY.

SHE CARRIED THREE MASTS AND A RIP-ROARING CREW, AND GERALD McBOING BOING AND HIS FAMILY, TOO!

HER CAPTAIN WAS JAUNTY, AS OLD AS CAN BE --- HIS BEARD HAD TURNED GREEN FROM THE SALT OF THE SEA!

THEY WERE SAILING FOR OG, IN THE CANNIBAL ISLES-- BUT THE DANGER INVOLVED JUST MADE EVERYONE SMILE.

FOR OF SHIPWRECKS AND CANNIBALS NONE WAS AFRAID -- GERALD'S DAD HAD A MAP AN OLD PIRATE HAD MADE!

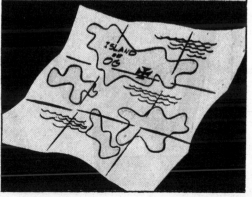

THE WEATHER HELD FAIR, WITH BLUE SEA AND BLUE SKY, AND GERALD GREETED ALL OF THE GULLS THAT FLEW BY.

SCREEE!

SOME PORPOISES FOLLOWED FOR MOST OF THE TRIP -- THEY SPLASHED AND THEY JUMPED AS THEY RACED WITH THE SHIP.

HUNTRESS

THEN ONE NIGHT THEY CROSSED THE EQUATOR WITH EASE, AND THE SOUTHERN CROSS SHOWED THEY WERE IN THE SOUTH SEAS.

THEY BEGAN PASSING ISLANDS, THROBBING WITH DRUMS, THE CAPTAIN EXPLAINED THAT IT MEANT, "GOOD FRIENDS COME!"

BOOM BOOM BOOM!

SO GERALD WOULD SIT AT THE MASTHEAD ALL DAY, ANSWERING DRUMS THAT HE HEARD FAR AWAY. "BOOM-BOOM-BOOM!" DRUMMED OUT GERALD, "BOOM-BOOM-BOOM, BAM-BAM-BAM!", AND THE GREETINGS CAME BACK FROM THE DRUMS ON THE LAND!

BOOM-BOOM-BUBBA-BOOM

AND SO THE DAYS PASSED ···
WITH EVERYONE WISHING
SO HARD FOR THE TREASURE,
THEY NEGLECTED THEIR FISHING!

TILL FINALLY, AT LAST
THE LOOKOUT SPIED LAND,
AND GERALD'S SHRILL WHISTLE
SUMMONED ALL HANDS.

WHOOOEEE
EEEEEEEEE

THE ENTIRE CREW RUSHED
TO PEER OVER THE RAIL,
SO THE LITTLE SHIP LISTED,
AND TIPPED ONE SAIL.

HUNTRESS

LOOK ALIVE, THERE, YA LUBBERS!
HARD A-PORT! HARD A-LEE!
WE'LL LIE OFF THE BEACH
TILL IT'S DARK AS CAN BE!

AND LET'S HAVE IT QUIET!
NO NOISE IN THE DARK!
THE FIRST BLOKE I HEAR
WILL GET FED TO THE SHARKS!

BUT BEFORE HE COULD FINISH,
THE TERRIBLE SCREECH
OF AN AMBULANCE SIREN
INTERRUPTED HIS SPEECH!

RRRP
RRRRRRRRRRRP

TWO HANDS WERE DISPATCHED TO THE YARDARM FOR GERALD-- HIS EARSPLITTING SHRIEK PUT THE SHIP IN GREAT PERIL!

SO GERALD WAS LOCKED IN HIS CABIN TO STAY... IT HAD BEEN 'SPECIALLY SOUNDPROOFED SO GERALD COULD PLAY.

THEY WERE TAKING NO CHANCES, WHEN THE CREW WAS ON LAND, OF GERALD ATTRACTING THE CANNIBAL BAND!

THEY LOWERED THE DINGHIES, AND ROWED FOR THE BEACH, WHILE, GERALD, UNHEARD NOW, CONTINUED TO SCREECH.

HE PRACTICED HIS SIREN, AND DRUMS THAT WENT *BOOM!* BUT THE SOUND NEVER WENT PAST THE WALLS OF HIS ROOM..

HE CLANGED AND HE CHUGGED, HE TOOTED AND YELLED, AND MADE A CRACKED NOISE LIKE THE LIBERTY BELL!

But all was not well with his friends on the land, for they had been caught, by the cannibal band!

When they didn't come back to the ship the next day, Gerald knew that they needed his help in some way.

From his cabin, the island looked easy to reach, so he dived out the porthole and swam for the beach!

SPLASH!

The island was dark -- there wasn't a sound! Gerald stood in the jungle, and peered all around!

Only one little monkey called from a tree. Gerald answered him back with a frightened...

CHEE! CHEE!

Then Gerald remembered that he ought to send a drum message saying that he was a friend!

BOOMITY - BUBBITY - BOOM! BOOM! BOOM! BUBBITY BOOM! BOOM! BOOM!

BUT THERE WASN'T AN ANSWER, NO DRUMS IN REPLY-- NO SIGNAL FIRES LIT--- JUST THE DARK EVENING SKY!

SO HE MUSTERED HIS COURAGE, AND SET OUT ON FOOT, AND TWO PACES LATER-- HE TRIPPED ON A ROOT!

HE PITCHED OVER FORWARD, AND FELL WITH A FWAP! NOT ON THE GROUND, BUT INTO A TRAP!

THE CANNIBALS HAD DUG THIS TRAP TO CATCH MEN -- AND GERALD WAS CERTAIN THAT THIS WAS THE END!

FWAP!

TO SUMMON ASSISTANCE HE BEGAN TO MAKE SOUNDS, AND THE WEIRDEST OF NOISES CAME OUT OF THE GROUND. KITTENS AND FOGHORNS AND ELEPHANT HOWLS, THE ROARING OF AIRPLANES, THE SCREECHING OF OWLS!

BEEOOOP! HOOOOT! WOOOM! EEEYAH! MEOW!

HAVING ONLY HEARD SOUNDS
LIKE THE SURF AND THE THUNDER,
THESE STRANGE SOUND EFFECTS
MAKE THE CANNIBALS WONDER.

BEEEOOP!
EEEYAH! MEEEOW!
HOOOT! ROARRRRRR!

THEY RAN TO THE TRAP,
AND THE THING THAT THEY SAW,
MADE THEM FALL TO THEIR KNEES
IN WONDER AND AWE.

FOR WHAT KIND OF DEVIL,
OR GOD COULD THIS BE,
WHO MADE MORE STRANGE SOUNDS
THAN THE RAIN AND THE SEA?

THEY HAULED GERALD OUT
WITH THE GREATEST OF CARE,
AND BORE HIM IN TRIUMPH
TO A HUGE GOLDEN CHAIR.

THE CANNIBAL KING
TOOK HIS CROWN FROM HIS HEAD,
AND GAVE IT TO GERALD
TO RULE IN HIS STEAD!

GERALD, IN HIS PLEASURE,
FEELING FULL, FAT AND SASSY,
MADE A SOUND LIKE A TROMBONE,
BAWDY AND BRASSY!

WAH! WAH! WAH!

BUT LOUD CRIES OF HELP
BROUGHT HIS JOY TO AN END,
AS HE HEARD THE LOUD CRIES
OF HIS FAMILY AND FRIENDS!

HELP!
HELP!

HE LEAPED FROM THE THRONE
AND RACED 'CROSS THE CLEARING,
DOWN A DARK JUNGLE PATH
TOWARD THE SHOUTS HE KEPT HEARING!

HELP!
HELP!

GERALD STOPPED WHEN HE SAW
THE SEVEN HUGE POTS!
..WITH THEIR FIRES ALL GOING,
AND THE WATER GETTING HOT!

AND STUFFED IN THE POTS
WAS THE "HUNTRESS'S" CREW,
HIS MOTHER, HIS FATHER,
AND THE OLD CAPTAIN, TOO!

THE CAPTAIN WAS BOILING,
WITHIN AND WITHOUT--
BUT HIS BEARD TURNING RED
WAS WHAT MADE HIM SHOUT!

THE CREW BEGAN CHEERING
WHEN GERALD HOVE TO,
GERALD'S MOTHER AND FATHER
BEGAN CHEERING, TOO!

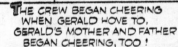

HURRAH!
HURRAH!

GERALD RAN UP
AND KICKED SAND ON THE FIRE,
THEN WENT TO HIS MOTHER
AND BEGAN TO UNTIE HER.

THEN GERALD HELPED OTHERS
GET OUT OF THE POTS,
WHILE ALL OF THE CANNIBALS
HELPED UNTIE KNOTS.

THEY RETURNED TO THE VILLAGE
FOR A GREAT CELEBRATION,
WITH CANNIBALS AND SAILORS
JOINING IN THE OVATION.

THEY SHOUTED AND SANG,
AND CHEERED THEMSELVES HOARSE,
AND GERALD JOINED IN
WITH HIS NOISES, OF COURSE!

THEY WHOOPED IT UP
AND DOWN UNTIL DAY,
AND THE SOUND THAT THEY MADE
CARRIED CLEAR TO BOMBAY!

THE NEXT DAY THEY SLEPT,
TILL THE SUN HAD CLIMBED HIGH--
THEN GERALD AND HIS FAMILY
TOLD THE NATIVES GOOD-BYE.

THEY WENT BACK TO THE SHIP
WITH THE CAPTAIN AND CREW--
THEY HOISTED THE SAILS,
AND THE BIG ANCHOR,TOO.

THEY TURNED THE SHIP 'ROUND,
AND SAILED INTO THE WIND--
BACK TO THE PORT,
WHERE THIS STORY BEGINS.

THEY BROUGHT BACK NO TREASURE,
NOR ANYTHING ELSE,
BUT GERALD'S GOLD CROWN,
THE SHIP AND THEMSELVES.

FOR THE MAP GERALD'S FATHER HAD
TURNED OUT A FAKE,
AND THEY DROPPED IT ASTERN
IN THE "HUNTRESS'S" WAKE !

BUT WHAT GREATER PLEASURE
COULD GOLD EVER BUY--
THAN A BRAVE OCEAN TRIP
'NEATH A FAIR, SUMMER SKY ?

THREE QUESTIONS ANSWERED ABOUT ROBERT CRUMB

BY TOM CRIPPEN

1. What about "When the Niggers Take Over America" and "When the Goddamn Jews Take Over America"?

They're shocking because, yes, white supremacists believe these things. In fact, white supremacists believe exactly these things. The only twist here is that Robert Crumb doesn't.

Crumb has produced many other works that don't have this twist. From the 1980s onward, he has written and drawn a series of comic-strip essays that are entertaining and ably put together, intelligent and well written. They give his point of view on one topic or another. He steps up and says what he has to say, and he does so with narrative captions that take you from little box to little box while the drawings flesh out the caption contents. You won't find a lot of surprises, and that applies to the thoughts being conveyed. Just as "Niggers" and "Goddamn Jews" represent the standard attitudes of racist trash, "I Remember the Sixties" is a greatest hits of what Baby Boomers were saying about their salad days as the 1980s began. "Where Has It Gone, All the Beautiful Music of Our Grandparents?" deplores the same trends deplored by the introductions to Lonely Planet Guides.

Well, why not? But the value added tends to be the comic strips' greater pithiness and the incidental pleasures of their presentation: Look at that

OH I'M TELLING YOU PEOPLE, THERE'S GONNA BE HELL TO PAY...

WHEN THE NIGGERS TAKE OVER AMERICA!

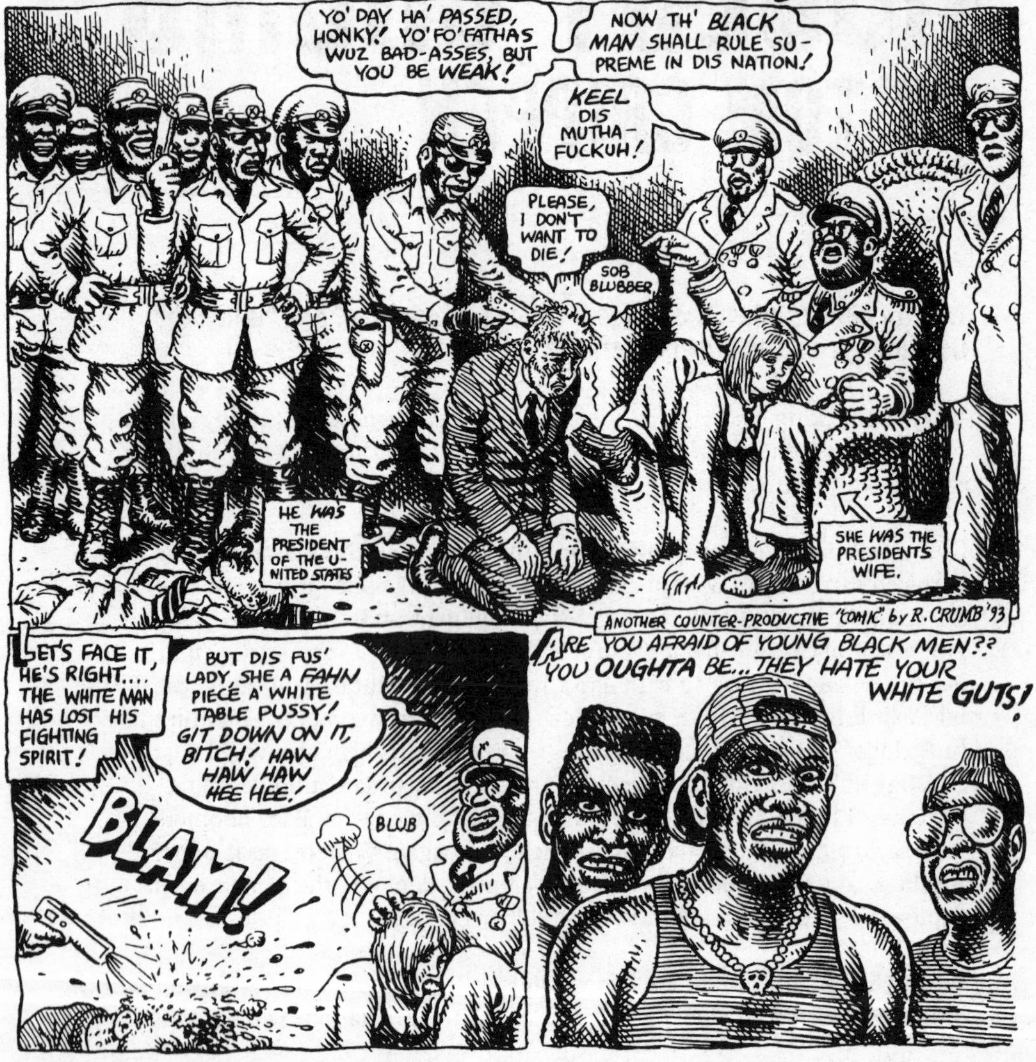
YO' DAY HA' PASSED, HONKY! YO' FO'FATHAS WUZ BAD-ASSES, BUT YOU BE WEAK!
NOW TH' BLACK MAN SHALL RULE SUPREME IN DIS NATION!
KEEL DIS MUTHA-FUCKUH!
PLEASE, I DON'T WANT TO DIE!
SOB BLUBBER
HE WAS THE PRESIDENT OF THE UNITED STATES
SHE WAS THE PRESIDENTS WIFE.
ANOTHER COUNTER-PRODUCTIVE "COMIC" by R. CRUMB '93
LET'S FACE IT, HE'S RIGHT.... THE WHITE MAN HAS LOST HIS FIGHTING SPIRIT!
BUT DIS FUS' LADY, SHE A FAHN PIECE A' WHITE TABLE PUSSY! GIT DOWN ON IT, BITCH! HAW HAW HAW HEE HEE!
BLAM!
BLUB
ARE YOU AFRAID OF YOUNG BLACK MEN?? YOU OUGHTA BE... THEY HATE YOUR WHITE GUTS!

face, dig that line of dialogue. A smarmy schlockmeister, face pursed with emotion, gets pious about the big bands ("This is the great music of America!"). To be very good at writing and drawing comic strips is no small thing. But the strips themselves are no big deal.

When the time came for a magnum opus, Crumb produced his *Book of Genesis Illustrated*, the most beautiful study aid ever published. The work inspired Robert Alter, the translator whose text Crumb used, to suggest that matching pictures with words is bound to flatten out a story, iron away its possibilities. If the text is the Bible, he said, you lose the shimmer produced by enigmatic quirks of translation. If it's a great novel, he continued, you give up "the deft slide in and out of the point of view of the characters, the subtle play of irony, the nice discriminations of the narrator's analytic observations." Those are serious losses to absorb. You have to hope that Alter is wrong, perhaps point him to captioning tricks by Alan Moore and others that could ease his mind regarding comics' use of irony and point of view. But his doubts are perfectly natural. He had just read the Crumb Genesis, and Crumb's Genesis is so exactly everybody else's Genesis, served up on a plate and with a big-thighed woman held in its mouth.

For an original, Crumb has a gift for being conventional. He grew up by fitting himself to a series of frameworks: pious Catholic, obedient little brother, conventional free-your-ass hippy, by-the-book promoter of appropriate technology. In his mid-30s he modified that last structure by downplaying the optimism; no more oats, now just the anomie. He's stayed in that groove ever since, and it suits him. But original it isn't. For me, everything Crumb has to say about the non-fun of modern times, about the reduction of life and joy to electrified twitches, is summed up by the progression from the "Keep on Truckin'" boobs to the fools on the cover of *Hup #4*. All right, that's plenty, but it leaves many pages of standard opinion nicely presented. Who else with his talent could have invented a character as boring, as completely unimaginative, as Mr. Appropriate? The soul would revolt.

2. What did drugs do for Robert Crumb?

There's Mr. Natural, of course, and the "Keep on Truckin'" guys and the sex fantasies on paper and all the trippy stuff that made him a star when he and his audience were ripped on the same shit — "the brilliant work of yours that we all got high off of back in the late 'Sixties," to quote the *High Times* interview with Robert Crumb. Crumb doesn't have a lot of original thoughts, but he

LEFT

From *Weirdo* #28

[©1993 R. Crumb]

"To be very good at writing and drawing comic strips is no small thing. But the strips themselves are no big deal."

draws original pictures. Drugs took Crumb and his readers, or potential readers, by the scruff of the neck and dropped them all on the same wavelength. That can help an original break on through to the big time a lot faster.

Nowadays it's easy to dismiss any psychedelia as the first goofy wave that led to ELO concept albums. But blowing minds is an honorable thing to do, and Crumb did it better than most. The skill and imagination shown in "The Old Pooperoo Pauses to Ponder" are still wonderful, with special reference to the "I Wanna Go Home!" parade of grotesques and the second page's allegory of debauched consciousness. It's a hell of a trip, and a lot of its appeal comes from the concept-album standby of loading the surface with detail, whether sensory or allegorical ("messages").

For all the liberation or pseudo-liberation that they spread, drugs caused a good deal of people to spend a good deal of time staring very closely at things that earlier they would not have looked at nearly so hard. For instance, candles, album covers and comic books. Going into the grain, whether of the moment or a drawing, became a hallmark of the period. Crumb and his audience were ready to take that step. The "Can the mind know it?" cover of the *East Village Other* features a tenement building that's as psychedelic as the picture's grimacing sun. The psychedelia, the extra dimension, lies in how much of the building is present: Every scratchy line seems to wiggle like a live thing. The

Keep on Truckin'...

dense crosshatching, and a line that would keep getting heavier, evolved into the style that we know today as standard Crumb, the style Robert Alter has in mind when he mistakenly says Crumb "has always been an artist with a single style." It's seen at its best, its warmest and most comfortable, in works like the cover of *Zap* #1 ("I wish somebody would tell me what 'diddy-wah-diddy' means . . .") and the famous shot of Mr. Natural as vacuum-cleaner salesman ("Let's just say this dirt is your conscious mind . . ."). Let's say that an overexcited college student, writing in 1971 for a local underground paper, might have put it like this: "The oatmeal-and-wool, scritchy-scratchy combination of crosshatching and lumpy forms can wheeze into an unexpected, insinuating rasp that works itself into the nervous system with minimal appeal to beauty. Whacked out on drugs, Crumb has taught himself a style that reconfigures old funny-animal comics and older flat-panel gag strips into an odd music similar to Robert Johnson's guitar duetting with a banjo, if Robert Johnson's guitar weren't so boring."

"Flat-panel strips" is a reference to Tijuana bibles and '20s and '30s humor strips. Crumb's line became denser during his drugs period, but in certain places it also became thinner and sketchier, and the two brands could coexist in the same drawing. As the months and years passed, the sketchy line was seen less and Crumb settled on a more uniform approach, one that started heavy and became heavier. I have to say I prefer the styles he was experimenting with before he took drugs. The cartoon portraits he did at age 18 and 19 sometimes outshine his later portraits, right up to the work in *Book of Genesis*. The line is freer and uncluttered; often enough actual people seem to be there, face to face with you. When he draws the racer Barney Oldfield, it's like the man is looking you in the eye even though his own eyes are hidden by ink. Crumb's Della Fox and Laura Hope Crews, his outrageously cartoony but

617

TOP

From "Keep on Truckin'" in *Zap* #2 (November 1967) [©1967 R. Crumb]

Mr. Natural, disguised as a vacuum cleaner salesman, talks to the Housewives of America.

vivid J. Harold Murray (these are all stage personalities from long ago), his pastry cook drawn from a collection of prewar German photographs — they register in a way that later Crumb portraits don't. Crumb never stopped drawing vivid people, but they seem like people trapped behind a screen of cross-hatching, their head and shoulders fastened atop structures that are a lot like bodies but also like sturdy furniture that could take the skin off your knee.

Freedom is a hallmark of the pre-psychedelic Crumb. It's odd because he was trapped and miserable, a prisoner in his parents' house and then at American Greetings, the company where he worked in Cleveland. But the panels of his comics back then have more air to them, and the eye is given greater range between foreground and background. The pages of R. Crumb's Comics and Stories, from 1964, have a sort of lilt that works from the loose figures to the freehand panel borders to the open page design. Some of the installments of his Roberta Smith, Office Girl series of apprentice comic strips done for American Greetings pack their little rectangles with shifting foreground-background dynamics, galleries of caricatures, and subtly balanced patterns of black and white, and they do it without seeming crowded.

Along with the air, there's a variety of approach to early Crumb that's a relief when placed next to psychedelic and post-psychedelic Crumb. The eye spends less time locked in the middle ground, less time locked on bulky figures that could fit together like wood carvings, less time locked on the crosshatching and heavy lines. The Crumb we know today could snap your neck; that's how much weight drags the eye

toward the page. It's an odd thing to find with a man who lived out a classic '60s liberation story: Hello to the open road, to the inner being, to artistic breakthrough, stampeding girls, international fame — and the damn weight. But all that staring into the grain is going to catch up with you.

3. Could Robert Crumb have survived during the premodern era?

Yes. The unspoken message of *Crumb*, Terry Zwigoff's documentary about Crumb, is that some people make it and some don't, and the difference lies in spine and appetite. Crumb and his big brother, Charles, grew up in the same house of horrors and were both under the thumb of bullies at high school. But Charles broke, Robert didn't. Charles sat around the house his whole life and then killed himself at age 50. Robert got out by means of comic fandom's underground railroad, then found himself a job, a wife, a psychic transformation, and on and on. He was a downtrodden, limp-wristed boy who looked like a string of snot, but he grabbed himself an adulthood pretty much made to order for a kid eager to make art and to fuck any girl he wanted to fuck. (The reason cartoonists can't get laid is that Robert Crumb used up their share.)

Crumb the boy suffered plenty, but Crumb the artist grew like a weed. He learned to crosshatch after looking at Thomas Nast cartoons in the ninth grade. Then, in his late teens, as Crumb told Peter Poplaski: "I started looking at the old masters in books ... Leonardo, everybody. I thought I wanted to draw like that, so I drew like a motherfucker!" His brother had him churning out funny-animal comics, a good training ground in itself, but nobody told him to draw like Leonardo. That was Crumb's idea, and he went at it hard

LEFT TOP
From *The East Village Other (EVO)* Vol. 3 #43 (Oct. 4, 1968) [©1968 R. Crumb]

LEFT BOTTOM
[©1968 R. Crumb]

TOP
"You're Going to Get There Anyway" *EVO* Dec. 1-16 1967 [©1967 R. Crumb]

during a time in his life when he thought he might as well die.

So, yes, Crumb most likely would have made it back in the days when peasants tossed hay, made music and dropped dead, the days before the modern blight that he hates so much. But he wouldn't have been Crumb. He would have been some guy getting by: a clockmaker, an engraver. He might possibly have been an artist, but one who took jobs and expressed himself through them, not an artist who drew what he wanted and made the works into a showcase for the weird sort of creature he happened to be. Crumb was born as the great age of "Dig Me" was moving toward a crest that has never dropped. He hit manhood in the 1960s, just when the distance between wave and beach had started to get dizzy. It's no accident that drugs became the world's new pastime during those years, or that Crumb used them plenty. Drugs became a popular short-cut for the stampede toward an illuminated consciousness, toward lighting up your own private self like it was the world's brightest Christmas tree.

And it's no accident that a good movie was made about Crumb, one with some dodges here and there (apparently that photo shoot with the porn models was not quite as presented) but with not much left uncovered of its subject's work and accomplishment. The movie did what Crumb has done with his work: It put him on display. Much as he likes to voice ideas, Crumb doesn't have anything all that new to tell us. But he himself is pretty catchy, as are his drawings. He's a talented man, and his personality and art make for quite a novelty — a conventional sort of novelty, a bit kickier than Woody Allen but in the same mold.

The modern age loves the idea of the artist, it loves display, it loves novelty. It's made quite a nice place for Robert Crumb. Much as he hates modern times, his particular deal seems to suit him. None of which means he's a hypocrite. But any coin has at least two sides and his coin landed lucky side up. ∎

TOP
Above From
"Roberta Smith,
Office Girl" American
Greetings Corporation
Late News Bulletin
(Nov. '63-April '64)
[©1963, 1964
R. Crumb]

RIGHT
(March 1966) [©1966
R. Crumb]

Mr. Natural OUTWITS FLAKEY FOONT

Below is a sampling of TCJ back issues available from our warehouse for your perusal. Visit tcj.com to read your favorite TCJ critics every day of the year, plus in-depth interviews, international comics coverage, audio, video and much, much more!

LIBRARIES AND SPECIALS

Before you regain your senses... Subscribe to *The Comics Journal!*

Yes, it is probably unfair to hit you with a sales pitch when you are still reeling from the glory and ginormousness of the "magazine" you are holding in your hands — but, what the hell, while you're still in this state of critical and intellectual euphoria, imagine getting future volumes of *The Comics Journal* in your mailbox when you (and we) least expect it. One day it's there and you're the better for it. (If you can heft it out of the ol' mailbox and haul it inside, that is.) We cannot tell you when exactly the next edition will be published, but we can promise you that it will respect your intelligence and publish the best critical and historical writing about comics available anywhere. And: Save money. Pre-paying for future issues will always cost you less than the retail cover price. Subscribe to the *Journal* — or pre-pay for the next issue — and strike a blow against the digitization of the entire planet: Subscribe to a printed journal.

Not that we have anything against digital media. No, no, never. We love the Web and invite you to visit our website at TCJ.com, where we feature, every day, everything you have come to expect from the print magazine — interviews, columns, critiques and debates covering the entire range of cartooning — from editorial cartoons to graphic novels, from 20th-century newspaper strips and comics to contemporary Web comics. Plus audio files, video clips, comics and a new international hub of exclusive bloggers from around the world.

"Still the best and most insightful magazine of comics criticism that exists."
— ALAN MOORE

"You ignore it at your peril."
— NEIL GAIMAN

Please Send Me: *(fill in issue # or check option below)*
NOTE: All subscriptions include online access to back issues from #277 forward.

☐   Send me the next issue — **$20**
    CAN. $30 / INT. $45

☐ Send me the next three issues — **$50** / CAN. $80 / INT. $120
Special Offer! Get a free copy of any TCJ Special or TCJ Library volume with every three-issue subscription!
TCJ Special or TCJ Library volume: _____

Back Issues: #_____ QTY:_____   #_____ QTY:_____   #_____ QTY:_____   #_____ QTY:_____   #_____ QTY:_____

Name: _____

Address: _____

City: _____   State: _____   Zip: _____

Method of Payment: _____   Amount Enclosed: _____
    (WA residents add 8.8% sales tax):

Visa/MC#: _____   Exp. Date: _____

Signature (for credit card orders): _____

Daytime phone (for credit card orders): _____

E-mail (required to access special website features): _____

Order toll free with Visa or MasterCard: 1-800-657-1100 or mail to: 7563 Lake City Way NE, Seattle, WA 98115 or visit: http://www.tcj.com

TCJ.COM

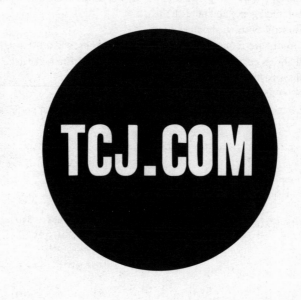